William J. Fay

P9-CMD-733

PAUL VI
THE FIRST MODERN POPE

PAUL VI

THE FIRST MODERN POPE

Peter Hebblethwaite

The deepest feature of Montini's spirituality was his desire to seek a relationship with the modern world. He had a modern sensibility; he knew by intuition the complexity and contradictory nature of the modern world. Jean Guitton, who knew him from close at hand, said: "In Paul VI we meet a complex modern personality, having a deep affinity with modern men and women whose aspirations and torments he shares."

(ANDREA RICCARDI, *Chiesa e Papato*, quoting Jean Guitton)

Paulist Press
New York/Mahwah

First published in Great Britain in 1993 by HarperCollins*Religious*

Copyright © 1993 by Peter Hebblethwaite

Peter Hebblethwaite asserts the moral right to be identified as the author of this work.

All rights reserved. No part of this book may be reproduced or transmitted in any form or by any means, electronic or mechanical, including photocopying, recording or by any information storage and retrieval system without permission in writing from the Publisher.

Library of Congress Cataloging-in-Publication Data

Hebblethwaite, Peter.
Paul VI: the first modern Pope/by Peter Hebblethwaite.
p. cm.
Includes bibliographical references and index.
ISBN 0-8091-0461-X
1. Paul VI, Pope, 1897–1978. 2. Popes—Biography. I. Title.
BX1378.3.H433 1993
282'.092—dc20
[B] 93-6475
CIP

Published by Paulist Press
997 Macarthur Boulevard
Mahwah, New Jersey 07430

Printed and bound in the
United States of America

In memory of John F. X. Harriott,
casualty of *Humanae Vitae*, who would
have reviewed it so spiffingly

CONTENTS

ACKNOWLEDGEMENTS

Acknowledgement is given to the following for permission to use their photographs in this book.

Marietti Editori, Turin, for the first eight pictures of the first section.

Religious News Service, New York, for the remaining pictures, with the exception of those mentioned below.

Topham Picture Source, London, for the picture of Paul VI with Graham Greene, July 15, 1965.

Catholic News Service, Washington, D.C., for the picture of Paul VI outside the Waldorf Astoria, October 4, 1965.

INTRODUCTION

The Fluctuating Image

An introduction that is also a conclusion

> St Augustine had a saying, *Nemo nisi per amicitiam cognoscitur*, you need to be a friend of a man before you understand him. So by analogy is our relationship to men of the past, societies of the past, even documents in the archives . . . You need no white paint, you need to see things as they were. But you need to be inside their minds and to forget the future which they could not know, and to come towards them with the openness of mind, the readiness to listen, which a man gives to a friend.
>
> (OWEN CHADWICK, Inaugural Lecture as Professor of Modern History, Cambridge, 27 November 1968)

Why write about Giovanni Battista Montini, the future Pope Paul VI? Because he straddles the twentieth century and contributed importantly to its history. He had first-hand knowledge of Modernism, Futurism, Fascism, Nazism, Communism, Third Worldism, Feminism, Ecology – all the movements that shook and shaped the century now closing. And because he was a good and holy man who in 1975 proclaimed the need for a "Civilization of Love" which prefigured the "New World Order" so desperately needed in the 1990s. Because he was, in short, a modern man and "the first modern pope".

Paul VI was "modern" in another sense. He concluded, and implemented, the Second Vatican Council inaugurated by Pope John XXIII in 1962. The Council can be seen as the Church's response to "modernity". It was the first Council in Church history to be devoted to *aggiornamento* (bringing up to date) rather than reform or doctrine. This, of course, implied reform and renewal, but as part of the process of *aggiornamento*; and it implied doctrine too, since one cannot make pastoral statements except on the basis of doctrine; but unlike previous Councils it was not called in order to refute errors.

The official title of its pastoral constitution, *Gaudium et Spes*, is *De Ecclesia in Mundo Hujus Temporis* (On the Church in the Contemporary World), which showed clearly what it was about. The Council was aware of "new forms of culture (mass culture) which give rise to new ways of thinking, acting and making use of leisure".[1] In his first encyclical, *Ecclesiam Suam*, Paul announced that he wanted to complement the Council by opening a dialogue with the contemporary world in all its aspects. This did not mean jettisoning tradition or blessing indiscriminately every modern trend or fad. It involved "discerning the signs of the times".[2] Paul's fifteen-year pontificate was one long exercise in discernment – and discernment means seeing in difficult circumstances. The story needed to be told before all the witnesses die off.[3]

There was also a less elaborate reason for writing a biography of Pope Paul VI: response to popular demand. Reviewers of *John XXIII: Pope of the Council* (in the USA *John XXIII: Shepherd of the Modern World*) urged me to follow it up with a life of his successor, Giovanni Battista Montini. The work was already half done, they said, in that casual throw-away style reviewers affect. Little did they know.

John was at first sight a more attractive subject for a biographer. Anecdotes about him abounded, though on inspection they mostly proved unfounded or *ben trovato* (aptly invented). There were hardly any anecdotes about Paul VI, reliable or not; and little of his playful self-deprecating wit survives translation.

When Karl Rahner reminded him that he was once forbidden by the Holy Office to write about concelebration, and that now the Pope himself concelebrated, Paul VI "smiled gently and replied: 'Yes, there is a time for laughter and a time for weeping.' What he really meant in this context, I don't know."[4] He liked historical anecdotes like the remark of Pope Paul II: "When I was called Piccolomini, no one knew me; now that I am Pope, everyone is my nephew."[5] An example of non-verbal humour: on the day neo-cardinals receive the congratulations of their supporters he sent one of them a gift-wrapped kitten in a basket, complete with ribbons in papal gold and white. But since it was to his

1 *Gaudium et Spes*, 54.

2 Ibid. 4 and 44.

3 Not everyone agrees. I submitted chapter 37 to Archbishop Luigi Barbarito, pro-nuncio to Great Britain. He replied: "It seems to me that your interpretation of some of the facts is too personal. You are obviously aware that it is impossible to write a true and objective life of a Pontiff until access to all the documents is obtained. This will mean waiting until the next century" (letter of 24 February 1992).

4 Karl Rahner, *I Remember: An Autobiographical Interview with Meinhold Krauss*, tr. Harvey D. Egan SJ, 1985, p. 72.

5 Jean Guitton, *Paul VI secret*, 1979, p. 75.

Oratorian friend Giulio Bevilacqua, who thought being a cardinal was something of a joke, perhaps the credit should go to him.

Again, while John's secretary, Msgr Loris F. Capovilla, eased my task a great deal by providing memories and documents, Msgr Pasquale Macchi, Paul's secretary, offered help, but within strict limits of discretion. What he had to say was contained in a short Memoir published in 1979.[1] He did not launch a "Montini industry" to rival Capovilla's regular output of Pope John *inédits* and memoirs.

Part of the reason was that the Istituto Paolo VI in Brescia took over this function, and did it better than any individual could have done. Its *Notiziario* is the basic source for the life of Paul. But another reason for Macchi's taciturnity could be that he was Paul's link with the shady financiers of Milan, Michele Sindona and Roberto Calvi. This implies no guilt: but were he to tell all, too many skeletons might perhaps come rattling out of Milanese cupboards.

Yet I shall argue that Montini is a better subject for a biography than Roncalli because he was a richer and deeper personality, had more worldly contacts, and because his pontificate – fifteen years compared with four and a half – was of more decisive importance for the long-term future of the Church.

Nor is documentation lacking. The Paul VI Institute gives some idea of the immense correspondence that he kept up throughout his life. As pope, he continued to write personal letters. In 1969 Julien Green, the French-American novelist, wrote complaining that in the new liturgy he found all the bareness and lack of mystery that led him to abandon the Calvinist Church so many years before. Paul replied that he shared Green's grief at the loss of Latin, but insisted that the change was necessary for pastoral reasons. He justified it with a favourite quotation from St Augustine: "I prefer to speak ungrammatically and be understood by the people, rather than appear learned and not be understood."[2] He tried to console Green with a Pauline text: "No one is made to stumble

1 Pasquale Macchi, *Ricordo di Paolo VI*, Milan 1979. In April 1991, as the work was nearly finished, I had a moment of anxiety when Don Gino Belleri, head of the Libreria Leoniana in Rome, drew my attention to Carlo Cremona's *Paolo VI*, Rusconi, Milan 1991. Msgr Macchi contributed a preface in which he praised the author's "extraordinary narrative capacity". "This is," he declares, "an account that is extremely faithful to the man and his times, and a fascinating portrait." By now I was distinctly worried. Carlo Cremona is a priest, Vaticanologue for GR2, an Italian radio network, for many years. I began to read. The second sentence read: "Every time a Pope dies, the world seems to tremble" (p. 11). Over the page Don Cremona says of John Paul I: "His was not a reign, but the apparition of an angel with a short message of light for humanity." I relaxed. The biographer's task was still to be done. Which is not to say the Cremona book is not useful: he provided the beribboned kitten. But where the desire to edify prevails, there can be no history.

2 Carlo Cremona, *Paolo VI*, p. 233.

[is scandalized] without me feeling the pain" (2 Corinthians 11:29b).

Paul also had a fine collection of manuscripts, most of them gifts to him as pope, though some dating from earlier. I will give three examples. He treasured the complete manuscript of Giovanni Papini's *Letters to the Men of Pope Celestine*. Particularly moving were the two prayers written by Antonio Fogazzaro on the death of his son, that the novelist carried in his wallet till his death in 1911. There was the manuscript of Georges Bernanos' booklet on St Dominic.

These three items were significant to him in different ways. Celestine was the last pope to have resigned. Fogazzaro's novel, *Il Santo*, was absurdly put on the Index of Forbidden Books in 1906 where it remained: it envisages a pope who "comes out" of the Vatican and visits Roman prisons. The last sentence of Bernanos' *Saint Dominique* is "there is only one sadness – not to be a saint."

The collection also contained personal letters from artists and writers. They included the prison diaries of his friend, the painter Aldo Carpi, director of the Brera Academy in Milan, who survived to write about the Nazi death camp of Gusen.[1] He liked to meditate before Carpi's oil painting: it showed a boat about to cast off from a cove or inlet, with the boatman encouraging a pope, exhausted and hunched on the deck, with a wave of the arm. It made a change from the cliché of the pope as fearless helmsman.

Paul was a writer himself, good enough to have studies done of his literary style.[2] Like all writers he read a lot, and collected books with passion. His six thousand volumes, often annotated and still in the order he arranged them, are also in the Istituto Paolo VI.

Though a writer, he had none of the affectations of the "man of letters". A book, he told his students in 1930 (in *La Conscienza universitaria*), is not a dead, inert thing in your hands. It should spring alive, overleap obstacles of time and distance, and prove the continuity of tradition. Yet in his will he directed his literary executor, Msgr Macchi, to destroy his personal papers. He was not entirely obeyed, except for "conscience matters" to which, rightly, we have no access anyway.[3]

1 Paul VI recalled Carpi's *Diario di Gusen* in his address for World Peace Day 1974, remarking that the eighty-year-old painter had died "some months ago" (*Insegnamenti*, XII, 1974, p. 9). He set Carpi alongside Gandhi and Albert Schweitzer as "one of the individuals who changed the world". Carpi taught him "the possibility of love in the midst of hatred, and a sense of justice that transcends merely making claims to become the self-giving service of others, with patience, humility and sheer goodness".

2 The most sophisticated is Fabio Finotti, *Critica stilistica e linguaggio religioso in Giovanni Battista Montini*, Edizioni-Studium, Rome, Saggi/1 for the Istituto Paolo VI.

3 Pasquale Macchi's explanation: "In his will he said I should destroy all his personal papers. Yet I have used here unpublished notes. I explained to Pope Paul that it would be impossible to carry out his will so drastically, and with his permission I undertook

Enough remains to form a picture of what Montini was like, not just in his pontificate (1963–78) but in the sixty-seven years that preceded and – as I believe – explain it. My role is to act as the midwife who allows Montini to be reborn. He had his limitations. Maybe he became pope too late in life and lived far too long – far longer than he ever expected to live. I hope the reader will be able to say, adapting Blaise Pascal, "We expected to meet a pope, and we found a brother."

But there is a message for the sisters too. Montini, like all those of his generation, used "sexist" language wholly unconsciously. He said man (*uomo*) when he meant the human person, female or male. This usage extended into his pontificate and up to his death. His attitude to women was courtly and very Italian. Italian women, it has been said, do not aim at equality because they already feel superior, fulfilling themselves as wives and mothers, or as nuns (another sort of "mother").

Battista Montini had no sisters but grew up in a household dominated by three mature women: his mother, paternal grandmother, and an unmarried aunt. Between them they ruled the household and fussed over him. From his student days in 1919 he welcomed women at conferences, and was always on the look-out for talented women to serve the Church in what today would be called "ministry". He gave Margot Pompe, former Minister of Education in the Netherlands, and British economist Dame Barbara Ward (Baroness Jackson) a key role in the International Justice and Peace Commission. He was delighted to be the first-ever pope to appoint a woman to the Pontifical Academy of Sciences. As a Nobel prize-winner it would have been hard to keep Rita Levi Montalcini out. Still, it was an important first.[1]

Giulio Andreotti, the durable Christian Democrat politician who early in 1992 was Prime Minister in the fiftieth Italian government since the war, credits Pope Paul with the remark that "women make up more than half the human race and make up more than half of the faithful in the Church".[2]

This truism was probably borrowed from the Belgian Cardinal Léon-Joseph Suenens who, until he fell under the spell of the charismatic renewal movement round about 1973, was the most notable advocate of an alternative "logic of Vatican II", and therefore the most assiduous thorn in Pope Paul's side. Yet Paul did what he could for women. In 1970 he made Sts Catherine of Siena and Theresa of Avila the first

to read through his entire correspondence and his numerous writings, assuring him that I would follow his criteria so as to satisfy his wishes. That is what I have done", *Notiziario*, 1, p. 42.

1 Cremona, *Paolo VI*, p. 222.

2 *Notiziario*, 13, p. 41.

women "doctors" of the Church, officially ratified as "teachers" and theologians. He meant well towards women. He tried.

Even if in 1976 *Inter Insigiores* the CDF (Congregation for the Doctrine of Faith) said "no" to the priestly ordination of women, it was not presented as a definitive statement for all time and was wholly devoid of the male chauvinist vehemence found in some clerics.

That brings us, inevitably, to the question: worked upon in the pontificate of Pope John Paul II, is not any biography of Paul VI bound to look like a critical tract directed against his successor? But to concede that would be to despair of writing history. It ought to be possible to tell the story of Paul VI without overt comment on the present.

I intend to follow the example of Cardinal Agostino Casaroli, close friend of Paul VI and former Secretary of State under John Paul II until 1990. Unveiling Lello Scorzello's statue of Paul VI in Brescia cathedral on 26 September 1985 Casaroli said:

> Man is made for dialogue: this deep conviction accompanied G. B. Montini throughout his whole life. The interior life, spiritual and material progress, all are nourished from this same source. The story of human progress is nothing other than the chronicle of the results obtained by dialogue with other people, with the environment, with the people who have preceded us and, in a sense, with those who will come after us. The person who does not converse with his fellows, who is shut off from reality, who neither listens nor responds, withers like a plant in dry soil. He cuts himself off from the course of history in barren isolation, where he risks atrophy of both intelligence and heart.[1]

This is a fine description of Montini's attitude to dialogue. However, on the strength of it right-wing zealots accused Casaroli of "criticizing the Holy Father". All one can say is that if the cap fits, by all means put it on. Feel free.

Yet two factors make it difficult to maintain complete imperturbability.

The first is that so many actions of John Paul II's pontificate imply a repudiation of the policies of Paul VI such that one is bound to construe it as a critique of Paul VI. Officially praise is lavished upon "our Venerable Predecessor", who is occasionally quoted with respect, but more often presented as a "tragic figure" who couldn't quite cope. Rhetoric aside, John Paul's actions say clearly that he considers Paul VI to have been weak, vacillating and mistaken on priestly identity, religious life,

1 Agostino Cardinale, "*Paolo VI e il dialogo*", *Il Regno*, 19/84, 11 November 1984, p. 594.

dangerous theologians, episcopal collegiality, ecumenism, the *Ostpolitik* and Vatican II. The Extraordinary Synod of 1985, with its abandonment of "the People of God" as the key concept in understanding the Church and its "pessimistic" re-editing of "the signs of the times", is further evidence of the dismantling of the heritage of Paul VI.

History is silently rewritten. I became aware of this when a Roman personage took me aside and assured me that towards the end of his life Paul VI deeply regretted the mistakes he had made on ecumenism, collegiality and so on. Everything we hitherto thought was admirable about his pontificate was now a matter for regret. Paul VI's many achievements were to be mere tinder for his funeral pyre.[1]

I refuse to play this game. Certainly Paul VI worried about some of his actions because he was scrupulous and a worrier; but he never wavered in his commitment to the full implementation of Vatican II. A similar legend was put around about John XXIII. Cardinals take you by the arm and assure you in confidence that, towards the end of his life, he told his intimates that he wished he had never called the Council. The only reply to that is that John XXIII would not have offered his death-agony for something he thought so wrong. Paul lived long enough to see that some effects of the Council were unforeseen and disturbing; but that does not mean that he rejected any of its positive achievements.

So it is important to capture the mind and heart of Paul VI before all those who knew him personally die off. But he himself will be our principal source. Though he did not keep a diary in the manner of John XXIII he lived with pen in hand and covered innumerable pages with his fine script. In 1975, when he was seventy-eight and beginning to weary, he made the following note:

> What is my state of mind? Am I Hamlet? Or Don Quixote? On the left? On the right? I don't feel I have been properly understood [*Non mi sento indovinato*]. I have had two dominant feelings: *Superabundo gaudio*. I am filled with comfort. With all our affliction, I am overjoyed. (2 Corinthians 7:4)[2]

1 This judgement is found in circles close to Communion and Liberation. For example, a certain Alan Robinson of Milton, Oxfordshire wrote to *Thirty Days* saying that "many objective commentators have described him and his reign as the worst in the recent history of the Church" and that "his sad reign is best forgotten". Robinson does not quote any of these "objective commentators" and they would be hard to find. Even *Thirty Days* found this too strong meat. Their reply is: "Our judgement is that Paul VI, especially after 1968 (the year of *Humanae Vitae*) gave an extraordinary testimony of faith and of love for the Church. He became profoundly aware of the dead-end to which a certain post-conciliar trend was leading the Church. He confided to Jean Guitton a year before his death that 'a non-Catholic mentality was increasingly dominant in the Church' ", *Thirty Days*, April 1969, p. 81. Tosh and QED.

2 *Notiziario*, 1, p. 50.

From the heading we know that the two dominant feelings are *Certezza e Gioia* (Certainty and Joy). In Italian culture Hamlet is the symbol of indecisiveness. "To be or not to be" is the only quotation anyone knows. Don Quixote tilts at imaginary windmills. Legend – though not history – has it that John XXIII taxed Montini with "*amletismo*", though this term was not in his vocabulary.

We will have to discuss whether Montini's analysis of late-twentieth-century problems was faulty – that is the substance of the Don Quixote charge. For either he was Don Quixote attacking the wrong targets, or he was "prophetic" in the strict sense that he correctly diagnosed his present and thus prepared our future.

The encyclical *Humanae Vitae* poses this problem acutely. Paul VI was generally pooh-poohed when he said that the widespread availability of contraceptives "could open the way to marital infidelity and a general lowering of standards" (*Humanae Vitae*, no. 17). His Catholic critics insisted they were talking only about the *responsible* use of contraceptives to space births within Christian marriage where children already existed. He also warned against government intervention in this private family area. "Don't be afraid," he reportedly told Edouard Gagnon on the eve of his encyclical, "in twenty years time they'll call me a prophet."[1]

Paul VI was not utterly wrong about this. Later the feminist use of the ecology theme (why should I stuff my body with harmful pills with uncertain consequences?) as well as the fear of AIDS suggested that Paul's teaching was not wholly crazy. It has also been remarked that once the link between the procreative and unitive goals of marriage has been broken it becomes more difficult to condemn buggery or bestiality. Others think it would have been wiser for *Humanae Vitae* to have drawn the line at abortion.

My purpose is not to defend Paul VI come what may or prove that he was "prophetic". I insist only that he should not be written off until he has been seen in context. The quotation about Hamlet and Don Quixote tells us something else about Montini: he was lucid about himself, and perfectly aware of what was being said behind his back.

Indeed this lucidity and self-awareness shaped the personal cross he had to carry. A less sensitive man might have ridden roughshod over his critics. Pope John XXIII was too old to do more than shrug at them (though they could hurt him deeply) while John Paul II simply brushes them aside as hostile, ill-informed and irrelevant. Paul was the first pope

1 *National Catholic Reporter*, 26 August 1988, p. 10.

to have taken his critics seriously. He made this astonishing statement in 1967: "The Pope – as we all know – is undoubtedly the gravest obstacle in the path of ecumenism."

He often thought his critics had a good point; and if they did, he took it. Cardinal Suenens objected that *Humanae Vitae* should have involved collegial consultation and not just the exercise of the primacy. As though responding to this criticism, Paul issued no more encyclicals after 1968, and his major literary work, the wonderful *Evangelii Nuntiandi* of 1975, was the fruit of his mature reflection on the muddled and indecisive Synod of 1974.

Nor was he the remote authoritarian bully he was sometimes portrayed as. Like Newman's gentleman, he did not like voluntarily to inflict pain. Though he could be firm, as with the Dutch, there were no excommunications in his pontificate. Nor was any theologian condemned, though several were carefully vetted. The only real condemnation was the suspension *a divinis* of dissident Archbishop Marcel Lefebvre in July 1976, and that was forced upon him by Lefebvre's intransigence.

He was the most naturally talented man to become pope in this century. That is obviously difficult to prove; but what can be shown is that the range of his reading and friendships extended far beyond the bounds of what an Italian cleric was expected to enjoy. An hour's meeting and you could be a friend for life. He kept his friendships in good repair, never forgetting anniversaries or feast-days.

He had, for example, many Anglican friends, like John Dickinson, chaplain of Pembroke College, Cambridge, in the 1950s and an outstanding historian of the Austin canons regular,[1] and Colin Hickling, later lecturer at King's College, London. No one suspected he knew such people or that he exchanged Christmas greetings with them and asked for records of Anglican religious music.

One has to admit, however, that among his friends was one who was privileged to know him better than anyone else. The French philosopher Jean Guitton first met him on 8 September 1950, shortly after the publication of *Humani Generis*, Pius XII's shock encyclical which "condemned" as far as anyone could judge the "new theology" developed by the French Dominicans and Jesuits who were Montini's masters. Guitton, four years younger than Paul VI, then met him annually at the same date for the rest of his life. From their first meeting

1 John Compton Dickinson died on 23 July 1991 at the age of seventy-nine. His last work was on *The Priory of Cartmel* in the English Lake District, one of the best-preserved of English mediaeval monasteries, near which he was born, lived and died.

Guitton consciously decided he was going to be Boswell to Montini's Johnson or Eckermann to his Goethe. One can wonder how far he edited his memories without detracting from his role as a witness. On their last meeting, at Castelgandolfo in September 1977, Paul VI, kneeling beside a pool, said to him: "Get away, you're frightening my carp."[1]

Guitton, member of the Académie Française, was every inch a French intellectual capable of transmuting the most banal observations by the brilliance of his style. He was also a keen amateur painter. Celebrating his ninetieth birthday on 19 October 1991, Guitton recalled that Msgr Montini had encouraged him to paint not as a hobby or diversion but out of *duty*. He should "want everything", that is, seek the highest and deepest level of synthesis between faith and art.[2] That is the explanation for Paul's art collections.

But Guitton was French, like-minded and arch-Catholic. Montini's friends were not confined to those he agreed with. He was the least clerical of modern popes. His last audience was for a socialist President of Italy, Sandro Pertini, and his last letter for Giuseppe Prezzolini, an unbelieving writer, professor of Italian Literature at Columbia University, New York from 1930, whom he addressed as "my *maestro*".[3] Literature and art were his way into the modern world. Nothing human was foreign to him. He "wanted all".

He makes dear old jug-eared Roncalli, the predecessor who won the hearts of the entire world, look narrow, frowsty, lacking in taste and distinctly old-fashioned. The difference could be seen in the physical appearance of his Vatican. He consigned John's heavy damask brocade and gilded furniture to the lumber-room and introduced tones of pale grey, then fashionable in Milan.

Yet throughout his pontificate he suffered from the comparison with his predecessor whose spontaneity and charm he could not – in public at least – recapture.

Paul's pontificate might have been much happier if he had brought in his own team straight away. But that did not happen. Retirement at seventy-five was only imposed in 1967, four years into the pontificate. One can argue that Amleto Cicognani, Secretary of State, was a shrewd old bird who knew the United States well, that Giuseppe Pizzardo at Seminaries was gaga and harmless, and that Alfredo Ottaviani at the

1 Jean Guitton, *Paul VI secret*, p. 167.

2 *Notiziario*, 22, pp. 75–79. The full text of all the speeches delivered in the Palazzo della Loggia, Brescia, on 19 October 1991 are announced for *Notiziario*, 23.

3 Ibid. 7, pp. 26–27, 20. Prezzolini, born on 22 January 1882, was fifteen years older than Montini yet outlived him. His *Diary* records how, back in Italy after many years in the United States, he just dropped in one day on the Archbishop of Milan and became a friend for life.

Holy Office was as blind as a bat. Yet they all provided trouble in a big way.

Ottaviani devoted his old age to recovering from the humiliation inflicted on the Curia during the first sessions. His I-told-you-so revenge was *Humanae Vitae*. But Montini could not deal harshly with colleagues he had known since the 1920s. Besides, as a connoisseur of the Roman Curia, he knew that unless he won them over he could not implement the Council at all.

So he left everyone in place – the old, the halt, the lame and the blind. Yet at the same time he made a thunderous speech on 21 September 1963, demanding that the Curia should reform itself – or else. He said:

> People everywhere are watching Catholic Rome, the Roman pontificate, the Roman Curia. The duty of being authentically Christian is especially binding here. We would not remind you of this duty if we did not remind ourselves of it every day. Everything in Rome teaches – the letter and the spirit, the way we think, study, speak, feel, act, suffer, pray, serve, love. Every moment, every aspect of our life is surrounded by a glow that can be beneficial if we are what Christ wants from us, or harmful if we are unfaithful.[1]

Maybe asking the Curia to reform itself is like asking the Mafia to change its spots. The speech illustrates Montini's optimism and touching disposition to think well of all.

But as soon as he decently could, he brought in his own chums, tough-minded no-nonsense bureaucratic pros like young Giovanni Benelli. Then the real reform of the Curia could begin. So successful was the reforming Benelli that the tyres of his Alfa-Romeo were slashed more than once in the Vatican car park.

But Pope John also left behind another legacy that was a source of embarrassment: many people thought he was a "liberal". Had he lived on, it was believed, he would have cheerfully endorsed contraception, the priestly ordination of married men, women priests, abortion, gay marriages, Marxism and whatever else figured on the liberal agenda.

Paul knew this was nonsense. He wrote in a private memo: "Serious harm is done to the memory of Pope John when people attribute to him attitudes he did not have. That he was good, yes; that he was indifferent, no. How firmly he stuck to (traditional) doctrine, how much he feared

1 *Insegnamenti*, 1, 1963, p. 150.

dangers etc."[1] This protest laid down the main lines of the pontificate.

Because Paul VI could by definition never fulfil the expectations aroused by this mythical Pope John, his own real achievements would remain unappreciated until after his death. He knew this perfectly well:

> Pope John was not weak, was not a compromiser, was not indulgent towards erroneous opinions or towards the so-called inevitability of history etc. . . . His dialogue was not goodness leading to cowardly surrender. As far as understanding the modern world and drawing close to it go, I think I am on the same lines as Pope John.

In understanding the modern world Montini actually boasts that he is rather better at it than good Pope John.

This is naturally introduced by the observation that he is "not going to brag", but then qualified by saying that "in the field of work, of culture, of human and diplomatic relations, perhaps our life is characterized more clearly than anything else by the love of our own time, and our own world". This may be why he abandoned this draft. He didn't want to boast.

But Montini's claim to understand the modern world is at the very heart of his pontificate. His address to the final session Council on 7 December 1965 stated this theme passionately – and drew criticism from the right wing for its alleged "humanism":

> At the Council the Church has been concerned not just with herself and her relationship of union with God, but with man – man as he really is today, living man, man wrapped up all in himself, man who makes himself not only the centre of his every interest but dares to claim that he is the principle and explanation of all reality.[2]

He invited those who called themselves "secular humanists" to give the Council credit for recognizing "our own new type of humanism: we too, in fact, more than any others, honour mankind". This was his version of *Gaudium et Spes*' observation that "we are the witnesses of the birth of a new humanism, one in which man is defined first of all by his responsibility towards his brothers and towards history".[3]

Montini tried to exercise this ministry of dialogue and listening, unprecedented for the papacy, throughout the fifteen years of his pontificate. As an historian he knew that a pope, any pope, has about five

1 *Notiziario*, 13, p. 16.

2 *Insegnamenti*, 3, 1965, p. 720.

3 *Gaudium et Spes*, no. 55.

creative years after which he tends to mark time. He clung to office, not because this gratified some power-complex but because precedent nailed him to this cross: this was the ideal of service he derived from his family and ecclesial education. That is why I will spend so much time on them.

His hesitations and scruples, his *amletismo* in short, now begin to look rather winning. They demonstrate his sense of complexity. Convictions divide people more than doubts. It is only with hindsight that Montini's life looks like a steady, orderly progression up the ecclesiastical ladder until he finally reaches the topmost rung. As he lived through his life he went through doubt, perplexity, bafflement, uncertainty and depression.

Indeed his life had no pattern at all: ordained priest without having been a seminarian, he was made archbishop of the most prestigious diocese of Italy without having been a parish priest, and his name was put forward as a candidate for the papacy in 1958 though he was not even a cardinal.[1] His election as pope in 1963 was the single "logical" event in his life.

Even in the United States the "image" of Paul VI has changed since his death and – why not admit it? – the pontificate of John Paul II has made some nostalgic for Paul's tortured subtleties. This trend is illustrated by Eugene Kennedy, a Chicago psychologist. In 1984 he wrote:

> Paul VI lived through fifteen difficult years, the heart of the Vatican transition, and may finally be perceived as the most extraordinary Pope of the century. He understood that transforming an institution like the Catholic Church was the most delicate of tasks. It demanded the exhausting pastoral art of encouraging change while holding it steady at the same time, something like giving a haircut to a drowsy lion.[2]

In the end what Kennedy calls Montini's "genius for the pastoral art" is what matters most about him.

He managed to complete the Council without dividing the Church. He reformed the Roman Curia without alienating it. He introduced collegiality without ever letting it undermine his papal office. He practised ecumenism without impairing Catholic identity. He had an *Ostpolitik* that involved neither surrender nor bouncing aggressiveness. He was "open to the world" without ever being its dupe. He pulled off the most difficult trick of all: combining openness with fidelity.

But Gene Kennedy was not very close to Paul VI. Few were closer

1 See Josef Coppens in *Notiziario*, 9, p. 72.

2 Eugene Kennedy, *The Now and Future Church: The Psychology of Being an American Catholic*, 1984, pp. 104–5.

to him in the early 1950s than Mario V. Rossi. From 1952 Rossi was the head of the Catholic Students in Italy – a papal appointment. At one point, provoked by the right-wing antics of Catholic Action headed by the Pope's trusty, Dr Luigi Gedda, he decided to resign in protest. But resignation was out of the question in the case of papal appointments. Wondering what to do, Montini kept the resignation letter on his desk, and thus was accused of "withholding information from the Holy Father". That was the pretext on which he was exiled to Milan without the cardinal's hat that went with the job.

In a book published in 1975 Rossi praises Montini for his courage in backing him up twenty years earlier. Then he goes on:

> This was when I began to understand his drama, though never to accept it. There was a conflict between the role and the man, between the priest who wanted to lead a hidden life and the public *persona* who worked within a regime of absolute power. He served it faithfully while understanding the need to revolt against it. This led to a deep conflict within himself which had the further handicap of a failure to understand the ordinary world, a remoteness from everyday life and a consequent lack of balance. He was always tempted by abstraction and idealism.[1]

This is a harsh judgement from someone who wished Paul VI well. It poses the gravest problem of all. Rossi is really saying that in the 1950s Montini, the Vatican diplomatic and bureaucrat, had deeply Christian instincts but was not able to express them in his pastoral work. He showed spurts of courage but then allowed apologetic and defensive considerations to prevail.

This 1950s analysis becomes even more poignantly true when Montini is elected pope. Now he is utterly trapped. There is no possibility of escape. Hence the anguish. His desperate earnestness to communicate the Christian Gospel is locked within a system that leaves him with little room for manoeuvre. What room he has he uses brilliantly. But the strain shows.

Everyone who holds high office in the Church will appreciate this problem. Those who say "no problem" are spinning fairy tales. Montini, the first *modern* pope, tried to be the second *Christian* pope after Pope John. It broke him.

After the psychologist and the psychiatrist, the novelist. Among the hundreds of possible witnesses to Paul VI I end this introduction with

1 Mario V. Rossi, *I Giorni della Onnipotenza, Memorie di un esperienza cattolica*, 1975, p. 117.

Graham Greene. In 1948 he had a nasty experience which showed the power of the institution. Cardinal Bernard Griffin summoned him to Archbishop's House, Westminster, and read out a letter from the Vatican condemning his recent novel about the whisky priest, *The Power and the Glory*. Why? Because it was supposedly "paradoxical" and dealt with "extraordinary circumstances".

The condemnation was not made public, but the London Catholic intelligentsia knew, rallied round Greene and mocked this latest example of fatuous Roman intransigence. Griffin was more embarrassed than anything else, and treated Greene gently "when I refused to revise the book on the casuistical ground that the copyright was in the hands of my publishers".[1]

There the matter ended, but controversy over Greene's orthodoxy was rekindled by *The Heart of the Matter* and *The End of the Affair*. Pius XII read *The End of the Affair*, and said to Fr John Carmel Heenan of Greene: "I think this man is in trouble. If ever he comes to you, you must listen."[2]

Montini recommended Greene to Pius XII. At this time he was making unsuccessful attempts to persuade *l'Osservatore Romano* to get Greene to write for it. But they did not meet until July 1965 when Greene, at Paul's invitation, had a private audience:

> When I met Pope Paul VI he mentioned that he had read *The Power and the Glory*. I told him that it had been condemned by the Holy Office.
>
> "Who condemned it?"
>
> "Cardinal Pizzardo."
>
> He repeated the name with a wry smile and added: "Mr Greene, some parts of your book are certain to offend some Catholics, but you should pay no attention to that."[3]

Advice I intend to follow as his biographer. Greene added another detail about this audience: "Instead of the conventional medal, he gave me a valuable Boldoni limited edition of the Gospels. 'If you would *like* to have it,' he said shyly."[4] The whole of Montini is contained in the

1 Graham Greene, *Ways of Escape*, 1980, p. 86.

2 Ibid. p. 139.

3 Ibid. p. 87.

4 Graham Greene, letter to the author, 8 October 1986. There is a memorable photograph of this meeting, much reproduced on Greene's death on 7 April 1991. Often captioned "The sinner and the saint can meet", Paul would not have accepted that discrimination. We all stand in need of the mercy of God, pope and novelist: that is why he appreciated the lines so often quoted by Greene, "Between the stirrup and the ground/He salvation found."

wryness and shyness of this remark. He does not impose. To understand him we need to go back to the beginning in 1897, and the love-match of Giorgio and Giuditta.

I

Formed in Brescia
(1897–1914)

> I think that to understand destiny you have to fathom that initial mystery: why am I here and not there? why have I sprung from this man and this woman? Simone Weil said with great truth: "Meditation on the chance which brought my father and mother together is even more salutary than meditation on death."
>
> (Paul VI in JEAN GUITTON, *Dialogues*, p. 56)

Giorgio Montini first met his future bride, Giuditta Alghisi, coming out of St Peter's, Rome, in 1883 after receiving Pope Leo XIII's blessing on the twenty-fifth anniversary of his episcopal ordination. They had gone on pilgrimage from Brescia to Rome for the most traditional of reasons: they wanted to see the Pope, *videre Petrum*, then hailed melodramatically as "the prisoner of the Vatican" when not "the Pope-King". Though moved by the papal blessing they also had eyes for each other. They fell in love.

Giuditta knew more about Giorgio than he knew about her. Now thirty-three, he had been editor of the local Catholic paper, *Il Cittadino di Brescia*, since 1881. Giuditta, nineteen, was fresh from a French-speaking convent in Milan. Apart from the age difference their love had another stimulating obstacle: Giuditta was an orphan – though not a poor one – and a ward of Giuseppe Bonardi, an old Garibaldian of 1859, now mayor of Brescia. He was an ally of Giuseppe Zarnadelli, the fire-eating radical and anti-clerical who dominated Brescian politics and played an important role in national life for forty years.

Giuditta's black-hearted guardian naturally refused permission for her to marry his political rival, Giorgio Montini. Unable to forbid them seeing each other, he restricted their meetings to twice a week, with Aunt Catina Rovetta acting as chaperon.[1] Giuditta cleverly strung her

1 Fappani-Molinari, *Montini Giovane*, pp. 16–18. Montini remains "young" in their eyes until the death of his parents in 1943.

guardian along, attending Radical Party dinners to keep him sweet.

But Bonardi was to be doubly discomfited: in May 1895 the Radicals lost the local elections and he ceased to be mayor; on 17 July when Giuditta reached her majority she announced her engagement and he was powerless to stop her.

Thus Giovanni Battista Montini, the future Pope Paul VI, owes his origins to a Victorian love story. It recalls the world of Antonio Fogazzaro's novel, *Il piccolo mondo moderno*, which depicts the prosperous and cultivated *haute bourgeoisie* (in fact of Verona) with their intense political rivalries pitting Catholic heroes against anti-clerical villains. Giuditta was swept away on Giorgio's white charger. If her knight in shining armour wore a wing-collar and pince-nez, that was the fashionable thing to do.

The bells of Santi Nazaro and Celso rang out for their marriage on 1 August 1895.[1] For Brescia it was the society wedding of the year. *Il Cittadino di Brescia* devoted the whole of page one to a graphic celebrating its editor's marriage, full of scrolls, flowers, a quill pen and "greetings from the heart". Giuditta's former guardian accepted his defeat and did the decent thing by dying shortly afterwards, "reconciled with the Church". Giuditta always piously believed that the blessing of the aged Leo XIII had done the trick. It was, she wrote ten years later, "the seed of so many other blessings which the Lord has heaped on me in giving me your heart, your whole self".[2]

That shows they hardly needed a copy of Léon Gautier's *L'amour chrétien dans le mariage* that an intellectual friend, Luigi Bazoli, gave them as a wedding present. He had just translated it. So after a honeymoon that included a stay in the guest-house of the Benedictine Abbey of Einsiedeln in Switzerland they began their married life at via Dante 7, conveniently opposite the offices of *Il Cittadino*, on the feast of the Assumption, 15 August 1895.

Their first child was born on 8 May 1896 and christened Lodovico after Giorgio's deceased father. The second, also a boy, was born on 26 September 1897 at Concesio, their country house five miles from Brescia. He was baptized four days later[3] and called Giovanni Battista in memory of his grandmother's father. He was also landed with the names Enrico, Antonio and Maria, but mercifully seems to have forgotten them. He

1 *Familiari*, p. xi.

2 Fappani-Molinari, *Montini Giovane*, pp. 16–17.

3 That same day in Lisieux, France, a Carmelite nun called Thérèse happened to die at the age of twenty-four. Jean Guitton, *Paul VI secret*, p. 137. When Montini in maturity pointed out the coincidence the Carmelites said that on her death-bed Thérèse had promised to "come back to visit the cribs of newly baptized babies".

used the initials GBM not GBEAMM. He was known in the family and to his friends as Battista. That is what I will call him until further notice.

In naming their children after these figures from the past the Montinis were not just being sentimental. They were making a point about family tradition. The only one of the four grandparents still alive was Giorgio's mother, the formidable Francesca Buffali Montini. She had had a hard life. Widowed at thirty-six, she had to bring up six children. Giorgio was her third-born and favourite son, and it was thanks to her drive that he had been able to study jurisprudence at Padua University. Her husband, Lodovico, was a medical doctor who had fought the Austrians in 1848 and 1849 and tended the wounded in the great battles for the liberation of Lombardy at Magnenta and Solferino in 1859. He won praise from Garibaldi's second-in-command, General Nino Brixio. Being Catholic never stopped the Montinis from being patriotic Italians.[1] Grandfather Lodovico caught pneumonia during a strenuous round of mountain visits and died on 4 December 1871.[2]

So Francesca, the grandmother, *la nonna*, remained as the witness and matriarch. Not that she bullied her son or intimidated her daughter-in-law. But she took charge, especially in "feminine" matters like childbirth. Giuditta, she judged, had been weakened by the birth of Battista. So the infant Battista was provided with a wet-nurse, a sturdy thirty-year-old peasant woman with four children of her own, who no doubt needed the money. Clorinda Zanotti lived at Peretti, five miles from Brescia.[3] So Battista spent the first fourteen months of his life in a rustic cottage half way up a hillside, surrounded by vines and chestnut trees. Back home in Brescia he missed his nurse, and she briefly came to stay at via Dante 7.

But he was weaned and survived. The earliest snap shows him on his grandmother's knee, wearing an abundant, frilly collar and a frock. At three and a half, still befrocked, he wears a straw hat against the sun.

1 Swiss historian Victor Conzemius relates that Lodovico Montini, Pope Paul's elder brother, was still enthusiastic for the cause of Italy at the age of ninety. "The entry of Italian troops into Rome through the Porta Pia in 1870," said Conzemius, "saved Vatican I from disaster." "I couldn't agree more (*Sono d'accordissimo*)," Lodovico replied. Lodovico Montini died in the family home at Brescia on 12 February 1990 at the age of ninety-four. A collection of his writings, ranging from 1919 to 1985, shows his commitment to the Catholic movement in Italy and, in the post-war world, the building of the European Community. *Lodovico Montini 1896–1990*, Centro di documentazione, Brescia, 1991.

2 This is what Vian says in *Familiari*, p. vii; but on p. 3 fn. 1, he gives 16 February 1872 as the date of death, and speaks of eight children. One assumes two died in infancy.

3 Ibid. p. xi.

The big ears are the most notable feature.[1] As is the way of things, most of the photographs were taken on holiday and in the country, either at Concesio, his birthplace, or at Verolavecchia, the house where his mother was born and which was her contribution to the family fortunes.

Usually they went to Concesio for Easter and Verolavecchia in the autumn. Giorgio could easily get to Concesio by pony and trap after putting his paper to bed. No matter how late he was Giuditta always waited up for him. Though not grand, the house is substantial. It had been in the family since 1830 when it was bought by Gaetano Montini, the local doctor and Battista's great-great-grandfather. The garden stretches to the foot of a steep hill covered with aromatic pines.

Battista had two very precise memories of Concesio. He remembered the mottoes on the clock-tower of the village church. "Time is gold for eternity," it warns, and on the other side, "Every hour is a gift from God." The clock still peals every quarter of an hour, even though the old church is now converted into apartments. The Montinis helped build the new church nearby in 1928.

Battista's other memory of Concesio was of the children of his father's tenants. He was always ready to share a dish of *polenta* with them and they remained his friends. Thirty years later on a visit to France he looked up Gabriele Gregori who was working as a barber in Versailles.[2] Others had emigrated to Australia but stayed in touch. He had his roots in Concesio.

By contrast his mother's property at Verolavecchia, known as "Il Dosso", was more suited to study and convalescence. It was thirty kilometres south-west of Brescia on the railway line to Cremona (the station is confusingly called Verolanuova). "This wonderful place of rest and recreation during the summer season" (as he called it in 1963)[3] was gently hilly and watered by two streams. The caretaker was an old peasant who kindled the imagination with droll, fantastic tales about royal palaces.[4] His mother loved it because she could show her three boys – Francesco had been born on 22 September 1900 – the hidden wayside shrines she had known as a little girl.

But to escape the heat of August they took refuge in the mountains to the north. This was a return to the family origins. For some time in the fifteenth century the Montinis came down from Valsabbia (or possibly Savallese) in the Alps to the plain and city below. Their name at this point was Benedetti or de Benedictis, which shows they were close to

1 Fappani-Molinari, *Montini Giovane*, between pp. 128 and 129.

2 *Familiari*, p. 645.

3 Ibid. p. 12.

4 Ibid. p. xiii.

some monastic foundation. Montini was a nickname that stuck. They remained the people from the mountains.[1]

The mountains and the foothills, the city and the plain summed up the four features of the province that Brescians, whatever their political views, never tire of extolling. Bounded to east and west by Lakes Garda and Iseo, to the north by the rich dairylands of the Alps and the south by the fertile Po valley, it seems a miracle of diversity reconciled. "Geography," wrote the anti-clerical Giuseppe Zarnadelli in 1857, "inclined Brescia to an idyllic self-sufficiency."[2] In truth its industrial wealth since the Renaissance had been based on steel, arms and armour. In 1981 Lodovico Montini echoed Zarnadelli, adding that the province of Brescia was a microcosm of Italy. In 1992 Brescia was still regarded as the political barometer of Italy.

From 1901 onwards the Montini spent their summers at Pezzoro high up in Val Trompia. Giorgio had other things in mind besides walks among the pine forests. He had been campaigning for a statue of Our Saviour on the two thousand metre high summit of Monte Guglielmo.[3] It was inaugurated in August 1902. Battista, nearly five, was carried up the mountain on tough peasant shoulders. His name was in the papers for the first time: with his brother Lodovico he served the bishop's Mass.[4]

By putting up their statue the Catholics of Lombardy sought to consecrate the new century to Christ. They wanted to say goodbye to the glum nineteenth century and start afresh. Their optimism was shared by Barnabite Fr Giovanni Semeria, the most celebrated preacher of the day. A friend of all the leading "modernists", including Baron Friedrich von Hügel, he greeted the twentieth century as the dawn of the new age in which science and religion would work in harmony, and Italian Catholics would contribute to social and political life.

Fr Semeria was brought along to say just that. For it was exactly the policy Giorgio pursued in *Il Cittadino di Brescia*. He expressed it in the formula *prepararsi coll'astensione*: Italian Catholics, excluded from national politics by the papal *non expedit* which said they should be "neither electors nor elected", should actively prepare for their return from political exile. When the time came they would be knowledgeable, competent and ready.

In the summer of 1902 they felt they were nearly there. Optimism was in order in the last years of Leo XIII, the pope who had opened the

1 *Anni e Opere*, 1978, p. 5.

2 Quoted in Alice A. Kelikian, *Town and Country under Fascism*, 1986, p. 7.

3 *Familiari*, p. xiii.

4 Fappani-Molinari, *Montini Giovane*, p. 39.

Vatican archives and said that the Church had nothing to fear from truth. Leo XIII was an old man who rejuvenated the Church. The election of Cardinal Sarto, Patriarch of Venice, in 1903 was a blow to these hopes. Pius X would return to the policies of Pio Nono. The novelist Antonio Fogazzaro noted: "In my opinion the people happiest with the new Pope are the anticlerical Zarnadelli and his crew; and outside politics all those who find an enlightened Catholicism harder to oppose."[1]

But Battista had other things on his mind in autumn 1903. He was six and starting school. He went to the Jesuits at the Collegio "Cesare Arici". He appears in his first school photograph in his black *grembulie* or apron, arms folded and sitting next to Andrea Trebeschi, who, eleven years later, became his best friend. But at the time Lionello Nardini was his *amico di cuore* – an expression Italians find natural.[2]

It was inevitable that Battista should go to school with the Jesuits. For Giorgio had campaigned for the right of Catholics to set up private schools in Brescia, and helped Giuseppe Tovini found Arici (as it was usually known) in 1888. It was a battle he had to win twice, for the school was closed down on government orders and reopened again only after public pressure in 1894.[3] Giorgio sent his three sons there as a matter of principle. Anyway, it was handy: from 1899 they lived at via Trieste 37, in the same street as the school and just two minutes away. Battista could see it from his bedroom window.

Primary school hours were from 9 to midday, and 2 to 4. Battista was a particularly "spirited" child (*vivace*) and was ordered to sit in front so he could be supervised more closely. He met few Jesuits at this stage: laymen and women taught the younger children. One of them, Ezechiele Malizia, lived long enough to see his old pupil become Pope and, at well over ninety, gave an interview inevitably entitled "How I taught the Pope to read".[4] Anyone unfortunate enough to be called Malizia would have been mercilessly ragged by the "spirited" Battista.

Home was a more important influence than school. It was the "nest", and Battista calls it that until well into his twenties. It was an open, welcoming household. Grandmother Francesca was constantly crying, "Lay another place at table," as an unexpected guest – they tended to be clerics, lawyers, politicians or writers – arrived. If she was out sampling sermons, her favourite occupation, Giorgio's unmarried sister Maria (1872–1951) provided an alternative, more soothing feminine presence.

Family discipline was strict though not harsh, punishments few but

1 Donatella and Leone Piccioni, *Fogazzaro*, p. 376.

2 Fappani-Molinari, *Montini Giovane*, p. 54.

3 *Anni e Opere*, p. 11.

4 Ibid.

irrevocable. Battista learned the habit of caution. At the holiday homes the children were allowed to pick only a stated number of fruits: Battista always took one less to be on the safe side. The severest sanction was that Giuditta withheld her goodnight kiss, the only one of the day.[1] Nello Vian uses this example to illustrate the undemonstrative self-restraint (*contengo*) of the Montini family. It is also reminiscent of the fate of the young Marcel Proust, except that his mother *forgot* the goodnight kiss when she had guests.

The going to bed routine was rigid. Before setting off to *Il Cittadino*, Giorgio would stretch the boys' imagination by reading them Jules Verne or Sir Walter Scott.[2] Giuditta read to Battista in French, in which he was at ease from an early age. Grandmother Francesca read Cardinal Nicholas Wiseman's *Fabiola or the Church of the Catacombs*, which had a great success in Italy, running through six editions before 1860.[3]

But that was a special treat in preparation for his first visit to Rome in April 1907 and his first communion on 6 June of the same year. Francesca had a hand in both events. She saw the visit to Rome as the continuation of a family tradition. For in June 1871 she had gone with her husband and young Giorgio to see Pope Pius IX.[4] It was within eight months of the breach of Porta Pia and the final collapse of the Papal States, yet Pio Nono cheerfully remarked to the eleven-year-old Giorgio: "So my little member of parliament is here as well."[5] This was regarded as a "prophetic" remark.

However it had not yet been fulfilled by 1907 when Giorgio took his wife, mother, sister and three boys to Rome for a private audience with Pope Pius X. They had a very precise purpose. Giorgio had helped prepare the centenary celebrations of St Angela Merici, canonized by Pius VII in 1807.[6] There was more to this event than met the eye.

For although St Angela was regarded as the Foundress of the Ursulines, one of the largest women's teaching orders, her original intention had not been to start another religious order but an association of laywomen living in the world and earning their own living. Canon lawyers drove them back into the enclosure. In 1866 two sisters, Maddalena and Elisabetta Girelli, revived the original plan and founded in Brescia the Company of St Angela. Grandmother Francesca

1 *Familiari*, p. 12.
2 Ibid. p. xii.
3 Ibid. p. 55.
4 Ibid. p. vii.
5 Fappani-Molinari, *Montini Giovane*, p. 48.
6 Ibid. p. 49.

had been at school with the Girelli sisters and remained close to them.[1] Pius X did not seem very interested in St Angela.

He had more urgent matters on his mind in 1907 – the year in which the errors of "modernism" were condemned in *Lamentabili* and *Pascendi*. But because these were "sensitive" topics Giorgio tactfully steered the conversation towards the deplorable state of the Church in France – he read *La revue des deux mondes* – where the religious orders had been suppressed. Thus it was just possible to portray Pius X in 1907 in the same light as Pius IX in 1871: the hapless victim of an unjust world.

To mark the continuity Francesca went to pray at the tomb of Pio Nono at San Lorenzo outside the walls. She begged that "the blessing which came down on their daddy (*babbo*) when he was orphaned at eleven, a blessing that had brought fruits beyond all expectations and made him a model of civic and religious virtue", might now descend upon Lodovico, Battista and Francesco.[2] Francesca and all the Montinis believed in the efficacy of papal blessings. It was part of their concept of the office as one of universal paternity.

However, Battista's memory of his first visit to Rome was disappointing and vague. He says nothing about the pope, and laments the tumble-down state of the basilica of St Mary Major. But he had acquired a taste for rail travel – on the way down they stopped at Florence and Siena – and did not dispute his grandfather's maxim as reported by Giorgio: "The Montinis love the smell of axle-grease."[3]

Back in Brescia he and Lodovico were prepared for their first communion by the Company of St Angela. He did not forget this. One of his first Masses after ordination in 1920 was said in and for the Girelli household.[4] In 1971 when they had been turned into a new-fangled "secular institute" he told the members of the Company of St Angela (he preferred the old name) that they were the "deaconesses of our time".[5]

The two boys were confirmed in the afternoon of the same day in the chapel of the Jesuit college. Francesca penned an edifying note for them to keep: "May society, which needs outspoken and sincere Catholics even for its material prosperity, find you always prepared for the struggles to preserve intact the faith you have received. You have the

1 *Familiari*, pp. 196–97.

2 Fappani-Molinari, *Montini Giovane*, p. 49.

3 Ibid. p. 48.

4 *Familiari*, p. 197.

5 22 September 1971. Here after *Voce*, autumn 1972, p. 10; I am indebted to Dr Dorothy Latz for this reference.

good fortune to have the best of fathers: always follow his example."[1] She was thinking of a vocation "in the world".

Then the Montinis moved house for the last time. Tradition said the house in via Trieste had once been a hospital; some thought their new home at via Grazie 17, with its ten green-shuttered windows, had the air of a convent. It has an enchanting courtyard garden and was then in a tranquil part of the city. But its main advantage was that it lay just across the street from Santa Maria delle Grazie, Brescia's most famous shrine. It had been founded by Bishop Berardo on 8 September 1290, was given the baroque treatment in the sixteenth century, and had been tended by religious orders who made a habit of being suppressed: the Gerolamini in 1668 and the Jesuits in 1773. Giorgio insisted that all his sons should be present every year for the feast of Our Lady's birthday. Battista naturally said his first Mass there.

The move to via delle Grazie also brought them closer to the Oratorians who looked after the church of Santa Maria della Pace. Oratorians in Italy are usually called Filippini (after their founder, St Philip Neri), but in Brescia they were known simply as "the fathers of Peace" (*Padri della Pace*). The Oratory was as characteristic of Brescia as the Trevi Fountain of Rome.[2] They were both eighteenth-century creations.

La Pace provided an intellectual and sporting centre for the boys and young men of the city. It became the second home of the Montini children, their innumerable cousins and their school friends. Much fierce, sweaty football was played in too confined a space, on too small a pitch. La Pace's essential function was to give them a deeper and more articulated view of Christian faith. Lodovico Montini said: "At La Pace we found a virile Christianity, without sentimental escapism, hypocrisy or calculation, a Christianity of which one could be proud, that could be professed without either triumphalism or inferiority complex."[3]

It was the Christianity, he adds, of their grandmother and parents.

It is hard to avoid the suspicion that Lodovico was contrasting this robust version of Christianity with what was available at their Jesuit college. He says as much when he explains that "the educational approaches of La Pace and Arici were notably different, and we used to have heated discussions about this".[4]

Though Battista remained in the Sodality of Our Lady at Arici and held high office in it, Jesuit piety in the restored Society remained rather

1 Fappani-Molinari, *Montini Giovane*, p. 48.

2 Ibid. p. 48.

3 Ibid. p. 76.

4 Ibid.

formal and systematic, a matter of leaping through a series of hoops. There were duties for every day, every week, every month. Virtues were carved up and handed round: purity this month, next month humility. We will make sure we have all the "approved" devotions to the Sacred Heart and Our Lady of Sorrows. Even the "charity" Battista learned in the Sodality remained rather self-conscious: at Christmas time these sons of the bourgeoisie served a Christmas dinner for forty poor old men. Battista preached his first trial sermonettes in the Sodality Chapel, and was described as "the soul" of the Sodality when he eventually left it in 1917.[1] Yet when he felt the need for a spiritual director he turned to the Oratorians.

This was partly a matter of individual availability. *Nonna* Francesca came back from La Pace one day and announced that a remarkable new priest had arrived. His name was Giulio Bevilacqua. Born in the Verona province in 1881, he was impulsive and unconventional. He disliked learning not backed up by experience. He recounted with glee how, after one exam, he had thrown all his useless school manuals into the river Adige.[2] He had a doctorate in social sciences from the University of Louvain in Belgium on Italian Law and the Workers. He already saw the link between the Church's social teaching and the liturgy, and over the years made La Pace in Brescia the model for parish liturgy. His Latin remained approximate rather than accurate, but that didn't matter. He joined the Oratorians because he admired their freedom of spirit.

Bevilacqua constantly extended Battista's cultural and intellectual horizons. He taught him to look for the signs of the Holy Spirit in the modern world. He remained the "master and friend", as Paul VI put it when making him a cardinal in 1965. The old man accepted the honour, but only on condition he could stay on as parish priest in a working-class suburb of Brescia. He is buried in the crypt of La Pace. As a young man he had appeared as a tornado of fresh air in Brescia.

Paolo Caresana, from the Pavia province, was a year younger than Bevilacqua and had a different temperament. He was calm, had a mellow voice and a reassuringly disorderly mop of hair.[3] He had worked as a diocesan priest among the oppressed rice-growers of his province, whose cause he defended. After long, agonizing conversations under the plane trees in the courtyard of La Pace he joined the Oratory in 1912 at the age of thirty. He became Battista's confessor and spiritual director and – so far as circumstances allowed – remained so for life. Not only that but he involved Battista in all his varied apostolic works, and later, when

1 Ibid. p. 73.

2 *Familiari*, p. xi.

3 Ibid. p. xv.

war broke out, employed him as his unofficial, unpaid secretary.[1] The extent of his influence on Battista will never be fully measured because the relationship was confidential. Judging by results, it was deep and real. He too lived to see his protégé become pope, dying in 1973.

But this makes the Oratorians sound altogether too solemn. Bevilacqua and Caresana – there were others too – were young and fun. They shared Battista's passion for cycling, the sport he most enjoyed. In 1912 when he was fourteen he "inaugurated" a new bike[2] by riding sixty kilometres, mostly uphill, to Bagolino. This epic ride alarmed Giuditta, and nearly killed him. In 1915 Bevilacqua cycled with Battista and Lodovico to Verolavecchia, not a comparable feat but still a respectable performance. Battista felt the need, typically, to rationalize his passion. Cycling was "a symbol of romance and idealism . . . because it involves risk, ardour, abnegation and fraternity".[3]

But cycling priests were a rarity and they were often suspected of "modernism". The austere Jesuits of the Arici College did not indulge. Nor did they approve of the Oratorian openness to friendship, being keenly aware of the perils of "particular friendships".

At home Lodovico and Battista were increasingly being drawn into adult conversations – as listeners. One of their most regular visitors was Giovanni Maria Longinotti, a colleague of Giorgio's on *Il Cittadino*. A chemist from Parma University, he led the Catholic trade union movement, setting up worker and consumer co-operatives and welfare and insurance societies.[4] This was the "social Catholicism" the Oratorians also defended. Longinotti – he was usually known in the Montini family as Signor Nì[5] – was one of the first Catholics to enter Parliament in 1909 when the *non expedit* was allowed to lapse because Pius X feared an upsurge of socialism.

In May 1911 Signor Nì was due to make an important speech in Parliament on freedom of organization and workers' councils. He wanted to try it out on some real farm workers first. Giorgio invited him to Verolavecchia where Battista was convalescing – he spent his time hunting crickets and designing a kite which actually worked. But he enjoyed the adult company and Giorgio wrote to Giuditta: "Battista has been an excellent companion here, and has done the honours of the house as a fine little fellow."[6] He was also beginning to join in grown-up

1 Ibid. p. 66.

2 He still remembered in 1972 that it was a Bianchi, in 1912 the very latest thing.

3 Fappani-Molinari, *Montini Giovane*, p. 50.

4 Ibid. p. 37.

5 *Familiari*, p. 72.

6 Fappani-Molinari, *Montini Giovane*, p. 53.

talk. Lodovico says that Battista always preferred to be last in any discussion. He would listen, and then sum up.

Summing up the respective influence of his parents many years later, Battista claimed that to Giorgio he owed "the example of courage . . . My father did not know fear. His whole life can be put in a word: be a witness." Of Giuditta he said: "To her I owe the sense of recollection, of the interior life, of meditation that is prayer, of prayer that is meditation. All her life was a gift. To the love of my father and mother I owe the love of God and the love of people."[1]

Giorgio tended to overshadow Giuditta. He was a journalist "of the old school".[2] But old-fashioned as he was Giorgio responded to events as they happened, treated opponents with respect and remained unfailingly courteous despite provocation. There was a lot of Giorgio in Battista. Giuditta has remained characteristically in the background. She translated French romantic novels as fillers for the paper, conferring with Don Defendente Salvetti, her spiritual director and chaplain to *Il Cittadino di Brescia*. She shrank from a public role but placed great confidence in the guidance of the Holy Spirit. There was a lot of Giuditta in Battista.

So that is what happens when lovers meet on the steps of St Peter's.

1 Ibid. p. 15, quoting Jean Guitton.

2 Paul VI admitted as much in his first address to journalists, 29 June 1963, *Anni e Opere*, p. 8.

2

The First Best Friend

> An optimal sense of identity . . . is experienced as a sense of psychosocial well-being. Its most obvious concomitants are a feeling of being at home in one's body, a sense of "knowing where one is going", and an inner assuredness of anticipated recognition from those who count.
>
> (ERIK H. ERIKSON, *Identity, Youth and Crisis*, p. 165)

Giorgio and Giuditta decided in the summer of 1914 that Battista should leave the Jesuit college of Arici for health reasons and finish his education privately, taking his exams at the state high school, Arnaldo da Brescia.[1]. That meant he would be parted from his newly-rediscovered friend, Andrea Trebeschi. Andrea invited him to write a page in his diary, a singular intimacy. Underneath, Andrea wrote:

> Battista Montini, my good friend, wrote this memento in my book. What a wonderful soul he has! What an example his life is, inspired entirely by the good; what a precious and dear warning is conveyed in his words! He is offering his life to God: *he is going to be a priest*. We will always be friends.[2]

It was St Andrew's day, 30 November 1914. They had both just turned seventeen. There was a war on but elsewhere. Apart from confessors it was the first time Battista had revealed that he would be a priest. Like a declaration of love, which in effect it was, this "avowal" marks an important stage in a vocation: no turning back once you are committed. Keep your hands to the plough. Demand the "grace of perseverance".

Battista's call to the priesthood was no surprise, but neither was it inevitable. In childhood he had no such thoughts and never claimed he had "always wanted to be a priest". Proof was to hand. One September evening the three Montini boys were cavorting in the square outside the

1 *Anni e Opere*, p. 13.

2 G. Battista Montini, *Lettere a un giovane amico*, 1978, p. 23.

church of San Rocco while Giorgio said his Rosary within. As he came out a group of seminarians passed by. The curate introduced them to Giorgio as "the future hope of the Church".

Giorgio gathered his sons about him: "Look," said the distinguished editor of *Il Cittadino di Brescia*, "these young men are going to be priests. Would any of you like to be a priest?"

"Not me," said Lodovico.

"Not me," echoed Battista.

"Not me either," Francesco piped up.[1]

Grandmother Francesca's constant exhortations to the boys all implied a vocation "in the world". Her spirituality was based on St Francis de Sales who stated clearly in the Preface to his *Introduction to the Devout Life*: "My purpose is to instruct those who live in towns, within families, or at court, and by their ordinary state of life are obliged to live an ordinary life as to outward appearances."[2]

That is what she envisaged for her grandsons; and in fact Francesco emulated his grandmother's husband by becoming a doctor, while Lodovico followed more directly in Giorgio's footsteps as far as the changed political situation allowed. Battista alone was the sore thumb, departing from the family tradition of medicine or public service.

He had dreams of becoming a writer. In his Easter greeting to his parents in 1907 he announced that "from now on I am going to 'do a Vittorio Alfieri' ".[3] This was an odd remark from a budding first communicant. For Vittorio Alfieri (1749–1803) was an Enlightenment author who derided confession, pooh-poohed clerical celibacy and denied the immortality of the soul.[4]

One of Battista's school essays in 1911 was on patriotism. At fourteen years of age he wrote:

> What shall I do for the *Patria*? *Patria*! How sweet is the name *Patria* to those who love her! And I love her, love Italy, love her more than anything else in the world; more than my own life! More than my own life, I repeat, because if one day, beset by threatening enemies, she should ask her sons to defend her, I would hasten under her noble banner to help her, save her, make her feared, make her triumph, at the cost of any sacrifice, any fatigue, any travail, and even of my very life. But Italy needs not only the arms of her sons: she needs their virtue,

1 Fappani-Molinari, *Montini Giovane*, p. 134.

2 St Francis de Sales, *Introduction to the Devout Life*, tr. and ed. John K. Ryan, p. 33.

3 *Familiari*, p. 997; Vian, p. xv, for its supposed significance.

4 Giovanni Fallani, *Letteratura Religiosa Italiana*, p. 79.

> their culture. Italy has been formed, said a great patriot, now we have to form Italians.[1]

This effusion continues for another two paragraphs. It would not rank in an anthology of Montini's finest prose. The point, however, is that though ready to die for his *Patria*, Battista expects to stay alive and serve her not with the sword but "with the pen".

He had to be modest in his aims. For with the onset of adolescence came the knowledge that he was an invalid. During a strenuous cycle ride with his brother Lodovico he suffered a minor stroke or heart flutter (*stretta di cuore*) that left him gasping for breath by the side of the road, looking deathly. "Your boy is suffering from a rather serious cardiac imbalance (*scompenso*)," the doctor told Giuditta, "he will have to take things easy."[2]

The weakness remained, aggravated from time to time by gastric and throat troubles. He spent more and more time off school. In 1911 he was at Verolavecchia for most of April and all of May, and that pattern was repeated in subsequent years. He prepared for exams with private tutors, taking them at the state high school in Chiari in 1913 where, it was whispered, they were less demanding. The natural adolescent question, what *shall* I do with my life? merged with another: what *can* I do with my life?

This was when the idea of the priesthood began to crystallize. Battista later confessed that these long periods of enforced solitude were more fruitful than any regular course of study could have been.[3] And he told Guitton that when he was ordained in 1920, "I didn't have much hope of a long life. I was so ill."[4] Part of the reason he became a priest was that, whatever he may have thought at fourteen, by sixteen he did not expect to live long.

Giorgio was one of the first to guess what was preoccupying his second son. But he did not put pressure either way. When Battista made a retreat at the Oratorian house of San Antonio in September 1913 Giorgio wrote:

> Dearest Battista
> It seems good, that you should profit from this occasion and open yourself to Padre Caresana about your future; he is the best person to give you advice, and in matters of such importance the advice of sensible and holy people is never without

1 Fappani-Molinari, *Montini Giovane*, pp. 58–59.

2 Ibid. p. 53.

3 *Familiari*, p. xvi.

4 *Notiziario*, 9, p. 8.

value. So I leave you completely free to decide what you will.
And may the Lord inspire, keep and bless you.[1]

Padre Caresana was equally non-directive. He was confessor not only to Battista but also to his soul-mate Andrea Trebeschi. No doubt he saw the faith-potential of their friendship.

There was another key factor in Battista's vocation. In 1910 the Benedictine monks of Sainte-Madeleine, Marseilles, expelled from France, were made welcome in Chiari, a not too difficult bicycle ride to the west of Brescia.[2] They had the use of the old Franciscan convent of San Bernadino which belonged to the Menna family. Msgr Domenico Menna was a friend of the Montinis and later Battista's professor of canon law at the Brescia seminary.

The solemn inauguration of the new Abbey on 10 July 1910 was a great event. Giorgio celebrated at length in *Il Cittadino di Brescia*. Welcoming the exiled French monks was a political act: they had taken refuge from a "Godless" regime and their reception proved that, despite the unresolved "Roman Question", Italy was both "more liberal" and "more Catholic" than France.[3]

Battista's interest in the exiled monks was different. Though the cradle of the Benedictines was in Italy, at Subiaco and Monte Cassino, their nineteenth-century revival was largely the work of French monks. The first-phase "liturgical movement" was monastic in character. It was inspired by Dom Prosper Guéranger's *l'Année liturgique* and the alleged rediscovery of the original rhythms of plainsong by the monks of Solesmes. Battista often went to Chiari, especially for Compline, sung by heart in a chapel darkened except for the candles before the Lady statue.

Montini still remembered this in 1973 when he told the Benedictine Abbots gathered in Rome: "I was in ecstasy: it was no doubt there that God planted in my heart the first desire of a life consecrated to his service."[4]

He wanted to become a Benedictine monk at Chiari. But the Abbot and Dom Denys Buenner, his confessor, dissuaded him: he did not have the strength to cope with the rigours of monastic life, and they could not molly-coddle a passenger. But they must keep in touch, and there would always be a room for him in the guest-house. The organist Dom Jules Jannin sent him his edition of *Mélodies Syriennes et Chaldéennes*

1 *Familiari*, pp. xv–xvi.

2 Ibid. p. 5.

3 *Notiziario*, 9, p. 7.

4 Ibid. p. 8.

when it appeared in 1921. These were songs in the language closest to Jesus' own language. So they had talked music before then – Battista was a passable pianist until he went to Rome and was forced to give it up.

Syrian and Chaldean melodies on the tinkling piano might seem self-indulgent as the First World War broke out in August 1914. Yet Battista and Andrea, still intent on their friendship, seemed oblivious to it. It was still possible to retreat into the private world. Andrea's diary for 9 October 1914 records their reunion:

> I've finished my exams, and hope for a good result. Now I am writing to my good friend, Battista Montini: we were together in the first two classes of the primary school and then we were cut off from each other although we used to say hello; now we have come together again, and I hope our friendship will last for ever; he is so good and intelligent.[1]

So Andrea made the first move. But it was as though Battista were waiting for him. He replied from Verolavecchia on 29 October 1914:

> Dearest Andrea
> I rejoice in your news and am glad that you are happy with your studies at Arici. Dearest, I've been wondering if your friendship will continue . . . Why not? Since your ideals of goodness and the apostolate are the same as mine, since our life within the family and outside it coincides with my ideals, why not walk the same road together and give each other a helping hand? All the more since through special circumstances the Lord has raised the simple awareness of childhood to the level of friendship? Dearest, I beg you, continue this friendship which has opened up for me, so withdrawn and alone, a living ray of goodness and a holy example.[2]

Mawkish, adolescent, embarrassing? But to censor it out would be to miss an essential aspect of the young Montini: he knew the need of love, took the risk of love, was passionate and deeply vulnerable. Friendship pulled him out of himself. Without some such experience it is difficult to know what God's love means.

Nor were they just gazing fondly into each other's eyes. This first letter is brimful of literary projects for a little magazine. One of Andrea's Jesuit teachers will write an eloquent introduction, Andrea himself will explain how the project came about, another friend will do theatre

1 Battista Montini, *Lettere a un giovane amico*, p. 12.
2 Ibid. p. 17.

reviews while Don Francesco Galloni will do a press review. And Battista? He shyly offers "a short story or a sketch" (*novella o bozzetto*). His cousin Lodovico Uberti would do the photographs.[1] It soon came unstuck and the little magazine, *Numero Unico*, proved aptly named.

Battista's life was like that: bursts of intense activity followed by periods of extreme inertia. He liked Lacordaire's maxim: "If only we knew how to waste time opportunely."[2] His enforced indolence disposed him towards an experience that is quite common in adolescence. It came while contemplating the stars at Verolavecchia.

He described it in the text he wrote for Andrea Trebeschi's diary in November 1914:

> I was out walking one night and as I looked up at the stars became aware of the hugeness of creation: and I understood that all the heavenly bodies themselves were mere specks of dust compared with the immensity of space; human thought is confined within this world which seems so vast to us and yet is a microscopic atom compared with the stars and space; and seeing above me thousands of unknown worlds representing beauty and fantastic prospects so greatly superior to anything to hand in this world, I felt a vivid longing for a happiness not tied to the wretched clay of this earth.

But this yearning for a happiness beyond this world, for a heaven beyond the heavens, did not make him disdain the everyday human realities. On the contrary:

> The prose of human life seemed to me more intense as I looked about me . . . Then there came to mind the long story of love and sorrow: the Redemption. I understood that this is the way, the truth and the life . . . And the prospect of suffering and humiliation that human wretchedness has to bear, and that would leave deep and lacerating traces in me, no longer seemed so horrible and monstrous, since it brought me face to face with the Martyr of Calvary who remains holy, calm and desirable despite the sorrow and the scorn.[3]

Unlike the young Angelo Giuseppe Roncalli, Battista Montini did not keep a private journal of his soul-states. If he wanted to express his deepest thoughts, he wrote to a friend.

His priestly vocation did not come about in a vacuum. Apart from

1 Ibid. pp. 17–18.

2 *Notiziario*, 8, p. 9.

3 Montini, *Lettere a un giovane amico*, pp. 21–23.

Andrea Trebeschi, he also confided in his earliest school friend, Lionello Nardini, now about to enter the seminary and thus become another "elder brother in the Christian life".[1] But the war could not for ever be kept at bay.

1 *Familiari*, p. xviii.

3

The Mysterious Call

> I firmly believe that our works are born in us before we are aware of them, and lie there fermenting in darkness until they come to maturity later in life.
>
> (Antonio Fogazzaro in an interview with Renato Simoni, quoted in *Il Santo*, Mondadori edn, p. 22)

The world had not been standing still while Battista wrestled with his call and decided to be a priest. What contemporaries called the Great War broke out that very August. Pius X died on 20 August. His successor, Giacomo della Chiesa, Archbishop of Bologna, belonged to one of the oldest families in Italy. Consciously breaking with recent tradition, he chose the name Benedict to show he was a man of peace.

Benedict XV made it clear from his first encyclical, *Ad Beatissimi*, that his main aim was to put a stop to the anti-Modernist campaign his predecessor, Pius X, had encouraged. But the war filled the horizon of his pontificate and diverted him to other ends. He worked hard to keep Italy neutral, not only because popes are generally for peace and Austria-Hungary was the leading "Catholic" power, but because he feared for the autonomy of the Holy See in a war-torn Italy.[1] He had some success. Italy remained neutral until May 1915. But people could talk of nothing but the war. God's call to Battista risked being drowned out by the call to arms.

The Montini family discussed these grave issues. But there is little trace of it in Battista's letters. In August 1914 Grandmother Francesca was all agog over the arrival of a new curate at Concesio. Don Francesco Galloni was twenty-four and freshly ordained.[2]

He was full of plans. He was going to build an oratory and make contact with the young people in the outlying villages. Battista thought

1 Christopher Seton-Watson, *Italy from Liberalism to Fascism*, p. 437.

2 Fappani-Molinari, *Montini Giovane*, p. 84, ordain him on 4 August 1914, while *Notiziario*, 8, p. 7, says that "by August he had been ordained for over a month". Not that it matters.

this a wonderful idea. Grandmother Francesca, an authority on clerics, summoned Don Galloni to run the rule over him. He found her reading St Francis de Sales in the garden. She explained that she kept her name-day twice, once on the feast of St Francis de Sales himself, and again on the feast of St Jeanne-Françoise de Freymot de Chantal, the Philothée for whom the *Introduction to the Devout Life* was written. Could he be her St Francis de Sales?

Don Francesco was not quite on that level. But he satisfied her. So much so that she "adopted" him as her "twenty-second Godchild". With Giorgio calling him "my fourth son", Don Francesco Galloni soon became an honorary member of the Montini family, welcome to stay at via delle Grazie 17 whenever he liked.

But though Don Galloni delighted the grandmother and Giorgio, he made the greatest impression on Battista. For this curate was no country bumpkin. He was an authority on Alessandro Manzoni, the nineteenth-century Italian novelist, and had tramped around all the sites associated with *I Promessi Sposi* between Lecco and the river Adda.[1]

This keen sense of place led him much later to make Antonio Fogazzaro's villa, La Montanina at Velo d'Astico, the centre for the ecumenical work, *Pro Oriente*, which he later founded.[2] For Battista it was a joy to discover a priest barely older than himself who was zealous, cultivated and pious. When they parted Galloni inscribed a copy of *Lettres aux Jeunes* by Henri-Dominique Lacordaire, the restorer of the Dominicans in France after the Revolution.

In his thank you letter Battista says he regards Don Galloni as "a wonderful elder brother, who has already passed his first test".[3] He now had another priestly role-model.

Throughout the winter of 1914–15 a "great debate" raged in Italy between "interventionists" and "neutralists". Giorgio, as a newspaper editor, could not afford Battista's luxury of silence. Mostly he took the common Catholic line – if so wobbly a position can be called a line – defended by his friends Filippo Meda, Member of Parliament since 1909, and Count Giuseppe Dalla Torre, President of the Unione Popolare, a pre-political Catholic group.

They argued for neutrality – *provided* Austria recognized Italian interests by ceding the province of Trentino and the right bank of the river Isonzo. "Thus," as Christopher Seton-Watson remarks, "while

1 *Notiziario*, 8, p. 8. Archibald Colquhoun, introducing *I Promessi Sposi*, said it was "not only the first modern Italian novel; for Italy it is all Scott, Dickens and Thackeray rolled into one". *The Betrothed*, Dent, London 1951, p. 575.

2 *Familiari*, p. 7.

3 *Notiziario*, 9, p. 8. Letter dated 1 October 1914.

continuing to oppose war, they left themselves a door open, and showed that they would not blindly follow the Vatican's lead."[1]

This satisfied neither the nationalists who wanted war to prove Italian virility nor the Futurist artists who announced from their armchairs that "war is hygiene" nor the socialists who wanted no part in a conflict that could only reinforce the monarchy, capitalism and militarism. The Catholics were too warlike for the socialists, too unheroic for the nationalists, and irrelevant for the artists. But their compromise served its purpose. They neither wanted nor sought war, but if it came they would not be lacking in patriotism.

Giorgio hedged his bets. On 15 May 1915, with war only a week away, *Il Cittadino di Brescia* ran two pieces on the subject: a front page editorial urged participation, while a page two feature praised peace.[2]

Too late! Italy was at war with Austria – though not, oddly, with Germany. Brescia was within forty miles of the border with Trentino, and the boom of big guns was heard in the city. The Italians had to fight a literally uphill battle almost all the way along the S-shaped 400-mile front. Gains were small and costly. The Oratorian retreat house of San Antonio, where Battista had made his annual retreat since 1913, became a military hospital.[3] Soon La Pace also housed the wounded.

Uniforms were everywhere. Andrea's elder brother, Giovanni, was called up.[4] Lodovico awaited his turn. There was no clerical exemption. Don Francesco Galloni enlisted in the 5th Alpine Regiment, which caused nervous mirth in the Montini family. Giorgio, "while praising his martial bearing, did not find him at all intimidating".[5] As the Duke of Wellington said of his troops: "They may not scare the enemy but, by God, they scare me."

Partly to say farewell to Don Galloni, Battista thought of making a retreat with him at a very special place he had come across in his Manzoni studies: the Camaldonese hermitage of San Genesio tucked away among the Brianza mountains. Padre Caresana, who needed a break and was also the spiritual director of Galloni, joined them. This retreat in August 1915 is one of the best documented in Battista's early life.

They had a hard time getting there. There was no transport from Lecco and they had to climb the last stage, "carefully trying to eke out the half-litre of generous wine," as Battista reported to Andrea.[6] When

1 *Italy from Liberalism to Fascism*, p. 438.

2 Alice A. Kelikian, *Town and Country under Fascism*, p. 43.

3 Fappani-Molinari, *Montini Giovane*, p. 139.

4 Montini, *Giovane amico*, p. 27.

5 *Notiziario*, 8, p. 10.

6 Montini, *Giovane amico*,. p. 27.

they knocked on the door of the Hermitage they got a chilly reception from the Polish monks. The two priests could stay, but the enclosure was off-limits to a mere layman. Galloni got the porter, Padre Matteo, to consult his superior who decreed that the young layman could at least sleep in the woodshed. That was Galloni's version many years later.[1]

Battista's contemporary letters to his mother and grandmother tell a different story. The monks were technically aliens – those from Galicia in Austrian Poland *enemy* aliens. They were not allowed to receive strangers without permission of the mayor of Cagliano, the neighbouring village; and they had only one spare room anyway. So the visitors spent the night in the village and next day persuaded the mayor to let two of them stay there longer. Battista is very clear: "Only one could stay with the brothers."[2]

Was the woodshed episode invented? Or did Battista suppress it so as not to alarm his grandmother? Whatever happened there can be no doubt that the retreat in the mountains was a period of "true joy and zest" (*allegria e brio*), as he wrote to Andrea. Naturally he hopes that "next year", 1916, Andrea will join them: "You will come, won't you? If the *Patria* forgets about us and *rejects* us. Meantime, let's make a plan; we've already got so many; we've got the Rome plan, remember?"[3]

But this was not a time when non-combatants could travel at will. Battista's remark about the *Patria* rejecting them was prompted by his medical inspection, now imminent. He expected to be turned down, and so he was, because of chest weakness and a liability to bronchitis (*insufficienza toracica*).[4]

So he was condemned to live the war by proxy and from a distance. He tries to imagine what barracks life is like, doesn't get very far, and is happy to be reassured by Don Galloni that "no obstacle is strong enough to prevent you leading a priestly life".[5] The eager, naïve patriotism of the essay he wrote at fourteen gave way to a more critical judgement. He wrote to Don Galloni on 28 February 1916:

> We will see each other again. Keep well, and remember us all. May the good Saviour be the gentle bond which unites those who are parted. Writing to his mother Giosué Borsi said that

1 Fappani-Molinari, *Montini Giovane*, p. 140. On 9 December 1968 Pope Paul VI wrote to Msgr Francesco Galloni: "We still remember with emotion and gratitude the panorama of the sites associated with Manzoni, expounded by one who had such a long and spiritual experience of them", *Notiziario*, 8, p. 26.

2 *Familiari*, p. 997, letter of 17 August 1915.

3 Montini, *Giovane amico*, p. 27, from Pian di Borno, 28 September 1915.

4 Fappani-Molinari, *Montini Giovane*, p. 65.

5 *Notiziario*, 8, p. 10.

> spiritual unity is no less real than physical unity; and do we not in fact all lead the same lives? with the same desires? with the same *patria* ahead of us? Oh! how the thought of the earthly *patria* for so many minds hides, veils, changes and relegates into second or third place the future *patria*! How wonderful it would be to unite them both in "practical Christianity". We will see each other again. I am just off to La Pace.[1]

Not a text to appeal to a recruiting sergeant. And *patria* has lost its capital letter.

Battista found the "practical Christianity" he was looking for at La Pace as an aide to Fathers Caresana and Luigi Carli. Carli might have lost his voice but his room became the news- and nerve-centre for a whole generation of Brescians.[2] La Pace could be trusted. It was home to soldiers on leave. Here the casualty lists mounted. So far as exams and health allowed, Battista kept people in touch. In the letter to Don Galloni just quoted he worried about his elder brother:

> Lodovico is still in Turin. He has asked to be sent to the Artillery College, but he hasn't yet been accepted and the gunnery course starts on 1 March. Poor Lodovico! He seems to me a bit disillusioned, a bit out of place, while remaining confident and resigned. The Lord has asked of him a career of sacrifice, and He surely will not fail to help him and those of us who are distressed to see him shunted about from digging trenches to the orderly office, which is in a sort of cow-shed, without a job of serious work in which he could use his talents for the *patria*.[3]

Lodovico was still trying to get into the 16th Artillery Regiment in late July. He begins to fear accusations of "shirking" (*imboscato*). Far from urging him into battle or sending white feathers, Giuditta thanks God this delay keeps him safe from harm.[4]

But war is a cruelly unjust affair, and if anyone was exposed to the charge of "dodging the column" it was Battista rather than Lodovico. Yet he seemed blithely unaware of this. Brescia was to have its first air raid and Ludovico finally joined his regiment,[5] while Battista was intent

1 Ibid. pp. 11–12.

2 Fappani-Molinari, *Montini Giovane*, p. 77.

3 *Notiziario*, 8, p. 11. Dated 28 February 1916.

4 Ibid. p. 12.

5 *Familiari*, p. 999.

on his summer holiday at Viareggio, the Mediterranean resort west of Lucca. He told Don Galloni on 9 July 1916:

> Tomorrow I set off with P. Luigi Carli for Viareggio. I hope to do some sea-bathing. If only I could be properly restored to good health, then I could set off with great energy along the road of duty and sacrifice! . . . I commend myself to the Lord especially during these holidays in which decisions will be taken on which the whole course of my life depends.[1]

Giorgio added a postscript which explains this self-absorption. Though unable to do much close work, Battista had prepared for his final exams alone and been successful. Giorgio goes on: "When one thinks that he couldn't even read newspaper headlines and for two years has been unable to do practically anything, then one sees that his improved health is a miracle. We consider a real grace."[2]

So much depended on this holiday: if proved really fit, then the army would claim him; if not, the Seminary.

So Battista, Padre Carli and four companions set off by train for Viareggio. It was a tough wartime journey with a four-hour wait in Parma. They struggled up the Appenines – the wooden trains hauled up one carriage at a time – but on arrival were rewarded by the sight of "the immense blue of the sea, a feast of light and colour". Viareggio was then the most fashionable Italian resort, one of the first to emulate the English passion for sea-bathing. Its leading hotels, the Prince of Piedmont, the Excelsior and the Grand, were among the most luxurious in Europe. Before the war they had been the haunt of Russian aristocrats celebrated for their drunkenness, gambling and debauchery.

The Carli party settled in the presbytery of St Paulinus' Priory for seven lire a day. The other guests were a young medical student, an artillery sub-lieutenant on leave, and two young priests including a Dominican who was, reports Battista, "very jolly, very fat, and very Florentine".

It was like a school outing. The voiceless Padre Carli woke them up at seven by hurling cushions at them, and roused them again after the siesta by the same method. The horseplay seems sometimes to have got out of hand: Battista's hair was ruined by his cheerful companions, so he had his head shaved and looked like a Buddhist monk.[3] The long walks along the beach and through the pine woods, and "good well-flavoured cooking" were restoring him to health, and he could

1 *Notiziario*, 8, pp. 12–13.

2 Ibid. p. 13.

3 *Familiari*, p. 999. What did they put on his hair? Jam? Honey?

feel it. He had his first swimming lessons, learning at least to float.

He writes enthusiastically to his mother: "You will see how black I have become – I who was always rather dark."[1] When the sun clouded over, a rare event, they played cards.

Padre Carli confirmed to Giuditta the improvement in Battista's health, adding, "I have never seen him so joyful, though his joy has a self-contained quality."[2] He liked it so much that he asked to stay on for another week. Giuditta, noting his return to health with mixed feelings, left the decision to him. He stayed. He was, after all, nearly nineteen.

"We do not forget the war," he wrote on 23 July 1916, "amid the peace we enjoy here."[3] Three days later he said the thought of the troops at the front kept on breaking into their recreations. This was a premonition, for the next day he heard that Andrea Trebeschi's brother, Giovanni, had been killed. He didn't write to Andrea because he didn't know what to say.[4]

But the spell of Viarreggio – the only real holiday he had in his life – was broken. He packed his bags gloomily. It was raining. He would see Andrea on his return to Brescia. Some things are better said than written down.

Yet he did try to write what-can-I-say letters on 29 July and again on 9 August 1916.[5] But it was no good. Andrea was inconsolable. Battista then wrote a "dark night of the soul" letter, a first sketch of his own developed spirituality. He too has known, in his own limited way, the mood of "a despair in which any comfort and any action, internal or external, become a form of torture, in which life seems weighed down beneath a heavy and terrible burden, in which every colour seems black, everything we used to enjoy bitter, and what should sustain us morally crumbles away".

One cannot battle one's way out of such desolation by an act of will, nor should one try.

Battista's advice is just to let go: "What is needed is that we should quietly close our eyes and gently, softly, peacefully, serenely, lovingly abandon ourselves to the current of our sorrow, whatever storms rage within or without us." In other words neither apathy nor revolt nor evasion nor repression can deal with suffering, but only – and maybe not straight away – an act of acceptance. "The secret of all Christianity

1 Fappani-Molinari, *Montini Giovane*, p. 64.

2 Ibid. p. 64.

3 *Familiari*, p. 999.

4 Ibid. p. 1000.

5 Montini, *Giovane amico*, pp. 34–35.

lies here," says Battista: "It does not take away hurt, it explains it, accepts it, takes it on its shoulders and, with Christ's help, bears it."

Then he quotes *The Imitation of Christ*: "Carry your cross, and the cross will carry you." He tries a modern metaphor: "The cross is like an aeroplane that carries us above." He hopes that the meaning of the experience will remain with Andrea all his life long. And he apologises: he did not mean to suggest that he had himself reached these mystical heights. So: "Don't do what I do, do what I say."[1]

Andrea carefully preserved the letter. Did he remember it in his last months in 1944–45 as concentration camps became his stations of the cross: Dachau, Mauthausen, and Gusen where he died on 24 January 1945?[2]

Battista's attempt to console Andrea for the loss of his brother coincided with his final *decision* to enter the seminary. Up to now he had been thinking about it. It seems that he told his father when he was in Rome on political business in September 1916. Giorgio took Battista along, and they were agreeably surprised to be met at the station by an official car which swept them to the Ministry of Finance where Filippo Meda now presided. Signor Nì was also on hand.

The war brought Catholics into the mainstream of public life for the first time since 1870. Within an hour they were at lunch together and installed in the Hotel Minerva, looking out on the elephant on which Sarah Bernhardt once climbed to denounce the hotel as stuffy. (It wouldn't take actresses.) After lunch they prayed at the shrine of St Catherine of Siena in the nearby Dominican church of Santa Maria sopra Minerva. Giorgio reported Battista's decision to Giuditta.[3]

She replied effusively on 16 September 1916: "Let us thank the Lord, yes, let us thank the Lord, and pray that he may make us worthy of the graces he has given us." She returned early from Verolavecchia to get things ready for him. Classes began on 20 October.

But to say Battista "entered the seminary" is rather misleading. By special dispensation of Bishop Giacinto Gaggia he became an "external student" allowed to live and study at home. This was not so much a privilege for the son of a prominent Catholic intellectual as a result of the war. The regular seminary of Sant'Angelo was being used as a storehouse for a military hospital. Classes had to be held at San Cristo at the foot of the castle which dominates Brescia. But fifteen seminarians had been called to the colours and when Battista started there were only five left. In 1917–18 they were reduced to Battista and one other,

1 Ibid. pp. 38–39.

2 Ibid. p. 11.

3 Fappani-Molinari, p. 142.

Giovanni Pelizzari. After that the place filled up again as the soldiers were demobbed. (But Battista never knew the hearty gregariousness of "normal" seminary life.)

On the day his classes began he wrote to Andrea to say that his decision, which made him tremble, would not outwardly change anything in his life, and that he hoped their friendship would endure and grow.[1] It not only survived – it flourished. Battista was also mercifully dispensed from wearing the soutane that was otherwise insisted on in seminaries at that time.

Giorgio, anxious that Battista's freedom should not leave him free-floating, devised a programme that would occupy him usefully from his rising at 7.30 to lights out at 10. His spare time would be devoted to piano practice.[2] But with, in principle, twenty lectures a week to be undergone, there was not a lot of spare time and most of it was devoted to charity.

1916–17 was the cruellest winter of the war. The poor were hardest hit. Battista worked in the *Cucine Economiche* (low-price kitchens – one of his father's enterprises). One witness says that for Battista it involved much more than ladling out soup: "He listened patiently, was interested in their trials and problems, and with a word made them feel they were his brothers in Christ."[3]

In April 1917 Padre Giovanni Semeria gave a lecture at the Seminary to *La Fionda* (The Sling), a Catholic student group, and burst in on the Montini household. His friendship with the leading modernists now overlooked, Semeria had become Chaplain to the Italian High Command and exuded an uncomplicated patriotism. He thought young Battista was shaping up well, and ventured the sort of pompous prediction that "great men" like to throw around: "One day from Brescia will come a cardinal – or more than a cardinal."[4]

The object of this prediction had never felt so low. Another medical in March had the same result as before: redeferred. One of Battista's contemporaries, Mario Martinelli, sketched the following portrait of him at this time:

> He seemed shut in on himself and shy . . . as though concentrating strongly on the interior life which preoccupied and sometimes frightened him. Yet he did not wallow in sadness or self-pity about his physical weaknesses, but managed to

1 Montini, *Giovane amico*, p. 40.

2 Fappani-Molinari, *Montini Giovane*, pp. 143–44.

3 Ibid. p. 86.

4 Ibid. p. 144; and *Giovane amico*, p. 59.

> enter into the lives of others, even though always at a certain distance, as though he were a "spectator".[1]

He felt relegated to the touch-line of existence. In May he wrote to Lionello Nardini, now a machine-gunner, quoting Boethius: " 'In order to be happy one needs to know how to suffer' for 'the normal state of man here below is a series of continually unfulfilled expectations'."[2]

He was reading a lot, but not the books usually recommended to young seminarians. Adam Mickiewicz's *Book of the Polish Nation* would do at a pinch. Tolstoy's manifestos, *The Troops* and *To the Workers*, were much read at the time and announced the October Revolution later that year. Goethe's *Dichtung und Wahrheit* posed the problem concerning the way literary language modifies the truth about oneself; but Battista read it as a conflict between realism and idealism.

His most surprising reading was Oscar Wilde's *De Profundis*. He had, however, only the sketchy version available to Italians in 1917. Wilde's aesthetic Christ, based on Ernest Renan's *Vie de Jésus*, is above all an enemy of the uncouth Philistines and his morality is all sympathy. His Christ remains a fuzzy figure. Battista marked a passage on how the poor react to prison: "The poor are wiser, more charitable, more inclined to good, more sensitive than we are. In their eyes prison is a tragedy in a man's life, a misfortune, a misadventure, something which calls for sympathy."[3]

Who are *we*? One wonders if Battista knew *why* Wilde was in Reading Gaol.

In a Wilde short story he underlined the following sentence: "A day without lamentation is a day in which one has had a closed heart, not a day about which one can be happy."[4] But when Wilde says that "a single London suburb contains enough unhappiness to demonstrate that God does not love men," Battista argues back censoriously in the margin: "Or that men do not love God?"

Padre Bevilacqua might have guided him through this reading jungle. But Bevilacqua left Brescia on 5 February 1917 to join the 5th Alpine Regiment (the same as Don Galloni) as chaplain; he was soon taken prisoner.[5]

But from Bevilacqua Battista had already learned that the act of reading was not a self-indulgent retreat into an aesthetic ivory tower but

1 *Familiari*, p. xxi.

2 Ibid. p. xix.

3 Ibid. p. xx.

4 Ibid.

5 *Giovane amico*, p. 47.

a way of *listening* to the contemporary world. Reading was the first stage towards what would become dialogue. Later he would present Bevilacqua himself as the figure of "*modern man*, the modern thinker, with all the energy, the weariness, the doubts, the struggles, the discouragements and the hopes that the philosophical, scientific, religious and social crises have caused in the exhausted soul of modern man".[1]

But it was Bevilacqua's Oratorian colleague, Padre Caresana, who really pulled him through 1917 and what he called in a letter to Andrea Trebeschi "the most critical period of my life so far".[2] Caresana now had an added reason for frequenting the Montinis: he was helping out in their parish church of San Giovanni. "His fatherhood was my seminary," wrote Battista succinctly.[3]

He needed someone at his side for there was crisis in the air. Benedict XV's appeal to all the belligerents to stop the "useless slaughter" (*inutile strage*) in August 1917 was indignantly rejected: it was said to have weakened Italian morale and some of the troops retreating from Caporetto cried out "for peace and the Pope" – until they were disarmed and decimated. Caporetto was a catastrophe, the biggest Italian defeat in the war, later compared to the collapse of France in 1940. Battista felt it keenly as a "misfortune for Italy", for now the war was on its own territory.[4]

In October he had the joy of a visit to Rome with Giorgio and Andrea Trebeschi. Giorgio had an audience with Benedict XV who treated him nicely (*familiarmente*).[5] He emerged as the President of the Unione Popolare.

Battista found it hard to pray "amid the pomp and ceremony" of the eternal city. He preferred the Catacombs. They met the Prefect of the Vatican Library, Cardinal Achille Ratti, who would precede him in Poland, Milan and Peter's chair. He made these contacts not as an insignificant second-year seminarian from Brescia, but as Giorgio Montini's son.

After the grim winter of 1917–18 Battista's spirits began to lift if not to soar. Andrea was back in Brescia after legal studies in Bologna. Injured in an accident, the army gave him a long leave. Together they began to plan a student magazine, to be called *La Fionda* (The Sling). It was aptly named, for they felt rather like David taking on Goliath. Why should they presume to lead the youth of Italy? Why not!

1 *Notiziario*, 3, p. 9.

2 *Familiari*, p. xx.

3 Ibid. p. xxi.

4 Ibid.

5 *Familiari*, p. 1001.

The first number of *La Fionda* appeared on 15 June 1918.[1] It was a remarkable success. It appeared "once or twice a month" depending on their ability to pay the printer. Andrea's home in via Battaglia was the "editorial office" but they got a lot of technical help from *Il Cittadino* as well. They soon had correspondents in Rome, Naples and elsewhere. By 14 September 1918 Battista was able to report: "Subscriptions up, articles in hand down."[2]

As editor of *La Fionda* Battista not only revealed hitherto unsuspected organizational abilities but learned to work under pressure. His productivity was remarkable for an invalid: twenty identifiable articles in the six months of 1918, and as many again in 1919.[3]

La Fionda succeeded because it caught the mood of a generation that had seen so many contemporaries killed or maimed. They were conscious of being escapees, survivors. Andrea had adopted his dead brother's name and became Giovanni Andrea Trebeschi (which gave rise to jokes about his initials GAT – *gatto* or cat). What Benedict XV had called "the useless slaughter" went on to the end: Lionello Nardini, Battista's other "best friend", was killed on 4 November 1918, the day the Italian armistice was signed. This generation did not have a lot of confidence in their elders who ran "official" Italy.

There is a touch of the defiant "angry young man" about the Montini who declares in *La Fionda*: "We don't care a hoot (*ne infischiamo*) about all these pedagogues, with or without their doctorates . . . and we will make a fresh start with the Master, the Rabbi. Yes, a fresh start, however laboriously, and on our own."[4] This was a mood with which members of FUCI (the *Federazione Universitaria Cattolica Italiana*), the Catholic Student Movement, the main readers of *La Fionda*, could easily identify.

But the same post-war impatience could lead in other directions. One of the early members of the *Fionda* team, Alessandro Melchiorri, soon left and joined the ex-*arditi* now known as Fascists.[5] Benito Mussolini was far from being their undisputed leader at this stage, what he stood for was as yet unclear and he had no electoral success.[6] But the methods he would use were already evident. First *La Fionda* was

1 Ibid. p. xxi.

2 Montini, *Giovane amico*, p. 103.

3 *Familiari*, p. xxi. Over fifty of his articles were published as *Scritti giovanili*, Quericiana 1979, ed. Cesare Trebeschi, Andrea's son.

4 Quoted in Vittoria Peri, *Archivum Pontificiae Historiae*, 1985, p. 316 CHK.

5 Fappani-Molinari, *Montini Giovane*, p. 99.

6 Denis Mack-Smith, *Mussolini*, pp. 41–2.

attacked in a crude polemical style.[1] Then on 12 October 1919 Andrea was beaten up in the middle of Brescia. Violence of language followed by violent deeds.

Elections were set for November 1919. Benedict XV had allowed Don Luigi Sturzo, a remarkable Sicilian priest, to found a political party. The *Partito Popolare Italiano* (PPI or *Pipisti*) – inspired by *Rerum Novarum*, Leo XII's social encyclical of 1891 – was the heir of the Unione Popolare of which Giorgio was President, and the direct ancestor of the modern Christian Democrats.[2]

Giorgio and his friends were all standing for Parliament on a programme of post-war reconstruction. Battista supported them, naturally, but with a certain scepticism about how politics worked. He wrote in *La Fionda* on 21 June 1919:

> It only remains to start all over again. But how? With others? No, with myself. This is the whole point: so long as we are not convinced that our value depends on ourselves and on God, and not on numbers, wealth or power, then we will not be able to rebuild anything. I believe in the responsibility of the individual for social catastrophes, whether great or still to come. I believe in that solidarity by which I, just one small citizen, embody all the duties of my immense country (*patria*). I am convinced that my own thinking, issuing from my own soul, is worth more to me than anything in the world; that money can never out-weigh my freedom and my conscience; and without the fulcrum of faith and the lever of grace no law, no illusion of philosophy, and no sanction can make me free of passions, lies and egoism.[3]

Politics moralized, no doubt. But it was an antidote to Fascism. Padre Bevilacqua put it more trenchantly after the beating up of Andrea: the Gospel and the truncheon are incompatible.[4]

Battista found this ceaseless activity stimulating, but it left him dog-tired. In March 1919 Brescia played host to a student "Victory Conference" which *La Fionda* exploited. His minutes of the meeting begin with the disclaimer: "I'm no good. My studies are getting me down. I'm rather tired. I'm practically alone."[5] He begins to weary of the high spirits and horseplay inseparable from student activities.

1 Fappani-Molinari, *Montini Giovane*, p. 99, for examples.

2 On Sturzo, see Nicholas S. Timasheff, *The Sociology of Luigi Sturzo*, Helicon Press, Baltimore 1962. One can predict a revival of Sturzo studies in the 1990s.

3 Fappani-Molinari, *Montini Giovane*, p. 101.

4 Ibid. p. 99.

5 *Familiari*, p. xxii.

When Andrea poured a pot of jam over the head of Gerolamo Martinelli, Bishop Giacinto Gaggia laughed so much that he fell off his chair.[1] Battista got a big bucket of water to drive the wasps away.

As he approached ordination he felt increasingly the need and the pain of solitude. On 18 June 1919 he wrote: "I want only to know how to live as the Lord wants me to live . . . from now on I will be, out of obedience and necessity, the one who is absent, from everything. It's tough."[2] But he was not yet counted out. In September 1919 the national chaplain of FUCI, Msgr Giandomenico Pini, organized a retreat at Monte Cassino.

It was a retreat *sui generis*, as Paul VI recalled when he consecrated the reopened abbey church in 1964, as the Benedictines put up with the student rowdiness with centuries-old patience. The Brescia contingent – there were fourteen of them including Battista, Lodovico and Andrea – got all their resolutions through. They were in favour of "the right to freedom in education" and wanted "a great Catholic University in Italy" along the lines of Louvain in Belgium. This had already been proposed by Battista in *La Fionda*. He thought it should be sited in Trent, recently recovered, and therefore symbolic both of the Italian victory and the Counter-Reformation.[3]

From Monte Cassino Battista wrote his first substantial letter home. He was enchanted by the place. It brought him "so close to the heart of a civilization that *must not* disappear but which must be regenerated, turning men's minds to the things that are above, but then returning and restoring to the nation (*patria*) its culture, its faith, its *ora et labora* (pray and work)".[4] Should a new "dark ages" descend upon Europe, Benedictine abbeys, above all Monte Cassino, would resume their traditional role as guardians of civilization.

Monte Cassino came second only to Rome: "After Rome I believe no other shrine evokes so strongly the Christian tradition, and makes self-evident the desire not to be unworthy of it, but to be its humble, alert and convinced continuators."[5]

Monte Cassino meant something else too for Battista in 1919. It was his last retreat before embarking on the "minor orders" which led straight to priestly ordination.

1 Fappani-Molinari, *Montini Giovane*, p. 107.

2 *Familiari*, p. xxii.

3 Fappani-Molinari, *Montini Giovane*, p. 103.

4 *Familiari*, p. 2.

5 This explains why he regarded the Allied destruction of the Abbey in 1944 as a tragedy that nothing could justify. One does not defend civilization by destroying its works.

He donned the soutane on 21 November 1919, the feast of Mary's Presentation in the temple, one of the Joyful Mysteries of the rosary. Before the ceremony in Santa Maria delle Grazie he sought the blessing of his grandmother Francesca, as a sign that he was her spiritual heir.[1] Guitton remarks that, given the age at which people are elected pope, "the mother of a pope never knows she is the mother of a pope".[2] That is even truer of papal grandmothers.

Battista was tonsured on 30 November and became doorkeeper and lector on 14 December 1919, and Giorgio said he was "as happy as could be".[3] He received the sub-diaconate on 28 February 1920. It was his irrevocable commitment to chastity. He wrote to Andrea four days later:

> I am now a sub-deacon, and this comes after fervent days of meditation as calm and strengthening as I have ever experienced. I feel joy in this step which separates me from the past and human desires, and imposes the promises and tasks that go with complete consecration . . . I cannot tell you how happy I am.[4]

To Don Galloni he wrote that his heart was filled with "the vibrations of the *Magnificat*".[5] The dizzy-making pace continued with ordination to the diaconate on 8 March and there was a slight *rallantando* while he got used to handling the Breviary and reached the peak of priestly ordination on 29 May 1920.

One urgent task remained before priestly ordination: to say farewell to Gian Andrea Trebeschi. He wrote on Whitsunday:

> *Carissimo*
> I entrust my ordination to your prayers in a special way. I know and cannot forget and hope to repay through the sacrifice (of the Mass) all that I owe to you, to your friendship, to your example, to your words of comfort in times of darkness and doubt. If ever in all these years in which we have lived in such intimacy you have ever found in me anything you did not want to find in a friend, a true Christian friend, then blot out the

1 *Familiari*, p. xxii.

2 Jean Guitton, *Dialogues*, p. 56. Guitton adds a remark which appears strange to those unfamiliar with Italian culture: "But her son knows and he suffers because he is unable to thank her or kneel before her to receive her blessing."

3 Virgilio Noè, "*Su le Ordinazioni 1930. X Anniversario di Messa*" in *Notiziario*, 11, pp. 7–37.

4 Montini, *Giovane amico*, p. 116.

5 Fappani-Molinari, *Montini Giovane*, p. 149.

> memory with fraternal forgiveness . . . Have the charity of compassion, and remember that God in his goodness chooses as his ministers not only human beings, but human beings who are too weak for the mission entrusted to them, and draw from that grounds for greater praise and boundless hope in the Lord's goodness. I will be very close to you in these days for this reason: if I want to go to meet Christ with a love that is young and ardent and the promise to seek him in his brethren, then how can I forget the people from whom I learned such feelings? You must tell our friends what has *not changed*, and that I still feel *one of them* even though my life is turned upside-down; then ask them to call down on me light, strength and courage.
>
> Remember me to your mother, whom you will ask for the blessing that only a mother can give.[1]

It was signed simply "B".

It was farewell to Andrea, and farewell to adolescent love. The important thing was that his heart had been broken open. If he was letting Andrea down he did it in the gentlest possible way. "What is attractive about the commitment to celibacy at twenty," he said many years later, "is the desire for an almost superhuman effort, a truly total gift of self."[2]

Andrea set his sights less high. Within three months he met his future wife, Vittoria di Toni, on the beach at Riccione – an apt place since her father, professor at the University of Modena, was an authority on *algi*. Battista thought Andrea was right to shave off his beard: "You are on the road to metamorphosis, and I like that."[3]

His own metamorphosis on 29 May 1920 was a major social event in Brescia. *Il Cittadino* reported it at length.[4] It had something of a party rally. Besides Giorgio, two other PPI deputies, Giovanni Longinotti and Luigi Bazoli, were present; and the leader, Don Luigi Sturzo, sent a telegram of congratulations from Rome.

Giuditta took her wedding dress out of the wardrobe and got the nuns to turn it into a chasuble. One tends to forget that Battista was only one of fourteen priests ordained that Saturday in May 1920. The war had opened up gaps in the ranks of the clergy and Bishop Giacinto Gaggia, with four hundred parishes to care for, was anxious to plug them.

1 Montini, *Giovane amico*, p. 122.

2 Jean Guitton, *Paul VI secret*, p. 115.

3 Fappani-Molinari, *Montini Giovane*, pp. 128–31.

4 Ibid. p. 153.

The next day Don Battista said his first Mass in the Sanctuary of the Madonna delle Grazie. Giorgio offered lunch just across the road. There were speeches and gifts. *La Fionda* gave him the most practical gift: a copy of the *Dictionnaire de Théologie Catholique*. The heat was intense, mitigated only by an enormous cloudburst on the night of 31 May.[1] His ordination card had a copy of Rubens' *Last Supper* and this prayer: "Grant, oh my God, that all minds may unite in the Truth, and all hearts in Charity." It carried an indulgence of 300 days, courtesy of Pope Pius X.

1 Ibid. p. 155.

4

Might-have-beens

Footfalls echo in memory
Down the passage which we did not take
Towards the door we never opened
Into the rose-garden.

T. S. ELIOT, *The Four Quartets*

But what was Don Battista, ordained at twenty-two, going to *do*? His Bishop, Giacinto Gaggia, robustly answered seminary professors' anxious enquiries about his health, "Very well, I'll ordain him for paradise."[1]

But he still had to decide what to do *next*. Gaggia did not want to risk him in a country parish, and accepted the family suggestion of further studies in Rome. The Montinis believed the Roman climate was milder; Lodovico was already there; and Giorgio's parliamentary duties meant that he commuted to and fro. But for a clerical student from Brescia, Rome, alas, meant the Lombardy Seminary, now reopened after the war.

Both Gaggia and Giorgio wanted to spare their delicate charge its notorious rigours. They used the old-boy network. The Prefect of the Ambrosian Library in Milan, Luigi Gramatica, was a Brescian. He asked his friend Giovanni Mercati, Prefect of the even more prestigious Vatican Library, to find room in his flat for Giorgio Montini's newly ordained son who proposed to study literature at Rome's Sapienza University, after which he would "do a doctorate in history".[2]

History was Gaggia's idea. An historian himself, he advised Battista to avoid scholastic manuals and instead study Hefele's *History of the Councils*.[3] Karl Joseph Hefele, a Tübingen professor, disciple of Johann Adam Möhler and later Bishop of Rottenburg, had been among the minority at Vatican I. His history of the *councils* brought out the collegial nature of the Church. Gaggia advised Battista: "Read Hefele – all

1 Fappani-Molinari, p. 146.

2 Nello Vian in *Familiari*, p. xxv.

3 Published in German in nine volumes, 1855–90; Montini used the French edition with important additions from H. Leclerq and others, which began appearing in 1907.

18 heavy tomes – he's got it all. In him you'll find theology, philosophy, spirituality, politics, humanism and Christianity, errors, debates, truth, abuses, laws, the virtue and the holiness of the Church. His *History of the Councils* is an encyclopaedia of the Church."[1]

This was recklessly daring advice in 1920. It bore fruit, but only in the long-term: Montini contributed another chapter to Hefele's history.

If Mercati had found room for him in 1920, remarks Nello Vian, "the daily contact with one of the most learned men in the Church, whose ministry was scholarship," would have marked him for life. We might have had Msgr Montini a man of letters (his reviews of George Bernanos' *Diary of a Country Priest*[2] and other novels prove his talent) or Cardinal Montini the celebrated historian.

But Mercati had no room. So Montini had to go to the Lombardy Seminary. Each day he saw the aged Louis Duchesne, the greatest living Catholic historian, shuffle by on his way to the *Ecole Française*.[3] Duchesne, still hoping for rehabilitation, had been put on the Index of Forbidden Books in 1911. Being a Church historian was dangerous.

The Lombardy College had been refounded by Cardinal Carlo Andrea Ferrari, Archbishop of Milan, as the first part of his educational reforms. The second part, the setting up of the Catholic University of the Sacred Heart in Milan, began this same year, 1921.[4] So Battista lodged at via del Mascherone 58, the former palace of the Teutonic Knights.[5] He did not like it. He counted 120 steps up to his room. With no piano to practice on his promising musical career was abruptly cut short. Ah well, he sighed, quoting the title of Giuseppe Verdi's opera, it's *La Fuerza del Destino* 'The Power of Destiny'. There was no central heating and Battista, who "expanded like a lizard in the sun",[6] froze. Conditions were primitive. He had to write home for a shaving brush and mirror.

Still, fascinating Rome was now his milieu, his home. One of his very first letters was, naturally, to Andrea Trebeschi on 19 December 1920: "For me Rome provides a continual subject for meditation,

1 *G. B. Montini e la societa italiana 1919–1939*, *Acta* of a seminar held at Brescia, 21–22 October 1983. Centro di Documentazione (CE.DOC), p. 61. Montini quoted this remark again in a 1962 lecture on "the Councils in the History of the Church", in *Discorsi e scritti sul Concilio 1959–1963*, p. 119, adding the contemporary comment: "This shows the place Councils have had in the life of the Church: they pervade its life, sum up its meaning, clear its way, direct its course."

2 Reproduced in "*Le Journal d'un Curé de Campagne*", *Notiziario*, 8, pp. 29–35.

3 *Familiari*, p. 27.

4 Pope John Paul II beatified him in 1987.

5 *Familiari*, p. 25–26.

6 Ibid. p. 31.

because the threads of my dearest memories are bound up with it."[1] *Meditation*: he chose the word with care. Whenever he thinks about Rome he stresses its mysterious double vocation, human and Christian: Rome as the centre of civilization and Rome as the centre of the Church. The thought of Rome is "the golden thread" running through his life. From now on he will be proud to say *Civis Romanus sum* (I am a Roman citizen), while completing it with the other maxim: "No one is a stranger in Rome."

He was at first assiduous at the Sapienza lectures where he had enrolled for courses in history, ancient and modern, literature, Italian and Latin, Greek and Latin grammar, Christian archaeology, not to mention exercises in geography, Latin literature and paleography.[2] Those were the *compulsory* courses. There were also optional extras.

It took Battista less than three months to admit to himself that his studies were in a mess and that he had bitten off more than he could reasonably chew. He wrote home on 13 January 1921 complaining of the contrast between what he expected and what he found. He wanted to study history – but he finds himself in a houseful of philosophers. He is happiest in a library or his study – but at the Lombardy College he is surrounded by a horde of young men who are "much healthier than me, and therefore capable of arousing me unconsciously to emulation or envy".[3] Contemporaries thought he was being unduly cosseted because of his father's political importance.

They were not altogether wrong. Friends from Brescia kept him going during his first months in Rome. The nineteen-year-old Carlo Manziana was there to study literature. They had a lot in common. Carlo was an old boy of the Collegio Cesare Arici, had lived in the same street as the Montinis, via Trieste, and frequented the Oratorians of La Pace whom he was to join in 1924. Pope Paul VI consecrated him Bishop of Crema on 2 February 1964.[4]

His brother Lodovico was already in Rome, toiling over his thesis on "Trades Unions in Civil Law":[5] this reflected the concerns of Bevilacqua whose own Louvain thesis had been on "Social Legislation in Italy", and it was controversial at a time when both the Liberal government and the Fascists were threatening to "take on the Unions". Lodovico

1 Montini, *Giovane amico*, p. 135.

2 *Familiari*, p. 27 fn. 4.

3 Ibid. p. 48.

4 Ibid. pp. 51–52. Bishop Carlo Manziana reached the age of ninety on 26 July 1992, having written a life of Montini.

5 *Familiari*, p. 68.

was on the left of the PPI (*Partito Popolare Italiano*), further left than his more cautious father.

Ireland was the touchstone of progressive Italian thinkers at this time. Terence McSwiny, Mayor of Cork, had died while on hunger strike on 25 October 1920. The Gibraltarian Archbishop of Southwark, Peter Amigo, gave him a spectacular funeral in his cathedral in South London.[1] This made a great impression on international opinion.

The PPI took up the Irish cause. So did Giorgio in *Il Cittadino di Brescia*. Just before Battista arrived in Rome, Roberto Murri cried out in the Chamber, "What about martyred Ireland?" whereupon "deputies all over the Chamber rose enthusiastically to their feet shouting 'Long live the Irish Republic'."[2] In March 1921 Alcide De Gasperi, the future leader of the PPI and post-war leader of the Christian Democrats, addressed a meeting on Ireland at the Teatro Eliseo. Lodovico Montini was in the chair.

On 4 March 1921 Battista Montini advised his friend Trebeschi to get hold of *La Revue des Jeunes*, organ of the French Dominicans. "There you will find," he writes, "invaluable documentation on the cause of Ireland, and the address of its office in Paris."[3] He also knew Msgr John Hagan, Rector of the Irish College in Rome, a tireless propagandist against British colonialism.[4]

Battista could hardly escape the rough-and-tumble of politics. His brother and his father were both committed to the PPI. Giovanni Longinotti, family friend and his patron in Rome, was Under-Secretary at the Ministry of Commerce and Labour.[5] Battista often dined with the Longinotti who provided him with the substitute family he needed. He became an honorary uncle to their children, baptizing them as they came along. Longinotti tried to mobilize the Catholic workers especially in Brescia, which led to tensions with the Socialists.[6] But he refused to deal with the Fascists. This reflected the attitude of Brescian Catholics generally.

There were strikes and lock-outs throughout Italy. Some Marxists – though not their leading thinker, Antonio Gramsci – said that Italian capitalism was in that terminal state technically dubbed "pre-revolutionary". In March 1921 student unrest suspended lectures at La

1 Michael Clifton, *Amigo, Friend of the Poor*, p. 80.

2 *Irish Independent*, 7 November 1920.

3 *Giovane amico*, p. 136.

4 Dermot Keogh, *The Vatican, the Bishops and Irish Politics 1919–39*, p. 249 fn. 54.

5 *Familiari*, p. 37.

6 Kelikian, *Town and Country under Fascism*, p. 114.

Sapienza.[1] The general election of 5 May 1921 resolved nothing. Fr Caresana, Battista's confessor, addressed a meeting at Sarezzo on 27 June at which shots rang out and a policeman was killed.[2] Don Francesco Galloni, now active among the textile workers, was accused of the murder by the left-wing.[3]

This was untrue, but Battista found Galloni increasingly disconcerting. He now loved wearing uniforms. He had taken part in Gabriele d'Annunzio's Fiume adventure – the poet seized the Slovenian city (now called Rijeka) with a handful of raggle-taggle volunteers like Don Galloni and held it for two years.[4] This was the first of a series of subversive acts which by demonstrating the weakness and indecisiveness of the Italian state called the Anglo-French bluff, undermined the Liberal government and so paved the way for Benito Mussolini's Fascist lawlessness. It was also the first appearance of the self-dramatizing poet-hero, the man of letters as man of action.[5]

Battista found Don Galloni quite impossible, and thought arguing with him a waste of time.[6] Galloni, always a literary priest, had fallen for d'Annunzio's overblown style, replete with unusual adjectives and archaic forms. He was John the Baptist to Mussolini, though at this date people of Montini's class were inclined to dismiss him as that classic Italian figure – the embittered intellectual down on his luck.[7] More menacing on the local level was the *ras* or chief of Cremona, Roberto Farinacci, another ex-revolutionary socialist who followed Lenin in turning violence into a political method.[8]

Battista tried to sound cheerful in his letters home. "I feel in exile," he reported on 20 October 1921, as his second year began, "but I also feel that Rome is the home of the spirit and the hearth (*focolare*) of the highest affections."[9]

But already the direction of his life had been changed without his lifting a finger. Longinotti dined with Cardinal Pietro Gasparri, Secretary

1 *Familiari*, p. 64.

2 Ibid. p. 69.

3 Kelikian, p. 111.

4 Seton-Watson, p. 540.

5 See Lino Pertile, "Fascism and Literature" in *Rethinking Italian Fascism, Capitalism, Populism and Culture*, ed. David Forgacs, Lawrence and Wishart, London 1986, p. 164.

6 *Familiari*, p. 90.

7 Martin Clark, *Modern Italy*, p. 214.

8 Denis Mack Smith, *Mussolini*, p. 81. Farinacci started his lucrative legal career by copying down, word for word, someone else's thesis – a crime in Fascist legislation.

9 *Familiari*, p. 91.

of State.[1] He put it to Gasparri that young Montini was languishing at the Lombardy College, and that he would be better off at the Academy for Noble Ecclesiastics, the school for Vatican diplomats.[2] Wheels within wheels.

Battista was unaccountably summoned by Msgr Giuseppe Pizzardo, substitute at the Secretariat of State (that is, number two to Gasparri), on 27 October 1921 and told to hold himself ready to enter the Academy. He went straight from the diminutive Pizzardo to Longinotti, and realizing that they were in league, acknowledged defeat (*la mia partita era perduta*).[3] He did not want, and had not sought, a diplomatic career. But with Church and State bearing down upon him he had no option. He wrote sadly home:

> Now I am waiting for the decision, and you can imagine how I feel. I have to do a complete *about-turn*: this is the first condition for serving the Church, yet this comforting phrase involves a bitter renunciation.
>
> My studies have been quite simply turned upside-down: literature is cut short, philosophy suspended; I have to do a novice's course in law. My academic specialization, that I considered a form of apostolate and after a year began to imagine could be quite fruitful, is over.
>
> Now I have to do practical studies for a year or so. From one moment to the next I pass from being a student to a . . . man of action.[4]

He asked his father for his copy of the *Code of Canon Law* which he is clearly going to need. It is a small, black book that he thinks is on his prie-dieu in Brescia.[5]

Thus on 18 November 1921, two weeks late, Battista Montini entered the Academy of Noble Ecclesiastics (the requirement of nobility was none too stringent) and began to study canon law with the Jesuits at the Gregorian University.[6] His brother Lodovico, meanwhile, started teaching at the newly founded Catholic University of Milan, where a colleague from 1921–27 was the Dominican Mariano Cordovani. He became a firm friend of both brothers.[7]

1 Ibid. p. 92.

2 Founded in 1701. Pius XII wisely changed its name to Pontifical Ecclesiastical Academy on 26 May 1939.

3 *Familiari*, p. 92.

4 Ibid.

5 Ibid. p. 93.

6 Ibid. p. 97.

7 Ibid. p. 98.

Battista moved to his new abode on a rainy Sunday afternoon in November 1921. It was (and still is) at Piazza Minerva 74, just opposite the Dominican church of Santa Maria sopra Minerva. He spent his time putting his gear in order and piously hoping that from now on there would be more "order" in his life. On 20 November 1921 he wrote home:

> I haven't yet been able to form a clear judgement on what coming here means or on the atmosphere and the studies; but my first impression is that there is some hope of a certain independence and discreet isolation.
>
> This consoles me, because *solitude charges up the energies that are dispersed in company*. I think back to two years ago when I put on clerical dress, and I feel that I have been flung head over heels and am still dizzy, not knowing which is the right way up. Perhaps I need another somersault to get back on my feet. However, I have the experience of God's grace which helps me, even when he "turns me inside out" and so, despite the vertigo, I remain calm.[1]

Not everyone thought he had done the right thing. Fr Bevilacqua strongly disapproved. Using First World War jargon, he told Giuditta that Battista would become a professional regular soldier, far too regimented for Bevilacqua who preferred to serve the Lord among the guerrillas and the free-lance operators.[2]

Battista no doubt agreed. But he was trapped. He spent an entire hour one afternoon sewing buttons on his soutane, and joked: "To be well buttoned up is an essential characteristic of the diplomatic life."[3] But perhaps it was an insight rather than a joke. His "worldly" brother, Lodovico, meanwhile, acquired a *smoking*, a dinner-jacket.

Battista attended lectures at the Gregorian, then at via del Seminario 120 (now the College for graduate Jesuits). His professor of moral theology was the Basque Antonio Maria Arregui SJ, notorious for discussing the distance from which one might properly view copulating animals.[4]

Battista was distinctly unhappy with the canonical approach to life. He wondered whether it was possible to translate the Gospel into terms of canon law: "The further one is from the external forms of the Gospel,

1 Ibid. p. 99.

2 Ibid. p. 102.

3 Ibid.

4 It depended entirely on the size of the animals: flies could be observed from relatively close range, elephants only from afar (ibid. p. 105). "This is the sort of thing," said one of my teachers, "that gives pornography a bad name."

the more one must insist on its *spirit*; but since the practice of the paradoxical Christian virtues is difficult enough, it is almost impossible to practise them by means that are contrary to their very nature."[1]

This was the reason why he was mistrustful of the Academy from the outset. Its natural pathway was one of ambition and honours. Three of his fellow students bore the title of "marquis". If he could not pretend to be a proletarian, at least he could claim to be rooted in a provincial village.

Then Pope Benedict XV lay dying. Battista headed for St Peter's basilica, "because it is there that one goes when prayer has to become as huge (*gigantesco*) as the wall of the Temple".[2] Confined to his bed on 17 January 1922, Benedict died five days later of a flu that unexpectedly turned into pneumonia. He was sixty-seven.

The high-flying students of the Academy were well placed to pick up edifying gossip about his last moments. Battista had the inside story from Cardinal Giovanni Tacci who said that "sometimes the Pope spent the entire night reading and writing without ever touching his bed, and he would allow no one else to read or deal with his immense correspondence".[3]

Battista refused to speculate on the succession – he left that to the newspapers. He waited until the VIPs were out of the way. He viewed the body as a member of the ordinary People of God. He indulges in an *exercise de style*:

> How majestic and calamitous is the death of a pope! . . . He dies, and it seems that the whole of humanity undergoes in him its own death-throes. He dies, and while a whole edifice of government collapses, another is awaited with an impatience that brooks no delay because the resurrection, projected from the beyond on to the screen of human destinies, must needs have its victory straight away.[4]

Pure Bossuet.

When he visits the body laid out in the Blessed Sacrament Chapel of St Peter's he switches to "psychological realism" in the manner of Paul Bourget. It rained hard on 22 January 1922. The trams were jam-packed. The people of Rome waited patiently in St Peter's Square beneath a tormented sky. The square was black with umbrellas. The crowd began to shuffle forward. Then:

1 *Familiari*, p. 104.
2 Ibid. p. 119.
3 Ibid. p. 120.
4 Ibid.

> Behind the closed bars of the chapel, at the height of a man, placed at an angle and dressed in red pontificals, with a gold-encrusted mitre: only one majesty remains, that of death.
>
> The face, pale, angular, emaciated (*smunta*), has not lost its character: the black hair tumbles over the brow and heightens the pallor of the wax-like face. He is dead, and the right hand, weary from blessing, lies inertly upon the august breast. Unconsciously one feels in the presence of a symbolic death.[1]

Battista snuffled with flu, his annual visitor, during the conclave. Giorgio and Lodovico reported on the succession of "black smokes".

From his sick-bed Battista sketched out a portrait of the "sort of pope" that was needed:

> The Church is about to be embodied (*sta per personificarsi*) in a man who after twenty centuries should represent not only the powerful Christ but the Christ who is evangelical, peace-loving, holy and poor. Let us pray that we may merit a pope who is very like Jesus; and for that he will have to be crucified by the world that hates what is not its own; its salvation demands as much.[2]

Fappani and Molinari claim that this passage breathes the spirit of Antonio Rosmini. They say that Luigi Bazoli had put this "dangerous" book, *The Five Wounds of the Church*, into the hands of the young Montini.[3] True: but he could have worked it out for himself from his daily meditation on the Gospels.

It looks forward to John XXIII, elected in 1958, but hardly to Achille Ratti, elected on 6 February 1922. Montini had met him the previous June when Ratti, fresh from his mission of saving Poland from Bolshevism, called in at the Lombardy College on his way to Milan as Archbishop.[4] Ratti, the compromise candidate, split the difference between Gasparri, the Secretary of State, and La Fontaine, Patriarch of Venice.[5] One of the criteria of his election was that he should have "a correct attitude to the Italian government". Translate: he should resolve the "Roman Question" by reconciling the Vatican and the State.

Ratti, who took the name Pius XI, personified the Church of his period: tough-minded, unyielding and vigorous in the defence of the

1 Ibid. p. 124.
2 Ibid. p. 128.
3 *Montini Giovane*, p. 384.
4 *Anni e opere*, p. 33.
5 See Giancarlo Zizola, *Quale Papa?*, pp. 138–41.

institutional rights of the Church in the age of dictators. Battista did not comment on this election. He sent his aunts flowers from the altar at the Coronation Mass on 12 February 1922.[1] Lodovico, recovering from an unhappy love affair, got a temporary post in Geneva at the International Labour Office (ILO, *Bureau International de Travail*, BIT).

Within a month the students of the Pontifical Academy had a private audience with the new Pope at 11.30 a.m. on 6 March 1922. Was Battista impressed? Moderately. Knowing him already, he writes home, "took away much of the awe which usually accompanies such visits".[2] Pius XI asked who was the youngest, and on being told Montini, enquired about Giorgio and regretted that, as Pope, he would not now be able to attend the first National Liturgical Week in Brescia. This was a Bevilacqua scheme. Don Emanuele Cavonti of Turin, who founded the *Rivista Liturgica* in 1914, regarded La Pace in Brescia as a model for parish liturgy and Bevilacqua as the great expert on *pastoral* as distinct from monastic liturgy.[3]

Battista was undergoing "moments of depression" not unconnected with his state of health. He had digestive troubles. Longinotti sent him to a leading Roman consultant, Pietro Borromeo, who "gave me a great deal of advice and some prodigious remedies, but I fear they will not work".[4] His regular doctor was Andrea Amici, known jokingly as the Blessed Andrea because he had been Pius X's doctor. It was a small world. Battista took the Longinotti children to Mass and enjoyed being their honorary uncle. He passed his second-year canon law exam with relief.[5]

To relieve his loneliness Battista wrote a long lament to his fallen hero, Don Francesco Galloni, dated 19 June 1922. He had heard nothing for eight months, *eight whole months*! He feared that Don Francesco was becoming increasingly eccentric. He divined he was one of those maverick priests who would never settle down to conventional parish work, and hoped he would find "a vocation within a vocation". "I suppose you're off looking for the hundredth sheep," he says desperately.[6] The truth was stranger than he could have guessed. Galloni had become obsessed with the number of unblessed corpses on the battlefields of Europe and went about giving them a decent burial. This mission had led him to Bulgaria. Battista lost touch with him for thirty-two years.

1 *Familiari*, p. 131.

2 Ibid. p. 139.

3 See Godfried Danneels, *Notiziario*, 10, p. 57. Forty years later Bevilacqua represented Montini, Archbishop of Milan, on the liturgical commission of Vatican II.

4 *Familiari*, p. 141.

5 Ibid. p. 156.

6 *Notiziario*, 8, pp. 22–23.

Battista left Rome as soon as he decently could, on 1 July 1922, not imagining that he would be away until 4 January 1923. In his absence Mussolini became Prime Minister. Although leading a rebellion against the State and despite the countless atrocities of his private army, Mussolini was invited by King Vittorio Emanuele to form a government. The myth of the "march on Rome" was a later invention. Mussolini arrived by train. "We defended Rome much better in 1870," said an ageing prelate.

Battista missed all the excitement because he was having his first experience of "abroad" in Austria and Germany. He was supposed to be learning the language but found German "every day more convoluted and incomprehensible".[1] His Latin sense of "order" made him very critical of German art, which "fails to understand the general principles of civilization". Its idea of "perfection" is a gross, grotesque and clumsy caricature. It took him a long time to understand the "Gothic".

Germany was undergoing hyper-inflation. Prices soared by 1000 or 2000 per cent while he called on Eugenio Pacelli, Nuncio in Munich (he was out), saw the Oberammergau Passion Play, and took a steamer down the romantic Rhine from Mainz to Bonn.[2] The only good thing about Germany was the companionship of Mariano Rampolla, a Sicilian, a distant relative of the Cardinal Rampolla who nearly became pope in 1903.

Then while Mussolini was supposedly "marching" on Rome in October 1922, Battista was ordered by Msgr Pizzardo, substitute at the Secretariat of State, to "get his canon law studies over as soon as possible".[3] The best way to do that was to live at home in Brescia and commute to the Canon Law Faculty of the Milan Seminary. The Sacred Congregation for Seminaries and Universities dispensed him from exams in "special subjects". Thus he was awarded a meaningless doctorate in canon law on 9 December 1922. Though he scored 32 out of 40 he was not fooled, and never had the gall to use the title of Dr Montini.

Back in Rome on 4 January 1923, Pizzardo had another surprise for him. He should "hold himself ready" to enter the Secretariat of State. Giorgio wrote resignedly that the family "would have preferred to see you here (in Brescia) in pastoral work or as a seminary professor".[4] But it was not to be.

While Battista waited for Pizzardo to make up his mind how best to employ him he marked time by attending the "in-house courses" at the

1 *Familiari*, p. 165.

2 Ibid. pp. 169, 173.

3 Ibid. p. 178.

4 Ibid. p. 183.

Pontifical Academy for Noble Ecclesiastics. He forbade his parents to use this pompous title in the address. They were to write simply to Piazza Minerva 74.

His eclectic education now took a new twist. He wrote an essay on "The influence of the Great Schism between East and West in preparing minds for the Protestant Reformation" – but it was only six pages long.[1] Another exercise was an imaginary report from the Paris Nunciature on the elections that were due later in 1923. That was a mere three pages long. Battista was learning the art of the diplomatic memo which pares down to the would-be essential, rather than the academic essay which expands and has to produce evidence. He buckled down to this task, but admitted that he was "most upset" (*dolentissimo*) at having to abandon his study of literature.[2]

To keep his literary hand in, he contributed articles to *La Fionda* and *Il Cittadino di Brescia*. After three weeks, however, his judgement is harsh: "This course annoys me: it is a parody of serious matters that can only serve self-deception."[3] He felt as though he was merely jumping up and down on the spot.

On 24 January 1923 Msgr Pizzardo informed him with "breath-taking *naïveté*" to steel himself to go to Poland or Peru or just possibly Hungary where he would have no other duty than "to observe how a nunciature works". This made Battista really angry. "You can imagine my objections and protests," he writes confidentially to his father, insisting that his mother must *not be told* since "there is no point in alarming her unduly".[4]

By 18 February 1923 he was feeling miserable: "Though I go on working, I don't know why I do."[5] As usual he was saved by his friends. He did his first baptism, in St Peter's, of the child of his German tutor: German would come in handy in Poland or Hungary (though not in Peru). He was pleased to see Carlo Maziana again, and innocently told his parents: "With all of you so far away, the sight of a familiar face does one good, and brings the consolation of living for someone and for something, even if the long term goal of the action is to seek the exclusive will of God."[6] He made new friends too. He was intellectually stimulated

1 Ibid. p. 184. This was a topic of the utmost ecumenical importance. Yves-Marie Congar OP later developed the idea that if the 1054 schism had not occurred, then the Western Church would not have been allowed to develop along narrowly juridical lines, and so the Reformation would have been unnecessary.

2 *Familiari*, p. 184.

3 Ibid. p. 187.

4 Ibid. p. 189.

5 Ibid. p. 191.

6 Ibid. p. 182.

by Giuseppe Domenico Allegri, an engineer of poetic temperament who had translated Paul Claudel's *L'Annonce faite à Marie*.[1]

Yet by March 1923 personal uncertainties compounded by political developments drove him near to despair. He dreams of the simple, uncluttered life in contrast to his own that is "varnished over with so many sterile desires, empty aspirations, base depressions, and silly external chores".[2] He understands Penelope, for ever unravelling by night what she has woven by day.[3]

He was home on 10 March, returning to Rome on 15 April. On the night train from Brescia to Rome he had first-hand experience of Fascist nastiness. Roberto Farinacci, soon to be Secretary of the Fascist Party, was aboard with his armed bodyguards. The Fascists changed compartments at every station, ostensibly as a precaution against bomb threats but in fact as a way of showing their arrogant power. It meant that the sleep of the other passengers was constantly disturbed. Farinacci, the *ras* of Cremona, was thirty, barely older than Battista himself, for whom the episode illustrated "the weakness of the powerful".[4]

Despite being shoved around he managed to read on the train the decisive speech made by Don Luigi Sturzo, founder of the PPI, at the last congress of his party he attended. It was held in Turin on 12–14 April. Sturzo signed the death-warrant of the PPI when he declared that there was a "substantial difference" between the Fascist concept of the state and that of the PPI. The *Popolari* would fight to the death the Fascist idea that "the state is the source of morality and its absolute, pantheist or deified embodiment".[5] Just as well Farinacci and his crew didn't know what he was reading.

Yet Don Battista, while admiring Sturzo's dialectical skill, seemed not altogether persuaded by his argument. Sturzo's position depended, he thought, on accepting the validity of "popular sovereignty" as the basis of political life; but if one started from "aristocratic sovereignty" (the rule of the best) then one might get a different answer. This was a slippery slope which could end in Fascism. His brother, Lodovico, would have none of this clerical élitism. He made his own Giovanni Longinotti's maxim: "I will not become a Fascist, nor will I approve of anyone who kneels down before Fascism."[6]

But there was soon not really much difference between the two

1 Ibid. pp. 15, 195.
2 Ibid. p. 197.
3 Ibid. p. 203.
4 Ibid. p. 199.
5 Ibid.
6 *Notiziario*, 9, p. 52.

brothers. Don Battista's first act on getting back to Rome after the Farinacci incident was to call the *onorevole* Longinotti with the news – his first recorded use of the telephone, a device that drives historians to despair. Longinotti treated Battista as one of the family and sustained him during the long "dark night" of Fascism. He was his second father.

May 1923 – though no one knew it then – was the time at which the fates of Don Battista and of Italy were sealed. He wrote to Msgr Pizzardo asking for a decision, and restating his desire to return to his diocese.[1] No answer. Rome, meantime, was in a state of high excitement because of the state visit of King George V and Queen Mary. Parades and fireworks, gleaming breastplates and nodding plumes marked what the papers called an "English week". Though it had a distinctly commercial purpose, the royal visit looked like a consecration of Mussolini. Don Battista ignored the royal visitors, preferring to attend instead the beatification of the Jesuit St Robert Bellarmine.[2]

The really bad news, however, was that after the Turin Congress the right-wing of the PPI, the so-called "nationalists", soon to be "clerico-Fascists", began to think of secession. Their leader, Egilberto Martire, craved an audience with Mussolini and walked straight into a honeyed trap. Giorgio was more disconsolate than furious at this betrayal. By 5 June 1923 Battista was in Vienna and on his way to Poland.

1 *Familiari*, p. 207.

2 Ibid. p. 208 fn. 1.

5

Polish Intermezzo

> Had Pilsudski and Wegand failed to arrest the triumphant advance of the Soviet Army at the Battle of Warsaw in 1920, not only would Christianity have experienced a dangerous reverse, but the very existence of Western civilization would have been imperilled.
>
> (Lord d'Aberon, British Ambassador to Warsaw, quoted in NORMAN DAVIES, *God's Playground*, vol. 2, p. 401)

Poland was barely five years old when Battista Montini got there in the sweltering heat of June 1923. Only one bridge across the river Vistula was usable; the Poniatowski bridge lay in ruins from the Russian attack of August 1920. The Russian Orthodox cathedral, hated symbol of tsarist rule, was destroyed shortly after he arrived.[1]

The new nation was cocky, insecure and aggressive. Twice as big as the Versailles Peace Conference anticipated, it played a mean, rough game. It seized eastern Galicia with its capital Lvov from the Ukrainians. It fought the Czechs over Teschen (Cieszyn), unsuccessfully. It attacked its small, peaceful neighbour Lithuania. A plebiscite turned their historic capital Vilnius into Wilno and incorporated it into Poland. The Lithuanians made Kaunas their temporary capital and smarted under this injustice.[2]

An offensive against the Bolsheviks, already weakened by internal splits, brought in yet more territory to the east. Lenin signed the decree packing off the books from the sometime Petersburg Catholic Theology

1 *Familiari*, p. 217. The baroque church of the Piarists was transformed into the Orthodox cathedral in 1833, no doubt as a punishment for the uprising of 1830. It stood on the north side of what is now Victory Square where, in June 1979, Pope John Paul prayed that the Holy Spirit might "renew the face of the earth – of this earth, of this land". Montini's first postcard home showed the Orthodox cathedral before it was destroyed: a hint of ecumenism?

2 They built a house for the papal nuncio who never came, and a museum for their greatest composer and painter, Mikolajus Cerulionis. Vytautis Landisbergis, the future (1989) President of Lithuania, wrote his thesis about Cerulionis as well as many articles illustrating his importance.

Faculty to the newly-founded Catholic University of Lublin (KUL).

After 126 years of partition this Polish peacock truculence, understandable enough, stored up future troubles. Culture, language and Catholicism had ensured the survival of the Polish nation during the partitions which wiped it off the map. The nation survived the dissolution of the state. So Polish political thinking stressed the "nation" at the expense of the "state". The first thing Montini noted was that the partitions had weakened the sense of "civil virtue".[1] But that was only half the problem: the expanded Poland resurrected in 1920 had to cope with minorities, accounting for one-third of its population, who did not belong to the Polish "nation": West Ruthenians (Ukrainians), Belorussians, Germans, Lithuanians, and three million Jews.[2]

As if that challenge were not enough, in 1920 Poland had to weld a nation out of fragments that had lived under four disparate legal dispensations, six currencies, three railway networks and three tax and fiscal systems. It made little economic sense. Vast discrepancies opened up between the once German-speaking Pomerania, culturally advanced and industrially prosperous, and the primitive rural subsistence economies in the ex-Russian zone. The rich industrial belt of Silesia was the economic motor of the nation. But like Galicia, once the granary of the Austro-Hungarian Empire, it was cut off from its friends and, more crucially, its markets.[3]

Maybe because of its many problems, Poland won many friends in the 1920s and 1930s. Poles had the right human values. They were nonchalant and coolly brave. They loved horses. One episode summed up their attitude. In August 1920 the Prime Minister, Witos Wincenty, a farmer, insisted very properly on gathering home his harvest before tackling the Bolshevik hordes who were hammering at the gates of Warsaw.[4] Catholics abroad found this "Catholic nation" very sympathetic, and compared it with Ireland.

Yet not every one admired the new Poland. "Poland," declared Lloyd George, "is drunk with the new wine of liberty supplied by the Allies, and fancies herself as the resistless mistress of Central Europe."[5] From a distant "ally", that was ominous. The Soviet foreign minister, Molotov, a likely enemy, sounded even more ominous, and inaccurate, when he dubbed Poland "the monstrous bastard of the Peace of Versailles". The 1939 scenario was already being put together.

1 *Familiari*, p. 244.

2 Paul Johnson, *A History of the Modern World from 1917 to the 1980s*, p. 39.

3 Adam Zamoyski, *The Polish Way*, p. 347.

4 Norman Davies, *God's Playground: A History of Poland*, vol. 2, p. 397.

5 Ibid. p. 393.

Montini wanted to be genuinely friendly on his first and, as it turned out, only diplomatic posting. But there were ill-feelings between Pius XI, who sent him there, and the Polish bishops. They had rebuffed him in 1919 and still resented his behaviour. They thought him too pro-German.[1]

The Vatican had followed its usual practice of changing ecclesiastical boundaries only when the political frontiers were recognized in international law. Thus Silesia was given Polish bishops only after all the problems concerning the 1921 plebiscite were cleared up. Danzig (Gdansk to Poles) was separated from the German episcopal conference only when it was formally made an independent city-state; but even then, in view of its German character, Danzig was given an ecclesiastical administrator of German birth who was not linked to the Polish hierarchy, as the Polish bishop wanted.[2] Catholic though it was, Poland did not enjoy untroubled relations with the Holy See.

On arrival in Warsaw on 10 June 1923 Battista was plunged head first into these problems as Ratti's successor, Lorenzo Lauri, a Rome diocesan priest, greeted him. The Nuncio was brooding over the draft Concordat with Poland – eventually signed in 1925 – and the disposal of Church property confiscated by Prussians, Russians or Austrians.[3] But after that initiation Battista saw little of Lauri: in July the Nuncio was taking the waters at Marienbad in Czechoslovakia "on his way" to Rome. He came back in late September.[4]

The Nunciature at ulica Ksiazeka 21[5] was part of the parish plant and overlooked the early-nineteenth-century church of St Alexander.[6] It was an island of *romanità* in the middle of Warsaw. Lauri insisted on Italian food and an Italian timetable for meals.[7] "All the conversation

1 Fappani-Molinari, *Montini Giovane*, p. 210. When Poland was reunited the bishops met at Czestochowa to plan the future. Msgr Achille Ratti, as Apostolic Visitor, hastened to the shrine. He was met by Prince (a secular title) Bishop Adam Sapieha of Kraków, who brusquely shut the door on him: the *Polish* bishops did not need the papal representative at their meeting. Elected Pope in 1923, Pius XI never forgot this snub, and Sapieha did not get a red hat in his pontificate. He became a cardinal only in 1946.

2 Stewart A. Stechlin, "The Emergence of a New Vatican Diplomacy during the Great War and its Aftermath, 1914–1929", a paper read at the conference on Vatican Diplomacy in the Nineteenth and Twentieth Centuries, University of New Brunswick, Canada, 13 October 1991, p. 7.

3 Fappani-Molinari, *Montini Giovane*, p. 210.

4 *Familiari*, p. 229.

5 Ibid. p. 217.

6 Ibid. The dedication of the church was designed to flatter the tsar.

7 Ibid.

is about Rome and the Romans," Battista wrote home on 16 June 1923, "and by Saturday Monday morning's papers have arrived."[1]

Despite this weekly lifeline from Rome, he felt marooned. For two months he said Mass in the Nunciature chapel: no one came. He told Andrea Trebeschi that although physically all right, "morally, this is a trial, just office routine and professionally tedious".[2] With Lauri away the *uditore*, the Tuscan *bon viveur* Carlo Chiarlo, took charge. He was a "character" – the clerical word for an eccentric. He was kind to Montini. Though full of good humour and common sense, he was distinctly odd.

Montini was well disposed towards him and described him to his family: "He likes photography, charades, the Jewish quarter – where he goes for long walks, in defiance of the scandalized, miracle cures, cigars from Tuscany, tunes from operas and popular songs, the comedies of Stentorello, children, walking, freedom."[3] These were a few of his favourite things. Naturally he was also very pious, and Montini offers as evidence the fact that Gemma Galgani, to be canonized in 1940, once lived in his house. Back in Rome he sent this *bon viveur* fifteen to twenty bottles of wine, "Chianti or something similar," he ordered. This suggests he was not a connoisseur.[4]

There was someone else in the Nunciature who, though unlikely to play charades, could tell Battista a lot about recent history. Fr Giovanni Genocchi, a missionary of the Sacred Heart, had been an outstanding scripture scholar. In the early years of the century his library was the meeting place for a body called, with deliberate vagueness, *l'unione per il bene*, which included the Baron von Hügel, Msgr Louis Duchesne, the novelist Antonio Fogazzaro and Padre Giovanni Semeria, last met in chapter 3.[5]

Genocchi, now seventy-three, had only three more years to live. He treasured a letter from Leo XIII who said he "was loath to proceed against Catholic scholars by means of condemnations", preferring "where necessary, more courteous and less insulting methods".

The "Modernist" scare wrecked his scholarly career, and the scripture scholar was sent first to New Guinea and then to Patagonia to

1 Ibid. p. 216.

2 *Giovane amico*, p. 165.

3 *Familiari* p. 248. Warsaw's Jewish population came to 30 per cent of the total population in the 1931 census. Wearing long black gaberdines, side-locks and beards, speaking Yiddish rather than Polish, the Warsaw Jews were all too visible. See Zamoyski, *The Polish Way*, p. 346.

4 *Familiari*, p. 391. Pope John XXIII made Chiarlo a cardinal in 1958, at the same time as Montini.

5 Piccioni, *Fogazzaro*, 368.

report on the ill-treatment of the Putulayo Indians.[1] Warsaw was nearer home, but he was only there because as Apostolic Visitor he was denied access to the Ukraine after its brief adventure of independence, and was obliged to concentrate on the Uniates (or Greek Catholics) of Galicia who numbered some four million. They were led since 1901 by Metropolitan Andrew Szepticky, a striking figure over seven feet tall.[2] This was Montini's introduction to the "Uniate problem".

Genocchi knew a great deal about the chancy nature of Vatican appointments. His assessment of Battista was swift and shrewd. He argued with Pizzardo, his superior, that Montini should not remain in Poland, since its cruel winter would ruin his already fragile health. He recommended that as a talented young man Fr Montini should be allowed to resume academic work.[3]

But where was the budding diplomat Montini? He tried hard to learn Polish but his head soon felt like "the tower of Babel".[4] Battista, he told his astonished parents, came out as "Chrzciciel" in Polish. The number of case-endings and declensions baffled him. As for pronunciation, his teacher said that to speak Polish you had to make train-like whistles and puffs.[5] Even after three months he could only "stammer a few phrases" like *Dzień dobry, jestem Jan Montini* (Good day, I'm Giovanni Montini). "This damn language" (*questa dannata lingua*), he called it.[6]

It was much easier to have 200 visiting cards printed – in French[7] – and go to parties. He attended a gala dinner in the vacant Royal Palace for the King and Queen of Romania. A military review on an airfield impressed him as "a splendid display of the energy and national will of Poland."[8] Marshal Józef Pilsulski, he explained, was "the creator of this army, the Garibaldi of the Polish nation". This was kindly meant. He lunched with the Primate, Cardinal Aleksander Kakowski (1862–1938), a giant of a man who seemed "cordial and affable".[9] It was the usual diplomatic routine, with many contacts and little communication. Every-

1 *Familiari*, p. 212.

2 Sonya A. Quitsland, *Beauduin, a Prophet Vindicated*, Newman Press, New York 1973, p. 85. He survived till 1944, and Nikita Khrushchev attended his funeral.

3 *Familiari*, pp. 260–1.

4 Ibid. p. 252.

5 Ibid. p. 255.

6 Ibid. p. 217.

7 Ibid.

8 Ibid. p. 252.

9 Ibid. pp. 215, 217.

one seemed to be very tall. "Are they all supermen?" he wondered.[1]

While Montini was finding his feet in Warsaw dramatic events were taking place in Italy. On 11 July 1923 Don Luigi Sturzo "resigned" as leader of the PPI, the party he had founded with a papal blessing in 1919.

At the time Don Sturzo's "resignation" was incomprehensible. Less than two months before, on 15 May 1923, the council or governing body of the PPI *unanimously* re-elected him as Secretary-General. Surprise turned to shock as the evidence mounted that Sturzo had probably been dumped by the Vatican. But one could not be sure in this murky area. An article by the philo-Fascist Don Enrico Pucci in *Il Corriere d'Italia* warned Don Sturzo "not to embarrass the Holy See". Pucci built a successful Roman career on gossip and knowing the way the wind was blowing.[2]

His remark would have been innocuous but for the fact that it was exactly the line plugged by the Fascist press. *Il Giornale d'Italia* alleged that Sturzo was "dragging the nation into obscure adventures that could only lead to a political upheaval" (23 June 1923). This really meant that the Vatican was trying to sweeten the Fascists so as to make possible "the resolution of the Roman question". Sturzo was sacrificed on the altar of reconciliation.

From Warsaw Montini had little chance of understanding what was really happening. He lacked the *retroscena*, the necessary background. From his distance Sturzo's resignation "looks like a defeat, but a decidedly unheroic one".[3] He thinks, however, that Sturzo's resignation is "a lesser evil than the dissolution of the party" and explains it by "internal disagreements rather than hostile external pressures". Every one of these statements was demonstrably wrong.

Giorgio, his father, in the thick of the parliamentary battle, was better placed to know the truth. He told Battista on 16 July 1923 that "after weeks of torment, yesterday was the bitterest, most emotional and difficult day of my life".[4] It was the day of the "vote of confidence" when official PPI policy was abstension. But ten *Popolari* opted for Mussolini. At issue was "electoral reform" which most of the *Popolari*, including Giorgio, believed would lead to dictatorship. They were right.

To perceive this required little more than an ability to count: for the Fascist proposal was that the party that won a quarter plus one of the votes should have two-thirds of the seats. Giorgio felt stabbed in the

1 Ibid. p. 214.

2 He was the unofficial "source" for many journalists well into the 1950s.

3 *Familiari*, p. 230.

4 Ibid. p. 230.

back by some of his *Popolari* friends. He warns Battista about editorials in *Corriere d'Italia*. It is part of a chain belonging to Count Giovanni Grosoli, a PPI founder present at Battista's ordination. He is now beginning to wobble towards Fascism.[1] Giorgio charitably explains that Grosoli wants to get back on the board of the Banco di Roma to finance his many good works.[2]

Yet the real wrecker of Sturzo and the PPI was Battista's own superior, Msgr Giuseppe Pizzardo, at the Secretariat of State. Battista was not slow to grasp the real meaning of the Pucci article. The sacking of Sturzo prefigured the liquidation – to use Lenin's word – of the *Popolari*. Sturzo went into exile in London in October 1923, telling everyone that he was on a study trip and would soon return. He even tried to persuade his brother Mario, Bishop of Piazza Armerina, that London was "his own idea".[3] In fact he had been "advised" (that is, ordered) to depart by the Cardinal Secretary of State, Pietro Gasparri, and at the same time "sworn to secrecy" about the real reasons for his exile.

These Italian events may not have seemed very relevant to Montini in Poland. Yet there was a link. The Church, according to current Catholic teaching, neither approved nor disapproved of this or that political regime: yet it mattered enormously whether a "Catholic country" like Poland chose democracy or swung to the right where Fascism already beckoned. Sturzo disagreed with the official teaching: he believed that democracy had a moral content.[4] This gave him ground to stand on in his anti-Fascism; it also exiled him for twenty years.

1 Giordani-Sturzo, *Un Ponte fra due Generazioni, carteggio 1924–1958*, Revista Milanese di economia, serie quaderna no. 12, 1986, p. 161.

2 *Familiari*, p. 230 fn. 4.

3 Luigi and Mario Sturzo, *Carteggio*, 4 vols, Edizioni di Storia e Letteratura, Rome 1985, vol. 1, p. xi. Mario, the elder brother, was Bishop of Piazza Armerina throughout the Fascist period. Luigi was in London, living at 213B Gloucester Place. There he was spied on by Msgr Umberto Benigni who, having first served in the *Sapinière*, which uncovered "modernists", transferred his talents to OVRA, the Fascist secret service. He reported on the London situation in 1926 just before the General Strike, which he said would not happen. He also denounced Fr Cyril Charles Martindale, the famous Farm Street Jesuit, as a crypto Christian Democrat (Benigni's report is in the Archives of the Italian Foreign Ministry, a copy of which is at St Anthony's College, Oxford).

Sturzo, object of this report, a resolute anti-Fascist whose works included *The International Community and the Right to War* (1928); *Society: its Nature and Laws* (1935); and, decisively, *Church and State* (1939), lived in London until 1940 when he was threatened with arrest as an "enemy alien". He understandably preferred New York to internment camp on the Isle of Man. Wickham Steed, a pundit from *The Times*, held him in high regard.

4 Sturzo was prophetic. A Polish Pope, John Paul II, declared: "The Church values the democratic system inasmuch as it ensures the participation of citizens in making political choices, guarantees to the governed the possibility both of electing and

Battista had not yet seen much of Poland. He set off by train on 19 August. His first stop was at Auschwitz (Oświęcim in Polish). Within twenty years it became notorious as the place of the *Shoah* or Holocaust. Battista was innocently there to celebrate the twenty-fifth anniversary of the arrival of the Salesians in Poland. Their founder, Don Bosco, was Milanese and most of them spoke Italian. The next Primate, August Hlond, would be a Salesian. Their technical school seemed "very modern". Battista made a sweeping judgement about national character: "Poles, like Slavs generally, are better at feeling than in practical affairs, unless they happen to be educated by Germans."[1]

Prince Bishop Sapieha presided, unveiling a statue of Don Bosco and blessing three church bells inscribed *una voce dicentes Sanctus, Sanctus, Sanctus* – "a lovely symbol," Battista noted. It was more than that. The occupying forces had stolen all the church bells so that the *Angelus* could no longer ring out across the Polish countryside. That the bells should first be rehung at Auschwitz was an eerie premonition.

From Auschwitz he went with Sapieha to Kraków. Sapieha was Italian-speaking, having worked in the Secretariat of State before the War. Kraków enchanted Battista. It was so like a "southern city" and so much more interesting than Warsaw.[2] His parents would have felt at home there. All the kings of Poland except Stanislaw Augustus, the last, he tells them, are buried in the cathedral crypt. The cathedral itself is Gothic but it is enfolded within a castle (*Zamek*) built in a jumble of borrowed styles from Venetian to Florentine Renaissance. It has a touch of "our own baroque, giving an impression of contorted heaviness".[3]

Every tomb bears a history of piety and heroism. Tadeusz Kosciuszko, who took part in the American revolution before declaring the anti-Russian insurrection in the Kraków market square in 1794, is the greatest of all Polish heroes. No Polish home was complete without a picture of him. At Czestochowa, which Battista dubbed "the Polish Loreto", the "traditional piety of this most religious people, so oppressed and humiliated", heartened him.[4]

holding accountable those who govern them, and of replacing them through peaceful means when appropriate" (*Centesimo Anno*, 1 May 1991, no. 45). See Rossana Carmagnani and Antonio Palazzo, *Mediazione culturale e impegno politico in Sturzo e Maritain*, Massimo, Milan 1985.

1 *Familiari*, p. 244. This was a widely accepted view. Posnania in the East had prospered under Prussian "colonization". Hipolyt Cegielski founded a factory for making agricultural machinery at Poznań (German, Posen) in the 1870s and went on to set up sugar refineries and a huge industrial complex (Adam Zamoyski, *The Polish Way*, p. 305). It still exists, though in other hands. Its workers revolted in July 1956 – the first example of workers rising against a "workers' state".

2 *Familiari*, p. 242.

3 Ibid. p. 245.

4 Ibid. p. 246.

Then it was home to the tedious routine of the Nunciature. Occasionally Lauri took a landau to lunch with a suburban parish priest. They were struck by the fact that so many of the houses and churches were built of wood.[1] Their own parish priest returned from Rome with a bunch of grapes. Pius XI had enquired about Battista's health, he reported, flattered.[2]

Uncertain about his future – to stay or not to stay – Battista was miserable on 2 September 1923:

> I am inept, inadequate, and what's more impatient; my health means that, like Penelope's web, my life will humanly speaking have no continuity, and that it is presumptuous of me to live with the idea that I am as capable as others of doing some serious work; so much so that sometimes the spring of desire for any activity at all simply snaps.[3]

Yet, assuming he is going to stay, he appends a list of things he wants. He needs linen and pills, Pascal's *Pensées*, Jacques Maritain's *Introduction à la Philosophie*, and Prat's *Théologie de Saint Paul*.[4] A week later he asks for "humorists" like Gandolin (Luigi Arnaldo Vassallo) and Paolo Farrari who "cheer one up when bad blood threatens"; but then ruins everything by adding that they are not really for him. Obviously Msgr Carlo Chiarlo needed a regular dose of humour.

On 19 September Battista was in Poznan and Gniezno to visit the tomb of St Adalbert (Wojciech) who, in 966, had baptized Miesko I. But his mind was not on tourism or history. His father and Padre Genocchi pulled strings to get him back to Italy before winter came. Giorgio saw the Warsaw Nuncio, Lorenzo Lauri, in Rome at five o'clock on 14 September. Giorgio had to be punctual because Lauri had an audience fixed with Pius XI. The Nuncio was sympathetic, writes Giorgio, and promised to include Genocchi's letter in the dossier for the Holy Father. Giorgio saw Lauri next morning at 9 to hear the Pope's decision: Battista would stay in Warsaw.[5]

He took his "sentence" with humour and sent for his warm winter longjohns. Antonio, servant at the Pontifical Academy, knows where they are. But he will need to buy a fur hat and coat. He wishes Giorgio had not intervened so soon. Pizzardo's letter with the "sentence" was not very friendly. The academic reasons for returning, Pizzardo loftily

1 Ibid. p. 248.
2 Ibid. p. 249.
3 Ibid. p. 251.
4 Ibid.
5 Ibid. p. 259.

advised, "should be entrusted to the conscience and responsibility of your superiors", while the medical factors "should be considered very calmly after consultation with local doctors". But, the substitute concluded, "Sincerely I would be very happy if the medical advice is that you should stay put."[1]

It is extraordinary that Pope and Curia should be bothering about the fate of a twenty-six-year-old priest who was in Warsaw "without official nomination, precise duties, or salary".[2] But so it was. Pius XI knew Warsaw: he had seen the Bolsheviks driven back from the gates of the city in "the miracle of the Vistula".

Battista was by now an "expert" on Poland. He wrote four articles in *Il Cittadino di Brescia*. Because of his position half in and half out of the Vatican diplomatic service, they were unsigned, but in Brescia "everyone knew" he was the author.[3] The titles reveal his interests: "The Queen of Poland", "The Demographic Context in Poland", "Polish Men and Parties" (signed "Nemo"), and "France and Poland". They are competent articles reflecting what he was learning in Poland, even as he learned it. Like many journalists he was writing at the outer edge of his knowledge.

A later article in Trebeschi's student magazine, *La Fionda* (5 September 1925), relates his Polish experience to the wider world. "Polish Patriotism" kept one eye on the Italian scene. It was an attempt to sort out concepts such as people, nation, nationality, country (*patria*), state, government, patriotism. Then as now these are the basic "building blocks" of political science.

Montini defended patriotism as a fundamental Christian virtue, the concrete expression of "love of one's neighbour". It can be corrupted or go horribly wrong, but patriotism as neighbourly love is the right place to start. He actually calls it "fraternal *solidarity*".[4] Naturally he expects Polish patriotism to take a Catholic shape. This enables him to make an anti-Bolshevik point, reinforced by the murder of a Polish priest and the arrest at 4 a.m. of the auxiliary bishop of Mohilew, Jan Cieplak.[5]

1 Ibid. p. 261.

2 Nello Vian, Introd. in ibid. p. xxxvi.

3 *Familiari*, p. 253.

4 Fappani-Molinari, *Montini Giovane*, p. 406. Heinrich Pesch SJ had already written a three-volume work on Catholic social teaching which enjoyed a vogue in Poland. "*Solidarismus*" was for Pesch the key-concept that overcame both "socialist" collectivism and "liberal" individualism. See Franz H. Mueller, *The Church and the Social Question*, American Enterprise Institute for Public Policy Research, Washington 1984, esp. pp. 101–3.

5 *Familiari*, p. 224. Cieplak was condemned to death in 1923, saw his sentence commuted to ten years in labour camp, and was freed in March 1924, dying in 1926. The "cause" of his beatification has been started.

Bolshevism, as developed by Lenin, involved the suppression of feelings traditionally known as patriotism: since class struggle was primary in Marxist ideology, national sentiment was vain and illusory. Six years after "the" revolution, Marxism invited not the nations but the workers of the world to unite. These were very real questions in the Poland of 1923. Were Communists patriotic? If not, should they be put in gaol?

Montini reflects Polish opinion picked up in many conversations. The Bolsheviks had been thrown out of Poland in 1920, the year Karol Wojtyla was born. Poland could not seriously be expected to give up its new-found independence in pursuit of some vaguely Utopian internationalist ideal. Hence the long-term dilemma of that pantomime horse, the Polish Communist Party.

Having established the validity of patriotism, Montini notes how easily it can be corrupted. The first distortion comes from the party spirit. He quotes a Polish proverb, "Three Poles, four parties."[1] He summarizes the tragic history of Poland with its elective monarchy constantly being "plagued by conflicts, plots, counter-plots, power struggles, abuses, treachery – all done in the name of Poland, but in fact all contributing to its downfall".[2]

These are not "racist" slurs, for Montini finds the same pattern in the Italian city-states of the Middle Ages: "There comes a moment when a party loses the idea of the *patria*, bringing in the foreigner, if it is weak, or oppressing the nation, if it is strong."[3] But partisanship, though not absent from the Poland of the 1920s, was not for Montini the immediate threat. The real danger was exclusive nationalism:

> A second and excessive form of patriotism is that which regards one's own nation as the unique motherland in the world. This form of nationalism, which characterizes not only young Poland but all modern European states, especially the former Central Powers (remember the *Deutschland über alles* of Nietzsche) and France today. This is born of a lack of social and historical perspective.
>
> The vision of one's own greatness not only belittles the greatness and dignity of other nations, but casts dark shadows

1 Fappani-Molinari, *Montini Giovane*, p. 404.

2 Montini gets his idea of Poland largely from Montalambert and from Adam Mickiewicz's lectures at the Collège de France from 1835. Both make much of the "Slav soul" which, despite material backwardness, is superior to what passes for "progress" in the West. In 1848 Mickiewicz went to Rome to raise a Polish legion, and pestered Pio Nono with his revolutionary ideas. He once seized the Pope's sleeve and yelled, "Let me tell you that today the Holy Spirit resides beneath the shirts of the Parisian workers." Adam Zamoyski, *The Polish Way*, p. 297.

3 Montini, *Giovane amico*, p. 404.

> over them. Moreover this form of nationalism habitually treats foreigners as enemies – especially the foreigners with whom one has common frontiers.
>
> Then one seeks the expansion of one's own country at the expense of its immediate neighbours. Thus a people grows up with a feeling of being hemmed in, and with an instinct for premeditated aggression. So peace becomes a transient compromise between two wars.[1]

That may seem an insensitive remark which ignored the potential industrial and military strength of Poland's neighbours. Poland would never have freely chosen to sit on a plain between Germany and Russia. But the point of geo-politics is that one does not have such choices. And Montini's conclusion was sadly verified within fifteen years.

He did not get a chance to deepen his knowledge of Poland. The Nunzio, Lorenzo Lauri, was back by 29 September 1923 and found a doctor for Montini's check-up. But on 2 October a telegram arrived out of the blue from the Secretary of State, Cardinal Pietro Gasparri. It read: "MONTINI AUTHORIZED RETURN ROME".[2] There was no explanation for the change of plan.

"Thus concludes," Battista wrote, "this episode in my life which has provided useful though not always joyful experiences, from which only later and with maturity I may profit according to the designs of Providence."[3]

He underestimated himself. At the very least he had learned to read the map of Poland, could visualize the scenes of wartime horrors, understand the significance of the millennium celebrations of 1966, and appreciate the emergence on the international scene of Karol Wojtyla, successor of Sapieha in Kraków. He also bought somewhere in Poland the alarm clock that went off the moment he died.

1 Ibid.

2 *Familiari*, p. 264.

3 Ibid. p. 265.

6

Roman Apprenticeship

> And the flags. And the trumpets. And so many
> eagles.
> How many? Count them. And such a press of people.
> We hardly knew ourselves that day, or knew the city.
> This way to the temple . . .
>
> T. S. Eliot, Coriolan,
> *Collected Poems 1909–1962*, p. 139.

After a night in a sleeper from Warsaw, Don Battista was back at the Pontifical Academy by 13 October 1923. The next day he was due to go *lassù*, up there, the usual Vatican term for the papal apartments. In fact he had to wait until the following 20 January 1924 for his audience with Pope Pius XI.[1] In the meantime his immediate superior, Msgr Pizzardo, behaving with "his usual *désinvolture*", told him the Holy Father had named him "ecclesiastical assistant" (in plain English "chaplain") to the Catholic students of Rome. He was immediately plunged into a round of meetings with the Cardinal Vicar of Rome and other FUCI chaplains. Their purpose was to decide how to cope with the new Fascist regime.[2]

His new post was no bed of roses. He had been brought in to remedy a crisis. There had been intrigues, petty disputes and what he calls "a parody of democratic procedures" which led to the resignation of the President, Gino Andreotti, after only a year in office.[3]

The Tiber was in full spate that winter, barely passing under the bridges, threatening St Paul's without-the-walls. This may have suggested his punning metaphor: "My own little barque is doing a barcarole (*la mia barqua procede un po' barocollante*), but at least it's on the move."[4] But his first attempts to tackle the problems of FUCI in Rome

1 *Familiari*, p. 289.

2 Ibid. p. 269.

3 Ibid. p. 272 fn. 5. Parody it may have been, but many Catholic students had their first, and only, experience of democracy in FUCI.

4 Ibid. p. 275.

left him feeling somewhat limp, and also reveal what his instructions were:

> My days are filled with sterile toil and taken up in the silly tasks imposed by my situation. It's all very well to say that our action should be confined to spiritual formation; would that it were. I have had to break myself in to the manoeuvres of practical politics even more than in Warsaw . . . and the terrible downdrag of Rome paralyses, exhausts and overwhelms me.[1]

He bade farewell to 1923 without regret, and prayed the early Christian prayer found in the *Didache*: *Maran atha*, Come, Lord, come.[2]

Montini's headquarters was at via della Scrofa 70. He spent the mornings at the Pontifical Academy and the late afternoon and evenings at the chaplaincy. It was difficult to find the neutral, non-partisan topics demanded of him. Almost anything could be given a political twist. He arranged a lecture on "Dante and Italy": but Dante had denounced tyrants, so that was politically explosive.[3]

To heighten the tension Parliament was dissolved and new elections were fixed for 5 April 1924. With the PPI now thoroughly confused, Giorgio Montini tried to explain to a provincial congress of the party just how the mould of Italian politics was being shattered and reshaped:

> The Fascist Party, proud of its strength and its victories, scorns all collaboration and wants to stifle all opposition. In this it makes a double mistake, because an honest minority always serves and improves the workings of the majority which holds power. Instead of being weakened by distrust, we should be honoured as the only party which has kept its identity and had the courage to assert its own ideas, its own faith, its own confidence in the future.[4]

But this public confidence was matched by private misgivings. Giorgio was pessimistic about the outcome, fearing that the election would not really be free.[5]

Battista admired his father's doggedness but was gloomy about the future. Italy was relapsing into fourteenth-century individualism. He

1 Ibid. p. 276.

2 Ibid. p. 278.

3 Ibid. p. 283. The academic year began with a Mass at Santa Maria sopra Minerva. Pietro Fedele gave the lecture on Dante. A reception followed.

4 *Il Cittadino di Brescia*, 26 February 1924. Don Battista saw to it that copies of his father's paper were available at via della Scrofa 70.

5 *Familiari*, p. 298 fn. 1.

saw through Mussolini: "The heroic poses make one weep when one thinks of the egoism and wretched personal virtues on which they are based."[1] Though he rejects the idea of "inner emigration" – resorting to Dante and Bach in private – he fears it may be forced upon them. In a St Patrick's Day letter, 17 March 1924, he offers his own strategy for survival: "He who has faith sows for a better time than the present. Will it not be one day understood that the best apologetic, the only one that is truly Christian, must convince in order to overcome (*per vincere, deve convincere*)?[2]

It was a formula for the long haul. They needed it, for the Fascists were sweeping all before them. In the Brescia province, for example, the PPI polled 28,221 votes (compared with 45,000 in 1921) while the Fascist "block", with the help of intimidation, soared to 76,255.[3]

On 12 April Battista reported a long conversation on the Italian situation with Msgr Pizzardo. The reason he could break confidence was that Pizzardo had a role for Giorgio. Battista writes: "The Church has high hopes of *our* group, and does not like it to be taken in tow by anyone else; he wants it to be the engine of the shattered party."[4] On this analysis the "Brescia current" represented the "balanced centre", while the left-wing under Guido Miglioli was restless and the right-wing was already supporting the Fascists. That may throw light on why Don Luigi Sturzo was sacked: he was considered too left-wing. He was briefly replaced by an uneasy triumvirate and then, on 19 May 1924, by Alcide De Gasperi. One could not hold out strong hopes for him.

On 23 April 1924 Don Battista addressed the FUCI Conference at Orvieto. He became a regular speaker at these meetings for nearly a decade. His theme was the need to grasp the inner meaning of the liturgy:

> A good liturgy does not consist in the correct observance of the rubrics and the rules; it involves the Christian soul and calls it really to take part in this act of adoration and homage to God. This is what the Church intends. It is not enough to follow the ceremonies with physical eyes, one needs to plumb them with the deepest spiritual sense. It is a waste of time to be present at Catholic worship unless the soul reaches out beyond the gestures and externals.[5]

1 Ibid. p. 292.

2 Ibid. p. 294. He would use a similar play on words during the Council. He wanted *des convaincus, pas de vaincus*. People cannot be forced to believe.

3 Ibid. p. 297.

4 Ibid. p. 299.

5 Maria Cristina Giuntella, " *Montini assistente*," in *G. B. Montini e la Societa Italiana 1919–1939*, Centro di Documentazione, Brescia, p. 134. Montini much admired

While Montini was addressing the Catholic students in Orvieto, Giacomo Matteotti, the Socialist leader in Parliament, denounced the violence, intimidation and fraud that had dominated the election, and demanded that the chamber should pronounce the result invalid. As he sat down he said to his friends: "Now you can get my funeral oration ready ."[1] How right he was. He was kidnapped on 10 June. His body, stabbed to death, was discovered only two months later. The assassins acted on the orders of Cesare Rossi, Mussolini's press officer. The Matteotti murder showed that the Fascists would stop at nothing. It caused a wave of revulsion against them. The government briefly tottered.[2]

Don Battista formally left the Pontifical Academy that same June. This meant he would have to find a flat. His brother, Lodovico, announced that he would be marrying Giuseppina Forlonari in October, so he too was flat-hunting. Meanwhile Battista prepared the Longinotti children, Mario and Alessandro, for their first communion: they received the sacrament from Pius XI at a private Mass in the Vatican on the feast of Corpus Christi.[3] Coming just a week after the "Aventine secession", when a hundred deputies including De Gasperi, Giorgio Montini and Longinotti resolved to have no more dealings with this morally tainted government, this mark of papal favour was significant. There would still be a role for Longinotti should Mussolini fall.

Don Battista escaped for the summer to France. He stayed with the monks at Hautecombe from 21 July to 4 August. Since these were the Benedictines he had known at Chiari, now home again in Savoy, this was hardly a very adventurous move. A last-minute decision took him to Paris where he spent the rest of August with the Benedictine sisters at rue Monsieur 20.

Seeking to show the deep influence of France on Montini, Jean Guitton exaggerates the significance of this first visit to Paris. He turns a stay of three weeks into one of "several months", and attributes to Montini the following remark: "I said Mass in the chapel where, on

Romano Guardini's pioneering work, *Vom Geist der Liturgie* (1922) ET, *The Spirit of the Liturgy* (1930). Montini's own language here anticipates Pius XII's encyclical, *Mediator Dei* (1947) which emphasized "active participation" in the liturgy. He parted company with those Jesuits who said they were concerned exclusively with the *training* in faith, hope and charity, of which the liturgy was merely the outward *expression*.

1 Christopher Seton-Watson, *Italy from Liberalism to Fascism*, p. 650.

2 Ibid., pp. 660–61. In 1945, towards the end of his life, Mussolini told a journalist that he had thought of resigning in June 1924, and recommending to the King that Filippo Turati, a reformist Socialist, should form the next government.

3 *Familiari*, p. 311. Mario was with his father on 13 May 1944 when the car in which they were travelling was machine-gunned. *Notiziario*, 9, p. 56.

Sundays, several of your writers, your converts, used to come together."[1] But this cannot be true of his 1924 visit. In August Paris is deserted. Even Josef Coppens, who at that time lived in the Benedictine convent and looked after Belgian clerical students in Paris, forgot this basic truth.

Coppens speculates that Montini *might have* met Jacques Maritain then at the Institute Catholique or gone to hear Loisy lecture at the College de France or crossed rue Monsieur to meet Léonce de Grandmaison SJ whose monumental *Jésus-Christ* "was considered the best reply to Modernism".[2] All this is unfounded guesswork.

Montini, however, did meet Maurice Zundel, a Swiss priest who was lodging with the Benedictine nuns at rue Monsieur. Zundel, from the French-speaking canton of Neuchâtel, a fellow student with Charles Journet at the Fribourg seminary, had "tried his vocation" with the German-speaking Benedictines of Einsiedeln. He now lived in great poverty with barely enough money to pay for the hand-rolled cigarettes he chain-smoked. Montini took to him straight away. Since leaving Einsiedeln he had devoted himself to writing and rewriting *Le Poème de la Sainte Liturgie* that would eventually make his name known throughout Europe. But here he was in Paris, living in the equivalent of a garret.

Montini had heard about Zundel through his brother Lodovico who met him while working at the ILO in Geneva. A common friend was Henry Ferrero, another Swiss, who broke his Protestant mother's heart by becoming a Catholic, later a priest. Zundel reveals another side of Montini's character. They were the same age, twenty-seven, and in conversation Montini said how saddened he was by "the mediocrity of so many priests who fail to live up to their vocation". Zundel consoled him:

> We're still young. But at forty, fifty, or sixty, won't we be more indulgent when we have gone through the same difficulties in being faithful? A priest who seems mediocre to us may have passed through the fire of trials we don't know about. And if

1 Jean Guitton, *Dialogues avec Paul VI*, Fayard, Paris, p. 139. The legend of a first meeting with Jacques Maritain has had a long life. Thus Domenico Paoletti in *La Testimonianza Cristiana nel Mondo Contemporaneo in Papa Montini*, 1991: "The beginning of this companionship-encounter between Montini and Maritain is to be placed in Paris in 1924. Although it is not certain that Montini heard lectures by Maritain – then professor at the Paris Institut Catholique – yet the frequentation of the intellectual milieux of the French capital undoubtedly put him in touch with the work of the French intellectual", pp. 59–60.

2 Josef Coppens, "*Sa Sainteté Paul VI, In Memoriam*", in *Notiziario*, 9, p. 73.

he's remained, on the whole, faithful to his vocation, that is already something.[1]

Montini's answer is not recorded.

He stayed in touch with the maverick Zundel, of whom even his sympathetic bishop said, "*C'est un franc-tireur, et l'Eglise n'aime pas les franc-tireurs.*" He welcomed him in Rome in 1925–27 when Zundel wrote a thesis on nominalism at the Angelicum, and arranged for the Italian translation of *Le Poème de la Sainte Liturgie*. During his second period at rue Monsieur, 1927–29, Zundel was his point of contact with the intellectuals who went to Mass there: Louis Massignon, already an expert on Islam, the literary critic Charles du Bos, the philosopher Henri Gouhier, and Jean Guitton himself.[2] As pope he quoted Zundel's lapidary, "God is not an invention but a discovery,"[3] and invited him to give the annual retreat to the Roman Curia in 1972.[4]

Pere Yves de la Brière SJ, who came over every morning at 7 a.m. to say Mass for the nuns, was no maverick. The Jesuits, though still officially illegal in France, had returned to live in small communities. Apartments were advertised as having "gas, heating, Jesuits and electricity on all floors". De la Brière was the political chronicler of the Jesuit monthly, *Etudes*, then at rue Monsieur 15.

Relations between France and the Holy See were at a delicate stage. Montini's first call was at the newly acquired Nunciature, avenue Wilson 10. Despite conciliatory gestures on the part of Pius XI, the "cartel of the left" (an alliance of Radicals and Socialists) defeated the Bloc National in the 11 May election (on which Montini had written an essay the previous year). This gave rise to fears of a new wave of anti-clericalism. Everyone waited to see which way Action Française would jump.[5]

1 Claire Luques, *Maurice Zundel, Esquisse pour un portrait*, Medias Paul 1986, p. 94. Clerical mediocrity is one of the themes of Georges Bernanos' novel, *L'Imposture*, which is set in the Paris Montini knew.

2 Ibid. pp. 103–6. Montini paid another visit to France in the summer of 1926 but he does not seem to have gone to Paris and spent most of his time in Strasbourg – learning German. See *Familiari*, pp. 423–6, for a long description of the cathedral.

3 *Insegnamenti*, 1968, p. 1024. The quotation comes from Zundel's *Recherche du Dieu inconnu*, which includes a discussion of Paul in the marketplace (Acts 17:23), always a key text for Montini.

4 Published in 1976 under the title *Quel homme et quel Dieu*. I am indebted for information on Maurice Zundel to André Kelly, the Swiss TV journalist. See also Marc Donzé, *La Pensée théologique de Maurice Blondel, pauvreté et libération*, Tricorne/Cerf 1980/81. Zundel spent 1929–30 as assistant chaplain to the Assumptionist Sisters at Kensington Square, London where, says Donzé, "*il etudiait avec grande sympathie l'anglicanisme*".

5 Oscar L. Arnal, *Ambivalent Alliance: The Catholic Church and the Action Française, 1899–1939*, University of Pittsburg Press 1985, pp. 93–95. It was a terrible period

The Nunciature, previously the palace of Prince Albert of Monaco, bought the previous January, was embarrassingly grand. De la Brière loyally tried to rationalize its purchase: "To acquire such a building in the present circumstances is a public and courageous act of faith in the future stability of Franco–Vatican relations."[1] Montini found its atmosphere sinister and "heard scarcely veiled accusations against its policies, which only goes to show how difficult it is to work for others".[2] France boasted of being "the eldest daughter of the Church" but she was a very troublesome daughter.

Montini spent his short time in Paris neither hobnobbing with intellectuals nor discussing high politics but improving his French. He was enrolled at the Alliance Française on the boulevard Raspail where most of the students were upper-class English girls. The clerics formed a group apart. They had grammar classes and did practical exercises. They heard lectures on art at the Louvre and on literature back at boulevard Raspail.

René Doumic, director of the Alliance Française and also secretary of the French Academy, was a brilliant lecturer. Montini would "never forget his lectures on Baudelaire, Flaubert and Maupassant".[3] The first encounter with a dazzlingly brilliant French lecturer can linger in the mind for ever; Montini learned by heart passages from *Cyrano de Bergerac*, from Victor Hugo and Verlaine; he read the novels of Paul Bourget, especially *L'Etape* and *Le Disciple*.[4]

From Paris he wrote a moving letter to his brother Lodovico on his forthcoming marriage. Dated 15 August 1924, close to the feast of St Louis, King of France and Lodovico's patron, it was first published in 1986:

> Dear Lodovico
> Just a couple of lines for today's feast . . . You are now the heart of our household, and the two months yet to elapse before your marriage arouse in us all the tremor of anticipation that goes with life-making events.

for the bishops and the Catholic press, reduced to a rabid patriotism which denounced Communism, Freemasonry, Judaism and Protestantism. Novelist Georges Bernanos satirized it in *L'Imposture*, a novel Montini greatly admired.

1 *Familiari*, p. 327.

2 Ibid. To understand this cryptic remark one needs to know that the Nuncio, Bonaventura Cerretti, was a close associate of Cardinal Pietro Gasparri, Secretary of State. They felt hamstrung in the efforts to devise a proper legal status for the Church in France because Roman theologians like Alfredo Ottaviani were still teaching that the separation of Church and State was contrary to Catholic doctrine. For Ottaviani at this time, see Vittorio Peri in *Archivum Pontificiae Historiae*, 1985, p. 316.

3 Jean Guitton, *Dialogues avec Paul VI*, pp. 140–41.

4 Jean Guitton, *Paul VI secret*, p. 93.

Looking at it selfishly, I can say that the happiness of the family now depends on you, for it is in you that the family is renewed and starts again. We who stand on the touchline are glad you are happy. You know that being happy is a difficult business. But the Lord has made it easier for you by giving you the lessons taught so simply and sublimely by our parents – the joy of love, that is, of understanding and being understood, of giving and receiving, of sacrificing oneself to be recreated, of pouring out the treasures of one's own heart only to find them multiplied endlessly.

You have the blessing of having found a lovely woman, privileged and – you know this better than I – unique. *Inventa una pretiosa* [having found a precious pearl] see to it that your soul is vested in a new personality; just think that now you are sealing for ever the means and the measure by which for your entire life you will communicate with another spirit in the mutual quest for human life [*vita humana*] and divine life. Mark well the providential design nature has implanted in you in this time of waiting, gentleness, self-giving, energy, generosity, abiding patience and immense desires. Use the plasticity of your soul in this period to create in yourself a new man, a new character, a new goodness, a new strength, and a new style as you seek the ideal offered by the Companion you await. Lay in a stock of love, yes indeed, for life is long and difficult, like winter, and the nest must always be warm and protected. Maybe in God's mind you have a sovereign right to expect that your marriage will grow and prosper. This is the grace I ask for you. Farewell. D.B.[1]

Lodovico treasured this letter from his celibate brother. It reveals a highly idealistic and uplifting view of marriage. It was based on the experience of their parents. Giuseppina bore Lodovico seven children, making Battista an uncle seven times over, nine times if we add the two daughters of his younger brother, Francesco. Perhaps this had some bearing on *Humanae Vitae*.

So Montini's real concerns in Paris were with Lodovico's marriage and his own future. Only in Guitton's mirror does his first Parisian sojourn become "the experience of modernity". He certainly did not think of it in that way at the time. On 9 August 1924 he got a letter from Pizzardo that decided his future: from October he will enter the Secretariat of State. It meant the end of Agostino Gemelli's attractive

1 *Notiziario*, 12, pp. 99–100.

scheme that he should be student chaplain at the newly-founded Catholic University of Milan, where he would have been a colleague of the just-married Lodovico, hired to teach Catholic social doctrine.[1]

At long last Don Battista had a proper job, though only on the lowest rung of the ladder. His entire future depended on this move. An *adetto* in the Secretariat of State is little more than a glorified office boy, but at least he writes with pride he will be a true *civis Romanus* (Roman citizen). The new intake at the Secretariat also included Alfredo Ottaviani, already famous for his lectures on canon law at the Lateran. Montini knew he was not on that level. His own appointment did not make headlines. Giorgio only put a local-boy-makes-good story in *Il Cittadino* in April 1925 when Battista became a "domestic prelate", assigned to the "second section" of the Secretariat which dealt with foreign governments as *minutante*.[2] This meant he had to take an awesome oath that his biographer could have done without, never to divulge anything. He began to work incessantly, even going into the office on Christmas Day.[3]

His superior was Cardinal Pietro Gasparri, Secretary of State. But more immediately he had to deal with Msgr Francesco Borgongini Duca,[4] Secretary for Extraordinary Affairs; the dwarf-like Msgr Giuseppe Pizzardo, *sostituto*; Domenico Spada, Chancellor of Apostolic Briefs: and Pietro Ciriaci, Under-Secretary for Extraordinary Affairs. Of his colleagues in 1925 Pizzardo, Ottaviani and Ciriaci would all be present at the conclave of 1963 in which he became Pope. They did not vote for him in the first ballot. Montini did not use his title *monsignore* and felt "transplanted into soil where the majestic oak and the parasitical ivy grow well enough, but where I find putting down roots hard work".[5]

Lodovico married Giuseppina on 22 October 1924 in the church where their parents were married. The auxiliary bishop presided at the wedding, but Don Battista said the nuptial Mass in the vestment made out of his mother's wedding robe for his ordination.[6] Thus were their complementary vocations conjoined. The newly-weds came to see him a week later in Rome, chaperoned incongruously by the bride's father. They visited the Carmelite convent of the Tre Madonna where Giusep-

1 *Familiari*, p. 329. The Franciscan Gemelli was the founder and first Rector of the Catholic University of the Sacred Heart.

2 Ibid. p. 369.

3 Ibid. p. 351.

4 A close friend of Angelo Roncalli, he became the first nuncio to Italy after the Lateran Pacts of 1929.

5 *Familiari*, p. 377. Who did he think were the mighty oaks? And who the parasites?

6 Ibid. p. 334.

pina's sister, Francesca, had been an enclosed nun since 1914. They prayed at the tomb of Pius X.[1] And when no one was looking, they made a baby.

Pius XI declared 1925 a Holy Year. Msgr Angelo Roncalli, the future Pope John XXIII, worked hard collecting "artefacts" from missionaries for a universal exhibition. Much of it was pious junk. Battista said the same in more diplomatic language: "It was more edifying than pleasurable."[2]

Montini's pastoral care of the students settled down into a pattern. When not disrupted by political interference, it went like this. The academic year was solemnly inaugurated at the Dominican church of Santa Maria sopra Minerva. A star preacher was secured, in 1925 the Latin Patriarch of Jerusalem (who at that date was inevitably an Italian); he was the second choice after Angelo Roncalli had been disconcertingly packed off to Bulgaria – it was the start of a lifelong friendship. There were regular visits to the Catacombs and St Paul's-without-the-walls where Ildefonso Schuster, the great historian of the liturgy, was abbot.[3]

Still only twenty-eight, Don Battista felt closer to his students than did the distinguished and greying guest speakers he had to invite. His younger brother Francesco, now twenty-five and a medical student in Siena, was another link with the younger generation. Battista suffered from the chronic condition well known to university chaplains: every year a host of apparently similar faces swam before his eyes, and yet they were all different. But he found this pastoral work much more satisfying than shifting paper in the Secretariat of State.

He was reading hard to prepare his own lectures for the students. Three works are worth mentioning from this Holy Year 1925 to illustrate how haphazard his theological reading was at this date. He read Fr Giulio Bevilacqua's translation of a Catholic Truth Society pamphlet by London Oratorian Alan Ross on Robert Hugh Benson. In the Chester–Belloc era Benson was sometimes hailed as a great Catholic writer.[4]

1 Ibid. pp. 366–67.

2 Ibid. pp. 349–51. In 1970 Montini, now Pope, inaugurated the new Ethnographical Museum in the Vatican. In this way he realized a project of Pope John that reached back to the 1925 exhibition. When Pope John Paul II was planning a visit to Australia in 1984 some Aborigines asked for their boomerangs and bark-paintings to be returned. This did not happen. "What we have we hold," said Dr Walter Perseguati, a Vatican museum official.

3 Ibid. p. 349. In 1930 he became Archbishop of Milan, where he was succeeded by Montini in 1954.

4 Ibid. p. 336. Nello Vian's touch deserts him when he has to deal with the English language. He says that Benson was the son of Edward White, the future Archbishop of Canterbury: he was Edward White Benson, and had already been Archbishop of Canterbury. Referring to C. C. M. Martindale's two-volume *Life of Robert Hugh*

A more substantial influence was Vita Fornari (1821–1900), a learned priest who had written a three-decker *Della Vita di Gesu Cristo*. Montini told Guitton he had read Fornari from his youth onwards and that Fornari "belonged to the school of St Augustine which expatiates on themes to the point of exhaustion".[1] More alarming was his remark that a colleague at the office urgently wanted Fornari volume I "so that he could copy it out and thus fix it in his mind".[2] This throws a curious light on the academic habits of the Roman Curia. It is difficult to see how an anti-Modernist writer like Benson (converted in 1903) and a pre-Modernist author like Fornari could answer the questions of 1925.

But Montini's third author in 1925, the Tübingen Professor Karl Adam, represented the best of Catholic thinking at the time. He devoured Adam's *The Essence of Catholicism* and it left a permanent mark on his ecclesiological thinking.[3] Its final chapter, called *Catholicism in its Actuality*, descends from the level of the ideal and frankly discusses the place of sin in the Church; from this contrast between the "essence" of the Church and its existential reality Adam deduced that the Church was in need of constant reform. This was a controversial theme in the 1920s. The book was later censured.

Montini felt lonely during his first year in the Secretariat of State. There was little social life apart from occasional feasts for departing nuncios like Gaetano Cicognani, off to Bolivia.[4] He begins to find the whole curial life-style "too grand", producing people "incapable of dealing with ordinary everyday life". This scruple partly reflects his own "learned helplessness". He is still writing home to mother when he needs clean socks. He casts envious glances at Lodovico, now installed with his pregnant wife on the first floor of the family home at via della Grazie. He is morose. He feels a "secret need" of family life and complains about the chancy impersonality of his own domestic arrangements.[5]

The canonization of St Theresa of Lisieux in May 1925 was the high point of the Holy Year celebrations. Don Battista knew about this

Benson, he calls this great Jesuit "Charlie Martindale". Anyone who called him that would have been quickly shown the door.

1 Jean Guitton, *Dialogues avec Paul VI*, pp. 146–47.

2 *Familiari*, p. 356.

3 Published in German in 1924, it was designed as a reply to Adolf Harnack's *Essence of Christianity*. The English translation, done by Justin McCann OSB, Master of St Benet's Hall, Oxford, was called *The Spirit of Catholicism* (Sheed and Ward 1929).

4 *Familiari*, p. 353.

5 Ibid. p. 366. He was cheered up, slightly, by a visit from Msgr Angelo Roncalli, now irrevocably doomed to go to Bulgaria. Roncalli invited him to visit his native village, Sotto il Monte, during the summer.

Carmelite nun who died in 1897 at twenty-four on the very day he was baptized. Without intellectual pretensions she had great influence over French intellectuals, like the novelist Georges Bernanos and other survivors of the trenches of what was still called the Great War. He was assailed on all sides for tickets for the canonization. Just as well his parents decided not to come. St Peter's was floodlit for the first time since 1870.[1]

The night was moonless, the scene spectacular, and the ex-*Popolari* turned clerico-Fascists concluded that "the Roman Question" was on the verge of resolution. St Peter's was floodlit again a few days later for the canonizations of the Curé d'Ars, St Jean Marie Vianney, and St Jean Eudes. The Pope was trying to woo France by canonizing so many French saints. Montini describes the floodlighting as "a marvellous spectacle which shows how light can symbolize the realities of the beyond".[2]

But then the tough, real world broke in with a vengeance. Don Montini was denounced to Pius XI for "having allowed his club (*circulo*) to be used for political ends". He had done nothing more than organize a "week of social studies", addressed by his brother Lodovico, to commemorate Leo XIII's *Rerum Novarum*. The choice of speakers, said the police informer, was disgraceful. It allegedly proved that "Catholic Action had fallen into the hands of the PPI".[3] From now on, until the collapse of Fascism, the whole Montini family was tarred with the same brush.

Don Battista replied to this charge. "The lectures," he explains, poker-faced, "had a purely historical character, without any political implications."[4] He gave the game away, however, by admitting that his students were "passionately interested in political matters and wished to be involved in them". But he saw his own task as that of restraining rather than egging them on. He took the entire blame for what he called the "somewhat eccentric choice of speakers", and absolved his superior, Pizzardo, from any responsibility. A shrewd ploy, but it did not prevent Pizzardo from proposing, a week later, a three-month stay in the Brussels nunciature "to give you the chance to have a rest". That was ominous. Once it made up its mind the Vatican could act swiftly. Here is your ticket for Brussels. *Arrivederci*. And three months could have turned into twenty years.

But he did not go to Belgium. He stayed in Rome as the conflict with

1 Ibid. p. 371.

2 Ibid. pp. 371–72.

3 Andrea Riccardi, *Roma "citta sacra"? Dalla Conciliazione all'operazione Sturzo*, Milan 1979, pp. 74–75.

4 *Familiari*, p. 373.

the Fascists intensified. On 11 June, the feast of Corpus Christi, a gang of Fascists belaboured with truncheons a group of his own students as they processed towards Porta Pia, scene of the Vatican defeat in 1870. Next day Catholic students were beaten up as they went about the university. The message was that there was room for only one student movement.

Pius XI reacted. On 18 June, receiving pilgrims from Perugia, among them one of the injured students, he deplored the incidents, piously hoping their perpetrators would be punished. The worst thing, he implied, was that they were spoiling the Holy Year when Rome should be a city open to all the world. Montini's own chief, Pizzardo, as the man responsible for Italian affairs, was scurrilously abused in the Fascist press.

By now Don Battista had had enough. He could no longer go on working at the chaplaincy "with energy and serenity". In mid-July he wrote a resignation letter to the Cardinal Vicar of Rome, Basilio Pompilj, to whom he had been denounced. He offered vague "health reasons". This was the only time in his life that he tried to resign. He showed the letter to Igino Righetti and Frederico Alessandrini, the newly elected president and secretary of the Rome FUCI.[1] He was not to know that these two would provide him with moral and spiritual support during his remaining eight years as university chaplain (still less that Alessandrini would edit *l'Osservatore Romano* during his papacy). Nor was he to know that in 1933 he would be sacked from the post from which in 1925 he had vainly tried to resign.

He did not go abroad that summer. He stayed with his family instead. He had missed them. In their absence, he wrote cryptically, he felt "the difficulty of virtue", and was "less strong in sacrifice, less resolute in the abandonment of human hopes".[2]

He returned refreshed to find Rome full of pilgrims and Pius XI determined to end the Holy Year in dramatic style with a display of Catholic muscle. First came an international jamboree of Catholic scouts, 10,000 of them, then the pilgrimage of Italian Catholic women, and finally 30,000 from the Catholic youth movement. To minimize the chance of incidents Pius addressed the young people in the Belvedere courtyard, safely within the Vatican walls. His message was clear. If the Fascists wished to win over Italian youth they would have to reckon with the cohorts of Catholic Action, which Pius always called, to the bafflement of foreigners, "the apple of our eye".[3] Don Montini would continue to be needed in the front line of this battle.

1 Ibid. p. 364.
2 Ibid. p. 366.
3 Ibid. pp. 381–82.

But this picture of a solid united front was shattered by an absurd incident which showed Pius XI's touchiness. The FUCI annual congress ended at Bologna on 8 September 1925. Next day 700 of them descended on Rome and prepared to march on St Peter's to demonstrate their loyalty to the Pope. Don Montini had the melancholy task of telling them the Pope would not receive them.

Why this snub? Simply because the organizers of the Bologna Congress had placed it under the patronage of King Victor Emmanuel III. So long as the "Roman Question" was unresolved the Italian royal family was not officially recognized by the Holy See. The FUCI students had jumped the gun. They found this legal fiction hard to swallow, went to St Peter's all the same, chanted *Viva il Papa* below the papal window and bellowed their song *Noi siam la giovinezza*, as they marched, unblessed, away. Songs played an important role in Fascism and anti-Fascism.

But FUCI was now in crisis. Its first elected president resigned straightaway. The second choice, Giuseppe Bacchi, organizer of the Bologna congress, declined the post. Msgr Luigi Piastrelli, the national chaplain, after vague accusations of "Modernism", resigned. Pizzardo intervened, made Montini temporary national chaplain and ordered him to convene a fresh meeting of the executive committee and to present two names (excluding members of the old committee) for president. The Holy See – in practice, Pizzardo – then accepted Igino Righetti as president, though only "provisionally". So while in mid-July Montini had tried to resign from the Rome FUCI, by mid-September he found himself national chaplain to the whole movement, besides retaining his Rome base. He had no illusions about this new responsibility. It was a hot seat. He feared it would all end in tears.[1]

The news from home got worse and worse. Giorgio's paper, *Il Cittadino di Brescia*, was seized on 5 November 1925, for the tenth time that year. It did not appear the next day because of attacks on the printing presses. The editor, Carlo Bresciani, forced out of his office, left Brescia altogether.[2] Clearly its days were numbered. What happened in Brescia was typical of what was happening all over Italy. Mussolini moved resolutely towards a personal dictatorship. In his own homely phrase, he was "plucking the chicken feather by feather".[3]

1 Ibid. p. 383. To lend strength to his arm he was given the title of *monsignore* and became, believe it or not, a "private supernumerary attendant" (ibid. p. 386). His students sent him the traditional bunch of white roses and continued to call him Don Battista (ibid. p. 388).

2 Ibid. pp. 389, 392.

3 Denis Mack Smith, *Mussolini*, p. 116.

A whole clutch of feathers was plucked out in this grey November 1925. All political parties except the Fascists were dissolved. All democratic associations or groups were outlawed. There were arrests and deportations without trial – 522 by the end of the month. The death penalty was reintroduced for catch-all "political crimes". The country was ruled by emergency legislation in which the ordinary rules of justice were suspended. No appeals were allowed. Italy was put on a war footing though there was not the slightest threat of war.

Giorgio felt out of his depth. He was too gentlemanly for such ferocious times. The national role to which he once aspired was now taken over by his son. Don Battista took charge of the Catholic student movement throughout Italy. It was the chief opposition group still in business. Other dissidents, like Don Luigi Sturzo, were in exile or, like the Communist thinker Antonio Gramsci, in prison. Thus, accidentally, at the age of twenty-eight Msgr Montini became the covert leader of the intellectual opposition to the Fascists. The Vatican blew hot and cold, thus complicating his task. But he did not waver.

7

Dictators Dig In

> To define Fascism . . . is above all to write its history.
> (A. TASCA, *Nascita e avvento del Fascismo*, vol. II, Laterza, Bari 1965, p. 553)

> Take away justice and what are kingdoms but mighty bands of robbers?
> (ST AUGUSTINE, *De Civitate Dei*, Book IV, ch. 4)

Student movements do different things at different times. Between 1926 and 1933 when Battista Montini was its national chaplain, the *Federazione degli Universitari Cattolici Italiani* (FUCI) was the only serious opposition to the Fascists in the university. Its Congress at Pavia in April 1926 began with a brisk address from Fr Giulio Bevilacqua, Battista's Oratorian friend, who declared: "We are not above the mêlée but in the thick of it." Bevilacqua opposed dual membership of FUCI and GUFI (the Fascist student movement) because they were "two incompatible schools of thought".[1] This cleared the air: Montini began to feel better. He was the leader of a potentially dissident movement. In the winter of 1926 he was too busy even to have flu.

But he had one hand tied behind his back. Despite his work in the Secretariat of State he was unaware that the Vatican was already secretly negotiating with the Fascist government to resolve "the Roman Question". Work with the students was more congenial. After a morning at the Secretariat of State he would arrive at his office at Piazza San Agostino 20/A on the dot of five o'clock every afternoon. San Agostino was close to the Senate and the university. The ground floor had a restaurant and a meeting room always full of milling Catholic students. On the top floor, more than 100 steps up – lifts had not yet become commonplace – were two rooms where the leadership of FUCI – Montini, Igino Righetti, Frederico Alessandrini – worked in cheerful chaos. They had two publications: *Studium*, a monthly intellectual review, and *Azione Fucina*, a bulletin directed to more practical matters.

1 *Familiari*, p. 411.

Guido Gonella recalled:

> The most interesting place was Msgr Montini's "corner". There he spoke, wrote, listened, and sometimes chided (in the gentlest way). He gave FUCI a precise intellectual and spiritual character. There he wrote his articles for *Studium*. Without them, written so neatly in exercise books with scarcely any corrections, *Studium* could never have been published. But this was only a tiny fraction of the work done in those distant and laborious afternoons half a century ago.[1]

Most of his articles in *Studium* were either reviews of French works or texts of his lectures. He learned as he taught. He was introducing theological thinking to lay young people from the provinces nonplussed on arrival in Rome, mixed up about Fascism but with an instinctive sense that something was wrong about it.

Montini began with essentials. His first theology course in 1927 was on the mystery of Church (as was his first encyclical, *Ecclesiam Suam*, in 1964). In 1928 he tackled Faith and Christology. He was in touch with the latest ideas. His friend Emilio Guano was already talking about the "pilgrim Church", still short of its eschatological goal, and thus far from being the "perfect society" on which Ottaviani learnedly discoursed at the Lateran University. Montini was no apologist: he provided a theology for committed lay people, giving them a sense of spiritual direction in a confused world.

The Church to which he introduced his students was in need of reform. One could not be complacent or triumphalistic about it. This theme he found in Karl Adam, the leading German Catholic theologian, professor at Tübingen University. *The Spirit of Catholicism* implied a "reform" project which was why the Holy Office, ever alert, "censured" it, that is, had it withdrawn from Roman bookshops.[2] Montini got hold of the remaindered copies, and handed them out to trusted friends.[3] This was a courageous, risky act that an ambitious curialist would have avoided.

Montini believed that intellectual activity was in itself deeply spiritual. He was inspired by the French Dominican Antonin Sertillanges'

1 Guido Gonella, "*Amico Maestro*" (Master and Friend), in *Notiziario*, No. 9, p. 64. Gonella was a member of the Constituent Assembly of 1946, and Secretary (that is, leader) of the Christian Democratic Party 1950–53.

2 Mario Bendiscioli, a Brescian who was a student of Montini at the time, tells the whole story in a *Festschrift* for the former Bishop of Bergamo, Adriano Bernareggi, *Studie e Memorie*, 7, Edizioni di Seminario, Bergamo 1979, pp. 95–147.

3 Jacques Prévotat, "*Les Sources françaises de G. B. Montini*", in *Modernité*, p. 119. Lodovico Montini is the source.

La Vie Intellectuelle (translated into Italian in 1925). It developed a "spirituality" of intellectual work. Research was to be done in an atmosphere of dialogue and sharing. Friendship was an intellectual virtue, not just an escape from loneliness. Montini would come to prefer the Thomism of the French lay professor, Etienne Gilson, who went back to the original texts of Aquinas, to that of the neo-scholastic Agostino Gemelli, Rector of the Catholic University in Milan, for whom Thomism was an all-embracing and self-sufficient "system".[1]

Jacques Maritain, destined to have a greater influence on Italian Catholicism than either Gemelli or Gilson, was still struggling to emerge from neo-Thomism. Maritain's *La Primauté du Spirituel* rejected Charles Maurras' Action Française with its pragmatic slogan, *la politique d'abord!* Prompted by Montini Guido Gonella had made the 1926 condemnation of Action Française the subject of his thesis for the Catholic University of Milan.[2]

Montini translated and introduced Maritain's *Three Reformers* to Italian readers. Maritain's trio, Martin Luther, René Descartes and Jean-Jacques Rousseau, were rudely treated as "so-called" or pseudo-reformers. The modern world had taken a wrong turning when Luther cast off church authority; the "rationalist" Descartes with his "methodic doubt" compounded the Protestant error of private judgement; finally the "romantic" Rousseau, wallowing in waves of sentiment, made subjectivity the norm. Together they produced the French Revolution and the "modern world". Though Maritain had abandoned Charles Maurras he retained his account of European intellectual history since the Renaissance.

Frederico Alessandrini was a colleague of Montini's in the FUCI office from 1926 to 1934. He gives a glimpse of another side of GBM. These student activists were all young and part-timers, like Montini himself. They were all very busy and sometimes met only for supper at the restaurant Il Passetto, just across the square. As chaplain he insisted their academic work had priority over everything else. "I don't want anyone to say: FUCI ruined me," he said.[3] With study went works of charity. He accompanied them in the work of the St Vincent de Paul Society in the poverty-stricken quarter of Porta Metronia. Getting there meant passing the Jewish ghetto on the banks of the Tiber. "Remember," he told Alessandrini, "the word of Jesus came to Rome through this people, and in a setting like this."[4]

1 Based on Maria Cristina Giuntella's paper to the FUCI 90th anniversary conference, "*Influenze culturali nella riflessione dei movimenti intelletuali negli anni '30*", Rome, 27 November 1986.

2 Giorgio Campanini, "*Montini e Maritain*", in *Società Italiana*, p. 92.

3 *Notiziario*, 3, p. 60. Righetti was writing a thesis on the natural law.

4 Ibid. p. 62.

After theology, art, study and charity, it was Montini's personal touch that made FUCI different. Gianbattista Scaglia recalls, "FUCI was a small world, always threatened by cliques and tensions: but Montini imbued it with a new mood of confidence, security and freedom."[1] He created a space of freedom under Fascism. Bevilacqua always said that the trouble with Italy was that no one could imagine any alternative to Fascism.[2] FUCI did just that; but in envisaging "post-Fascism" it had to be radically subversive.

This conclusion, however, emerged only slowly. On 26 August 1926 Montini was made well aware of what was at stake. The FUCI Congress at Macerata, 34 miles south of Ancona on the Adriatic coast, was fraught from the start. The Fascist students were spoiling for a fight. They beat up some Genoese on the way from the railway station. They stayed in the same hotel as Montini and his committee, singing rowdy songs throughout the night. When the congress began next morning in the seventeenth-century theatre, Lauro Rossi, the Fascists gate-crashed the meeting and took umbrage at the innocent remark Dominican Mario Cordovani addressed to the local bishop: "Be our teacher, our open-hearted father, and if need be our defender."[3] To avoid further trouble Montini and his committee wanted to call off the university meeting, but its Rector insisted and treated them to "an ultra-patriotic lecture that was ultra-applauded".[4]

As the *Fucini* left there was some shoving and jostling, rival anthems were bawled, fists flew, banners were torn to shreds, FUCI students were belaboured with photographers' tripods. The *carabinieri* looked impassively on. That afternoon Montini and Righetti – who displayed "remarkable cool-headedness for his twenty-two years" – had "a long and dramatic conversation" with the Prefect of the city. While they were talking one of Montini's best friends, Renzo Enrico de Sanctis, was hauled away to the Fascist militia (MVSN) HQ where he was beaten with rifle butts.[5] The Prefect ordered the FUCI students out of Macerata at once "for reasons of public order".

They obeyed. They took the train to Assisi where they had planned to end their congress anyway. Far from being downhearted, Montini

1 Ibid. p. 57.

2 Roy MacGregor Hastie, *Pope Paul VI*, Frederick Muller, London 1964, p. 107.

3 *Familiari*, p. 434.

4 Ibid.

5 Ibid. p. 435. The previous month, July 1926, de Sanctis had been with Montini in Strasbourg where they tried to learn German. An authority on French and Spanish literature, always known as REDS (after his initials), small and bearded, he was literary critic and features editor of *L'Osservatore Romano* 1934–44 (ibid. p. 423).

and his students were elated by the experience of persecution, and the five-hour journey together in third-class carriages gave them a sense of "togetherness" which – said his report in *Studium* – "buoyed up all our hearts in a most remarkable way for our pilgrimage to Assisi".[1]

It was Montini's first taste of violence. He was torn between contempt for the Fascist bully-boys and admiration for the bearing of his own students. They could laugh at their trials. They were recklessly brave and had a gift for improvisation.

They would need both. In Bologna on 31 October 1926 a fifteen-year-old boy tried to assassinate Mussolini. He was shot dead. This was the pretext for a wave of repression against Catholic organizations and independent newspapers throughout Italy. Brescia was particularly hard hit. The presses of *Il Cittadino* were gutted, the headquarters of Catholic Action was sacked, the Oratory of La Pace was invaded after defiant sermons from Fr Giulio Bevilacqua. "Obviously the aim is to intimidate us," Battista wrote home, "they are trying to lock up all the free spirits who elude their grasp." He predicted that Fascism would "die of indigestion, and be defeated by its own overbearing pretentiousness".[2]

His father Giorgio thought it wiser to move the family to their country home at Concesio. He warned Lodovico that the house in via delle Grazie could be searched at any time. They all became conspiratorial. Battista typed his letters, used plain envelopes, avoided names, and wherever possible sent them by hand.[3] "Lon", he reported on 11 November 1926, is well – though he already knew that Giovanni Longinotti was in danger of imprisonment. This threat hovered over all the *Popolari* (the ex-PPI) who did not support the Fascists. Their political careers were at an end.

On 9 November 1926 the Chamber approved a motion declaring that the mandate of 120 opposition deputies had "lapsed".[4] Longinotti retired to his model farm at Ronciglione. Battista urged his father to use his sabbatical to set down his memories of "the glorious battle fought in Brescia" as guidance for his grandson, Giorgio junior, Lodovico's first child.[5]

If there is a symbolic moment when a son takes over from his father

1 Ibid. p. 435.

2 Ibid. p. 440.

3 Ibid. p. xxv, Nello Vian, in Introd. He would continue this practice for the next seventeen years.

4 Ibid. p. 443.

5 Ibid. p. 505. Giorgio never wrote his memoirs. But he did produce an autobiographical letter on the origins of the formula *Preparazione nell'astensione*, significantly dating it Vatican City, 19 March 1940. So he finished it while staying with his eldest son. It was published in 1952, with a preface by Don Battista.

and continues his mission, then for the Montinis it was now. Yet Battista was only twenty-nine. He tried to console his father for the wrecking of his paper and the ending of his political career. The success of Fascism, now in command of Italian society, posed *the problem of evil*. Why should the wicked prosper? What was worrying was that Italian democracy had such thin roots. He distinguishes between "indifference and resignation", and recommends "bearing witness to the justice of the kingdom of God, even if only ineffectually and silently".[1] But what is the use of a "silent and ineffectual witness" to God's justice?

There was no more poignant twentieth-century question. Montini put his trust in "the idea of the hidden fruitfulness of the good, the steady charging up of moral energy, the chance to expiate for others, the deep-down victory of the good even when it seems that evil triumphs – this is the idea that Redemption alone brings to full and perfect realization". Montini confronted Fascism from his prie-dieu.

Back in the everyday world he finally abandoned his den at the Pontifical Academy and moved to via Aurelia 106. A tram ride away from the Vatican and his FUCI headquarters, other Catholic Action chaplains provided company. What seems strange about this period is the way Montini was left to make up FUCI policy on the nod. There is no record of any instructions from Msgr Pizzardo, his chief, still less from Pope Pius XI.[2]

But this freedom also made for insecurity. His appointment as national chaplain of FUCI was still "provisional", though Righetti was confirmed as President. "This lack of interest is a worry," he wrote to Renato de Sanctis, "but if no one in particular can be blamed for it, everyone is a little involved."[3] Montini was charitable as usual. But, unbeknown, he was trapped in the Vatican dilemma: what concessions would have to be made to Mussolini to secure "reconciliation" between the Holy See and Italy?

His eyes were opened when Giulio Bevilacqua suddenly turned up at via Aurelia 106 on the eve of the Epiphany 1928. His anti-Fascist outspokenness had got him thrown out of Brescia. Cardinal Camillo Laurenti, Prefect of the Congregation of Religious, summoned Bevilacqua to Rome – he said – to prevent worse harm. His Eminence unctuously explained: "This means that the Roman Church sees that you are in danger; it calls you to Rome so that you can be put under its protection; from now on you will be covered by the red of my cardinal's robe."[4]

1 Ibid. p. 443.
2 Ibid. p. 475. There is talk of a papal audience, but it is postponed infinitely.
3 Ibid. p. 496 fn. 1.
4 Ibid. p. 517.

The plain truth, however, was that Bevilacqua had been *silenced* by his own side.

It was a blow for Brescia, and a blow for the Church in Italy. "It is the worst form of oppression," wrote Battista, "because we don't know what to do abou tit." Bevilacqua, meanwhile, stayed remarkably "calm and without resentment" and was given a token job as consultor in the Congregation of Religious.[1] Those who knew him found the idea of Bevilacqua as a Vatican bureaucrat ludicrous, but he stuck it for the next four years. His main job was keeping Don Battista cheerful, well-informed about France, and resolute.

This was all the more necessary since – for the first time in his priestly life – Montini began to doubt the wisdom and rightness of Vatican policy towards Italy. The tide was clearly set for what in Italy was called "reconciliation", though elsewhere it was often seen as appeasement. Destroying what was left of the shattered *Popolari* and silencing independent minds like Bevilacqua was a high price to pay for "reconciliation". But Montini was loath to condemn his superiors. He states the problem clearly: having defended the rights of the Holy See as an absolute principle, and suffered for them, it is now disconcerting to hear talk about the need for "flexibility and relative adaptability". He concludes that "though the barque of Peter can't sink, it can seem to ship water".[2] He thought it safer to have this letter of 22 February 1928 delivered by the hand of Fr Caresana, his confessor, with whom he had no doubt discussed these matters.

That summer Montini was due to travel around the Middle East on semi-official business for the Secretariat of State. He was glad that they still considered him employed there, but didn't go because "at the last moment, I didn't feel very well".[3] After a day in bed he reverted to his original plan and toured Benedictine abbeys in Belgium with Msgr Angelo Grazioli, FUCI chaplain in Verona. Their main interest was in the liturgy. Maredesous Abbey had published *La Revue Bénédictine* since 1884; Mont César was famous for its Gregorian chant and being burnt down by German troops in August 1914; and Saint-André near Bruges had produced the Dom Gaspard Lefebvre Roman Missal which went round the whole world, as well as the first *Bulletin paroissial liturgique*, ancestor of many inferior "missalettes". Montini was still thinking of parish liturgy as an adapted version of monastic liturgy.[4]

On the way back they visited a vast International Press Exhibition

1 Ibid. pp. 517–19.
2 Ibid. pp. 523–24.
3 Ibid. p. 546.
4 Ibid. pp. 552–56.

organized by the mayor of Cologne, Konrad Adenauer.[1] *Pravda* and *Izvestia*, Soviet newspapers available for the first time, aroused much curiosity among those who could understand them. The Catholic press was well represented too. Montini wrote about the Exhibition in *Studium*.[2] He did not share the optimism of Fr Paul Doncoeur SJ who looked forward to a new era of international understanding thanks to the press. Rarely was the press so blatantly ideological and outrageous as in Fascist Italy.

Back in Rome in late August 1928 he got the warning he had been half-expecting: his frequent absences on FUCI business were interfering with his work at the Secretariat of State; from now on he must cut down on conferences and retreats outside Rome. "My vagabond life is over," he writes.[3] But by now he had a good enough network of friends around Italy for this travel ban not to prove too tragic. More worrying was that his superiors did not appreciate the value of his work with the university students. They didn't seem to understand that he was more interested in his ministry than building a career.

But at least, at the age of thirty-one, he had managed to rent a place of his own. It was a solid three-storey house on the Aventine Hill. It had belonged to a painter. It cost 1000 lire a month. It was an enchanting place, close to the Benedictine house of San Anselmo. Fr Bevilacqua would join him there; two paying guests would help with the costs; there would be a spare room for any of the Montini family when they came to Rome. Bevilacqua had found a cook, a fifty-six-year-old Piedmontese called Giulia Bussolino, a woman of "strong temperament" who had spent some time in Brazil and thus knew – ask not why – English and French. Montini called her (in English) "the nurse".[4] But there was not much time for domesticity.

For the first time the Fascist press attacked Don Battista by name. *Il Resto del Carlino* accused him, as Giorgio's son, of being a PPI sympathizer and "meddler in politics". *L'Osservatore Romano* replied with a "precision", denying the charges.[5] Yet it is true that Battista judged Catholic Action to be "listless and spineless", and that this was a political judgement.

Thanks to him, FUCI alone still had some energy and backbone. Pope Pius XI then made one of his periodic "strong statements" to which Montini clutched as at a straw. At the end of a FUCI study week Pius

1 During the war Adenauer took refuge with the Benedictines of Maria Laach where he used his leisure to study *Rerum Novarum* and Catholic social doctrine.

2 *Familiari*, p. 557.

3 Ibid. p. 561.

4 Ibid.. pp. 569–71.

5 Ibid. pp. 576–77.

received Montini's students in audience and said, speaking of himself in the third person:

> To call things by their name, there are not lacking those who want to reduce the number of Catholics in the university and who would perhaps wish to suppress their organizations in favour of others. This seems to his Holiness to be ungenerous, in the sense the ancient Romans gave to this word – uncivilized; and in such a moment, it is particularly painful for his paternal heart. Nothing so afflicts the spirit of the Pontiff as monopolistic tendencies in such lofty, delicate and sacred matters.[1]

The Pope quoted Aquinas to the effect that "greater virtue is required to know how to suffer than to know how to act and react". This was hardly a stirring call to action. Even had it been, few would have known about it for it appeared neither in *L'Osservatore Romano* nor in the official edition of his *Discorsi*. The "tough speech" was no more than an impotent gesture made at a time when the prospect of "reconciliation" was imminent.

Montini spent a miserable Christmas in his new home. He was aware of "the bleakness with which the modern world surrounds the Christian mystery, and this desolation is my crib". The nearby church of St Prisca, where he said Mass, was empty save for a handful of nuns. "Midnight Mass was spoiled by dreadful hymns," he wrote, "made doubly gloomy by the bleak interior of St Prisca." Christmas is a lonely time for a celibate cleric. Battista made it more endurable by dining with the Longinotti family.[2]

In January 1929 St Peter's Square was covered in snow. Lads from the English and Scots College pelted each other with snowballs on the way to the Gregorian. It had never been so cold.[3] The pressures on FUCI intensified as the rumours about "reconciliation" became more and more insistent. On 19 January 1929 Battista wrote to his father:

> There's a lot of talk about resolving the Roman Question; and this, though long-awaited and desired by both sides, has a faintly ridiculous air for both of them: was it worth sixty years of protest to arrive at such a meagre result? Was it worth making such professions of independence, only to give way on the territorial principle? True, this is not the whole story: it might be one of the greatest and finest moments of our history.

1 Ibid. p. 580. This was on 22 December 1928.

2 Ibid. pp. 579–81.

3 Ibid. p. 583. The late Cardinal John Carmen Heenan is the source for the snowballs.

> How odd that the good and honest people who have waited most for this moment are now the least inclined to enjoy it – not because they are habitual grumblers, but because they suspect further and worse conditions. If the freedom of the pope is not guaranteed by the strong and voluntary confidence of the people, especially the Italian people, what territory or treaty could secure it?[1]

This was the "Brescia line". No one could accuse Brescian Catholics of being unpatriotic or not longing for reconciliation. Bevilacqua had been one of the first to run up the tricolour from the church of La Pace.

But the "reconciliation" they saw coming was with the wrong government, at the wrong time and without the consent of the Italian people. It would therefore be seen, at home and abroad, as the simple embrace of Fascism and the Holy See. Giorgio shared Battista's apprehensions. His heart was heavy, he wrote, and prayer his only consolation.[2]

The cold spell continued into February as did the rumours. On 4 February 1929, just a week before the event, Battista shares the latest gossip with Giorgio:

> It looks as though the Treaty on the Roman Question will be accompanied by a Concordat, of which the strangest things are said. It seems that, among other things, civil marriage will be abolished. All of which supposes a completely new direction in ecclesiastical policy and consequently in the attitude of Catholics. You can easily guess my feelings . . . The atmosphere of expectation and intrigue is almost entertaining. They say that the first news of the event will be released in St Peter's on 12 February. But who knows?[3]

Montini had good sources but he was not to know that detailed haggling went on right up to the last moment on 10 February. The Lateran Pacts, as they were comprehensively known, were signed the next day by Benito Mussolini and Cardinal Pietro Gasparri. Simultaneously Pius XI announced the news in his traditional pre-Lent address to the parish priests and preachers of Rome.

There were two treaties, one dealing with the territorial status of the newly-created and minuscule Vatican City State, the other with the financial compensation owing to the Holy See for the loss of the Papal

1 Ibid. p. 584.
2 Ibid. p. 584 fn. 4.
3 Ibid. p. 586.

States in 1870; and there was, as predicted, a Concordat which governed the relationship between the Holy See and Italy.[1]

Great was the official enthusiasm for the Lateran Pacts in 1929. *L'Osservatore Romano* claimed that "God has been given back to Italy, and Italy back to God." Mussolini, it was said, had achieved what no "liberal" government could have done (a very dubious proposition). The Duce was, said Pius XI, "the man whom Providence put in our path". The end of anti-clericalism was announced, the start of a new era prophesied.

Archbishop Angelo Roncalli, then Apostolic Delegate in Bulgaria, was overjoyed and saw here the vindication of the hopes of his ancestors: now at last it was possible for good Catholics to be uninhibitedly good Italian patriots. Even those close to Montini, like Igino Righetti, were taken in. "We can now look forward," Righetti wrote on 14 February, "with greater calm to the future of our association (FUCI)."[2]

Msgr Montini remained sceptical. "Ordinary people," he pointed out, were untouched by euphoria, and most of the enthusiasm was drummed up "by the artificial clamour of the press". The commonest reaction was "to note the facts without comment and move on to something else". Fascism actually *depoliticized* Italians by both disfranchising them and dictating how they should feel about it. Their only recourse was silence or indifference. "Thinking people", on the other hand – and here Montini included Longinotti and Bevilacqua with whom he lunched the previous day – "are all, or almost all, full of reservations and forebodings."[3] For Montini and his friends the Lateran Pacts were essentially an exercise in Fascist public relations.

As such they were successful. Montini told the FUCI committee in a private memorandum that the "conciliatory attitude" recommended by the Lateran Pacts had in effect disarmed Catholic Action.[4] Though the principle that one could not belong simultaneously to the Catholic (FUCI) and the Fascist (GUFI) student movements was not officially discarded, it became increasingly difficult to explain to the next generation of students just why it should be maintained.

After all if Pope and Duce could be reconciled, why should not Catholic and Fascist students? Furthermore, penalties were imposed on those students who did not belong to the Fascist organization, and

1 In 1976 Paul VI began the process of "revising" the Concordat of 1929, which was concluded under his successor on 18 February 1984.

2 *Familiari*, p. 589. See Nicola Antonetti, *La Fuci di Montini e di Righetti, Lettere di Igino Ringhetti ad Angela Gotelli (1928–33)*, A. V. E., Rome 1979, p. 104.

3 *Familiari*, p. 589.

4 Ibid. p. 618.

Montini was sure that efforts were being made to infiltrate FUCI.[1] It did not help that he was now forbidden to attend FUCI congresses, and there was talk of sending him to the Nunciature in Berne which, though it fell through, did not indicate any great confidence in him.

He felt better understood by Msgr Domenico Tardini who came to dinner – Bevilacqua regaled him with an Alpine *salame*. Their careers would intertwine in the Secretariat of State for the next twenty-five years. There were great differences between the combative, blunt Roman and the aesthetic, tortured Brescian, but at this point they were agreed on the essential: the Corcordat made it more than ever necessary for Catholics to brace themselves for suffering and to be ready to "bear witness to the beauty of our moral position".

Yet only a week after Montini wrote this gloomy letter Pius XI received King Victor Emmanuel and Queen Elena in the Vatican. Since Pius IX had always considered the Italian King a "usurper", this was regarded as a great boost for "reconciliation".

On 27 January 1930 Montini lunched at the Pontifical Academy with Eugenio Pacelli, the future Pius XII, who had been made a cardinal just six weeks before. It soon became clear why Pius XI had brought him back after four years as Nuncio in Berlin: on 9 February 1930 he replaced Pietro Gasparri as Secretary of State. Pacelli was tall, thin, princely in bearing and manner.

There is some evidence that Gasparri felt roughly treated by Pius XI. But he had confidence in his successor.[2] However, Pacelli's long absence from Rome meant that the combative Pizzardo had virtual control of Catholic Action. Moreover, as the British Ambassador to the Quirinale remarked, "Gasparri's resignation was a great misfortune, the Pope is too impulsive, too undiplomatic . . . and Pacelli has been unable to moderate his actions and utterances."[3] It was not difficult to predict quarrels and disputes ahead. The Concordat had not brought concord. The Reconciliation had failed to reconcile.

The main grounds for conflict concerned Montini directly. The secret police, OVRA, were aware of the presence of ex-*Popolari* in the Vatican, and they kept a sharp eye on Battista as Giorgio's son. The ex-*Popolari* were particularly important in *l'Osservatore Romano*, and Alcide De Gasperi was working in the Vatican Library. It must have seemed to the Fascist Police that with Vatican connivance the ex-*Popolari* were regrouping in preparation for the expected fall of the regime.[4]

1 Ibid.

2 John F. Pollard, *The Vatican and Italian Fascism 1929–32*, p. 134.

3 Ibid. p. 135.

4 Ibid. p. 153.

But not all ex-*Popolari* were opposed to Fascism. Fr Agostino Gemelli OFM, Rector of the Catholic University of Milan, believed the Lateran Pacts had made possible a new era for the Catholic Church in Italy. In 1930 he launched a survey on "Catholic culture" in *Vita e Pensiero*, the university journal, to develop this theme. Gemelli, a psychologist and convert from atheism, wanted to use the social sciences to win back souls for Christ. The Catholic University would play a key role in this reconquest of Italian society.[1] Lodovico, who taught at the Catholic University, told Battista that there was now little hope for the Catholic Social Weeks (of which he was Secretary). Their meetings were "sluggish and academic".[2] Gemelli's policy was to exploit Fascism in the Catholic interest.

Montini did not believe that to be a serious long-term option. Nor did he believe in the "drop-out" solution adopted by Don Giuseppe De Luca. They had been good friends in 1927 when De Luca introduced him to southern Italy and its traditions. According to De Luca, St Alphonus Liguori, whose tomb was at Nocera, "was for southern Italy what St Charles Borromeo was for the north, that is, the teacher of the most elementary truths and at the same time the most sublime doctor of the faith".[3] De Luca was the leading authority on Italian spirituality.[4] He was highly cultivated and revelled in it. Though his grandmother had been an illiterate peasant, he was the complete clerical man of letters.

These were the grounds for Montini's quarrel with him. Though temperamentally close and with a common interest in literature and the arts, Montini could not accept De Luca's aesthetic detachment from what was happening in Italy. The crunch came when De Luca refused to do any more cultural work for FUCI. Montini thought he was deserting the front line with the battle at its height. He wrote an angry goodbye letter:

> Dear De Luca
> So it's farewell, and with great bitterness . . . What makes me so sad is the deliberate abandonment of our work together . . . You have thought of "action" as something that can be

1 See Maria Cristina Giuntella, *Influenze culturali nella riflessione de movimenti intelletuali negli anni '30*.

2 *Familiari*, p. 613. This remark refers to the 1929 Congress. It was not a propitious moment to be developing "Catholic social doctrine", though *Quadragesimo Anno* of 1931 attempted, fifty years on, to update Leo XIII's *Rerum Novarum*.

3 Fappani-Molinari, *Montini Giovane*, p. 249.

4 His nephew, Archbishop Eugenio Cardinale, called him the "Msgr Ronnie Knox of Italy", though others called him the "Henri Bremond of Italy" and certainly there are analogies between Bremond's *Histoire du sentiment religieux* and De Luca's work as editor of the *Archivio italiano per la storia della pietà*.

> drummed up at will, but you have not understood it was a cry of help coming from people of good will . . . If your solitude were merely tactical and a matter of simple fidelity to your chosen work and vocation – and it is both – I would have no right to complain. But you seem to have turned it into a theory which cuts us off from the poor and sweaty threads of charity which should clothe afresh the glory of the Church in the twentieth century . . . Take care that your expertise and erudition do not make love grow cold, eliminate sacrifice, and fragment the Body of Christ. *You choose books, I prefer to choose souls* . . . In the courage that comes from loving Christ above all else, I will continue to be, if you will allow me, your most affectionate friend Don Montini.[1]

Montini loved books and literature. But, in a time of crisis, he would not abandon those for whom he felt responsible.

If only De Luca had stayed in touch he would have realized that Montini's commitment to art was as deep as his own. Through all the turmoil of this period he was trying to develop an aesthetic based on Thomistic principles. Jacques Maritain had opened up this question with his *Art and Scholasticism* – the very title was a challenge to modernity. Maritain's concern was practical. Art was to do with *poesis*, making. His Russian-born wife, Raissa, was a poet, and artists and writers like Georges Rouault, Henri Ghéon, Stanislaus Fumet and Emmanuel Mounier frequented their salon at Meudon.

Montini made a serious study of religious art, and set up a study group within FUCI devoted to its historical and philosophical aspects. He took endless notes on the literature in preparation for a 1931 article "On the Future of Sacred Art".[2] He read everything relevant from Romain Rolland to Benedetto Croce. Part of his concern was with the place of art in the liturgical reform and priestly formation. "How can one say the divine office (Psalms, responsories etc.) without an artistic education?" he asks.[3]

1 Full text in Fappani-Molinari, *Montini Giovane*, pp. 308–9. If De Luca is to be thought of as an Italian Henri Bremond, then there is a curious literary parallelism between this letter and Georges Bernanos' novel, *L'Imposture*. The protagonist of the novel, the abbé Cenabre, was modelled on Bremond. Bernanos blamed him for replacing charity with "curiosity" about mystical states, and devastatingly concludes: "His real gift, however, is to conceive of a spiritual order robbed of its crown of charity" (*L'Imposture*, Livres de Poche, p. 29). Both Montini and De Luca were reading Bernanos at this time.

2 They were published in *Notiziario*, 22, 1992, pp. 7–26, as "*Note sull'arte*", ed. Pier Virgilio Begni Redona.

3 Ibid. p. 9.

His summary of the history of religious art concluded that modern religious art would be necessary *different*:

> *On Christian Art of the Future*
>
> The Middle Ages (see Emile Mâle, *Art et artistes du Moyen Age*, 1927).
>
> The Renaissance tried to turn Christian truth into human perfection (suggested by classical antiquity). Dominance of humanist and decorative trends.
>
> Baroque strives for expressive effects (see the review of Croce's Italian Baroque in *La Revue des deux Mondes*, September 1930).
>
> Romanticism appealed to sincerity of feelings.
>
> New Christian art should aim at the ontological *realism* of Religion.[1]

What "ontological realism" meant was the subject of impassioned debate at the time.

For the neo-Thomists "beauty" already existed "out there" as the reflection of God in creation. Montini noted the definition of Réginald Garrigou-Lagrange OP in a book called with admirable simplicity *Dieu*: ". . . the *beautiful*, in the created order, is the splendour of all the transcendentals together, of the one, the true and the good; more especially it is the *éclat* derived from a harmonious unity of proportion and the integrity of the parts. See *Summa Theologica*, 1a.q.39.a.8."[2]

It was more economically put by Stanislaus Fumet in *Procès de l'art*: "*Le beau c'est le bien qui se donne en spectacle pour faire aimer l'être*."

Fumet's title, *Art on Trial*, indicated a polemical attitude towards modern artists like Pablo Picasso and others who had abandoned any concept of "representativity", leaving the attempt to reproduce the world to photography. Montini had a formidable opponent in Italy. Benedetto Croce had been minister of Education in the Giolitti government and was now brooding in anti-Fascist isolation in Naples. In 1903 he had founded the review *Critica* and edited it for the next forty-one years. Croce held that there were two forms of knowledge: the conceptual, studied in logic, and the intuitional, studied in aesthetics. Thus "art" had a central place in his system. Croce was a thoroughly secular thinker who ruled out religion and metaphysics. So art could not be "useful" either to political regimes or the Church. It was an end in itself, the intuitive expression of the gifted individual.

1 Ibid. p. 16. Italics and capitals as in the original.

2 Ibid.

Montini's notebooks show him grappling with Croce's thought. Croce *defines* art as "successful expression", so it does not "correspond" to any pre-existent "beautiful thing". But what is *successful* expression, Montini pertinently asks?[1] He is prepared to grant that "intuition" is the artist's way to truth and beauty, but thinks it needs to refer to some pre-existing objective reality. Otherwise the artist can express nothing but himself. And that was what the modern artist so frequently did. In the neo-Thomist scheme, he observes, the artist knows when he has "successfully" expressed objective beauty – *id quod visum placet* was the scholastic word for it – because he experiences joy (*gaudium*). So art and spirituality were closely linked. Georges Rouault in painting, Paul Claudel in poetry and Francis Poulenc in music showed the way ahead for Christian "ontological realism". In France there was talk of a "Catholic Renaissance" in the arts.

In Italy the attacks on Catholic Action intensified in the spring of 1931. They were accused of preparing cadres to take over from the Fascist cadres.[2] All FUCI congresses were now cancelled. There was a sense of moving towards a denouement that obstinately refused to come. On 21 May 1931 the headquarters at Piazza San Agostino 20A was surrounded by Fascist police. Within the FUCI students recite their rosaries in the semi-darkness. Montini begins a letter home and asks: How long can it last? Is there a difference between heroism and bravado? Menace hovers in the air. The "only relief is in prayer and the innocent diversion of friendship".[3]

How long can it last, Montini asked on 21 May 1931. The answer was about a week. FUCI premises were violently attacked in Venice, Florence, Milan and Genoa. On 29 May *all* Catholic youth movements in Italy, FUCI specifically included, were dissolved. Their property was sequestrated. Montini in Rome only had to wait until the next day when, at 14.42, as he puts it in his memo:

> FUCI has been dissolved by the vice-commissar of police of San Eustachio, Rome, after a search made by the police at first in the absence of anyone from FUCI. They made another search in the presence of Righetti and myself. I remained seated during the inspection, saying my Breviary and contemplating the painting of San Tarcisio above the entrance.
>
> Then Righetti and I went outside while they carted off

1 Ibid. p. 19.

2 *Familiari*, p. 675. This is what they were in fact doing, or would eventually do; but it couldn't be admitted.

3 Ibid. p. 679.

> boxes with our papers. The doors were not locked but all access was forbidden. I removed Righetti's FUCI badge immediately after the reading of the order of dissolation. There was no mention of any warrant. The *palazzo* was now empty and all our friends gone. Shortly before the same thing had happened at the Rome chaplaincy. I saw a policeman emerge with a mattock for forcing open the doors. At 13.30 we met the officers of the Catholic Youth Movement, likewise dissolved. We embraced each other with emotion.
>
> When this sad operation was over Righetti and I went to pray at St Peter's. Then we looked for our friends. That evening four of us went to pray at San Filippo. Then I went with them to the Church of San Eustachio to return the keys of San Ivo (the university church) left me by Msgr (Amleto) Cicognani. *Roma non perit si Romani non pereant* (St Augustine).[1]

It was the most bitter and dramatic day of his life so far. The phrase of St Augustine – "Rome will not perish provided the Romans survive" – was based on hope rather than experience. A week later he was still reeling from the shock of these events, bewildered that something so obviously good and healthy should be destroyed. "From all over Italy," he wrote home, "there comes the discreet and grieving lamentation of our devastated groups."[2]

But ahead loomed an even greater danger: that of resignation to the *fait accompli*. Not all of Montini's student friends were supported by their families. Parents told them to give in to the inevitable. There was every likelihood that FUCI, already dissolved, would soon be *dead*. He blames himself for having been "too tepid and too tired to serve the cause". He felt sustained by others. They judged he was sustaining them.[3] Much depended on how Pius XI reacted.

He had reacted, in fact, with a vigorous encyclical called *Non abbiamo bisogno* (We do not need this). Officially dated 29 June 1931, the feast of Sts Peter and Paul, it was not released in Italy until 7 July. On 25 June Montini telegraphed Giorgio: PLEASE HAVE JACKET AND HAT TOMORROW MORNING AT VERONA 8.45. Giorgio duly set off at five to meet Battista at Verona station where he exchanged his

1 Ibid. p. 686. This MS is kept in the Paul VI Archives in Brescia. Amleto Cicognani (1883–1973), from the diocese of Faenza, was sent to Washington as Apostolic Delegate in 1933 where he remained, the forgotten man of Vatican diplomacy, until 1958 when Pope John XXIII recalled him to Rome. Later Pope John made him Cardinal Secretary of State, a post he also occupied under Paul VI until 30 April 1969.

2 Ibid. p. 688.

3 Ibid.

soutane for civilian dress. He was on his way to deliver the encyclical to the Nuncio in Munich. Francis J. Spellman, one of the rare Americans in the Secretariat of State, took it to Paris.[1] The idea was to diffuse the encyclical abroad so that it would be known even if the Fascists banned it in Italy.

Montini and FUCI were both reassured and disturbed by the encyclical. It was good when it condemned the "spontaneous" acts of aggression against Catholic Action, and pointed out that the police raids had produced no incriminating evidence. It was shakier when it said that the idea that the *Popolari* dominated Catholic Action was a downright lie, and was dangerously specific in claiming that "in all there are only four cases where ex-leaders of the *Partito Popolare* have become leaders of Catholic Action". Whatever criterion one uses in defining a PPI "leader", this statement was dubious, as the Fascist press hastened to point out in the coming weeks. One of their main targets was, yet again, Battista Montini.[2]

The encyclical was also ambivalent. It denounced the regime for its "out-and-out pagan worship of the state", and for educating Italian youth "in hatred, violence, and even irreverence towards the Pope himself". What most upset the Fascists was the papal recommendation that the Fascist oath could be taken provided one added the mental reservation, "saving the laws of God and the Church, or saving the duties of a good Christian".[3] At the same time the encyclical did not rule out hopes of an accommodation: "We do not wish to condemn the Party and the regime as such, but we do mean to draw attention to policies that are contrary to Catholic theory and practice." That was hardly enough to make a dictator tremble.

Montini never discussed his Secretariat of State work in his letters to his parents. It remained confidential. He appears in a photograph taken in August 1931 at the Villa Bonaparte, then the German Embassy to the Holy See, with Pacelli, the Cardinal Secretary of State, Heinrich Brüning, the last strictly parliamentary German Chancellor before Adolf Hitler. The German Ambassador, Diego von Bergen, and his wife, Vera, smile dutifully for the camera. The lay people wear evening dress.

Montini is away to the right, looking neither happy nor miserable. He is simply there on parade. Even if he had views on Germany he would not be expected to voice them. After all, Pacelli, his chief, was the expert on Germany. But he could well have anticipated that the

1 John Pollard, *The Church under Fascism*, p. 157.

2 *Familiari*, p. 693.

3 John Pollard, *The Church under Fascism*, p. 158.

Centre Party in Germany would go the way of the *Popolari* in Italy, and thus prepare the advent of Nazism.[1]

Montini's boredom and sense of foreboding, however, thrust him back on *hope*: "Never before have I felt so strongly that the word of Truth, stripped of any kind of internal props, has to rely on hope based on intrinsic reasons and on the Providence who in the end rules the world."[2]

But if it lacks external props, neither can the word of God be bound. *Verbum Dei non est alligatum* (2 Timothy 2:9): this text from the pastoral epistle was inscribed in the two works of St Augustine, *De Magistro* and *De Vera Religione*, presented to him on his feast day, St John the Baptist, 24 June 1931. It was signed by a great number of FUCI friends including Renzo de Sanctis, Igino Righetti, Ugo Piazza and Maria Faina.[3]

There were all kinds of subtle messages here. In 1930 he had written in *Studium* on "The Heritage of St Augustine" – it was the fifteen-hundredth anniversary of his death in 430 – and warned of the need to face a new barbarism. The FUCI offices near the church of St Augustine had been emptied. And the "word of Truth", though not bound, was seeking an accommodation with the men of power.

Gasparri, though out of office, was active in promoting reconciliation. Mussolini felt the dispute was damaging Italy's interests abroad. The Jesuit historian Fr Pietro Tacchi-Venturi pursued his "shuttle diplomacy" between the Vatican and the Palazzo Venezia (involving twenty-two papal audiences and thirteen encounters with Mussolini)[4] so successfully that by 2 September 1931 agreement was reached. The key point was that henceforward Catholic Action would come under *diocesan* rather than *national* control. In practice this meant that the remaining *Popolari* were rendered largely impotent, and Montini's days as national chaplain of FUCI were numbered.

No one put it quite so crudely. Instead Ernesto Ruffini, Secretary of the Congregation of Seminaries, invited him to lecture on the history of papal diplomacy at the Lateran University. Montini pleaded incompetence and lack of time, "but ended up by accepting, the first to be surprised by this whole affair".[5]

Another and more disturbing surprise was about to fall upon him.

1 Stewart A. Stehlin, *Weimar and the Vatican, 1919–1933: German-Vatican Diplomatic Relations in the Interwar Years*, p. 434.

2 *Familiari*, p. 693.

3 Ibid. p. 691.

4 Ibid. p. 700.

5 Ibid. p. 706.

On 9 March 1933 he received a letter from Msgr Giuseppe Pizzardo, head of Catholic Action, curtly informing him that he was relieved of his post as national chaplain of FUCI. He was thanked and sacked at the same time. The reason given was that his work at the Secretariat of State was now so important that it demanded his full-time attention. The irony was, as Righetti pointed out to the Pope, that Montini, worried about straddling two jobs, had asked to be relieved of his office work at the Secretariat of State in order to concentrate on the student chaplaincy which seemed, in the circumstances, much more urgent.

That was not an argument calculated to appeal to Pius XI. He "paternally" replied: "Msgr Montini has gifts destined to permit him to render services to the Church on a much higher level."[1] This was later regarded as a "prophetic" remark. Montini accepted this "trial" as a station along the *Via Crucis*, the way of the cross. But he could not disguise his hurt.

1 Fappani-Molinari, *Montini Giovane*, pp. 284–91.

8

The Barbarians Advance

We are destroying our ancient edifices to make ready the ground on which the barbarian nomads of the future will encamp in their mechanized caravans.

(T. S. ELIOT, *Notes Towards a Definition of Culture*, 1946)

Msgr Montini's traumatic dismissal from the post of national chaplain of the Catholic Students (FUCI) was the result of an intrigue. Already in March 1932 he had been denounced to the Cardinal Vicar of Rome, Francesco Marchetti Selvaggiani, notoriously a "friend of the Jesuits". There had long been demarcation disputes between the Jesuit student organizations (the Marian Sodality and the Roman Association) and FUCI. The argument was also about whether the traditional methods of the Jesuits, who emphasized the apologetic defence of the faith, were to be preferred to FUCI's more liberal approach. Montini wanted his students to explore and deepen their faith.[1]

He briskly defended himself against what he considered false accusations. He wrote a full account of the whole affair for Giacinto Gaggia, Bishop of Brescia; it was never delivered – for Gaggia lay dying, and Montini destroyed the letter. However, a draft survived in the FUCI archives.[2] It ends with the text: *Qui autem judicat me Dominus est.* It was the Lord's judgement that mattered, not that of the Cardinal Vicar of Rome.

Nevertheless he sought out Marchetti Selvaggiani to plead his case. To no avail. The Cardinal Vicar was "irreconcilably hostile".[3] A nervous Montini wrote home: "I have decided to accept this trial the Lord sends me; I don't think it will reach the point where my superiors will lose confidence in me; but it could damage the revival and sense of direction found in recent FUCI congresses."[4] And that was the point: a vigorous

1 *Familiari*, p. 726.

2 Fappani-Molinari, *Montini Giovane*, pp. 285–91.

3 *Familiari*, p. 727.

4 Ibid.

FUCI would disrupt the harmony now officially reigning between Church and state. The new chaplain, Msgr Roberto Ronca, was a more skilled political manoeuvrer.[1]

In his unsent letter to Bishop Gaggia Montini reveals that the pretext for his dismissal was a two-page memorandum on preparing for Easter put out in February 1933 to all FUCI branches:

> It proposed a number of Gospel readings, giving them priority over all other texts, and suggesting they should not be read moralistically or uncritically. It laid great emphasis on personal prayer, and advised avoiding churches with too many plaster statues, pious old ladies, candles, flowers, shrines and collection-taking sacristans. It was better not to recite the rosary in public. The Our Father, said slowly and meditatively, was preferable.[2]

Montini's modest proposals met the needs of Catholics who for the first time in their lives found themselves invited to choose between an anti-Christian ideology and a personally appropriated Christian faith. Yet these remarks were considered insulting to "popular piety" and – worse still – inspired by "Protestant methods". The thirty-six-year-old Montini was a dangerous liberal.

He got little sympathy from the Cardinal Secretary of State, Pacelli, as he explained to Gaggia:

> Cardinal Pacelli had only an imperfect grasp of the Lenten circular, and the business of the Roman Association. He made a number of remarks. It wasn't difficult to explain myself, and he seemed satisfied with what I told him. But along with paternal praise for my work in the Secretariat of State, he could not hide his amazement that I was involved in matters so remote from my official duties. I had to tell him I had done this work as student chaplain for the last ten years not by choice but at the behest of Msgr Pizzardo, a decision confirmed by the Holy Father. But I gathered he wanted me out of Catholic Action altogether.[3]

The Cardinal Secretary of State saw the question in bureaucratic terms. So did Montini's immediate superiors, Ottaviani and Pizzardo.[4] They

1 For an account of the crisis see Maria Luisa Paronetto Valier, "*Una fiera contesa per cosa da nulla. La crisi del Circolo romana della FUCI nel 1933*", in *Studium*, 22, 1981, pp. 25–44. The Jesuit "opposition" included Fr Agostino Garangnai.

2 Fappani-Molinari, *Montini Giovane*, p. 292.

3 Ibid. p. 289.

4 Ibid. pp. 289–90.

dismissed it as a storm in a teacup (*una fiera contesa per nulla*). No one seemed to understand why he cared about FUCI.

Montini's family had a much shrewder grasp of what was really happening. Giorgio and Giuditta came to Rome in February to be with him in his hour of need. Writing to Lodovico on 10 March 1933, the day after the axe fell, Giorgio explains that the reason given – the need to concentrate on his work in the Secretariat – at least removed the "malicious charges" against Battista and thus freed him of any blame. But Giorgio knew perfectly well that this was a pretext:

> There remains the painful hidden fact that, through underhand influences and for obscure reasons, a blow is struck at FUCI in the person of its leading exponent. Is this meant to destroy it? To transform it utterly? To throw away the only branch of Catholic Action that is really effective? Who knows? . . . Don Battista has been sacrificed to placate the storm. But the result is that gradually a wave of sympathy and support, complaints and condolences, has arrived to comfort the resigning chaplain, making even more bitter his removal from the work of which he was the undisputed Master and Friend. Let us accept, as he accepts, in a submissive spirit what Providence through his superiors permits. He will undoubtedly find good in it.[1]

This was an accurate judgement. Giorgio knew Battista backwards, and was franker than his son could ever be in public.

Life in the Roman Curia was not all sweetness and light. There would be crises of conscience and crises of integrity. How to lead a Christian life in the midst of careerists was his most urgent problem, and he had already faced it.

In 1930 on the tenth anniversary of his ordination he made a retreat at the abbey of Monte Cassino. He reflected on the minor and major orders of the Church one by one. By the sub-diaconate he was committed to celibacy; by the diaconate to service. The priestly ministry was not like a ladder you kicked away once you had reached the summit of ordination: it recapitulated and enfolded all the stages towards it. So in 1930 he resolved: "To chose the humblest offices in the Church, because they are closest to the kingdom. Not to aim to have a career; to prefer the apostle to the canon lawyer, the parish priest to the cathedral canon or religious; the missionary to the bureaucrat; the teacher to the scholar."[2]

1 *Familiari*, p. 748.

2 *Notiziario*, 11, p. 21. John Henry Newman had spoken in very similar terms.

But this is precisely what he was not allowed to do. He had offices thrust upon him.

He had anticipated that too. In his Monte Cassino retreat he stated a principle to which he would remain faithful throughout his life – including his pontificate:

> *Authority* in the Church is a service, not an honour. Vanity plays an important part here, also within the Church; one should not encourage it, still less make it one's own. When one has an office one should (1) carry it out with firmness and courage; neither being depressed nor crawling (*avvilirsi*), one should not confine one's actions merely to what is possible but should try, dare and risk doing as much good as possible. All evasions – whether out of laziness or exhaustion – go against the Holy Spirit. Mental desertion is not allowed; reasonable abstention is. One should therefore learn how to give orders, and how to put up with the unsuccessful results of one's efforts. (2) one should study the real needs of people and the works on which one is engaged, and try to meet them. One should feel the sufferings of others, and the suffering in others, and uncover the resources of good that God has placed in souls, or at least try to discover them.[1]

Such were his principles: do the good one can, within the inevitable limitations of the office.

But one result of Montini's transformation into a reluctant full-time bureaucrat was that he becomes almost invisible. He is so immersed in his work that his head rarely emerges above the parapet. Diplomatic lunches were a burden (*corvée*). He was not supposed to have ideas of his own. He was a technician whose task was to draft and redraft until he had satisfied the Cardinal Secretary of State, Eugenio Pacelli, and his chief assistant, Alfredo Ottaviani. They were both sticklers who wanted "executants rather than collaborators".

Montini was overawed by Pius XI who always made him think of the *Dies Irae: Rex Tremendae Majestatis* (King of Awesome Majesty). The Pope was fussy, pedantic and given to unaccountable rages. Once his mind was made up he would not budge.[2] He was thought of as a

1 "*Su le ordinazioni 1930: X anniversario di Messa*", with a commentary by Virgilio Noè, in ibid. pp. 7–21. There were seven orders: Montini took one a day, meditating on the text of the *Pontificale Romanum*. At that time it was unusual to use liturgical books in this way. These notes – the key to Montini's spirituality – were not published until 1985.

2 Jean Guitton, *Paul VI secret*, pp. 72–73. These are admittedly memories from 1966, filtered through Guitton, but they fit with other evidence. Pius XI was a choleric man. Even his official biographer grants him "holy obstinacy", René Fontanelle, *His*

"modern man". He once induced a timorous convent to install a telephone. "Use it," he ordered the nuns, "and make good use of it. All gifts of God are good; but by how many are they ill-used!" But he influenced Montini on one point: "Learning – for *life*" was his motto.[1] He was against "pure" scholarship. History was the *magister vitae*, the teacher of life.

The main diplomatic activity of his pontificate consisted in making Concordats. A record number of eighteen were concluded – with, for example, Germany (1933), Austria (1934), Yugoslavia (1935) and Latvia (1938). From the point of view of the nations the advantage of a Concordat was that they could settle the frontiers of ecclesiastical jurisdictions to their own advantage: Prussia's Concordat of 1929 strengthened Germany's ecclesiastical position by turning Breslau into an archbishopric; France's lack of a Concordat made it more difficult to extend its influence in the Rhineland.[2] Yet none of these Concordats proved either durable or creditable and they wholly failed in their aim of safeguarding the institutional rights of the Church. Europe was entering a period in which such agreements were regarded as mere scraps of paper.[3]

In particular the Concordat signed with Nazi Germany on 20 July 1933, though an extension of earlier Concordats with Prussia and Bavaria, seemed more like a surrender than anything else: it involved the suicide of the Centre Party – the German equivalent of the *Popolari*. Montini looks wretched in the photograph that recorded this event.[4]

In July and August 1933 he stood in for Ottaviani, the substitute. He had never been so close to the peak of power. Yet it was just the same as working anywhere else:

> If I were expecting in this work some satisfactions that would bring refreshment to the spirit, then I would have to admit that besides being tired, I am very bored (*molto annoiato*). But since it is a sound rule not to look for any satisfaction here, I think I can say that I am discreetly happy, not having too great troubles nor, I believe, being the cause of them for others.[5]

Holiness Pope Pius XII, Pref. C. C. Martindale SJ. Fontanelle was in the Secretariat of State with Montini.

1 C. C. Martindale SJ, ibid.

2 Stewart A. Stehlin, "The Emergence of a New Vatican Diplomacy", *The Holy See in the Modern Age*, p. 8.

3 This explains why, as Pope, Montini did not try to make new Concordats though he revised old ones. For Agostino Casaroli, at the Secretariat of State, what mattered was concord, not concordats.

4 See Stewart A. Stehlin, *Weimar and the Vatican*, p. 438.

5 *Familiari*, p. 760.

Montini was like Newman's "gentleman" in his reluctance to inflict pain. But by this policy of nil-expectations he admits that he is not really in the right place. His heart was elsewhere.

His isolation was enhanced by the fact that he now lived inside the Vatican. The villa on the Aventine had not been a success: the Montinis did not use it much, there were difficulties with the paying guests, Bevilacqua preferred to be elsewhere, and it was too far from the office. He was now installed in a ten-room apartment (with services) at the back of the Belvedere Palace inside the Vatican. Confessing his helplessness in matters domestic – he still couldn't sew on a button – he persuaded his Aunt Maria to set him up in his new place.

This took her two weeks and in his thank-you letter he admits that "my company cannot have been very satisfactory for you". He is becoming "a bit of a bear" (*un po'orso*).[1] He begs his parents to please, *please*, send him some photographs *in large format* of his dearest friends. "My new house lacks pictures," he moans.[2]

Though now a workaholic confined within the Vatican Montini stayed in touch with life outside. First he took very seriously his teaching of Church history at the Pontifical Academy. His parents must send him von Pastor's *History of the Popes*, left behind in Brescia, along with the volumes of ex-Cardinal Louis Billot SJ who lost his red hat for showing too much enthusiasm for *Action Française*.[3]

Notes survive of some of his courses between 1930 and 1937. He ranged widely from Gregory the Great in 1933–34 to the pontificate of Pius VI in 1936–37. This was less remote from the 1930s than might be imagined. Pius VI (1775–99) had to deal with Napoleon, who could be considered as a forerunner of Hitler and Mussolini.[4] In 1935–36 his lectures were on the Lutheran and Anglican Reformation. This was history "for a purpose" but he tries to distinguish between the "apologist" who rebuts objections and the diplomat who has to use history

1 Ibid. pp. 745–46.

2 Ibid. p. 748.

3 Ibid. Billot subsequently lived quietly in the Jesuit noviceship at Aix-en-Provence, and died in 1931. In 1932 there appeared in a limited edition a book by a Holy Ghost Father, Père le Floch, superior of the French College in Rome. Called *Le cardinal Billot, lumière de la théologie*, it was an anti-modernist tract in which the French Revolution was presented as the "satanic" source of modern errors, and Christian Democracy as a blasphemy. The young Marcel Lefebvre was a student at the French College and soon after joined the Holy Ghost Fathers. Montini would have been aware of this background when the conflict with the dissident Archbishop Marcel Lefebvre came to a head in 1975. See *Cultures et Foi*, Lyons, September–October 1988, p. 8.

4 See Gian Ludovico Masetti Zannini, "*G. B. Montini docente di storia della diplomazia pontificia*" in *G. B. Montini e la società italiana 1919–39*, pp. 105–6.

"operationally". "The apologist defends the truth," he says, "the diplomat defends the institutions which diffuse the truth."[1]

Montini turned to the past as a refuge from an uncongenial present, but also as a pointer to the future. Though FUCI was now practically powerless it had decided at its 1932 congress at Cagliari in Sardinia to found a graduate section, the *Movimento Laureati*. This would continue the work of FUCI as its members entered professional and academic life. Many of them became historians as the only relatively "safe" profession under Fascism. Igino Righetti ceased to be President of FUCI in September 1934.[2] He married Maria Faina on 8 October in the feudal splendour of Perugia. From now on they would be jointly responsible for the graduates or *Laureati*.[3]

This was a real FUCI marriage, announced to applause and blushes at the Cagliari Congress. Battista wrote to Maria:

> I didn't say much to Igino; but I'm sure he understood my fraternal joy on his behalf . . . For years I've followed him day by day, shared his work, his thinking, his feelings. I have noted his subtle, strong, and deep goodness and so I have no worries about his future.[4]

Montini had encouraged Maria to get on with her doctorate on St Francis de Sales.

Marriage was all the rage. Montini rejoiced when his fellow-Brescian, Emilio Bonomelli, wedded Teresa Battaglini.[5] To call Bonomelli a "gardener" is like calling Michelangelo a house-painter: he was an historian who presided over the restoration and reorganization of the papal gardens at Castelgandolfo. Montini loved the place and liked to feed the carp.[6] He also introduced his friends to the Bonomelli household, including Msgr Angelo Roncalli, on leave from Istanbul, on 31 October 1935.[7]

Montini was always appreciative of the wives of his friends. And they of him.[8] The net effect of his removal from FUCI was that his

1 Ibid. p. 107.

2 *Familiari*, p. 813.

3 *Notiziario*, 8, p. 129.

4 Ibid. 7, p. 80. Letter dated 28 May 1933.

5 *Familiari*, p. 784.

6 Jean Guitton, *Paul VI secret*, pp. 167–8. Of course, in order to feed the carp, he had to become pope.

7 Loris Capovilla, *Giovanni XXIII, Quindici Letture*, p. 563.

8 Most of his friends met their wives through FUCI. Montini was opposed to the measure – welcomed equally by the Church and the Fascist state – which decreed that only 15,000 women students would be allowed in Italian Universities. Under Fascism

former students, now older and more mature, were bound to him by scholarship and friendship. He sustained their hope in a time of darkness. He sustained their marriages and baptized their children. He sustained their widows. When Igino Righetti died prematurely in 1939 Battista wrote an article called "Leadership Quality" in *Studium* to commemorate him.

It was an accurate title at a time when "leaders" were would-be charismatic demagogues calling themselves in Germany the Führer and in Italy the Duce. Between the years 1935 and 1939 Righetti and Montini had worked hard to develop an alternative style of leadership "in waiting". The graduate group (the *Laureati*) met annually from 1936 in the Camaldolese Abbey at Fiesole above Florence for "study weeks". Montini addressed the first meeting on "The God of the New Testament". In 1937 there were over 130 present.[1] It was in this monastic redoubt that the principles of post-Fascism were developed. The common good was to be the norm, genuine democracy the means, and Jacques Maritain the prophet. They appealed to Maritain partly for tactical reasons: Luigi Sturzo and Alcide De Gasperi shared the same ideas. But both had been silenced by the Fascists.

So Maritain was to some extent a "flag of convenience". He was free to say what the Italians could not say. A new Maritain was beginning to emerge from the chrysalis of the old. He had been a keen supporter of *Action Française*. After its condemnation he still thought that the Protestant Reformation had brought about the crisis of the modern world. The "anti-modern" Maritain of *Three Reformers* did not change, but his onslaught on the dictators who claimed to embody Jean-Jacques Rousseau's "general will" was ever more topical as Hitler and Mussolini strutted the world stage.

It was also more dangerous. After a series of lectures at the Catholic University of Milan in 1930 Maritain was no longer welcome there. His 1934 lecture on "Religion and Culture" at the Dominican Angelicum University in Rome had been tried out in Santander, Spain, earlier that year, and recycled at Gniezno, the Canterbury of Poland, the following year. It was a sketch for his 1936 book *Humanisme Intégral* ("Integral Humanism"), the key work for the future of Europe.[2] It was also his

Italian women were supposed to be passive, cheerful and monogamously good breeders. See Miriam Mafai, *Pane nero: Donne e vita quotidiana nella seconda guerra mondiale*, 1988.

1 *Familiari*, p. 837.

2 *Humanisme intégral: Problèmes temporels et spirituels d'une nouvelle chrétienté*, Aubier, Paris 1936; this was beyond question Maritain's most influential work in Italy, contributing to the formation and development of Christian Democracy during the war and after it.

last appearance in Italy until he returned as French Ambassador to the Holy See in 1945.

Maritain provided Montini and his friends with a vision of a "Christian civilization", a "new Christendom". It would not be a revival of mediaeval Christendom which was clerically dominated and could not be restored in the twentieth century. What was "new" about Maritain's Christendom was that it was lay rather than clerical, democratic rather than authoritarian, and capable of inspiring a mass political party in which all who shared "Christian values" could participate.[1] The Church's influence would be indirect rather than direct, accepting autonomous institutions (like political parties and trade unions) and imbuing them with a Christian spirit. In ecclesiology Maritain used the work of a young Swiss theologian, Fr Charles Journet, who also influenced Montini's doctrine of the Church.[2]

But in the mid-1930s thinking about Christian democracy was, as Maritain said, like planting trees for the future.[3] In 1935 Italian "Christendom" was engaged in a "crusade" against the defenceless Abyssinians (many of whom were Christians of ancient lineage). 1936 saw the outbreak of the Spanish civil war, widely perceived as the dress-rehearsal for the major European war that now came inevitably closer. Maritain protested against describing the Spanish Civil War as a "crusade". War is a secular reality and to call it a crusade was sacrilege or blasphemy.[4]

Montini did not show his hand in these events. He had been away from the office for so long that he had an alibi for silence: the doctors ordered "complete rest" from February to July 1935. Ottaviani was most solicitous, sent him to recuperate at Nettuno overlooking Anzio

1 Giorgio Campanini, "*Montini e Maritain*" in *G. B. Montini e la Società Italiana 1919–39*, pp. 83–95.

2 The key work was *La Juridiction de l'Eglise dans la Cité*, Paris 1931. See Daniele Menozzi, "*L'Eglise et l'Histoire*" in *La chrétienté en débat*, p. 60. Journet later published his *L'Eglise du Verbe Incarné*, Paris 1941. Paul VI made him a cardinal.

3 "Master foresters work for a future state of their forests which is calculated precisely but which neither their eyes nor those of their children will ever see", *True Humanism*, p. 256.

4 Maritain was not alone in this view. Georges Bernanos was revolted by the Nationalist massacres on the island of Majorca, where he wrote *Le Journal d'un Curé de Campagne*. François Mauriac and leading French Dominicans including Yves Congar and Jean-Marie Chenu also opposed the war in Spain. So the Catholic opposition spanned both right (Bernanos was a monarchist) and left, and marked this generation. They remained mistrustful of Franco's Spain and therefore of Opus Dei.

(where the 1944 beachhead happened) in his "magnificent motor", and paid his salary even though he was doing no work for the Secretariat of State. He returned feeling "rustic and foreign".[1]

In his absence Pius XI had been making statements which, for sheer diplomatic obscurity, would have put the Delphic oracle to shame. Had Italy the right to establish an empire in Africa by invading Abyssinia? The Pope replied on 28 July 1935, in anticipation:

> Clouds darken the sky over Italy and Abyssinia; no one should deceive himself that dire events may not come. We hope and believe always in the peace of Christ and his kingdom, and we have complete confidence that nothing can happen which is not consistent with Truth, Justice and Love. One thing, however, appears certain to us: namely that if the need to expand is a fact, we must also consider the right to self-defence, which also has its limits, and a moderation which is to be observed if the defence is to remain guiltless.[2]

No one quite knew what this baffling statement meant; both sides sought solace in it; diplomats accredited to the Vatican decoded papal statements rather than simply transmitting them.

The Foreign Office in London found it harder than ever to distinguish between the Vatican and the Italian government. But when it circulated all its embassies to discover whether local Vatican diplomats were supporting the Italian cause, the answer was almost unanimously negative. This showed that the Vatican was not so much subscribing to the Italian position as desperately seeking a peaceful solution which Mussolini would accept. Hugh Montgomery,[3] the British *chargé d'affaires*, confirmed this by showing how upset the Vatican had been at the keenness for the war displayed by certain Italian bishops. Cardinal Schuster of Milan had been rebuked by *l'Osservatore Romano* for ordering churches in his diocese to send their superfluous gold to Fascist headquarters. He really meant they should be given to the poor, the Vatican paper explained, stretching a point.[4]

Montini wrote home on 14 November 1935, six weeks after

1 *Familiari*, pp. 810–20. What was he suffering from? Nothing clear emerges. "Overwork" might have been a clerical euphemism for "depression".

2 Anthony Rhodes, *The Vatican in the Age of the Dictators 1922–1945*, p. 70. Sir Samuel Hoare noted: "The Pope appears so timid as to give the impression that he supports Mussolini", ibid. fn. 2.

3 After studies at the Beda College in Rome he was ordained priest.

4 See Peter C. Kent, "Catholics and the Italo-Abyssinian War", a paper delivered at the Canadian Historical Association meeting, McMaster University, 5 June 1987, pp. 11, 15.

the invasion: "Nothing of note here. We live in a kind of suspended animination (*una certa sospensione d'anima*) concerning the events which affect our country; but here, whether by habit or design, a certain calm optimism prevails. I hope, God willing, it is justified."[1] The note of "calm optimism" was hardly borne out by events. In a secret memo to Hugh Montgomery the Pope said that he knew that he was accused of inaction but preferred to face unfavourable criticism rather than prejudice his chances of stopping the war.

Pius XI explained that in article 24 of the Concordat the Pope had undertaken "to remain outside temporal conflicts unless the parties concerned jointly appealed for the pacifying mission of the Holy See". But this had not happened.[2] This apologia was pregnant with consequences for the future. It was the basis of the Holy See's "neutrality" during the Second World War.

And it made no sense. The conflicting parties – Italy and the Emperor of Abyssinia – were hardly likely to come together to ask the Pope to mediate. Diplomats don't like proposals that lead only into the quicksands. Montini was critical of the Vatican policy on Concordats and saw the need for strong international organizations. In the 1930s the view of the Secretariat of State was that the League of Nations had usurped the papal prerogative as mediator in international disputes. By its very existence it marginalized the Holy See. It was also believed to be a den of Freemasons.[3]

Moreover there was mileage in the contrast between papal interdicts, which once made kings and nations tremble, and the ineffectual sanctions imposed by the League of Nations. *Il Messagero* was not too far off the Vatican line when it declared that the League of Nations "mimics and adulterates a function which for centuries has been the Pope's – replacing the Universal Church's administration of Justice by a typically Anglo-Saxon substitute."[4]

1 *Familiari*, p. 820. His friend, Msgr Mariano Rampolla del Tindaro, who would be with him in England and Scotland in 1934, looked after the teaching of the lay students at the school of canon and civil law.

2 Rhodes, *The Vatican in the Age of Dictators*, p. 78, quoting FO 371/19136.

3 "*Une ruche de franc-maçons*": Joseph Joblin SJ, "*Paul VI et les Institutions Internationales*", in *Modernité*, p. 533.

4 7 October 1935. Anthony Rhodes, *The Vatican in the Age of Dictators*, p. 71. *Il Messagero* grotesquely simplified the Holy See's position. Though at first sceptical of an arrangement which gave the French hegemony and imposed impossible reparations on defeated Germany, by 1932 these fears were dissipated at the Locarno Conference and the Vatican began to see the League of Nations as a possible instrument of international reconciliation. Its sovereignty restored by the Lateran Pacts of 1929, the Holy See *could* have joined the League; but preferred to stay outside to

There were two aids to sanity amidst the intensity of desk-work: charity and travel. Montini tried both. On being sacked from the national chaplaincy of FUCI he joined his friend Dr Ugo Piazzi from Faenza, now working in a poor quarter of Rome where he led the local St Vincent de Paul Society.[1] Primavalle was one of the newest and poorest suburbs. People thrown out of the city centre as a result of Mussolini's grandiose urban schemes were dumped in damp jerry-built one-storey houses lacking decent sanitation and water. The Primavalle St Vincent de Paul Society first met in the convent of Polish Ursulines, but in August 1934 they moved to the new church of St Philip Neri, via Pineta Sachetti, much closer to the really poor. They had financial difficulties. Montini suggests approaching "the American uncle", Amleto Cicognani, Apostolic Delegate in Washington. "If you ask him for a signed photograph of himself," says Montini slyly, "he might send some money for our poor." Cicognani obliged with 1,200 lire.

This is the first appearance of Montini the "fixer", a role that flourished under Fascism when the deep Catholic sub-culture was able to come to the aid of those whom the regime discarded as hopeless.

Then there was travel. In England there was a revival of interest in "Christendom" as a counter to Fascism and Communism. Maurice Reckitt, an Anglican, directed the review *Christendom*. Back in 1922 G. K. Chesterton's last essay before becoming a Roman Catholic was called *The Return of Christendom*. In 1932 he had dashingly addressed the Dublin Eucharistic Congress on the same theme.[2] It was all rather vague but Christendom was what had to be defended against the new barbarians.

Pius XI was taking an interest in England too. In 1934 he made G. K. Chesterton and Hilaire Belloc Knights of St Gregory. The convert Chesterton loved this: it appealed to his Lepanto side. The cradle-Catholic Belloc left the invitation on his desk, unanswered, muttering: "Why should I accept an honour from some greasy Italian *monsignore*?"[3]

In fact two punctiliously dressed Italian *monsignori* were, unknown to Belloc, visiting England and Scotland that same summer of 1934: Montini and his Sicilian friend Mariano Rampolla da Tindaro, grand-nephew of the Cardinal Rampolla who narrowly failed to become pope

preserve its impartiality and ability to mediate. See Stewart A. Stehlin, "The Emergence of a New Vatican Diplomacy", pp. 8, 10.

1 Piazzi had arrived in Rome in 1925 wearing baggy trousers and a disconcerting black shirt. At first he wanted to be a vet because his working-class father drove carriages between Faenza and Bologna. But he qualified as a doctor, *Notiziario*, 11, p. 11.

2 Menozzi, op. cit. p. 57.

3 Andrew H. Wilson, *Hilaire Belloc*, p. 330.

in 1903 – foiled by the veto of the Cardinal Archbishop of Kraków. After a few days in Quarr Abbey on the Isle of Wight they crossed over to Portsmouth where they were joined by Msgr Antonio Riberi, since 1930 counsellor at the Nunciature in Dublin. In a hired car Riberi led them on a helter-skelter tour of Britain that included Benedictine abbeys, Anglican cathedrals, Glastonbury and Stonehenge. Montini provided an estate agent's description of Downside:

> Downside Abbey is a relatively recent monastery, magnificently built though not quite complete, with a most beautiful Gothic church. It is one of the leading colleges of England. It stands on a hill, surrounded by trees and meadows and offers superb views. At Quarr Abbey the atmosphere was French. Here everything is English, the language, the customs, the food, everything. But meeting and understanding have been greatly helped not only by the presence of Msgr Riberi, who is known here, but by a simplicity and cordiality that owe much to Englishness and, even more, to the ever courteous and hospitable Benedictine tradition of kindness.[1]

They visited the Italian church of St Peter's, Clerkenwell, saw Canterbury Cathedral, and were present in the House of Commons on the day Sir John Simon, Foreign Secretary, announced that armed Nazis had seized the radio station in Vienna and murdered the Austrian Chancellor, Engelbert Dollfuss, on whom the Vatican had pinned some unrealistic hopes as an exponent of neither-left-nor-right "Catholic social doctrine".

Far away central European events they must have seemed as Peterborough, Lincoln, York, Durham and, somehow, Cambridge flitted by. He mentions no less than nine Anglican cathedrals, and was impressed:

> They are monuments on a vast scale, very well preserved, rather austere, with huge fantastic spaces, full of history, mystery and piety, veritable ships of the spirit where matter has not only a use but a meaning, whose lines are not only harmonious in their proportions but strive upwards in aspiration, and where glorious and sorrowful memories of the past are brought into living contact with the present. They are marvels that only music can express, and music there is, gentle and grave, and as the great organs resound the entire buildings vibrate with the marvellous sound of hymns and canticles.[2]

So he must have attended Evensong at least. But his appreciation of

1 *Familiari*, p. 790.
2 Ibid. p. 794.

Anglicans was at this date limited. People are drawn to the cathedrals, he thinks, for aesthetic rather than religious reasons and he laments the feeling of "emptiness, the great void in the absence of Christ, the priesthood and the faith".[1] Belloc would have liked that.

Scotland he found "poorer but more picturesque than England". They reached Fort Augustus Abbey by way of Loch Ness where – it was the silly season – there had been sightings of the monster. Fort Augustus, he declared, "was a welcoming oasis of prayer and Catholic education in a Protestant country", and they joined in a sung Mass that inspired thoughts not so much of home but of the heavenly home (*casa nostra quassù*). They spent four days at the Nunciature in Phoenix Park, Dublin, where the first Nuncio was an Irish Franciscan, Fr Paschal Robinson.

What was the effect of this visit to the Western Isles? Montini could now read the map and knew where places were, he discovered Gothic as a genuinely Christian art form, had his first inkling that Anglicans were not just Protestants, and was disposed to like the English at a time when they were unpopular in Italy. In Scotland and Ireland as well as in England he "felt what a great thing is the brotherhood of the Catholic Church". He added: "We talk and travel about, we discuss and think, we pray and discover how big the world is and how small we are."[2]

An important discovery for a member of the Roman Curia. His colleague, Domenico Tardini, did not need to travel to sharpen his mind but surveyed the world from this imperial centre. In December 1935 Tardini became "substitute" to Pacelli, while another stay-at-home, Ottaviani, went as "assessor" to the Holy Office, the watchdog of doctrinal orthodoxy. He was still barking thirty years later when Montini became Pope. Battista advised Giorgio to congratulate Ottaviani, now much more "cardinable", he said.[3]

He got on well with Tardini, his new immediate superior. Tardini spared him much office work to allow him to concentrate on his teaching of Vatican diplomatic history.[4] Tardini also promoted his career by getting Montini to stand in for him when he went on vacation. During these periods he saw Pacelli, Secretary of State, every morning. He also got to know Pius XI better, finding him in November 1937 "always very friendly and most clear-minded".[5] One historian maintains that Pius

1 Ibid.

2 Ibid. pp. 791–95.

3 Ibid. p. 823.

4 Ibid. p. 827.

5 Ibid. p. 874. November 1937.

XI's "greatest weakness lay in his tendency to select worthy mediocrities, whose loyalty and industry were undoubted but whose ability was questionable".[1]

One could not question the abilities of Tardini or Montini, the two high-fliers in the final stage of Pius XI's pontificate. They saw themselves as priests who were professional diplomats in a severely overstretched service. Hence the need to train future diplomats at the Pontifical Academy. The study of diplomatic history, Montini insisted, is not a merely academic exercise: it flowers into a study of the way God works through history and the signs of the times:

> If it is true that history turns our gaze towards the past, it is equally true that history . . . reveals the present more than the past; it shows us what has been in order to enable us to foresee what must and will come to pass in the future; it confidently projects the life of the Church into the future. The Church may experience innumerable vicissitudes but she still has the future before her.[2]

So far, so vague.

His 1936–37 course of lectures was on Pius VI's *Responsio super Nunciaturis* of 1786. This is the classic defence of Vatican diplomatic activity against German-speaking Prince Bishops who thought Vatican nuncios redundant and powerless. Montini follows Pius VI in the not wholly convincing claim that the principle of "representativity" is found in the New Testament itself: Paul sends envoys like Barnabas who can speak in his name; the Council of Jerusalem involved the same idea. Pius VI was really arguing for papal primacy against Gallicanism and Febronianism.[3]

Montini's conclusion is that the Vatican diplomatic service's first function is to serve the internal unity of the Church. It deals in an organized way with governments only in the second phase. What then is its relationship with the local Churches? Vatican diplomacy, says Montini in 1937, "does not set out to undermine the local bishops, or to substitute itself for them in their inalienable duties, but rather to

1 Rhodes, *The Vatican in the Age of the Dictators*, p. 215.

2 G. B. Montini, address on the 250th anniversary of the foundation of the Pontifical Academy, 25 April 1951. Quoted in Eugenio Cardinale, *The Holy See and the International Order*, p. 303.

3 *Società Italiana*, pp. 109–12. Gallicanism was the name for the French Church's attempt to state its relative autonomy from Rome. Febronianism in Austria was the policy followed under the Emperor Joseph II which involved complete religious toleration, the subjection of Church to state, and the restriction of papal intervention to the spiritual sphere.

watch over and strengthen them in their work and to act as a shield against the inevitable hostility, incomprehension or ambitions of states".[1]

This was the official line. In the age of dictatorships it made a lot of sense. On such questions the ever-reliable Montini was soundness itself. As Pius XI woke up to the realities of Fascism his *Popolari* contacts were no longer held against him. The Church was clearly being persecuted in Nazi Germany.

The Berlin–Rome "axis" was sealed on 21 October 1936 during the visit of Hans Frank to Rome. The Vatican riposte to Nazi persecutions was drafted by Cardinal Michael von Faulhaber of Munich in January 1937 and *Mit Brennender Sorge* (*With Burning Concern*) was secretly distributed and read in German churches the next Palm Sunday.[2]

On 13 December 1937 Montini was appointed "substitute" at the Secretariat of State. He took over from Tardini who became Secretary (that is, head) of the Extraordinary Ecclesiastical Affairs Section (which dealt with governments). At forty Monsignore Montini was now, in effect, the chief executive officer to Pacelli, Secretary of State. Other tasks went with the job. He became a consultor of the Holy Office, which vetted orthodoxy, and of the Consistorial Congregation, which vetted future bishops.

He jokes with his father about his membership of the magnificently pompous Segnatura – a sort of supreme court – noting that it carries with it the right to "use a portable altar". But he does not even mention another of his offices, Secretary of the Cipher, about which one did not joke.[3] There is some evidence that he tried to decline his new post. His confessor, Fr Caresana, sent a telegram to the parents who had heard rumours: EDIFYING RESISTANCE FINALLY OVERCOME.[4] It does not sound as though he struggled very hard.

A new apartment went with the job – this time in the Apostolic Palace, the papal residence itself. Tradition said it had been used by St Charles Borromeo. Approached through "the old salon of the Swiss Guards", it was adorned with huge allegorical figures of the fifteen virtues. He said Mass next door in a room used by the Renaissance Pope Julius II (a man described as "ruthless, violent, forceful").[5] His old servant, Giulia, a misfit in the gossipy Vatican, departed. Her replacement, Teresa Pastrello, was a taciturn peasant from the Padua region.

1 Ibid. pp. 111–12. Talk of the "local Church" was unusual in the 1930s.

2 Rhodes, *The Vatican in the Age of the Dictators*, p. 205.

3 Nello Vian, *Anni e Opere*, pp. 32–33; *Familiari*, p. 846.

4 Fappani-Molinari, *Montini Giovane*, p. 336.

5 *Anni e Opere*, p. 33.

She performed well at the frequent dinner parties.[1] Montini would remain inside the Vatican for the next seventeen years. It was his longest stay in any one place.

The ex-*Popolari* were particularly pleased by his appointment. Alcide De Gasperi wrote: "Your excellency, a lofty title can add nothing to a good man," and he quoted Schiller: "*Der Mensch Wächst mit seinen höhen Zwecken*" ("A person grows as he is set higher goals"). Don Luigi Sturzo sent congratulations from his exile at 231A Gloucester Terrace, London.[2] Emilio Bonomelli reports that a reception to honour Pizzardo, created Cardinal, in fact turned into a celebration of Montini's appointment.[3] That stored up trouble for the future. The inevitable "prophet" assured Giorgio that his son would be a cardinal and, more boldly, that "one day a Brescian would sit on Peter's throne". Giorgio knew Battista better, imagining Christ's words ringing in his ears: "Are you able to drink my chalice?"[4]

Montini was now in a position of influence if not authority. But his manner did not change. Jacques Martin, newly arrived in the Secretariat of State in 1936, described the system. The younger officials had to leave their reports on Montini's desk when they left at 1.30 p.m. Montini would study them, correct them, then pass them upwards for signature. His ante-room was always crowded, the telephone rang incessantly, the dossiers mounted up on his desk. Yet in conversation Montini always made you feel that you were the most important person in the world. He treated his colleagues not as mere "employees" but as human beings, fellow-priests, brothers. He was always ready to "listen to his staff, to give advice and eventually explain some decision, and he knew how to give a word of encouragement which eased the daily burden of hard work".[5] Though this may seem banal, it was not the habitual style of

1 *Familiari*, p. 846.

2 Fappani-Molinari, *Montini Giovane*, p. 337. The correspondence of Luigi Sturzo with his brother Mario, Bishop of Piazza Armenia, is published in Gabriele De Rosa, *Carteggio*, op. cit. The correspondence was mostly on literary and philosophical questions such as Benedetto Croce's works. But Mario also asks how to pronounce the following English names, "Smiles, Byron, Pusey, Tyrrell", and rejoices that "poor Puccini" received the last Sacraments on his death-bed.

3 Fappani-Molinari, *Montini Giovane*, p. 337. Bonomelli added the significant remark: "I've been in the service of the Vatican for eight years now and I have never seen a less 'Vatican' event. Not much was said, but the smiles and the handshakes had real meaning – something that does not come easily to Vatican insiders."

4 Ibid. pp. 336–37.

5 Jacques Martin, "*Da Minutante a Sostituto*" in *Notiziario*, 11, p. 83. This article first appeared in *L'Osservatore della Domenica*, 28 June 1970, by which time Msgr Martin was "Prefect of the Apostolic Palace" where he remained throughout the pontificate of Paul VI. He was made a cardinal in 1988.

the Roman Curia. Tardini, for example, turned rudeness into a policy, never apologizing, never explaining.

Montini was trying to lead a Christian life in the Curia – the problem that had exercised him in his 1930 retreat. Martin remarks that so many visitors to Montini, irritated by the long wait – interviews invariably overshot their stated time – would then be surprised and moved at the welcome he gave them. He "saw his work as a form of apostolate".

But he did not neglect other forms of ministry. He heard confessions of the women in black who crowded the church of Santa Anna. He stayed in touch with Ugo Piazza's St Vincent de Paul Conference. He lived simply, preferring the tram to the official car. But he saw his professional diplomatic work – which could easily seem so secular or bureaucratic – as his main ministry and vocation.

Montini took up his new post just as Pius XI fell ill and retired to Castelgandolfo for the first six months of 1938 suffering from a combination of cardiac weakness, arteriosclerosis and asthma. Pius XI, who had never in his life consulted a doctor, now announced that "suffering was a new and necessary experience".[1]

Montini's first foreign journey as "substitute" was in company with the papal legate Pacelli to Budapest for the 34th International Eucharistic Congress in May 1938.[2] Montini's letter home has a touch of self-mockery. The Vatican delegation was lodged in the Royal Palace and "it was as though we were all archdukes, or just slightly less, living in a setting of such regal splendour that it seemed almost as though the imperial tradition had never ended".[3] As dusk fell there was a marvellous procession of boats along the Danube, all fairy lights and hymns and devout and recollected crowds, that went on till well past midnight.

But the fairy lights were going out all over Europe and there were some notable absentees. Where were the Spaniards? Engaged in a bitter civil war. And the Austrians? Annexed and humiliated by Hitler in the *Anschluss* of 11 March 1938. It was the last big international Catholic meeting before the war everyone expected. The mood was gloomy. Hitler and Mussolini were now firm allies. One might laugh at Mussolini, but Hitler was no laughing matter. Pius XI, though terminally ill and with less than a year to live, roused himself for a letter to the people of Hungary in which he "thanked God for being allowed to live in these stirring times when the forces of good and evil were engaged in titanic

1 Rhodes, *The Vatican in the Age of the Dictators*, pp. 215–16.

2 *Anni e Opere*, p. 33. So Budapest was visited by two future popes. John Paul II was the first reigning pope to go to Hungary, 16–20 August 1991.

3 *Familiari*, p. 889.

combat".[1] Many would have preferred to live in less exciting times.

Back in the Vatican Montini reports home that "our cardinal" – Eugenio Pacelli – had made a good impression (*una bella figura*) in Hungary. He also talked enthusiastically about an article by the Jesuit liturgist, Josef Jungmann, that he never forgot. It was a turning-point in his ecclesiology. It presented a different vision of the Church: "One no longer thinks of the Church first of all as an hierarchical organization, standing over against the Christian; instead one becomes aware that it is the community of believers, a warm, living, compact environment (*milieu*) in which each one is plunged."[2]

A banality today, it seemed like a brilliant insight in the 1930s. He quoted it just as he received a letter from Angelo Roncalli, Apostolic Delegate in Istanbul, congratulating him on his new post and his feast day. "If I'm not mistaken," said the future Pope John XXIII, "*aspera per vias planas*, make straight the ways of the Lord is the daily task of the Secretariat of State."[3]

Other tasks went with the job. Msgr Montini was the first to be called to the death-bed of Pius XII at 4 a.m. on 10 February 1939. He was present as Pius was anointed, and reflected on the contrast between the grandeur of the décor and the ordinariness of death. In death the Pope rejoined the human race. Montini's future was now problematical. It depended on the conclave.

1 D. A. Binchy, *Church and State in Fascist Italy*, p. 82.

2 See *Notiziario*, 13, pp. 25–26. Joseph Jungmann SJ, "*L'Eglise dans la vie religieuse aujourd'hui*" in *Nouvelle Revue Théologique*, 65, 1938, pp. 1026–43. Montini dug it out again in 1963 when preparing *Ecclesiam Suam*.

3 *Giovanni e Paolo, Due Papi, Saggio di Correspondenza 1925–62*, Istituto Paolo VI, Brescia 1982, p. 28. Msgr Loris F. Capovilla, who edited this correspondence, points out that the reasons Roncalli gives for liking the name John – it was the name of his father and the dedication of his parish church – anticipate the speech he made on the day of his election, explaining why as pope he chose this discredited name. But from that to call the letter prophetic is a big jump. It is more significant in showing that Roncalli thought that in Montini he had a friend at court. In this he was not mistaken.

9

Backwards into War

> The news shows no prospects of peace. The Pope's appeal was in terms so general and trite that it passes unnoticed here [in Britain], where no one doubts that peace is preferable to war. Perhaps it may have more meaning in Italy, where they have not heard such sentiments every day of their lives.
>
> (EVELYN WAUGH, *Diaries*, 25 August 1939, p. 437)

Sixty-three cardinals entered the conclave on 1 March 1939. After two inconclusive ballots the next morning, by 5.45 p.m. a thin trail of white smoke[1] crept from the Sistine Chapel chimney. An hour later the slim, ascetic figure of Eugenio Pacelli appeared on the balcony. It was his sixty-third birthday. He took the name Pius XII. It was a promise of continuity: all over within a single day. For Montini it meant there would be no question of returning to Brescia. There was still work to do in Rome.

Pacelli's election was predictable. But it was not as unanimous as immediate rumour said. According to an anonymous Vatican "source" (no doubt the arch-gossip Msgr Enrico Pucci),[2] Pacelli had gained sixty-two out of the sixty-three votes cast in the third ballot. Obviously he

1 Max Bergerre, a young Swiss journalist on his first assignment in Rome, found it hard to make out against the brilliant sunlight. See *Six Papes et un Journaliste*, Téqui, Paris 1979.

2 Bergerre, ibid., has a photograph of Msgr Enrico Pucci talking to bow-tied journalists outside the *Portone di Bronzo*; another picture, between pp. 96–97, shows the "office" Pucci shared with the Vatican fire brigade.

had not voted for himself. However Pacelli's majority had not been quite so solid.[1]

Once validly elected, a pope is a pope is a pope whatever his majority. Yet the existence of this irreducible opposition to Pacelli affected his pontificate: fourteen Roman cardinals thought he was not the right man for the time. The foreigners were more easily impressed by Pacelli's brilliant diplomatic career: he had travelled widely, not only in Germany but – by aeroplane – in North and Latin America. He was therefore a "modern" man in an acceptable way. He had lunched with President Franklin D. Roosevelt. He had been tipped by his predecessor. He learned German by reading Goethe. With war clouds menacing, why not do the obvious thing?

The Italians knew a different Pacelli.[2] His colleague in the Secretariat of State, Domenico Tardini, makes a revealing remark in his memoir of him: "He was by temperament gentle and rather shy (*timido*). He wasn't a fighter . . . His great goodness led him to wish to please everyone, and to prefer the path of gentleness to that of severity, to persuade rather than to impose."[3] Nor was this mere hindsight. Tardini quotes an Austrian diplomat who said in 1934 that Pacelli was "handicapped by a caution that was the result of anxiety, and also by a lack of drive (*slancio nella initiativa*)".[4] These traits help explain Pius XII's famous "silences".

Tardini, who loved a scrap and was never inhibited by doubt, was here drawing a self-portrait. Montini was much closer temperamentally

1 Giancarlo Zizola, *Quale Papa?* pp. 145–47. The truth leaked out in characteristic Roman fashion. Cardinal Alfred Baudrillart, historian and Rector of the Institut Catholique in Paris, grew impatient with those who went about exclaiming, "How wonderful that the vote for Pacelli should have been unanimous!" "Unanimous," he growled, "you're quite wrong." It only remained to elicit from the Cardinal some indication of the strength of the opposition. "I hear Cardinal Pacelli had fifty-two votes," said someone at the French College, plucking a figure out of thin air. "Forty-eight," snapped Baudrillart. Baudrillart would soon become a great supporter of Marshal Pétain and urge young Frenchmen to volunteer for the Russian front. It was perhaps just as well that he died, old and senile, in 1942. See Rhodes, *The Vatican in the Age of the Dictators*, pp. 324–25.

2 The Italian cardinals' alternative to Pacelli was not a diplomat at all but Cardinal Elia Dalla Costa, Archbishop of Florence, "a pastor with extraordinary spiritual, human and leadership qualities". See Giulio Villani, *Il vescovo Elia Dalla Costa*, p. 244. At the 1958 conclave Dalla Costa, by then eighty-four, said to Angelo Roncalli, "You'd make a good Pope." "But I'm seventy-six," the Patriarch of Venice objected. "That's ten years younger than me," replied the ancient. Zizola, *Quale Papa?* pp. 151–52.

3 Domenico Tardini, *Pio XII*, p. 72. The frontispiece shows Pius XII with eyes aloft and arms extended in the form of a cross. Throughout his pontificate he cultivated the image of the *Pastor Angelicus* (the Angelic Pastor) who was above ordinary human needs.

4 This was probably Ludwig von Pastor, author of a multi-volume history of the popes, who was Austrian Ambassador to the Holy See until the *Anschluss* – the Nazi seizure of Austria.

to Pacelli than was Tardini. Perhaps that was the trouble. Pius XII kept them working in strict tandem. Montini alone would have reinforced his tendency to temporize, delay and look indefinitely at all sides of a question. Tardini, smart, quick and decisive, provided the grit in the machine.

In March 1939 it seemed natural that Pius, modern man, would choose one of them as his Secretary of State. They knew the ropes. They had worked with him intimately. Though only forty-two, Montini was a serious candidate. The British Minister to the Holy See, Francis D'Arcy Godolphin Osborne, who already had three years experience of the Vatican, minuted: "I should have thought Montini is too junior to be considered, though he is first-class and the Pope is very fond of him."[1]

In the event Pius made Luigi Maglione, former nuncio to France, Secretary of State, because the French cardinals had supported him in the conclave. But Pius soon regretted this appointment. Maglione was pro-democracy and anti-dictatorships whatever their colour. He detested Hitler and thought Mussolini a clown. Maglione was exuberant where Pius XII was reserved. Tardini insinuates that Maglione presumed too much on his old friendship with Pacelli and forgot that their relationship had changed. "Pius XII," Tardini's biographer remarks, "always remained scrupulously aware of the difference." Pius remained "His Holiness" even when fast asleep.[2]

The result was that Maglione was effectively side-tracked. Pius wanted "excutants not collaborators" (*Io non voglio collaboratori, ma esecutori*) – and indeed this became the watchword of his pontificate.[3] On the domestic side the Pope relied on the Bavarian nun Madre Pasqualina. When he wanted secretarial help he turned to the Jesuit General, who provided him with Robert Leiber. The fact that he reserved important diplomatic matters to himself merely increased the workload of Tardini and Montini. For them Pacelli becoming pope made little difference. They continued to see him daily at the same time. His desk, white typewriter, habits of work, gestures and thoughts remained as before.

1 Owen Chadwick, *Britain and the Vatican during the Second World War*, p. 52. The Osborne diaries, now in the possession of Owen Chadwick, are an invaluable source for the wartime Montini.

2 Giulio Nicolini, *Il cardinale Domenico Tardini*, p. 145. Though born in Concesio, Montini's birthplace, Msgr Nicolini worked closely with Cardinal Tardini and inherited his papers. Later he became Secretary of the Congregation of Bishops and then, in 1987, auxiliary Bishop of Turin with the title of Alba.

3 Tardini, ibid. p. 79. It is true that Pius XII made this remark to Tardini on 5 November 1944 to explain why Maglione, who died in August, would not be replaced. But it was equally true in 1939. Maglione wanted to thrash things out in discussion; Pius XII did not. His remark is as characteristic of him as Pio Nono's "*Io sono la tradizione* [I am Tradition]" uttered during Vatican I.

"We never heard the majestic 'we'; only the familiar 'I' we knew so well," boasts Tardini. The only difference, he admits, was that compared with the protracted waffly meetings they used to have with the Secretary of State, their discussions were now snappier.[1]

Montini never hints at anything remotely so critical. Working so closely with the Pope compensates for all the hardship it involves. On 2 May 1939 he wrote: "Every day I have the good fortune and . . . the trepidation of meeting the Holy Father who is always so good to me."[2] By 29 June the apprehensions had gone: "He is always very good and patient, with me especially. For my feast day he sent me five bottles of wine, a mark of kindness and confidence that embarrasses me."[3] The death of Cardinal Domenico Mariani meant that he had a new flat with a terrace overlooking St Peter's Square.

There was private grief. Igino Righetti died on 17 March at the age of thirty-five. Montini had carried his love letters to Maria (née Faina) to avoid the Fascist police. They had been married a mere five years. Maria, whose thesis had been a study of St Francis de Sales, had a young son, Francesco, and was pregnant again. The posthumously born son was baptized Giovanni Battista in honour of Montini. She continued his work by becoming, from January 1940, the editor of *Studium*. She was Montini's closest woman friend.[4]

But Montini was overworked, ate too many diplomatic lunches and had too little time for his friends. To congratulate his father on embarking on his eightieth year he had to burn the midnight oil. Giorgio nobly replied: "Your wishes and prayers are the *viaticum* that I need for the last stages of my life, that will be neither long nor many, but yet decisive."

One of Montini's main tasks was liaison with the diplomats accredited to the Vatican. By 1939 there were theoretically thirty-four of them, though the Nicaraguan was senile and the Panamanian had not been seen since 1929. The Honduran Ambassador was unpaid, while the Estonian preferred Paris and the Latvian stayed in Riga to run the foreign ministry.[5] The Ambassadors of France, Italy, Germany, and the British Minister, D'Arcy Godolphin Osborne, were the ones who counted. They took their duties very seriously.

1 Fappani-Molinari, *Montini Giovane*, p. 347.

2 *Familiari*, p. 909.

3 Ibid. p. 913.

4 *Notiziario*, 8, p. 128. Maria Righetti was editor of *Studium* from 1940 to 1977, and secretary of the *Laureati* from 1946. Even as Pope, Montini continued to help and comfort her. He wrote her over fifty letters that are now lodged in the Istituto Paolo VI in Brescia.

5 Chadwick, op. cit. p. 1.

Once regarded as a gentle sinecure on the downhill slope to retirement, the post of British Minister to the Holy See had acquired political importance as the British government realized that if anyone could stop Mussolini joining Hitler in his military ambitions it was the Pope. Since Osborne was both a friend of Montini and a consummate diarist he provides glimpses of Montini at work not otherwise available.[1] But Montini appears in French and Italian diplomatic reports, in which his even-handedness appears. He also figures in the German diplomatic reports from the formidable Diego von Bergen, the senior Ambassador, a Weimar republic hangover who remained *en poste* until 1943.

Pius's immediate concern after his election was to avert the war so many feared. Characteristically he believed he could stop Hitler by following the precedent set by Leo XIII in 1878: he inaugurated his pontificate with a message of peace to Germany. So with the German cardinals who had elected him he discussed the protocol for addressing the Führer: should he be "most Illustrious" or merely "Illustrious"? Was it to be the intimate *Du* or the impersonal *Sie*? The German cardinals thought "Dearly beloved son" would be going too far, and that it would be better to use German since Latin infuriated Hitler.

None of this, of course, implied the slightest approval of the dictator. Pius simply wanted to demonstrate that he had left no stone unturned: "The world shall see that we have tried everything to live at peace with Germany."[2] Pius was right to be preoccupied with Germany: it was the country most likely to disturb the peace of Europe. Within two weeks of Pius's election Hitler annexed Bohemia and Moravia.

Montini did not specialize in German affairs and gladly left them to the Pope and Leiber. He was more concerned with Italy. There were good contacts with the army and the Italian Foreign Minister, Count Ciano, Mussolini's son-in-law. The Rome rumour-mill said Italy would not join in because Ciano had a French mistress, the film star Corinne Luchaire.[3] In June Marshal Enrico Caviglia told Maglione that the only properly equipped army was the French, and that Mussolini would be mad to go to war. Since Caviglia was chief of staff his views carried weight.[4]

Military analysts shared this judgement. Italy was ill-equipped in tanks, planes, motorized vehicles and ships. Italian military theory relied greatly on statistical fictions such as the "eight million bayonets"

1 See ibid.

2 Rhodes, *The Vatican in the Age of the Dictators*, pp. 226–30.

3 Barbara Wall (née Lucas) reported this from Rome in the *Catholic Herald*, but without naming the film star.

4 Rhodes, op. cit. p. 231.

frequently evoked by Mussolini, which "did not exist and would have made no difference even if they had".[1] This, however, was not enough to discourage the Duce: his bellicose propaganda machine continued to glorify war.

From Berlin Ciano brought some good news on 13 June 1939. He assured the Nuncio to Italy, Borgongini Duca, that "there was no danger of war for the next six months because Germany has no intention of attacking Poland". It would all be settled by diplomacy – provided the Poles did nothing rash or impetuous. In any case, Ciano reported, "Germany will make no move without our consent. And neither Mussolini nor I want war."[2] So the Nuncio in Warsaw, Msgr Filippo Cortesi, was instructed to urge the Polish government to "moderation".

But this looked more and more like a misreading of the situation. Throughout August German "tourists" crowded the city of Danzig while their troops massed on the Polish frontier. The French Ambassador to the Holy See, François Charles-Roux, begged the Pope to condemn this threat of aggression on a Catholic nation. The Germans, not the Poles, were to blame for the dangerous situation. The French Ambassador was mortified when Maglione, the Secretary of State, tired and overworked, went on holiday on 18 August.[3] Tardini "covered" for him in his absence.

This was the background to Pius's 24 August appeal for peace. Montini was the chief author of the document.[4] Tardini and Montini supplied the Pope with four different drafts varying in outspokenness and toughness. The Pope chose the least "political", the vaguest and most "pastoral". So Montini's words echoed round the world:

> Standing above all public disputes and passions, I speak to all of you, leaders of nations, in the name of God . . . I appeal again to all governments and their people; to governments that they lay aside threats and accusations and try to settle their differences by agreement; to peoples that they may be calm and encourage the efforts of their governments for peace.
>
> It is by force of reason and not by force of arms that justice makes progress. Empires not founded on justice are not blessed by God. Immoral policy is not successful policy.

1 Martin Clark, *Modern Italy 1871–1982*, Longman, London 1984, p. 287. In one department the Italian army was strong: in 1939 there were over 600 Generals.

2 Rhodes, op. cit. p. 232.

3 Chadwick, op. cit. p. 73. Yet Maglione was back by 29 August just in time to witness the débâcle of all their hopes.

4 Burkhardt Schneider SJ, "*Der Friedensappel Papst Pius' XII vom 24 August 1939*" in *Archivum Historiae Pontificiae*, 6, 1968, pp. 415–24.

> Nothing is lost by peace; everything may be lost by war . . . Let men start to negotiate again . . . I have with me the soul of this historic Europe, the child of faith and Christian genius.[1]

It was an eloquent and a moving appeal. But it bore little relation to the real world and came too late. The die was already cast.

Unknown to the Pope and indeed to anyone else Ribbentrop and Molotov signed the Nazi–Soviet pact partitioning Poland and assigning the Baltic Republics to the Soviet Union the day before Pius made his appeal. It was the most spectacular and unexpected diplomatic coup of the century. Hitler had cast himself as Europe's defender against Bolshevism, while Stalin claimed to be the leader of the anti-Fascist crusade. It was the most striking instance of "personal rule" the modern world had seen.[2]

In any case, after the Munich humiliation of September 1938, to call for negotiation was to support a policy of appeasement: negotiations favoured only those who wanted to change the status quo. The Poles felt insulted and betrayed.

Yet even after the revelation of the cynical Nazi–Soviet pact Pius suggested to Colonel Joseph Beck, the Polish leader, that ceding Danzig would save the peace. "I replied," says Beck in his memoirs, "that the publication of this proposal would offend the most sensitive feelings of the Catholic majority of citizens in our country."[3] Montini knew that from his Polish experience. But he was the ghost-writer not the architect of papal policies. So to war and, within a month, devastation from the air, defeat and another partition of Poland.

With the outbreak of war the object of Vatican policy was to prevent Italy joining in on the German side. Since this was also the aim of British and French policy Montini drew closer to D'Arcy Osborne and Charles-Roux. Mussolini invented the term "non-belligerent" as a mask to hide his unpreparedness: it sounded slightly more heroic than "neutral" with its overtones of 1914–15. The Italian people were greatly relieved. Montini was able to spend two days with his family at Verolavecchia on 3–4 November and then made his retreat at Gardone Riviera.

1 *Documents of British Foreign Policy 1919–1939*, Third Series, vol. vii, pp. 230ff. Tr. in Owen Chadwick, op. cit. pp. 73–74.

2 Alan Bullock, *Hitler and Stalin: Parallel Lives*, HarperCollins 1991, which explains "personal power": "Stalin's power, like Hitler's, was personal and arbitrary. The mistake is to suppose Hitler and Stalin decided everything – an impossibility in a large modern state. What personal rule meant was that both were able to decide not everything, but anything they chose to; that their interventions were unpredictable, and that there were no rival centres of power or opposition to challenge them."

3 Joseph Beck, *Dernier Rapport: Politique Polonaise, 1926–1939*, Editions de la Baconnière, Neuchâtel 1951.

"I need these days of silence, quiet and solitude," he wrote, "to put some order into my interior life and, if God wills, to recover some of the fervour that gets lost in the rush and bother of my Roman business."[1] It was a very brief respite.

The fact that Italy was not yet at war did not mean there were no conflicts with the Vatican. On the contrary there were endless arguments about *L'Osservatore Romano* and Vatican Radio. Montini's friend Guido Gonella, chief columnist of the *L'Osservatore Romano*, was arrested on the outbreak of war, released only after the most energetic protest by the Secretariat of State, and spent the rest of the war under close police surveillance although given Vatican citizenship for the duration.[2]

Montini's role at this stage was to soothe angry diplomats without yielding an inch on principle. On 19 January 1940, after an audience with Pius (*ex audientia Sanctissimi* was the formula), Montini minuted the papal decision that the German language service of Vatican Radio was "to give some information about the state of Poland". Fritz Menshausen, German *chargé d'affaires*, was up in arms as soon as this order came into effect. The scandal was that this was happening on the *German* language service. The other language services were less inhibited in reporting Nazi atrocities in Poland, so much so that the *Manchester Guardian* editorialized on 24 January 1940: "Tortured Poland has found a powerful advocate in Rome . . . The Vatican Radio emission is a warning to all who care for civilization that Europe is in mortal danger." Menshausen threatened unspecified reprisals. Montini assured him that Maglione, Secretary of State, had asked Vatican Radio to desist.[3]

That looked like surrender but it was only a temporary withdrawal, as Tardini's minute shows: "The Holy Father told me he'd given orders to stop the broadcasts. I replied that I hoped they would soon begin again. His Holiness smiled and agreed."[4]

The Vatican could also point out, somewhat disingenuously, that Vatican Radio was run by the Jesuits – though this did not reassure the Nazis who regarded the German Jesuits as their main enemy within and Pius's Secretary, Robert Leiber, as a traitor. Nor could they expect the Polish count, Wladimir Ledachowski, Jesuit General since 1915, to applaud the destruction of his people and nation.

But the Vatican line was that the head of Vatican Radio, the Italian Jesuit Philippe Soccorsi, co-ordinated its news policy directly with the

1 *Familiari*, p. 923.

2 Ibid. p. 921.

3 *Actes et documents*, 3.1, p. 9.

4 Ibid.

Secretariat of State. Maglione's view was that with propaganda thickening the air Vatican Radio should eschew comment and "let the facts speak for themselves". They could indeed be devastating. Montini's role was to murmur sweet nothings at von Menshausen after Tardini had given him short shrift.[1]

However, these brave words about Poland were undermined by a tragic mistake the Vatican made in the early days of the war. On 19 October 1939 the Vatican Nuncio to Berlin, Orsenigo, proposed that the *German* Bishop of Danzig, Splett, should become Apostolic Administrator of the nearby diocese of Chelmno-Peplin in the "Polish Corridor", its Polish Bishop having fled. Pius approved this move and Bishop Splett soon found a hundred German priests to replace the vanished Poles. This was a disaster for Polish–Vatican relations. It set a precedent for the replacement of Polish priests by Germans in the Warthegau, the Polish lands annexed by Germany. And it meant that Polish affairs would be dealt with through the Nuncio in Berlin who could be expected to understand the German position better than the dismemberment and agony of Poland. The Poles felt betrayed. They could communicate with the Vatican only sporadically and informally. The proper channels were German-controlled.[2] This fuelled Polish resentment.

The German diplomatic documents showed Montini trying to make the best of a weak hand. The Vatican anti-German? Nonsense: to rebut this charge it was enough to recall the time spent by the Pope in Germany. A more shameful argument was that the Pope had urged Poland to make concessions over Danzig (thus trying to exploit what had been a mistake).

When von Bergen complained of the Francophile tendencies of Giuseppe Dalla Torre, editor for twenty years of *L'Osservatore Romano*, who – he alleged – wrote articles about the Germans in Poland "as if he were writing for a Polish paper", Montini counter-attacked. The Pope was deeply offended, he said, by the German government's refusal to allow the Church to undertake charitable and relief work in occupied Poland. This appeal to the Pope's feelings had some effect. Von Bergen reported to Berlin that if they continued to exclude the Vatican charitable organization from Poland "we shall lose all influence in Rome to our enemies".[3]

1 Ibid. 4, p. 25.

2 *Le Saint-Siège et la situation religieuse en Pologne et dans les pays Baltes (1939–1945)*. Discussion in Joseph H. Crehan SJ, "The Papacy and the Polish Holocaust", *Month*, November 1967, pp. 253–59.

3 Rhodes, *Vatican in the Age of the Dictators*, pp. 238–39, quoting *A. A. Pol III Beziehungen des heiligen Stuhls zu Polen*, vol. I.

This was already happening, so Montini did not need to work so hard on the British Minister. D'Arcy Osborne was getting to know him, as these two diary entries attest:

> 18 March: Monsignor Montini to luncheon, wearing his squeaky shoes and charming, as always.
> 6 April: To see Cardinal Maglione who was precariously optimistic. Also to see Montini whom I like so much and who will be, in my opinion, next Pope but one, or possibly next.[1]

Osborne and Montini had just welcomed a new figure on the Roman diplomatic scene: the personal representative of President Franklin D. Roosevelt, Myron Charles Taylor, arrived in February 1940. His rooms at the Hotel Excelsior became the natural *rendezvous* for anti-Fascists. Montini was one of the first to greet him.[2]

It proved more difficult to reassure Italy than the "Anglo-Saxons". On 10 April 1940 Ciano lodged an official complaint with Maglione that in so many churches there were "sermons about peace and peace demonstrations, perhaps inspired by the Vatican". Maglione drily replied that there was no need for Vatican instructions "to explain the need for more insistent prayer for peace, since" – and this was the telling point – "the desire for peace was deep and widely diffused in Italy".[3] This was true enough and it began the process by which the Church became the spokesman for an Italian people disenchanted with propaganda.

Still in April 1940, the new Italian ambassador to the Holy See, Vittorio Alfieri, protested that *L'Osservatore Romano* saw the democracies through rose-tinted spectacles. Maglione pointed out that *L'Osservatore Romano* was not an Italian newspaper and that it would be credible only if free. Alfieri then had a meeting with Montini on which he reported to Ciano:

> Monsignor Montini showed himself particularly understanding and repeated that he believes we have the right to ask for an attitude in Catholic journals that does not hurt Italian public

1 Quoted in Chadwick, *Britain and the Vatican*, pp. 95, 97.

2 *Familiari*, p. 931. Montini met him in the evening of 25 February 1940, the day on which he had lunch at the Romanian Embassy ("My poor stomach"). Roosevelt announced the despatch of his "personal envoy" on Christmas Eve 1939. In 1936 he had invited Eugenio Pacelli to his Hyde Park home, and on this basis addressed the Pope as "a good friend, better, an old friend". This breach of protocol was soon forgiven. Wilton Wynn, *Keepers of the Keys*, pp. 183–84.

3 Francesco Malgeri, "*La Chiesa di Pio XII fra guerra e dopoguerra*" in *Pio XI*, ed. Andrea Riccardi, pp. 102–3.

> opinion at a particularly delicate time in the international situation. He added that the Holy See never had the least intention of interfering in Italian affairs . . . But he also said that we could not ask the Church to adopt an attitude contrary to its eternal principles of humanity and respect for all peoples.[1]

Once again Montini was required to present a bland diplomatic front while leaving the Pope an escape route.

But such diplomatic niceties were soon to be swept away in the rush of events. On 3 May a German anti-Nazi, Josef Muller, told Leiber that an attack on Holland and Belgium was imminent. It might also include Switzerland. It would probably involve parachute drops to secure lines of communication. Maglione telegraphed in code to the Nuncio in Brussels and the inter-Nuncio in The Hague with this intelligence. Italian counter-espionage knew the contents of the message as soon as it was transmitted. On 6 May Pius committed a rare imprudence. He spoke to Crown Prince Umberto of the imminent attack on Belgium. Umberto told Mussolini who said it was not true. The Germans regarded the Pope's behaviour as equivalent to espionage.[2]

Princess Maria José, Umberto's wife, adds another detail. When she learned about the imminent attack from the Pope she informed her brother, King Leopold of Belgium. Two days later the Belgian Ambassador to the Holy See told her she could sleep tranquilly for this was a piece of misinformation spread by a German spy in the Vatican.[3] Next day, 10 May, Germany invaded Belgium, Holland and Luxembourg, thus circumventing the French defences of the Maginot Line.

Montini found time in the thick of these events to write home to his parents. No doubt despairing of ever seeing him, they broke with the habits of a lifetime and stayed with him in the Vatican in April.[4] Now late on 6 May 1940 he tries to distract his parents (and perhaps himself) with an account of a Mass celebrated by the Pope at Santa Maria sopra Minerva to honour St Francis of Assisi and St Catherine of Siena as the two co-equal patrons of Italy. They may have heard it on Vatican Radio. It became a "national" occasion thanks to the presence of Princess Maria José.[5] Was this the occasion of the fateful meeting?

Of course to ask Sts Francis and Catherine to "protect" Italy was to

1 Owen Chadwick, *Britain and the Vatican*, p. 108, quoting *Affari Esteri*, Santa Sede 1940, Busta 49.

2 Owen Chadwick, *Britain and the Vatican*, pp. 109–10.

3 Interview in *La Repubblica*, 7 September 1983.

4 *Familiari*, p. 932.

5 Ibid. pp. 933–34.

make another "peace demonstration", since they were both notable for reconciling enemies and St Francis tried to halt a crusade. St Catherine was relevant in another way. Pius told Alfieri, the Italian Ambassador to the Holy See, now on his way to Berlin, that there were times when a Pope had to speak out: "He had been reading the letters of St Catherine of Siena, when she threatened the Pope of the fourteenth century with the judgement of God if he failed in his duty. How could he be so guilty as to say nothing when all the world expected him to speak."[1]

On 6 May 1940 St Peter's was festively illumined for the last time for five years. "The sight was enchanting from my terrace," Montini writes. The terrace had a flourishing peach tree, splendid geraniums, and Giorgio, an expert rose-grower, had added rose bushes.[2] But then he pulls himself up suddenly, as though reproaching himself for his superficiality, and says: "Such is the painful burden of human events that we cannot enjoy things without feeling the burden of present misfortunes and the threat of future ones, and thinking too of the kingdom of God that must 'suffer violence'."[3]

Pius XII's willingness to emulate St Catherine of Siena's outspokenness was soon tested. The invasion of Holland, Belgium and Luxembourg on 10 May had the French Ambassador, Charles-Roux, demanding a condemnation of the aggressor. In private Pius confided to Montini: "We would like to utter words of fire against such actions; and the only thing that restrains us from speaking is the fear of making the plight of victims worse."[4] This was plausible enough. But if the democracies considered Pius's protests inadequate, the Fascists found his telegrams of sympathy with the Low Countries inflammatory and provocative.

On 13 May 1940 Montini noted the following conversation between Pius and Alfieri:

> The Italian Ambassador said that the messages addressed by the Holy Father to the sovereigns of Belgium, Holland and Luxembourg were a cause of serious displeasure to the head of the Italian government, who saw in them a move against his policies. The Holy Father explained that this evaluation was quite wrong, the more so in that it was impossible to find in these messages an offensive word against Germany – while it

1 *Actes et documents*, 1, p. 454. That proves that Pius XII had thought at least as deeply about the problem of "speaking out" as some of his armchair critics, then and later.

2 *Familiari*, pp. 938, 941, 944.

3 Ibid. p. 934.

4 *Actes et documents*, 1, p. 454.

> would have been his duty to affirm the same principles and to make the same statements if the violation of the neutrality of those countries had been committed by the Allies.
>
> The Italian Ambassador let it be understood what this meant. The Holy Father showed himself very tranquil and serene. He said he would not be in the least afraid of falling into hostile hands or going to a concentration camp. "We were not intimidated," he said, "by pistols being pointed at us in the past, and we will be even less frightened next time."[1]

Pius was referring to the Spartacist incident in Munich in 1919 when he faced revolutionary violence in the Nunciature.

Pius did not lack courage. Montini's report continues:

> "The Pope," Pius XII said, "on certain occasions cannot remain silent." How could he remain the uninterested spectator of such heinous acts when the entire world was waiting on his word? The Italian government could not insist that the Pope remained silent just because it suited them. What sort of freedom would the Pope then enjoy?[2]

Montini had to defend a paradoxical position: Pius evidently believed that he had "spoken out" but at the same time carefully drafted his telegrams so as to avoid the word "invasion" because it had "political" connotations. Vatican neutrality meant walking a diplomatic tightrope and using language that would make the Delphic oracle look crystal-clear.

As the German tanks raced across France Mussolini grew impatient to join in the war that seemed already won. His advisers had said Italy was unprepared for combat in September 1939: now there was the prospect of a brief war with few risks, a place at the negotiating table and territorial gains. Italy declared war on France and Britain on 10 June. On 14 June Montini found time to write a brief note to Jacques Martin, the young Frenchman working in the Secretariat of State since 1936:

> Dear and Reverend Friend
>
> I didn't have time to see you today to talk about the terrible trial that your great country is undergoing. I would have liked to tell you how close I feel to you and how I pray that the Lord will transform the painful sufferings of your country into blessings for France, for the Church and for the world.

1 Ibid.

2 Ibid.

> I hope and pray that will happen, and say this with all my heart, also because you know the friendship of
>
> Yours, G. B. Montini.[1]

That is the kind of gesture that is never forgotten.

One immediate consequence of Italy's entry into the war was that the Allied diplomats accredited to the Holy See could no longer live in "enemy territory" and had to take refuge in the Vatican. D'Arcy Osborne moved into the spartan Palazzo Santa Marta which had no bath. To take a bath he walked over to Montini's flat, and he entrusted his valuables to Montini's safe.[2]

By July D'Arcy Osborne was settled in. His diary records:

> 8 July 1940: (Montini at tea) I like him enormously and greatly admire his qualities and his character. Among other things he has vision, courage, and a very nice dry wit. How he can work as hard and unceasingly as he does I cannot conceive.[3]

Montini supervised the removal of his diplomatic "refugees" and felt responsible for them. They had great symbolic importance: the right to receive diplomatic representation was one of the last attributes of sovereignty possessed by the Vatican, which became a claustrophobic island of neutrality in a nation at war.

Pius's diplomatic initiatives were all in tatters. He had failed to prevent the war, failed to keep Mussolini out of it and now, in June 1940, was accused of failing in neutrality as he urged Britain to make peace with Germany. This well-intentioned move was resented in London: it looked as though the Vatican was playing the game of the Italian government. In fact it was not: Maglione's reasoning was that if Britain fought on alone it might well be defeated, and the consequences for the whole of Europe would indeed be dire. So negotiate while the fleet remained intact and the Commonwealth was still strong.[4] It was a sensible proposal but it misread the mood in Britain. The cliché Montini had put in the mouth of Pius a year before, "Nothing will be lost by peace", no longer applied.

1 *Notiziario*, 11, p. 84.

2 Owen Chadwick, *Britain and the Vatican*, p. 124.

3 Ibid. p. 128.

4 Ibid. pp. 137–38.

10

Darkness over the Earth

In moments of supreme crisis, the whole nation can suddenly draw together and act upon a species of instinct, really a code of conduct which is understood by almost everyone, though never formulated. The phrase that Hitler coined for the Germans, "a sleep-walking people", would have been better applied to the English.

(GEORGE ORWELL, "England your England", originally in *The Lion and the Unicorn*, 1941, in *Inside the Whale*, Penguin 1957, p. 66)

Italy's entry into the war on the Nazi side enormously increased the pressure on the Vatican. It was a pocket-handkerchief state entirely dependent on Italy for food, gas, electricity, water, banking arrangements and international communications. Its inhabitants shared the privations of the Italian people: the rationing of oil and butter, then of bread and pasta.[1] Italy's entry into the war made the Fascist government even more touchy. Montini was the favourite target of Roberto Farinacci, Mussolini's propaganda chief. In *Regime Fascista* he screamed abuse at the allies of the Anglo-Saxons and the Jews within the Vatican.

In Bernardo Attolico, Italian Ambassador to the Holy See, Montini had a much shrewder opponent. His pious wife impressed the Curia and the couple dined frequently with the Pope's two Pacelli nephews. Attolico argued fairly plausibly that the Pope should have a purely religious role, not a political one. Translate: he should not be a nuisance to the regime.

Moreover the Fascists could count on ardent sympathizers within the Vatican, like Cardinal Nicola Canali, Governor of the City State, who did not have the Secretariat of State's obligation of neutrality.[2] The pro-Fascist Canali encouraged the "spies" who swarmed about the Vatican, often in the guise of "servants". Montini found it difficult to replace Maria, his maid, because he knew that OVRA, the secret police,

1 Owen Chadwick, *Britain and the Vatican*, p. 128.

2 Ibid. p. 124.

would try to plant someone on him.[1] But he could not say so directly because, as Giorgio says, his letters were regularly intercepted. These pressures meant that all who worked in the wartime Vatican were under continual strain and tension.

D'Arcy Osborne's diary goes as far as to suggest that already, by September 1940 while the Battle of Britain raged over southern England, with the Pope silent and Cardinal Luigi Maglione, Secretary of State, on holiday, Msgr Montini appeared "exhausted and near to breakdown".[2] There is no evidence for that in his letters home or in the wartime documents of the Vatican. Most of his time was spent in fielding complaints from the opposing sides.

On 17 August 1940 Montini noted Fritz Menhausen's protest against the founding of The Sword of the Spirit in London.[3] This was quick work on the part of the German envoy, for the meeting at Archbishop's House, Westminster, which launched the joint Christian anti-totalitarian campaign, took place on 1 August.[4] On 4 August Cardinal Hinsley broadcast a robust Yorkshire attack on the Nazis as "soldiers of Lucifer". Menshausen complained that the new movement attacked Nazism for "seeking to rid Europe of Christianity and lead it to racist paganism". Montini thought this a fair summary of the Nazi movement but diplomatically held his peace.

Christopher Dawson, then editor of the *Dublin Review*, explained that The Sword of the Spirit was founded to embody "the dynamic and prophetic element within the Church", destined to work out "the general realization that social and political issues have become spiritual issues – that the Church cannot abstain from intervention without betraying its mission".[5] This could have been a hint to Pius XII, who cast himself in the role of *Pastor Angelicus* hovering above the mêlée.

D'Arcy Osborne had a more practical turn of mind. He reported to

1 *Familiari*, pp. 943, 939.

2 Owen Chadwick, *Britain and the Vatican*, p. 137.

3 *Actes et documents*, 4, p. 113.

4 Adrian Hastings, *A History of English Christianity 1920–1985*, p. 393.

5 *Dublin Review*, January 1941. Christopher Dawson was just the sort of European intellectual who appealed to Montini, and The Sword of the Spirit was the kind of movement he liked: ecumenical in spirit, predominantly lay, and concerned with the social implications of faith. That same year, 1941, Jacques Maritain published articles in the *Dublin Review*, and his influence could be seen in A. C. F. Beale's Penguin Special on *The Church and the International Order*. It was reviewed in the *Dublin Review* by a brilliant twenty-seven-year-old economist, Barbara Ward (later Lady Jackson). As Paul VI he made her a member of the Justice and Peace Commission. (I should explain that the *Dublin Review* was not published from Dublin but London: its name was chosen as a conscious Catholic *riposte* to the *Edinburgh Review*, which represented Whig views).

Montini on 13 September that incendiary bombs had fallen on Buckingham Palace while King George VI and Queen Elizabeth were in residence. Protocol demanded that the Pope should send a telegram to congratulate the royal family on their narrow escape. Montini hummed and hawed: true, the Pope habitually sent telegrams to victims of floods, earthquakes and other *natural* disasters, but an air raid was not an "act of God" and any comment would be politically exploited. Osborne insisted that the attack on Buckingham Palace was deliberate and marked a new notch of barbarism: no one could pretend that the King and Queen were military targets.

On this occasion the Pope was less hesitant than Montini and the Apostolic Delegate in London, Archbishop Thomas Godfrey, was told to send a message of deep sympathy. It was gratefully received. Pius wanted Rome declared an "open city" and needed bargaining chips, all the more since Mussolini boasted that his air force took part in the raids on London.[1]

Many of Montini's friends were caught up in the war. Fr Giulio Bevilacqua, now in his sixties, became chaplain of a hospital ship, the *Arno*. Montini scrounged him a pyx and humeral veil (for carrying the Blessed Sacrament) and kept him posted on the arrangements for general absolution: on the eve of battle troops could be collectively shriven if there was no time for individual confession.[2] Bevilacqua had always stressed the principle, much needed in wartime: *sacramenta propter homines* (sacraments are for people).

Antonio Riberi, who had guided Montini on his visit to England in 1934, had a humiliating war. Patriotic Franciscan missionaries in Egypt used the confessional to put across Italian propaganda. The British resented this and considered Riberi, Nuncio to East Africa, an Italian agent. Heated memos flew back and forth. Tardini, who could turn the most trivial dispute into a matter of fundamental principle, argued that to recall Riberi would:

1 infringe the freedom of the Holy See;
2 displease the HF (Holy Father) who remembers that as papal nuncio to Germany in 1917 he was free to come and go and carry out his duties.[3]

1 *Actes et documents*, 4, p. 149. The bombing of Buckingham Palace was a great psychological mistake. Liberal MP Clement Davies said: "If the Germans had confined their air raids to the working-class East End of London, there might have been a revolution." Queen Elizabeth herself remarked: "Now I can look the East Enders in the face." See Susan Briggs, *Keep Smiling Through: The Home Front 1939–1945*.

2 *Notiziario*, 3, p. 10. Letter dated 29 September 1940. This was an early instance of "General Absolution".

3 *Actes et documents*, 4, p. 150.

This was not tactful. Nor did Tardini's defence that Riberi was born in the principality of Monaco carry much weight. Montini noted on 2 October 1940 that Pius, while insisting that "the objections to him are unfounded", reluctantly agreed to lose his envoy.[1] Riberi spent the rest of his war in Montini's office tracing Anglo-Saxon prisoners of war.

Montini was directly responsible for the Vatican Information Office which brought news of vanished prisoners of war and, where possible, relayed to them messages from their families. The work expanded rapidly as Italian forces suffered more and more reverses. The campaign against Greece – launched symbolically on 28 October, anniversary of the March on Rome – turned out to be a catastrophe quite unlike the anticipated pushover. The Greeks resisted fiercely, occupied half of Albania and sank three cruisers and two destroyers at Cape Matapan in March 1941. It took the arrival of the Germans to retrieve the situation.

It was the same story in Africa. In December 1940 General Graziani's army was driven back into Libya with the loss of 130,000 prisoners: Rommel's Afrika Corps intervened to stop the rout. In spring 1941 Italy lost Eritrea, Somalia and Ethiopia, the Duke of Aosta's army of 250,000 surrendered to the British.[2]

How did Montini feel, as an Italian, about these defeats? Writing to his mother he avoids the topic and tells her he had Bevilacqua, Alcide De Gasperi and Clemente Micara to dinner. Micara is going to Brescia for an ordination. She must welcome the former Nuncio to Brussels who is "the kindest of men", has a fine stamp collection and is "on his way up".[3] But this idle chit-chat seems rather forced.

On 12 December 1940 he heard Giuseppe Verdi's *Requiem* in Santa Maria degli Angeli. It was the fortieth anniversary of the death of the composer, and his *Requiem* had been written to honour Alessandro Manzoni, the finest Italian novelist. Nello Vian says that "Montini felt his Italian nature (*italianità*) in these tragic days".[4] But what this meant was that his pride in Italy did not depend on military victories so much as on works of compassion, culture and humanity. "Much hard work, very satisfying in its motives, less so in its results," he wrote home on 28 March 1941.[5]

1 Ibid. 4, p. 170.

2 Martin Clark, *Modern Italy*, pp. 285–86.

3 *Familiari*, p. 947. Letter of 4 December 1940. "Due for honours" is Montini's phrase. Micara had to wait for his honours: created Cardinal 18 February 1946, he became Vicar of Rome in 1951 until his death in 1965. In this wartime period Montini liked the man, "but did not have excessive confidence in him".

4 Ibid. p. 948 fn. 2. Verdi's *Requiem* was also sung at Theresienstadt in Czechoslovakia, the concentration camp for artists and musicians, in a performance that can only be imagined.

5 Ibid. p. 956.

He was talking, among other things, about the work of tracing prisoners of war. On 9 February 1941 he tells his parents that yet another room in his apartment has been given over to this "exhausting (*affannosa*) and often unsuccessful search for those who are far away". Montini prays that "the intense sufferings of our compatriots may help them to find a deeper and more fraternal sense of living together and of Christian solidarity".[1]

Many Italians began to feel the same. Triumphalist they were not. Already in December 1940 the chief of military intelligence spoke privately of "a state of mind similar to that which overcame the French on the eve of their catastrophe . . . Most people want the war to end come what may."[2] The more the Fascist propaganda – now in the hands of Roberto Farinacci – tried to whip up enthusiasm for this unpopular war the more the Vatican's reputation for competence and reliability grew.

So the patriotic exuberance of Fr Agostino Gemelli, Rector of the Catholic University of Milan, became an embarrassment. Sunday, 2 February 1941 was fixed as a day of prayer for the troops. After the Libyan defeat that was about all one could do for them. Gemelli stuck to his Fascist guns: "Pray," he exhorted the nation, "and God will grant Italy a dazzling (*fulgida*) victory." What to pray for was a crucial question. The German bishops prayed for "peace"; they could not bring themselves to pray for "victory". In Britain The Sword of the Spirit, the newly founded ecumenical movement, prayed uninhibitedly for "victory".

Pius was very doubtful about the day of prayer. First he decreed that *L'Osservatore Romano* should not even mention it. Then he accepted that it should appear as a simple news item without commentary. Readers of the Vatican paper learned that on 2 February 1941 "there would be an hour of exposition of the Blessed Sacrament in all parishes".[3] Montini handled this matter. Like so many items in *Actes et documents* it is marked *Ex. Aud. SS.mi* (after an audience with the Most Holy Father).

Another audience about the same time suggests that Pius, despite his obsession with diplomatic neutrality, could recognize and welcome "prophecy" in others. On 26 January 1941 a pastoral letter from the Dutch bishops condemning Nazism was read out all over the Netherlands. The practical consequences that followed were published next day in *De Tijd*. Montini sent them in code to Amleto Cicognani, Apostolic delegate in Washington, with instructions to publicize this

1 Ibid. p. 953.

2 Martin Clark, *Modern Italy*, p. 290.

3 *Actes et documents*, 4, p. 366.

condemnation. It duly appeared in NCWC, organ of the American bishops, in its 10 February bulletin.[1]

The fact that this coded message got through does not mean, however, that it was not intercepted by Fascist intelligence. It added to the catalogue of complaints that the Vatican was openly supporting the enemy. Farinacci, no fool, considered Montini the chief opponent of the regime within the Roman Curia and began to look for hard evidence against him.

The first attempt misfired. On 20 April 1941 Pius gave a speech to the *Laureati*, the post-graduate group formed by Montini and Righetti. He said nothing subversive. But a week later the Italian Foreign Minister, Count Galeazzo Ciano, Mussolini's son-in-law, complained that 1500 copies of an anti-Fascist tract were allegedly circulated during the audience.[2]

The Vatican reply came in a letter from the Nuncio to Italy, Borgongini Duca, to Ciano dated 26 April 1941. It is a masterpiece of eyebrow-raising indignation. In view of the seriousness of the accusation, Borgongini Duca grandly begins, the Secretary of State, Cardinal Maglione, personally summoned Tardini and Montini to his office: he makes this sound like a most unusual and impressive event.

Both men, however, totally baffled, declared they could not begin to imagine what Ciano was talking about. Then Borgongini Duca put the boot in: the papal audience had been very crowded and there were so many Pontifical Guards not to mention Italian police in mufti present that "if such a document had been distributed, it would have been known immediately, and those who passed it round would have been arrested on the spot". He concluded that the document was a fake designed to discredit the Holy See.[3]

Forgery or not, it summed up well enough the aspirations of Alcide De Gasperi, Giovanni Maria Longinotti, Guido Gonella, Giorgio and Lodovico Montini and the other ex-*Popolari* condemned to lie low. Giovanni Battista was the bridge between two generations, the ex-PPI members or *Pipisti*, as Lodovico calls them, and the younger Catholic graduates who had been in FUCI. According to the supposedly subversive document the members of University Catholic Action "sought the defeat of Italy, a revolution against the Fascist regime, and to be the future masters of the state (*impadronarsi della cosa pubblica*)".[4]

The document may well have been a forgery, for it would have been

1 Ibid. p. 419.

2 Ibid. p. 471. One would love to know who was present: it would have been a roll-call of Montini's former FUCI students.

3 Ibid.

4 Ibid. p. 472.

folly to set down such ideas on paper when there was no need to. Borgongini Duca tried to brush aside the charges by quoting Pius XII on the strictly non-political nature of Catholic Action. Its members, the Pope had declared when promulgating its new statutes on 4 September 1940, "are fervent Christians who are also perfect citizens, lovers of their country (*patria*), even ready to give their lives for it whenever the legitimate good of their country requires this supreme sacrifice".[1]

That sounded fine. Many Italians doubted whether the occupation of Slovenia, Albania and Greece really was a noble cause meriting the supreme sacrifice.

The Balkans were in ferment. In March 1941 German, Italian, Bulgarian and Hungarian armies fell upon Yugoslavia. Prince Paul, the Regent, gave way to overwhelming pressure and signed a pact with the Nazis on 25 March 1941. Two days later, overthrown by a *coup d'état*, he fled to London. Young Peter II was proclaimed King but he was soon bundled into exile as the Fascists or *ustaci* (from the verb *ustati* = leap to one's feet, rise up) came to power. Their leader, Ante Pavelic, was known as the *Poglavnik* (Serbo-Croat for Duce or Führer). He had been groomed by Mussolini for his role as puppet dictator, returning to Zagreb behind the German troops to set up the Independent State of Croatia infamously known as NDH (*Nezavisna Drzava Hravtska*).[2]

Pavelic was anxious to get diplomatic relations and a Vatican blessing for the new "Catholic" state. Neither was forthcoming. The Royal Yugoslav Legation to the Holy See was still in business and complained via Montini of "the arbitrary and unjustified elimination of Serbs in the enemy-occupied territories".[3] This pre-emptive strike came on 17 May 1941. The next day Montini had the task of explaining to Pavelic that *de jure* diplomatic relations were out of the question since the Holy See does not recognize frontiers that have been changed by force. Pavelic's "suite" turned up unannounced at St Jerome's College and, to the delight of the students, insisted that the Rector, Msgr George Majgerec, should run up the Croatian flag. A frightened Majgerec explained to Montini by phone that he had no choice.[4]

Montini's more serious problem was what to do about the Duke of Spoleto and his mother. Before setting off for Albania on 10 May King

1 Ibid.

2 Stella Alexander, *The Triple Myth: A life of Archbishop Alojzije Stepinac*, p. 59.

3 *Actes et documents*, 4, p. 499.

4 Ibid. At the start of the next academic year the Croatian students started a riot when they appeared in the handbook of the Gregorian University as hailing from the *natio* of "Yugoslavia". The Rector, Fr Paolo Dezza (the very one who became a cardinal in June 1991), diplomatically decreed that henceforth only the diocese of origin should be given. Carlo Falconi, *The Silence of Pius XII*, p. 360.

Victor Emmanuel III phoned the Duke to tell him he had been "designated as King of Croatia". The Duke had provisionally accepted the mediaeval Croatian "crown of Zovimir".

Pius XII, Montini explained, was willing to receive the Duke and his team in private audience but only *before* he became King; otherwise they could attend a public audience as ordinary members of the faithful.[1] Later Pius relented and granted Pavelic half an hour *alone*, insisting that he was being received as a *private person*. Montini's minute records:

> As for recognizing the new state, the practice of the Holy See does not permit it to pronounce until a peace treaty has settled the territorial questions. The Holy See must be impartial; it must think of all; there are Catholics on all sides towards whom the HS [Holy See] should be respectful.[2]

Pius also wondered why the Duke was in such a hurry to accept the poisoned crown: the Nazis would run the show anyway. That was on 18 May 1941. On the streets of Rome Pavelic and his men were coldly received.[3] The Duke of Spoleto thought better of the plan and stayed at home.

Fr Giulio Bevilacqua, the naval chaplain, turned up in Montini's apartment early in June 1941. He was exhausted, slept a lot and didn't stay long. Montini made an official protest in his name to D'Arcy Osborne about the "deplorable behaviour" of British convoys who left shipwrecked seamen to their fate.[4] He did not mind this display of even-handedness for he had just been called in public an enemy of Italy.

This episode began in May 1941 when Fritz Menshausen said Montini had been hatching plots against the Fascists in an apartment in the Borgia Court (there was no such place) with Harold Tittman, Myron Taylor's assistant, Msgr Ludwig Kaas, former leader of the German Centre Party, Giuseppe Dalla Torre, editor of *L'Osservatore Romano*, and D'Arcy Osborne.[5] Roberto Farinacci embroidered the story in *Regime Fascista* for 3 June accusing Montini of being "anti-Italian" and

1 *Actes et documents*, 4, p. 498.

2 Ibid. p. 500.

3 Galeazzo Ciano, *Diario*, p. 514: "*Per le strade, poco folla e freddina.*"

4 *Notiziario*, 3, pp. 10–11. It is not clear whether Italian or British sailors were abandoned to their fate. The protest, dated 11 July 1941, speaks of "other facts of wartime inhumanity, committed by both sides".

5 *Actes et documents*, 4, p. 539. Kaas had been put in charge of the excavations in the crypt of St Peter's. Not an archaeologist, he had noticed a heap of bones in the cavity (or *loculus*) associated with St Peter since 321–326 when the Emperor Constantine and Pope Sylvester ordered them to be put there. Kaas had them tidied away in a box and then forgot about them. They were then discovered in 1952 when Dr Margherita Guarducci was given permission to work on the *graffiti* on the tombs under St Peter's. See Guarducci, *La Tomba di San Pietro*, Rusconi, Milan 1990.

in league with the Anglo-Saxons.[1] This was the most menacing attack on Montini so far. It put his position in the Secretariat of State in jeopardy. But the Vatican backed him up.

On 10 June 1941, the first anniversary of Italy's entry into the war and just ten days before Operation Barbarossa, the Nazi attack on the Soviet Union, Msgr Francesco Borgongini Duca made his way to the Italian Foreign Minister, Galeazzo Ciano, to lodge a formal protest against these charges. A third person lurked in the corner. Ciano introduced him as "someone who would like to meet you". It was Roberto Farinacci. Borgongini Duca pulled the offending article in *Regime Fascista* out of his briefcase and waxed indignant.

"You have attacked Msgr Montini," he began, "an official of the Vatican foreign ministry." (He used "secular" language so that Ciano would understand.)

"Yes," said Ciano, "he's Under-Secretary."

Borgongini Duca, every inch a nuncio, went on:

> He is received twice a day by the Holy Father, and by his eminence Cardinal Maglione up to three times a day. If someone attacks you, Ciano, this affects Mussolini who gave you your high position. Likewise when you attack Msgr Montini you attack the Pope and the Secretariat of State. Signor Farinacci, you are an Italian: you must surely realize that to provoke a Church–State clash just now would do great harm to Italy.

Farinacci replied that Montini's links with the PPI were well known, and that he was plotting with foreign diplomats against Italy. He said he could prove these charges – his information came not from the elegant salons frequented by Borgongini Duca but from below-stairs, in short, from spies. Unimpressed, the Nuncio said he knew the Vatican cellars (what André Gide called *Les Caves du Vatican*) better than Farinacci. With that he swept away.[2]

Borgongini Duca threw a smokescreen around the crucial question. He could not deny that those named actually met from time to time, though not as a group. And they can hardly have met without discussing "what comes after Fascism", given that it was in a terminal state and that Italy's future would depend on the United States and Britain. In such a complex situation it was difficult to distinguish between swopping the latest news, wondering what would happen, imagining "scenarios" for the future and "plotting". However June 1941 was a little early to

1 *Familiari*, p. 959.

2 *Actes et documents*, 4, pp. 539–41; see also introd. p. 37ff.

be taking such charges seriously. Whatever may have been true in 1943, at this date they were largely a projection of Farinacci's fears.

Montini brushed them aside in a letter home:

> My work here is exhausting and varied as ever. I am the target of some nasty shafts, as you have no doubt seen, in the same old newspaper. But I have been sustained by the customary kindness of my superiors and the serenity that comes from a good conscience. In my position I can't expect anything better.[1]

It was all in a day's work. Farinacci's attacks merely reinforced the sense of solidarity and loyalty among those who served Pius XII.

Montini needed this reassurance from the top, for he felt lonely in the Vatican. He welcomes letters from home, "because they bring me the comfort of the domestic atmosphere, something that is totally lacking here".[2] He often eats solitary meals, with only the two canaries for company. When he can he crosses the Tiber to hear confessions at la Chiesa Nuova or to go to confession himself to Fr Paolo Caresana, the Oratorian superior.[3] He is mistrusted by Cardinal Canali and his henchmen although one of them, the arch-gossip Msgr Enrico Pucci, cultivates him in the hope – says rumour – that Montini will help him get a bishopric.[4]

The atmosphere was better in the Secretariat of State, but the problems were no less. In September 1941 Fr Cherubino Seguic of Zagreb appeared in Montini's office. The Ustaci had been in power for four months. The Vatican was not a priori unsympathetic to a new Catholic nation, especially one so close at hand and so persecuted in the 1930s. Only two years before, on 14 October 1939 when the Croats came to Rome begging for the canonization of their martyr, Franciscan Nicola Tavelic, the Pope seemed to bless and encourage the belief that Croatian nationalism was praiseworthy as "one of the most important bulwarks of Christian civilization". He looked forward to 1941, due to be celebrated as the thirteen-hundredth anniversary of Croatia's bond with the chair of Peter.

But by late 1941 the defenders of Christian civilization were best known for the horrendous tortures and massacres they inflicted on the Serbs. Hasty enforced conversion to Catholicism was the only way the Orthodox Serbs could stay alive. Croatian visitors to Rome were constantly taken by surprise as their interlocutors seemed more inter-

1 *Familiari*, pp. 958–59. Letter dated 5 June 1941.

2 Ibid. p. 964. 22 October 1941.

3 *Notiziario*, 3, p. 11.

4 Owen Chadwick, *Britain and the Vatican*, p. 156.

ested in their crimes than their Catholicism. Fr Cherubino Seguic, a patriarch of over eighty, was in Rome on a secret mission in September 1941. Croatians, he records in his *Diary*, are calumniated and made out to be "a bunch of barbarians or criminals". Unable to reach Cardinal Maglione, Secretary of State, he had to content himself with Montini who showed no enthusiasm for the cause:

> Right at the beginning of the talk he [Msgr Montini] asked me, "What on earth is going on in Croatia? Is it possible that so many crimes have been committed? And is it true that prisoners are being ill-treated?" I was not short of words. He listened with great interest and attention. The calumnies have reached the Vatican and must be convincingly exposed.[1]

On the contrary they were convincingly confirmed. Unlike Poland, where there were few sources of information, Croatia had too many. The Vatican's policy was to strengthen the hand of Alojzije Stepinac, Archbishop of Zagreb, in his rejection of forcible conversions and brutalities.[2]

This meeting with Fr Seguic left no trace in the Vatican diplomatic documents. The continuing presence of the Royal Legation of Yugoslavia saved the Holy See from believing Croatian propaganda.

The weakness of the Polish Ambassador to the Holy See, Casimir Papée, was that he had no such access to his homeland. The Poles resented the fact that information about the Church in Poland had to be channelled through the Papal Nuncio in Berlin, Archbishop Cesare Orsenigo. His house at Rauchstrasse 21 was under constant surveillance. He was expected to deal with the affairs of Warsaw, Brussels and The Hague, from which his colleagues had been expelled. He could do nothing for Poland.

Throughout August and September 1941 Papée tried to persuade the Vatican that the runaway Polish Primate, Cardinal August Hlond, should go to the United States. The Secretary of State, Maglione, opposed the idea and delegated Montini to give the answer: "Such a journey could easily take on an air of political propaganda for which the Holy See would be made co-responsible. The difficulty is all the

1 Quoted in Falconi, *The Silence of Pius XII*, p. 307. Seguic wrote his *Diary* in Italian but only 100 copies of it were printed. Falconi found one in Zagreb Library.

2 Stella Alexander, *The Triple Myth*, p. 72. Pavelic was well aware what Stepinac's true thoughts were: "He told Ribbentrop, the Nazi Foreign Minister, that the lower clergy supported the *ustace* but that the bishops and in particular Archbishop Stepinac were all opposed to the *ustaca* movement not because they were pro-Serb but because of Vatican international policy" (Krizman, *Pavelic izmedju Hitlera i Mussolinjia*).

greater in that Poland has made a pact, though a purely political one, with Russia."[1]

But couldn't Hlond go as the "grand almoner" of the Polish people in the time of their greatest affliction, Papée plaintively asked? Another negative.

That Montini at this point dealt with Polish and Croatian affairs illustrates the fact that there was no clear division of labour between his own Second Section and the First Section headed by Domenico Tardini. In theory "Tardini was concerned with high political matters, while Montini busied himself with everyday practical administration."[2] But this was a distinction without a difference: there was chronic under-staffing, matters had to be dealt with as they arose, and papal whim often decided who did what. For much of the time they overlapped.[3]

Montini differed from Tardini in one respect: far-sighted as ever, he was already thinking about the archives (the *fondi*). On 17 November 1941 he comments on an exchange of correspondence between the British government and the Holy See and says: "In view of future publication I have prepared a full and complete memorandum bringing out the principles and attitude of the Holy See."

Owen Chadwick marks the contrasts between Montini and Tardini, as seen through the eyes of the Allied diplomats accredited to the Holy See:

> Where Tardini was forcible and decisive, Montini was gentle, persuasive and indecisive; very sincere and frank, likeable as a man and yet they found in him something elusive. Far more than Tardini he bore the stamp of the professional diplomat. He had the self-control and never failing balance of the professional. He too had a horror of Nazism. They liked him greatly and were pleased with his views. But he would not speak with the *élan* of which Tardini was capable. He was always kind and they knew him to be on their side. He would bring them fish from the lake at Castelgandolfo, or baskets of fruit from its orchards.[4]

1 *Actes et documentes*, 5, p. 251. The meeting was at noon on 26 September 1941. The "pact" with Russia was made with the London-based government in exile.

2 Robert Graham SJ, *Pio XII*, ed. Andrea Riccardi, p. 268.

3 Ibid. In the *Actes et documents* their presence has to be deduced either from the initials of Tardini or Montini or the indication Aes (*Affari ecclesiastici straordinari*) or Ass (*Affari segretario di stato*). They cannot be distinguished by their contents. Fr Graham tells the story of a monsignor rushing in to Tardini to inform him that Cardinal X had just run off with his housekeeper. Without looking up from his papers Tardini said: "Tell Montini – he deals with ordinary affairs."

4 Owen Chadwick, *Britain and the Vatican*, p. 55.

But however consoling, these were professional relationships, in which he had to remain on his guard.

Meanwhile the whole course of the war had been transformed by Hitler's attack on the Soviet Union on 22 June 1941. It was the first anniversary of the day of Pétain's signature of the armistice in the railway carriage at Compiègne. The long-planned onslaught was code-named "Barbarossa" after the nickname of the most popular German Emperor, Frederick I, drowned in 1190 while leading his legions to the Holy Land.[1] For Montini this meant opening up a vast new field of relief: the Catholics of Lithuania as well as the five million Uniates of the Ukrainian Catholic Church soon fell under Nazi rule. Keeping in touch with them was even more difficult than communicating with Poland.

By opening this second front Hitler had overreached himself. Von Weizsäcker, a diplomat of the old school, thought it absurd. England was not a natural ally of the Soviet Union and therefore "to fight England in Russia – this is no programme".[2] Von Weizsäcker was soon named Ambassador to the Vatican.

Throughout these events Montini was sustained by his genuine love and admiration for Pius XII. He meant what he said to his parents in January 1942:

> Sometimes I feel the burden of my office; but that does not mean that I don't relish my privilege in being able to receive from the lips of the Holy Father so much enlightenment and strength. More than ever one lives in the hope of divine mercy: the conditions of the world intensify in everyone the sense of suffering and bewilderment. *Sursum corda.*[3]

"Lift up your hearts": this was not a "political" or "diplomatic" reading of the war.

If Montini felt lonely he could appreciate the still deeper solitude of Pius, cut off by war from the non-Italian cardinals, alone with his canaries and his conscience. One vignette sums up Montini's almost mystical regard for the papal office. On the evening of 9 February 1941 Pius took Montini down to the crypt of St Peter's where the tomb of Pius XI had just been completed, two years after his death. The Pope lingered a long time, Montini wrote, "praying and commenting on what he saw". Then he prayed at the tombs of Pius X and Benedict XV. Montini reflects:

1 Alexander Dallin, *German Rule in Russia 1941–1945*, p. 15.

2 Ibid. p. 17.

3 *Familiari*, p. 969.

> Never had the communion of saints and the spiritual genealogy of the successors of Christ been given, it seemed to me, a more moving expression. And that is very consoling. The Church, this living reality, spiritual and visible, is more present than ever, more modern and necessary than ever; may God who unites and teaches us all be praised.[1]

Pius knew he would be entombed here in this crypt alongside his predecessors; Montini did not yet know that he would be buried here too. But this experience affected Montini's idea of the papacy for ever. It was an exalted idea of the papal office that other Christians found hard to understand: it placed the pope at the heart of the communion of saints. If anything good were to come out of the tragedy of war, it would be a Church purified and "more modern and necessary than ever". What on earth did he mean?

1 Ibid. pp. 953–54.

11

The Silences of Pius XII

> It appears from the Vatican's wartime diplomatic documents that Pius XII was holding back an outright denunciation as a card-player might hold back an ace of trumps when he knew he had but little of the same suit to support it. However much provoked, he would not go to the limit.
>
> (JOSEPH CREHAN SJ, "The Papacy and the Holocaust", *Month*, November 1967, p. 255)

While Pius XII was communing with old popes, the European war became a world war as the Japanese bombed the American fleet at Pearl Harbor on 7 December 1941. It was instant war without a declaration of war. This "Day of Infamy", as it was known in the United States, actually served the purposes of the Roosevelt administration very nicely. Feeling in Congress and generally was such that America could not make a pre-emptive strike nor enter the war unprovoked. But once it did, the final result was certain.[1]

As another vast area in which prisoners of war would have to be traced opened up, Montini was overwhelmed with work. "Time is passing with incredible swiftness," he wrote on Palm Sunday 1942. He spent a "secular Easter" with too much paper work and too few helpers.[2] For him the Russian front was no abstraction: it meant old friends like Fr Ottorino Marcolini, the son of a Brescia postman whose Oratorian vocation he had encouraged in the 1920s, setting off as air force chaplain

1 This was the judgement of Admiral Yamamoto, the Japanese commander who launched the attack on Pearl Harbor. "If I have to fight," he said, "in the first six months of the war against the US and England I will run wild, and I will show you an uninterrupted string of victories. I must add that should the war be prolonged for more than two or three years, I would have no confidence in our ultimate victory." As to whether Pearl Harbor was infamous or not, one should note: (1) the State Department had cracked the Japanese code and should have known it was coming; (2) the Japanese used the same tactic against the Russians at Port Arthur on 29 January 1904; and (3) they learned it from Nelson who destroyed the Danish fleet at Copenhagen in 1801 without declaration of war. Julian Critchley, "On the Lessons of Pearl Harbor", *Independent Magazine*, 16 November 1991.

2 *Familiari*, pp. 973, 975.

for the unknown.[1] He admired the quiet heroism of the chaplains but was silent about their cause.

In this he was following the official Vatican line. As usual Mussolini had miscalculated: he expected a short campaign and a quick victory in Russia and insisted on sending an expeditionary force that by 1942 counted 227,000 ill-equipped men, most of whom never came back.[2] Farinacci presented the Russian venture as a crusade against the godless Reds, and had reprinted *Divini Redemptoris*, Pius XI's 1937 encyclical, which declared Communism "intrinsically evil" and contrary to "Christian civilization".[3]

This stroke had a certain success among Italian bishops and in the Curia. Msgr Celso Constantini, Secretary of Propaganda, the missionary Congregation, joined in the crusade, calling down God's blessing on the Italian soldiers who defended the ideal of Italian liberty against Red barbarism.[4] After floundering for over a year, Italy had at last found a plausible war aim.

But Pius remained silent on the question, implacably silent. Tardini explained why to Bernardo Attolico, Italian Ambassador to the Holy See:

> It is said that the Vatican has been placed in such a position that it can only keep silent. Yet the persecution of the Church in Germany has been so severe that if the Pope had talked about Bolshevism, he could not in conscience have kept silent about Nazism. He preferred to say nothing at all . . . The swastika can hardly be presented as a crusader's cross.[5]

Pius's silence, therefore, did not give consent to anything at all.

Maglione explained to Myron Taylor the Vatican's "plague on both

1 Ibid. pp. 973–74. Marcolini's correspondence with Montini is published as *Saggio di corrispondenza (1923–1977)*, CIDOC, Brescia 1985. He returned from Russia in May 1943, joined the Alpine regiment, was taken prisoner by the Germans on 8 September 1943 and passed through various concentration camps. His post-war ministry in Brescia was devoted to providing housing for the poor. He was killed in a car crash in 1978.

2 Martin Clark, *Modern Italy*, p. 286.

3 *Divini Redemptoris*, 58.

4 Owen Chadwick, *Britain and the Vatican*, p. 194. Yet Constantini proved a great man, in many ways comparable to Pope John XXIII who revered him. As Nuncio to China he persuaded Pius XI to ordain six Chinese bishops in 1926. Missionaries like Pierre Teilhard de Chardin thought the Chinese were "not yet ready" for such advancement. Constantini, inspired by the Belgian missionary Vincent Lebbe, said that unless the Chinese ran their own Church the mission would fail. See Claude Soetens, "*Chinois avec les Chinois*" in *Louvain*, the review of the Catholic University of Louvain, July–August 1990, pp. 46–48.

5 *Actes et documents*, 5, p. 182. This throws further light on Pius's "silences".

your houses" approach: the hope was that the two enemies of Christianity, both equally pernicious, materialist and oppressive of human rights, would knock each other out. The best result would be for Communism to be defeated and Nazism to be so weakened that it too would soon be destroyed.[1] But that was a private judgement confided to a US diplomat. It was not for public consumption. The effect of the silence, whatever its motive, was that guesses and suppositions filled the gap and both sides claimed the Pope was on their side.

Montini was both silent and silencing. In March 1942 he dealt with the case of Fr Ettore Civati, an over-enthusiastic military chaplain who wrote in *La Regime Fascista*:

> England is anti-Catholic and anti-Roman, with the morals of a pirate; a country of vast possessions and rich bankers, where poor miners are left to rot in the mines. Her armies are composed of mercenaries of every colour, and she has taught the Australians to pillage. England's motto is, "First me, then my horse, then my dog, then everyone else".

Montini, Osborne reported to the Foreign Office, was "most embarrassed and duly mortified". Fr Civati was suspended from priestly duties by the Bishop of Como.[2]

Montini was rescued from such routine chores by an "absolutely confidential" letter from his friend Msgr Angelo Roncalli, Apostolic Delegate in Istanbul. Roncalli felt sure he was on to something important. Franz von Papen, German Ambassador to Turkey since 1939, and his associate Baron Kurt von Lersner were searching for ways to bring about a negotiated peace.

Von Lersner was planning to go to Rome and hoped to persuade the Pope to mediate. Could Montini help? Roncalli recommends von Lersner as a sincere Protestant and patriot who was not a party member and opposed the anti-Christian theories propagated by the Nazis. Roncalli knew he would be criticized by Tardini,[3] so he added: "If this is going to be seen as a gesture of excessive goodness on my part, it would be better if it remained between ourselves." Roncalli infiltrates a doubt

1 Ibid. 5, no. 78. Tardini took the notes on this occasion. This was usually Montini's task.

2 Foreign Office 371/33414, report from Mr Osborne. Quoted in Rhodes, *The Vatican in the Age of the Dictators*, p. 298.

3 Tardini had once scrawled in the margin of a Roncalli report: "This fellow knows *nothing*." That is one of the reasons in 1958 he was reluctant to accept the post of Secretary of State under Pope John. John persuaded him.

about von Papen: "Is he acting under orders? Is he deluded? I can't say."[1]

Lersner was received by Maglione on 21 May 1942 in cloak-and-dagger style. Lersner knew he was being tailed by OVRA, the Fascist secret police. He nonchalantly visited the Vatican Gardens where he came upon Msgr Giacomo Testa, formerly Roncalli's Secretary in Istanbul. Together they "paced up and down between the flower beds, from path to path, until they arrived (what a coincidence!) at the apartment of his eminence the Secretary of State who was waiting for him".[2] But Maglione offered him no comfort. Von Papen was not trusted in the Secretariat of State.

Later the same day Lersner said his piece before Montini, claiming to speak as someone "obsessed with peace". He said he had been encouraged by both Msgr Roncalli and von Papen. At the mention of von Papen, Montini's face clouded over, just as Maglione's had, and Lersner concluded that von Papen was very definitely *persona non grata* (*ingrata*, he writes) hereabouts. But he plunged on: "I stressed once again von Papen's religious nature, and his whole family's integrity, piety and loyalty to the Church. To this Roncalli had always replied that he knew that von Papen was a faithful son of the Church. But Bishop Montini kept up his eloquent silence."[3]

Montini was not a bishop but Lersner was not to know that. The argument that had impressed the good-hearted Roncalli fell on stony ground in the Vatican.

Nor did von Lersner realize that what he was proposing was out of the question. What he was really asking for was a separate peace between Germany and the Western Allies that would give the Nazis a free hand to complete their conquest of the Soviet Union.

Lersner found Montini typically courteous – "Come back any time, day or night" – but also completely unyielding. He left Rome complaining that "the Pope is more a diplomat and politician than an apostle whose supreme goal would be to bring peace to poor humanity".[4]

One good reason, however, for not accepting Hitler's "New Order" was the disturbing news that was beginning to filter out of Poland. The Primate, August Hlond, had hurriedly fled his homeland arriving in

1 *Giovanni e Paolo, due Papi, Saggio di correpondenza (1925–1962)*, Paul VI Institute, Brescia 1982, pp. 31–32.

2 Peter Hoffmann, "*Non silet caritas inter arma*: Archbishop Angelo Roncalli and Ambassador Franz von Papen in Turkey during the Second World War", MS, pp. 24–25.

3 Ibid. p. 26, quoting Lersner's *Memoirs*.

4 Ibid. p. 27.

Rome on 18 September 1939. Pius XII – and the Polish people – judged him faint-hearted. Fiery broadcasts on Vatican Radio ensured that he could not possibly return. Thus in its hour of crisis the Polish Church was leaderless.[1] Such leadership as existed fell to Prince Adam Sapieha, Archbishop of Kraków, in whose diocese was Oświęcim (better known as Auschwitz). In February 1942 Sapieha sent news about concentration camps whose inmates were "deprived of all human rights, handed over to the cruelty of men who have no feelings of humanity. We live in terror, continually in danger of losing everything if we attempt to escape, thrown into camps from which few emerge alive."

Sapieha, who had worked in the Secretariat of State before the First World War, entrusted this letter to an Italian chaplain whose hospital train was returning to Rome via Kraków. But then, thinking even that channel too risky, he got the chaplain to destroy the letter after committing it to memory.[2]

Though Sapieha wanted the Vatican to be informed, he warned that the publication of information could "give rise to further persecutions. In any case we are already suffering on account of our secret communications with the Holy See."[3] But Sapieha pointedly does not mention Jewish sufferings which he could observe on a stroll through the city: the Jews of the wealthy Kasimierz quarter were crammed in the ghetto across the Vistula or in Oskar Schindler's factory at Plaszów.[4] Note too that although Sapieha was giving reasons why *he* had to be silent and why the sources had to be concealed, this also entailed the silence of the Vatican.

Twenty years later, on the eve of the conclave in which he became Pope, Montini wrote a letter to the editor of the *Tablet* in which he made this point in response to Rudolf Hochhuth's play *The Representative*:

> It is not true to say that Pope Pius XII's conduct was inspired by a calculating political opportunism . . . As for his omitting to take up a position of violent opposition to Hitler in order

1 Carlo Falconi, *The Silence of Pius XII*, p. 142. He remarks that Pius XII was gentler with Hlond than with a later – 1948 – fleeing cardinal, Tien-Ken-Sin, Archbishop of Peking.

2 Rhodes, *The Vatican in the Age of the Dictators*, pp. 288–89. The Polish bishops could hardly communicate with each other, still less with the Vatican, for the Nazi order was that they should not use Polish. One can wonder why Sapieha, who knew what was happening in the Jewish ghetto across the Vistula, did not mention Jews. Karol Wojtyla, twenty-one at the time, was working in a stone quarry; but in October 1942 he entered the clandestine seminary and was moved into Sapieha's residence on ul. Franciszkanska 3, that was his home in 1958–78.

3 Ibid. p. 289.

4 For a fictional account, Thomas Keneally, *Schindler's Ark*, 1982.

> to save the lives of those millions of Jews slaughtered by the Nazis, this will be readily understood by anyone who avoids Hochhuth's mistake of trying to assess what could have been effectively and responsibly done *then*, in those appalling conditions of war and Nazi oppression, by the standard of what would be feasible in normal conditions – or in some hypothetical conditions arbitrarily invented by the young playwright's imagination. An attitude of protest and condemnation such as this young man blames the Pope for not having adopted would have been *not only futile but harmful*: that is the long and short of the matter.
>
> Let us suppose that Pius XII had done what Hochhuth blames him for not doing. His action would have led to such reprisals and devastations that Hochhuth himself, the war being over and he now possessed of a better historical, political and moral judgement, would have been able to write another play, far more realistic and far more interesting than the one he has in fact so cleverly and ineptly put together: a play, that is, about a *Stellvertreter* who, through political exhibitionism or psychological myopia, would have been guilty of unleashing on the already tormented world still greater calamities involving innumerable innocent victims, let alone himself.[1]

A sledgehammer to crack a nut. The emphasis on Hochhuth's youth – he was thirty-two at the time – is no doubt a way of saying that he was a boy of twelve when these events were taking place.

If Hitler's attack on the Soviet Union made the war more acceptable to some Italians, the Japanese attack on Pearl Harbor and the enforced entry of the United States into the war on the Allied side turned many more against it. It completely changed the balance of power and the Italian perception of the conflict. But at first there was a diplomatic move that disconcerted the United States.

The Japanese had been actively seeking diplomatic relations with the Vatican – first mooted in 1922 – from July 1941. Within two months of Pearl Harbor they had overrun Malaysia, the Philippines, Hong Kong, Guam, Borneo, Singapore and Sumatra. Eighteen million Catholics had fallen within the Empire of the Rising Sun. Diplomatic relations between the Holy See and Japan were announced in February 1942.

President Roosevelt was flabbergasted. "Knowing the Pope as I do,"

1 *Tablet*, 29 June 1963, pp. 714–16. Also in *Notiziario*, 17, pp. 69–75, with *L'Osservatore Romano* version which calls the author "Hockhut" throughout. My italics. In the US the play was entitled *The Deputy*.

he claimed with his customary mix of chutzpah and charm, "I find the news incredible."[1] The other Allies were equally incensed. Osborne protested vigorously, saying, "it created a most unfavourable impression".

The Japanese Ambassador presented his credentials on 9 May 1942. For Montini that meant more diplomatic lunches. "You would have thought they would have been abolished," he wrote to his father, "and yet they are still offered, even though with wartime austerity, with ever greater insistence and obligation."[2] To lunch or not to lunch became a matter of great political significance. Lunches would get Montini into hot water later.

However dismayed Roosevelt might be, the Vatican claimed to be observing the strictest protocol: diplomatic relations did not imply approval of Japanese policies. For the Vatican diplomatic relations were a defensive move. Already there were reports of a Japanese Bishop, Paul Yoshigoro Taguchi of Osaka, being sent to Manila in the Philippines along with a team of Japanese sisters. He was to replace the Irish-born Archbishop Michael O'Doherty. The apostolic delegate Paolo Marella intervened to get Taguchi sent back home. That would not have been possible without diplomatic relations.[3]

Italian opinion was tilting towards the United States. The millions of Italians with North American relatives were unlikely to be persuaded by propaganda that simply abused the "Anglo-Saxons". They were more inclined to view the US as the goal of emigration and Americans as their liberators.

Thanks to his regular contacts with Harold Tittman, Myron Taylor's deputy, who had received the diplomatic title of chargé d'affaires, Montini was well placed to know about American intentions towards Italy. In the summer of 1942 Princess Maria José, wife of the heir to the throne, involved him in plans for a *coup d'état*. She went to see Marshal Badoglio at Cogne in the Val d'Aosta. He said the army would be prepared to move against Mussolini if the King gave his blessing. It would be enough for a regiment of grenadiers to surround the Villa Torlonia, Mussolini's residence, for the deed to be done.

Princess Maria José then approached Guido Gonella of *L'Osservatore Romano* who put her in touch with Montini. She saw Montini "many times, especially at the beginning" to determine how the Allies

1 Rhodes, *The Vatican in the Age of the Dictators*, p. 308.

2 *Familiari*, p. 975.

3 This information is in James Henessey SJ, "American Jesuit in Wartime Rome: The Diary of Vincent A. McCormick SJ, 1942–1945", in *Mid-America; an Historical Review*, January 1974, p. 34. Fr McCormick is an exceptionally valuable witness.

would respond to a *coup d'état.* He appeared to know that the Italian frontiers would be guaranteed, and that the Allies would defend Italy against a German attack. "Montini," she remembers, "said that what we were doing was right. Badoglio should lead the *coup d'état*, but then the government should pass to a civilian, Ivanoe Bonomi."[1] Bonomi and Gonella were among those who for at least six years had been meeting Montini at Longinotti's country retreat at Ronciglione.[2]

The plan passed into other hands and Montini faded into the background. In September 1942, however, there was a warning that getting Italy out of the war would not be easy. Myron Taylor arrived in Rome on 17 September, driving through the city in a closed car. The Germans were aghast that Mussolini should have allowed this. Taylor brought a letter from President Roosevelt with his assessment that – barring a miracle or some improbable "secret weapon" – the Allies were going to win the war.[3] The tide had definitely turned.

The letter also asserted profound harmony between the Pope's Christmas message of 1940 and the Atlantic Charter setting out Allied war aims. The Pope should not find it too difficult to support the moral basis of the Allied cause. It was also made clear that the Pope should drop any idea of a compromise peace – news of Lersner's "personal mission" had been picked up despite the amateurish cloak-and-dagger business in the Vatican gardens. So Italy could not hope for a separate peace. It was an adumbration of the policy of "unconditional surrender" formally stated at Casablanca the following January.

Myron Taylor also brought a request from Roosevelt that the Pope should condemn the atrocities being committed in Nazi-occupied Europe.[4] Throughout the summer of 1942 Jews were rounded up in occupied France, then in Vichy France and Holland. While Taylor was in Rome solid news arrived in Washington about the killing of the Jews in the Warsaw ghetto.[5] Relayed to the Vatican, this reinforced Taylor's argument that "it was now necessary for the Pope again to denounce the inhuman treatment of refugees, and above all the Jews, in the occupied countries. Not only Catholics want the Pope to speak but also Protestants."[6]

1 Interview with Nicola Caracciolo in *La Repubblica*, 7 September 1983. The interviewer had it from Guido Gonella that in meeting Badoglio he was not acting on his own but in the name of Alcide De Gasperi, "who was already considered the leader of what would become the Christian Democratic party".

2 Fappani-Molinari, *Montini Giovane*, p. 372.

3 *Actes et Documents*, 5, nos. 472, 374.

4 Owen Chadwick, *Britain and the Vatican*, p. 211.

5 Ibid. p. 214. See also Martin Gilbert, *Auschwitz and the Allies*, London 1981.

6 *Actes et Documents*, 5, p. 721.

Easier said than done, and Montini knew the difficulties involved in speaking out, as we have seen. But on the facts of the case his file was already bulky. On 12 May 1942 the Pope was informed for the first time about the system of *mass* extermination (*uccisioni di massa*) of Jews from Germany, Poland and the Ukraine. This was based on first-hand reports from Fr Pirro Scavizzi who several times traversed occupied Poland and the Ukraine as chaplain to a Knights of Malta hospital train.[1] Count Malvezzi, who had been in Poland for IRI,[2] confirmed these reports.

Fr Scavizzi later said that when he reported these crimes to Pius XII "I saw him weep like a child".[3] Military convoys passed close by the death camps. Another Knights of Malta chaplain wrote:

> . . . in our regular journeys through Auschwitz, only a few yards separated us from the infamous enclosure. At night we could see the searchlights from the watch-towers slowly turning in an unnecessary search for impossible escapees, while the acrid smell from the crematoria reached us in nauseating whiffs. We were hopeless in our impotence and in that of the whole world, and we felt an overpowering need to rebel.[4]

Sapieha in Kraków of course knew about the ghetto and Auschwitz: but when he received information from Pius XII – actually Montini – he stuffed it hastily into the stove, saying, "if I give publicity to this and it is found in my house, the head of every Pole would not be enough for the reprisals *Gauleiter* Hans Frank would order . . . It's not just the Jews . . . Here they are killing us all."[5]

Sapieha's next remark is crucial. Fr Quirino Paganuzzi had seen "the apocalyptic spectacle" of the removal of the Jews from the Kraków ghetto, and worried about it. Sapieha replied:

1 *Actes et Documents*, 8, no. 374.

2 Istituto per la Riconstruzione Industriale controlled most of the banking system and investment. Founded by the Fascists in the 1930s it continued after the war, and played an important part in the post-war economic "miracle".

3 Quoted in Hansjakob Stehle, *Eastern Politics of the Vatican 1917–1979*, p. 214. This was in 1964, the year Fr Scavizzi died. Carlo Falconi, not an easy man to impress, wrote that despite the countless Knights of Malta who attended his funeral, he was "the priest of the poor, and the confessor of prisoners" (ibid. p. 150). Pope John asked him to give the Lenten retreat to the Roman Curia in 1961.

4 Quoted in Carlo Falconi, *The Silence of Pius XII*, p. 148. Since the Knights of Malta are usually presented as a right-wing if not quasi-Fascist organization in the left-wing press, it is good to be reminded that there was another side. The fact that they were a *sovereign* order gave them a certain leeway.

5 Ibid. p. 149. The bearer of the information was yet another Knights of Malta chaplain, Msgr Quirino Paganuzzi.

> The worst thing of all is that those unfortunates are left without help, cut off from the whole world. They are dying, deprived of even a comforting word. We cannot, we must not say so for fear of shortening their lives. We are living through the tragedy of those unfortunate people and none of us is in a position to help them any more . . . There's no difference between Jews and Poles . . . They have taken away our bread and our freedom . . . but at least we have our lives, and with life there's hope of seeing the end of our Calvary.[1]

It would be wrong to see this as an anti-Semitic remark: when it comes to comparing the circles of hell no distinctions make much sense. The Jews were further along the road for which the Poles were destined.

These were some of the documents in Montini's dossier. But what is astonishing is that the Cardinal Secretary of State was unaware of them. When Myron Taylor demanded action on Nazi atrocities in Poland, Maglione wetly replied: "I don't think we have any corroboration of this serious news, do we?"

"Yes," said Montini, "there is: we have Count Malvezzi's report."

Montini was told to say that "the Holy See has received news of severe treatment of the Jews, but cannot check the accuracy of all these reports".[2] That too was feeble: Auschwitz was only forty miles from Kraków, and the first gas chambers, built late autumn 1941, were already at work. The problem lay in imagining it. Death had never before been industrialized.

Yet Taylor's visit to wartime Rome was a success, despite Tardini's sardonic jokes about ignorant Americans wanting to reorganize Europe "as they think fit" and making a mess of it.[3] In his 1942 Christmas message Pius was more forthright than he had ever been before. He condemned the idolatry of the State and alluded to "the hundreds of thousands of innocent people, put to death or doomed to slow extinction, sometimes (*talora*) merely because of their race or descent".[4] The Pope judged this a "strong" statement. So did the Germans.

When Ribbentrop instructed von Bergen, his ambassador, to

1 Ibid. pp. 149–50. He also discusses (p. 152) the hypothesis that there were other Italian intermediaries possibly connected with the Royal Italian Mission in Kraków set up early in 1942 to take the place of the Italian Embassy in Warsaw, shut down in September 1939. In his account of a year spent in the Monowitz *Judenlager* that was part of the Auschwitz complex, *If This is A Man*, Primo Levi says that the sense of not being heard, and not being believed if they had been heard, was used by the SS to taunt their prisoners.

2 *Actes et Documents*, 8, no. 496.

3 Rhodes, *The Vatican in the Age of the Dictators*, p. 267.

4 Actes et Documents, 7, p. 161.

threaten the Holy See with retaliation for this breach of neutrality, von Bergen replied that "Pacelli is no more amenable to threats than we are". The German Foreign Office considered the speech and concluded: "God, the Pope says, regards all peoples and all races as worthy of the same consideration. Here he is clearly speaking on behalf of the Jews . . . He is virtually accusing the German people of injustice towards the Jews, and makes himself the mouthpiece of the Jewish war criminals."[1]

That is an important witness to the effectiveness of Pius XII's interventions. Was he really so silent? Yet McCormick found the 1942 Christmas message "much too heavy, ideas not clear-cut and obscurely expressed". He discussed it with Leiber, who had worked on it, and confided to his diary that "the Pope should get away from German tutoring; have an Italian or a Frenchman prepare his text".

That, one suspects, would have been Montini's view. Throughout the dramatic events in the autumn of 1942 his mind kept straying to Brescia where his father lay dying. At midnight on 11 October 1942 he wrote a gently affectionate letter to Giorgio, who was confined to bed or, when he did get up, slumped in a wheelchair. "I'm sorry I can't be with you," he writes, "I don't say to help you, because I wouldn't be any good as a nurse, but simply to share with you and your dear ones everyday concerns, small or big." He reflects on his own work in the Secretariat of State:

> Let me tell you something about my life, but by now you know what it's like: there have been no changes worth mentioning . . . I have become broody with my friends and see little of them; I hardly ever go out; and as for books, their spines stare down at me from the silent shelves; I've stopped writing and I've very little time to think and pray (at least that would do some good). But patience. God will provide.[2]

Turin, Genoa and Milan were bombed on the nights of 27–29 October.[3] There was great indignation in Italy, especially when twenty churches were hit in Genoa. The Vatican feared that Rome would be bombed. The Americans opposed it but the British refused to rule it out on the grounds, "let 'em sweat".

Rome braced itself for air raids. Piles of sand dumped along the main streets and all along the Corso Vittorio Emanuele made a fine playground for children until the sandbags were all filled up. As Vatican

1 Owen Chadwick, *Britain and the Vatican*, p. 219.

2 *Familiari*, pp. 983–84.

3 Owen Chadwick, *Britain and the Vatican*, p. 233.

territory, the Cancelleria remained unprotected. Yet from the air it was quite impossible to distinguish it from military targets.

As Montini walked around Rome he could see the German war command installed in the Hotel Minerva and the naval command across the street in the Hotel Santa Chiara. If these were legitimate targets, then the church of Santa Maria sopra Minerva, the French College and the Pontifical Academy would all be at risk.[1]

Montini wrote to his father again on 1 December 1942. You sometimes read about me in the papers, he began, but they give an imaginary picture of my life. The day to day experience was different:

> So many things seems to me grey and monotonous, even though I am engaged in great things for the Pope, but always in such humble and ministerial form that I no longer have time to enjoy the uniqueness and distinction of my position. I say this without personal vanity. I have been in this post for five years almost to the day; I seem to have piled up more responsibilities than merits, and have the same feeling now that I had at the start: that of being here thanks to some improper trick (*indebita combinazione*) while waiting to go back to something simpler and more myself. I think of the way my studies have been abandoned, my priestly ministry reduced, my prayer curtailed; but when one thinks about it more deeply, this feeling is common to every state of life once one becomes aware of its precariousness compared with the insatiable desire of the human soul. We are on a pilgrimage, and there's nothing more to be said.[2]

That was the last letter he ever wrote to Giorgio, his father.

A week later Montini was embroiled in a diplomatic furore which showed he was a reluctant bureaucrat. On 7 December 1942, the first anniversary of Pearl Harbor, the Irish Ambassador to the Holy See, T. J. Kiernan, hosted a party that was attended by the ambassadors or ministers of Germany, Italy and Japan. He also invited Msgr Walter Carroll, responsible for the USA desk in the Secretariat of State, who declined when he discovered what company he would have to keep. Vincent McCormick was "livid" when he learned that Montini had attended the reception.[3] But he had to maintain the façade of Vatican

1 Vincent A. McCormick, *Diary*, p. 35.

2 *Familiari*, p. 985.

3 See Vincent A. McCormick, *Diary*, p. 36. Also Gerald P. Fogarty, *The Vatican and the American Hierarchy from 1870 to 1965*, p. 286.

neutrality. A sense of duty, not the prospect of enjoyment, took him there.[1]

After Christmas he spent three days in Brescia and saw his father for the last time (26–29 December). As 1943 began Giorgio took a turn for the worse. In his eighty-third year he survived a prostate infection and an operation. In the morning he chatted amiably with two Brescian priest contemporaries – their combined ages came to over 240 – but in the afternoon was struck down by a heart attack. He asked for the sacrament of anointing (then called extreme unction) and with perfect lucidity spoke his last words: "I die in the Catholic, apostolic and Roman Church, wearing the scapular of St Francis . . . I ask forgiveness. *Ciao* Giuditta."[2] It was a wonderful farewell to the woman he had met and loved on the steps of St Peter's in 1883.

Montini specially cherished two letters of condolence. One was from Alcide De Gasperi and the other from Angelo Roncalli, the Apostolic Delegate in Turkey. Roncalli said that diplomatic duties had prevented him from being present at the deaths of both his parents, and that he knew how Montini felt. But on hearing of Giorgio's death he had celebrated not a *Requiem* but the Mass of the two Brescian saints, Faustino and Giovita.

Montini became Battista again as he tried to comfort Giuditta. "Why can't I manage to write?" he asked in a letter to his mother dated 7 February 1943. He answered himself, "because it is more difficult than ever to tell you what is in my heart, and I only feel at ease with silence". There was a Mass for Giorgio at the Chiesa Nuova, Don Lorenzo Perosi played the organ and directed the choir. Cardinal Luigi Maglione said another Mass for the officials of the Secretariat of State in the Pauline chapel. On 15 March Giovanni Maria Longinotti gave a lecture, "*Giorgio Montini nel suo tempo*", that was later published by the Vatican Press as a 32-page booklet.[3]

1 The legend of Montini the secret agent begins here. See R. Harris Smith, *OSS: The Secret History of America's First Intelligence Agency*, University of California Press 1972, pp. 84–85. According to Smith, Montini and OSS conspirator Earl Brennan "master-minded" the Vessell Project. Agents in Japan collected information on the effects of American strategic bombing and sent it to the Vatican; with the approval of President de Valera it was then transmitted by diplomatic pouch to Dublin and finally by naval code to Washington. "This circuitous process," says the optimistic Smith, "took only a matter of days and provided Washington with vital Japanese intelligence in the spring of 1943." Irish historians like T. Ryle Dwyer accept that Irish "neutrality" was "a neutrality against the Axis and for the Allies". So the least that can be said is that the lunch at the Irish Embassy was an elaborate cover-up for something.

2 Fappani-Molinari, *Montini Giovane*, p. 366.

3 *Familiari*, pp. 989–90. Longinotti's presentation of "Giorgio Montini in his time" showed how the Brescians responded to "the Roman Question" and the *non expedit*.

Battista tries gently to lead his mother through the process of mourning, encouraging her to express her grief but not to dwell on it. "I remember you every hour, with your dear ones, in the Lord, and ask you always to bless your little boy (*figliolo*). D.B."[1] Those were the last words he addressed to his *carissima mamma*. On 17 May she was gathering roses in the garden for a friend. She died suddenly at 3.15. Her prayer book was open on her desk.[2] Though seventeen years younger than Giorgio, she outlived him by only four months. *Ciao* Giuditta, he said on his death-bed. Now she had gone to rejoin him.

Montini hastened to Brescia the next day – he had, like Roncalli before him, "missed" the death of both parents – and stayed till 23 May 1943 clearing up and gauging opinion. In her will he found she recommended to him "the encounter with God" as the *unum necessarium*, the one thing necessary.[3]

A psychoanalytic cliché says that you only really become an adult on the death of your parents. If so Msgr Montini became an adult in the spring of 1943 at the age of forty-five. With his brother Lodovico, now lodging with him in the Vatican, he provided a bridge between the old *Popolari* of Giorgio's generation who had simply dropped out of politics during Fascism, and the new generation of Christian Democrats formed by Montini in the student and graduate movements.

1 Ibid. p. 992.

2 Ibid. Giuditta had equal rites with her husband: a *Laureati* (graduate) Mass in the Chiesa Nuova and another said by the Cardinal Secretary of State in the Vatican.

3 Pasquale Macchi, in *Notiziario*, p. 45.

12

Bridging the Generation Gap

> We are young and old people who want to build a bridge between two generations. The generation of those who tried to block the way to Fascist totalitarianism, fighting in the ranks of the *Popolari* for freedom against dictatorship; a battle in which we failed because of unequal weapons.
>
> The other generation is made up of those young people who lived through the twenty years of Fascism without being contaminated, retaining a heart that rejected the oppressive regime, and preparing themselves through works of culture and social brotherhood for the day of the inevitable resumption (*ripresa*).
>
> ("Demofilo", in GIORDANI and STURZO, *Un Ponte tra due Generazioni, Carteggio 1924–1958*)

Demofilo was none other than Alcide De Gasperi, successor of Don Luigi Sturzo, founder of the PPI, when Sturzo went into exile in 1924. De Gasperi had had a quiet war so far, discreetly preparing the future in the Vatican Library. The gap to be bridged was between the two generations of Christian Democrats, between those like De Gasperi now poised to emerge from the obscurity of the Vatican Library, and those like Aldo Moro and Giulio Andreotti coming from FUCI and the graduate movement. Battista Montini was the conscious link between the two generations.

But he had to be discreet. Back from his father's funeral, he found that his enemies within the Vatican had arrested Anton Call, the security man who guarded the Allied diplomats immured in the Palazzo Santa Marta. Knowing that the Vatican security service was infiltrated by OVRA, the Italian equivalent of the Gestapo, Montini had instructed Call to report only to himself or Belardo, his lay assistant. When Call's superiors complained, "You give us no news," he was to reply that he took orders only from Msgr Montini. This obviously exposed Call to danger, and he knew it.

Montini's chief enemy within the Vatican was the pro-Fascist Cardinal Nicola Canali, Governor of Vatican City State. "Corpulent, bewigged and by temperament cantankerous,"[1] Canali ordered Call's arrest on trumped-up charges, handing him over to the Italian police. Call spent a few months in the Regina Coeli prison emerging unscathed with a lowly job as German interpreter with the *carabinieri*. He was lucky to get off so lightly. What this meant was that although Msgr Montini was able to "fix" some things, his position in the Vatican was vulnerable and precarious. All his ingenuity would have to be devoted to protecting the Allied diplomats whose presence was the last fig-leaf of Vatican "sovereignty". With OVRA inside the Vatican any plotting for the future of Italy would have to be discreet and well-covered.

So Montini had to watch his flanks and rear. He worked on the humblest as well as the highest levels of diplomacy. The Secretariat of State followed the quarrels between Hitler and Mussolini with great interest, correctly judging their relationship a key factor in the war. The dictators disagreed about Yugoslavia, and Mussolini wanted Hitler to settle for what he had gained in Russia so as to be free to pursue the war in the Mediterranean with greater zest. Hitler refused.[2] Mussolini was in bad health and increasingly desperate for some way out.

On 12 January 1943 his son-in-law and Foreign Minister, Galeazzo Ciano, lunched at Princess Colonna's; Montini just happened to be there. They talked privately for an hour. Montini did not have to report on a private conversation, but the nervous Ciano confided to his diary:

> Long conversation at the Colonnas with Msgr Montini who, if gossip is to be believed, really is an intimate associate of the Holy Father. He was prudent, balanced and *Italian*. He offered no judgement on the military situation: he merely said the Vatican thinks the conflict will be long and bitter. He added that if it were possible to do something for our country, he would be fully at our disposal. I spoke about the importance, in any case, of internal order in the country and he took my point. The Church will always work along such lines. Clearly anti-Bolshevik though also marvelling at what Stalin has been able to achieve, he said: "Whatever the future, this people of ours has given proof of its remarkable qualities of strength, faith, discipline and courage. These are *resurrection qualities*."[3]

That was code: Montini at the Vatican would help towards the orderly transition to post-Fascism. On top of the political point came the

1 Owen Chadwick, *Britain and the Vatican*, p. 125.

2 Elizabeth Wiskemann, *Europe of the Dictators*, p. 198.

3 Galeazzo Ciano, *Diario 1937–1943*, ed. Renzo De Felice, pp. 688–89.

spiritual judgement: defeat, and its concomitant changing sides, would be a resurrection – the Christian name for a new *risorgimento*.

A month later, on 8 February 1943, Ciano was sacked after six years as Foreign Minister. Mussolini, a one-man Fascist band, became his own Foreign Minister as well as Minister of the Interior. Ciano was named Ambassador to the Holy See. This appointment was regarded as "a slap in the face for the Pope". Harold Tittman, President Roosevelt's man in Rome, remarked to Fr Vincent A. McCormick that he found it "very hard to swallow the idea of Ciano and Edda [Mussolini's daughter] in the Sistine Chapel".[1] It was as though he expected Michelangelo's *Last Judgement* to fall off the wall. The Croatian envoy to the Vatican, Prince Erwin Lobkowicz, reported:

> The appointment of Count Ciano as Ambassador to the Vatican has caused a revolution in official Vatican circles. The main reason for the shock is the new Ambassador's wife, who is very immoral. All the same, approval for this appointment was given a few days after it was asked for . . . Some people assert that the aim is to get Ciano inside the Vatican so as to be better able to carry out a special mission there . . .[2]

What special mission? Ciano, always the least hawkish of Mussolini's ministers, was widely expected to "intrigue for peace".

As Ambassador to the Holy See he now had every reason to meet Montini formally, and there are minutes of their first meeting.[3] Montini probed away at Ciano's obscurities and evasions. What exactly did Ciano mean by saying that this was not the time for party politics but for *patria* politics? How should one read his remark that the Pope's mission, though now unclear, "would in time be recognized for the Pope would certainly have great tasks to perform in these historic moments"? Ciano liked *Pastor Angelicus*, a saccharine-schmalzy film on the Pope's charitable works, and thought the Pope's last Christmas message very good because "he didn't beat the big drum".

After prospecting Ciano's thought processes, Montini reviewed the topics that came up with every new Italian Ambassador to the Holy See. Top of the list was the status of the Allied diplomats locked up in the Vatican. Together with the Institute of Religious Works, commonly known as the "Vatican Bank", set up in January 1942, the diplomats

1 Vincent A. McCormick, *Diary*, p. 40.

2 Quoted in Carlo Falconi, *The Silence of Pius XII*, p. 364.

3 There are two accounts of this conversation, Ciano, *Diario*, vol. 2, pp. 212–13; and R. Guargiglia, *Ricordi 1922–46*, pp. 528ff. Discussion in Owen Chadwick, *Britain and the Vatican*, pp. 179–80.

were the last token of Vatican sovereignty. Mussolini, Ciano reported, wanted to stop the Vatican fraternizing with traitors and becoming what many Italians believed it already was, "a den of spies" (*un covo di spione*). By "traitors" Mussolini meant the ex-*Popolari* intent on preparing post-Fascism.

But since Ciano did not seem to have any precise or reliable information on this score, Montini dropped the question of "Italian traitors" (it was too near the bone), and homed in on the safer ground of the Allied diplomats. They were suffering from claustrophobia. Since they could not send messages in code, they were useless for intelligence work and posed no threat to the Italian government.

Then, according to Ciano's report to Mussolini, Montini made a prediction that was almost a threat. The more the Italian government showed itself hostile to the diplomats accredited to the Holy See, the more difficult it would be after the war to resist the pressure to "internationalize the Curia". Inevitably it would become "less Italian". "Msgr Montini," Ciano noted, "said that he spoke from the heart as an Italian and a priest; and he implied that such internationalization was not in the interests of the Church."

Since Montini was on record as holding the opposite view, it is hard to take this seriously. Either Ciano's leg was being pulled or he was humouring his father-in-law, Mussolini. The latter explanation seems more likely, for, by the time Ciano made his report in May 1943, Mussolini was in bad shape and incapable of thinking very straight. He was told what he wanted to hear.

By now the Fascist state was crumbling from within. "The Party is impotent and absent," wailed Roberto Farinacci, the leading demagogue, as a wave of strikes rippled through the northern factories in March 1943. The Grand Council, the ruling body of the Fascist Party, had not met since December 1939; it would meet again only to arrest Mussolini. Having no victories to report, the Duce had not addressed the crowds in the Piazza Venezia since June 1940, when, in Churchill's phrase, he had "fallen like a jackal" on an already defeated France.

Fascism was now discredited. Its fall seemed imminent. What part did the Vatican play in its demise? A British historian says that Pius was an ineffectual Pope to whom no one paid any heed, and goes on: "Nor did he have any hand in the ousting of Mussolini and the collapse of Fascism."[1] But by this time Fascism was going to collapse anyway. The best way the Vatican could contribute was by preparing the future. The

1 Denis Mack Smith, reviewing Owen Chadwick, *Britain and the Vatican*, in *The Times Literary Supplement*, 23 January 1987, p. 78.

Pope could not be too obviously involved in this task and thus much of the clandestine work fell to Montini.

The Vatican prepared the transition on a number of levels. First there were meetings at the Catholic University of Milan. Given the pro-Fascist tendencies of its founder and President, Agostino Gemelli, that may seem odd. But Gemelli, no fool, sensed the changing wind. Many Catholic University teachers were "absent" (code for with the resistance) on full pay. The Catholic University plotters included Amintore Fanfani, Carlo Colombo, who would be Montini's personal theologian from Milan onwards, and, when available, Giuseppe Lazzati.[1]

On 29 April 1943 they sent a request for "clarifications" to the Secretariat of State, and Montini replied on 27 May just after returning from his mother's funeral.[2] Pius worked on it personally. At issue was democracy. Was the separation of powers into legislative, executive, judicial, in accord with natural justice? Should "people normally participate in legislative activity by means of representatives freely elected"?

These may seem rather simple-minded questions but Pius agonized over them because at that date Church teaching did not have a preference for democracy. That would come only in his Christmas message of 1944; these deliberations contributed to it.

But the group that met at Camadoli, the monastery where FUCI and the *Laureati* had been in the habit of going, was even closer to Montini. Laymen present included Franco Costa, president of FUCI in Genoa 1925–27, Enzio Vanoni, Pasquale Saraceno, Aldo Moro and Giulio Andreotti. Among the priests involved were Carlo Colombo (ubiquitous as ever), Mario Cordovani OP, Montini's ally in the Curia, and Emilio Guano, future Bishop of Livorno. They worked through the summer drafting the *Codici de Camaldoli*. With De Gasperi's *Idee reconstruttive* it is the founding document of Christian Democracy.[3] Monasteries were places where you could breathe a purer air. It was a common idea in the war years that the great abbeys like Monte Cassino would once again "save European civilization".

1 Lazzati was a remarkable example of the dedicated layman who grew up under Fascism without being affected by it. He did a thesis in patristics on Theophilus of Alexandria. From 1934 to 1945 he was president of Youth Catholic Action in Milan. For them he wrote popular works with titles such as . . . *l'avete fatto a me* (You did it unto me) (1940), *La Volunta del Padre* (The Father's Will) (1942) and *La tua battaglia* (Your Combat) (1944). See Tomasso Turi, *Laicità e Laicato nel Pensiero de Giuseppe Lazzati*, Pontificia Universita Laterenense 1990. We will meet Lazzati again.

2 Sandro Magister, *La Politica Vaticana e l'Italia*, pp. 19–20.

3 Ibid. pp. 108–9. Magister stresses that Jacques Maritain was an invisible honorary member of this group. Their names will recur in Montini's life, many of them during the Council.

Rome was increasingly tense and hungry. Nuns dug up roots to have something to gnaw on. Vincent McCormick quoted a lugubrious saying that if you used the black market you ended up in a concentration camp, and if you didn't you ended up in the graveyard.[1] Bus services were greatly reduced and Rome became preternaturally silent. It took schoolboys five minutes flat to get from the Piazza di Spagna to the Vatican on their bikes. Montini walked. The German troops installed in the Hotel Santa Chiara and the Hotel Minerva near the Pantheon made a mockery of the papal plea that Rome should be treated as an "open city" because it contained no military targets.

Yet Romans continued to put their trust in Pius XII as the only one who could save the city. This idea was strengthened when the Vatican film on Pius's work for peace, *Pastor Angelicus*, was shown throughout Italy. The title came from a Belgian visionary or fraud, Arnold Wion of Douai, who in 1595 attributed characteristics to future popes based on communications allegedly received from St Malachy.

Pius XII qualified as *Pastor Angelicus* by virtue of being the 292nd pope after St Peter. D'Arcy Osborne considered "Angelic Pastor" a hopeless title because it reinforced Pius's tendency to inhabit another world altogether. He should have been cast as *Leo Furibundus* (a raging lion) because that was what the world needed.[2] McCormick thought packaging the Pope like a Hollywood star was undignified but noted: "Here in Rome it ran for only a few days, and was ordered off the screen by the civil authorities. The Pope became too popular, it is said; it occasioned shouts for peace."[3]

But shouts for peace were scorned as "defeatism". Allied leaflets were dropped to drive home the lesson. Hitler was depicted "fighting to the death of the last Italian". A map of future bombing raids asked: "Must Rome be Coventryized?" A wedge was driven between Italians and Germans as it was hinted that the doctrine of unconditional surrender would not be too rigorously applied to Italy: "Remember that your Alliance with Germany is the only cause of Allied bombs on Italy. Demand peace! Demonstrate for peace!" The idea was to sap civilian morale and detach Italy from Germany.

In the midst of this turmoil and uncertainty Pius XII chose to publish his first encyclical, *Mystici Corporis*, on the nature of the Church, dated the feast of Sts Peter and Paul, 29 June 1943. Then on 30 September 1943 there appeared another encyclical, *Divino Afflante Spiritu*, on biblical studies. This looked like a deliberate attempt to defy the world. The

1 Vincent J. McCormick, *Diary*, p. 46.

2 Owen Chadwick, *Britain and the Vatican*, p. 210.

3 Vincent A. McCormick, *Diary*, p. 37.

critics said the Angelic Pastor was fiddling in Rome while the world exploded and burned. Montini never shared this judgement. The Vatican thinks in centuries, and the two encyclicals will be remembered when the events between June and September 1943, dramatic though they were, have faded from memory.

Pius was pursuing the programme for his papacy that he had thought up while Secretary of State (1930–39).[1] He believed it would bring the Church into the twentieth century. He set himself three goals: to excavate the tomb of St Peter in the crypt of the basilica, revise the Latin Psalter and define the Assumption of Mary into heaven. These three aims were in the practical order.

They were balanced by a *theological* project involving the renewal of ecclesiology (*Mystici Corporis*), of biblical studies (*Divino Afflante Spiritu*) and of the liturgy (though *Mediator Dei* did not appear until 1947 and the reform of the Holy Week liturgy had to wait till the 1950s). These were indeed the key issues, and they shaped the Church's thinking until Vatican II. This was what Montini had to "get beyond" to accept the Council.

Pius XII was not a theologian. He was a canon lawyer. Montini recognized this in a memo written in 1942 for Gilla Gremigni's projected *Life of Pius XII*. Montini analyses Msgr Eugenio Pacelli's first work, *La personalità e la territorialità delle leggi specialmente nel diritto canonico*.[2] Pius XII did not venture into theology and entrusted the drafting of his encyclicals to others. The principal author of *Mystici Corporis* was the Dutch Jesuit Fr Sebastian Tromp,[3] while the German Jesuit Augustin Bea, then Rector of the Biblical Institute, worked on *Divino Afflante Spiritu* along with the Dominican, Fr Jacques Marie Boste. They also passed through the Secretariat of State in case there were any political implications.

Pius's encyclicals were a judicious combination of liberalism and conservatism; while opening some doors they shut others; essentially they let Catholic theologians know "how far they could go".

Divino Afflante Spiritu, though by no means a radical document,

1 In his commemoration of Pius XII in St Peter's on 6 October 1983 Cardinal Giuseppe Siri stated that Pius's grand plan came about by design rather than accident: "*Questa opera magistrale fu disegno e non pure casualita*", Vatican Press Office Bulletin, p. 2.

2 Published by the Vatican Press in 1912. Pacelli's study was about how Church-State relations were to be conducted where the old arrangement of concordats had broken down or was trampled underfoot. See *Notiziario*, 20, pp. 25–26. This seems to have been his only scholarly work before he became Pope. As Pope he was notorious for mugging up topics the night before, revealing an intimate knowledge of, say, the gas industry gained from encyclopaedias.

3 We know this because Fr Tromp, in his lectures at the Gregorian, used to say: "As we observed in our encyclical" – and then correcting himself to, "Excuse me, as the Holy Father observed in his encyclical." Oral tradition.

liberated Catholic biblical scholars from the worst anti-modernist shackles by permitting them to take seriously the study of "literary forms". This innocent phrase meant simply that to understand the Bible one should not interpret in the same way a narrative, a canticle, a parable, a psalm, a law-text, a genealogy and so on. The biblical fundamentalists in the Roman Curia never forgot that Augustin Bea and Jacques-Marie Boste had introduced these new-fangled ideas, and that they had got them from German theologians like Martin Dibelius and Rudolf Bultmann.

Germany was also involved in the genesis of *Mystici Corporis*. Conrad Gröber was Archbishop of Freiburg-im-Bresgau, an important intellectual centre in Germany because it boasted a University with a Catholic Faculty of Theology and a prestigious publisher, the house of Herder. Gröber might well have examined the thought of the ex-Jesuit novice Martin Heidegger, who held that Germany would realize in the modern world what the Greeks could only aspire to in the ancient world – a thesis highly congenial to the Nazis. Gröber, however, ignored this intellectual threat, obsessed as he was with the way modern theologians were allegedly ruining the Church.

One might have thought that a German bishop, in 1943, should have had priorities other than unorthodoxy. But that would be to underestimate Gröber. In an unprecedented address to the Greater German episcopacy (that is, including the bishops of Austria as well as those of Germany) he denounced the increasing lack of interest in natural theology, the widespread contempt for scholastic theology, the growing influence of Protestant theology, the ecumenical movement, the liturgical movement and the exaggerations of those who talked of the Church as Christ's Mystical Body.[1]

Who precisely did Gröber have in mind in this Europe that had been unified by the jackboot? Karl Barth, now safe in Basle, Switzerland, was famous for declaring "natural theology" impossible and, in his very early works, blasphemous. The "opposition to scholasticism" was believed to be particularly rife among French Jesuits and Dominicans in Lyons – also the place where Nazi anti-Semitism was opposed most honourably.[2]

Nearer home, Gröber perhaps had in mind Dom Odo Casel as an exponent of errors on the Mystical Body and Romano Guardini as wrong about liturgy. An inquisitor is never too fussy about details. But these were authors Montini read, esteemed, revered even. Happily Gröber's complaints found very little echo among the "Greater German"

1 See Bruno Schwalbach, *Erzbischof Conrad Gröber und die nationalsozialistische Diktatur*, pp. 150–52.

2 Henri de Lubac SJ, *Résistance chrétienne à l'antisémitisme: Souvenirs 1940–1944*, 1988. This was the great man's last book.

bishops, and even Cardinal Theodor Innitzer of Vienna invited the young Jesuit, Karl Rahner, to draft a crushing reply on his behalf.[1]

Mystici Corporis took the sting out of Gröber's worries about the Mystical Body. It taught that the Church is indeed the Mystical Body of Christ, and that all its members are alive through their union with its head, Christ. That was a massive step beyond the juridicial approach to ecclesiology hitherto prevailing which saw the Church as a "perfect society" needing nothing outside itself to attain its goals and standing over against a corrupt "world". *Mystici Corporis* had important consequences for the liturgy, the community expression of the Body of Christ, and the theology of the laity since all the baptized were potentially equal in grace. Giuseppe Colombo would later say that "as far as the intimate nature of the Church was concerned, the ecclesiology of *Ecclesiam Suam*, Pope Paul VI's first encyclical, was the ecclesiology of *Mystici Corporis*".[2]

That is not wholly matter for praise. For *Mystici Corporis* had two major weaknesses the Council would have to correct and Montini would have to overcome.

First it erected a huge ecumenical obstacle simply by identifying the Mystical Body of Christ with the Roman Catholic Church. At a time when Catholics and Protestants were meeting each other and dying together in concentration camps, *Mystici Corporis* contradicted their ecumenical experience. Hitler did not distinguish between Dietrich Bonhoeffer and Alfred Delp SJ, hanging them both on meat hooks. Why should anyone else?

Second, the too solid identification of Christ and the Church made it difficult to see how sin could worm its way in, as it empirically and manifestly did and does. Karl Rahner wrote not only about "the sinful Church" but even "the Church of sinners – and was censured by the Holy Office for this reason.[3]

1 Schwalbach, op. cit., p. 152. "Even" because Innitzer was famous for welcoming the *Anschluss* with a handwritten message signed "*Heil Hitler*!" His successor, Cardinal Franz König, apologized for this behaviour: Hans Küng, *Judaism*, SCM Press, London 1992, p. 676. See also *I remember: Karl Rahner, an Autobiographical Interview with Meinhold Krauss*, tr. Harvey D. Egan SJ, SCM Press 1965. Rahner said: "The German Bishops had concerns other than Conrad Gröber's and after the war, when Germany and Austria were divided, no more was heard about it" (p. 53).

2 Giuseppe Colombo, "*Genesi, storia e significato dell'enciclica 'Ecclesiam Suam'* ", in "*Ecclesiam Suam*", Brescia 1982, p. 142. But note the qualification. Congar makes the same point when he remarks that Cardinal Montini, in his critique of the draft schema *de Ecclesia*, quotes *Mystici Corporis*, but only to stress the mystical as distinct from the juridical nature of the Church (ibid. p. 80).

3 Herbert Vorgrimler, "Karl Rahner: the Theologian's Contribution", in *The Council by those who were there*, ed. Alberic Stacpoole OSB, Chapman, London 1985, p. 47. To progress, Montini would have to "get beyond" *Mystici Corporis*: the Council provided him with the key concept of *koinonia*, communion. Yves Congar in *Problemi ecclesiologici*, p. 89.

Mystici Corporis raised in acute form the question posed by Karl Adam's *The Spirit of Catholicism*: how did one get from the "ideal" Church depicted in ecclesiology to the "actual" Church? How, to make the question more precise, did one get from this dream-Church to the one that, in the German-speaking lands, had dealt so feebly with Nazis?[1] Or, with another twist of the screw, how did one get from the heights of theology to the "actual" world in which Jews were being murdered on an industrial scale?

In July the British and Americans invaded Sicily. Part of the plan was that 500 American bombers should attack the Rome railway station and marshalling yards. The sirens sounded in Rome at 11 a.m. on 19 July. Montini was with Harold Tittman. They watched the attack from the windows of Palazzo Santa Marta with mixed feelings. Mrs Tittman and the boys had seen wave upon wave sweeping over the city, counting 100 planes in the last one.[2] Five hundred people were killed – one per bomber – and many more wounded, while San Lorenzo – one of the seven basilicas of Rome – lost its roof and a portico. Casualties were particularly high because crowded trams happened to be parked outside San Lorenzo as the raid came.[3]

Pius went to the shattered basilica of San Lorenzo that same afternoon, accompanied by Montini, and stayed for two and a half hours. It was the first time the Pope had been outside the Vatican since mobs had hooted him in 1940. He knelt among the ruins and recited the psalm *De Profundis* (Out of the Depths, O Lord). A crowd gathered to pray with him. He comforted the wounded and tried to console the bereaved. His white soutane was soon flecked with blood. The Pope had failed to save Rome from the bombs but he was closer to the people of Rome than ever Mussolini had been.

Where *was* Mussolini on this 19 July 1943? He was meeting Hitler at Feltre in northern Italy.[4] The symbolic contrast with the Pope was striking. Mussolini had never visited any of the bomb-damaged cities of Italy, though he had twice gone abroad, to Libya and Albania, bay horse in the wings, in expectation of victory parades that never happened. McCormick thought the bombing of Rome a mistake and "the greatest

1 Karl Rahner admitted later: "In Vienna I had contacts with people, including Jesuits, who put themselves in grave danger to care for Jews. But by and large it remains true that we endured this madness rather passively." *I remember*, p. 52.

2 Vincent A. McCormick, *Diary*, pp. 48–49.

3 Owen Chadwick, *Britain and the Vatican*, p. 242.

4 Denis Mack Smith, *Mussolini*, p. 341.

American defeat of the war",[1] though he admired Pius XII's subtlety: instead of emulating Fascist propaganda and denouncing the barbarous Anglo-Saxons as criminal assassins, he simply wrote a letter to Cardinal Francesco Marchetti Selvaggiani, his Vicar for Rome, expressing sympathy and solidarity with the people of Rome.

One can argue that the bombing of Rome achieved its objective: Mussolini's position became untenable and within six days he fell. The Grand Council demanded that he forfeit all his powers, whereupon King Victor Emmanuel arrested him and appointed Marshal Pietro Badoglio, chief of staff, to succeed him. Badoglio publicly declared that "the war goes on" while privately engaging in negotiations for a separate peace with the Allies. On 25 July Montini went to the Propaganda Fide building where Alberto di Stefano informed him of the Grand Council's vote, and tried to enlist the Vatican's help in negotiating with the Allies. Montini was not unwilling, but said he could do nothing without an official request to the Holy See from the appropriate authority – whatever it was. It was evident now that Italy's only hope was to change sides swiftly.[2] But the tortuous negotiations dragged on throughout August 1943. On 11 August Dr Luigi Gedda offered Badoglio the support of the two and a half million members of Catholic Action, though this was a private initiative.[3] There was confusion about who was authorized to negotiate. It was compounded on the Allied side by relics of the old "unconditional surrender" theory which said there was nothing to negotiate.

The dithering gave the Germans time to flood troops into Italy and around Rome. The planned landing of Allied parachutists on Rome airfield was cancelled at the last minute. The chance to save Rome and avoid war in the south was missed.[4] General Dwight Eisenhower cut through Italian hesitations by releasing the news that they had signed a

1 Vincent A. McCormick, *Diary*, p. 48. McCormick was critical of Pius XII for denouncing only the bombing of Italian cities and not referring to anywhere else.

2 *Actes et documents*, 7, pp. 520–21. Montini's involvement is discussed in Elisa A. Carillo, "Italy in Vatican-US relations", a paper read at the conference, *Vatican Diplomacy in the Nineteenth and Twentieth Centuries*, University of New Brunswick, Canada, 13 October 1991, p. 18.

3 Sandro Magister, *La politica Vaticana*, p. 25.

4 Bedell Smith, one of Eisenhower's aides, wrote to General Giuseppe Castellano three months later: "I have given a great deal of thought to our abortive plan for landing an airborne division near Rome . . . I remain convinced as do the officers of our planning staff that had there been in command of the Italian divisions around Rome an officer of courage, firmness and determination convinced of success, the plan could have been carried out." That was also the judgement of the German High Command. See Richard Lamb, *The Ghosts of Peace*, p. 203.

secret armistice on 3 September. This went out on Algiers Radio on 8 September 1943, feast of the Nativity of Our Lady, always a great day in Brescia. Announced on the Assumption, 15 August, an armistice would have found Italy wide open to the Allies and the Italian campaign would have been far less costly.

The political future could not wait upon the military events. That summer Lodovico Montini argued with De Gasperi against the use of "Christian" in the name of the new party. The arguments valid against it in 1919 still applied: if you have "Christian" in your title, you will get a confessional party from which a great number of Italians would feel excluded.[1]

De Gasperi replied that the shock of Nazism and Fascism had changed the ground rules. After the war Europeans would want political parties with a well-defined identity that rejected, utterly, Nazism and Fascism. By calling themselves "Christian Democrats" they would appeal to this resistance to state totalitarianism of left and right and take their place as "heirs to a great tradition". The party would be "Christian" not in any exclusive sense, but would be "a party of Christian inspiration" open to those who shared Christian values if not Christian faith. This echoed conversations De Gasperi had often had with Giovanni Battista Montini. It was Jacques Maritain's *Humanisme Intégral* applied to the Italian situation. Maritain himself was in the United States, producing a series of works which presented the war as a crisis of Western civilization.

As Italy came closer to switching sides, the mood in the Vatican was tense and anxious. On 4 August 1943 Secretary of State Cardinal Luigi Maglione told the cardinals resident in Rome that the Italian government's view was that the Pope would be seized and taken away to Munich. Rome was bombed again on 13 August and Pius was once again first on the scene with Montini.

Montini and Tardini supervised the last-minute preparations. Papers were shredded and diaries misleadingly composed to limit the damage.[2] Heads of religious orders were told to destroy papers connected with Nazi Germany. Vatican Radio had already shredded compromising material. The members of the Secretariat of State were told to have their bags packed and be ready to go with the Pope into captivity.

Since Pius XII never became Hitler's hostage, there is a tendency to believe that the threat was never real. Yet the Nazis undoubtedly thought of kidnapping Pius XII and hauling him away to Germany. Goebbels's

1 *Notiziario*, 9, 1984, p. 52.

2 Owen Chadwick, *Britain and the Vatican*, p. 260.

diary for 26 July 1943 has Hitler talking with great violence about seizing the Pope and taking over the Vatican.[1]

On the day German troops occupied Rome, 9 September 1943, Hitler blustered: "I'll go into the Vatican when I like. You think the Vatican worries me? We'll just grab it . . . After the war there won't be any more concordats. The time is coming when I will settle my accounts with the Church."[2]

But one did not need to eavesdrop on Hitler's table-talk to know the danger was very real. Though the Germans halted at the Vatican frontier when they took over Rome, they now had the Vatican at their mercy.

The other immediate effect of the German occupation of Rome was that Pius was now irremediably "silenced". At least the Fascists were Italians who left him a little room to manoeuvre. The Germans would have dragged him off at the first sign of protest.

1 Ibid. p. 259.

2 *Table-Talk*, quoted in Joseph Lichten, "*Pio XII e gli Ebrei*", *Il Regno-Documenti*, 3/88. An American Jew who stayed on in Rome after the Council, Joe Lichten did much to foster Jewish-Catholic relations. His judgement on Pius XII was very positive.

13

From Nazis to Anglo-Saxons

> The other evening I heard on the radio the account of Monte Cassino's destruction, told by the Abbot, an old man of eighty. Without a single adjective, quietly and in a tired and saddened voice, he told the story as if it happened a hundred years ago. It was terribly moving and I can hardly imagine what the Benedictines from that monastery, now scattered all over the world, must have felt on hearing this quiet, heartfelt account of the end of this cradle of civilization – now after fourteen centuries of religious life, buried forever.
>
> (IRIS ORIGO, Diary, 28 February 1944. At her villa in Tuscany)

The final judgement was premature but this captures the mood of the times, especially in Italy. Hitherto, for all its devastation and disasters, the war had been taking place somewhere else. Now it came home on the Italian peninsula.

In Rome it was soon evident that life under Nazi occupation would be nastily different. The news from Brescia was bad too. The family home at via delle Grazie 17 was requisitioned by the Germans who casually destroyed part of the Montini archives.

Montini's elder brother Lodovico was on the black list provided by Mussolini's puppet republic of Salò. After Mussolini's spectacular rescue – German parachutists spirited him away from the hotel in the Apennines where he was being held – the ex-duce was a virtual prisoner at Gargano, a small town on Lake Garda not far from Brescia.

Lodovico made his way to Rome and stayed with Battista in the Vatican. Back in Brescia his wife, Giuseppina, was arrested, while their seven children were looked after by Agnese Bedussi. The rest of the family fled to Grumone in the province of Cremona.

Francesco, Battista's younger brother, held the fort at via delle Grazie in Brescia and never left it. For a whole month in 1944 Francesco, a medical doctor, hid Don Peppino Tedeschi in the room where, in May 1943, he had given the last sacraments to Giuditta. "Her chest of drawers became my altar," said Don Peppino. The fact that there were

Germans in the house paradoxically made him feel extra-secure. It also illustrates the cool courage of Battista's younger brother, Dr Francesco Montini.[1]

On 14 September 1943 Franciscan Fr Carlo Varischi, chaplain of the *Laureati* of the Catholic University of Milan, boarded the 22.15 express for Rome. It was packed with Italian troops fleeing German occupation. They were profiting from the general chaos and confusion to melt away before it was too late. Next evening Fr Varischi was with Montini who "prepared" him for his papal audience. As Varischi knelt before Pius XII, the Pope "looking alarmed and anxious" asked: "Are you Fr Gemelli's secretary? How are things in Milan? Are you prisoners? Just look: I am a prisoner here too. Tell Fr Gemelli to carry on as best he can and keep the University alive, without making any fuss and without engaging in politics of any kind."[2]

This was not crystal-clear, so after the audience Varischi met Montini again who spelled out – in case he had not understood – just what the papal message was. Montini's advice was to "manoeuvre deftly" (*destreggiarsi*). That seemed rather redundant advice to someone like Gemelli who had done little else all his life. But Montini's conclusion was a warning to the enthusiastic Gemelli: above all "he should avoid all value-judgements on governments of yesterday, today or tomorrow". In short, he should shut up.

Probably there was little real danger that Gemelli would endorse the republic of Salò. He had already sensed the prevailing wind. Within a short time he was hiding the Socialist Sandro Pertini (a future President of Italy) in his psychology lab, and those of his staff who were "away in the hills" were kept on full pay.

This episode also illustrates the relationship between Pius and Montini. Montini sometimes helped the Pope know his own mind. Hence the Vatican "joke": you needn't go to the *Monte* (the mountain) if you can get to the *Montini* (the foothills).

Montini certainly anticipated Vatican policy on the attitude to Mussolini's Salò Republic. On 27 September 1943 Cardinal Luigi Maglione, Secretary of State, stated officially that there would be no recognition, either *de facto* still less *de jure*, of Mussolini's new republican government in Salò.[3] Mussolini could not appeal to the Lateran Pacts of 1929: they had been signed not with the Fascist party but with the Italian state.

1 Fappani-Molinari, *Montini Giovane*, p. 368. Francesco, the forgotten Montini, was a thoughtful doctor who spent most of his life in research at the Fatebenefratelli Hospital in Rome. After a heart attack in 1963 he slowly returned to work until his death on 8 January 1971.

2 Sandro Magister, *La politica Vaticana e l'Italia, 1943–78*, p. 33.

3 Ibid. p. 34.

The fear that the Pope would be arrested intensified. On 15 September the Brazilian Ambassador, acting as spokesman for the diplomats now completely trapped in the Vatican, assured the Pope that if he were kidnapped they would demand the right to go along with him. "The Pope was touched," remarks Owen Chadwick, "but he cannot have found it a comforting message."[1] Quite. It suited the Nazis to keep the Pope on tenterhooks. Pius instructed the German Jesuit Fr Robert Leiber to enquire discreetly among *Wehrmacht* officers whether he was likely to be kidnapped.[2]

The racial laws had been applied in Italy since 1938, but in lackadaisical fashion. In Italy the concept of "racial purity" was hardly serious. Italians in the main were not blond-haired, blue-eyed Aryans. They had magnificent opera, but it was not Wagner: they thought the winds that blew from the north presaged or brought disaster. Throughout 1943 the reluctance of the Italians to hand over their Jews was a cause of friction between Mussolini and Hitler.

Jonathan Steinberg goes as far as to say that "no Jew under the protection of the Italian army was ever surrendered to the Nazis". The Italians might be Fascists but they inhabited a different moral universe from the Nazis. Steinberg says that in 1942–43 the Vatican was recognized as the chief obstacle to the anti-Jewish policy. In Croatia Archbishop Stepinac was regarded as *Judenfreundlich*.[3]

The collapse of Fascism in Italy left the Jews with no defender except the Vatican. They began to be rounded up on 16 October 1943 and 2900 Roman Jews perished in concentration camps along with 6000 Jews from the rest of Italy. Shocking as it is, this was a lower proportion of the Jewish population than in any other occupied country. The Vatican was largely responsible for this difference, but only because it could count on Italian instincts.[4]

By Christmas 1943 it was possible to foresee the liberation of Italy if not the end of the war. What would Italy's status be as an enemy who had changed sides? Technically this was a question for Tardini rather than Montini. Involving relations with a foreign power, the USA, it belonged properly to the Extraordinary Affairs Section. But that did not mean that Montini was not concerned with this question. Far from it.

Lodovico Montini's presence in his apartments gave Battista an

1 Owen Chadwick, *Britain and the Vatican*, p. 273.

2 See Appendix to Chapter 13 (p. 711) for more details on escape plans.

3 Jonathan Steinberg, *The Axis and the Holocaust 1941–43: All or Nothing*, Routledge 1990. The quotations come not from the book but from a lecture at the Italian Institute, London, on its publication, 28 July 1990.

4 See Susan Zuccotti, *The Italians and the Holocaust*, 1987.

insider's view of the backstage political development. The German occupiers were powerless to prevent political figures of every stripe from coming together. The Rector of the Roman Seminary, Msgr Roberto Ronca, played host at the extra-territorial Lateran Palace to 180 political figures including Christian Democrats like Alcide De Gasperi and Guido Gonella, Liberals like Alessandro Casati and the anti-clerical Meuccio Ruini, and Socialists like Pietro Nenni and Giuseppe Saragat.[1]

Ronca was ecumenical to a fault. The only reason he did not have any Communists was that, accustomed to clandestinity, they had made their own arrangements and did not need the Church. But they came to lunch. Ronca also thought the Church could usefully dialogue with Freemasonry which, banned under Mussolini, would inevitably be restored by the "Anglo-Saxons".

Though not an agent of the Secretariat of State, Ronca's initiative needed its approval. He got on well with Tardini, and his broad-minded open-house policy admirably matched Tardini's view that the Church should stand "above" political parties in the new post-Fascist Italy. Neither Tardini nor Ottaviani at the Holy Office had been enamoured of the *Popolari*. Their department indeed had connived (at the very least) in crushing it. They thought it past history, so much water under the Tiber bridges.[2]

They had no reason to think of De Gasperi as the natural leader of a Christian Democratic Party that would take up where the *Popolari* had left off. This brought them up against Montini and Count Giuseppe Dalla Torre, editor of *L'Osservatore Romano*. But Montini had an advantage over his curial colleagues: he had a network of friends who would actually set up and control the political arrangements of democratic Italy, while Tardini's thoughts moved on a more rarefied level of principle and Ottaviani's contacts were restricted to the clerical world.

But while the future coalition governments of Italy were being secretly stitched together on Vatican territory, it was essential that the Germans should be made to believe in the Holy See's "scrupulous neutrality". This affected its attitude to the resistance movement that came into being as a result of the armistice. The Vatican's case was summed up by Ambrogio Marchioni, Secretary at the Nunciature to Italy, on 18 October 1943.

Evidently the Vatican could not do what the Germans wanted and condemn the partisans and their "terrorist" depredations; but neither could it issue a stirring call to resistance, already seen as "a second

1 Andrea Riccardi, *Il "Partito Romano" nella secondo dopoguerra (1945–1954)*, p. 14. Nenni became the leader of the Socialist Party, Saragat President of Italy.

2 Ibid. p. 13.

Risorgimento". So it sat mugwump on the fence declaring that "the clergy fulfil their priestly duty by recommending calm, tranquillity and order so that 'special operations' [the dreaded *Sonderaktionen*] do not lead to reprisals against the innocent".[1]

Yet the Catholic contribution to the resistance movement was not negligible, notably in the north where parish priests did not wait on orders from the Vatican. Almost every hamlet, city and diocese had a story to tell about the underground battle against Fascism.

Typical was Don Giovanni Nardini of Livorno whose most memorable feat was to destroy a list of 400 villagers about to be deported to Germany: he poured out glass after glass of *grappa* to the four *Wehrmacht* officers in charge of the operation. As they staggered out of the village they were incapable of remembering anything.[2]

Yet as Sandro Magister put it: "Though militant anti-Fascism was an option taken by many Catholics, it was never in any sense a decision of the Church as such."[3] One reason for holding back was that the Communists tended to cast themselves as the leaders in the struggle against Fascism. But Montini and De Gasperi both believed that the Communists were as anti-democratic and totalitarian as the Fascists and Nazis.

On 5 November 1943 the Vatican was bombed. It was a very small raid causing no casualties and little damage. Tardini ordered an investigation, only to find that nothing resembles an exploded bomb so much as another exploded bomb. The bombs were unsigned though the evidence later pointed to an American plane dropping them by accident. The Vatican view was that Roberto Farinacci had organized this provocation, and that the planes came from the Viterbo air base.[4] Montini knew the road well. The via Cassia was on the way to the Longinottis at Rociglione.

Tardini's December 1943 memorandum to Myron Taylor was a vitally important document. It was a firm commitment to democracy as the best of political systems. This would have been unremarkable were it not for the fact that the Church's "official teaching" was still stuck in the groove of Leo XIII's encyclical, *Libertas*, of 20 June 1888. This settled for a prudent agnosticism about political arrangements, observing that "the Church disapproves of no form of government that is *per se* adapted to preserving the good of its citizens".[5]

1 *Actes et documents*, 7, pp. 674–77.

2 Maria di Blasio Wilhelm, *The Other Italy*, Norton, London 1989.

3 Sandro Magister, *La politica Vaticana e l'Italia*, p 37.

4 *Actes et documents*, 7, p. 705.

5 *Pio XII*, ed. Andrea Riccardi, p. 109.

That could be used to defend almost any regime from monarchy to benevolent despotism. It was too vague to be of any practical use. Tardini, by contrast, was characteristically crisp and clear:

> No doubt Italy should return to democracy. Only this kind of consent offers sufficient guarantees for the control of government by the people; it accustoms people to self-discipline; it makes it possible for everyone, from whatever class they come, to enter public life; it embraces all the vital forces of the country; it can gradually educate the Italian people towards the habit of moderation in political rivalries so that the general harmony of the country will not be impaired.[1]

Tardini had just rewritten – admittedly in a private note for President Roosevelt's personal representative – the Catholic tradition on democracy. Though his remarks carried no magisterial punch, they were in fact adopted by Pius XII in his Christmas message for 1944.

Tardini drew the practical consequences of the "return to democracy". "Fanatical Fascists" would have to be eliminated from public life, and the "exploiters would need to undergo exemplary punishments". (In fact no Italian "war criminals" ever stood trial, though they existed, especially in Slovenia.) The government that replaced the Fascists should be "civil rather than military" – Tardini had a low opinion of Italian generals.[2] Although he mentioned Alcide De Gasperi as a possible leader, he also expressed doubts about him.

Tardini says De Gasperi had "had no experience of government, and it is not possible to say whether he will be successful". Though De Gasperi had represented Trieste in the Austrian Parliament before the First World War and led the PPI after Sturzo's exile, it was true that he had "no experience of government". But very few had. Tardini wondered whether an experienced pre-Fascist politician might not be preferable while the next generation "played themselves in".[3]

Montini, who had known De Gasperi for over twenty years, harboured no such doubts. De Gasperi was just the man to "play in" the next generation. After twenty years in the wings his hour had come. As for Tardini's fears that De Gasperi, as the first serious Catholic to lead Italy since 1870, would endanger the Holy See's impartiality, Montini knew that De Gasperi, like all those schooled on Maritain, believed in the legitimate autonomy of the laity in politics.

1 Francesco Malgeri, "*La Chiesa di Pio XII fra Guerra e Dopoguerra*", in *Pio XII*, ed. Riccardi, p. 110.

2 Ibid.

3 Ibid. p. 13.

But no whisper of these discussions reached German ears. Security was good in occupied Rome. On 8 February 1944 the politicians were secretly whisked away from the Lateran Palace to Propaganda Fide where their host was Msgr Celso Constantini, Secretary of Propaganda Fide, the missionary congregation.

By early 1944 20,000 partisans had emerged from Catholic Action. They were known as "Green Flames". What the Vatican thought about them was immaterial. The northern clergy were sympathetic towards them. In Udine the provincial clergy pronounced the Germans "unjust invaders" whom it was lawful, indeed meritorious, to repel.[1]

Bishops tended to be more cautious, but the Cardinal Archbishop of Turin, Maurilio Fossati, visited partisan units in the mountains, heard their confessions and said Mass for them. Convents and Catholic hospitals provided food and shelter, and sometimes stored arms.[2] Those who helped the partisans also helped allied airmen escape. One bicycled into the Vatican. They also concealed Jews. Franciscan Rufino Niccaci organized the convents of Assisi so that they not only concealed Jews but were the link in the escape-line to Florence.[3]

A high price had to be paid for all this: reprisals (the Defregger case) and arrests. The Fascists of the Salò republic used the Germans to settle old scores. On the feast of the Epiphany 1944 Montini's "best friend" in adolescence, Andrea Trebeschi, was arrested and put in the Arsenal on via Crispi in Brescia. He was then transferred to the Verona prison where he found his two uncles, Franco and Roberto. Peppino Pelosi, another mutual friend of Andrea and Battista, was on death-row. He went before the firing-squad forgiving whoever had betrayed him (they were all there because they had been betrayed) and crying *Viva l'Italia*!

Andrea Trebeschi was last seen alive by his grandmother and aunt who said his hands were black and his eyes swollen from beatings.[4] All Montini knew in this bleakest winter of the war was that his friend Andrea was in prison. Only later did he learn he had died in the concentration camp of Guthausen.

Montini defended Pius XII, and said he had shown "courage and goodness" in wanting to protect Rome "even in its most dangerous and tragic moments". Pius had assured him that he would never, never leave Rome: "Pius XII did what was humanly possible to save human lives

1 This, for priests in their fifties, was the way the First World War had been legitimated in 1917.

2 Martin Clark, *Modern Italy*, p. 313.

3 Alexander Ramati, *While the Pope kept Silent: Assisi and the Nazi Occupation*, 1978.

4 Cesare Trebeschi, Introd. to Montini, *Giovane amico*, p. 11.

and alleviate unspeakable sufferings, even when the swift course of events stifled at birth any chance of success for his charitable activities."[1]

Montini looked up the address given to the vast crowd of refugees assembled in St Peter's Square on 12 March 1944. Pius had exclaimed, from the self-same window at which he, Paul VI, was speaking twenty-one years later: "Beloved people of Rome! In the whirlwind of so many misfortunes and hazards, we feel and admit the bitterness of our spirit at the way all human resources are unequal and inadequate compared with the excess of an unspeakable wretchedness." It was a typical piece of Pius XII rhetoric. But it needs a context.

The claim to "have done what was humanly possible" should be read in the light of the plight of the Jews and the Ardeantine Caves Massacre in which on 24 March 1944 250 hostages were shot in cold blood as a reprisal for the killing of a few German soldiers the day before. Pius was blamed for not intervening. Montini's mature judgement on Pius came in his 1963 reply to Rudolf Hochhuth:

> It is utterly false to tax Pius XII with cowardice: both his natural temperament and the consciousness he had of his authority and the mission entrusted to him speak clearly against any such accusation.
>
> Nor is it true that he was a heartless solitary. On the contrary he was a man of exquisite sensibility and the most delicate human sympathies. True, he did love solitude: his richly cultivated mind, his unusual capacity for thought and study led him to avoid all useless distractions, every unnecessary relaxation. He wished to enter fully into the history of his own afflicted time: with a deep sense that he was himself part of that history, he wished to participate fully in it, to share its sufferings in his own heart and soul.[2]

He concluded by quoting Sir Francis d'Arcy Osborne: "Pius XII was the most warmly humane, kindly, generous, sympathetic (and, incidentally, saintly) character that it has been my privilege to meet in the course of a long life."[3]

In spring 1944 Pius was still trying to get Rome declared an "open city" to spare it the horrors of Monte Cassino where allied troops, it

1 *Insegmamenti*, 1975, p. 219. This was at the Angelus of 2 March 1975, when Paul VI recalled that Pacelli had been elected on 2 March and crowned on 10 March 1939.

2 *Tablet*, 29 June 1963.

3 D'Arcy Osborne, letter to *The Times*, 20 May 1963. The former British Minister to the Holy See stayed on in Rome, and inherited the title Duke of Leeds later that year. He died on 20 March 1964 and was buried in the Protestant cemetery in Rome. See Owen Chadwick, *Britain and the Vatican*, p. 317.

was said, had behaved with unparalleled barbarism in destroying the cradle of Western monasticism. In so doing they had forfeited any claim to moral superiority. The fact that Monte Cassino barred the road to Rome, that it was surrounded by German troops, and that its movable *objets d'art* were stored in Roman vaults, went for nothing.

Armchair critics later contended that Pius should have been more concerned with the fate of the Jews than with the fate of Rome. But did he really have much choice? John Conway described the mood in Rome at the start of 1944: "German troops encircled the tiny Vatican territory on all sides, and a feeling of impotent claustrophobia tinged the panic-filled atmosphere."[1] They were also very hungry. The tunnel under the Gianiculum was filled with refugees and beggars. But the Germans were equally apprehensive.

As the time for their withdrawal from Rome came closer, von Weizsäcker had a private conversation with Montini in which he "explored avenues". He wanted to "return to active politics" so as to be able to "work for peace". On 26 April 1944 he politely enquired as a private citizen whether the Vatican thought there was any chance of a deal to end the war. He got a dusty answer: "The present German regime *will not* negotiate with Russia, and *cannot* negotiate with the English [*sic*] because they do not want it."[2] Tardini speaking. Yet such discussions were becoming academic.

There was one ironic twist of the tail of history before Rome was liberated. Giovanni Maria Longinotti's house at Vico was occupied by the Germans while the family took refuge in a farm on the estate. They spent the first weeks of May 1944 in Rome where rumbling artillery fire could be heard almost continuously. Longinotti judged it safer to go back to his farm. His last hours were spent in Montini's apartment – Lodovico was also there – and he set off with two of his sons towards eight o'clock on the evening of 12 May having cadged a lift in a Fiat 1100 with a soldier. Travel by day was impossible because whatever moved on the roads was mercilessly machine-gunned.

There were no witnesses to what happened, but Montini reconstructed the event in a letter to his brother Francesco in Brescia, and a report that formed the basis of an article in a Milan newspaper, *L'Italia*, dated 7 June 1944. The driver, scared and in a hurry, drove as fast as he could. Five or six kilometres from home they crashed into an oncoming German lorry. There they lay unconscious for two hours. No one

1 John S. Conway, "Records and Documents of the Holy See relating to the Second World War", *Yad Vashem Studies*, vol. xv, Jerusalem 1983, p. 337. Perhaps I should add that Professor Conway is an Anglican and an Ulsterman.

2 *Actes et documents*, 7, pp. 674–77.

stopped until a German soldier took pity on them. Longinotti was already dead, his sons Mario and Giulio gravely injured. Montini was greatly affected by the loss of Longinotti. He was sixty-eight, still fit, and would have played an important political role in post-war Italy.[1]

Rome was liberated on 4 June 1944. Half a million Romans walked – there was no other transport – to St Peter's Square and cheered themselves hoarse with cries of *Viva il Papa*! Pius was acclaimed as "*Defensor Civitatis* (Defender of the City)". He acknowledged the cheers, his outstretched arms sawing the air, but his rhetoric was restrained: "We must give thanks for the favours we have received. Rome has been spared. This day will go down in the annals of Rome." The *New York Times* correspondent captured the mood while renewing some old clichés:

> The world has been changed for Rome, but the Vatican goes on imperturbably as it has through so many other conquests in centuries gone by. It is neutral in fact and in spirit. Except for the tanks and armoured cars running along the street in front of St Peter's, one would never have known what had happened today.[2]

Old Father Tiber keeps rollin' along, down to the tideless sea. But Pius remained impartial as ever, thanking both belligerents for sparing Rome.

Despite the adulation of the Allied troops – Protestant and Catholic – who flocked to St Peter's Square for his blessing, the first tangible fruit of victory, Pius tried hard to sound even-handed. So now that he was safe from it, he denounced the Allies' bombing of Rome, though it had been insignificant compared with what was even then happening to Cologne, Dresden and Hamburg.[3] Tardini continued to deplore the doctrine of unconditional surrender which took the war "into a particularly cruel and harsh phase, which can only get worse".[4]

Francis J. Spellman, Archbishop of New York, was the first American Church leader to visit Rome after its liberation. He had secured a pledge from President Franklin D. Roosevelt that allied troops would not be stationed in Rome, but would use it only for "rest and recreation".[5]

1 *Notiziario*, 9, pp. 52–59. Lodovico Montini, commenting on his brother's report, says that in fact they were caught up in a machine-gun attack on the Hermann Goering division that was being moved by night to Monte Cassino. He believes that Battista concealed this fact to get the article past the Milan censors (ibid. p. 56).

2 *New York Times*, 6 June 1944.

3 *Pio XII*, ed. Riccardi, p. 217.

4 Ibid. p. 221.

5 Gerald P. Fogarty SJ, *The Vatican and the American Hierarchy from 1870 to 1965*, p. 307. If the curial officials had known what was meant by "rest and recreation" they might not have been comforted.

Spellman, an old Secretariat of State hand, had an hour and a half with Pius XII on 31 July, another on 4 August 1945, during which the Pope "wept", and yet another long audience on 20 August at which he appeared "restless and nervous".

Spellman was receiving all this attention not simply as Archbishop of New York. Maglione, Secretary of State, was not expected to live much longer, and Pius wanted to make Spellman his Secretary of State. Harold Tittman reported this in a cable to the State Department on 5 July 1945. Montini had explained the many reasons why. The Pope wanted to show gratitude for the friendship the USA had extended throughout the war, to ensure the continuation of the Myron Taylor mission, to strengthen the Church's hand against Communism, and to facilitate co-operation on displaced persons "who were victims of political, religious and racial persecution". Pius may also have wanted to put down Churchill and the British who, he believed, had shown a "lack of comprehension" of the Holy See throughout the war.

Spellman never became Secretary of State; and Pius XII never appointed one. It may be that the two facts are connected. Disappointed that he could not get the man he wanted, Pius preferred to act as his own Secretary of State. Why was Spellman not appointed?

Because the news leaked out prematurely in September 1944: with the war still on it would be impossible to give to an archbishop from one of the belligerents so high a post without abandoning "neutrality". There is another, perhaps overlapping explanation. Everyone was still expecting Pius to name a Secretary of State, but on 5 November 1944 he told Tardini, "*Io non voglio collaboratori, ma esecutori*" ("I want people to do what I say, not to help me think").[1] Being his own Secretary of State was, according to Tardini, "an act of courage". It is difficult to see why.

Montini welcomed the liberation of Rome because it took pressure off him. He no longer needed to wear a mask. There was a general about-turn of the diplomats he was answerable for. The Allied diplomats emerged blinking from the Vatican and returned to their traditional haunts in Rome, while the Axis diplomats, including the Finns and the Japanese, experienced the claustrophobic rigours of the Palazzo Santa Marta.

Montini was glad to get a chance to practise his English. He dropped in most evenings at the club for British servicemen in Rome run by the Catholic Women's League. Their President, Mia Woodruff, wife of

1 Domenico Tardini, *Pio XII*, p. 79. Tardini says this remark was addressed to *him* personally. Perhaps Pius would not have said quite the same to Montini, whose mind and culture he respected.

Douglas Woodruff, editor of the *Tablet* 1936–67, had devised their uniform and ran a very tight ship. Novelist Evelyn Waugh found her looking "very young and pretty and thin".[1]

Montini said to her one evening: "I don't understand how you operate, one couldn't organize Italian women like this. What's your secret?" "Englishwomen," Mia Woodruff grandly replied, "are natural nannies. They are used to clearing up messes. They have done this all over the empire. They take over when the chaps don't know how to cope."[2] Montini was amazed. D'Arcy Osborne had warned him about English nannies.

Through Hugh Montgomery, first secretary to D'Arcy Osborne at the Legation, Montini met many other English Catholics as they passed through Rome. Evelyn Waugh turned up to report on the situation in Yugoslavia. He found Rome "short of water, light and transport. The few restaurants madly expensive. Ranieri open for luncheon only. Most of the hotels taken over for various messes." Waugh noted that Hugh Montgomery was "neurotically anti-Italian and anti-clerical from his confinement in the Vatican".[3]

Though the war was not yet over, it was still important to prepare the *dopoguerra*. Charles de Gaulle led the way on 30 June 1944. Familiar with *grandeur*, he was impressed. "Pius XII," he wrote, "judges everything from a point of view that transcends human beings, their enterprises and their quarrels." From that lofty height the Pope feared that liberated France would soon relapse into its age-old feuding, grieved over the sufferings about to befall the German people, but "it was the action of the Soviets in Poland today and in the whole of Eastern Europe tomorrow that filled the Holy Father with anxiety".[4]

That anxiety was intensified in August 1944 when, with Russian troops poised on the other side of the Vistula, Moscow Radio broadcast

1 Michael Davie, ed., *The Diaries of Evelyn Waugh*, Weidenfeld and Nicolson 1976, p. 617.

2 Mrs Woodruff recounted this over lunch at Marcham Priory in the summer of 1988. Though well over eighty and half-blind, her mind was as alert as ever. Earlier in 1944 her brother John, Lord Acton, took part in the battle for Monte Cassino with his medium artillery regiment. General Sir Oliver Leese, his army commander, had him slip through the enemy lines to assure Pope Pius XII that Rome would not have to undergo the bombardments that were being inflicted on Monte Cassino. Pius later confided that he regarded Monte Cassino as the necessary sacrifice that saved Rome. See Alberic Stacpoole OSB, "Montecassino 1989", in *Priests and People*, May 1990, pp. 177–91.

3 *Diaries*, op. cit. pp. 619, 577. Montgomery was not remotely anti-clerical. He was later ordained priest and ended up a *Monsignore*. But having been abusively arrested in Naples by the Italians he was at the time feeling rather anti-Italian.

4 Charles de Gaulle, *Mémoires de Guerre*, vol. 2, pp. 233–34.

an appeal urging the inhabitants of Warsaw to rise against their oppressors. The Russians then sat on their hands while Warsaw was savagely and systematically destroyed. This cynical act of treachery destroyed whatever credibility the Soviets might have had in Poland, and meant that whatever regime they installed would be an alien usurpation.[1]

Winston Churchill had an audience on 23 August 1944 and found the Vatican in mourning: Luigi Maglione, Cardinal Secretary of State, had died the day before. Montini briefed the Pope on what to expect with the help of D'Arcy Osborne and Myron Taylor, whom Evelyn Waugh described as "elderly, handsome, obtuse".[2] The Pope admired the great political and intellectual gifts of Churchill. In conversation with Babuisco Rizzo, Italian foreign minister, Montini was happy that all the main topics had been dealt with and that Pope and Premier were "particularly satisfied with the way the conversation went". Churchill himself laconically noted: "This morning I was received in audience by the Pope. The conversation was very cordial and touched on in general all the usual topics. On each one I gave an appropriate response."[3]

For Churchill the Vatican was not very important. Of course it could help Italy to avoid the fate of Greece where the Communist Party had filled the vacuum left by the departing Germans, resulting in a bitter civil war. But the other points on the papal agenda – the way Italy was treated by the Allies as an occupied country, and the fear of "Protestant proselytism" – left him cold.

Churchill stayed with Sir Noel Charles, the British High Commissioner, in the restored British Embassy, the Villa Wolonsky. D'Arcy Osborne and Hugh Montgomery felt miffed that no one consulted them about the role of the Vatican.

Churchill had a long conversation with Marshal Badoglio, his old foe. They agreed that "given the enormous Moscovite advance into the centre of Europe, Italy could turn red overnight". Churchill was prepared to be forgiving to exorcise the red peril: "There is nothing between the King, and those patriots who have rallied to him, and rampant Bolshevism. It is vital to build up their position." Admiral Ellery Stone, the US High Commissioner, agreed.

The Vatican may have felt that the Americans were more sympathetic than the British. But they too were to prove disappointing. Montini was charged with finding out about the plans for an organization that would

1 See Norman Davies, *God's Playground: A History of Poland*, vol. II, *1795 to the Present*, p. 474.

2 *The Diaries of Evelyn Waugh*, p. 617.

3 Italo Garzia, *Pio XII e l'Italia nella seconda guerra mondiale*, p. 330.

safeguard world peace (what became UNO). Cordell Hull replied that it would be "premature to inform His Holiness about trends in the debate and the drafting that is going on".[1]

Clearly the Holy See was never to be a member of UNO. Cordell Hull explained that "the other great powers, including the Soviet Union, were agreed that the Vatican, as a tiny little statelet, would be unable to fulfil all its responsibilities as a member of an organization whose primary aim was the maintenance of peace and security".[2]

However, as a small crumb of comfort, the Holy See could take part in the humanitarian aspects of the international organization. It was better than nothing. But the Holy See was frozen out of the post-war settlement, just as it had been in 1919.

In December 1944, the last Christmas of the war, Montini wrote a letter, or rather drafted a letter for Pius XII, that won him great favour in French theological circles, especially in Lyons, during the war the intellectual capital of France, the recently liberated France. The letter was to Maurice Blondel, whose "philosophy of immanence" (grace is *in* nature but not *of* nature) was behind the renewal of theology of the Jesuits of Fourvière and the Dominicans of Le Saulchoir. The letter to Blondel was significant, for much of the attack already brewing on *la théologie nouvelle* took Blondel to task for allegedly "undermining the gratuity of the supernatural order".

Though the letter also recalled "the abiding philosophical relevance of Thomism" and regretted in Blondel "some expressions that theological rigour would have preferred to be more precise", it contained no hint of condemnation. It brought comfort to the aged Blondel in Aix-en-Provence – he was eighty-three and lingered on for another five years. Montini told Jean Guitton that "several people, here in Rome, attacked me for the letter".[3] His enemies brandished it in subsequent controversies.

Knowing where friends were in the chaos was not easy. Montini received a letter from his poet-doctor friend Ugo Piazzi, who was in a shack somewhere near Forlì on the Adriatic. With his wife and five children they were still close to the front line. The British (he calls them

1 Italo Garzia, "*La diplomazia vaticana e l'assetto post-bellico*", in *Pio XII*, ed. Riccardi, pp. 225–26.

2 Ibid. p. 226.

3 Etienne Fouilloux, "G. B. Montini face aux débats ecclésiaux de son temps 1944–1955", in *Modernité*, p. 96 fn. 37. Montini later – 8 September 1950 – somewhat relativized his letter by remarking that although he said, on behalf of the Pope, that Blondel's philosophy was valid (*valable*), he added the qualifying clause, "although not everything in Maurice Blondel's philosophy is accepted by theologians". Jean Guitton, *Paul VI secret*, p. 42. But that was after *Humani Generis*.

the "English") had just liberated them, and had shifted what was left of the bombed-out church and presbytery to rebuild the road – or so they said. He was still waiting for the vital pass guaranteeing he was bi-lingual that he hoped would save them.[1] That was on 12 December 1944. Montini replied on 28 December, urging him to come to Rome where "everything generous and new is rapidly picking up again: newspapers, organizations, works of charity. We feel the need to reawaken Catholic militancy and effectiveness after so many years of sleep and reduced activity."

He blesses the children, especially the latest one, Antonina, only six months old. Piazzi and his family returned to Rome in February 1945 in a Vatican lorry that had taken supplies to the Bishop of Forlì.

Spring and the end of the war in the West came with a rush. Montini learned of Mussolini's death and humiliation on 28 April. Hitler committed suicide on 30 April. Von Kesselring, commander of the German forces in Italy, surrendered on 1 May, a prelude to VE Day, the unconditional surrender on 8 May. In Italy hostilities officially ceased on 2 May.

But the war against Japan continued. The OSS, predecessor of the CIA, was already at work in Italy. They had noted that the head of the Japanese mission had taken refuge in the Vatican in the Palazzo Santa Marta that had housed D'Arcy Osborne until the previous year. This interested Martin S. Quigley because before he left Washington his chief, General William ("Wild Bill") J. Donovan had given him only one precise order: "Be alert at the right time to attempt to open up communications to Tokyo looking to the surrender of Japan. After all, the Vatican is one of the few possible points for such contact."[2]

But how? Quigley rejected Fr Vincent A. McCormick on the grounds that an American citizen could not be seen with a Japanese and Jesuits were noted for intrigue. He settled on Egidio Vagnozzi, protégé of Alfredo Ottaviani, who had served in the Apostolic Delegation in Washington. His mind was made up when he discovered that a Japanese priest, Benedict Tomizawa, ecclesiastical adviser to the Japanese mission, lived in the same palazzo as Vagnozzi and shared meals with him. Tomizawa talked with Ken Harada, the Japanese Ambassador. Vagnozzi saw Quigley next day and reported that Tokyo wanted more information. What about? About surrender terms. "I have no authority to negotiate," said Quigley, "only to try to arrange a channel of peacemaking."

Vagnozzi accepted this, but thought it would be tragic if this channel

1 *Notiziario*, 11, p. 41.

2 Martin S. Quigley, *Peace without Hiroshima: Secret Action at the Vatican in the Spring of 1945*, p. 80.

remained closed. They had to be imaginative. "Unconditional surrender," Quigley thought, "is a propaganda term." However severe the defeat, there are always some conditions. "Speaking personally," Vagnozzi said, "I believe the Japanese will never surrender but will prefer to die to the last man and woman if their Emperor is going to be deposed or punished as a war criminal." So Quigley drew up a list of "major points that a surrender document is likely to include: (1) Occupation of Japan by American forces; (2) No permanent transfer of territory to the United States; (3) No change in the status of the Emperor, unless decided by the Japanese people."[1] A message along these lines was received in Tokyo on 2 June. It was intercepted and circulated in Washington as the lead item in the "MAGIC" diplomatic summary no. 1177, 15 June 1945. It mentions "a Vatican official, Msgr Vagnozzi" and "an unknown American". Quigley wisely remained anonymous, for his superior in Rome, Earl Brennan, did not know what he was up to.

Neither Montini nor Tardini was informed *at the time* about what, had it succeeded, would have made the horror of Hiroshima and Nagasaki unnecessary, because Vagnozzi was unsure of his ground and feared his involvement would offend against Pius XII's concept of neutrality.[2]

Montini's final contribution to the *Actes et documents* is a rather dry memo to Franklin C. Gowen, who had replaced Tittmann as Myron Taylor's assistant, about the plan for a "non-sectarian" religious service to be held in the Piazza Venezia within forty-eight hours of the official end of hostilities in Europe. Montini wrote:

> If the celebration is to be a civil or military ceremony there is no reason why Catholics should not take part. If, on the other hand, it is to be a religious ceremony, it will be necessary, according to the provisions of canon law, for Catholics to conduct their service separately, just as they did on the occasion of the death of the late President Roosevelt.[3]

This does not sound very ecumenical. Nor was it. The age forbade the expression of ecumenical convictions. The end of the war in Europe

1 Ibid. pp. 134–35.

2 Ibid. p. 152. Robert Graham SJ took up the story in "*Contatti di pace fra Americani e Giaponesi in Vaticano nel 1945*", in *Civiltà Cattolica*, 1971, Quaterno 2899, pp. 18–30. Harada was still alive, and thought his messages from the Vatican proved fruitless because Tokyo was already seeking peace through Moscow and because "it was considered a most difficult matter to persuade the Japanese army to agree to terminate the war".

3 *Actes et documents*, 11, p. 738.

virtually coincided with the twenty-fifth anniversary of his priestly ordination on 29 May 1920. He would die on the thirty-third anniversary of the bombing of Hiroshima, 6 August 1945, an event witnessed by a young Jesuit called Pedro Arrupe.

14

Christian Democrats and the Cold War

> If the western democracies stand together in strict adherence to the principles of the United Nations Charter, their influence for furthering those principles will be immense, and no one is likely to molest them. If, however, they become divided or falter in their duty ... catastrophe may overwhelm us all.
>
> (WINSTON S. CHURCHILL in his Iron Curtain speech at Fulton, Missouri, 6 March 1946)

Diplomats considered Msgr Giovanni Battista Montini the most important person in the Vatican after Pope Pius XII. For the US State Department he was "the perfect diplomat who achieves his goals quietly and without annoying people". It pronounced him "far and away the most authoritative person in the Vatican, and the most likely candidate to be the next Pope".[1] Such predictions were usually the kiss of death.

Domenico Tardini had a different estimate of Montini's importance. In the absence of a Cardinal Secretary of State they were theoretically co-equal under-secretaries. Both were subordinate to Pius XII who declared that he did not want "*collaboratori, ma esecutori*" – obedient executants who would suppress their own opinions. As *sostituto* Montini specialized in Italian affairs. Tardini, with a hint of sour grapes, declared: "The truth is that I dealt with the more important matters. Montini was responsible for contacts with the outside world, so people thought he *did everything*. Poor chap! He wouldn't be happy to be thought of as an *éminence grise*."[2] In other words, when the crunch comes, go to Uncle Domenico.

They had contrasting styles, and American diplomacy had accurately probed their strengths and weaknesses: "Where Tardini gets results by strength, energy and a refusal to compromise, Montini attains his ends

1 Andrea Riccardi, *Il "Partito Romano" nel secondo dopoguerra (1945–1954)*, p. 39.
2 Ibid. p. 39.

by logic, the clever understanding and manipulation of his adversary." Montini's brief included "dealing with the Italian bishops and being informed through their parish priests of what people were feeling".[1]

That was in January 1946 when Italians shivered and went hungry. After eighteen months of civil war half a million homeless refugees were on the move, political oppositions were bitter, and the financial and industrial disruption was immense. In Emilia armed bands professing allegiance to Communism and hatred of the Church murdered fifty-two priests between 1944 and 1946.[2] Italy was like a Third World country, with the *scugnizzi* of Naples and other southern cities scavanging for food and selling their sisters to Americans.

Tardini implied that Montini was the front man who grappled with the Italian realities, while he beavered away at vaster international problems. This was broadly true, as relations with Italy ceased to belong to the "international" section of the Secretariat of State.[3]

Two post-war changes enhanced Montini's role. First Catholic Action was restored to papal control. In 1940 it was thought wiser to let it pass to the Italian bishops to spare the Vatican direct involvement in the hurly-burly of political conflict. With the war over there was no longer any need to keep a distance. Catholic Action was centralized more than ever before, with all its leaders being directly appointed by the Holy See. This enormously strengthened Montini's hand. His FUCI friend Vittorio Veronese became the first head of Catholic Action in the new dispensation.

There was a similar concentration of charitable work in the Vatican. The head of the Pontifical Aid Commission, Msgr Ferdinando Baldelli, managed American aid and food programmes in Italy which the US government entrusted to the Church rather than the State.[4] This gave him an immense power of patronage, greater than that of the political parties. However, Baldelli ran his own show and had his doubts about Montini.

On the other hand Montini had a friend in Mario Cordovani, Master of the Sacred Palace from 1942. This "civil Dominican", as Evelyn Waugh called him,[5] was the official papal theologian. His influence was seen chiefly in the wartime encyclicals on Scripture and the Mystical Body; but he was also a sound anti-Fascist and committed to democracy. He was a useful ally in the post-war period, able to counterbalance

1 Ibid.

2 Owen Chadwick, *The Christian Church in the Cold War*, p. 15.

3 Andrea Riccardi, *Le Chiese di Pio XII*, p. 26.

4 Giancarlo Zizola, *Il Microfono di Dio*, p. 89.

5 *The Diaries of Evelyn Waugh*, p. 618.

Ottaviani at the Holy Office. But Cordovani's influence waned gradually until his death in 1950.[1] Montini's network of friends – already dubbed *Montiniani* – included Sergio Pignedoli and Giovanni Urbani within the Curia, while among the Vatican diplomats he trusted Clemente Micara and Angelo Roncalli. He was also training younger men like Giovanni Benelli who at twenty-six became his secretary in 1947–50.

But Montini's most important ally remained his spiritual director, the Oratorian Paolo Caresana, now superior of the Chiesa Nuova just across the Tiber from the Vatican. Caresana, as it were, delivered the lay *Montiniani*. He was spiritual guide to a group of young Catholic members of the Constituent Assembly who had distinctive views on the direction Christian Democracy should take. They all found lodgings close to the Chiesa Nuova. Chief among them were Giuseppe Dossetti, Giorgio La Pira and Giuseppe Lazzati. Dossetti gave his name to the group: the *Dossettiani* acted as a left-wing ginger-group within the Christian Democratic Party who agreed with the Communists in seeing the resistance movement as a second *Risorgimento*.

Pius XII, a belated convert to democracy, did not hold that view. But at this time he made the famous statements which non-Italians always tend to take out of context. Pius begins to say to the laity, "*You* are the Church," he concedes that there is a role for "public opinion" within the Church, and he dusts down Pius XI's concept of "subsidiarity" (never put up to a higher level what can be dealt with on a lower level) without saying whether it applied also to the Church. (It didn't.) Renato Moro concludes that Pius XII was for democracy in Italy – provided it was led by Catholics.[2]

The Constituent Assembly, elected on 2 June 1946, had the task of drafting a new constitution. A national referendum held the same day determined whether Italy was to continue to be a monarchy or become a republic. The vote went narrowly against the monarchy.[3]

The Constituent Assembly formed a committee of seventy-five to produce a text by the end of January 1947. It was signed by the leaders of the three anti-Fascist forces, the pre-Fascist Liberal Enrico Di Nichola, the Christian Democrat Alcide De Gasperi, and the Communist Umberto

1 Andrea Riccardi, "*Governo e 'profezia' nel pontificato di Pio XII*", in *Pio XII*, p. 41.

2 Renato Moro, "The Catholic Contribution to the Constituent Assembly", a paper to the FUCI conference, La Chiesa Nuova, Rome, 27 November 1986.

3 One effect of this synchronization was that the first clause of the Constitution – "Italy is a democratic republic" – was sanctioned directly by the people, not imposed by their elected representatives. That, at least, is what most Italian politicians say. Monarchists claim that peasants cast their vote against the monarchy under the mistaken impression that the lady figuring *la Repubblica* on the ballot paper was the popular Belgian Queen, Maria José.

Terracini, President of the Constituent Assembly. The presence of Terracini, who had spent most of the inter-war years in gaol, meant that the Communists were "locked into" the Italian political system; they could not properly be described as "subversive", still less as "revolutionary".

After their electoral success the *Dossettiani* began to plan Italy's future. They set down their programme in a document called "*Questa che domandiamo*" (What we Demand).[1] Italy had ceased to be a Catholic country. Like France, it had become a mission territory. A gap yawned between committed Catholics and those who were merely conventional or routine. That gap must be closed by remedying the "defective education" of the clergy and transforming Catholic Action. With the creation of a Catholic political party came the danger that political power might be sought at the expense of pastoral effectiveness: the Church could appear subordinate to the Christian Democrats, with the clergy acting as party recruiting agents. This would lead to the charge and reality of clericalism.

To avoid this the *Dossettiani* stressed the autonomy of politics, by which they meant its freedom from clerical interference. The new Christendom they hoped to inaugurate was inspired by Jacques Maritain's *Humanisme Intégral*. To quote Maritain at this date was highly provocative, since he was heartily disliked by Alfredo Ottaviani at the Holy Office as dangerously "liberal". Ironically enough Maritain was now in Rome as French Ambassador to the Holy See and closer to Montini than ever before. Maritain gave them moral support, explaining that his "new Christendom" differed from the mediaeval version by being lay-led and open to all men and women of good will. It was inclusive rather than exclusive. A prophet without honour in his own country, he knew it had more chances of realization in Italy than in France.

The new Christendom was conceived of as a "third way" between Communism and liberalism, between the models proposed by the Soviet Union and the United States. The strength of Communism, they believed, came from the errors of Christians: they had tolerated injustices, they had encouraged an other-worldly spirituality without any social commitment and they had neglected to study Marx and Lenin to understand how Communism worked.[2] The Christian Democrat radicals did not believe that the Italian people were seriously attracted by Communist atheism or the Marxist interpretation of history. Giuseppe Toniolo, the Catholic sociologist at the turn of the century, had predicted that one day the workers would "take their place" in society.

1 Given in Giancarlo Zizola, *Il Microfono di Dio*, pp. 77–81.

2 Ibid. p. 76.

Now in 1946 that day had arrived. So the Christian Democrats would be a party committed to practical justice and social reform. Inevitably they would fall short of this ideal; and inevitably there would be opposition. The Vatican was not alone in wanting the Christian Democrats to be merely the Italian Conservative Party at prayer.

The manifesto of the *Dossettiani* was anti-Communist but not bigoted. That was Montini's position too. Yet he has been accused of being so blinded by anti-Communism that he helped Nazi criminals escape along the "Ratline" (the USA code-name for it) to Latin America. The story goes that Martin Bormann and Heinrich Mueller, two Gestapo chiefs, vanished from Germany in May 1945, reached Rome where they were hidden by "the Vatican", and were then passed on to various Latin American dictators who sheltered them to a ripe old age.

That such clandestine activities went on in Rome is not in question. The Austrian Bishop Alois Hudal, notoriously pro-Nazi, who was Rector of the Anima, the hospitality house for German-speaking students, could have been one link in the chain; but he was interrogated by British counter-intelligence at the time and no action was taken against him.[1] The Croatian College, then on Piazza Colonna, was a refuge for many of those whose return "home" would mean certain execution. Behind them both lurked Msgr Krunoslav Draganovic who is alleged to have spirited away to Latin America some 30,000 Croatians including Ante Pavelic, the fallen dictator himself, and most of his government. Down the same Ratline scuttled other war criminals such as Klaus Barbie, the "butcher of Lyons".[2] Montini, say his critics, "must have known" what was going on. It doesn't follow.

Ante Pavelic, for example, was not even in Rome at the relevant time, being hidden in a Salzburg convent until the spring of 1948. Then Draganovic, who was a law unto himself and ran his own show, brought him to Rome and lodged him at the Collegio Pio Latino

1 Robert Graham SJ, "Foreign Intelligence and the Vatican", in *The Catholic World Report*, March 1992, p. 50.

2 Penny Lernoux, *People of God: The Struggle for World Catholicism*, p. 252. Lernoux "explains" Montini's behaviour in the following manner: "He *apparently* shared Pius XII's conviction that Pavelic and his Ustaci troops might overthrow Marshal Tito's government and re-establish a Catholic state in Croatia" (ibid.). This is nonsense. We have seen what Pius XII's attitude to Pavelic and his crimes was (above, pp. 156–7). No sane person would have wanted to restore *that* regime. Lernoux had swallowed the left-wing view that Pius and Montini were so blinded by anti-Communism as to be indulgent towards Fascism and Nazism. No matter how often it is refuted, this hydra-headed monster keeps on sprouting new heads. See Mark Aarons and John Loftus, *Unholy Trinity*, Heinemann 1991. A BBC programme with the same title went out in the United Kingdom on 28 November 1991.

Americano disguised as "Father Gomez" until Perón *invited* him to Argentina.[1]

Montini had no part at all in the Pavelic story. His position was accurately described in a despatch to the British Foreign Office. Mr Simon Cocks reported on 20 September 1947 that Msgr Montini was well briefed on Yugoslav problems:

> Msgr Montini added however that the Vatican must act circumspectly, because Italy under the peace treaty was obliged to return Yugoslav refugees to Yugoslavia, and because the Yugoslav government would interpret charitable activities of the Vatican on their behalf as a hostile act and would be liable to take reprisals against Catholic clergy in Yugoslavia.[2]

If he took that prudent view about refugees then he is unlikely to have risked the lives of Yugoslav priests by helping war criminals escape.

A sense of proportion is called for. During the Nazi occupation of Rome Montini had helped save Jews and assorted left-wing political opponents. That in the hour of victory he should oppose immediate vengeance on those who were seeking safety is a tribute to his judgement. The Vatican was under no illusions about what was happening in Yugoslavia. In March 1945 Evelyn Waugh had written a paper for Fitzroy Maclean at the Foreign Office on "Church and State in Liberated Yugoslavia". Waugh concluded that the Tito regime "threatens to destroy the Catholic faith in a region where there are now some 5,000,000 Catholics", adding however that Tito, if subjected to Allied pressure, "might be induced to modify his policy enough to give the Church a chance of life".[3] Waugh gave Pius XII the gist of his report in an audience on 2 March 1945. Pius thanked Waugh for his work "for the Church and civilization" and urged him to carry on (*Continuez!*).[4]

1 Carlo Falconi, *The Silence of Pius XII*, p. 408, quoting a Serbo-Croat biography by Sime Balen. When Perôn fell Pavelic fled Buenos Aires and led a wandering, hunted existence. An assassination attempt in 1957 led him to take refuge in Franco's Spain where he died the following year. As for Fr Krunoslav Draganovic, who once had a reputation for omnipotence, he stayed quietly on in Rome until 1967 when he mysteriously disappeared. He was later found in Sarajevo in the hands of the secret police. Had he been kidnapped? Or had he returned voluntarily to his native Bosnia? Or had the "protocol" signed between Yugoslavia and the Holy See in 1966 permitted his return? He died in 1983. See L. Nevistic, "*La Muerte del Prof. Krunoslav Draganovic*", *Studia Croatica*, Buenos Aires 1983, pp. 90–1.

2 PRO, Kew, FO 380/117. These hitherto unpublished documents somehow escaped the fifty-year rule imposed by the Foreign Office on all Vatican material.

3 *Diaries of Evelyn Waugh*, p. 620. This report is in the PRO. A summary of it can be found in Christopher Sykes, *Evelyn Waugh*, pp. 273–76. It also provides the background to *Unconditional Surrender*, the final volume of Waugh's *Sword of Honour* trilogy.

4 *Diaries*, p. 618.

A year later any notion that Tito might yield to pressure had evaporated. As Harold Macmillan found, the risk of handing over the innocent was greater than the danger that some of the guilty should escape. In March 1946 the Vatican broke the news of a secret clause in the Yalta agreement by which Russians who had left the Soviet Union after 1929 were to be handed back and, for obscure reasons, given the status of prisoners of war.[1] An Anglican historian says: "The silence of the Vatican, when apprised of the atrocities of the war-mongers, was a deliberate policy aimed at preventing future opportunities for revenge."[2]

This had a bearing on Italy too, where the "purge" of former Fascists was a kid-glove affair compared with the German "de-Nazification" process and the French *épuration*. Montini, like most Italians, thought Fascism had not bitten very deeply into the minds of his fellow-countrymen and he was more concerned with rebuilding than with revenge.

The trial of Archbishop Alojzije Stepinac in Zagreb started on 28 September 1946. A show-trial for dramatic effect with the verdict decided in advance, it had nothing to do with justice or evidence.[3] It was keenly followed in the West because it was feared other countries falling under Communist rule would go the way of Yugoslavia – the only country to have "liberated itself". The others had all been liberated by the Red Army.

That did not help Archbishop Stepinac who played the game according to the international norms so recently proclaimed. His defence of Croatian nationalism was based on the Atlantic Charter principle that all nations, even small nations, have the right to exist. Charged with blessing the Ustace terrorist gangs he imprudently said: "I give my blessing to everyone who asks for it."[4] But as the trial wore on he repeatedly refused to defend himself, saying only: "I did everything according to the Catholic moral law."

Cardinal Francis J. Spellman, Archbishop of New York, was sure Stepinac would be condemned to death. Instead he got sixteen years. If this could happen to the innocent Stepinac what would happen in more ambivalent cases? In Slovakia Msgr Josef Tiso was hanged overlooking the Danube at Bratislava, on 18 April 1947. Drugged and tortured into making a confession of spying, treason and currency manipulation, Jöszef Mindszenty, as anti-Nazi as he was anti-Communist, got life

1 Edmund Wilson, *Europe without Baedeker*, p. 148.

2 John S. Conway, *Yad Vaschem Studies*, vol. XV, p. 335.

3 Stella Alexander, *The Triple Myth: A Life of Archbishop Alojzije Stepinac*, East European Monographs, 1987.

4 Owen Chadwick, *The Church in the Cold War*, p. 66.

imprisonment. The function of these trials was to dramatize the new political realities and show who was boss. They were the prelude to the Cold War.

The Italian situation was shifting rapidly. The Communists formed part of the provisional government until May 1947. They were still sharing power when the Constitution was approved by 453 votes to 62. But the future already cast its dark shadows: Europe was bieng carved up into two spheres of influence with grave consequences for the Church in Eastern Europe, especially in Poland, Hungary and Czechoslovakia. Despite Yalta's promise of "free and fair elections" they all fell under Communist sway. This was the overture to the Cold War.

It is remarkable how restrained De Gasperi was in not exploiting these events in his internal debates with the Italian Communist Party.[1] The Vatican showed a similar restraint. It went out of its way not to pre-judge the situation in Eastern Europe. In September 1947 Montini wrote to Cardinal Jöszef Mindszenty before his trial, about the crown of Hungary.[2] The Vatican, unwilling to give unnecessary offence, adopted a cautiously accommodating attitude towards the Communists.

In June 1947 Count Giuseppe Dalla Torre, veteran editor of *L'Osservatore Romano*, wrote optimistically: "For those who see things in the light of the divine order, there is always room for peaceful accommodation even in the gravest clashes of human and national interests."[3] Dalla Torre showed understanding of Russia's quest for secure frontiers to the West: to believe that Russia's policy was "sheer aggressivity" was as absurd as to imagine that the "Anglo-Saxons" sought imperialist expansion in Europe.

The editor of *L'Osservatore Romano* thought East and West should shelve their ideological differences, just as they had done during the war, and learn how to live together in peace (*convivenza*). Everything must be done to avoid an East–West confrontation, which could only have the direst consequences for Europe. In 1947 Churchill's Iron Curtain had not yet descended. The object of Vatican foreign policy was to try to ensure that it never did.

But it failed and the Soviet *niet* to the Marshall Plan marked the true outbreak of the Cold War. It created insurmountable difficulties for the Italian Communist Party. Under Palmiro Togliatti it claimed to have

1 Donald Sassoon, *Contemporary Italy: Politics, Economy and Society since 1945*, 1986.

2 Facsimile in Hans-Jakob Stehle, *Eastern Politics of the Vatican 1917–1979*, p. 234. The Latin letter, dated 9 September 1947, transmits the negative decision of the US War Department to Cardinal Francis Spellman. The Vatican expresses no opinion. The crown was returned to Hungary in 1977.

3 *Weekly Political Intelligence Digest*, for internal FO use, July 1947, p. 17 (PRO).

transformed the idea of revolution as the violent seizure of state power into the long march through democratic institutions. Togliatti called it "progressive democracy" and it was to be only the first stage on the road to socialism.[1]

The Vatican, noting the Communist seizure of power in Poland, Hungary and Czechoslovakia, concluded simply that Communists "said one thing when out of power and another when they attained it". Togliatti was simply not believed. The Italian Communist Party, said Enrico Manfredini, a typical Italian bishop, was "contrary to our history, to our beliefs, to our culture, to our needs, and to our interests".[2] But then one had to explain its eight million votes, usually attributed to its organizational power and skill at propaganda. Like would have to be met by like. Propaganda and organization would be the main tasks of Catholic Action.

Luigi Gedda, a Turin-educated doctor, now forty-five, had already reached this conclusion. In 1947 he founded the *Comitati Civici* (Civic Committees) whose purpose was "to fill the organizational vacuum of the Catholic world and to counter (*contraporre*) the Communists with as active and far-reaching (*capillare*) a presence as theirs".[3]

Montini did not take to Gedda. The *Comitati Civici* were an uncontrolled engine that could go off or explode anywhere. Montini and Vittorio Veronese, fearing the *Comitati* might come to rival Christian Democracy, managed to hold up their formation in the summer of 1947.

But once the Communists and Socialists were excluded from the government in May 1947 the Holy See frankly adopted the Christian Democratic Party, since no other Christian party had any hope of success, and used Gedda's organization to drum up votes. The *Comitati Civici* became part of the Christian Democratic electoral machine. The doctrine of "the unity of Catholics" (a euphemism for "all Catholics should vote the same way") was drummed in to the faithful.

1 Paul Ginsborg in ASMI (Association for the Study of Modern Italy) *Newsletter*, 17, Spring 1990, pp. 19–20. The opening of the ex-Soviet secret archives in 1992 caused an uproar in Italy, demoralizing the Party of the Democratic Left (as the Communist Party had rebaptized itself). For it was now revealed that Togliatti had refused to help save the lives of tens of thousands of Italian prisoners of war in Russian hands.

2 Enrico Manfredini, "*Le scelte pastorali dell'arcivescovo Montini*", in *Montini Arcivescovo di Milano*, p. 90. The article occupies pp. 46–155 of this volume, and Manfredini, a Milanese priest whom Montini made Bishop of Piacenza in 1969, presented it in abbreviated form at the Milan colloquy, 23–25 September 1983. He died suddenly on 16 December 1983 without being able to revise his MS. The discussion on his paper was chaired by Giuseppe Lazzati, Rector of the Catholic University of Milan. No one challenged Manfredini's judgement on the Communist Party of the late 1940s.

3 Sandro Magister, *La Politica Vaticana e l'Italia*, p. 98. Gedda made this speech in Bologna on 20 September 1947.

With the Communists forming the chief party of the opposition the elections of 18 April 1948 could be presented as a battle for Christian civilization. In the mind of Joseph Walshe, Irish Ambassador to the Holy See, who took his cue from Gedda, this battle could well be armed. Walshe fully expected a civil war to break out before Easter 1948, although he thought the Communists would not attempt a *coup d'état* until they were sure of electoral defeat.[1]

To calm the excitable Irishman Montini arranged an audience with Pius XII on 26 February 1948. The ambassador found the Pope "looking very tired indeed and, for the first time, I saw Him in a mood of deepest pessimism". Pius was "hunched up, almost physically overcome by the weight of his present burden". He spoke of "the imminent danger to the Church in Italy and the whole of Western Europe".

"If *they* have a majority," the Pope asked, leaving no doubt about who *they* were, "what can I do to govern the Church as Christ wants Me to govern?"[2] Walshe offered the Pope a safe refuge in Dublin. Pius was grateful, said he would feel alright in Phoenix Park but insisted his duty was to stay put: "My place is in Rome and, if it be the will of the Divine Master, I am ready to be martyred for Him in Rome."[3]

Montini meantime took steps to win the election so that papal martyrdom would not be required. He saw to it that Gedda's campaign was soundly financed. He got the IOR (the "Vatican Bank", founded in 1942) to provide a "start-up" fund of a hundred million lire earned from the sale of surplus United States war material: this was a special concession granted to the Vatican for the anti-Communist campaign. Montini also put Gedda in contact with John McKnight of the US Embassy, probably a CIA man, and with the leaders of *Confindustria* (the Italian employers' organization).[4]

While the old Roman Tardini joked about American support Montini welcomed it as a factor in the Italian political equation. He had grounds for not sharing Pius XII's chronic pessimism early in 1948. On 17 February Montini assured Graham Parsons, who had succeeded Gowen as Myron Taylor's assistant, that the mass of the people already knew "that in this election there were but two alternatives, Communism and anti-Communism".

1 Dermot Keogh, "Ireland, the Vatican and the Cold War", a paper prepared for the Smithsonian Institute, Washington, April 1988, pp. 21–22. Thanks to Professor Keogh for making his MS available.

2 Ibid. p. 34. The capital letters come from Walshe's Diary.

3 Ibid. p. 35.

4 Sandro Magister, *La Politicà Vaticana*, p. 114 fn. 48. This collusion with the Americans, though often asserted at the time, could not then be proved.

It was the "civic duty" of Catholics to vote, Montini went on. Though these were early days he was sure the "Demo-Christians would come out with a 'relative majority', even though the margin might be small".[1] In the event the Demo-Christian-led coalition gained 48.5 per cent of the votes while the United Front of Communists and Socialists had 31 per cent.[2]

Yet still there were fears that the Italian Communist Party would try to recover by insurrection what the ballot box had denied it: that had been, after all, the experience of Poland, Hungary and Romania. The Communists responded to the failed assassination of Togliatti in Palermo on 14 July 1948 with a general strike: it looked like the first stage of a coup. It made the divorce of ACLI, the Catholic trade union, from the general union movement CGIL inevitable.

The US Embassy wanted to set up an anti-Communist trade union and provided funds for it, channelled through Gedda. The Vatican did not like this. US Embassy official Edward Page summed up the situation on 11 October 1948. No problem about Gedda: he assured Page he could "sell" the idea of the Western alliance to the Italians through his 20,000 *Comitati Civici*. However, Page goes on, "broad sectors of the Italian population, among them many Christian Democrats, don't view favourably Italy's adhesion to the Western bloc, preferring to follow a policy of equidistance between East and West".[3] That was the policy the Vatican would have preferred to follow.

Unwilling to forgo its traditional neutrality the Holy See was reluctant to endorse the Atlantic Pact. Yet it was already committed *de facto* by its stance in the election campaign and its reliance on Gedda. This worried Tardini who saw the USA as an economic giant with a pigmy political brain. Italians high-mindedly criticized the US as "liberal" in politics and Protestant in religion. But Montini with De Gasperi took the pro-American view that Italy's future depended on building up Europe in firm alliance with the United States.

In Church terms this meant strengthening American Catholicism, drawing it into the universal Church and finding a role for Americans in the Curia. Montini worked on this in Rome and his August 1951 visit had it in mind. But to have any hope of success there would have to be not only ecumenical friendliness towards other Christians but a serious attempt to tackle the question of religious freedom along the lines that Fr John Courtney Murray SJ was already sketching out in *Theological Studies*. For in the US Paul Blanshard was thundering away about the

1 Dermot Keogh, "Ireland, the Vatican and the Cold War", p. 31.

2 Robert Leonardi, *Italian Christian Democracy*, p. 59.

3 Sandro Magister, *La Politicà Vaticana*, p. 126.

Vatican as an authoritarian system comparable only to the Kremlin.[1]

There was truth in Blanshard's charges. Ecumenism and religious liberty were anathema to the Holy Office so long as Alfred Ottaviani was in charge. The Pope was technically the head of the Holy Office and Ottaviani was merely its pro-Prefect: but the Roman joke said Pius reigned while Ottaviani ruled.

Montini was awkwardly placed: as consultor to the Holy Office since 1937 he knew its secrets but was powerless to influence its decisions, a fact the French never understood. The most advanced ecumenical ideas at the time came from them. Montini had the first two volumes of the *Unam Sanctam* collection edited by the French Dominicans: Johann Adam Möhler's *L'Unité de l'Eglise* and Congar's work, *Chrétiens désunis.*[2] *Chrétiens désunis* had appeared in 1937; its validity was tested in prison and concentration camps. Though Montini had read it he had not yet assimilated its message. So far his ecumenism was spontaneous and improvised.

The French, conscious of their pre-eminence in Church renewal, knew that priest-workers and other "dissidents" were sympathetically received in Rome by Montini's friend Jacques Maritain, French Ambassador to the Holy See. Maritain put the French case in a swan-song speech in 1948:

> France is light-years ahead of other countries. Hence the ambivalence of the Holy See in its regard; if the Holy See slams on the brakes, this is not because France is in error, but because France is way ahead. But one knows that it is opening the ways

1 Paul Blanshard, *Communism, Democracy and Catholic Power*, Cape, 1952. George Orwell had already noted the resemblance between what he called "the smelly little orthodoxies", while the KGB was commonly said to have learned its techniques of sensory deprivation and tough/soft guy interrogation from the Spanish Inquisition. Rightly: see *Le Manuel des Inquisiteurs*, ed. Louis Sala-Moulins, Mouton, Paris, 1973.

Blanshard himself claims his eyes were unsealed by Harvard Professor George La Piana's article in *The Shane Quarterly* (1949), "A Totalitarian Church in a Democratic State: the American Experiment". La Piana was an Italian priest who had left the Church in the Modernist crisis, but was later reconciled.

There was a sharp exchange of letters between Spellman and Montini on the subject of Blanshard. Spellman sought Vatican help in refuting him; Montini thought that "entering into controversy with a writer of this kind, thereby giving him further importance and publicity, would be of doubtful value at this time; and would in all likelihood bring about a new attack upon the Church, with the rallying again of its adversaries to his support". Blanshard objected to American citizens acting as diplomatic representatives of the Holy See. Montini commented that the way to avoid that charge was not to appoint Americans. See Gerald P. Fogarty, *The Vatican and the American Hierarchy*, p. 367.

2 Jacques Prévotat, "*Les Sources françaises de G. B. Montini*", in *Modernité*, p. 121.

> of the Lord, and that the rest of Christendom (*chrétienté*) will follow where France has gone.[1]

France, claimed ambassador-philosopher Maritain, evoked admiration and astonishment even as it disconcerted its friends by its pioneering boldness. Such arrogance was breathtaking. Yet Maritain did not even notice it.

Though Montini was well-disposed towards France he had little freedom and had to carry out orders. He used what discretion he could to modify or humanize the system.

Montini started off with the advantage of being considered pro-French. His translations of Maritain and Léonce de Grandemaison, the 1944 letter to Maurice Blondel, his appreciation of the abbé Godin's 1945 book, *France, Pays de Mission*, persuaded the French he was their friend. Though pro-French, Montini sometimes lost patience with their quarrelsomeness. "Of two theologically-minded Frenchmen," he told Guitton, "one is having an original idea and the other is on his way to Rome to denounce him."

This lesson was soon brought home to him. Montini used the French Jesuit Charles Boyer, Professor at the Gregorian University in Rome, as his contact man in matters ecumenical. This was logical enough. In 1945 Boyer had founded the *Foyer Unitas* in Rome as an ecumenical centre. The fourth floor of via Santa Maria dell'Anima 30 was soon known as "the Foyer Boyer". Boyer, a Toulousain, was pious, discreet and prudent, qualities needed in what was still often a cloak-and-dagger operation.

The French Dominicans judged Boyer a timid ecumenist inhibited by paranoiac caution, so "prudent" as to be motionless. They knew he had links with Montini. Their own experience of Montini was that though he might be well-disposed it fell to him to give them bad news or no news.

Thus on 21 May 1946 Montini told Yves Congar and Féret that Pius XII did not like what *Maison-Dieu*, the review of pastoral liturgy, had said about the new version of the Latin Psalter. Montini tried to explain the Pope's *mens* or mind: designed to be more accurate than the Vulgate, this new version was meant to be the harbinger of further improvements in the text of the Bible.

Their cold-waterish welcome of the new Psalter would have the effect of "putting a stop to further reforms". It would have helped if Montini had been able to explain that the Latin Psalter was one of the Pope's

1 Quoted by Emile Poulat, "*Chiesa e Mondo Moderno*", in *Pio XII*, ed. Andrea Riccardi, p. 298.

pet projects.[1] Yet he was not always so negative. In July 1947 he told Aimé Martimort, editor of *Maison-Dieu*, that the "teaching part of the Mass" would one day be in the vernacular. Martimort said that would take a hundred years. "No," said Montini, "a development that once would have taken a century can now be realized in twenty years."[2]

Montini oscillated. On 27 January 1947 he replied to Christophe-Jean Dumont OP about a memo on ecumenical matters. The letter is a model of bureaucratic evasiveness:

> Given the importance of your memorandum, I thought it my duty to lay it before the HF [Holy Father] who is thus informed of your efforts and your projects. Then I forwarded it to the appropriate dicastery for study and examination. Naturally, as is usual in such cases, I do not know what its fate will be.[3]

Dumont's memo was indeed important: it proposed the creation of a body in Rome which would specialize in dealing with non-Catholics and which would have corresponding bodies to carry out the same task on the local level. In other words Dumont was proposing the chrysalis of what, in 1961, would evolve into the Secretariat for Christian Unity. But in 1947 it simply disappeared into the maw ("the appropriate dicastery") of the Holy Office and got lost.

Montini and Maritain worked together to prepare an "oil on troubled waters" audience with Pius XII for French Dominicans Dominique Dubarle and Pierre Maydieu, chief editors of the Maison du Cerf, their Parisian publishing house. Back home they received a telegram from Pius XII blessing them and their work. They hastened to publish it to silence their detractors. It had, of course, been drafted by Montini. They were astonished to receive a letter from the Dominican Master-General, Emmanuel Suarez, explaining that the papal telegram should not be construed as "approval of everything published by the Editions du Cerf".[4]

At Easter 1947 lay theologian Etienne Gilson, worried by the threat of theological trials and condemnations that were in the air, met Montini and found him strangely unconcerned. In his judgement, "*L'Eglise condamne très peu.*" He disclaimed any inside knowledge of the 1942 con-

1 Giulio Nicolini, *Il Cardinale Domenico Tardini*, Messagero, Padua 1980, pp. 144–45.

2 Aimé Georges Martimort, "*Le rôle de Paul VI dans la réforme liturgique*", in the eponymous *Le rôle de G. B. Montini*, p. 59. The study day of which the book is the fruit was held at Louvain-la-Neuve, 17 October 1984.

3 *Modernité*, p. 70.

4 Etienne Fouilloux, "*Les débats ecclesiaux*", *Modernité*, p. 96.

demnation of the French Dominican Marie-Dominique Chenu's work, *Le Saulchoir: Une Ecole de Théologie*. Yves Congar, the source for these conversations, noted after a meeting with Suarez, the Dominican Master-General:

> Once something reaches the Holy Office, nothing more can be done. The HO controls everything, including the Secretariat of State and the Pope himself. That is why, as soon as the HO is involved, everyone in Rome is afraid – it doesn't matter whether they are Cardinal [Eugène] Tisserant or Msgr Montini.[1]

So to the young French Dominicans Montini appeared biddable but powerless. They wondered whose side he was on. Could they count on him to avert or draw off the thunderbolts?

Another French witness was the Oratorian Pierre Dabosville, university chaplain at the Sorbonne:

> It is difficult to give an idea of the impression made by this eminent prelate. He seems at first to hide behind his office. The Holy See's man listens to what his many visitors, often eminent and with heavy responsibilities, have to say. He listens and passes the information upwards. Will we manage to convey the whole of our message? . . . As we spoke his face was alive with intelligence and sympathy. No doubt we were meant to understand that behind the prudent referral of all questions to the judgement of the Holy Father, his tone was saying that he personally desired to guide and help us.[2]

That was the general French view at this time.

The "Anglo-Saxons" had another way of assessing Montini's importance. They looked not so much at his present as his potential authority. Gossip and rumour suggested that he would be the next-pope-but-one. Archbishop David Matthew, formerly auxiliary of Westminster and at this date (1949) Apostolic Delegate to East Africa, had introduced the Anglican theologian George Leonard Prestige to Montini. Mathew, who had a Dominican brother, Gervase, wrote to Prestige on St Stephen's Day 1949: "I am happy that everything went so well and particularly that you liked Msgr Montini. He (and in a sense he alone) is the key to the situation. It is difficult to overestimate his significance as he may so easily be Pius XIV."[3]

1 Ibid. p. 90.
2 Ibid. p. 89.
3 MS in Foreign Relations Office, Lambeth Palace.

By Pius XIV Archbishop Mathew meant the next-but-one successor to Pius XII. He was, of course, right about this but wrong in thinking that the name Pius had become inevitable. Anglicans, instructed by their Catholic friends about Montini's role, were flattered to be received by him at all and delighted to find him so friendly.

The first Anglican visitor was Canon Herbert Waddams on 23 February 1948. He was the Archbishop of Canterbury's secretary for foreign (that is ecumenical) relations.[1] The visit was arranged by Sir Victor Perowne, British Minister to the Holy See. Waddams was touched that Montini, though suffering from his usual bout of winter flu, got out of bed to see him at 6.30 in the evening. Montini listened carefully and then asked "whether I had any specific proposals to make or points to carry forward, or whether I simply wished to discuss the question in general". Waddams wanted closer consultations but otherwise had no very precise ideas in mind.

Montini asked him about Anglican participation in the Amsterdam Conference, coming that summer, which would set up the World Council of Churches (WCC), and about the Lambeth Conference, a gathering of 350–400 Anglican bishops later that year. Waddams found Montini knowledgeable about Anglican matters such as the South India scheme, a union of Anglicans and free churchmen which infuriated Anglo-Catholics. Montini also knew that the Archbishop of York had been to Yugoslavia and told Tito that Anglicans were much exercised about religious liberty for Roman Catholics there. Sir Victor Perowne was evidently doing his job.

It was Montini's habit (though Waddams was not to know this) to listen hard during the first part of an interview, and then to deliver his carefully prepared little speech. He now told Waddams that Catholics could never regard dogmatic questions as unimportant. He thought "co-operation" with other Churches should be "on the basis of the natural law". Difficulties in practical co-operation should be referred to the "experts", specifically to Fr Charles Boyer.

On his return Waddams should get in touch with Thomas Godfrey, Archbishop of Westminster; and Montini would be glad to meet George Bell, Bishop of Chichester, a key player on the ecumenical scene. Montini stressed, Waddams concluded, "his desire to see a spirit of charity and spoke of the many who were devoting themselves with many sacrifices

1 See Alberic Stacpoole OSB, "Cordial Relations between Rome and Canterbury", *One in Christ*, 1987, 3, pp. 212–34.

to the cause of unity. He said he prayed constantly for Unity and I said I did too and our prayers met in God."[1]

The great ecumenical question of 1948 had been barely touched upon. Should Catholics take part in the crucial Amsterdam conference? And if so, who? A list of fourteen names was circulating. The Archbishop of Utrecht, Cardinal Jan de Jong, wanted to see it and intimated that some names would be refused, "since their writings are under discussion". On 18 June 1948 the Holy Office issued a "note" saying that no Catholic could attend the conference without permission of the Holy See and that this permission would not be granted. However Boyer just "happened" to be in Amsterdam for a philosophy congress and although not a direct participant in the ecumenical meeting he was given a press pass, along with three other priests. Thus he observed the meeting from outside, made many contacts and returned to the Gregorian with a wodge of papers several inches thick.[2]

But two Amsterdam-linked events created a furore. As the assembly began Yves Congar, whose position-paper had been rejected by the Roman censors, said Mass in the church of St François Xavier in Paris. He explained that despite the official Roman ban on observers, "the 'no' said to the ecumenical movement and the Amsterdam assembly was not the Church's last word, and that there were positive aspects in our attitude".[3] Congar was already convinced that the ecumenical movement would overcome the doctrinal "indifferentism" that had spoiled its beginnings in the 1920s and that the Holy Spirit was at work in the growing-together process. That was a Catholic way of saying it was a Good Thing. But that was not a common Roman view in 1948.[4]

Much more disturbing was the extraordinary keynote speech of the Swiss–German theologian Karl Barth on 23 August 1948. Shaking his

1 Canon Waddams' report, dated 23 March 1948, is in the archives of the Council for Foreign Relations at Lambeth Palace. Other correspondence relating to his visit is in the same file.

2 Gustave Thils, *Histoire Doctrinale du Mouvement Oecuménique*, Paris and Louvain 1962, p. 98.

3 Margaret Nash, *The Ecumenical Movement in the 1960s*, Ravan Press, Johannesburg 1975, pp. 232–33.

4 It seems that Montini, still under the spell of Père Charles Boyer, had not yet assimilated Yves-Marie Congar's *Chrétiens désunis*. Reviewing it in *Theology*, January 1938, Anglican theologian A. G. Hebert said, "a knowledge of it ought to be presupposed in all future discussions about Christian unity. It contains what is usually missing in those discussions, *a positive doctrine of the visible unity of the Church*". The "Protestant" ecumenism then in vogue was an attempt to introduce a certain unity into an already existing diversity; Catholics start from already existing unity and integrate diversity within it. In 1950 Montini asked Congar for a copy of *Vraie et Fausse Réforme dans l'Eglise* as soon as it appeared. This was a mark of trust at a difficult time. See "*Ecclesiam Suam*", 1982, p. 179.

fist like some Old Testament prophet he urged them to put *God first*. They could only be saved by God's plan, not by some Marshall Plan of human concoction. The fact that Rome and the Moscow Patriarchate refused to take part in their conference should not worry the true followers of Jesus Christ. Perhaps it is providential that Rome and Moscow can agree on not wanting to know us. In subsequent interviews Barth went even further: "The Orthodox are cloudy and vague; there is nothing vague about the Romans – they have a self-sufficient smugness that fixes everything once and for all in juridical forms."[1]

Anglican Bishop Stephen Neill had been seconded to the newly-founded World Council of Churches in Geneva. A year after Amsterdam, in June 1949, he ventured to Rome and though he saw only Boyer, in his confidential report to the Archbishop of Canterbury he assessed Montini's position in the Curia:

> It seems clear to me that Fr [Charles] Boyer wishes to be, and to be regarded as, the ecumenical link in Rome. In my judgement it is desirable that Fr Boyer should be humoured in this estimate of his own position, but that at the same time we should not take it ourselves too seriously. There is no doubt that at the moment he is in a very strong position.
>
> He is in close touch with Montini, and Montini sees the Pope every day without exception. I have no doubt that my visit and my conversations with Fr Boyer will have been reported to him, and I have strong reason to think that Montini will have informed the Pope in person of them.
>
> On the other hand the present situation is precarious. The death of the present Pope is bound to produce an inner revolution. Pius XI trained the present Pope, and there has therefore been continuity of policy. The present Pope will leave no tradition behind him.
>
> It is almost certain that on his death Montini will fall from power, and there is no indication at all as to what situation will follow.[2]

But, as Neill pointed out, Pius XII was seventy-four and in good health. And Montini's fall, when it came in 1954, had other causes.

Neill wanted to know what Rome really thought about what he called the "French group", by which he meant chiefly the Dominicans

1 Thils, *Histoire Doctrinale*, p. 100.

2 Report on a visit to Rome by Bishop Stephen Neill, 13 June 1949. Archives of the Council for Foreign Relations, Lambeth Palace. Neill's papers are kept at Wycliffe College, Oxford.

like Yves Congar but also some Fourvière Jesuits like Jean Daniélou. Boyer gave a straight answer:

> I have not heard anything said by those in authority, but Père Congar has sometimes used words which, though not actually heretical, would not be approved by authority. He has suggested sometimes that there are things which Catholics might learn from Protestants, e.g. on the subject of Grace as a free gift. It is permissible to say that certain individual Catholics have not realized the fullness of Catholic doctrine, and such individual Catholics might learn from Protestants, but it is not permitted to suggest that there is any defect in Catholic doctrine as such or in Catholic apprehension of the faith. The present Pope is very watchful and very exacting (*très exigeant*) in all matters of faith and dogma.[1]

Bishop Neill concluded that action against the French theologians "could not be ruled out". It was already being prepared, as Montini well knew. In September 1948 Montini transmitted a papal blessing to a Gregorian University study week that was "a veritable war engine aimed at French theological thinking".[2] It was a dress rehearsal for *Humani Generis*, condemning among other things "false irenicism".

Despite these rumblings on the horizon Montini agreed to see the formidable figure of Dr George Leonard Prestige, noted patristic scholar and secretary of the Church of England's Council for Foreign Relations, and a future Canon of St Paul's. Prestige was sent by Geoffrey Fisher, Archbishop of Canterbury, to explore whether there were any common topics that could usefully be discussed. Boyer gave him the phone number of Msgr Walter Carroll, Montini's English-language secretary, an American. Prestige felt he was being vetted before being passed onwards and upwards.

Prestige's appointment was for 12 moon but so many people wanted to see Montini that he had to wait an hour and a half. Prestige's diary gives the best pen-portrait of him at this period:

> Then at 1.30, Montini. He struck me as shrewd, good and lovable; a man of deep kindliness, high intelligence, and real wisdom. Slight, not very tall; dark, alert and laugh-capable eyes, both penetrating and bird-like – a strong face but not in

1 Ibid. MS p. 3. This inability to learn from others was the mark of pre-conciliar thinking.

2 Etienne Fouilloux, "*G. B. Montini face aux débats ecclésiaux de son temps*", in *Modernité*, p. 93.

the *least* hard – and very calm too; a man looking older than his years. He spoke partly in French, partly in English, I mostly in English, but he seemed to understand me. He was friendly and gracious in the best sense, and I frankly liked him no end. Carroll was present, but hardly spoke. [He was just making sure Montini and I were understanding one another; and he translated Montini's final remarks on my memorandum.]

I spoke my usual piece again . . . We agreed that one must pray for reunion, and work for it by building up contacts and creating understanding. He asked how long I was staying – could he do anything for me in the way of contacts? I thanked him and said I'd really got about all the introductions I needed . . . I thought the interview impressive and important. We parted in most friendly courteous fashion. It was now ten to two o'clock.[1]

So Montini said farewell, in this private and personal encounter, to the 1940s, the most tumultuous decade he had so far lived through.

None of his ecumenical partners in dialogue ever doubted his intransigence about Catholic faith and doctrine; but he combined this with an openness which surprised or even astonished them. If Rome is tough, he told Roger Schutz and Max Thurian, the founders of Taizé, who first visited him on 6 June 1948, this is its special vocation, its particular contribution to the ecumenical chorus. "The Church is built on the rock of Peter," he told them, "and sometimes the rock is hard."

Once that was recognized, however, he insisted that the Catholic Church had to recognize the wrongs done by its members in history and today.[2] Historical "truth" was not something Rome had privileged access to. Catholics are wrong if they fail to make their truth understood and loved. If the Catholic Church showed more humility it would make a better impression on the non-Catholic communities.[3]

Montini was here preparing Roger Schutz and Max Thurian for their first ever audience with Pius XII the next day. He would let the Pope know what they had told him. He paused on his threshold and added:

1 Prestige's Diary is kept in Lambeth Palace Library. It is quoted by permission of his two daughters. Square brackets [ ] indicate afterthoughts. Further extracts can be found in my article, "An Anglican in Rome", *Tablet*, 17 January 1987, pp. 57–58.

2 There may have been a subtlety here. The members of the Church might be sinful, but the Church "as such" (*an und für sich*) was not. Karl Rahner fell foul of the Holy Office over just this issue and about this time. Towards *Sancta simul et semper purificanda* of *Lumen Gentium*. See Vorgrimler in Stacpoole, *The Council by those who were there*.

3 Max Thurian, "Paul VI et les observateurs au Concile Vatican II", in *Paolo VI e i problemi ecclesiologici*, pp. 250–51.

"Christ go with you; you pray for unity, we too would like to pray."[1]

Though all these meetings were hush-hush there were sometimes leaks. The meeting with Prestige had not gone unremarked. A Tyrolean newspaper, *Volksbote*, alleged he had proposed to Montini that Rome should take the lead in uniting the Churches. In no time Prague Radio was reporting that they had agreed to set dogmatic problems aside and concentrate on fighting Communism.[2] It was like a game of "Consequences". *Démentis* were issued. People believed what they wanted.

It may seem that Montini's mind was concentrated on European or even Italian problems in this post-war period. This was inevitable because this was where the intellectual battles were being fought at the time. But he was not narrow. His openness to the world of Islam is the least-known and most surprising aspect of his life at this period.

Montini's interest in Islam was kindled by Louis Massignon, a friend of Maritain's who had great influence on his thinking. Massignon, explorer and Arabist, had founded "Badaliya" at Damietta in Egypt, the place where St Francis of Assisi had tried to convert the Sultan, Malik-al-Kamil, in 1219. "*Amici nostri sunt, quos multum diligere debemus*" (They are our friends, whom we must greatly love), said Francis in his Rule. In the post-war world "Badaliya" was devoted to Muslim-Christian understanding at a time when Italian Christians were handicapped by the memory of their occupation of Libya, and French Christians were beginning to feel threatened in Algeria.

In Rome, Paris and elsewhere Massignon had founded "Badaliya" groups which met on Friday evenings for prayer in solidarity with Muslims. The Rome group was organized by Msgr Paolo Mulla, Professor of Islamic and Turkish studies at the Pontifical Oriental Institute, a convert from Islam after reading Maurice Blondel. Their aim, said Mulla in a letter to Giorgio la Pira, the future mayor of Florence, was to sympathize with "the suffering of these anonymous members of Christ, and join in their prayer to lead it towards the *per Dominum*".[3] Montini joined the group whenever he could, and so knew Massignon's thesis about "the triple inheritance of Abraham". In so far as it shares in "the faith of our father Abraham" Islam participates in true revelation.[4]

1 Ibid. p. 521.

2 Owen Chadwick, "The Church of England and the Church of Rome from the beginning of the Nineteenth Century to Today", in *Anglican Initiatives in Christian Unity*, Lectures delivered in Lambeth Palace Library, 1966, ed. E. G. W. Bill, SPCK 1967, p. 96.

3 Giulio Basetti-Sani, *Louis Massignon (1883–1962)*, Alinea, Florence 1985, p. 275. This is also the source for Montini's links with Massignon.

4 This bore fruit in *Nostra Aetate* of Vatican II in 1965: "Upon the Muslims, too, the Church looks with esteem . . . They strive to submit themselves to God's inscrutable decrees, just as did Abraham" (3).

But Montini had little time to spare for Muslim or any other prayer. Preparations for the Holy Year of 1950 were time-consuming. The man in charge of the arrangements for the Holy Year, in Roman parlance its Secretary-General, was Sergio Pignedoli, Montini's closest friend. The time of preparation was over. On Christmas Eve Pius XII, with three stout hammer blows, unsealed the "holy door" of St Peter's through which thousands of pilgrims would pass, thus inaugurating a new decade, the last of his pontificate.

15

Holy Year 1950: Between Triumphalism and Reform

> Msgr Montini, as assistant secretary of state, was actually below (Domenico) Tardini in the hierarchy, but most people credited him with having more influence, especially with the Pope. That belief accounted for the number of those wanting to see him and the fevered state of his waiting-room. He had the enviable but potentially inconvenient gift of making each visitor feel that he was the person Montini had been waiting all his life to talk to . . . The first time I went to see him a knowing friend advised taking along a packet of sandwiches "because if your appointment is 11 a.m. or later, you'll almost certainly miss your lunch".
>
> (FRANK GILES, *Sundry Times*, John Murray, 1986, pp. 107–8)

Msgr Giovanni Battista Montini suffered from being too popular. His regular access to Pius XII, it was believed, lent him extraordinary power. Yet he remained detached, untainted, uninfluenced by power. Where possible he used it to good purpose.

Thus with Sergio Pignedoli as his executive officer Montini masterminded the Holy Year or Jubilee of 1950. The tradition started in the time of Dante: Pope Boniface VIII decreed a Holy Year once a century in 1300; in 1343 Clement VI preferred twice a century and in 1470 Paul II halved that, settling for every twenty-five years: this set the twentieth-century pattern.

The Holy Year was based on the Jewish answer to land distribution problems: cancel debts and free Hebrew slaves. None of this was particularly evident in 1950. The Holy Year was seen rather as a less threatening alternative to "the-Council-that-never-was".

The idea of an Ecumenical Council of the Church – a Vatican II – was the pet project of Cardinal Ernesto Ruffini of Palermo, Sicily, who got Msgr Alfredo Ottaviani of the Holy Office to propose it to Pius XII in 1948. An exploratory commission was set up. Its Secretary-General,

Pierre Charles SJ, was an expert on missiology known for his extreme conservatism. Its purpose would have been to condemn contemporary errors such as "existentialism" and "polygenism" (the denial of the view that the whole of humanity were descended from the single pair, Adam and Eve). Jean-Paul Sartre illustrated "existentialism" while the gagged Jesuit paleontologist, Pierre Teilhard de Chardin, was the scapegoat for "polygenism".

After banishing errors from the world the proposed Council would prove to it that warring enemies could become brothers and sisters in Christ. And it would define the Assumption of Our Lady into heaven, body and soul, by acclamation.[1]

Sixty-five hand-picked bishops were consulted. They replied enthusiastically and it was evident that, should a Council be called, many other topics would have to battle their way on to the agenda. It all began to look too difficult and too expensive. So the idea of a Council was shelved, and during the Holy Year the Pope acting alone did what the Council would have done corporately – defined the Assumption and condemned contemporary errors. This confirmed the widespread but misguided view that anything a Council could do the Pope could do better, more economically and more effectively.

The projected Council of 1948 had been a Ruffini–Ottaviani scheme with which Montini had not been in sympathy. It was finally abandoned even before the start of the Holy Year. Giovanni Caprile drily remarks that the labours of the "Commission on Modern Errors" were not in vain, since the same errors cropped up again in *Humani Generis*.[2]

So instead of a *conciliar* event the Church in 1950 had a *papal* spectacular, the first in the era of the mass media. Yet it took aboard one major theme of the Council-that-never-was: it dramatized the unity of the Church after the last and most terrible "European civil war". Its theme was "*Il Grande Ritorno*" (The Great Return). But who was returning and to what? Catholics were returning to Rome and the Pope, conceived as the "lighthouse" in the tempest-tossed seas.

Rome was the still centre of the turning world. For Montini Rome was the "universal city" twice over: first as the city which "promoted the political union of peoples under the empire of law, and so of liberty, culture and peace"; and second as the heart of the Catholic Church and see of the Bishop of Rome. So the "sacred" vocation of Rome was founded upon its "secular" destiny, and grace built neatly on nature.[3]

1 For the "Council-that-never-was" see Giovanni Caprile SJ, *Il Concilio Vaticano II*, vol. I, part 1, *Annunzio e preparazione 1959–1960*, pp. 16–24.

2 Ibid. p. 28.

3 See Giovanni Coppa, "*La Meditazione su Roma di Giovanni Battista Montini*", in *Notiziario*, 20, p. 62.

The three millions who flocked to Rome to gain the Holy Year plenary indulgence[1] may not have been aware of such depths of meaning. The majority were Italians brought up on Mussolini's bombast about Rome as the centre of world civilization. But official estimates showed there came 570,000 other Europeans, 46,000 North Americans, 16,000 Latin Americans, 6400 Africans, 3460 Asiatics and 1350 from Oceania.[2] That was a good symbolic representation not of the strength of the local churches, but of their influence in Rome.[3]

It was a marvellous display of the Church triumphant marked by spectacular canonizations (Maria Goretti and Domenico Savio), a brand-new dogma, the Assumption of Our Lady body and soul into heaven (1 November), and condemnations *ad libitum* in the encyclical *Humani Generis*.

Montini kept in the background using the Holy Year to make contacts. He gave special attention to Vatican Radio, twenty years old in 1950. Still in the hands of the Jesuits under their new General, the austere Belgian John Baptist Janssens, by 1948 Vatican Radio was broadcasting in nineteen languages. The Holy Year Committee decided to mark the anniversary by offering a sum of money for the expansion of Vatican Radio. Dutch Catholics collected a million florins to buy a short-wave 100kw Philips transmitter for "the Pope's Radio". They presented Pius with a model of it. They were famous for their loyalty, docility and skill in propagating Philips.

Montini wrote about "The New Vatican Radio" in the Holy Year bulletin. His article offers a "theology" of Vatican Radio. There was a profound inner match, he noted, between "this marvellous vehicle of word and thought" and the very nature of the Church, "so that one can see in it a belated but nevertheless vitally important response to the constitutional premise on which the Church is based". Vatican Radio embodied and expressed the universality of the Catholic Church.[4] No doubt this was substantially true. But Vatican Radio provided only for

1 From 1500 onwards, just eight years after Christóbal Cólon's discovery of America, the plenary indulgence could be obtained in churches throughout the Christian world. But the lure of Rome remained.

2 Giancarlo Zizola, *Il Microfono di Dio*, p. 217.

3 Of the sixty-four bishops consulted for the 1948 project for a Council, twenty-seven came from Europe (with a Czech as the sole East European), nine from North America, eight from Asia, seven from Latin America and one (an Australian) from Oceania. The numbers were made up by Patriarchs and religious superiors. Caprile, *Il Concilio Vaticano II*, I, part 1, p. 20.

4 These two paragraphs are based on a lecture by Roberto Tucci SJ on the forty-sixth anniversary of the inauguration of Vatican Radio (12 February 1931), given to the Circolo di Roma, 18 January 1977.

one-way communication and thus left another aspect of the Church unexpressed.

Under Pius XII the Jesuits wielded great influence. Robert Leiber, Church History professor at the Gregorian, who had known Pius since Munich in 1924 and had been his wartime secretary, continued to be consulted. Giacomo Martegani, Editor of *Civiltà Cattolica*, saw the Pope every two weeks and reported his views to the *consulta*, the meeting of the writers' college. They then wrote the articles the Holy Father desired. That was the idea, at least. The minutes of these fortnightly discussions are a precious source for understanding Pius XII.[1]

However the *Civiltà* Jesuits were not just meekly doing the Pope's bidding: Martegani and his colleagues had "a political and cultural agenda that appeared only partially in the pages of the review".[2]

What were the Jesuits up to in the wings of history? Their view was that De Gasperi was weak, complacent and made too many concessions to the left. They tried to induce the right-wing parties, in particular the Monarchists or *Movimento Sociale Italiano* (MSI), to become "more Christian" in order to woo and win over the Vatican. In short they were intriguing with the right-wing opposition to De Gasperi, and casting about for an alternative. They were therefore opposed to the left-wing of the Christian Democrats – Montini's friends like Guido Gonella, Minister of Education since 1946, and Giuseppe Dossetti who in 1949 had argued for "factions" within Christian Democracy and lost.[3]

Dossetti and his friends turned the review *Cronache Sociali* into a laboratory of new political ideas. For De Gasperi the unity of the party came first and "factions" were ruled imperiously out. There was dissension among Montini's old friends and pupils. Padre Antonio Messineo, *Civiltà Cattolica*'s leading political columnist, thundered away against Jacques Maritain and Christian Democrats indiscriminately. But none of these low-laid schemes came to much in the Holy Year. They would have their hour later.

Also residing at *Civiltà Cattolica* was Riccardo Lombardi, the most celebrated preacher of the age, known without irony as "God's microphone". His brethren regarded him as a gifted if slightly crazed prima

1 Roberto Sani, "*Un Laboratorio politico e culturale, La Civiltà Cattolica*", in *Pio XII*, ed. Andrea Riccardi, pp. 409–36. Not enough attention has been paid to the "college" of Jesuit writers at *Civiltà Cattolica*. It was rather like All Souls, Oxford, a group of scholars without any students to teach. Though the dominant view was as described, there were independent spirits like Fr Angelo Brucculeri who were still highly regarded in the Vatican.

2 Ibid. p. 409.

3 Robert Leonardi and Douglas A. Wertman, *Italian Christian Democracy: The Politics of Dominance*, pp. 98–100.

donna. He had a habit of saying in his sermons "As Jesus said to me", though his influence came from the fact that he had the ear and the confidence of Pius XII. His success was phenomenal. Charismatic he certainly was. Visiting Austria and Germany he found he could speak German "charismatically", that is, without actually learning it. This method of learning languages did not work in the United States. But in Italy Communists tore up their party cards (*tessere*) at his bidding, enclosed nuns emerged from their convents to teach catechism in the "red belt" of Bologna, young people took vows of chastity. Lombardi was a maverick with a plan. A whole fistful of plans.

He unveiled them in the Holy Year, steadily progressing up the Vatican hierarchy until, on 15 June 1950, he found himself in Montini's office in the Secretariat of State. Lombardi had already disconcerted curial cardinals by his habit of enquiring what Jesus would have done had he been sitting in their place. Eugène Tisserant, Prefect of the Oriental Congregation, claimed to be doing his best for reform – but in the Holy Year felt he could do nothing since "all audiences were suspended".[1] They might be suspended for cardinals. But not for Montini.

Lombardi's other encounters with Roman cardinals brought no comfort. They give one some idea of the level of Pius XII's Curia. Giuseppe Pizzardo, Congregation of Seminaries: "The problem of the clergy in Latin America is very grave. We need proposals." Lombardi: "Not just in Latin America." Clemente Micara, Congregation of Rites, gave him a cold shower: "I just want to do the will of God . . . I'll try to talk to the Pope." Adeodato Piazza, Consistorial Congregation (episcopal nominations): "To cut down on the number of dioceses in Italy would cause popular revolts from which only the Communists would profit." Benedetto Aloisi Masella, Congregation of the Sacraments, "But where can we find the men to do all this . . . the cardinals are old and few in number." Massimo Massimi of the Segnatura thought family rosary and catechetical education in seminaries were the answer. Lombardi did not feel he was getting through.[2]

So Lombardi came to his most crucial encounter: Montini was already more important than any cardinal.

We have only Lombardi's account of this meeting. Going along "discreetly" at 6 p.m. when the offices were deserted, Lombardi outlined his plan of reform for Italy and the Church. His idea was that the Roman Curia should be presided over by a group of four "wise men" enjoying papal approval with full authority over the Roman Congregations, bishops, religious, Catholic Action; in short, everyone and everything.

1 Zizola, *Il Microfono di Dio*, p. 234.

2 Ibid. pp. 234–35.

Only in this way, Lombardi maintained, would the Church be able to "guide the world" and encompass the collapse of Communism which, he believed, was imminent.

Montini listened patiently. He doubted very much whether one should present Jesus as an "earthly saviour, because this might give rise to unrealizable hopes". He thought that priests should not have a political role in society. No one today wanted Prince Bishops or clerical rulers.

Montini was more sympathetic towards Lombardi's proposals for the Roman Curia because he knew how badly it needed reform. Lombardi's survey of curial opinion revealed that with its bureaucratic stick-in-the-mud habits (*immobilismo*) the Curia would be incapable of reforming itself. Prefects of Roman Congregations had no retirement age, so they lingered on like mediaeval barons, building up their clientèle. Their junior officials played safe by doing nothing.[1] Even the simplest reforms such as reducing the number of dioceses in Italy sent them into a tizzy. Montini had seen enough spiritual aridity in the Curia to know that Lombardi had a case.

But his scheme was too Pope-centred. It involved reform from the top brought about by the Pope and his four special advisers. Montini thought that any plan of reform should respect "the vital liberty" that the Church enjoys according to the divine plan. The normal way "reforms" come about is through pressure from what Pius XII himself had called "public opinion in the Church". Authority in the Church may then take up movements arising from below, testing whether they are in accord with the Gospel and with the Church's constitution. The would-be reformer should avoid too rigid centralization. Montini had been reading Congar's *Vraie et Fausse Réforme dans l'Eglise*, just out.

Montini had strong feelings on the way Pius XII ran his Curia. The lack of retirement age was the greatest weakness: it meant that cardinals were able to go on empire-building until they died. Montini liked Lombardi's idea of men in their energetic prime directing the Church's work: the two of them were instances of it. But it was not the way things were done: "People shouldn't have the right to promotion on the basis of past services. The criterion for jobs should be their objective capacities *now*. But the system in vogue under Pius XII is based on an excessive concern for personal feelings."[2]

Montini was more than willing to dispense with the papal court – the flunkeys, chamberlains and ostrich feathers – which he saw as relics from the days of temporal sovereignty. "They're like an old cloak," said

1 Giancarlo Zizola, *Il Microfono di Dio*, p. 230.
2 Ibid. p. 232.

Montini, "but they will have to go and one day a pope will get rid of that old cloak."[1]

These were trivial matters compared with the basic truth that "Christianity is only just beginning so long as a Christian society does not exist." He advised Lombardi to temper his "combative optimism" with a sense of "gradualism" (the step-by-step approach). "It's a good thing that such ideas should be spread around," Montini concluded, "they will bear fruit in due course."

It was important that in the midst of the triumphalist Holy Year Montini should be thinking of an alternative style of papacy. Lombardi was half-way through the door when Montini launched into a vision of what might be:

> Let the Pope leave the Vatican with all those in it, let him leave them with their stipends and go off, at least for certain periods, to St John Lateran; there he would live with his seminarians, with his people, with a new ritual . . . He could return to the Vatican from time to time. And in St John Lateran he would begin a new way of governing the Church, like Peter who was a poor man.[2]

Lombardi departed, moved, impressed but a little doubtful.

What he had heard was subversive. Yet there was something lacking in Montini's reformism. Lombardi contrasted his reticence with Cardinal Giacomo Lercaro's enthusiasm. With Lombardi's help Bologna had become "the capital of the revolt of good sense against the devil".[3] Lombardi confided to his diary: "Pius XII can only *begin* the reforms. It will be up to the next Pope to be a *true reformer*." He was right. But he was wrong about the candidate. "Lercaro will be the pope of the New World," he wrote.[4] Just as there was a Tardini–Montini contrast in the Vatican's diplomatic world, in the papacy stakes there was a Lercaro–Montini contest.

As though confirming the wisdom of Lombardi's suspicions Montini

1 Ibid. He used the metaphor again in 1962 in his pastoral letter, *Pensiamo al Concilio*.

2 Ibid. San Giovanni is the cathedral church of the Bishop of Rome, and Popes lived in the Lateran Palace until 1367 (when they were not in Avignon). St Peter's belonged to all Christian peoples but it was not the "pope's church". It seems extraordinary that this text, so important for understanding the pontificate of Pope Paul VI, should not have been published until 1990. Paul VI ordered the restoration of the "Hall of Emperors" at St John Lateran; it was first used on 29 June 1991 for a reception given by Cardinal Camillo Ruini, the newly appointed Vicar of Rome.

3 Ibid. p. 320.

4 Ibid. By "New World" Lombardi meant not the Americas but the movement he was busily launching. Picking up a phrase of Pius XII to the Catholics of Rome (12 February 1952) he eventually called it the "Better World Movement".

had second thoughts the moment he left. He wrote the same evening begging Lombardi "not to make any use of what I said to you. I want to think these things through and pray a little."[1]

If Lombardi told his fellow-Jesuits at *Civiltà Cattolica* the news would soon be all over the Curia. Cardinal Francesco Marchetti Selvaggiani, Vicar of Rome, was such a "great friend of the Jesuits" that he decreed in his will that he be buried in a Jesuit cemetery.[2] He had combined with the *Civiltà Cattolica* Jesuits to get Montini ousted in 1933. A man of the extreme right, he had reconciled Action Française in 1939.[3] Now a shadow of his former self he soldiered manfully on with a gammy leg, ran the diocese of Rome from his office, and was grateful in the 1950s to have as his auxiliary Clemente Micara, a "great builder". This was just what Rome needed in the 1950s as Italy's "economic miracle" took off and the city extended devastatingly over the Campagna.

It was the "American era" in the Church. Evelyn Waugh saw Thomas Merton's conversion and autobiography (*Seven-storey Mountain*) as evidence of a religious revival.[4] But it was thin. Any Hollywood star that could claim some vestigial Catholicism went to Rome to collect the jubilee indulgence and to scoff at Maria Goretti, the thirteen-year-old virgin canonized amid great pomp. For a brief Roman holiday they could ignore the fact that in Korea the cold war had turned hot, while a tiny Pacific atoll called Bikini was devastated in the first hydrogen bomb tested.

The "American era", however, did not include Latin America, potentially the most "Christian" of the continents. Each episcopal conference, if there were one, was supposed to appoint a Secretary-General to organize the pilgrimage to Rome. Brazil named Dom Helder Câmara Pessoa. Ordained in 1931 he was one of the founders of the October Legion, a Brazilian Fascist movement that admired the European dictators for their stress on national unity, spiritual rebirth and anti-Communism. An expert on pedagogy, Helder Câmara had worked at the Ministry of Education. He had not yet discovered the "option for the poor".[5] He

1 Ibid.

2 Giacomo Martina SJ, *Revista di storia della Chiese in Italia*, January–June 1965.

3 Letter to Cardinal Verdier, 10 May 1939. Archives of Paris archdiocese. Quoted by Andrea Riccardi, *Pio XII*, p. 86.

4 For the British edition Waugh cut the book by a third and gave it a new title, *Elected Silence*, based on G. M. Hopkins' poem, "The Habit of Perfection": "Elected silence, sing to me, and beat upon my whorlèd ear."

5 Dom Helder Câmara's past is usually suppressed. Not, however, by Alistair Kee, *Marx and the Failure of Liberation Theology*, pp. 146–56. He went on to be Archbishop of Olinde and Recife in north-east Brazil.

was advising the Nuncio, Msgr Carlo Chiarlo, Montini's old *bon viveur* superior in Poland, when he was asked to lead the Holy Year pilgrimage to Rome.

Helder Câmara scrounged a battered old troopship from his government, packed it to the gunwales with 1350 people (it was meant to take 800) and preached vigorous sermons on deck, which converted at least some of the prostitutes who had come aboard thinking it the easiest way to get to Paris.[1] It was the first time Helder Câmara and most of his shipmates had left Brazil. He did not meet Montini at this point but the story of his heroic expedition went the rounds.

The encyclical *Humani Generis* appeared out of a clear blue sky on 12 August 1950. It merited the overworked phrase "theological bombshell". Though it may not have meant much to the pilgrims flocking to Rome for the Holy Year, theologians found it heart-breaking. It named no names but, as the example of *Pascendi* in 1907 proved, anonymity merely meant that everyone was under suspicion until the contrary was proved. *Humani Generis* was a catch-all net designed by the political and theological right-wing[2] to entangle anyone linked, however tenuously, with *la nouvelle théologie* developed by the French Dominicans and Jesuits.

All the French theologians Montini admired felt incriminated by *Humani Generis*, and they were not mistaken for very soon it was followed by "disciplinary measures" which threw them out of their professorial posts and in some cases exiled them. It was the most drastic and embarrassing action of Pius XII's pontificate. Its timing was particularly shrewd: in the middle of August when theologians were on holiday and could not organize protests (Congar was in Greece); and in the middle of the Holy Year when the complaints of intellectuals would seem churlish amid so much populist enthusiasm for the papacy.

It is hard to imagine Montini actually wanting *Humani Generis* or thinking it necessary. Yet on 8 September 1950 in the first of his annual conversations with the French thinker and pundit Jean Guitton he constructed a defence of the encyclical that is chiefly remarkable for its

1 Dom Helder Câmara, *Conversations with a Bishop: An Interview with José de Broucker*, Collins 1979, pp. 129–30.

2 Former Vichy supporters now got their revenge on the Lyons Jesuits Henri de Lubac and Gaston Fessard. The non-historical Thomists like Réginald Garrigou-Lagrange, the Angelicum's leading dogmatic theologian, who considered Jacques Maritain jumped up and dangerous, renewed the attacks on Marie-Dominique Chenu and Le Saulchoir. It is significant that Montini did not think it worth keeping any books of Garrigou-Lagrange in his library (see Jacques Prévotat, "Les Sources Françaises de G. B. Montini", in *Modernité*), and that the student Karol Wojtyla of Kraków did his thesis on St John of the Cross with this learned Dominican.

ingenuity.[1] Guitton said French intellectuals were distressed at the apparent anti-intellectual tone of the encyclical. Montini answered:

> I know what you mean. But [pause] just listen for a moment. At first some French Catholics may have had the impression you say they have. But I'm sure this impression will soon be dissipated. Anyway, we will be working to dissipate it. *Humani Generis* issues certain warnings. It sets limits, to left and right, so that one may go forward along the road of progress in safety, knowing that the sources are pure, so that a new age of cultural progress may be opened up for the Church. I would say it opens up a royal way, that is, an open and sure way (*une voie ouverte et sûre*).[2]

So *Humani Generis* does not mean what it appears to mean. What Montini provides is a how-to-read guide, a hermeneutic, if you will.

The first thing to note, he says, is that *Humani Generis* does not speak of errors (*errores*) but of opinions (*opiniones*). He claims this means that "the Holy See is not condemning errors *as such* but ways of thinking (*modes de pensée*) that *could* lead to errors but which in themselves remain respectable". He makes a distinction, not easy to grasp, between the duties of the French bishops who have *pastoral* care for their flock, and "Rome" which must be concerned with the purity of doctrine and keeping "the deposit of faith".[3]

Even so, Montini insists, the *tone* is so very different from *Pascendi*: "Indeed one could say that the Holy Father's intention is to avoid the need for another *Pascendi*. The Holy See would prefer to say nothing at all, but it cannot surrender this duty."[4]

This was rather muddled. Montini was a little clearer on why *Humani Generis* objected to attacks on Thomism:

> Thomism seems to us, from a pastoral and ecclesiastical point of view (especially in clergy education) to be an approximation to the "eternal philosophy". That is why we deplore the unjust

1 Jean Guitton, *Paul VI secret*, pp. 38–44. It repeats the version of their first conversation given in an earlier book, *Dialogues avec Paul VI*, 1967. There is however one difference: in 1967 the interview ends thus: "He vanished. Three o'clock was striking. The sun began to decline: The morning was finished" (p. 12). In 1979 he concludes: "He tells me that 8 September will always be an important date in his life. He gives me his blessing. It is ten past two" (p. 44). Since Guitton had the unrealized pretension of doing for Paul VI what Boswell did for Samuel Johnson (or, as he puts it, what Eckermann did for Goethe) one can never be sure how "creative" his reporting was.

2 Ibid. p. 39.

3 Ibid.

4 Ibid. p. 41.

> attacks of which Thomism has been the object and which give the impression that Thomism is merely a mediaeval philosophy, now completely *dépassée* and entirely explicable in terms of its sources.[1]

So much for scholars like Etienne Gilson and Marie-Dominique Chenu OP who had toiled to give Aquinas an historical context, which added to his prestige and made him more intelligible. Montini shows little understanding of this.

Guitton then asked about Henri de Lubac SJ, the Fourvière (Lyons) professor, famous in France as an anti-Nazi and leading intellectual. To sack him seemed sheer folly. Montini replied:

> We know him well, and you may be sure that Père de Lubac will do great things for the Church. We know all about his learning, his virtues and his influence. His thought is not in itself worthy of condemnation, but it has been deformed by some of his disciples. The return to the Fathers, especially the Greek Fathers, that Père de Lubac proposes is excellent; but given the nature of the human mind, in certain young religious it might have led to an anti-intellectualism which is regrettable, as well as to a mistrust of the present-day *magisterium* to which they prefer the study of the Greek Fathers, a complex and diverse realm in which anyone can project and find what he brings.[2]

Montini's apologia for *Humani Generis* is unconvincing. He must have known this himself for as soon as he was in a position to do so he remedied the injustices of the encyclical. But loyal as ever to Pius XII he became its apologist.

Yet only a month or so before, on 21 June 1950, he had remarked cryptically to Roger Schutz and Max Thurian of Taizé, the Protestant co-founders of monastic life near Cluny: "War, peace, respect, invitation:

1 Ibid. p. 43.

2 Ibid. As one of the "young religious" who fell under the spell of Henri de Lubac, I can truthfully report what blush-bringing nonsense this whole passage is. Who would not prefer the Greek Fathers to the *magisterium*, if *Humani Generis* is the most recent instance of it? The scrupulously scholarly approach of de Lubac and the Fourvière school which searched through *the whole* of Christian tradition, giving a privileged but not an exclusive place to St Thomas, was in stark contrast with current Roman requirements. In his Rules for Thinking with the Church, 11, St Ignatius said "we should praise both positive theology and the Scholastics". By "positive theology" he meant the Fathers of the Church who "rouse the affections so that we are moved to love and serve the Lord our God in all things". The Scholastics had the merit of clarity, and helped to "refute errors and expose all fallacies".

we must go further . . . *we* must go *towards you*."[1] But then, meeting the Lyons Marist Maurice Villain on 23 September 1950, he seemed ice-cold and two-faced. "He tried to leave me not a leg to stand on in the difficult situation created by the encyclical," said Villain, "and wanted very much to show his agreement with its severity towards the French."[2]

Did the Assumption, defined with much pomp on 1 November, the feast of All Saints 1950, involve him in similar gyrations of conscience? It was controversial for a variety of reasons. It raised the question of the relationship between the *magisterium* and history, and of tradition and Scripture. It stood out as an additional and unnecessary barrier to ecumenism. It seemed a gauntlet thrown down to the modern world. The definition of the Assumption, declared Cardinal Giuseppe Siri of Genoa, commonly held to be Pius XII's dauphin, "was an act of courage by which the Pope challenged with an infallible definition a world that preferred film stars and sporting heroes to true teachers".[3]

It is hard to believe that Montini saw the definition of the Assumption in that light, as an act of ecclesiastical self-assertion. It is more likely that he shared the view of the Theology Faculty of the Catholic University of Milan which, with its Benedictine Archbishop, Cardinal Ildefonso Schuster, thought the definition "inopportune" for ecumenical reasons.[4]

Ten years later Montini reflected on one "doubt" about the definition that had been rarely articulated. Many judged that Vatican I, by exalting the power of the papacy, had annihilated the effective authority of the bishops. No more councils would be needed, since anything a council could do the pope could do on his own.

The definition of the Assumption seemed to confirm this judgement on the irrelevance of councils and the collegial principle in the Church. Yet Montini used it to prove the contrary since "before undertaking this act of his supreme teaching office, Pius XII of venerated memory wished to consult all the episcopates to find out whether the truth to be defined

1 Etienne Fouilloux, "*G. B. Montini face aux debats ecclesiaux de son temps*", in *Modernité*, p. 93.

2 Ibid. This is the most hostile portrait of Montini ever drawn. Maurice Villain adds that he pushed the identification with Pius XII so far that the "*sostituto*" "substituted himself for the Pope".

3 Giuseppe Siri, address in St Peter's on the twenty-fifth anniversary of Pius XII's death, 8 October 1983, p. 4.

4 See Antonio Rimoldi in the discussion in *Montini Arcivescovo*, p. 303. Rimoldi says that Milan was the only Faculty of Theology to fail to request the definition. Carlo Colombo wrote interestingly diverse articles in *Scuola cattolica* before and after the definition.

was a matter of the faith of the Church".[1] It was not quite, however, an instance of "collegiality", since Pius consulted the bishops one by one, individually and by correspondence. There was no common process out of which a common mind might have emerged.

Yet by taking the initiative in consulting the bishops, which he did not strictly need to do, Pius showed he wanted to draw them into a quasi-collegial process. "The more the head recognizes himself as the head," Montini concludes, "the more does he feel the need to join himself to the members and to celebrate with them the mystery of the one organic life of the entire ecclesiastical body".[2]

Fine and edifying: but this remained a top-down view of the papacy that was soon to be challenged.

Montini himself added a nuance by organizing the first systematic form of consultation with lay people in the Church in modern times. The First World Congress of the Lay Apostolate was scheduled for 1951. In those days clergy were divided into those who thought the laity were there "to hunt, to entertain, and to pay up" (in the immortal words of Msgr Talbot) and those used to taking the laity seriously as partners in the apostolate. Montini, with his FUCI experience, was used to working with the educated laity.

On 19 December 1950 Montini addressed the preparatory meeting for the Laity Congress and stressed that "catholicity" was now an international concept:

> Today all human activity tends towards the international level, and the same should be true of the apostolate of the laity. But there are also more important and loftier reasons why the Church invites you to work on the international level: the aim is to extend the boundaries of charity (*élargir les frontières de la charité*). The Church wonders: will all these volunteers who have come to join the hierarchy be capable of inaugurating the festival of charity?[3]

1 Giovanni Battista Montini, *Discorsi e scritti sul Concilio*, p. 46. This came in a lecture, "*I Concili ecumenici nella vita della Chiesa*", given at Passo della Mendola, 16 August 1960.

2 The date of Montini's lecture was 1960, after the announcement that there would be another Vatican Council. So perhaps he was trying to defend Pius XII against the charge of acting "unilaterally" and imposing his own views on the Church. But the language is obscure. Looking forward, this discussion foreshadows Montini's agonizing over the *Nota Praevia* to *Lumen Gentium* and, even further ahead, *Humanae Vitae*.

3 Rosemary Goldie, "*Paul VI, les laïcs et le laïcat*", in *Modernité*, pp. 296–97. At about the same time, Pierre Teilhard de Chardin, friend of Henri de Lubac, was developing similar exciting thoughts about increasing interdependence and growing complexity ushering in a "new order" of human relationships. But Teilhard said it in

This is an instance of the way Montini could transform a bureaucratic arrangement (organizing a congress) into a spiritual truth. At the same time he is still, like Pius XII, using "Church" as a synonym of the hierarchy within Catholicism.[1]

This preliminary meeting on the Laity Congress brought Dom Helder Câmara back to Rome, bursting with ideas as usual. He noted that most of the position-papers for the Laity meeting ended with the formula: "None of this will be possible or effective unless there is a conference of Bishops in Brazil."[2] Helder Câmara determined to get the Holy See to set up a Brazilian episcopal conference. Knowing little about Rome he consulted his Nuncio, Msgr Carlo Chiarlo, who wisely told him Montini was the man to see. But Montini was very busy and kept Helder Câmara hanging about for several days until he received the curt summons: "Msgr Montini will receive you at the Vatican at 1 p.m. on 21 December."

Helder Câmara went along, worried about his rusty French and half-deaf from a bloody ear later diagnosed as "an incipient rupture of the ear-drum".[3] But Montini charmed him:

> I discovered that the reason Montini had delayed the interview was so that he would have time to study all the documents on the apostolate of the laity that I had sent him through the diplomatic bag – all of which concluded by saying that a national conference of bishops was essential. He could read Portuguese without difficulty.
>
> Strange how diplomats never cease to be diplomats . . . After we had been talking for half an hour, Mgr Montini decided to test me. Or at least that was how I interpreted his question: "Monsignor, I am now convinced of the necessity, indeed the urgency, of setting up a Brazilian national conference of bishops. But one thing troubles me. This is a conference of *bishops*. But from everything I have heard and from everything I know, the secretary of this conference of bishops has to be you, Padre Helder Câmara. No one else could do it. You are the natural choice for the position. But you are not a bishop . . ."
>
> He was trying to find out if there was some ulterior motive behind my plan – to see if I were putting myself forward as a

evilly printed mimeographed *samizdat MSS*; Montini's words went straight into *L'Osservatore Romano*.

1 See *Mystici Corporis*, 1943, and, of course, *Humani Generis*, which echoed it.

2 *Mystici Corporis*, p. 131.

3 *Conversations with a Bishop*, p. 134.

> candidate for the episcopacy. So I replied: "Forgive me, Msgr Montini, but you should not worry about that. Unless I am mistaken you are not a bishop, and yet in your work at the Secretariat of State the Lord uses you, in the service of the Holy Father, as a link between all the bishops of the world. So why should I not serve Christ and his Church by acting as a link between a small group of bishops in a little corner of the world – without being a bishop myself?" Msgr Montini smiled. After that we were friends.[1]

Helder Câmara was talking to José de Broucker early in 1976, so he may have unconsciously edited his memories to cope with the fact that Montini had in the meantime become pope. But it is a fact that Montini was instrumental in setting up the Brazilian Episcopal Conference in 1952 and that Fr Helder Câmara was its first General Secretary from 1952 to 1964, when Paul VI named him Archbishop of Olinde and Recife.

If Brazil needed an Episcopal Conference, then so did other Latin American countries, and once they were in place it was logical to proceed to the Council of Latin American Episcopal Conferences (CELAM) which was set up in 1955. So much depended on this meeting at the end of the Holy Year 1950. Next time Montini met Helder Câmara they would no longer be strangers. Already Montini liked Dom Helder's lack of fussiness and disdain for ecclesiastical honours. Whereas others saw him as a diplomat, Helder Câmara saw him as "a link between all the bishops of the world".

It was Christmas. The "holy door" in St Peter's was sealed up until 1974. Montini set off on Christmas Day along the Tiber to Trastevere to visit an old friend – a priest who had abandoned his ministry. He was living in great poverty; according to the Concordat lapsed priests could not be employed as teachers or in any government post. "I thought you'd be alone today," said Msgr Montini, the man closest to the Pope, "so I thought I'd visit you." They shared a frugal meal.[2] It was reminiscent of the closing chapter of Georges Bernanos' novel, *Le Journal d'un curé de Campagne.*

1 Ibid. pp. 132–33.

2 Daniel-Ange, *Paul VI, un regard prophétique*, p. 64.

16

Apogee and Fall
(1951–1954)

> Old people today shake their heads and ask, just what do these young people want? . . . They want to be sustained by the understanding of their fathers. Yet today's world is a world without fathers, and where fatherhood is lacking, paternalism takes over.
>
> (MARIO V. ROSSI, "*Queste generazioni nuove*", in *Gioventù*, XXX, 1953, p. 154)

Mario Rossi, author of these lines, succeeded Carlo Carretto as head of Catholic Youth Action (GIAC) in 1952. It was a papal appointment which meant that Msgr Giovanni Battista Montini was involved and that Rossi could not resign. They became very close, "thick as thieves" said their numerous enemies. The critique of "paternalism" in the writings of this period is really a critique of Fascism. Rossi says "dictatorships came from paternalism gone wrong". Their blood fathers were disgraced or dead, and if still present were discredited.[1]

By contrast Montini, now a skilled pedagogue, was a non-suspect, non-threatening father for young people like Mario Rossi. Unlike the literal fathers of the students of the 1950s he had opposed Fascism, and unlike them he knew how to leave an area of freedom – that freedom which is essential to the act of faith. Another generation was grateful to their spiritual father, while he was consoled by a spiritual paternity that made celibacy tolerable.

But such "liberal" ideas ran counter to the dominant line of Catholics in the pontificate of Pope Pius XII. Dr Luigi Gedda was still in charge of Catholic Action and his star was in the ascendant. His mission was to keep the Communists permanently out of power and prevent the Cossacks from watering their horses in St Peter's Square – a recurrent nightmare that haunted the Pope. To avert it and with the help of the

1 Maria Cristina Giuntella, "*Cristiani nella Storia, Il 'caso Rossi' e suoi reflessi nelle organizzaoni cattoliche di massa*", in *Pio XII*, ed. Andrea Riccardi, pp. 348–77.

CIA Gedda turned the parish churches of Italy into recruiting centres for the Christian Democrats, made parish priests its agents and thus "delivered" the Catholic vote. Fr Riccardo Lombardi ("God's microphone"), the Jesuit charismatic preacher, brought the same message to the streets and squares of Italy. Lombardi, as we have seen, was full of plans for reforming the Church and still had access to Pius XII.

Montini, Rossi, FUCI and the *Laureati* had a different view of Catholic Action and of how Christians should relate to the "world". The Church for them was not a mass movement in which individuals were lost. It was rather a community of common endeavour in the intellectual and spiritual sphere. Priests like Montini preferred to tutor talented individuals than to address vast crowds in demagogic fashion. *Witness* rather than *conquest* was their watchword. The "green berets" Gedda organized were all too reminiscent of Fascist youth movements, as was the slogan "Rome or Moscow".

Rossi accepted the "autonomy" of politics view of De Gasperi, though he was now out of favour with the Vatican: the Church's influence should be indirect – through *the action of Catholics* rather than *Catholic Action*. Italian Catholic Action divided people horizontally into age groups. Rossi was attracted by the French approach which stressed the apostolate of the like by the like, *milieu* by *milieu*. There were, in short, two models of the Church which worked out as two ways of doing politics. Inevitably opponents of the official Catholic Action line were accused of élitism. Cardinal Giuseppe Pizzardo, Secretary of the Holy Office, opened a file on Rossi which stressed not so much his "doctrinal deviations", though his friendship with banned French Dominicans such as Marie-Dominique Chenu and Yves-Marie Congar made him suspect, as his deviations from the Gedda line.[1] Pizzardo did not need to open a file on Montini: his dossier was already bulky.

Montini felt growing unease with the policies he was obliged to implement towards De Gasperi and the Christian Democrats. To ensure the defeat of the Communists Pius XII wanted the Christian Democrats to ally themselves with the extreme right-wing including the Neo-Fascists. This was contrary to all their traditions. The conflict came to a head in the spring of 1952 when the Communists devised a neutral list of moderate candidates for the Rome city council headed by F. S. Nitti, a veteran statesman of unimpeachable integrity. The right-wing parties warned Pius that if this move were not stopped the red flag would soon be flying over the Campidoglio, Rome's city hall.

To counter this threat the Pope got Gedda to prepare a spoiling "civic list" of his own, made up of acceptable non-Christian Democrats.

1 Ibid. pp. 350–6.

He made clear his belief that the Christian Democrats should ally themselves with the extreme right, including the neo-Fascists of MSI (Movimento Sociale Italiano). *L'Osservatore Romano* beat this drum, an attempt was made to persuade the veteran anti-Fascist Don Luigi Sturzo to support it, and the Christian Democrats were faced with the dilemma of denying their past traditions and allying themselves with the most reactionary forces in Italy, or being superseded by Gedda's list.

This manoeuvre (known as "operation Sturzo") was aimed at De Gasperi. Riccardo Lombardi was used to pressurize him. On Thursday, 12 April 1952 Lombardi arrived at De Gasperi's apartment, via Gregorio Settimo, hardly noticing the picture of St Theresa of Lisieux holding a bunch of roses that dominated the entrance hall. Lombardi came straight to the point: "I've come in obedience to a clear mandate from the Holy Father . . . If Rome elected a Communist mayor democratically, that would be a shame and scandal (*vergogna*) for the Church, for the Pope, for the whole anti-Communist world and so also for Christian Democracy and the government."[1]

De Gasperi said that if the Pope *ordered* him to enter into the proposed arrangement he would obey. But not otherwise. He would accept no form of co-operation with the MSI. Lombardi, whose powers of self-deception were considerable, thought he had persuaded De Gasperi to give way.[2]

That version, based on Lombardi's diary, appeared only in 1990. An earlier account by De Gasperi's daughter Maria is more brutal:

> In the course of an hour and a half, Fr Lombardi went from flattery to threats . . . He said things like: "The Pope would rather see Stalin and his Cossacks in St Peter's Square than the Communists victorious in the elections to the Campidoglio. Take care, for if the elections go badly we shall make him [i.e. my father] resign.[3]

In the end "operation Sturzo" was abandoned and the Christian Democrats won the day in Rome unaided. It was much ado about nothing.

But henceforward De Gasperi was regarded as a rebel, and when he asked for an audience on the thirtieth anniversary of his marriage, which was also the anniversary of his daughter Lucia's becoming a nun, he was refused. Montini felt the injustice of this but could do nothing about

1 Giancarlo Zizola, *Il microfono di Dio*, p. 300.

2 Ibid. pp. 300–1.

3 Carlo Falconi, *The Popes in the Twentieth Century*, p. 275.

it.[1] Rossi diagnosed in him a conflict between "faithfulness to a regime of absolute power and the need to rebel against it".[2]

At the time it was difficult, indeed impossible, to distinguish between politics and theology. Msgr Alfredo Ottaviani, all-powerful at the Holy Office, boasted that "you can say whatever you like about the divinity of Christ but if, in the remotest village in Sicily, you vote Communist, your excommunication will arrive the next day".[3] The hard line prevailed both theologically and politically. So long as the Dominican Mario Cordovani was alive there was a counterweight to Ottaviani. But on his death in 1950 Ottaviani was the unchallenged master of the Holy Office.[4] The paradox was that while Montini was being reproached for his French contacts, *they* were feeling disappointed in him, either because of *Humani Generis* or because of the condemnation of the priest-worker movement, already brewing, for which they held him responsible.

Of all the French theologians silenced by *Humani Generis* Henri de Lubac was the closest spiritually to Montini. Montini did not join the pack in comdemning him, but neither did he dissent from the condemnation.[5] De Lubac's response to his silencing was magnificent. He wrote a *Meditation on the Church* (1953) in which his love for the Church shone forth on every page. It put one in mind of the remark of Humbert Clérissac OP, quoted by Georges Bernanos: "It is easy to suffer for the Church: the difficult thing is to suffer at the hands of the Church."

"*The Meditation on the Church* was very dear to Msgr Montini," says Giacomo Martina SJ, "and his copy eventually became dog-eared."[6]

1 Ten years after the death of de Gasperi, Montini, by then Pope Paul VI, sent a signed portrait to the De Gasperi family with a message that was both an apology and a benediction: "To the family of the regretted Alcide de Gasperi, on the tenth anniversary of this exemplary man, this sincere Catholic, this strong and free statesman who by his example, words and actions wisely guided Christian Democracy towards its mission for the civil prosperity and the social order of the Italian people, and upon the ruins of war led us to peaceful reconstruction and international status, a remembrance and paternal blessing from the heart." *L'Osservatore Romano*, 19 August 1964.

2 Mario V. Rossi, *I Giorni della Onnipotenza*, p. 117.

3 Sandro Magister, *La politica vaticana*, p. 52.

4 Andrea Riccardi, *Pio XII*, p. 41.

5 In his eighties de Lubac, by then a cardinal, claimed that he had been silenced not by the Holy Office but by the Jesuit General, Fr John Baptist Janssens, "to protect him from further trouble". This comforting theory found its way into Avery Dulles' obituary of de Lubac in *America*. In April 1965 Père de Lubac told me that at the height of the crisis he received two sets of letters from Janssens, the first communicating the decisions of the Holy Office, and the second offering encouragement and signed "your old friend, J-BJ". This did not comfort de Lubac. "If Janssens really believed that," he said, "he should have defended me more stoutly."

6 Giacomo Martina in *Vatican II, Assessments and Perspectives*, Paulist Press, Mahwah 1988, p. 36.

It made a deep impression not only because of its vast patristic learning but above all for its deep *sensus ecclesiae* (an instinctive feel for what the Church really is). That one could suffer at the hands of the Church, as de Lubac undoubtedly had, and yet remain so free of bitterness and uncomplainingly loyal was indeed very remarkable. De Lubac's lesson was to stand Montini in good stead when a year later he was "exiled" to Milan.

Americans did not so much suffer for the Church as pay for it. They represented "modernity" with a price-tag. The "American era" took shape as real estate in Rome. In 1953 a magnificent new North American College rose on the Gianiculum from which the dome of St Peter's could be descried. It replaced the historic but shabby building on via dell'Umilità that now became the graduate student college. The new North American College could accommodate over 200 students destined, if they were lucky, to be bishops.

Cardinal Samuel Stritch's speech at the opening ceremony of the new North American College on 16 October 1953 was deliberately controversial. Stritch included a sentence about "American" values: "For us our country is above everything else a land of free men, conscious of their rights and dignity, collaborating together in a common spirit for the good of all."[1]

This upset Ottaviani: Stritch could be held to have contradicted or at least "gone beyond" the official position of the Church on freedom of religious propaganda and Church–State relations. To "go beyond" current teaching was almost as heinous as to dissent from it. But the Curia was not unanimous on Church–State relations. Montini assured Stritch that he had a perfect right to hold such views, and that Ottaviani was merely expressing a personal opinion and not official Church teaching. As Gerald P. Fogarty, leading historian of Vatican–USA contacts put it, "the Pope's utterances seemed to reflect whoever got his ear, men like Ottaviani or men like Montini. For the next few weeks, it appears as if the Pope listened more to Montini."[2]

But appearances could prove deceptive and it did not help that Claire Booth Luce, a spectacular convert to Catholicism and wife of the publishing tycoon Henry B. Luce, co-founder of *Time* magazine, now arrived as US Ambassador to the Republic of Italy (1952–57). No liberal, she

1 Gerald P. Fogarty SJ, *The Vatican and the American Hierarchy*, p. 376.

2 Ibid. p. 379. Montini's influence allegedly appeared in *Ciriesce*, an allocution to Italian jurists, 6 December 1953, which seemed to call for the recognition of pluralism not only between states but within them. But there was controversy about its exact meaning.

Above: Giovanni Battista's birthplace at Concesio, a village five miles north of Brescia. He was baptized the next day at the village church, a hundred yards down the road to the left.

Right: Battista's paternal grandmother, the determined Francesca Buffali, widowed at 36, who brought up six surviving children single-handedly. Battista is in the centre, Lodovico on the right.

Below: A Montini family holiday; Giorgio, father; Battista; Giuditta, mother; Lodovico, elder brother; and Francesco, younger brother.

Battista at 18 at La Pace, the Oratorian church in Brescia, declared unfit for military service, keeps in touch with those in uniform.

The editors of the irreverent student magazine *La Fionda* (the Sling) with Andrea Trebeschi, best friend, on the right. The 'invalid' Battista wrote over forty articles within twelve months in 1918–19.

After ordination on 29 May 1920 in Brescia. His ordination card bore the text: "May all minds unite in truth, and all hearts in charity."

Above: Don Battista at 29, barely older than the students whose chaplain he was; 1926 was the year his father withdrew from politics, his paper suppressed; FUCI was the germ of an anti-Fascist underground movement.

Left: Don Montini in Budapest in 1938 with Giacinto Tredici, Bishop of Brescia since 1934, for the last Eucharistic Congress before 'the lights went out'.

Left: From 1939 to 1954 Montini was Pius XII's right-hand man, ready with the pontifical speech that he may well have drafted.

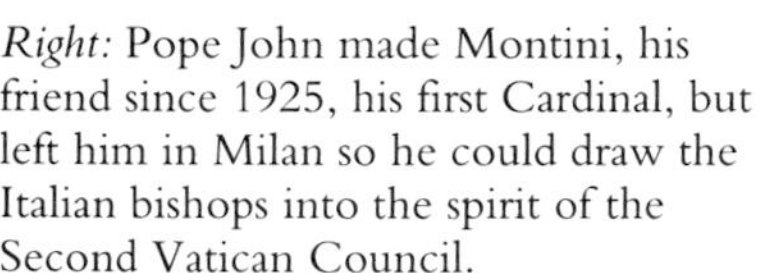
Right: Pope John made Montini, his friend since 1925, his first Cardinal, but left him in Milan so he could draw the Italian bishops into the spirit of the Second Vatican Council.

Below: An unsolved crime: in 1956 a home-made bomb was thrown through the window of his residence in Milan, Piazza Fortuna 5. Montini had right-wing enemies.

Cardinal Montini enters the conclave during which he told Cardinal Franz Konig: "I'm in darkness and cannot see anything clearly."

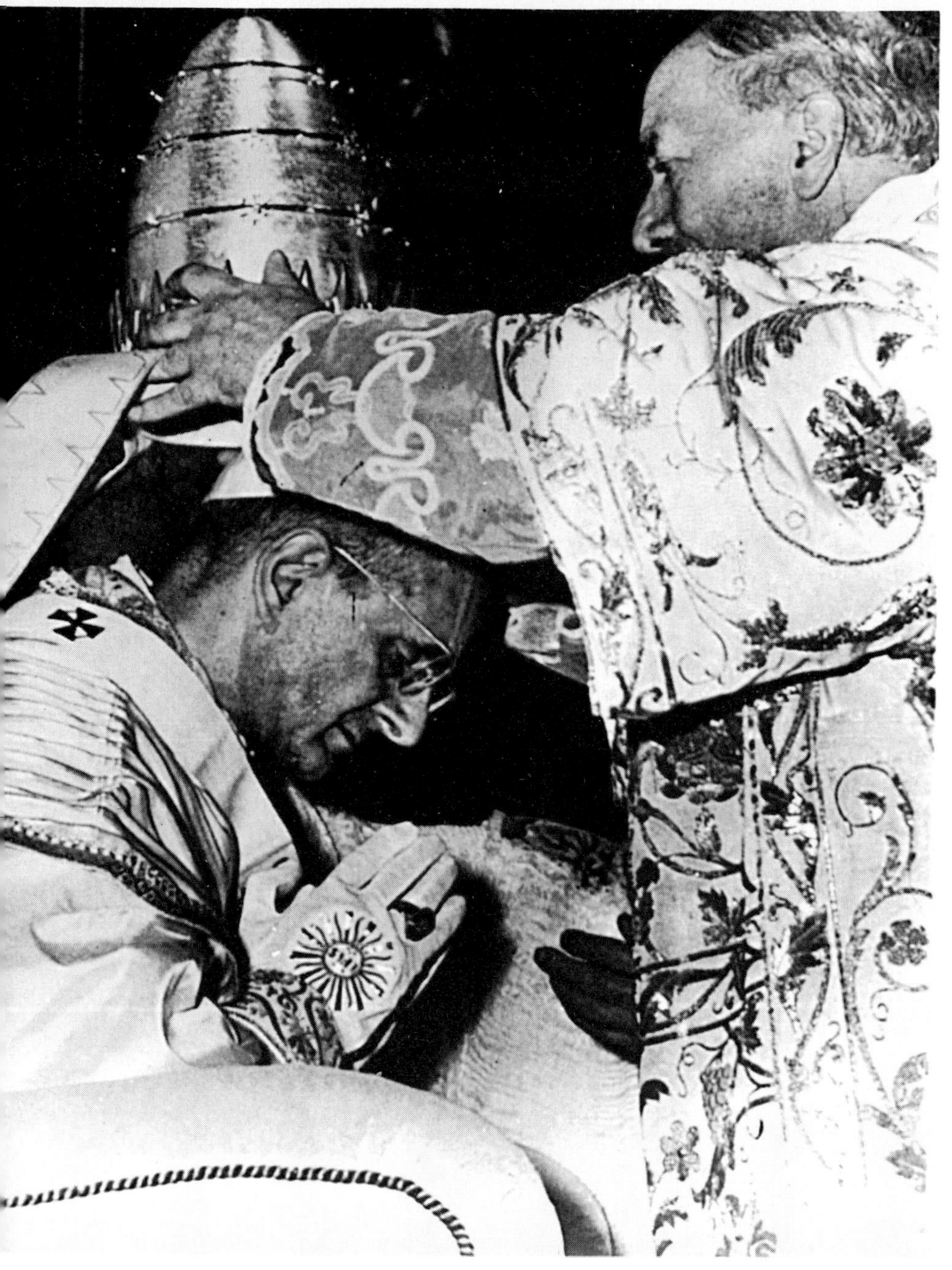

dinal Alfredo Ottaviani places the tiara on the head of Pope Paul VI. It was the last coronation
r.

First blessing of Paul VI from the central *loggia* of St Peter's, surrounded by the inherited curia among whom are Cardinals Eugene Tisserant (bearded) and Aloisi Masella (tucked away in dark glasses).

Cardinal Augustin Bea, the eighty year old Jesuit who was first president of the Secretariat for Promoting Christian Unity, confers with Cardinal Albert Meyer, archbishop of Chicago, who warned the Council would be a waste of time unless it produced positive documents on religious liberty and the Jews.

had been prominent in the "China lobby", the intellectual force behind the McCarthy witch-hunts which smeared State Department dissenters as "Reds".[1] But as the first Catholic to be appointed ambassador to Italy she naturally played host to Father John Courtney Murray SJ, who had advised her during the Senate confirmation hearings. His writings on Church and State set the agenda for the conciliar debate on religious freedom. Murray's advocacy of religious liberty got him into hot water with the Holy Office: he was silenced until the pontificate of Pope John XXIII.

Booth Luce, as the new ambassador, accepted that with feelings running high against having diplomatic relations with the Holy See at all, it would be wiser not to seek an audience with Pius XII. Her discretion was read as a snub by the Vatican. When she did eventually have an audience her convert's zeal led the Pope to say, "But I'm a Catholic too, you know." Undaunted she compounded her errors by inviting a group of Texan Pentecostals to Rome, where they openly proselytized. Meanwhile *America* magazine attacked the intolerance of the Franco regime in Spain. Nothing good seemed to be coming from the United States.

Yet Montini, in a famous lecture on the 250th anniversary of the foundation of the Pontifical Ecclesiastical Academy, his Alma Mater, seemed closer to "American" positions than to anything taught in Spain and Portugal, both under right-wing dictatorships boasting of fidelity to the Pope. Vatican diplomacy, he says

> looks like a system of self-defence which relies on the support of secular states and founds the welfare of the Church on relationships with powers that have become secular, alien, and sometimes hostile to her . . . Such props are not real supports but obstacles. The Church of today must expect her strength and prosperity to depend, not on the favour of established powers, but on the word and power which, by divine institution, she bears in her bosom. It is not links but liberty that she needs; it is not from outside but from within that her fortune must come.[2]

He seems quite carried away. It comes as something of a shock to find that he is here putting forward an *objection* that he is about to *refute*.

Of course the Church cannot sever all links with the political

1 See Penny Lernoux, *People of God: The Struggle for World Catholicism*, p. 261.

2 25 April 1951. The full text is in Hyginus Eugene Cardinale, *The Holy See and the International Order*, pp. 295–305. The quotation is from p. 297.

communities in which it exists. It cannot exist in a chemically pure state or soar away into some dreamland where it does not have to face the realities of power. Of course, of course. Yet Montini does not seem terribly convinced by his own argument. Have we an instance of *l'astuzia fortunata* (successful cunning) which he quotes as Niccolò Machiavelli's definition of diplomacy? Of course he denies that as well. But surely there were so many coded messages here. One example: "If I were asked which of the two careers, the army or diplomacy, were more a thing of the past, and was more out of date, I would point not to diplomacy but to the army."[1] Dazzling footwork.

He needed it, for there were many signs that Montini's position was shaky and precarious. He was connected with all the wrong people in the Christian Democrats from De Gasperi to Amintore Fanfani, Giorgio La Pira to Mario Rossi. Sister Pasqualina, Pius XII's handmaiden, muttered that "the Pope feels badly served by someone close to him".[2] But the signs were unclear. Did he, or did he not, have the ear of the Pope? Pius XII oscillated between Montini and Ottaviani.

A decisive moment seemed to have been reached when a consistory was announced for January 1953. "Everyone knew" (that is, it was widely assumed) Montini would be made a cardinal and Secretary of State. Tardini seemed to be fading from the scene. Yet when the list of twenty-four cardinals was published neither Montini nor Tardini was on it. Ten out of the twenty-four were Italian including Giuseppe Siri of Genoa, commonly regarded as the Pope's natural successor, and Angelo Giuseppe Roncalli, the future John XXIII, considered a genial old buffer delighted to be Patriarch of Venice in his retirement.

The absence of Montini and Tardini was a serious matter. For there had been no consistory since February 1946, and Teresa Neumann, the Munich mystic, was believed to have predicted that Pope Pacelli would have only two consistories in his reign.[3] So anyone who missed out in 1953 would have to wait for the next pontificate.

Pius, wondering how much longer he might live, agonized endlessly over his second and final consistory. By pointedly excluding Montini from the list of cardinals he ensured that Montini could not be a serious candidate in the conclave on his death. So Montini was deliberately ruled out as his immediate successor.

1 Ibid. p. 299.

2 Giancarlo Zizola, *Il microfono di Dio*, p. 333.

3 Derek Worlock, Archbishop of Liverpool, passed on this widely reported prediction. In Paola Giovetti, *Teresa Neumann*, there is no mention of Pius XII, not even of his time as Nuncio to Germany. One likely link was with Pius XII's confessor, Fr Augustin Bea SJ, who visited the famous stigmatic. According to Giovetti: "Like so many others he told her about his problems and said 'I rely on your prayers' " (p. 91).

Yet the legend of Montini's influence on the Vatican, cardinal or not, continued to grow. Derek Worlock, as Cardinal's secretary, accompanied Bernard Griffin to the consistory of January 1953, and captures well the atmosphere:

> Consistories in those days were grand affairs lasting a whole week from Monday to Friday. On the Monday the cardinals-designate were expected to dress in episcopal purple (for the last time) and, dotted about Rome, they formally "awaited the shock-news" that they had actually been named Cardinals. Since they already had a papal document assuring them of their appointment there was an element of make-believe about this hanging about and no real suspense.
>
> There was no new "British" cardinal on this occasion, but Cardinal Valerian Gracias of Bombay [successor of Archbishop Thomas d'Esterre Roberts SJ] was a member of the Commonwealth and that was a sufficient excuse for Griffin to go out. He had an interview with Montini. The ante-room was packed. It was like a dentist's waiting-room. The other visiting cardinals and prelates in Rome for the Consistory patiently awaited their audience with the great man. Cardinal Pierre Gerlier of Lyons reported that Msgr Montini was talking with an old friend, the French philosopher Jacques Maritain.
>
> The waiting visitors, anxious to speak with Montini, fidgeted and gossiped. Suddenly came sensational news. The decree *Christus Dominus* had been issued that very morning. It changed the rules for the time of fasting before Communion. Hitherto Catholics had been supposed to fast from midnight until Communion. This caused casuistical problems with brushing teeth and ruled out evening Masses. The new regulations were accompanied by other provisions which gradually eased the lot of Catholics, eventually making evening Mass feasible.
>
> The French, and Gerlier in particular, were cock-a-hoop. They claimed to have invented "liturgical renewal". So when Maritain eventually emerged they congratulated him on this "French victory". He had thanked Montini, it was whispered, for this pro-French initiative. Gerlier embraced the diminutive ex-French Ambassador to the Holy See.
>
> But there was something else: Maritain had congratulated Montini on *not becoming a cardinal*. He had declined this honour, it was said, knowing that the Pope did not intend to appoint a Cardinal Secretary of State, and therefore that the

> only way to remain in the immediate service of the Pope was to say "no" to the offer.[1]

That is more or less what happened. But one is still entitled to ask *why* Pius XII held only two consistories in nineteen years, especially given his alleged desire to "internationalize the Curia", and why he dispensed with a Cardinal Secretary of State. Why should the Bavarian mystic Teresa Neumann have held him in thrall?

But Pius XII had in fact put the names of these two prelates – Montini and Tardini – at the top of his list of cardinals in 1952 (*Iam erant nomina in primis a Nobis scripta*); however, both had refused the offer of a red hat with such vigour (*tam instanter*) that he felt bound to oblige them.[2]

Tardini offers a slightly different picture in his highly self-censored biography of Pius XII:

> The truth is that Pius XII was as good and sincere as ever. He not only offered red hats to both of us but for some months insisted on his kindly proposal. In the end he paternally acceded to our desire. His idea was to leave us at work just as before. "Nothing would be altered," he used to say, "except that you would wear a red skull-cap."
>
> The Pope added that he had devised a title that could be given to his putative non-cardinals: "For example," he said, "Montini could be put in charge of Ordinary Affairs while Tardini could deal with Extraordinary Affairs."[3]

That is what in effect they had already been doing.

Pius XII played around with titles such as "Pro-Secretary of State", which Tardini was perfectly happy to accept. In Tardini's biography of Pius XII there occurs the following exchange late in 1952:

> The Pope asked amiably, "*Monsignore mio*, why should you thank me when I have not done what you wished?"
>
> I answered, "But, your Holiness, I thank you for what you have done for me – far more than might have been expected."
>
> And the Pope smiled.[4]

Soft syrup. The plain fact is that both Tardini and Montini would have

1 Conversation with Archbishop Derek Warlock, 4 March 1988, at Mossley Hill, Liverpool.

2 Giulio Nicolini, *Il Cardinale Domenico Tardini*, Messagero, Padua 1980, p. 153. He refers to *Discorsi e Radiomessagi di SS Pio XII*, vol. 14, p. 458.

3 Nicolini, ibid. p. 155.

4 Ibid. p. 156. Tardini was probably being disingenuous here.

lost whatever influence they had on becoming cardinals. By staying put, they still counted.

Yet they were also losing ground, particularly to the Holy Office where Alfredo Ottaviani, now a cardinal, assumed the title of Pro-Prefect (the Prefect being, theoretically, the Pope). The question of priest-workers in France came to a head in the summer of 1953. Montini had long been familiar with this dossier. In May 1951 he had received a memo on the subject from Jacques Loew OP, the priest-docker from Marseilles.[1] Loew gathered that although Rome would take account of "the good of souls" (*salus animarum*) in judging this experiment, the real threat came from the alleged danger to the priestly ministry itself. This judgement was accurate.

If the priest-workers had paid more attention to the encyclical *Mentis Nostrae* (September 1950) they would have realized that its theology of the priest was incompatible with what they were doing. For while their concern was with relevance to the world of work, Pius XII's mind was set on orthodoxy: "Given a choice," he said, "between apostolic efficacy and the integrity of the priesthood, I opt for the integrity of the priesthood."

The decision to suppress the priest-workers was taken in the autumn of 1953. Montini certainly knew it was impending and did not disagree with it. He told d'Ormesson on 9 October 1953 that solving the problem was not a matter of correcting a few "individual lapses" but rethinking and reshaping the whole movement: "This initiative began badly. The first priests who volunteered for it were off-beam. For this reason Rome was very worried from the outset . . . Several of these priest-workers increasingly misunderstood the spirit of Christianity and put themselves on the same level as Marxists."[2]

This was particularly grave, Montini explained, as the Marxist persecution of the Church intensified throughout Europe. In September 1953, he pointed out, Cardinal Stefan Wyszyński had been imprisoned in Poland.

A letter from Cardinal Giuseppe Pizzardo, Secretary of the Holy Office, dated the next day, 10 October 1953, charged the Dominican Master General, the Spaniard Emanuel Suarez, with rooting out "the excessive spirit of insubordination and indiscipline" deemed prevalent among the French Dominicans (sometimes coming from other French Dominicans) in general. Suarez went to France in January 1954, sacked the three provincials (technically he "accepted their resignations"), silencing and dispersing theologians like Yves Congar and Marie-

1 François Leprieur, *Quand Rome condamne*, p. 313.

2 Ibid. p. 294.

Dominique Chenu. His motive, he explained, was "to save the Order". If he had not taken these measures, then worse would have befallen them: they might have been suppressed.

Pius XII had fallen gravely ill on 27 January 1954 and saw no one except his doctors and Montini and Tardini.[1] Jacques Maritain's successor as French Ambassador to the Holy See, Vladimir d'Ormesson, believed Montini was exercising a moderating influence. When the manifesto of the seventy-three priest-workers appeared on 3 February *L'Osservatore Romano* remained silent, but Montini "inspired" an article by Frederico Alessandrini, its deputy editor, in *Quotidiano*, the organ of Catholic Action. It expressed the hope that the Manifesto was not their last word on the subject and that further reflection would reduce the emotional temperature. D'Ormesson informed the Quai d'Orsay:

> I believe that Msgr Montini is doing everything in his power to see that nothing irreparable happens, that bridges should not be cut too soon, that every effort should be made to keep or bring back to the bosom of the Church those whom he still considers, in spite of their excesses or wanderings (*égarements*), the impassioned servants of Christ.[2]

But any hope of defusing the situation soon vanished. François Mauriac weighed in with a column in *Le Figaro* in which he asked, rhetorically, what are the priest-workers and the Dominicans but "the guardians of our hope"? The silence of the Dominicans should not mislead: the whole progressive wing of the French Church was mortally struck by this blow.

In conversation with d'Ormesson, Montini showed himself well aware of "the disastrous effects of the measures taken against the priest-workers and the Dominicans, and the dangerous consequences to which this crisis could lead". He told d'Ormesson that Pope Pius, though gravely ill, had read the press cuttings and was particularly affected by attacks on "his nuncio" (*sic*).[3]

Montini helped organize the mediating mission of Msgr André Baron, Rector of the French church in Rome, who was sent to Paris to assure the French bishops that the Holy See had not lost confidence in them and would trust them to arrange a new statute for the priest-

1 Ibid.

2 Ibid. p. 71.

3 Ibid. p. 126. Angelo Giuseppe Roncalli had by now gone to Venice, to be replaced in Paris by the hard-liner Paolo Marella.

workers.[1] He was happy with the pastoral letters of the French bishops, especially that of Cardinal Maurice Feltin, Archbishop of Paris, appreciating its "serenity, truth, justice and balance".[2]

So throughout the whole episode the role of Montini was to soften the blows, not to avert them. Yet in Vatican circles his reputation of being pro-French was not dented and did him no good. The French continued to believe that he understood them better than others in Rome.

These events had their repercussions in Italy, particularly in the youth section of Catholic Action, GIAC. Reflecting on the operation Sturzo and the elections of 1952, Rossi wrote that "religion should inspire politics, not be a substitute for it."[3] After an article supporting Giorgio La Pira, mayor of Florence, and Cardinal Giacomo Lercaro, Archbishop of Bologna, Don Arturo Paolo, chaplain of GIAC, was sacked. He wrote to Montini: "Two mentalities are at work, for today laypeople are adults in the Church, and the young don't want to be on the right wing."[4] Mario Rossi wanted to resign out of solidarity with Don Arturo.

Someone conceived the crazy idea of replacing him by Padre Virgilio Rotondi SJ, Lombardi's side-kick. Lercaro told Rossi: "They say I'm going to be pope. If so, the first thing I'll do will be to boot out (*allonatare*) Professor Gedda."[5]

Emotions were running high. Montini attended a secret meeting at Villa Carpegna which considered what to do next. He accepted Rossi's letter of resignation, but kept it on his desk. Whether his motive was not to distress Pius XII in his illness or to protect Rossi is unclear.[6] Anyway it was too late. Rossi was hauled before a three-man commission consisting of Pizzardo, Piazza and Urbani. This kangaroo court accused him of "options not in conformity with the directives of ecclesiastical authority and the Pope" and of being too pro-French.[7] Montini had the wonderful but hopeless idea of publishing Rossi's resignation letter, with its sincere protestations of loyalty to the Church and the Holy See, in *L'Osservatore Romano*. This led Rossi to speak of his "remoteness from everyday life . . . his abstraction and idealism".[8]

The Vatican paper simply announced in its 19–20 April number

1 Ibid. p. 34 fn. 198.

2 Ibid.

3 Ibid. p. 356.

4 Giuntella, p. 359.

5 Giancarlo Zizola, *Il microfono di Dio*, p. 333.

6 Giuntella, p. 360.

7 Ibid.

8 Mario V. Rossi, *I Giorni della Onnipotenza*, p. 117.

that Rossi had been replaced by Enrico Vinci, a Gedda candidate.

The attack on Rossi was a sighting-shot on Montini, the more imposing target. He was the *bête noire* of the Roman party. God's microphone, Lombardi, turned against Montini, dismissing him quite unfairly as a creature of Amintore Fanfani and all those who favoured an "opening to the left" (*apertura a sinistra*). Lombardi's diary for 1953 says that the way to save Italy is to "take away Montini's powers in relation to Italy and give them to Tardini (for Montini is too dependent on Fanfani)".[1]

This was, at the very least, ingratitude on the part of Lombardi. His Movement for a Better World owed its very existence to Montini's invitation to a "brain-storming" session at the Secretariat of State on 31 August 1953. Rotondi was there along with the Rector of the Jesuit Agnani College, Pasquale Biretti, a Gregorian University sociologist. Montini said the Holy Father was very upset and didn't know what to do, particularly about Rome.[2] There was agreement that the Gedda method of beating the Communists by pre-electoral pacts was inadequate: the Rome diocese needed something more – a spiritual renewal directed by an élite corps of priests and laypeople.

Montini recommended approval of the Better World Movement early in 1954. Lombardi was beginning to give courses for all-comers at Mondragone, a Jesuit College not far from Rome. The frugal simplicity of the primitive church was the norm: bishops and others carried their own bags to their rooms, and often had to share cubicles. This worried some Roman *monsignori* accustomed to the advantages of less egalitarian treatment.

Those priests or religious who joined the Better World Movement did not detach themselves from their own religious orders or dioceses. Lombardi's idea was that they would be an aristocracy of the Spirit who would go back and transform home-base. He used the *Spiritual Exercises* of St Ignatius, adding a social or community dimension that seemed wholly new at the time. He called it his University of the Holy Spirit.

On 14 August 1954 Pius XII, by now restored to health, praised Lombardi and Rotondi extravagantly: "To them we owe this action for the renewal of the world." Ottaviani himself had survived the Mondragone experience and declared that "Padre Lombardi has been inspired by God to find the right way" – high praise from this source. In October Pope Pius XII lauded the pair as "two great, sublime apostles".[3]

That was on 24 October. A week later Montini was sacked and

1 Zizola, *Il microfono di Dio*, p. 349.

2 Ibid. p. 331.

3 Ibid. pp. 341–42.

despatched to Milan. Milan was notoriously the richest, the hugest and the most awkward diocese of Italy. He was kicked upstairs. How did it happen?

Montini always knew how exposed he was. He had some *risqué* friends. He tried to get Graham Greene to write in *L'Osservatore Romano*. The crisis of the student movement swirled around Carlo Carretto, later to become a Little Brother of Charles de Foucauld and a well-known spiritual writer. What he really thought about Don Primo Mazzolari, the uncomfortable prophet of the Church of the Poor, is unclear, but he sensed his importance and subscribed to his reviews, *Adesso* and *Testimonianze*, from the moment they began to appear.[1]

Though he was perfectly loyal to the pope he served, he kept his ear to the ground and did not accept the package deal propounded by the "Roman Party", hoping that the future might be different from the past. But he had to be discreet in showing where his true sympathies lay. In this system you had to be pope before you could indulge in self-expression.

Invited by his friend the priest-poet David Maria Turoldo to write a preface to Don Lorenzo Milani's *Esperienze Pastorali* (*Pastoral Experiences*), a truly seminal book, he declined with the enigmatic remark: "We are going through difficult times, times in which prudence is not enough, but in which prudence must become cunning (*astuzia*)."[2] Machiavelli again.

But even prudence allied to low cunning could not save him now. In the summer of 1954 Cardinal Bernard Griffin, Archbishop of Westminster, in Rome for the canonization of Pope Pius X, went to see his old friend Cardinal Giuseppe Pizzardo. He had been at the coronation of King George VI in 1937, was the "Protector" of the Venerable English College, and was thus deemed to be Anglophile.[3]

Pizzardo assured Griffin that the Church was in grave danger. It was about to fall into the hands of "one extremely powerful man, who had very strong views on certain matters".[4] This dangerous fellow was none other than Montini. His downfall was already being plotted.

1 Pietro Scoppola, *La "Nuova cirstianita" perduta*, p. 70.

2 Ibid. p. 78. Don David Turoldo, priest and poet, spent his last years at Sotto il Monte, Pope John's birthplace. He died on 6 February 1992. He liked to relate how Antonio Rosmini, author of *The Five Wounds of the Church*, kissed the hand of Alessandro Manzoni, author of *I Promessi Sposi*; whereupon the novelist fell to his knees and tried to kiss the feet of the one priest he revered.

3 See Thomas Maloney, *Westminster, Whitehall and the Vatican*, pp. 88–89. Pizzardo had been "deeply impressed with the stability of the British constitution in its time of trial".

4 Archbishop Derek Worlock, interview, 4 March 1988.

He gave his enemies new material with a preface in the form of a letter to a two-volume compilation by Msgr Pierre Veuillot, from 1949 a colleague in the Secretariat of State. Veuillot, descended from the famous Louis Veuillot editor of the nineteenth century *L'Univers*, had simply gathered all the papal texts on the priesthood from Pius X to Pius XII.[1] That might seem an innocent enough occupation. But coming from a Frenchman and with the condemnation of the priest-workers still fresh in everyone's mind, Veuillot's book would inevitably be read as a conformist endorsement of Pius XII's positions or, worse, mere propaganda for them.

Montini's presentation is much subtler than that. He begins with praise for this synthesis which not only throws light on *the priesthood* but by the same token on *the Church*. Indeed it is in the priest that the nature of the Church appears "in its institutional features, its specific functions, and its perpetual effort to sanctify the world".[2] The priest discloses the Church. This theme does not come from his sources. It is the fruit of his personal reflection and prayer.

Equally personal are his thoughts on the "image" of the priest. Writing for a French audience, he has in mind French models. There is a world of difference between the conventional comic abbés of Flaubert and the priests of Georges Bernanos, "mysterious beings, whose experience of people is tinged with suffering and mysticism, and destined not to have much practical success not through any fault of their own but because of the deafness or hostility of the secular world that surrounds them".[3] That is at least better than the nineteenth-century anti-clerical positivist view of the priest as "the hangover from the Middle Ages, ally of conservatism, selfishness, bonze of an out-of-date liturgy, ignorant of real life – that's a priest for you!"

But, says Montini, there is no point in being defensive. The liturgical movement has focused on the essential role of the priest as the president of the Eucharist:

> Some have admirably devoted themselves to revivifying the liturgy from within, giving meaning and poetry to the prayers we use; the rites appear in their authentic austerity and beauty; the celebration of the mystery reawakens the sense of the ineffable union of divine and human in the sacramental action; a tremor of mysterious joy, of divine presence and human charity

1 Pierre Veuillot, *Notre Sacerdoce: Documents Pontificaux de Pie X à nos jours; Lettre-préface de son excellence Monseigneur Montini, Pro-Secrétaire d'Etat de sa Sainteté pour les Affaires ordinaires*, 1954.

2 *Notiziario*, 4, p. 13.

3 Ibid.

> ripples through the group praying round the altar; the priest is filled with joy; the springtime of the Church blossoms.[1]

This reflects Montini's own Masses celebrated for FUCI and the *Laureati*, based on the principles found in Romano Guardini and Pius Parsch OSB ("You shouldn't pray at Mass, you should pray the Mass'). The "dialogue Mass" for small groups was given a great boost in the 1950s by the relaxation of the fasting discipline.

But – and this is a most important admission – this experience is only open to the few who can call up a friendly priest:

> These meetings were for the most part restricted to élite groups. They didn't draw crowds. The people seemed, in their immense majority, indifferent. Would they come back? They didn't come back. So it's up to the priest to move, not the people. There's no point in ringing your bell if no one is listening to it. The priest has to listen to sirens from the factories, these temples of technology where the modern world vibrates. It's up to the priest to become a missionary, if he wants Christianity to remain and become the living leaven of civilization.

This was quite enough to confirm the worst fears of Cardinal Giuseppe Pizzardo about this dangerous man. Montini might have formally rejected the priest-worker movement, but here he was restating the very grounds on which it was based: if they don't come to him, the priest must go to the people.

In truth Montini, liberated by writing in French, was throwing more light on his own experience of the priesthood than on the priest-worker movement. For him pastoral work is an "art" rather than a "science". It involves a "certain apostolic relativism" – that is, the means are less important than the goals. He recognizes that Communists, here disguised as "atheists", can have ideals and that "fraternal service between brothers is the only lever that can lift the world". Ideals of sacrifice and redemption are at the heart of any authentic social and moral cause. Pizzardo would have said that he was conceding too much to these "anonymous Christians", and not felt much happier with his idea that the priest was someone who should "get drunk on God" (*s'enivrer de Dieu*). "Priesthood is a social service," he concludes, "the priest is a man for others. Priesthood and egoism exclude each other; priesthood and charity coincide."[2]

He dated his preface 23 August 1954. Then fate – or providence –

1 Ibid.

2 Ibid. p. 14.

took a hand. On 28 August 1954 Cardinal Ildefonso Schuster, the former Benedictine Abbot of the Roman basilica of St Paul's, Archbishop of Milan since 1929, lay dying. The last words he scribbled were an invitation to Angelo Roncalli, Patriarch of Venice, to replace him in crowning the statue of the Madonna del Bosco near Imbersago (Como) on the 29th. Roncalli was holidaying at Sotto il Monte, his native village, and gladly went to a shrine he had loved from boyhood. Schuster died the next day at 4.30 a.m. aged seventy-four.[1] Milan, the most prestigious see of Italy, graced by saints like Ambrose and Charles Borromeo, was now vacant.

There would be no "disgrace" involved in despatching Montini to Milan. The Pope was worked on. Feline arguments were used. Montini needed some pastoral experience. But shrewd observers like his friend Roncalli knew it was a defeat and noted the atmosphere of melancholy that hung like dust about Montini's flat after the news was announced on 3 November, appropriately the eve of the feast of St Charles Borromeo.

One parting shot proved that he departed under something of a cloud. He needed two removal vans for his luggage – mostly the 8000 volumes of his library. But the vans were carefully searched before he could leave. Why? For incriminating material? Did he know too much about certain cardinals? Was he removing information about candidates for the episcopacy that properly belonged in Rome? Impossible to say just yet. But whatever these suspicious minds thought about him, the friends he left behind in the Secretariat of State knew that he would be back.

In some ways it was a relief to be leaving, for Rome in the early fifties exuded a nasty odour. There was scandal when Prince Filippo Orsini, whose family shared with their rivals the Colonnas the title of assistants to the papal throne (all this meant was that on certain days they could bring up the cruets with wine and water at the papal Mass), slit his wrists. But he botched the job and survived. He explained his suicide attempt as the only way to break off his relationship with the English actress, the beautiful Belinda Lee. To hush up the affair the Vatican conspired with Orsini's wife to lock up the Prince in a psychiatric clinic. Whereupon the *la bella* Belinda fled to South Africa – where else? – to make a film on Lucrezia Borgia – who else? – which made the most of her relationship with the Prince. Fury in the Vatican. Storm in Italy. The Orsini were stripped of their ancient title, "assistants to the papal throne".[2]

It was a sign of the corruption of Rome. Another was that Montini's

1 *Due Papi*, pp. 118, 122.

2 Claudio Rendina, *Il Vaticano, Storia e Segreti*, pp. 389–90.

appointment to Milan was leaked to *Le Monde* on 22 October 1954, two weeks before its official announcement on 3 December.[1] After thirty-four years in Rome it was time to move on. Montini had always tried to bridge the generation gap, to be a father to the young without being "paternalist". Milan would test his resources of paternity and there he could listen to the call of the factory sirens.

1 Jacques Nobécourt, "*Le Monde et le personnage de Paul VI*", in *Modernité*, p. 260.

17

Pastor of the Secular City

I shall pray that the clatter of machinery may become music, and that the smoke of factory chimneys may become incense.

(G. B. MONTINI in Jean Guitton, *Dialogues*, p. 65)

Pius XII presented Archbishop Giovanni Battista Montini as his "personal gift" to Milan. When a stunned Montini timidly enquired, "Holy Father, do you think I am capable of this task?" the Pope's only answer was to raise him from his knees and embrace him warmly.[1] Yet Pius did not have a very clear idea about what he wanted Montini to do in Milan. At the final meeting before his departure, Pius, from his sickbed, simply "repeated paternally, *depositum custodi* [hold on to the deposit of faith]".[2]

Many tears were shed at this parting of friends. There were tears in the Secretariat of State where Msgr Angelo Dell'Aqua, a Milanese, remained as his friend and witness. There were tears among the diplomats gathered to bid him godspeed. Vladimir d'Ormesson, the French Ambassador, said that "what we have most respected and loved in you is that behind the diplomatic official, we have always found the priest".[3] Maria, Montini's housekeeper for many years, was bundled off to her native Abruzzi with a bicycle and a sewing-machine. No doubt she shed the odd tear too.

In his despatches to the Quai d'Orsay, however, d'Ormesson bluntly blamed Montini's departure on "the reactionary gang (*clan*) which had more and more influence over Pius XII as he grew older, weaker, more and more obsessed by Communism". Cardinal Giuseppe Pizzardo was the gang-leader. By removing Montini to Milan they had achieved their

1 John G. Clancy, *Apostle for our Time: Pope Paul VI*, Collins 1964.

2 Enrico Manfredini, "*Le scelte pastorali dell'arcivescovo di Milano*", in *Arcivescovo* (1985), p. 63.

3 Clancy, *Apostle for our Time*, p. 74.

first aim; the second aim was to stop him becoming a cardinal for as long as possible.[1]

Cardinal Angelo Rocalli, Patriarch of Venice, called on Montini on 4 December to express his sympathy. He was "struck by the air of departure, tinged with sadness, that already hung about the apartment".[2] Roncalli shook his grey head. He simply could not understand why Pius XII, in extreme old age, after the crippling illness of the previous spring, should deprive himself of his most accomplished aide. "Where," he muttered, "will he find anyone else as good at writing letters or drafting documents?" Perhaps the answer was that Pius XII considered his pontificate over.

Another visitor, Fr Anselmo Giabanni, was shocked at finding Montini so crestfallen: "His tone of voice was different. Plucking up courage, I said how full of joy I was at his promotion. He evidently did not share my joy. He said nothing. He seemed bewildered (*smarrito*)."[3]

A light drizzle was falling on 12 December, *Gaudete* Sunday, when Montini was ordained bishop in St Peter's basilica. Cardinal Eugène Tisserant, dean of the sacred college, stood in for Pius XII who had taken to his bed again. The co-consecrators were Giacinto Tredici, bishop of Brescia since January 1936, a family friend, and Domenico Bernareggi, capitular vicar of Milan: between them they represented his past and his future.[4] St Peter's was crammed with Milanese, well aware that in Montini they had the Vatican's highest flier. They applauded him out of the basilica, forgetting – perhaps with prescience – that only the pope may be hailed in this way.

But Archbishop Montini was in no hurry to get to Milan. Public applause masked private anxieties. He felt overwhelmed by the immensity of the task before him. He poured his heart out in a letter to Fr Giulio Bevilacqua:

> Dear Father
> I have gone through days of intense suffering. They made me think of the words of St Paul: *supra modum gravati sumus, ita ut taederet nos etiam vivere*. Then came dismay, bewilderment; not yet peace, confidence, abandonment; a sense of being invaded, overpowered by something immensely greater than

1 *Archives du Quai d'Orsay, Europe 1949–55, Saint-Siège*, b.8, despatch of 5 March 1954.

2 *Giovanni* e Paolo, Due Papi, Saggio di Corrispondenza (1925–1962), Quaderni dell'Istituto Paolo VI, 2, 1982, p. 15. It is Pope John's secretary, Msgr Loris F. Capovilla, who noted this.

3 Andrea Riccardi, *Le Chiese di Pio XII*, p. 40.

4 *Anni e Opere*, p. 38.

myself. Now I await the serenity of the ways of God, who guides even the most faltering and unskilled steps.

I feel the chorus of prayer all about me, and the atmosphere of piety and affection that surrounds an "I" transformed into a sign of Christ, and I find once again communion with the Master. How great, how deep is my need of him just now; it seems that only now am I just beginning to love him.

What will happen? I can see a tangle of problems, a host of difficulties enough to make me dizzy; and once again I am assailed by the temptation of faint-heartedness. But from now on I will have to give a real and positive assent to divine help. Continue to pray for me. Please share with me whatever ideas your experience and affection suggest. For you and the Oratorians the best blessings entrusted to my hands.

Most affectionately yours in Christ

D. Battista.[1]

He wanted Bevilacqua to tell him the truth. But Bevilacqua was not a man to encourage any illusions. For someone who had not even been a parish priest the move to the pastoral care of the Milan diocese, with its 1000 churches, 2500 priests and 3,500,000 souls, was distinctly alarming. Bevilacqua said he was moving "from diplomacy to nastiness (*brutalità*)".[2] No longer filtered through the Secretariat of State's reports, the world would hit him in all its rawness.

It seemed much easier to find an episcopal motto. His first choice was "*Cum ipso in monte*" (With him on the mountainside) from the synoptic account of the Transfiguration. But Msgr Antonio Maria Travia pointed out that this was more apt for a contemplative than an Archbishop of Milan. So he thought again and came up with "*In nomine Domini*" (In the name of the Lord), a better motto for his pastoral ministry.[3] But perhaps his first thought was more faithful to his nature. A true contemplative, he was to die on the feast of the Transfiguration.

Montini finally left Rome for Milan on 4 January 1955. He took the train to Lodi and spent the night with the Oblates of St Charles Borromeo at Rho. Next morning, in heavy rain, he knelt and kissed the sodden asphalt on entering his diocese near Melegano, and followed the traditional route from the basilica of Sant'Eustorgio to the spiky cathedral, standing in the open car in his soup-plate hat, waving and

1 *Notiziario*, 3, pp. 19–22 with facsimile. The letter is dated 18 November 1954.

2 Quoted by Giorgio Rumi, in *Arcivescovo* (1983), p. 19.

3 *Notiziario*, 3, p. 58.

blessing the workers who lined the streets.[1] The rain continued to fall.

"The first meeting between a bishop and his city," said one of Montini's successors in Milan, "is no chance matter."[2] From the outset Montini was determined to reach out to the Milanese working-class. They might vote Communist, and go to church only to be hatched, matched and despatched, but he wanted to show "the Church's love for those who are estranged from her".[3] Dell'Acqua predicted he would be "the cardinal of the workers".

Giving bishops such sobriquets was a clerical sport. Montini's seminary rector, Msgr Francesco Olgiati, dubbed his three predecessors the cardinal of youth (Bl. Carlo Andrea Ferrari), the cardinal of goodness (Eugenio Tosi) and the cardinal of prayer (Ildefonso Schuster OSB).[4]

These titles were not as complimentary as they might appear. In his long reign (1930–54) Schuster certainly prayed, but he had also blessed Fascism in its early days, and was disappointed to find Mussolini far from penitent just three days before he was executed and strung upside-down round the corner in the Piazzale Loreto.[5] Some said he had tried to turn Milan into a Benedictine abbey.

In the preface to a pamphlet about his predecessor, Montini, despite himself, damns him with the faintest of praise. He describes "the fascination this sacred, delicate, special, solitary figure" exercised, whom he had known since the 1920s when he was abbot of St Paul's-without-the-Walls.[6] Though Schuster could legitimately claim to have been a pioneer of liturgical reform,[7] never could he have been called "the bishop of the workers".

By the time Montini arrived in Milan in 1955 the city offered a microcosm of Italy. It was poised for the great leap forward dubbed "economic miracle"; it was undergoing rapid industrialization and

1 Nello Vian, *Anni e Opere*, p. 41.

2 Marco Garzonio, *Cardinale a Milano in un Mondo che cambia*, Rizzoli 1985, p. 11. The cardinal in question was the Jesuit Carlo Maria Martini, who entered the city on 10 February 1980, on foot, and in the midst of the faithful at prayer.

3 This is the title of a lecture he gave in September 1958 to the Eighth National Week of Pastoral Renewal. English in *The Mind of Paul VI*, ed. James Walsh SJ, G. Chapman 1964, pp. 22–33.

4 *Arcivescovo* (1983), p. 156. In England the titles given to dioceses were a little more malicious, the Cruel See, the Dead See and the Red See being particular favourites. When John Carmel Heenan was Bishop of Leeds, it was known as the Cruel See because of his habit of moving pastors without warning.

5 Denis Mack Smith, *Mussolini*, pp. 370–71.

6 Vincenzo Gremigni, *Il Cardinale Schuster come l'ho visto io . . .*, Maria Immaculata, Milan 1956. Gremigni was Bishop of Novara.

7 Carlo Colombo, "*Alcune Linee Pastorali*", in *Arcivescovo* (1985), p. 313.

attracted thousands of uprooted immigrants from the impoverished south. There was a danger, he soon realized, that there would be two Milans: the rich historic city centre, where he lived at Piazza Fontana 2 hard by his cathedral, and the higgledy-piggledy squalor of the new suburbs. "Milan must love Milan," he exclaimed in a letter to a suburban priest, "ancient Milan must love modern Milan."[1] The exhortation was addressed to himself in the first place.

Giorgio Rumor insists that Montini was not the only actor in the drama of Milan in this period. The principal actor was the city itself with its thousand and one institutions – Montini ticked them off on his fingers – cultural, social, political, financial, commercial, industrial. It would be wrong to see Milan as just another stage on Montini's inevitable rise to the papacy. His election was not inevitable, and the pastoral care of Milan mattered to him far more than personal ambition.

Montini's attempts to reach out to the workers sometimes caused mirth. He became a familiar sight in the city, approaching workers with sad smile and outstretched hand, despite their hoots and jeers. In the end they usually accepted *la main tendue*.

He put on a hard hat, went down mines, visited factories, toured Communist districts never penetrated by Dom Schuster. He took with him a portable Mass kit which he set up and used wherever possible. He preached a message of love "to the unfortunates who gather behind Marx", and assured the workers that "Jesus still loves you strongly, divinely, immensely."[2] If the workers had stopped coming to church, the church would have to go to them.

Msgr Carlo Colombo provides an important corrective to this picture of a man forcing himself to act against his nature. He insists Montini did not wait until he reached Milan to be interested in the workers. Secret documents in the Secretariat of State will one day illumine the part played by Montini in the setting up of ACLI (*Associazioni Cristiane Lavoratori Italiani*) in the summer of 1948.[3]

Montini attended an ACLI meeting and made favourable remarks about Ezio Vanoni, who had worked with his friends Carlo Colombo and P. Mariano Cordovani on the *Codice di Camaldoli* in the summer

1 Giorgio Rumor, "*L'Arcivescovo Montini e la società del suo tempo*", in *Arcivescovo* (1985), p. 21.

2 For this paragraph, see Xavier Rynne, *The Second Session*, Faber 1963, pp. 16–17. There can be few who do not know that behind the *nom de guerre* of Xavier Rynne lurks Fr Francis Xavier Murphy CSSR.

3 Carlo Colombo, "Discussione", in *Arcivescovo* (1985), p. 157. Sandro Magister, *La Politicà Vaticana*, p. 91, for the events of 1948. ACLI split from the Communist-dominated CGIL because it wanted to affiliate with the US labour unions who partially funded them.

of 1943.[1] He encouraged a new priestly association called the Missionaries of the World of Work – the best he could do after the banning of the French priest-workers. He helped a group of ex-FUCI students from the Augustinianum in the Catholic University to found *Relazioni sociali*.

They were soon nicknamed "the Archbishop's left-wingers". He left them completely free, his only advice being: "You must *believe* in what you *do*." But these were only sighting-shots for the great "Mission to Milan" that he was already thinking about: it took place in 1957.

Before then he had to clarify the relationship between the Seminary and the Theology Faculty. The purpose of the seminary at Venegono was to form "pastors", while the goal of the Theology Faculty was to promote research. His advice to his seminary professors was:

> You have to learn how to hand on the Christian message, formed and shaped by classical culture as it is, to young people who mostly come from a scientific background and technical schools, and so have a predominantly scientific outlook. I can't say that these problems have yet been resolved.[2]

But he was not averse to the Seminary transferring to Milan and the Theology Faculty. He opposed the subordination of the Theology Faculty to the Toniolo Institute, the governing body of the Catholic University of Milan, on the grounds that it should not be under university or lay control. The Theology Faculty should be subordinate only to the Church's *magisterium*, for "it is the Church as such that evangelizes the world, the Church as Jesus Christ founded it, not the way it would be if human beings had made it up".

Yet when the Toniolo Institute's president, Msgr Francesco Olgiati, died on 21 May 1962 Montini was invited to replace him. He tergiversated, saying the post was incompatible with his role as archbishop, and finally gave in when persuaded it was the best way he could help the Catholic University.[3]

Milan had its own Ambrosian rite – the only Church in the West with this privilege. Many of Milan's churches had been bombed in August 1943. Montini wanted the worship in the cathedral, the *duomo*, to be the model for the whole diocese. Church architecture, whatever its style, should carry the eye horizontally towards the altar of the Eucharist, and vertically towards God.[4] If the cathedral is unique, the

1 Sandro Magister, ibid. p. 109.

2 Carlo Colombo, in *Arcivescovo* (1985), p. 158.

3 Ibid. Carlo Colombo indicates that the archives of P. Agostino Gemelli contain traces of fierce debates on such matters from the time of Montini's arrival in 1955.

4 Ernesto Brivio, "*L'Azione per le Nuove Chiese*", in *Arcivescovo* (1983), pp. 186–87.

parish churches also serve a sociological as well as a religious function:

> The church is so often the only building in the area that doesn't serve some utilitarian purpose, the only original "monument" that doesn't strictly have to be there . . . Wherever a church is, it becomes a centre; it is not an encumbrance; it is the pivot of communication; a place where you can look out on modest houses or vast skyscrapers and get a comforting, ordering, inspiring perspective . . . It offers a host of people who don't know each other an assembly point where they can meet and make friends. It builds up unity between the local people and strangers; around it is vitality such that what is lumpish and profane becomes, in the church, consoling and sacred.[1]

So Montini became a great builder of churches. He increased the number in the diocese by more than 10 per cent, with forty-one in Milan itself and seventy-four dotted around the diocese.[2] He multiplied other places of prayer, reopening chapels in abandoned convents and abbeys. "The Milanese," he used to say, "don't need to be taught how to work and make money; but they do need to be taught how to pray well."[3]

He took immense trouble over his sermons, especially for the great feasts when the cathedral was crowded. He began his pastoral visitation of the whole diocese with the Duomo. The liturgy, he said, is

> the voice of the cathedral: it is prayer, action, the mystery of the Church in its true place, in its most glorious and mysterious epiphany. It is the liturgy that makes the stones speak, the liturgy that makes dead stones come alive. It is the liturgy that discloses and realizes the secret of the cathedral.[4]

Montini never recycled old material in his sermons. They flowed fresh from his prayer and his reading. At each feast he made notes on what he might say next year.

So after the Corpus Christi procession of 1963 he jotted down some thoughts under the heading "the psychology of the priest when saying Mass and the psychology of the lay person receiving the Eucharist".[5]

1 Ibid.

2 Ibid. p. 204. There are discrepancies in the statistics. This is because sometimes every kind of building at whatever stage is counted. Enrico Manfredini says that by the time he became pope in June 1963 he had blessed or consecrated thirty-four churches and work was in progress on eighty-one others. *Arcivescovo* (1985).

3 Carlo Colombo, in *Arcivescovo* (1985), p. 159.

4 Ernesto Brivio, "*Il Duomo nella sua vita e nel suo pensiero*", in *Arcivescovo* (1983), p. 176.

5 Carlo Colombo, in *Arcivescovo* (1985), p. 159.

He never gave the sermon on this novel theme. By Corpus Christi 1964 he was pope.

In talking about "the cathedral" Montini was wont to remark that he found "non-Catholic" cathedrals empty and desolate places. However this was not intended as an anti-ecumenical gibe. The proof is that he was already making Milan a centre for ecumenism. Bishop George Bell[1] in 1955 reported him as saying: "Although the Holy Father [Pius XII] has often urged collaboration between Catholics and the separated Brethren, he had never indicated how this should be done . . ." He was like a curate being discreetly critical of his Vicar, adds Bell.[2]

Bell was scouting, preparing the ground for a more substantial visit the next year. Bernard Pawley described its purpose:

> The object of the exercise was not the discussion of controversial topics but the exchange of basic information. The group showed books and photographs and answered endless questions. The Archbishop was clearly trying to build up for himself a picture of other Christians on the basis of what they said about themselves.[3]

Apart from Pawley, the party comprised Prebendary C.-L. Gage-Brown, Vicar of St Cuthbert's, Philbeach Gardens, London;[4] John Dickinson, Fellow of Pembroke College, Cambridge; Colin James, then chaplain of Stowe School, from 1985 Bishop of Winchester; and Colin Hickling, a student at Chichester Theological College, dragged in at the last moment for his Italian.

1 Bernard and Margaret Pawley, *Rome and Canterbury through Four Centuries*, 1974, p. 327. Bernard Pawley, an army chaplain in Libya, was captured in 1941 by the Germans who handed him over to the Italians. Thus he found himself Anglican chaplain to a POW hospital first in Parma, then in Piacenza and finally in Milan. Late in 1943 a RAF attack on the railway station devastated the POW hospital close by. Pawley and Cardinal Ildefonso Schuster were on the scene the following morning as bodies were hauled out of the ruins, and the cardinal attended the Anglican funeral service. Thanks to Margaret Pawley, letter of 14 November 1986, for these details. We will meet him again. George Bell was Bishop of Chichester from 1929 until his death in 1958. He was also chairman of the Council for Foreign Relations 1945–58 and Honorary President of the World Council of Churches 1948–58. A friend of Dietrich Bonhoeffer, he would have been Archbishop of Canterbury in 1944 when William Temple suddenly died at eighty-three, had not Winston Churchill blackballed him for his criticisms of the RAF's carpet-bombing of German cities.

2 Ibid.

3 Ibid. pp. 327–28.

4 His successor as Vicar of St Cuthbert's, Prebendary George Irvine, writes: "Gage-Brown was a zealous ecumenist before it became the fashion to be so; and as he had the advantage of being a considerable linguist, fluent not only in Germanic and Latin languages but also in Serbo-Croat, he was much used by Lambeth for inter-Church dialogue." Letter to the author, 24 January 1990.

The Anglican team – "delegation" would be too grand – was to have been led by the then Principal of Chichester Theological College, John H. R. Moorman,[1] an authority on the Franciscan movement. But his mother died on the day he was booked to leave.[2] His absence was a blow but not a tragedy. It meant the Anglicans carried less theological fire-power, but since the purpose of the meeting was not theological, that hardly mattered. For them what counted was to be taken seriously by an important continental Roman Catholic, the successor of St Ambrose and St Charles Borromeo. They were not used to such consideration at home.

The report of this visit gives us a rare chance to see Montini at work and at home in Milan. Headed simply "Visit to Milan", it was written by Prebendary Gage-Brown and intended in the first place for the Archbishop of Canterbury, Dr Geoffrey Fisher:

> I went with three other priests and a student from Chichester to Milan in September to stay for a week as the guest of Abp Montini. The party were all Italian-speaking and were, I understood, approved by the Bp of Chichester [George Bell]. We experienced the most generous hospitality, living in an excellent hotel and having all our meals with the auxiliary Abp Pignedoli next door.
>
> Three cars were at our disposal the whole week: we were shown all the main tourists sites but also the principal ecclesiastical institutions, always being received by the head. Everybody was cordiality itself and we were always thanked for the "honour of our visit".
>
> The outstanding places we visited were the Seminary, an enormous building with a thousand students and a big library with books in many languages, including some Anglican works, and a great many periodicals.
>
> We saw several "oratorios" and parish institutes, containing class-rooms for catechism, bars, TV, club rooms, a large chapel and sometimes extremely up-to-date cinemas, some of them holding 1200 people.
>
> There was an enormous institution dealing with imbecile children and senile old men, with everything in between of both sexes. It has 5000 inmates, all in separate buildings.
>
> We were received by the Rector of the RC University

1 Later Bishop of Ripon 1959–75, senior delegate observer at Vatican II, member of ARCIC 1961–81, author of *Vatican Observed: An Anglican Impression of Vatican II*, Darton, Longman and Todd 1967.

2 Letter to the author from Bishop Moorman, 5 January 1987.

[E. Franceschini], a very remarkable character, and the editor of the RC daily paper [*L'Italia*]. The Jesuits have an institution for press cuttings on a big scale of all sorts of social, scientific and artistic subjects. They also get authors, artists etc. to come and lecture about their most recent work. We were received by the Bp of Brescia [Giacinto Tredeci] who was conducting a conference on "God" attended by professors of theology.

The impression we got everywhere was of immense vitality and enthusiasm. We were treated rather like visiting RC bishops, and no word of controversy was uttered. Abp P[ignedoli] said once jokingly: "Of course we think we are the only true Church, but we do not think you are all going to Hell."

Abp Montini said to us that he realized everything was not as it should be, but that they were trying hard to improve things and he asked us for our advice and criticism. We dined with him three or four times and saw him at various functions, where we were always given the best seats.

We all got the impression that there was no scheme behind all this hospitality, but that he was genuinely anxious to promote friendly contacts. When asked whether we could talk about our visit in England, he replied that we could say, what was indeed the truth, that it was simply a visit of friends.

We said as tactfully as possible that relations with English RCs were not particularly friendly, and I said it could perhaps be understood by our past history of persecution of them, to which he replied that such history should be forgotten.

It was noticeable that the modern churches etc. were free from plaster statues and votive candles, were austere and well kept, though the BVM occupies an excessive place in public and private worship.

There was none of the sub-acid attitude or the patronizing condescension of many English RCs but an uninhibited friendliness; they seemed to forget we were foreign "heretics".

We came back loaded with presents and an invitation to visit them again. It seemed natural not to dwell on our differences but to enjoy their friendship without *arrière-pensée*. I invited some of the younger clergy to visit me, which they expressed themselves anxious to do.

Abp Montini said how much he had enjoyed being in

> England and praised our cathedrals and their music. His tours in the diocese were in the nature of royal progresses, yet he was modest and simple, without a trace of pomposity.[1]

He was already well on the way to becoming the Anglicans' favourite archbishop. There was no competition.

Colin Hickling adds some glosses. As the most junior member of the party he never sat close to Montini at meals. But he came to know Don Luigi Sala, Montini's secretary, and Don Angelo Cremascoli, Pignedoli's secretary. Sala made a remark that struck him. Someone said that "his excellency" (Montini) was not looking very well this morning. Sala replied: "He is never really ill, and never really well."[2] That could have been said of Montini at any stage in his life.

The Anglicans were very anxious to get the protocol right. Mostly High Churchmen, they kissed the Archbishop's ring at the slightest opportunity. But Montini adopted a swift downward movement of the hand to avoid this "osculation of homage". On one occasion the portly Prebendary Gage-Brown (irreverently known as Greengage) lost his balance while genuflecting "so that Montini with that well-known and very genuine solicitude had to help him to his feet".[3]

Sometimes Montini gave away his lack of experience in ecumenical encounters. "*Erà Cattolica*," he said of York Minster, unaware of Anglican claims to be in continuity with mediaeval Catholicism. But that was ordinary Roman Catholic usage at the time. He tried hard to enter into their ways of thinking. Hickling reports:

> On the last day he asked us for impressions and reactions. All fell silent, and though I did not intervene, I remember thinking that my elders and betters were being a bit feeble and missing a big chance. Montini tried to help us. What about our churches? You must have found much to shock you – "*tutti questi idoli* [all those idols]", and that was certainly the noun he used. These were early days.[4]

They did indeed miss a chance. For although Gage-Brown complained of "the excessive place in public and private worship" of Mary the Mother of Jesus, Montini was already accused by Milanese tradition-

1 Council for Foreign Relations Archives, Lambeth Palace. Thanks to the Librarian for permission to use this hitherto unpublished text. I have described the visit in greater detail in "An Anglican Visit to Milan: September 1956", in *Theology*, September 1989, pp. 374–82.

2 Letter to the author, 26 September 1986.

3 Ibid.

4 Ibid.

alists of "lacking Marian sensitivity". They thought he neglected the long-established expressions of Marian piety – such as processions in the month of May, public recitation of the rosary, pilgrimages to Loreto. Montini wanted a Christ-centred mariology. He was learning ecumenical sensitivity the hard way.[1]

This Anglican visit was a great success.[2] Its first result was that durable friendships were formed – Pawley, Dickinson and Hickling all stayed in touch before and after Montini became pope.[3] So Paul VI became better informed about Anglican matters than any of his predecessors.

But however important this intimate visit was for the future, it was in Rome that Montini had to prove himself. His "return" came in October 1957 when the Second World Congress of the Lay Apostolate was held, attended by over 2000 delegates. It was a spectacular event. Montini had helped organize the first Congress in 1951. In 1957 he was invited to speak, but was not the keynote speaker and not the only star.

In the main the clerical orators reflected late-Pius-XII pessimism. Cardinal Giuseppe Pizzardo shared an Augustinian vision of humankind as a *massa damnata* [a condemned mass]. Fr Sebastian Tromp, a Dutch Jesuit famed for drafting texts for Cardinal Alfredo Ottaviani and being the sworn foe of Henri de Lubac, came next. Riccardo Lombardi gave no hint that he was out of favour with the Pope and that his scheme for uniting the Better World Movement with the Focolarini of Chiara Lubich had failed.[4] The concluding address was given by Cardinal Giuseppe Siri of Genoa, whom the Roman Curia thought would succeed the eighty-one-year-old Pius. Siri, an arch-conservative, did nothing to discourage the idea.

The lay assembly was carefully stage-managed. There was no discussion, and the laypeople were mere spectators. Yet the control was not total. Some of the theologians who would emerge at the Council

1 Giovanni Battista Montini, *Sulla Madonna, discorsi e scritti 1955–1963*, ed. René Laurentin, in *Quaderni*, 7, 1988.

2 See Appendix to Chapter 17 (p. 714) for the correspondence between the Archbishop of Canterbury and the Archbishop of Milan.

3 Hickling regularly sent him Christmas cards until Msgr Jean-François Arrighi of the Secretariat for Christian Unity pointed out that this was not an Italian custom, and that a Christmas letter would be more appreciated. So Hickling wrote newsy Christmas letters telling him, for example, about the move of Heythrop College to London in 1970. Letter to the author, 26 September 1986.

4 In August 1957 Lombardi received a letter, in Latin, from the Jesuit General, John Baptist Janssens, warning him not to rely on his own judgement, because he interpreted everything according to his own convenience. Giancarlo Zizola, *Il microfono di Dio*, p. 400. Many bishops thought he was mad.

were on show. Msgr Gérard Philips of Louvain, soon to be secretary of the Theological Commission, dared to define the layperson (he said layman) as "the Christian *in the world*". This meant he was not just, as Abbot Christopher Butler of Downside Abbey, put it, "a monk in a bowler hat". Louis-Joseph Lebret OP, editor of *Economie et Humanisme*, was also present.

Then there were the laypeople, already friends of Montini, who would play an important role in Church or political life in the years to come. Aldo Moro, president, with Vittorino Veronese, Italy; Joaquin Ruiz-Jimenez, Spain; Joseph Folliet, France; John C. H. Wu, China; Jan Grootaers, Belgium; Douglas Woodruff, John Todd and Patrick Keegan, England; Frank Sheed, Australian by birth, British by marriage and American by vocation.[1]

So when Montini spoke on 9 October 1957 his words did not fall on stony ground. The question in many minds was: is this the next pope? Speaking in French, Montini displayed once more his gift for see-saw equilibrium:

> The Church shows herself under two aspects at the same time. One is of coherence, conservation, continuity, loyalty, presence; and it is symbolized by the stability of the rock.
>
> The second aspect is of movement, transmission, projection in time and space, expansion, dynamism, hope which looks to a final end; and it is symbolized by the body which lives and grows – the body of Christ.[2]

This was in fact a traditional trope of Roman rhetoric: the contrast between Peter, symbol of stability, and Paul, representing adventure and missionary zest.

But the hearers could take away from it whatever they wanted: who would not prefer dynamism to stability? So was Montini a "liberal"? Yes, said some: observe how he departed from his prepared script to quote in good part Jacques Maritain, attacked by Fr Antonio Messineo in *Civiltà Cattolica*.[3]

Yet on the definition of a layperson Archbishop Montini sounded distinctly traditional, or at least transitional. The argument was one which mere Anglo-Saxons stayed well clear of. It involved asking: Do you need permission from the bishop to engage in the apostolate? This

1 Jean-Guy Vaillancourt, *Papal Power*, p. 72.

2 Translation in *The Mind of Paul VI*, ed. James Walsh, pp. 8–9, where it is given the title, "The Church's Mission is the Continuation of Christ's." This evocation of Bossuet is not false. But the topic assigned to Montini was simply "The Church's Mission".

3 Jean-Guy Vaillancourt, *Papal Power*, p. 74.

permission was called a "mandate". From the time of Pius XI onwards, the necessity of the mandate had been stressed in those countries which knew about Catholic Action.

Yves Congar thought Pius XII, at this very Congress, had made a great breakthrough by talking of Catholic Action as *co-operation* with the bishops' apostolate rather than *participation* in it. It was the sort of nuance you needed a magnifying glass to detect.[1]

Montini made no comment on this issue. He sounded rather hard-line when he set up an essential link between "orthodoxy and the mandate": "Orthodoxy concerns the content of the message to be handed on; the mandate concerns the capacity to hand that content on."[2]

Yet Montini was only a semi-hard-liner and "anticipated Vatican II" when he asserted the basic Christian truth that every Christian by virtue of his baptism has the right (he says "capacity") to participate in the divine gifts conferred by the royal priesthood (see 1 Peter 2:9). But this freedom is qualified by the need for "discipline", the need to have a commission from those who are themselves commissioned, that is, the bishops.

Thus empowered, laypeople were totally free to go forth and transform the world through love. "Layperson" for Archbishop Montini was above all an "ecclesial" term. It is not that priests are "religious" while the laity are not. "Layperson" simply tells you *where* the Christian is: in the thick of the secular world. By the same token the layperson also represents "modernity" in the Church, and it is through the laity that the voice of the oppressed, the afflicted, the simply puzzled, can be heard.[3] Adopting an intimate tone Montini declared, "The secret of the apostolate is: to know how to love."

He had reached his peroration. It was a personal programme, a testimony and, one guesses, his examination of conscience in Milan:

> Let us love those near by and those afar; love our own country and those of others; love our friends and our enemies; love Catholics, schismatics, Protestants, Anglicans, the indifferent; love Moslems, pagans, atheists; love members of all social classes, particularly those most in need of help and support; love children; love the old, the poor and the sick; love those who deride or despise us, obstruct or persecute us; love those

1 Congar claimed it meant a shift from a hierarchical model of the Church to one of collaboration among equals. You could have fooled me. See Jan Grootaers, *Le Chantier reste ouvert, les laïcs dans l'Eglise et dans le monde*, Centurion, Paris 1988, p. 18.

2 Ibid. p. 11.

3 Rosemary Goldie, "*Paul VI, les laïcs et le laicat*", in *Modernité*, p. 300, remarks on the anticipation of *Gaudium et Spes*.

> who deserve love and those who do not; love our adversaries – we want no man as our enemy; love our own times, our modern civilization, techniques, art, sport, our world. Let us love and try to understand, esteem, appreciate, serve it and suffer for it. Let us love it with the heart of Christ.[1]

It was magnificent. Most of the two thousand delegates applauded enthusiastically. Curialists may have asked what he meant by loving atheists and persecutors: was he going to lie down and roll over before Communists like Nikita Khruschev who the previous year had suppressed the Hungarian revolution and was persecuting the Church even more savagely than Stalin? How did he propose to love Muslims who became more aggressive the more oil-rich they became? What did it mean to "love those who do not deserve love"? But all this was the fine print.

Theologians and pastors were described in this period not as conservatives or liberals but as either *fermé* or *ouvert*, closed- or open-minded. Montini was *ouvert*. He was telling the laity to love the world which, since the *Syllabus of Errors* in 1864, had been castigated as the cause of all the Church's woes. His optimism anticipated *Gaudium et Spes*.

It would be going too far to call this speech Montini's manifesto for the papacy: not being a cardinal he was not a serious candidate. But with his remark that "Rome is the centre of the apostolate" he set the agenda for Pope John XXIII's pontificate.

Montini also had a "hidden agenda" at the Laity conference. He had always wanted the Church represented in international organizations: the decision to have an observer at the FAO (Food and Agriculture Organization) in Rome and at UNESCO in Paris was his; in 1951 the Holy See joined the Universal Postal Union, the International Union of Telecommunications, the High Commission for Refugees, and in 1956 the International Agency for Atomic Energy.[2]

If these were more than token commitments, the Secretariat of State would need competent lay Catholics to make up its delegations; the clerical monopoly was broken. Mlle Edwige de Romer, a Polish diplomat stranded in Geneva by the war, set up the mechanism to encourage this trend. With Henri de Riedmatten, a Swiss Dominican from a diplomatic family in the Valais as chaplain, she founded an information centre which became OIC (*Organisations Internationales Catholiques*). De Romer realized earlier than most the importance of NGOs (Non-

1 Ibid. pp. 20–21.

2 Joseph Joblin SJ, *Modernité*, pp. 534–35.

Governmental Organizations) as pressure groups. She died in 1956, but Montini did not forget her.

Meantime in Venice Patriarch Angelo Roncalli was preparing to address the first ever National Congress of Archivists in the Vatican on 6–8 November 1957. It was on St Charles Borromeo to whose pastoral visitations Roncalli had devoted his scholarly labours.

We know this because Montini wrote to Roncalli on 12 November 1957 during the Mission to Milan, to thank him for his prayers. "Something is stirring," he wrote, "but *secundum hominem* [humanly speaking] I feel that we have hardly scratched the surface of the hard crust of indifference and hostility to religion in this chosen vineyard of Catholic tradition."[1] Such gloom was not for public consumption.

"People of Milan," cried the posters outside the Duomo, "from 10 to 24 November a thousand voices will speak to you of God." The statistics were certainly impressive: more than five hundred priests, twenty-four bishops, two cardinals and untold lay collaborators delivered more than 7000 sermons.[2] *Paris-Match* called it "the monster-mission". Pignedoli, who visited seventy-one establishments in the course of it, boasted that it "was the greatest experiment of its kind in the history of the Catholic Church".[3]

More interesting was that these sermons were delivered not just in churches, where one addressed the converted, but in the streets, in factories and in cinemas. Jean Guitton reported that 1283 sites were used to deliver the message, and that "the strategy was to give the city a functional shock, as a Protestant mission had done in the city of New York, to shake up atheistic indifference".[4]

But the emphasis on scale and statistics gets it wrong. The whole point of the Mission to Milan was to speak a *personal* word to people wherever they were. As Montini put it:

> The central theme of the preaching will be God the Father (*il Dio-Padre*), the basic truth of faith, the prime reality of the world and life . . . Churches will be opened up: halls, houses, courtyards, schools, offices, barracks, factories, hospitals, hotels, institutions, hospices; wherever people meet, there will come the good word.[5]

Montini had been dreaming and scheming his mission almost from the

1 *Due Papi*, p. 96.

2 *Anni e Opere*, p. 49.

3 Luigi Olgiati, "*La 'Missione' di Milano*", in *Arcivescovo* (1983), p. 245.

4 Jean Guitton, *Dialogues*, p. 62.

5 Olgiati, in *Arcivescovo* (1983), p. 244.

moment he arrived in Milan. He would be Paul on the Areopagus (Acts 17:15–34), unveiling the "unknown God" to the Milanese. If only we could say "Our Father" and know what it meant, he said, quoting Georges Bernanos, then we would understand Christian faith.

The Mission was also a triumph of organization. A secretariat of five full-time members worked with parish committees under the general direction of Pignedoli. Montini oversaw all the details. He fussed over the flags and banners fluttering from the dome. He arranged special missions for *ragazzi* (youth). He organized coaches to bring the seminarians in from Venegono. He tried to ensure that parishes – and parish priests – should not feel threatened.

He broadcast regularly in an effort to reach those furthest away. He found a new note of self-criticism that was far removed from the triumphalism so prevalent at the time:

> How empty the house of the Lord often is. If it were possible to cry out loudly enough to reach you, sons who love us no longer, I would first ask your forgiveness. For why has our brother separated himself from us? Because he was not loved enough. Because we have not watched over him enough, not taught him well enough, not initiated him into the joys of faith. Because he has judged the faith on the basis of what we are.[1]

It was a recognition of what later came to be called "secularization". In the 1950s it took the form of recognizing that modern Europe was *un pays de mission*, mission territory. It was a matter of realism, spotting the problems that were about to arise. "Woe to us," he told his priests during the mission, "if we blind ourselves with unjustified optimism."[2]

It was one temptation he resisted. One of his consolations, however, in Milan was meeting cultured people. On 13 May 1957, for example, he spent two hours with Count Giovanni Treccani degli Alfieri at via Montebello 32. In 1953 Treccani set up a foundation to promote historical studies about Milan. Montini had urged him to produce a critical edition of the life of St Ambrose. Now Treccani presented him with two more volumes of the History of Milan.

The twelve grandchildren romped about, undisturbed at having an archbishop in the house. Montini admired the manuscripts of St Alphonsus Liguori, St Charles and Frederico Borromeo, Michelangelo, Ariosto and others. There was also a copy – only a copy, alas –

1 Jean Guitton, *Dialogues*, pp. 62–63.

2 Olgiati, in *Arcivescovo* (1983), p. 246.

of the manuscript of Verdi's *Requiem*. The evening was a great success. It helped that Treccani was a fellow-Brescian.[1]

Montini, never wholly at ease when addressing the workers, felt most at home with people who loved Dante[2] and Alessandro Manzoni's *I Promessi Sposi*. Manzoni's novel was for him a breviary of Christian humanism. Commenting on the scene in which the young girl pleads with a man of violence, saying, "God forgives so many things for a single act of mercy", he said:

> This novel teaches us not to be afraid of people who have expelled God and his grace from their hearts; it teaches that no one is excluded from divine mercy; "*Puo esser castigo, puo esser misericordia*" [It could be punishment, it could be mercy]; it teaches us that behind every human event is concealed a gesture of the Providence of God; it teaches us, finally, to *be* Providence for those in greater need than ourselves.[3]

Manzoni, besides providing a spirituality for all seasons, could come in handy pastorally.

Cardinal Giovanni Colombo, Montini's successor in Milan, tells the story of a young man from the agricultural department of the Catholic University in Piacenza. Though engaged to be married, he felt he had a call from God to be a priest. He sought out the Archbishop who pointed out that something similar happens in *I Promessi Sposi.* Manzoni says that though you can offer your own will to God, you have not the right to offer someone else's to whom you are already bound. "So what happened?" Colombo asked, "Did you talk about the two characters in René Bazin's novel, *Magnificat*?" "No," said Montini, "I just quoted the words of Padre Cristofero in Manzoni: '*Tornate ai pensieri d'una volta* [Go back to the thoughts you once had]'."

There was a link between being rich and being cultured. Msgr Pasquale Macchi, one of Montini's secretaries in Milan, had written a thesis on the novels of Georges Bernanos. He was well connected in the world

1 Enrico Cattaneo, "*Il Rapporto con il Conte Giovanni Treccani degli Alfieri*", in *Arcivescovo* (1983), p. 318. There were other visits. On 11 March 1958, Archbishop Montini made a pastoral visitation at Vanzaghello where the count had a country house and a textile factory. He died suddenly on 6 July 1961 (ibid. p. 323). Montini went straight away to the house to pray with the family.

2 He encouraged Dante studies in the United States by making available photocopies to the Catholic University of Notre Dame, Indiana of all the documentation on Dante and the mediaeval period in the Ambrosian Library. Carlo Colombo, *Arcivescovo* (1985), p. 157.

3 Giovanni Colombo, Preface to *Arcivescovo* (1983), p. 6. Cardinal Colombo does not explain in what circumstances Montini made these remarks or how he manages to reproduce them so accurately.

of high finance. Montini needed such men (they were all men) to fund his church-building programme. Macchi introduced him to Massimo Spada, who later became accountant at the IOR. Spada brought along Michele Sindona who raised a million pounds for an old people's home, the Casa della Madonnina. Roberto Calvi came through the same network. Montini paid them ominously little attention.[1]

He was still only Archbishop Montini. He could not therefore take part in the conclave, though theoretically as a validly ordained cleric over thirty he could have succeeded Pius XII. By 1958 Pius was clearly dying despite the best efforts of Dr Paul Niehans of Montreux, who believed he could rejuvenate the Pope by his controversial "living cell" therapy – injections of finely ground tissue taken from freshly slaughtered lambs. The fact that Dr Niehaus was a Protestant was sometimes taken to prove that Pius XII had ecumenical dispositions.[2]

This was not the only example of Pius XII's bizarre behaviour. That the Archbishop of Milan, the see of Ambrose and of Charles Borromeo, should not have become a cardinal was not only unprecedented: it was unintelligible. Papal neglect of the college of cardinals moreover meant that by the time Pius died it had only fifty-one members, half of whom were over eighty: this was a serious restriction on the freedom of choice of the conclave. The full complement of the college of cardinals was at that time seventy, having been fixed by Sixtus V in 1588, the year of the Spanish Armada.

It seemed almost as though Pius *did not want* to be succeeded by Montini. One can only speculate about why that might be. Perhaps the aged Pope lost interest in or didn't care about the succession. "*Après moi le déluge*," he was supposed to have murmured.

On 2 March 1958 Montini had a long conversation with the Patriarch of Venice, Angelo Roncalli. It was not a private conversation: Sergio Pignedoli, Montini's auxiliary, was also present. It would be surprising if they had not discussed the imminent conclave. Everyone else was discussing it. Roncalli had twice, publicly and privately, predicted that Montini would succeed Pius XII. Answering a question put to him at a meeting of academics on Isola San Giorgio in Venice, Roncalli said: "If Montini were a cardinal, I would have no hesitation in voting for him at the conclave." To his Milanese cousins Giovanni and Candida Roncalli, who stayed with him in Venice, he said:

1 Sindona did not enter the Montini scene until 1962. See "The Sicilian who lost the Pope a Fortune", in *The Sunday Times*, 2 February 1975. Also Larry Gurwin, *The Calvi Affair*, Pan 1984, p. 26, for the links between Macchi and other Milan financiers. The Ambrosian liturgy was fine; the Ambrosian Bank was not.

2 Paul Hoffmann, *O Vatican!: A Slightly Wicked View of the Holy See*, Congdon & Weed, New York 1984, p. 24.

> Look what happened to your relative, little Angelo, the son of Giovanni Roncalli, a farm-worker: he became Patriarch of Venice and a Cardinal of the Holy Roman Church. The only thing left for him now is to become Pope, but that won't happen, because the next Pope will be your Archbishop [Montini].[1]

Both these predictions dated from 1955; but there is no reason to think that Roncalli changed his mind in the interim. On the contrary he was getting much too old himself.

Montini waited for the death of Pius XII, the man he had served so faithfully and who had treated him so shabbily, with mixed feelings.

1 Both quotations come from *Giovanni XXIII, Lettere 1958–1963*, ed. Loris F. Capovilla, p. 40.

18

The Cardinal from Milan

"Why is Cardinal Léon-Joseph Suenens like the football team, *Standard Liège*?"

"He wins away matches and loses home ones."

Belgian joke *c.* 1966

Though Archbishop Montini may have been the leading personality among the Italian bishops, nevertheless he was not their leader. They mostly took their cue from older cardinals like Giuseppe Siri of Genoa and Ernesto Ruffini of Palermo. These power-brokers were in league with the "Roman gang" that had exiled him. Yet, as Andrea Riccardi remarks, "Montini brought prestige and lustre to every institution in which he took part,"[1] and the Italian Episcopal Conference (CEI) did not mind having an eagle in its midst, provided it stayed caged.

Montini's horizons were never limited to Italy. He had proposed a meeting of secretaries of European bishops' conferences, the embryo of European equivalent of the Latin American Council of Episcopal Conferences (CELAM) he had worked towards with Helder Câmara. He entrusted his Euro-project to Carlo Colombo, his theologian, who proved too shy to get it off the ground.[2] The setting up of a European Conference of Bishops would have to wait for his pontificate.

Meantime Montini contributed to the "construction of Europe" (as it was called) by blessing a statue of Our Lady of Europe at Alpe Motta near Campodolcino (Sondrio) in the Italian Alps.[3] In this region a hundred years before the French armies of the Emperor Napoelon III had driven the Austrians out of Milan and defeated them at Magenta and, with the help of the Piedmontese, at Solferino. The battles of the First World War in which so many friends perished took place away to the east. The innocent-seeming Alpine peaks had known death and disaster.

1 Andrea Riccardi, *Le Chiese di Pio XII*, p. 41.

2 Carlo Colombo, "*Alcuni Linee Pastorali*", in *Arcivescovo* (1983), p. 303.

3 From 1923 onwards Don Luigi Ré, parish priest of St Francesca Romana in Milan, had organized a summer camp there for orphans under the slogan "Through the mountains to God". By 1958, the supply of orphans having dried up, Don Luigi gave the house to the diocese. Montini turned it into a cultural and training centre for Catholic Action. See Montini, *Sulla Madonna*, p. 83.

So Montini was not exaggerating when on 8 September 1958 as Pius XII lay dying, he surveyed Europe's recent past:

> It seemed that the entire soil of Europe was bloodstained, and that fire and hatred raged between peoples. Military war, civil war, social war, ideological war, cold war, hot war – these were the actors in the last act of the drama. We then looked at each other in astonishment and stupor, and understood that it was all great madness, useless slaughter, as the Pope said.
>
> But why should we fight when we are all sons and daughters of the same land. We look at past history, at the drama which brought us here, with feelings of horror and dread. And then just one word wells up from our heart, *Pace*! *Pace*![1]

Montini captures well the Italo-Franco-German reconciliation that was at the heart of the European Economic Community (as it was then known) created by the Treaty of Rome in 1957. All European wars were civil wars, fratricidal strife. That included the "wider Europe" that embraced the East Europeans.

The Europe that the Madonna could bring together was, of course, Catholic Europe. But without claiming with Hilaire Belloc that "Europe is the faith, and the faith Europe", that Europe had deeply Christian roots was the premise of his Euro-thinking.[2]

Pius XII was an unconscionably long time dying. On 9 October 1958 Montini was high in the Alps at Monteviasco, a village that could be reached only on foot. With his secretary Don Pasquale Macchi he listened to Vatican Radio's commentary broadcast from the bedside. Pius died at 3.52 a.m.[3] Not being a cardinal Montini had no place either in the conclave or the general congregations that preceded it. Yet he was an unseen influence on them. Cardinal Giuseppe Pizzardo, still on the warpath, refused to vote for Angelo Roncalli, Patriarch of Venice, because he feared he would bring Montini back to Rome. The shrewd old Patriarch "calmly replied that he did not and would not seek to be elected pope, and so the question did not arise".[4] Canon law forbade deals.

1 Ibid. p. 98. "Useless slaughter [*inutile strage*]" was the term used by Benedict XV in his 1 August 1917 appeal for peace. The Germans said he was a *Franzozenpapst*, the French a *Boche* Pope. Pope John Paul II revived the expression during the Gulf War of 1991. Some wondered how human slaughter could ever be "useful".

2 Hilaire Belloc's *Europe and the Faith*, Clarke, Wheathampstead 1962, originally appeared in 1920. It was a series of lectures Belloc gave during the First World War. That explains his view of history as "*Gestas Dei per Francos*" as the mediaevals said of the Crusades.

3 Pasquale Macchi, *Notiziario*, 1, p. 45.

4 Giancarlo Zizola, *Quale Papa?* p. 154.

Roncalli knew that some electors were prepared to "throw away" their votes on Montini to show their feelings about Pius XII. He told Giulio Andreotti:

> I received a good will message from General Charles de Gaulle, but that doesn't mean the French cardinals will vote the way he wants them to. I know they would like Montini, and he would certainly be very good; but I don't think the tradition of choosing from among the cardinals can be set aside.[1]

Others were furious at the very idea. Cardinal Siri thumped the table so violently at the preposterous notion of electing an outsider that he smashed the ruby in his ring.[2]

The last lay people Patriarch Roncalli saw before the veil of secrecy fell were Montini's friends Jean Guitton and Vittorino Veronese.[3] This was on 21 October. They might have proposed that Roncalli should keep the seat warm for Montini. At 5 p.m. on 28 October the white smoke indicated that we had a pope and that his name was John.

The election of Roncalli as John XXIII changed Montini's life. Not only did he immediately become a cardinal – that should have happened four years earlier – but he becamc the leading candidate for the succession of the rising seventy-seven-year-old Pope whom everyone saw as a stop-gap. Not all the *Montiniani* welcomed Roncalli's election. Pierre Veuillot wept openly when the result was announced.[4] He reflected the common view that Roncalli was an amiable old buffer who would do nothing much. But he wouldn't last long, and then Montini would be supremely *papabile*.

Though flattering, this scheme was not an unalloyed blessing. It meant that the same "enemies" who had encompassed Montini's removal in 1954 would work to prevent his election next time round. Besides, by making Domenico Tardini his Secretary of State, Pope John clearly indicated that he *wanted* Montini to stay in Milan: for John, who put pastoral work before diplomacy, this was not a mark of disfavour. On the contrary.

1 Giulio Andreotti, *A Ogni Morte de Papa*, Rizzoli, Milan 1980, p. 72.

2 Benny Lai, *Les Secrets du Vatican*, p. 60. Lai added that the suggestion that Montini, though not a cardinal, might be considered came from Clemente Micara and one of the French cardinals.

3 Loris Capovilla, *Giovanni XXIII, Quindici Letture*, p. 746.

4 Robert Rouquette SJ, *Vatican II, La Fin d'une Chrétienté*, vol. I, Cerf 1968, p. 316. *Mon cher maître* did not identify Veuillot, descendant of the nineteenth-century editor of *l'Univers*, but attributed the tears to "one of our great bishops, remarkable for his character and intelligence, who died too young". Only Veuillot fitted that description.

John was crowned on 4 November, feast of St Charles Borromeo. No modern pope had ever preached at his own coronation, but John insisted on it. In his homily he recalled that he had been consecrated bishop in the Roman church of San Carlo, close to where the heart of the saint is kept. He went on:

> The life of the Church has its moments of stagnation and renewal. In one such period of renewal Providence reserved for St Charles Borromeo the lofty task of restoring ecclesiastical order. The part he played in implementing the reforms of the Council of Trent, and the example he gave in Milan and other dioceses of Italy, earned him the glorious title of teacher of bishops (*maestro dei vescovi*), and as such he was adviser to popes and a model of episcopal holiness.[1]

Was Pope John intimating that he was about to resume the work of renewal and reform launched by St Charles Borromeo? And was he hinting that he expected St Charles's contemporary successor, Montini, to be his adviser and a teacher of the bishops of Italy?

The answer to both questions was "yes". On 17 November – the day the world learned that Montini would be Pope John's first cardinal,[2] John wrote saying that "the new pope is continuing his novitiate and so far, by God's grace, *ne va pas si mal*". He also asked a favour. He wanted Cardinal Montini to preface the fifth and final volume of his monumental study of the *Acta* of the Visitations of St Charles.[3] Montini could hardly refuse, all the more since he received the letter while at Pieve di Trezzo d'Adda, one of the places visited by St Charles himself.

When the following 25 January 1959 Pope John announced the calling of an Ecumenical Council, the special role he had for Montini became even more evident for, as a member of the Roman Curia, Montini could not have done what Pope John had in mind: to swing round the heavy mass of Italian bishops towards the Pope's understanding of the Council.

Antonio Rimoldi guesses that "Montini had been informed in

1 *Discorsi, messagi, colloqui del Santo Padre Giovanni XXIII*, vol. I, pp. 13–14.

2 The choice of the first cardinal is usually significant. Leo XIII said that the policy of his pontificate would be revealed in his first nomination: John Henry Newman.

3 *Gli Atti della Visista Apostolica di San Carlo Borromeo a Bergamo* (1575), L. S. Olschki, Florence 1936–57. John's letter is in *Giovanni e Paolo, Due Papi*, p. 107. Montini's text appeared not as a preface but as a testimonial to St Charles Borromeo's abiding influence. Though the work does not make for easy reading, he wrote, it was never "dull or boring, but was full of stimulating information about every aspect of the life of this people, the whole tending to reawaken religious, moral and civic virtues". No doubt the fact that the author was pope did more for the work than this encomium.

advance of his, Pope John's, intentions."[1] Pope John's secretary, Msgr Loris Capovilla, has no memory of this but thinks it quite likely since, with John's encouragement, the substitute, Msgr Angelo Dell'Acqua, "was often on the phone to Montini".[2] So we may take it that Montini had advance warning about the Council. But then there is a problem.

On the evening of the day the Council was announced Montini telephoned Fr Giulio Bevilacqua with the news and said, "This holy old boy doesn't realize what a hornet's nest he's stirring up."

"Don't worry, Don Battista," replied Bevilacqua, still calling him by his 1920s title, "*lascia fare*, let it be, the Holy Spirit is still awake and about in the Church."[3]

The two stories can be reconciled if we place this conversation not on 25 January but on the evening of the day (whenever it was) that he learned the staggering news. Whatever the explanation, by 26 January he produced a message to his diocese which he called the "Ambrosian echo" to the papal announcement. He wrote:

> This Council will be the greatest that the Church has ever celebrated in the twenty centuries of its history, the greatest in numbers and in spiritual impact, called in complete and peaceful unity with the hierarchy.[4] It will be the most "catholic" in its dimensions, truly reaching out towards the whole world and all civil societies.[5]

Once again, he says, "Rome, capital of our country, will be what the Apostles Peter and Paul made and still make it – the spiritual capital of the world."

It was a truly astonishing announcement. For some manuals of theology taught that, since the 1870 definition of papal infallibility, councils had become *unnecessary*. Opponents of the infallibility decree, like John Joseph Döllinger who drifted away into the Old Catholic Church, thought it had made councils superfluous.

The point of the hornet's nest anecdote is that Montini would never have called a council himself. The Church at that date appeared so well structured and secure that it seemed better to leave well alone (*quieta non movere*): striving to do better, oft we mar what's well. By the

1 "*La Preparazione del Concilio*", in *Arcivescovo* (1985), p. 204.

2 Letter to the author, 25 November 1986.

3 Fappani-Molinari, *Montini Giovane*, p. 171.

4 Montini means that the Council did not come about as the result of outside pressures, as in the "conciliarist" movement of the fifteenth and sixteenth centuries.

5 *Eco Ambrosiano*, in *Discorsi e scritti sul Concilio*, p. 25.

summer of 1960 Montini stood this argument on its head: this Council is different because it is *not* called to respond to a crisis:

> Neither heresies nor schisms nor dramatic difficulties within the Church call for the summoning of the bishops to gather round the Pope. Other reasons prompt them to come together: a desire to enjoy their own inner unity, a duty to exercise their healthy vitality more efficiently, a need for holiness and inner spiritual development.[1]

This Council, one can say, had the merit of being gratuitous: it was the Church discovering and expressing itself.

Montini quotes a remark of the Bonn Church historian, Hubert Jedin, about the Council of Trent which would apply even more to Vatican II – as it was already being called: "The Council's deepest significance does not lie in any one doctrine it defined, nor in any one reform it instituted: its importance consists in the fact that it was the true and proper expression of the Catholic concept of the Church."[2] The "Catholic concept" can be discovered by asking: Who will be present at the Council? Though laypeople and theologians[3] were present at earlier Councils, *bishops* alone have the right to be there by virtue of their episcopal consecration because "the episcopal body is the successor of the apostolic college to which Christ entrusted specific powers".[4]

Where there is a *college*, there is *collegiality* (though the term was not yet in widespread use). The relationship of the pope and the college would be a major theme of Vatican II. Montini acknowledges this by quoting Leo the Great's summons to the Council of Chalcedon in 451. Countless bishops assembled *per iussionem Leonis Romani Pontificis, qui est caput episcoporum* (by order of the Roman Pontiff Leo, who is head of the bishops).[5]

So already Montini was preparing to ally himself with the most "progressive" forces in the Council who would stress that the pope was not a solitary Atlas but could count on the college of bishops for support. Yet the judgement of the Milan clergy was that their cardinal would never have taken the initiative of calling a Council himself. Antonio

1 The address "*I Concilii Ecumenici nella vita della Chiesa*" was given at a summer school on "Pastoral *Aggiornamento*", Passo della Mendola, 16 August 1960. ET in *The Church*, p. 145.

2 *The Church*, p. 141.

3 Up to the sixteenth-century Council of Trent the laypeople present were "princes", a relic of when the emperor took an active part in councils. Theologians were present not as experts (*periti*) but as representatives of universities like Paris and Bologna.

4 Tr. in G. B. Montini, *The Church*, p. 133.

5 Ibid. p. 134.

Rimoldi goes so far as to say that Montini's acute sense of the difficulties involved in getting some 3000 people to work together would have made the idea of him calling a Council "impossible".

Rimoldi confirms this by remarking how reluctant Montini was to put into effect the plan for restructuring the Milanese diocese, even though it had been approved by a team of experts and involved widespread consultation with priests and laity. Why? Because he was so respectful of the opposition of certain inner city parish priests and did not want to upset them. He shrank from hurting people. So he adopted a policy of masterly inactivity and the eminently sensible scheme had to wait for his successor, Cardinal Giovanni Colombo, who realized it some fifteen years later.[1]

If Montini felt incapable of reforming the diocese of Milan, he was unlikely voluntarily to have taken on the task of reforming the whole Church. This is an important point, for to inherit a Council is not the same as to launch one.

Yet his initial misgivings soon turned to enthusiasm. He was determined to be as intellectually well prepared as possible. Just as Léon-Joseph Suenens used the back-up facilities of the Catholic University of Louvain (Leuven) to the full, so Montini involved his seminary, the Jesuit theologate at Gallarate and the Catholic University of the Sacred Heart, in study weeks and symposia. The whole Ambrosian Church was drawn in by pastoral letters and days of prayer. Few dioceses were so well prepared. No bishop was.

Though by now wearying of Milan, it would be unfair to suggest that he welcomed the Council as a chance to play a role in the Roman and international scene. He saw in it a unique chance to renew the Church and, in particular, to reform the Roman Curia. Business took him to Rome more and more often but he always stayed at the Lombardy College in Piazza Santa Maria Maggiore. This was the obvious place for the Cardinal Archbishop of Milan to stay, and he became a friend of its Rector, Msgr Ferdinando Maggioni. But it also enabled him to steer well clear of his old curial haunts where, as Rimoldi says, "the anti-Montinians watched like hawks for the slightest false move".[2]

The Ante-Preparatory Commission for the Council was set up on Whitsunday, 17 May 1959. A month later it got in touch with all the world's bishops and archbishops (2594) and major superiors of (male)

1 *Arcivescovo (1985)*, p. 205. Rimoldi was professor of theology at the "northern" seminary of Milan. His remarks should not be interpreted as "anti-Montini". Rimoldi, having compiled the bibliography of Montini's Milanese period, knew him as well as anyone else at this period.

2 Ibid. p. 241.

religious orders (156) as well as theological faculties of Catholic universities and other comparable institutes (62). They were asked what they thought should be on the agenda of the Council and 2150 or 76.4 per cent replied – a good "market response". Montini's answer, dated 8 May 1960, repays study. It gains enormously in significance if we set it in the context of the Italian bishops generally.

The vast majority did not attach much importance to the Council so their replies are bureaucratic, brief and belittling.[1] The Bishop of Montepulciano (where St Robert Bellarmine came from) wrote unctuously: "I do not dare to presume to think that any subject of importance has escaped the attention of the illustrious members of this most splendid commission."[2] The Archbishop of Trani and Barletta thought a Council "most inopportune". Most of them wanted yet more condemnations and called for a new edition of the Syllabus of Errors. Sixty-five wanted a denunciation of "laicism" and almost as many deplored its twin sister "theological neo-modernism".

Many sought condemnations for the French Jesuits Henri de Lubac and Pierre Teilhard de Chardin. Prompted no doubt by a damning article from Fr Antonio Messineo in *Civiltà Cattolica*, they also hoped to see Jacques Maritain's "Christian humanism" condemned.[3] They could not have known that a second article attacking Maritain was banned by the Vatican Secretariat of State,[4] which regularly censored the proofs of *Civiltà Cattolica*. There was a call for "a single, universal catechism" for the whole Church that was rejected by the Council (and resuscitated at the Extraordinary Synod of 1985).

Positively, if that's the right word, over a hundred Italian bishops called for a new Marian dogma, the "universal Mediatrix of all graces" being a strong contender. In the background was the Franciscan principle *De Maria nunquam satis* (You can never say too much about Mary). Not a few thought that the evils of the present day sprang from Luther's rebellion: this disinclined them to look favourably on the "separated brethren" whom they called "dissidents"; and some even detected a link between Protestantism and Communism, hoping that Vatican II would do for Communism what Trent did for Protestantism, that is, repel the oncoming tide.[5]

If the Italian bishops, in the main, remained incurably myopic,

1 See Giovanni Miccoli, "*Sul ruolo di Roncalli nella Chiesa italiana*", in *Papa Giovanni*, ed. Giuseppe Alberigo, esp. pp. 195–200.

2 Ibid. p. 196.

3 Ibid. p. 197.

4 This comes from Fr Roberto Tucci, then Editor of *Civiltà Cattolica*.

5 Miccoli, "*Sul ruolo . . .*" p. 198.

Montini's own proposals for the Council were remarkable for their far-sightedness. He was thinking about *after* the Council. It was still two years in the future, and yet he was already alive to its practical implementation.

He made two precise proposals, and issued a warning. He thought regional or partial Councils would be needed to bring the message down to the local level: this explains why he was so keen to be present at Medellín in 1968 where CELAM met to discover what the "new Pentecost" meant for Latin America.[1]

Second, he suggested that UNO and the other international bodies on which the Holy See had observer status should be "informed of its conclusions and invited to support its implementation, especially in matters concerning the defence of religion and the Catholic Church, and the universal acceptance of rights and duties according to the Christian idea of man".[2] This must have seemed a rather grandiose scheme at a time when the drawing-board was completely blank, but it explains his eagerness to visit UNO, the new emphasis on human rights and his desire that the pope should become a "transnational actor".

Third, Montini noted the possibility that the Council might *fail*. Commenting on Montini's *vota*, Carlo Cremona says that "for Montini a Council of the technological age should work like a perfect machine. Could it fail? That would be a terrible self-inflicted wound on the Church."[3] This distorts Montini's thought. He had ecumenism in mind and was reflecting on the immense obstacles which barred the route to Christian unity when he wrote: "Besides, a council to re-establish the unity of Christians, after the vain endeavours which history has seen – if it should fail in its sweep – would make the present state of affairs worse. The pundits in the media are all saying that this possibility has to be taken seriously."[4]

The date was 12 August 1960. The remark suggests that a year and a half after the announcement even someone so well-informed and close to Pope John as Cardinal Montini was still not quite sure whether the Council would be a "Council of reunion", like those of Lyons IV in 1274 and Florence/Rome in 1438–45, which tried to heal the breach between East and West, between Orthodox and Catholic. The ambiguity lay in Pope John's mind.

1 *Arcivescovo* (1985), p. 384.

2 Ibid. p. 284.

3 Carlo Cremona, *Paolo VI*, Rusconi, Milan 1991, p. 198.

4 *Discorsi e messagi sul concilio*, p. 34. Thanks to Dr Lawrence Moonan for translation suggestions.

The Council would be "an *ecumenical* Council", by Catholic computation the twenty-first in the series. But what did "ecumenical" mean here? Did it refer to the whole *Catholic* world or the whole *Christian* world? Père Charles Boyer SJ, supposedly an authority on such matters, argued for the narrow view: the Council was essentially a *Catholic* event and "ecumenical" was contrasted with "local" or "partial". As such it said nothing about inter-church relations.[1]

Montini was by now well beyond the judgement of his former adviser. The old reasons for timidity had gone. But the truth was that though Pope John clearly had a desire for Christian unity in its broadest sense, in his first encyclical, *Ad Petri Cathedram*, he had made the mistake of talking about "a *return* to unity", as though all the separated brethren had to do was to "come back" to Roman obedience. In 1960 Montini quoted Pope John naïvely without realizing that such appeals could offend other Christians: "May we, in fond anticipation, address you as sons and brothers? May we hope with a father's love for your return?"[2] The visit of Dr Geoffrey Fisher in December 1960 soon put the damper on such hopes. The Council would be a "Catholic" event but it would concern the whole Christian world, who would be present as "delegate-observers".

Yet elated though he was by the prospect of the Council, Montini seemed to go through another bout of depression. He cannot have seen it in those terms for he wrote to Pope John about it in a long Christmas letter dated 22 December 1959. What is going wrong? He lists five recent deaths of priests (including that of Msgr Francesco Olgiati) who "gave faithful and solid support to the cathedral chapter and the archdiocesan curia".[3] That confirms that not all the Milanese clergy gave him the support he needed.

In the secular world things are even worse, and his rhetoric takes on the dark hues of any Italian bishop flaying the modern world:

> The ranks of the enemies of God wax ever stronger; laicism and anti-clericalism are back imperiously in fashion; licence in customs, in the press and especially in the theatre and cinema (*spettacoli*) is widespread, abusive and unbridled; ideas and trends of dubious value trouble and divide the ranks of those who bear the name of Christian.[4]

1 Sir John Lawrence, Diary, MS p. 4. See Peter Hebblethwaite, *John XXIII, Pope of the Council*, pp. 327–28.

2 *The Church*, p. 147.

3 *Due Papi*, p. 116.

4 Ibid.

No wonder, with a sob in his voice, he begs a blessing from the Holy Father to give him the strength "to challenge (*fronteggiare*) this age of confusion and weakness".

It is hard to believe that Montini wrote such fustian. And – the thought occurs – if that is how he felt as Archbishop of Milan, how much worse would he fare as pope. For then, apart from God, he would have no one to turn to. There was a case against Montini as pope, not based on his "liberal" ideas but on his temperament. Would he be able to ride out the inevitable storms? Or, in more evangelical terms, would he be able to drink the cup, carry the cross?

Montini lived life at a great and worrying pitch of intensity. An analysis of his literary style may take us close to his inner state.[1] "Tension" is the dominant note of his spirituality, like a taut bow-string. So his prose, defined by Giuliani Vigini as "equilibrium in motion", never settles down comfortably. Here is a passage from an address to Milanese priests, which in both *form* and *content* illustrates Montini's "theology of tension":

> The priestly vocation is a call to a tense life (*una vita tesa*), to a life that is perpetual aspiration, that never turns in on itself, that never sits down along the road, but continually quickens its step; if tired, it is reassured; if limping, it is strengthened; if delayed, it is stimulated. Our minds should be ever vigilant, alert, active . . . More: we need to live at this high temperature. Why? Because the priesthood is a great reality that fills those who live it fully with great joy, that becomes burdensome only when the temperature falls and tepidity sets in. Why should that be? Because we have renounced so much; we have given up so many relationships in the natural and temporal order; we have forgone many, so many legitimate and sacred things in order to be in the *agone*, in the contest, to be athletes of the spirit.[2]

This passage is clearly autobiographical. This is his own ideal of the priesthood. The feeling of "exaltation" is the compensation for giving up marriage (dimly visible in the coy language about "so many legitimate and sacred things"). The "high temperature" (fever-pitch?) he rec-

1 What follows is inspired by Giuliano Vigini, "*Lo stile letterario nei discorsi e negli scritti pastorali*", in *Arcivescovo* (1985), pp. 231–41. Later there appeared Fabio Finotti, *Critica linguistica et linguaggio religioso in Giovanni Battista Montini*, Saggi (Essays) 1.

2 *Discorsi*, IV, pp. 171, 174. Quoted by Vigini, op. cit. p. 233. Though translations do not lend themselves easily to discussion of stylistic questions, *le style c'est l'homme même* even in another language.

ommends to the Milanese priests was traditionally called priestly ardour or fervour, that inner fire that burns without consuming.[1]

It is quite understandable if not all Milanese priests wanted to live their priesthood in such a state of perpetual tension and exaltation. Let Cardinal Montini live on that level of enthusiasm if he must. Many priests prefer to live their lives at a slightly lower temperature: even the much-dreaded "tepidity" is a long way down the thermometer. They still had a margin for virtue.[2]

Montini really believed what he said about spiritual alertness and constant tension. But it is risky to try to live at such heights. "The mind, the mind has mountains, dark, sheer, no-man-fathomed," said the Jesuit Gerard Manley Hopkins, a poet Montini could not read but would have loved. The higher one aspires, the greater the crash. Pascal should have taught him that "*Qui veut faire l'ange, fait la bête*". The loftier the spiritual ambition the deeper the plunge into the "vale of despondency". Montini really knew moments of depression of a depth and extent that hardly anyone noticed. It is not something a cardinal archbishop easily talks about. They become adept at covering up.

Nello Vian, layman and historian, dropped in on Montini on a Sunday morning, 12 February 1961. The cardinal was suffering from a cold – it was his annual fixture – but otherwise looked no worse than usual. Yet Montini's gloom shocked Vian:

> What most struck me was his pessimism about the Church, and in particular about his Church of Milan. He said that the phrase that best summed up his state of mind was Jesus' Agony in the garden, a painful intense suffering. In this half-hour he spoke of the gap between means and ends (60–70 churches to be built, three or four more every year because of the influx of immigrants), of the proportion of Mass-goers (a third, I think) in his and other archdioceses; of the incredible poverty of men and means compared with the wealth that grew and accumulated, almost effortlessly, in certain hands, especially in manufacturing.
>
> He spoke of the suffering caused by young lay people,

1 One of Montini's favourite authors, Romano Guardini, used this image in *Steps to the Temple*. Here is a little *florilegium* of texts from his exhortations to the priests of Milan: "I should have a spirit always ready to be exalted, to wonder, to admire." "We should always be as it were in a state of exaltation (*di esaltazione*)." "It is time to be on watch, it is the time of tension and toil." All in ibid. p. 238 fn. 5.

2 Montini's stress on high-wire heroism may owe something to the novels of Georges Bernanos. The French novelist abominated the "mediocre" clerics who ran the Catholic press and the "mediocre" *bourgeoisie*. Montini favourably reviewed the novel in which this theme made its first appearance, *L'Imposture*.

> rebellious (*riottosi*) and disobedient to the Church (he mentioned ACLI,[1] and the magazine *Adesso*;[2] of the bitterness he felt that people hostile to the Church were in a position to attack her.
>
> There were other minor causes of suffering – difficulties with the Ambrosian Library, the odd lack of interest in the great bishops of the diocese (the works of St Charles Borromeo were not even in the Library).
>
> He said, more than once, that he would have gladly passed through Milan *raptim*, without leaving a trace (he was thinking of Achille Ratti, Archbishop of Milan for just seven months before becoming pope); and I thought of the rumours that were going the rounds about him being called to Rome.
>
> The dominant impression I came away from the meeting with was that he felt alone, lacking in help and support, particularly from the clergy. He lamented the desolate state of catechetics, which was no longer done according to the historical tradition of the Milan archdiocese.
>
> He alluded, towards the end, to the renunciation he had made, to the barrier that he had to set up between himself and his old friends in Rome [the *Montiniani*, led by Dell'Acqua] in order to avoid hostile critics who – it seems to me he said this bluntly – have been denouncing him. He said he had great hopes for the Council, that would soon begin. He said nothing about Rome, not without a touch of bitterness. He insisted that I should pray for him.[3]

How much did Pope John know about Montini's depression? It is hard to say. He had sensitive antennae. Perhaps to get him out of Milan and his melancholy, Pope John suggested travel.

It seemed to have worked in 1960 when Montini spent a month in the USA and Brazil. In Brazil he visited São Paolo, Rio de Janeiro where

1 ACLI, acronym of the *Associazione Cattolica dei Lavoratori Italiane*, was to the left of the Christian Democrats, and wanted an "opening to the Left".

2 *Adesso* was the magazine of the Catholic Left, inspired by Don Primo Mazzolari, a "prophetic" figure who suffered at the hands of the Fascists and then of the Holy Office. Sent to a remote country parish at Bozzolo, he was forbidden to preach or teach outside his parish. Montini used Pignedoli to stay in touch with him. See Giacomo Lercaro, *Don Primo Mazzolari e la Chiesa dei poveri*, La Voce del Popolo, Brescia 1969, p. 82. Mazzolari's disciples, it was said, were uncontrollable.

3 Nello Vian, in *Arcivescovo* (1985), pp. 369–70. We must be grateful to Vian for his outspokenness. His remarks were made at the 1983 *colloquium* of the Istituto Paolo Sesto in Milan, 23–25 September 1983. It was a written submission, it came last, and so there was no chance to discuss it. But it is a remarkable document that takes us to the heart of Montini.

he met Dom Helder Câmara again, and Brasilia where he met Juscelino Kubitschek de Oliveira, Brazil's forty-first President (1956–1961) who dreamed up the new capital.[1]

In the United States he had fourteen flights in thirteen days. If it's Tuesday it must be Notre Dame, where he received an honorary degree along with President Dwight Eisenhower. Neither had been the first choice of Fr "Ted" Hesburgh, Notre Dame's ebullient President. Notre Dame traditionally had a cardinal for its graduation Mass: Montini was number five on the list, but he was not to know that. As for Eisenhower, his regard for Hesburgh was such that he agreed to give the commencement address at only a month's notice.

What happened next is best described in Hesburgh's own words:

> A day or two before graduation, Frank Folsom met Montini in New York and flew him out to Notre Dame. Most European cardinals would have turned up in a cassock and sash and beaver hat, but Montini never tried to impress people with his office. When he got off the plane in South Bend, he looked dapper, wearing a soft Borsolino fedora, a tailored black clerical suit, and Gucci shoes. His one problem was his English. During his years in Milan his English had deteriorated . . .
>
> He loved the campus and insisted on seeing all of it. At each residence hall he would go into the chapel and say a quick prayer. From the time he spent in each place, I figured him to be a three-Hail-Marys man.
>
> The new main library was just a hole in the ground at the time, and I described our plans for a new three-million-volume library. He remarked that there was a great library in Milan, the Ambrosiana. I told him how much we would like to microfilm the Ambrosiana collection and make it available to America through our new library. He promised to try to arrange it. Shortly after, Canon Astrik Gabriel, director of our Mediaeval Institute, followed through on Montini's offer.
>
> We wanted to make sure that Montini and Eisenhower had some time together during their relatively brief stay on campus, and so we arranged a meeting in a room at the Morris Inn[2] when the commencement ceremonies had ended. We presented both our guests with token gifts of appreciation. Ned Joyce

1 *Anni e Opere*, p. 54. Don Pasquale Macchi wrote "*Tredici giorni americani*" in *Diocesi di Milano*, August 1960, pp. 3–35. But he missed Brazil. Thanks to Francisco Pimentel-Pinto for Brazilian details.

2 The Morris Inn belongs to Notre Dame and is on the campus. It overlooks the golf course.

> had gathered some souvenirs for Ike, small things like Notre Dame caps and buttons and a few joke items like a putter that broke in half as soon as you swung it . . .
>
> When the President had thanked us for our gifts, Montini started speaking softly in Italian. He said that he, too, had something for Eisenhower. Then he produced a beautiful blue box and opened it. Inside was a block of marble with a bronze angel holding several severed chains. Montini said the statuette was symbolic of what Eisenhower had done for Europe. At the base of the statue was a scriptural quote in Latin from the Old Testament: *Et abstulerit vincula de medio eorum*, which in English is "He took the chains from their midst". Montini added his own comment: "You freed us and we are deeply grateful."
>
> Ike was very moved by this. For a moment or so, he choked up and could not speak. Finally he thanked the Pope[1] and their visit came to an end. Before leaving Notre Dame, Montini presented several gifts to the university. The ones I remember best were copies of sketches signed by Leonardo da Vinci, and some theological talks signed by himself.[2]

One implication was that a man who could deal with presidents so charmingly and effectively would make a good pope.

That unspoken question was in everyone's minds. Pope John had taken a great risk in calling a Council at the age of seventy-six. It involved setting in motion an immense consultative machine. Even if he lived to see it start, he was unlikely to see it through. From now on all Montini's efforts were directed towards ensuring that the Council got successfully under way. He did not neglect his diocese, but he spent more and more time in Rome. He became the archbishop from Milan rather than the Archbishop of Milan. In preparing the Council he was also offering himself as a candidate in the next conclave; but that was a by-product, not what he was about.

1 Presumably Fr Hesburgh means that the President sent his thanks to Pope John through Cardinal Montini.

2 Theodore M. Hesburgh, *God, Country, Notre Dame, The Autobiography of Theodore M. Hesburgh*, with Jerry Reedy, Doubleday, New York 1990, pp. 250–51.

19

Battle-lines at Vatican II

The meetings of the Central Preparatory Commission of the Council will be more important than the sessions of the Council itself, since greater frankness and sincerity may be expected in them.

(CARDINAL BERNARD ALFRINK, Archbishop of Utrecht, in *Herder Korrespondenz*, XVI, 2, 1962)

Cardinal Giovanni Battista Montini prepared for the Council on two levels. He composed lectures and pastoral letters in close collaboration with his own Theology Faculty and in particular with Msgr Carlo Colombo, from now on his chief theological adviser. Secondly, appointed to the Central Preparatory Commission of Vatican II on 6 November 1961, he attended as many of its meetings as he could.[1] If anyone imagined this was a board of honour for notables, they would soon be disabused: it involved unremitting hard work, digesting masses of paper, and endless voting on the question: is this worthy of a Council?

Montini's thinking was developing all the time thanks to the contacts these meetings made possible and his own reading. His lecture, "Councils in the Life of the Church", given at the Catholic University of Milan on 25 March 1962, and above all his pastoral letter in Lent 1962, *Pensiamo al Concilio* (Let's think about the Council), show how much he has assimilated and how far he has moved on since his first, "naïve" response to the calling of the Council in 1960.

For Montini the Council was above all an invitation to deepen the mystery of the Church. It would reveal, display, enact, true "Catholicity". He musters a cloud of witnesses who would have rejoiced: the Tübingen professor, Johann Adam Möhler, with his romantic vision of the Church as *Gemeinschaft* (community); John Henry Newman in his *Consulting the Faithful in Matters of Doctrine*, which does not mean, he explains, that the laity "are a normative source of faith, but that they are a sign of the religious faith that normally pervades the Christian

1 A complete list of these meetings, with the themes discussed and the votes cast, is found in Montini, *Discorsi e scritti sul concilio (1959–1963)*, Quaderni pp. 225–32.

people".[1] He noted Cardinal Bernard Alfrink's important contributions on collegiality and the local Church, and quotes the pastoral letter of the Dutch bishops on "The Meaning of the Council": "Conciliar decisions and decrees are a powerful manifestation of the active collaboration of the whole community of believers in matters of faith – pope, bishops, priests and lay people accompanied by the judgement of the hierarchy that, moved by the Spirit, examines, defines and adjusts everything."[2]

Whatever this means, it is certain that no Italian bishop other than Montini would have bothered to find out.

Montini expected the Council to deal with *collegiality* in the Church, the relationship between pope and bishops. This was the unfinished business of Vatican I, interrupted by war before it could move on to consider the role of bishops. The breach of Porta Pia by Italian troops in 1870 left the Church with a lop-sided ecclesiology. Correcting that would be the first task of Vatican II (as the new Council was already inevitably called).

Msgr Carlo Colombo would be Montini's trusted theologian now and throughout the Council. Montini summarizes Colombo's work on collegiality, reflecting the teaching of *Mystici Corporis* that though "bishops receive their full sacramental powers by virtue of the sacrament of orders, it is the supreme pontiff who invests them with jurisdiction over their dioceses".[3] He wanted to maintain that "papal authority, rather than reducing the bishop's authority, sustains it and finds its own honour in the dignity and stability of that authority".[4] He remarks that St Charles Borromeo – we are back in the Catholic University lecture – though an authoritarian figure (*autoritario com'era*), had the greatest respect for Synods and Councils and proved it in his pastoral action.[5] Like St Charles, his predecessor in Milan, Montini believed that synods and councils were both "providential and necessary"; and like him he would be *autoritario* but with a keen sense of constitutional propriety with respect to the Council.

1 "*I Concili nella vita della Chiesa*", in ibid. p. 114. Unfortunately Montini seems to have read Newman in French translation.

2 Ibid. pp. 114–15. The Dutch bishops already represented the most "advanced" thinking in the Church, emphasizing the "autonomy" of the "particular or local Church" and the role of the laity. See J. Y. H. A. Jacobs, "*L'aggiornamento' est mis en relief. Les vota des évêques néerlandais pour Vatican II*", in *Cristianesimo nella Storia*, June 1991, pp. 323–40.

3 "*Pensiamo al Concilio*", in *Discorsi e scritti*, pp. 82–83.

4 Ibid. p. 83. A famous letter from Gregory the Great to the Bishop of Alexandria was pressed into service: "My honour is one with the universal Church's honour. My honour is one with my brother's strength and prosperity."

5 "*I concili nella vita della Chiesa*", *Discorsi e messagi*, p. 118.

After *Pensiamo al Concilio* in spring 1962 one could not say there was nothing to do for the Council except wait for it. The pre-conciliar period was decisive. Some tough battles were fought in the Central Preparatory Commission. Precisely because they took place behind closed doors, said Cardinal Bernard Alfrink, they were marked by "greater frankness and sincerity".[1] In short, the gloves were off, there was much blood on the marble floors, and these preparatory meetings acted as a dress rehearsal for the conflicts of the Council. What happened at the first session would hold few surprises for anyone who had gone through this experience.

Montini's interventions in the Central Preparatory Commission were brief and usually effective. The 26 March to 3 April session focused on liturgy. Pope John insisted that Prefects of the corresponding curial dicasteries should chair the related conciliar commission: which process automatically made Cardinal Arcadio Larraona of the Congregation of Rites president of the liturgical commission.

Larraona, a notorious "friend of Opus Dei", aptly described by Annibale Bugnini as "a great jurist of conservative bent",[2] was opposed to liturgical reform. Montini defended liturgy in the vernacular on the grounds of 1 Corinthians 14:14 ("For if I pray in a tongue, my spirit prays but my mind is unfruitful"). Against Cardinal Joseph Frings of Cologne he insisted that the "Chrism Mass", celebrated in the cathedral church on Maundy Thursday morning, should be a concelebration; he already had the idea of making the Maundy Thursday evening Mass a celebration of the priesthood. He supported Cardinal Ernesto Ruffini's proposal to drop the "cursing psalms" from the recitation of the Divine Office.[3] It was a packet of reforms that would soon come to pass.

Montini sided with Pope John on another disputed question at the next session, 3–12 May 1962. John wanted a *pastoral* Council, but bans and excommunications would thwart that aim. Cardinal Paolo Marella, who had spent his war coping with the Japanese, presented a fiercely anti-Communist schema or draft, *De Cura animarum pro Christianis Communismo infectis* (On the Care of Souls for Christians infected by Communism). It called for the setting up of a special international commission to plan and direct the anti-Communist campaign. It sounded like, and was, a Riccardo Lombardi scheme. The old Holy Office firm of Ernesto Ruffini, the ex-curialist now Archbishop of

1 Bernard Alfrink, in *Herder-Korrespondenz*, XIV, 2, 1962.

2 Annibale Bugnini, *The Reform of the Liturgy*, p. 25.

3 *Acta et documenta Concilio Vaticano IIo apparando*, Ser. II, vol. II, pars 3, Vatican Press 1968, pp. 84, 135, 310, 340, 361.

Palermo, Alfredo Ottaviani and Giuseppe Pizzardo welcomed this crusading approach.

However bishops from Eastern Europe, such as Franjo Seper of Zagreb and Alfred Bengsh of East Berlin, knew that such inflammatory language would do unnecessary harm. Cicognani, Secretary of State, made the same point in diplomatic terms. But it was Montini's intervention that finally demolished the project: "Throughout the Communists are made to feel condemned and crushed by excommunications – nowhere are they seen as erring sheep. They experience our harshness, not our charity."[1]

Montini was here anticipating Pope John's remark that there was no need to condemn errors, since "today men are condemning them of their own accord". Montini asked two questions: Why was Communism so effective (*Cur communismus tam efficax evadit*?) and why were Catholic efforts to counter it so unsuccessful?[2]

But he went further,[3] mounting an attack on the Manichaean habit of condemning a whole lot of people *en bloc* as "a satanic body", adding prophetically: "It will need patience, but if we are patient enough our faith will be vindicated; time is on our side, and our patience in bearing persecution will be rewarded; perhaps Christ wanted us to bear this witness by carrying the cross."

Hearing this, a Council father from the East (almost certainly Stefan Wyszyński, the Polish Primate) remarked: "Communism is already on the wane." The date, remember, was May 1962.

One contemporary problem that the Council was expected to deal with was birth-control – or, rather, "artificial" birth-control, as it was always called in Catholic circles, in contrast to the rhythm method which was "natural". An older tradition deriving from St Augustine condemned the use of infertile days as a means of avoiding conception, but this was academic as long as the safe period could not be pin-pointed with any accuracy. So it was regarded as *progress* when in 1951 Pius XII said the rhythm method could be used, provided there was a grave reason, whether medical, eugenic or economic. The draft text for the Council, *De Castitate*, was written by Ermenegildo Lio OFM and it restated the doctrine of Pius XI in *Casti Connubii* in 1930 and Pius XII in his address to the midwives.

This was not a topic that greatly exercised Montini. He was not a moral theologian. Neither was Léon-Joseph Suenens, Archbishop of

1 Andrea Riccardi, "*Da Giovanni XXIII a Paolo VI*", in *Chiesa e Papato nel Mondo contemporaneo*, p. 217.

2 *Discorsi e scritta (1959–1963)*, p. 228.

3 Carlo Cremona, *Paolo VI*, p. 219.

Malines-Brussels, though Suenens understood why the laity cared so much about this question. The "pill" – a combination of progesterone and oestrogen – came on the market in Britain, for example, in 1961. As an oral contraceptive it did not "interfere with the act" as did condoms and pessaries. It was not an abortifacient. But did it sterilize? Such questions were considered "too delicate" for the Council floor.

Suenens made this anxiety work for him. Appalled by reading Lio's *De Castitate*, he set about persuading Pope John to set up a small commission of experts. By March 1963 he had succeeded, and what everyone called the Birth Control Commission – its correct handle was Pontifical Commission for the Study of Population, Family and Births – came into being. It had six members of whom four were Belgian, one English (Dr John Marshall), and one Swiss (Henri de Riedmatten OP). Three were doctors; none were women.

Remember Fr Lio's *De Castitate*. Though the Council threw it out its theses reappeared in 1965 in the papal *modi* or amendments to *Gaudium et Spes*' chapter on marriage; and his friends claimed in 1970 that his work was a dress rehearsal for *Humanae Vitae*, its first draft.[1]

The "seventh session" of the Central Preparatory Commission was certainly a dress rehearsal for the Council. The schema on religious liberty prepared by the Holy Office declared that it was something Catholics claimed when in minority but did not have to concede when in a majority. This schema was defended by Cardinal Alfred Ottaviani who also maintained that "error has not rights", and attacked by Augustin Bea, now a Cardinal and President of the Secretariat for Christian Unity. Ottaviani versus Bea, the old Holy Office versus the new Secretariat, became the classic conciliar contest. Usually Montini did not show his hand, but this provoked him:

> I don't like this text (*non mihi placet*) . . . If Catholic doctrine were presented in this form at the Council, great harm would be done to the Church and to the Council . . . The draft should make a better attempt to reconcile the rights of Catholic doctrine, on the one hand, and the rights of conscience and of the state so as to give Caesar what belongs to Caesar and to God what belongs to God.[2]

1 This new light on the controverted encyclical was cast by Jan Grootaers, "*Humanae Vitae*", in *Dictionnaire d'histoire et de géographie ecclésiastiques*, Letouzey, Paris 1992.

2 ASCV II, vol. II, pars IV, pp. 729–30.

At a critical moment when the fate of religious liberty hung in the balance, Bishop Emile de Smedt of Bruges drew Paul VI's attention to this passage.[1]

Birth-control apart, Montini was well prepared for the Council; few others were. As a former curial man he did not wish to appear a back-seat driver. But as the commission meetings wore on he was alarmed to discover that the Council had no overall plan and therefore would lack direction. Leadership was needed, and that *Pope John could not provide*.

Suenens had reached the same conclusion. In March 1962 he asked Pope John, "Who is working on an overall plan for the Council?"

"Nobody," said Pope John.

"But there will be total chaos. How do you imagine we can discuss seventy-two *schemata* (draft texts) *de omni re scibili et quibusdam aliis* (about all that is known and a few other things besides)?"

"Yes," John agreed, "we need a plan . . . Would you like to do one?"[2]

But Suenens had a preliminary question before setting to work: "Can I send you a note on the *idem velle* and the *idem nolle* – what the Council should do and what it should not do? The Council mustn't get bogged down in details and try to deal with everything: it will have to concentrate on precise themes."

Pope John readily agreed, and on 19 March 1962, the feast of St Joseph, he named Suenens a cardinal.

Suenens made a brave attempt to see the forest for the trees and, so as to win the good will of the Curia (*ad captandam benevolentiam*), tried to incorporate all their seventy-two drafts in a twofold plan, based on the nature of the Church (collegiality, for example), and the Church and modern problems (population explosion, war and peace, for example); or what he already called *ecclesia ad intra* and *ecclesia ad extra*.[3] Though criticized subsequently as superficial or unworkable, at the time the distinction was useful in drawing attention to the fact that the Council could not be merely a matter of introverted navel-gazing.

Suenens was clearly *l'uomo ascendente*, the coming man. There is always one such on the Roman scene. Were he Italian he would have been *papabile*. But Montini was not miffed; anyway Suenens sent him

1 Jan Grootaers, "*Paul VI et la déclaration conciliaire*, 'Dignitatis Humanae' ", p. 122.

2 *Arcivescovo* (1985), p. 178. English version in Cardinal Léon-Joseph Suenens, "A Plan for the Whole Council", in *Vatican II by those who were There*, ed. Alberic Stacpoole OSB, pp. 88–91.

3 Léon-Joseph Suenens, "*Aux origines de Vatican II*", in *Nouvelle Revue Théologique*, 107 (1985), 3–21, pp. 1–21. This gives the full text of the Suenens plan. It is almost certain that Suenens was advised by Msgr Gérard Philips of Louvain.

a copy of his plan directly, while others had to wait for xeroxed copies from Cicognani, Secretary of State.[1] Moreover Pope John advised Suenens to meet Montini, Julius Döpfner of Munich, Giuseppe Siri of Genoa and Achille Liénart of Lille, to think about the project: "Bring them together so that I will be able to say 'According to the wishes of a number of cardinals', while being a bit vague on the details. Then it won't just look like something I've cooked up."[2]

This was indeed the shrewd old peasant of the legend, delighting in a foxy scheme that would by-pass Ottaviani and the Curia.

But it also shows that Pope John had no idea what the *content* of the Council should be. He cherished the illusion that the Council would be over in a single session, lasting two months at the most.[3] His readiness to improvise got the Council under way but it could never have brought it to a conclusion.

So Suenens gathered his "gang of four" at the Belgian College, via del Quirinale, to save the Council from chaos. He was able to report to Pope John on 4 July. Döpfner defended the idea of letting the seventy-two *schemata* run on (and on) but was soon converted to the need for a plan. With a few grumbles from Siri, they all agreed on that. They agreed too that, while the first session should be "doctrinal" in content, focusing on the Church as the mystery of Christ (*de Ecclesiae Christi mysterio*), later sessions would have a more "pastoral" character.

The notion of other sessions alarmed Pope John: he wanted to finish the Council in a single session before Christmas. It was the start of the 400th anniversary year of the Council of Trent. Besides, on 21 September 1962 Pope John learned he had cancer. If there were more than one session he would not see it through to the end.

The real significance of the meeting at the Belgian College was that if, as this group suspected, the Council reached a procedural dead-end, an alternative plan would be available to rescue it. The group also had a place to meet or conspire: the Belgian College.

From 19 July to 20 August 1962 Cardinal Montini got away from it all with a long journey to the Lombardy missions, visiting priests,

1 That is what Cardinal Suenens says in ibid. Nr 1, 1985, p. 3: "Je crus utile de le communiquer à quelques amis, dont le cardinal Montini."

2 Ibid. p. 179.

3 The evidence given at Pope John's beatification process confirms this. Cardinal Agostino Casaroli said, "Pope John thought that all the conciliar problems could be solved in the space of two months." Cardinal Pericle Felici added: "He [Pope John] was very happy with the draft documents and thought the Council could be finished in a single session – two months – or, at the very most, given the difficulties that had emerged in the preparatory commission, two sessions", Carlo Cremona, *Paolo VI*, p. 195.

sisters and lay people in Zimbabwe (then Southern Rhodesia) and the Upper Volta. He also called at Nigeria and Ghana where his former auxiliary, Sergio Pignedoli, was apostolic delegate. Here Pignedoli had his first serious encounters with Islam. He told Montini that the further one got away from the cauldron of the Middle East, where anti-Zionism bubbled, the more Islam could be seen in its religious dimension. Montini had a special feel for the future Zimbabwe, where the mission was in the hands of the British Jesuits, and visited the Kariba dam project built by the Milanese consortium IMPRESIT. Many Italians worked on it.[1]

There were good objective reasons for this journey. He had given the Milan diocese a missionary dimension as never before. In 1961 he had laid the foundations for the Lombardy Mission and found priests from Milan and Lodi and the Sisters of Maria Bambina to run it. Finance was another headache. He remarked to Giovanni Colombo, one of his auxiliaries, "I'll leave you and the others in charge of the means; I'll remain the man of ends."[2] Colombo says that his message to Africa was: "Fear not, Africa, if the Gospel takes root among your people it will purify and safeguard both your faith and your freedom; and it will also protect and keep intact the heritage of your original culture on which your future surely depends."[3]

This was said just as the "winds of change" were blowing, indeed howling, through Africa.

Montini's extended visit to Africa meant that he missed some of the intrigues that preceded the Council. He didn't miss much. His successor in Milan, Cardinal Giovanni Colombo, reports two significant remarks as Montini set off for Rome on 9 October 1962. "We are not yet ready for the Council," he complained. But then he said, "I think the Church is ready (*matura*) for a non-Italian pope."[4] Unlike most of the bishops, he knew about Pope John's cancer and wondered about the succession. He set off thinking that perhaps the Council might fail and that Suenens might well become the next pope.

Cardinal Montini arrived in time to give a lecture at the Campidoglio, Rome's city hall, in the presence of President Antonio Segni and the Prime Minister, Amintore Fanfani. The purpose of the lecture was to "place" the event of the Council in the long perspective of Rome's

1 Bishop Donal Lamont, a fiery Irish Carmelite who opposed the Ian Smith regime, assures me that Paul VI "always had a particular interest in Rhodesia, as it was then called, as a result of this visit in 1962".

2 *Arcivescovo* (1983), pp. 10–11.

3 Ibid. p. 12. It seems extraordinary that this should be the only reference to Africa in the two stout books devoted to Montini in Milan. This does not reflect his own priorities.

4 *Arcivescovo* (1985), p. 193.

history and explain what the it meant for Rome and for Italy. Fascism had claimed the inheritance of ancient imperial Rome, master of the Mediterranean, while despising papal Rome, "sacred Rome", centre of Christendom. Democratic Italy had put an end to that absurd competition and the Holy See and Rome could live happily together. But they remained distinct. Far from challenging the reality of "Italian" Rome, he lives it and celebrates it even as he speaks in the Campidoglio, "which is the symbol of the glory that was Rome through the centuries".

But that is not the whole of Rome:

> Can Rome fulfil itself if it remains merely a national capital? Is the memory of its glorious past enough to satisfy its radical universalism? . . . We are saying nothing very new when we say that another Rome survives, on another level, the Rome of the Catholic faith, eternal Rome. Not only the Rome of the Emperors but the Rome of the Apostles. The comparison is made not to decide which is the more enduring but to note that they both combine to challenge the centuries.[1]

St Peter *chose* Rome as the place of his ministry, as though understanding that the "universality" that would characterize the Church needed to build on the "universality" that was Rome.

However, Cardinal Montini added, Councils do not have to take place in Rome, and in fact the majority of them were elsewhere. But there is a congruence between Rome and the very idea of an ecumenical council:

> Yet it is evident that Rome is the best seat of a Council, the place where its meaning is given sharpest relief and the most luminous setting. Rome is the city of unity, the city of authority, the city of catholicity, the city of universality, the city of truth, the city of charity. What is a council but the celebration of these human ideals that only the religion of Christ realizes, sanctifies and makes eternal? Rome is the city of the Church: a council is a time when the fullness of the Church is manifested. Rome is the city of Christ: a council is a time when Christ is made mystically and operatively present in his Church and in the world.

Giovanni Coppa says this peroration "reaches extraordinary theological and poetical heights".[2] It should have been better known. For it was

1 *Discorsi e scritti*, p. 175.

2 Giovanni Coppa, "*La Meditazione su Roma di Giovanni Battista Montini*", in *Notiziario*, 20, p. 64.

Cardinal Montini's chief contribution to the first session of the Council which began the next day.

Montini poured all of himself and his experience into the Campidoglio address, just as, next day, Pope John XXIII put all his experience into the opening address to the Council, which should be known by its opening words *Gaudet Mater Ecclesia* (Mother Church rejoices). It had five themes which lifted it above banality and shaped the future course of the Council: the idea of the Council as the *celebration* of faith, ever-old, ever-new; an optimism in the Spirit which involved a repudiation of the "prophets of misfortune"; a clear statement about what the Council was for and what not; a crucial distinction between the "substance" of faith and the language in which it was clothed; and a preference for the "medicine of mercy" in dealing with modern errors rather than "the rod of condemnation".[1]

Montini was special for Pope John. The Capidoglio speech proves it. They were discreetly in league, left hand, right hand, some punch. Another privilege was that of living inside the Vatican during the Council. He was not the only one. A few others were lodged in the austere Palazzo Santa Marta where D'Arcy Osborne had been holed up for the duration of the war. Logically Montini should have stayed at the Lombardy College on the Piazza Santa Maria Maggiore. He personally had decided the College must stay in the *centro storico* rather than move to the suburbs at via Casaletto where a plot of land had already been bought by his predecessor, Cardinal Ildefonso Schuster.

The disadvantages of staying at Piazza Santa Maria Maggiore – the racket, closeness to the *louche* hotels near Termini station – could be overcome by rebuilding and double glazing. He wanted his Lombardy students to have the full experience of Rome, its history, its libraries, its problems. The Rome he had talked about in his Campidoglio address was simply not available in the suburbs. Anyway the gutting and reconstruction of the Lombardy College began now, in October 1962, just as the Council opened.

1 See Peter Hebblethwaite, *John XXIII, Pope of the Council*, pp. 430–33. Also Giuseppe Alberigo and Alberto Melloni in *Fede Tradizione Profezia*, pp. 187–285, who study the successive drafts and provide the nearest we have to a critical edition. Discussion about "what Pope John really said" on the substance of faith and the language in which it was clothed flared up briefly at the start of 1992. The contest was concluded by Francis Sullivan SJ: "The crucial question remains: did Pope John approve of every word of the official Latin text (as John Finnis maintains), or was he made to say something by his Latin translators that was incompatible with what he meant to say (as Peter Hebblethwaite claims)? I do not know how Finnis can be so sure that Pope John approved of every word of the Latin text", which added Vatican I's formula *eodem tamen sensu eademque sententia* (in the same sense and with the same meaning), *Tablet*, 1 February 1992, p. 139.

Montini was given the first floor of the Archpriest's Residence (*palazzina*) on the left of St Peter's as you look at it. Ironically, it had been occupied for decades by Cardinal Nicola Canali, reputed financial wizard and Montini's wartime enemy, who died on 3 August 1961. Pope John's old Bergamo chum and fellow fat man, Cardinal Gustavo Testa, took it over, lived on the second floor and did not need the first floor. Canali had used them to store the archives for the canonization of St Pius X and the "process" of beatification of Cardinal Merry del Val, Pius X's Secretary of State.[1] Testa, now in charge of conciliar administration, put Montini's problem to Pope John, who said, "Let him have your first floor." The practical upshot was that while others were struggling across Rome to get to St Peter's, Montini only had to stroll across the Piazza Santa Marta to be home and back at work.[2]

His new home also had a more efficient telephone system than the Belgian College, which had only one line. All calls went through the Rector, Msgr Albert Prignon, who on 12 October 1962 logged 164 calls about the lists of candidates for conciliar commissions.[3] Soon the Belgian College installed a console with fifteen lines.

But at this stage Montini, though not unhappy that the Council should elect its own commissions and do so at the suggestion of Cardinal Achille Liénart of Liège, another member of the Belgian College group, he thought this solved nothing. He foresaw shipwreck if the Council were allowed merely to drift on rudderlessly. That was a not uncommon judgement. "No good can come out of the Council," said Dom Helder Câmara, "unless the Holy Spirit can produce a miracle."

Montini was constantly on the phone trying to contact the experts needed to legitimate liturgical reform on historical grounds. He begged Aimé Martimort to find out where Marist Fr Annibale Bugnini was – unaware that Bugnini was "disgraced" and sidelined for excessive liturgical enthusiasm.[4]

All eyes were fixed on the elections to the new commissions: they were a sign that the Council was master of its own fate. Montini obeyed the principle *in omnibus respice finem* (remember the goal).

1 Michele Maccarrone, *Arcivescovo* (1985), pp. 301–2.

2 The Archpriest's residence is unchanged. But in 1991 a third floor was added on top of the Palazzo Santa Marta, at enormous expense, and its first inhabitant was Cardinal Agostino Casaroli, who resigned as Secretary of State in December 1990, as soon as the Charter of Paris which concluded the Helsinki process and formally ended the Cold War was signed. He was then seventy-six.

3 *Evêques et théologiens belges au concile*, Louvain-la-Neuve, 1 October 1988, MS p. 13.

4 Aimé Georges Martimort, "*Le rôle de Paul VI dans la réforme Liturgique*", in *Le rôle de G. B. Montini–Paul VI dans la réforme liturgique*, p. 59.

The Council began in confusion and the chances were that this would continue. In his wonderful opening address, *Gaudet Mater Ecclesia*, Pope John indicated a general direction but offered no directives as to how it was to be achieved. Pope John provided the Council with inspiration; what it needed was a *plan*.

In a letter to Cardinal Amleto Cicognani, Secretary of State, dated 18 October 1962 and transparently intended for Pope John, Montini produced such a plan.

> Your most reverend eminence
> With deep humility and on the prompting of several other bishops whose wisdom is unquestionable and of the Lombardy bishops, I draw attention to a matter that seems very serious to me and to other Council fathers: the Council which has begun so well and which is followed so attentively by the whole Church and the secular world, does not have any organic programme; nor can one see a plan emerging, based on some particular idea or logic.

We were told, Montini goes on, that the first topic to be discussed was the sacred liturgy, whereas in the booklets we received it does not come first and there is no very cogent reason why it should; that confirms the idea that there is no coherent plan:

> Without some organic structure the lofty aims by which the Holy Father has justified the celebration of this extraordinary event cannot be realized. That is dangerous for the outcome of the Council; it diminishes its importance; it means that in the eyes of the world it forfeits the intellectual power and comprehensibility on which its effectiveness greatly depends. The material already prepared is not a harmonious and well-thought out piece of architecture, nor can it reach the height needed to be a lighthouse casting its beams on the world and time.

This was only a week after *Gaudet Mater Ecclesia*, which contains the gist of Pope John's "revolution".

But now Montini is saying that splendid though that speech may have been in getting the Council in the right frame of mind – ecumenical, merciful and so on – it did not deal with any of the practical questions that would have to be faced. The contrast between John's inspirational speech of 11 October and Montini's down-to-earth letter of 18 October 1962 illustrates the contrast between the two men more generally. Montini goes on:

> That is why, permit me, the least of all, to remind your most reverend eminence that several months ago and on your per-

> sonal invitation a number of cardinals discussed the need for the Council to be not a mere heap of disparate building blocks, but a thoughtfully constructed monument. We arrived at certain conclusions that seemed right and which, when submitted to the judgement of other prudent ecclesiastics, were deemed excellent.

Why, in short, wasn't the Suenens plan being taken seriously? Why was it ignored? Montini knows the probable answer: the Curia resented this "interference" from a foreigner, and would not be too worried by the "failure" of the Council.

The whole future of the Council hangs on this thread. Montini presents once more the "plan which *still* seems to be what we need", and presents it in more practical, operational terms. Suenens admitted his scheme was "an ideal plan". Montini envisages three sessions organically linked. Montini's programme may be paraphrased as follows:

1) The Council should focus on one theme: the nature of the Church. Why? Because it is the completion of Vatican I which had half-dealt with ecclesiological questions, and because in the twentieth century there had been a renewal of the Church's self-understanding, illustrated by Pius XII's encyclical *Mystici Corporis* (1943).

2) But while focusing on the Church, the Council should not be introspective. "Christ the Lord is the principle of the Church, which is the emanation and continuation of Christ. The image of Christ, like the Pantocrator of the ancient basilicas, should rule over the Church which gathers around him and in his name."

3) The Council should recognize the primacy of Peter and his successors as an "acquired certainty". After the 1870 definition of papal primacy and infallibility, "there were some departures" (he refers for example to Old Catholics like Johann Döllinger) "and some hesitations but now there is docile acquiescence". Since in order to "complete" Vatican I, they had to discuss collegiality and the complementary role of bishops, why not state "clearly, briefly and sincerely" that the papal office was in no way being called into question?

4) The Council should concentrate, in short, on "the mystery of the Church". Then it could move on to consider different roles or tasks in the Church in the light of this renewed self-understanding: bishops, priests, religious, lay people. The aim was to arrive at a vision of the Church that was not merely juridical – seeing the Church as a "perfect society" – but rather as "humanity living in faith and love, animated by the Holy Spirit, the Spouse of Christ, one and Catholic, holy and making

holy. It seems to me that this was the original intention of the Pope when he summoned the Council."

5) The *second session* should consider the mission of the Church, what the Church actually *does. Operatio sequitur esse* (action expresses being). Montini suggests this would be the proper place to deal with liturgy (the Church at prayer) and "the young Churches" (the Church as mission).

6) Finally, a *third session* would be needed to deal with the Church's relationships with other human groupings in the light of its renewed self-understanding. This would include:

i) Ecumenism. "To try to attend to relations with the separated brethren at the start of the Council would seem to me to make any solution impossible."
ii) Relations with civil society (peace and war, Church and State, justice, colonialism).
iii) Relations with the world of culture, the arts and sciences.
iv) Relations with the world of work and industrial society, social teaching, economics etc.
v) Relations with the enemies of the Church etc.

That was uncannily close to what actually happened at the Council.

So Montini took over the Suenens plan, reflected and prayed about it over the summer, re-imagined it and made it workable. Unlike Suenens he avoids controversial proposals on, for example, married sexuality or the restoration of the diaconate. Like Suenens he stressed the importance of post-conciliar commissions, but saw them differently: Suenens thought of them as shadowing or marking (as in soccer) curial congregations; Montini thought they should be *new* bodies opening up *new* questions. Unlike Suenens, he allows for the fact that Ottaviani and his ilk are going to fight every inch, and knows therefore they will have to be won over, not just elbowed out of the way with Belgian brusqueness.

It was a remarkable foreshadowing of the way he would run the Council when he became pope. Yet it cannot be said that in this plan was an election manifesto for the conclave that could not be long delayed, since only *a handful of people knew about it at the time*. Yet by proposing three sessions he was in effect raising the question of the succession, since Pope John clearly could not be expected to last that long.

Even without insider's knowledge, everyone realized that a new pope would soon be needed, and he was almost certainly among them. This accounts for Montini's reluctance to push himself forward at the first session. His dilemma was that if he spoke he would be accused of setting out his programme; if he was silent he would be accused of not showing his hand. As Suenens says, Montini "remained very reserved during the Council (*était resté très réservé au concile*").[1] His contribution was minimal. He spoke twice.

He first intervened on 22 October, stressing the point of liturgical change: it was so that the prayer of the Church might be pastorally more effective. That was the golden rule. He steered a middle course between "arbitrary innovations" and simply doing nothing. He had a criterion for innovation, borrowed from St Augustine: "It is better that we should be blamed by literary critics than that we should not be understood by the people."[2] Montini then fell silent in the *aula* until 5 December.

Montini did something no other Italian bishop thought of doing. He became a journalist, writing regular weekly articles on the Council in *L'Italia*, the Milanese Catholic daily, under the heading "From the Vatican". He explained in simple direct language how the two criteria of "simplification" and "comprehensibility" of rites might work, and gently prepared the Milanese for liturgical change.[3] *L'Italia* was his "own" paper. In 1961, when Aldo Moro was under attack for his "opening to the left", Montini had replaced its clerical editor with Giuseppe Lazzati, a friend since the Constituent Assembly of 1946. He was happy to have as columnist this authoritative voice from within the Council who "everyone knew" would be the next pope.

Indeed Pope John dropped the broadest of hints on 4 November, the feast of St Charles Borromeo and fourth anniversary of his coronation. It fell conveniently on a Sunday. Montini celebrated Mass in the Ambrosian rite in the presence of all the Council Fathers. Pope John preached the homily, and invited them to admire this instance of liturgical diversity which greatly enriched the Church. Never before had Mass been celebrated in the Ambrosian rite in St Peter's. The first hint was dropped to the conservatives in the Curia: the Pope favoured liturgical reform, a point he reinforced a week later when he added to the Roman canon the name of St Joseph – *beati Joseph, eiusdem Virginis Sponsi* – a pious ruse to show that the text was not immutable.

The other hint concerned Montini as much as Milan. Masses in the Coptic and the Chaldean rite had already been celebrated in St Peter's to display the riches of the Oriental Churches. But not in the presence of Pope John. In his homily Pope John said that Rome had learned from Milan: the *mandatum* or Maundy washing of the feet was not originally a Roman custom but came from Milan, as St Ambrose testifies in his

1 *Aux origines*, p. 5.

2 ASCV, I, 1, pp. 314–15.

3 *Discorsi e scritti sul concilio*, pp. 184–86.

De Sacramentis. Finally, by his presence and warm words about "the first cardinal whom we created", he seemed to be almost designating his successor. He knew he had no right to do so. But he was naturally concerned about the outcome of *his* Council. Montini reported the Ambrosian Mass in *L'Italia*, but otherwise maintained his prudent policy of silence. What was he waiting for?

The Council moved on to discuss the two sources of revelation – on how scripture and tradition fitted in with each other – where another Ottaviani-inspired text (*De Fontibus Revelationis*) came up for rude and rapid dismissal. On the eve of this debate Montini let the readers of *L'Italia* know that a crunch had been arrived at: "Only those who are familiar with the development of theology, the progress that has been made in biblical studies, and the controversial heat generated by these questions, both within and without the Church, can appreciate the apprehensions, hopes and fears which this new topic brings to the Council."

If that seems lordly, compare it with the sort of reporting the readers of *Time* and *Newsweek* devoured, in which the good guys, captained by Suenens, continually routed the bad guys, with Ottaviani as their fuming, impotent general who had stalked out of the Council in a huff on 30 October.

On 12 November it was announced that there would be a second and concluding session in 1963, from 12 May to 29 June. On 20 November the *De Fontibus Revelationis* was abandoned, or was it, no one quite knew. On 24 November Cardinal Bernard Alfrink was Montini's guest in Milan, and gave a lecture to mark the fiftieth anniversary of *L'Italia*. That gave them a chance to look ahead and think tactically. By 25 November, Pope John's eighty-first birthday, they were discussing the mass media in desultory fashion. And during the night of 25–26 November Pope John had a serious haemorrhage.[1]

Who was in charge of the Council now? Theoretically the grandly named Council of Presidents which took decisions about the agenda; but it didn't meet regularly. At least of equal importance was the almost unknown Secretariat of Extraordinary Affairs which met under the presidency of Cardinal Amleto Cicognani. Its members were Montini, Suenens, Confalonieri, Wyszyński, Meyer and Döpfner.[2] They had better contact with Pope John and with him helped to arrange the final week so that the session could end with the feeling that, even if not

1 Loris Capovilla, *Due Papi*, p. 150.

2 See Jan Grootaers, "*L'attitude de l'archevêque Montini au cours de la première période du Concile*", in *Arcivescovo* (1985), p. 259.

much had been achieved, at least they had got to know each other and could expect better forward planning in the future.

There was a division of labour between the three most authoritative figures of the Council: on 4 December Suenens outlined a plan and an approach to modern problems; next day Montini dealt with the Christ-centred nature of the Church; on 6 December Lercaro spoke on the "Church of the poor". Pope John got up from his sickbed to end the session on 8 December with some degree of optimism.

Though co-ordinated and complementary, these speeches could also be read – were read – as programmatic statements from candidates for Pope John's succession. Each stressed a different aspect of the Church.

Suenens on 4 December had the most exciting theme. His speech had been vetted by Pope John. He revived the distinction between the Church *ad intra* and the Church *ad extra*. The time would come when the Council would need to move from "the Church in itself" to "the Church in relation to the modern world". He listed four topics that clamoured for attention under the *ad extra* heading: everything concerned with human dignity – and that included "the population explosion"; social justice; the Church of the poor; war and peace. The proper treatment of this subject, Suenens went on, "involves us in a threefold dialogue: with the faithful; with our separated brothers; with the world". Following Pope John's tactical advice Suenens "brought in Pius XII", declaring that John was merely "continuing the brilliant magisterium [*magisterium fulgens*] of Pius XII". Against Pope John's advice, he advocated the setting up of a "Secretariat for the problems of the contemporary world".[1]

Pope John told him it would be better to talk of a "sub-commission" so as not to alarm people and keep the options open.[2] Suenens referred to Pope John's opening speech of 11 October (*Gaudet Mater Ecclesia*) and claimed to be merely expanding it.[3] He was applauded, partly out of relief at making some headway at last.

Montini's speech was an attempt to dispel the gloom that had invaded the Council, the feeling that – as a New York Auxiliary James H. Griffiths put it – "We have laboured all night and caught nothing." Montini carefully prepared the Milanese for his speech by his 2 November article in *L'Italia*. Loath though he was to be critical of the Council,

1 ASCV, I, 4, p. 224.

2 Caprile, II, p. 264.

3 Suenens was actually referring to Pope John's broadcast on 11 September 1962, which he had helped draft. It contained for the first time the distinction between the Church *ad intra* and the Church *ad extra*, which needed to be kept in balance. But when Suenens said on 4 December "there is nothing here that was not already contained in the speech already mentioned" (ibid. p. 247), everyone supposed he was referring to the better-known 11 October address, *Gaudet Mater Ecclesia*.

the basic mistake in his view had been to "heap up piles of disparate material of unequal value . . . without any logical, organic or architectonic plan to give direction to this immense labour". Of course, he added, the freedom and spontaneity of the Council should be preserved, but not if that meant it failed to realize the goals set out in the two papal speeches of 11 September and 11 October.

Now, on 5 December, Montini began by approving the Suenens *plan d'ensemble* of the previous day. That meant it had virtually won the day, for it was "generally understood that Cardinal Montini spoke not only with the approval of Pope John, but as his *porte-parole*".[1] Then he developed his Christo-centric theme and made very clear proposals for the way out of the impasse on the doctrine of the episcopacy. He proposed three chapters focusing on:

1) the college of the Apostles
2) the episcopal body that succeeded the college of Apostles
3) the tasks and faculties of individual bishops and the sacramental foundation of their ministry.

He thought this approach made more ecumenical sense. He recognized the problems posed by the way *Mystici Corporis* quite wrongly presented the pope as the unique source of episcopal jurisdiction. He recommended, finally, that further studies should be done conjointly by the Theological Commission and the Secretariat for Christian Unity.

That was the key. It unlocked the Council. Grootaers remarks that Montini's words had an intrinsic authority quite apart from the authority conferred by Pope John's blessing. Max Weber distinguished between an ethic of conviction and an ethic of responsibility. Montini possessed to a high degree the sense of responsibility that goes with a knowledge of what the exercise of real power means.[2]

It was less certain that Cardinal Giacomo Lercaro, Archbishop of Bologna, possessed this quality. His speech on 6 December, last of the series, was the most original. He took his cue from Pope John in his 11 October speech (*Gaudet Mater Ecclesia*) and the quotation from St Peter in Acts 3:6: "Silver and gold I have not, but what I have I give you." Lercaro, who had turned a diocesan villa into a home for orphans, exhorted the whole Church to follow Christ who "though being rich, became poor for us". The Church of the poor was the Church of *kenosis*, of utter self-emptying.[3]

Lercaro was speaking in the name of a Third World group in the

1 Jan Grootaers, "*L'attitude de Montini*", in *Arcivescovo* (1985), p. 276.

2 Ibid.

3 ASCV, I, 4, p. 330.

Council. Presided over by the ageing Cardinal Pierre Gerlier of Lyons, it included Dom Helder Câmara (not yet a bishop) and, as its theologian, Yves Congar. They took heart from a sentence in Pope John's 11 September broadcast: "Faced with the developing countries, the Church presents herself as she is and wishes to be, as the Church of all *and especially the Church of the poor*." The italicized phrase made its way into *Gaudium et Spes*.

But one cannot say that the Church-of-the-poor group made a great impact on the Council. This discourse had implications for the exercise of authority in the Church, which were drawn out by Congar in a lecture given in Rome at this time.[1] Congar was working his passage back.

Pope John had compared starting the Council to launching a mighty ship. Now, on 8 December 1962 as the session ended, it was temporarily in dry dock. Pope John insisted that the months between then and what he conceived of as the "final" session, far from being a holiday, would be a period of intensive work by everyone involved: modern means of communication and jet-travel would keep them in touch. But – correctly, in the event – few expected to see him again, so talk about the "next session" easily slipped into talk about the "next pope".

Had the first session been a success? No decrees had been approved, and for a section of the secular press that spelt failure. Pope John knew that "in spiritual matters quantitative judgements do not apply" and the Beatitudes overturn the usual worldly criteria of success or failure. The session had been "like a slow and solemn introduction to the Council, revealing a generous willingness to enter into the heart and substance of the divine plan".[2] Laborious and painful though it sometimes was, these two months had been a necessary exercise in group dynamics:

> Brothers gathered from afar took time to get to know one another; they needed to look each other in the eyes in order to understand each other's heart; they needed time to describe their own experiences which reflected differences in the apostolate in the most varied situations; they needed time to have thoughtful and useful exchanges on pastoral matters.[3]

But time was what they did not have. The pressures on the Council were intense. Astonishingly the first session had lasted only two crowded

1 Yves Congar, "The Historical Development of Authority", in *Power and Poverty in the Church*, pp. 40–79. The book is dedicated to "his eminence Cardinal Lercaro, the spokesman for the Church of the poor".

2 Giovanni Caprile SJ, *Il Concilio Vaticano II, primo periodo*, p. 270.

3 Ibid.

months – around the world Church in sixty days! Everything happened so swiftly, said Karl Rahner afterwards, that it was difficult to remember who said what or where a particular idea came from.

Fr Francis X. Murphy CSSR wrote his *Letters from Vatican City* under the *nom de guerre* of Xavier Rynne. With *Time* magazine writer Robert Kaiser's *Inside the Council* it popularized a version of the Council that sticks in the Anglo-Saxon mind to this day. Good Pope John chuckles over episcopal quarrels. Quipped he: "I don't expect them to behave like a lot of monks in choir."[1] Perfectly ordinary bishops become eagles as they assert themselves against the curial conservatives symbolized by the half-blind Alfredo Ottaviani, the butt of so many jokes. ("Take me to the Council": the taxi-driver takes him to Trent.) There was a mixture of myth and truth in all this. Truest of all was the positive reaction to the Council on the part of Protestants, the Orthodox, Communists and world opinion generally. Great expectations were aroused.

The end of the first session meant the intensification of work on the Council rather than the end of it. Though not a member of the new Co-ordinating Commission, which met from 21 to 27 January 1963, the influence of Montini's 18 October letter and memorandum remained. Cardinal Léon-Joseph Suenens exploited Montini's support to the full. He was the leading figure in the effort to reduce to manageable proportions the curially-prepared documents. With the aid of Occam's Razor (*Schemata non multiplicanda praeter necessitatem*), Cartesian logic (*toujours diviser les difficultés* – break the problems down), and some pushiness, Suenens reduced the number of drafts from seventy to seventeen.

Pope John urged them on, still confident that one more session would be enough to conclude. Suenens' re-ordering of the drafts in the light of Montini's memo was the decisive moment in the history of the Council. The whole Council was placed under the sign of *Ecclesia Christi: lumen gentium* (The Church of Christ: light of Peoples). There followed:

1 *De Divina revelatione* (On divine revelation)
2 *De Ecclesia* (On the Church)

1 "Xavier Rynne", *Letters from Vatican City*, p. 241. The articles on which this book, and its three successors, were based appeared originally in the *New Yorker*. Many sources supplied material (such as Fr Frank McCool SJ of the Biblicum) and many hands worked to lick them into breezy *New Yorker* style. To protect himself from curial retaliation, no imaginary danger, Redemptorist Francis X. Murphy denied authorship for about ten years. But the clues were there much earlier. "Xavier" was his middle name; and "Rynne" was his mother's maiden name.

3 *De Beata Maria Virgine, matre Ecclesiae* (On the Blessed Virgin Mary, mother of the Church)
4 *De episcopis et dioeceseon regimine* (On bishops and the ordering of dioceses)
5 *De Oecumenismo* (On ecumenism)
6 *De Clericis* (On clerics, that is, priests)
7 *De religiosis* (On religious)
8 *De apostulatu laicorum* (On the lay apostolate)
9 *De Ecclesiis orientalibus* (On the Oriental Churches)
10 *De Sacra liturgia* (On the sacred liturgy)
11 *De cura animarum* (On the cure of souls)
12 *De matrimonii sacramento* (On the sacrament of marriage)
13 *De sacrorum alumnis formandis* (Educating seminarians)
14 *De scholis catholicis et studiis academicis* (On Catholic schools and universities)
15 *De missionibus* (On missions)
16 *De instrumentis communicationis socialis* (On the means of social communication or media)
17 *De ecclesiae principiis et actione ad bonum societatis promovendum* (On the principles of the Church's action in promoting the betterment of society)

This is astonishingly close, in form and content, to the final tally of sixteen Council documents.

The last text, schema 17 as it came to be known, was the most important and controversial. It would be wrong to see it merely as Suenens' pet project; Montini was just as passionately concerned that the Council should, having evoked the mystery of the Church, enter into dialogue with the modern world. But Montini was not a member of the new Co-ordinating Commission, and withdrew into discretion. But not into silence.

At a meeting with priests of his diocese at Varese on 6 February 1963 Cardinal Montini was very critical of the Dutch bishops' pastoral he had quoted favourably a year before.[1] There had been controversy over the translation, so perhaps that was in his mind. But he had welcomed Cardinal Alfrink as a guest in Milan on 24 November and could have cleared up any misunderstanding there and then. Slightly ominous.

The more cheerful news was that at the end of 1962 Pope John was declared "Man of the Year" by *Time* magazine and a tasteful portrait

1 See p. 296 above.

by Pietro Annigoni adorned its cover. In February 1963 *Time-Life* invited Pope John to a spectacular top people's lunch for those who had previously made its cover: they included General Charles de Gaulle, Karl Barth and Pablo Picasso. Pope John didn't say no. But he was dying and anxious to get on with his encyclical, *Pacem in Terris*. He thought the first visit of a pope to the United States should be to New York, not for lunch but to visit the United Nations headquarters.

That was why on 13 May 1963 Cardinal Léon-Joseph Suenens was at the UN in New York "presenting" *Pacem in Terris* to its 119 member states. Suenens carried it off brilliantly, addressing a thronged assembly for over an hour. He called the encyclical "an open letter to the world". He summarized it economically: its theme is peace, and peace needs truth as its foundation, justice as its norm, love as its driving force and freedom as its setting. He quoted Antoine de Saint-Exupéry: "If respect for the person dwells within our hearts we can devise a social, political and economic system that will enshrine respect." Pushing his luck, he declared that like Beethoven's Ninth Symphony, *Pacem in Terris* could be called "a symphony for peace".

Asked the obvious question, does the Pope condemn Communism? Suenens replied with the encyclical's own distinction: as a doctrine Communism is wrong, but "people are always deserving of respect and have a value far above whatever views they may hold."[1]

Suenens' UN mission on behalf of the dying Pope John had some important consequences that Msgr Alberto Giovannetti, the Vatican's UN observer, did his best to work up. It confirmed the idea that papal documents could be of interest to the whole world. It set up a good working relationship with U Thant, the Buddhist from Thailand, UN Secretary-General, who thought religion was an important factor for peace. And it meant that there would be a standing invitation for the next pope. Without deviating a hair's breadth from protocol, Suenens managed to leave the impression that he might be that man.

That was not the view of the Roman Curia for whom Suenens represented a progressive faction; but the Church must be ruled from the centre. Pope John was far too shrewd to show his hand. He did say privately to Roberto Tucci on 9 February 1963 that everything must be done to prevent the conclave being "a conclave *against* me, for that would destroy all that I set out to achieve".[2] That presumably meant someone who would continue his line, but prudently, so that neither the progressives nor the conservatives could claim utter victory. So Montini rather than Suenens. Should an *Italian* progressive be needed, then Car-

1 Elizabeth Hamilton, *Cardinal Suenens, a Portrait*, pp. 90–92.

2 Sandro Magister, *La Politica Vaticana*, p. 294.

dinal Giacomo Lercaro of Bologna would be happy to be called forward.

Montini remained the favoured son. Pope John sought his advice and help in his conflicts with the Secretariat of State. The issue was nearly always the same: was he being soft on Communism by welcoming the visit of Alexis Adjubei, Nikita Khrushchev's son-in-law or by accepting the Balzan Peace Prize? The in-house view was negative on both questions. He should not receive Soviet Communists because that would lose millions of votes for the Christian Democrats in the forthcoming Italian elections. He should not accept the Balzan Peace Prize because it was beneath his dignity: popes didn't accept prizes for peace – they just worked for peace as their duty. "I only accepted the prize," Pope John told his secretary, Msgr Loris Capovilla, "to please Cardinal Montini."[1]

On 31 May 1963, a Friday, just four days before his death from cancer, Pope John summoned Montini to his bedside. The Cardinal Archbishop of Milan ushered in the old Pope's brothers, Zaverio, Alfredo and Giuseppe, and his surviving sister Assunta. They knelt in prayer until late into the night.

Canon law said a bishop must be in his diocese for the great feasts. 2 June was Whitsunday, Pentecost. So Montini goes back to Milan and takes his place modestly among the 20,000 young people praying in the Duomo. Asked to say a few words, he speaks with sadness and affection. We need, says Montini, "to gather up his heritage and his final message of peace". "Perhaps never before in our time," Montini goes on, "has a human word – the word of a master, a leader, a pope – rung out so loudly and won such affection throughout the world."[2]

The next day, at 7.49 p.m., Pope John was dead. He had lived eighty-one and a half years, been a priest for fifty-eight years, a bishop for thirty-eight years, and pope for less than five years – the shortest pontificate of the century till then. Yet in him the Church and the world had been prodigiously blessed.[3]

1 Giancarlo Zizola, *The Utopia of Pope John XXIII*, p. 154.

2 Loris Capovilla, *L'Ite Missa Est di Papa Giovanni*, Messagero, Padua, and Grafica e Arte, Bergamo 1983, p. 225.

3 The reader may recognize this paragraph. It is the final words of Peter Hebblethwaite, *John XXIII, Pope of the Council*, p. 504.

20

Contested Conclave Won

> Cardinal Montini's last sermon before the conclave was in the Milanese church of San Carlo on the Corso where the heart of St Charles Borromeo is preserved. His text was John 21:18, "Truly, truly, Peter, when you were young, you girded yourself and walked where you would; but when you are old, you will stretch out your hands, and another will gird you and carry you where you do not wish to go." He was not speaking of himself, but of the Petrine office. Yet he was in tears, and so was everyone else. They knew.

Pope John XXIII died on Whitmonday, at 7.49 p.m. on 3 June 1963. Election fever had been in the air for six months. Some though not all of the curial cardinals resident in Rome rubbed their hands as they mourned: now they could avenge the humiliation of the first session of the Council by blocking Cardinal Giovanni Battista Montini, the obvious "liberal" candidate. They knew Pope John's opinion was that "the votes of the college will converge on Montini",[1] but this was a private judgement that could not engage the future. As we have seen, Pope John had also told Roberto Tucci SJ, editor of *Civilità Cattolica*: "I don't have very long to live. I must therefore be very careful in everything I do to stop the next conclave being a conclave "against me", because then it might destroy the things I have not been able to achieve."[2]

He was not, however, as successful in this aim as he had hoped.

The first general congregation (as the pre-conclave meetings of the cardinals are called) was held on Wednesday, 5 June. To Roman astonishment, Cardinal Achille Liénart of Lille had dropped everything to rush to Rome. Though this involved nothing more strenuous than buying an air ticket, Liénart's prompt arrival aroused the suspicion that, flushed

1 Loris Capovilla, *Ite Missa Est*, p. 220.

2 Sandro Magister, *La politica vaticana e l'Italia 1943–1978*, p. 294. If the last part of the quotation differs from the Magister version, that is because Fr Tucci himself corrected it in a letter of 25 April 1991.

with the success of his *coup* at the opening session of the Council, he was now plotting the succession. Cardinal Eugène Tisserant, who had strong views on uppity French cardinals as on everything else, murmured felinely, "so you see, the Council has prepared the Conclave".[1]

The plain truth was that for the first time in history the non-Roman cardinals could affect the outcome of a conclave which, they rightly judged, would be of crucial importance for the future of the Church. They did not intend to miss this unique opportunity. There was no moral or theological reason why they should not try to break the monopoly of the curial cardinals.

It would certainly be the biggest conclave ever. In 1958 a mere fifty-one cardinals assembled to elect Pope John. In 1963 eighty-one cardinals were eligible to vote, provided they could get to Rome or be carried there on a stretcher. Fifty-seven were European (of whom twenty-nine were Italian). The European preponderance was symbolically challenged by twelve cardinals from Latin America, seven from North America, three Asians, two Oceanians and a solitary African, Laurean Rugawambwa.[2]

Hard on the heels of Liénart came Julius Döpfner of Munich, Giacomo Lercaro of Bologna and Paul-Emile Léger of Montreal, all equally determined, it was said, to get Montini elected. In truth, Lercaro had his own private agenda. Factors in Montini's favour were his Milanese "exile" heroically borne, the blessing of Pope John, his openness to "French" theology, the enthusiasm of his supporters in the Curia – Angelo dell'Acqua, for example – and, above all, his vast knowledge of the Church and his firm commitment to continuing Vatican II.

The subject of all this speculation remained in Milan writing a letter to the editor of the *Tablet*, Douglas Woodruff, with whom he had been in regular postcard touch since the war, when Mia Woodruff had so impressed him. Rudolf Hochhut's play *Der Stellvertreter* (*The Representative*) blaming Pius XII for his failure to speak out against the persecution of the Jews had opened in London in January 1963. But it was not old friendship that led Cardinal Montini to write to Woodruff at this precise moment. The Apostolic Delegate in London, Archbishop Gerald P. O'Hara, intervened, sending Montini copies of Woodruff's article in the *Tablet* of 13 May 1963, "Pius XII and the Jews: Could more have been done?" and George Steiner's review of the play in the *Sunday Times* of 5 May. Montini replied that he would help by writing an article for *Corriere della Sera* that the *Tablet* would be free to quote.

1 Benny Lai, *Les Secrets du Vatican*, p. 121.

2 Philippe Levillain, *La mécanique politique de Vatican II*. Pope John was inordinately proud of his first African cardinal, who was indeed tall and handsome.

He did not want to write in *L'Osservatore Romano* because it had already dealt cogently with the subject on 5 April.[1]

O'Hara then reported to Woodruff: "It was finally decided that he would take your present article and comment on it etc. for publication in the *Tablet*," adding that "Cardinal Montini's name, apart from any other consideration, would have an immense sentimental value in this country." "Sentimental" was an odd word to use. Probably O'Hara meant that by now everyone knew Pope John was dying and that Montini was widely tipped to succeed him.[2]

Pope John had died on 3 June, and the conclave assembled on 17 June. Montini wrote his letter to the editor of the *Tablet* between those two dates. It was his last act as Archbishop of Milan. As pope he would no longer be able to intervene in this personal way. It is the one indication we have that he expected to be elected.

Yet for one worldly-wise cardinal, Pietro Ciriaci, this early rallying to Montini merely illustrated the uncertainty of the "liberals". A desire to continue the Council could not of itself be the criterion for choosing the next pope, he pointed out, since "no one can halt the Council now". Ciriaci added: "Even if Ottaviani were elected he would not be able to do anything other than complete the Council."[3] Was Ciriaci, whose physical resemblance to the French comedian Fernandel was striking, joking? Probably not. His remarks masked the crucial issue: no longer a matter of deciding for or against the Council, the real question now was *what sort* of Council?

Another unguarded cardinal was Spanish Claretian Arcadio Larraona, a severe canon lawyer who was now in charge of the Council's liturgy commission. A friend of Generalissimo Francisco Franco and the Roman champion of Opus Dei, Larraona privately argued that Pope John's goodness and simple-mindedness had led him astray.[4] Cardinal

1 He may have had other reasons for not writing in *L'Osservatore Romano*. When Fr Robert Graham SJ of *Civiltà Cattolica* and one of the editors of *Actes et documents* wrote asking for help, he rather coldly replied that Graham should go through the regular channels in the Curia, that is, the Secretariat of State. Graham sent me copies of this exchange.

2 Thanks to Michael J. Walsh, Librarian of Heythrop College, University of London, who discovered O'Hara's letters in the Woodruff Archive now kept at Georgetown University, Washington.

3 Lai, *Les Secrets du Vatican*, p. 122.

4 Larraona had been active in Rome for many years. He had played a key role in 1943 when Opus Dei received its first *nihil obstat* as "The Priestly Society of the Holy Cross". It was he who in 1950 proposed the novel idea of "secular institute" as the best answer to Opus Dei's juridical status. He also defended its right to secrecy "the better to penetrate the world" (including the ecclesiastical world). See Giancarlo Rocca, *L'Opus Dei, Appunti e Documenti per una Storia*, p. 27.

Antonio Bacci, likewise linked with Opus Dei, thought Pope John's inspired rashness had proved a disaster for the Church.[1] Cardinal Giuseppe Siri of Genoa, of a more combative disposition, also believed "it would take the Church four centuries to recover from Pope John's pontificate".[2] During the conclave they kept such thoughts for themselves or the like-minded.

Larraona was their public spokesman. He pointed out that the "innovators" – a neatly "non-political" term – were divided among themselves. Asked if this indicated a Montini versus Lercaro contest, he changed the subject.[3] He had already had one major brush with Lercaro on the pace of liturgical change, and so sought to discredit him by every possible means.

This was not too difficult. The case against Lercaro was both shifty and shifting. For Larraona and Siri, he was the leopard who had changed his spots. A thorough-going "conservative" in the pontificate of Pius XII, Lercaro had thrown off the mask and revealed his true "leftist" colours only in the pontificate of the benign Pope John. Lercaro was alleged to be under the spell of a rather *louche* layman, Umberto Ortaloni,[4] officially titled his "gentleman" but in effect his fixer, fund-raiser and *homme-à-tout-faire*.

But he was not Lercaro's "grey eminence". Don Giuseppe Dossetti played that part. He had been an under-secretary of the Christian Democrats in the post-war period until falling foul of De Gasperi. Then he gave up politics to become a monk, founding the Institute of Religious Studies in Bologna.[5] Dossetti was credited with having "converted" Lercaro to the cause of "peace" and to the "Church of the poor". Since Lercaro in this pre-conclave period was lodged with the Sisters of Saint Priscilla, founded by Msgr Giulio Belvederi, uncle of the durable

1 Yet Bacci in 1958 had given the *de eligendo Pontifice* discourse, and sketched a portrait of an open-minded pope who could reconcile East and West. It seemed to point to Roncalli. For the rest Bacci spent his time thinking up Latin equivalents for zip-fastener and helicopter. On hearing Bacci described as a "Latinist", Peter Levi, later Professor of Poetry in Oxford, remarked that "a Latinist was someone who didn't know enough Greek to be a classical scholar". Bacci had been the *ponente* (or presenter) of the beatification cause of Isidoro Zorzano Ledesma. Zorzano, one of the earliest companions of Msgr Escriva de Balanguer, founder of Opus Dei, died in 1943 in the nick of time: all the other pioneers of Opus abandoned it.

2 He later relented a little, bearing witness at the beatification process that Pope John's portrait was in every home in Genoa, including Communist homes.

3 Benny Lai, *Les Secrets*, pp. 125–26.

4 Thirty years later Ortaloni became notorious as an associate of Licio Gelli, founder and Grand Master of the pseudo-masonic lodge P-2.

5 This is the *Istituto per le scienze religiose*, now – 1993 – directed by Giuseppe Alberigo. Dossetti devoted his later years to looking after the shrine for the victims of Nazism at Monteveglio.

Christian Democrat politician, Giulio Andreotti,[1] some saw him as the candidate of the Christian Democratic left.

Doubts having been cast on Lercaro's state of health, he had a check-up done by an independent Neapolitan physician who pronounced him fit enough. This was taken to be Lercaro's way of throwing his red hat into the ring.[2]

But the Cardinal Archbishop of Bologna declared he was up and running even more manifestly in a letter to his family of orphans. Dated 18 June 1963, the eve of the conclave, it was written "after a meeting with Cardinal Montini":

> I ardently hope and consider it probable that I will be returning to you; but with a little less certainty than I thought when I left Bologna for Rome. I would like to warn you against the rumours going the rounds which, as you will understand, are indiscretions (inspired or not) coming more or less from in and around the sacred college.
>
> If there were no such rumours, I wouldn't be troubled; but as it is, I am a little disturbed. However all any of us can do is to pray to the Lord as Jesus did: "Lord, let this chalice pass from me; not my will but thine be done." We should also ask Our Lady that she should not leave our family "orphans".[3]

Lercaro presumed too much. Only successful candidates beg the Lord to let the chalice pass from them. Yet Lercaro was a serious contender, and Montini's election was not a foregone conclusion.

Writing on 7 June 1963 the Anglican Canon Bernard Pawley, the representative of the Archbishop of Canterbury, surveyed the Italian weekly press and came up with this "depressing" conclusion:

> Two matters seem to be fairly well agreed on, and both are disappointing. One is that the election must take into account the political situation in Italy. The Christian Democrats were returned at the last election with a very much reduced majority, and now rely on co-operation from the Socialists. Their government is thus very tenuous. The last pope having caused a swing to the left, the reviews say, the new one must surely correct the tendency.
>
> The other thing on which the reviews agree is that Mon-

1 Giulio Andreotti, *A Ogni Morte di Papa*, p. 49.

2 Benny Lai, *Les Secrets*, p. 127.

3 *Modernité*, p. 672. Interestingly, Andreotti revealed this document for the first time not in his own contribution at the Ecole Française conference of 1983, but in response to Andrea Riccardi's paper on "The Holy See and the Church in Italy".

> tini's chances have grown much less in the past two years. He has become cautious and diplomatic, and has even involved himself in palpable contradictions. But they may be wrong about this, though I have heard it in other circles . . . They give a larger chance than I should have thought to Lercaro . . . The colourless Confalonieri is the favourite.[1]

This was Pawley's first (and last) conclave. In Rome for just over a year, he placed too much reliance on the Italian press.

On the very eve of the conclave, 19 June, Pawley reported that the conclave was becoming ever more a lottery like the Grand National, with a daily call-over in which the odds fluctuated wildly. This was bad news for the Cardinal Archbishop of Milan:

> Montini is played down while Lercaro is played up in his place. In public opinion Confalonieri the favourite. Urbani of Venice and Costaldo of Naples increasingly canvassed. So put them on a "long list" . . . In the present state of tension, almost nobody will get the candidate they really want, and they will have to agree on a "third man".[2]

Antoniutti now entered the race. Despite being extremely right-wing and friendly with Franco, he had botched the job of Nuncio to Spain and been kicked upstairs to Rome with a cardinal's hat only the previous year. The only thing he had to offer was his age: he was sixty-five – just the right "age-window".

While others hastened to Rome to intrigue, Montini, sixty-six, stayed pointedly in Milan until 17 June, just forty-eight hours before the start of the conclave. True, Dell'Acqua kept him in touch with the latest developments by phone. Yet he was as modest and discreet as could be. Arriving in Rome, he did not lodge at the Lombardy College, as might have been expected, where the building work was over. Instead, leaving his bags with the Sisters of Maria Bambina (he was their "protector"), he slipped quietly away to Castelgandolfo to stay for the last time with Emilio Bonomelli, administrator and historian of the papal villas.[3]

Nothing sinister about that. It was put about that Montini had chosen this retreat to be away from the intrigues and heat of the city. His future plans demonstrated his total lack of ambition: he was greatly looking forward to a visit to Norway once the conclave was over. Unlike Lercaro, he wrote no letter to Milan saying "don't expect me back".

1 Bernard Pawley, *Rome Report*, 72, 6 June 1963, 63. Canterbury Cathedral archives.

2 Ibid. 73, 17 June 1963.

3 Benny Lai, *Les Secrets*, p. 139.

Yet he preached the sermon alluded to in the epigraph to this chapter. Among the Milanese in their Roman Church, close to the heart of St Charles Borromeo, he could foresee being "girded by someone else, and led where he did not wish to go".

Yet there had already been a meeting of Montini supporters (*Montiniani*) at the Franciscan convent in Frascati near Castelgandolfo. Among those present were Cardinals Liénart, Frings, Suenens, König, Léger and Alfrink. This was substantially the group that met at the Belgian College during the first session – minus its Italian members Lercaro and Montini, who were the main candidates.

König later claimed that this group thought that a non-Italian might by now be acceptable to the Italians: that seemed to indicate Suenens. But the notion of Suenens as pope greatly alarmed the Curia. So the realistic consensus in this progressive group settled on Montini, who let them know that although he was unwilling to put himself forward, he was prepared to be drafted.[1]

But the uncertainty was such that new compromise candidates were still being put forward even at this late stage. The British Minister to the Holy See, Sir Peter Scarlett, fancied Cardinal Paolo Marella, during the war apostolic delegate to Japan. Pawley reports: "Sir Peter seems to be particularly attracted to his personality; he is friendly, devout, intellectual and a good linguist. Again I should have thought his physical limitations would have weighed against him. He is very small of stature, always wears dark glasses, and has a very feeble voice."[2] Apart from such misfortunes Marella was unlikely to be elected as the French were against him. As Nuncio to France after Roncalli he had bungled the winding up of the worker-priest movement.

On the morning of 19 June, eve of the conclave and still at Castelgandolfo, Montini received his old colleague in the Secretariat of State, Francis J. Spellman, a man whose mind was already made up. He promised Montini his vote. Spellman was more concerned with stamp-collecting and autograph-hunting: he showed Giulio Andreotti his Vatican stamps from the *sede vacante* period and the autographs of all eighty cardinals; and a great prize – the coat of arms used by Montini in the Sistine Chapel during the conclave. Spellman had clearly spent much of his conclave souvenir-hunting.

As the cardinals entered the Apostolic Palace later that afternoon and were sealed off from the world, they seemed to have only two options: continue the Council in the spirit of Pope John – which pointed to Montini or Lercaro – or conclude it as swiftly, economically and

1 Ibid. p. 131.

2 Report 73, 17 June 1963.

harmlessly as possible. That pointed to Cardinal Giuseppe Siri of Genoa, created a cardinal in 1946 and once the dauphin of Pius XII. The CIA spies, no better informed than most journalists, saw the conclave as a straightforward contest between the "liberal" Montini and the "conservative" Siri.[1]

The conservatives then proceeded to overplay their hand. The discourse *De eligendo pontifice* was given by Msgr Amleto Tondini. This was traditionally the last act before the cardinals were locked up for the conclave. It was supposed to provide a job-description of the sort of pope the Church needed.

In 1958 Cardinal Antonio Bacci had traced in advance the portrait of Pope John XXIII.[2] Now in 1963 Tondini, who bore the proud title of "Secretary of Latin briefs", savaged Pope John, barely cold in his tomb, with a venom and lack of "fair play" unparalleled in recent conclave history.

He mocked Pope John's optimism. He offered a gloomy and apocalyptic vision of a world hastening towards ruin. He was evidently exacting his revenge for the inaugural address to the Council of 11 October 1962 when Pope John denounced the "prophets of misfortune, who are for ever predicting disaster". Liberated from all scruples by Pope John's death, Tondini said that "doubt should be cast on the *enthusiastic applause* received by the Pope of peace, and one wonders whether the enthusiasm came from people who were true believers who accepted all the dogmatic and moral teachings of the Church".[3]

The answer to that implied question was "no": manifest unbelievers like Khrushchev and other riff-raff had eagerly welcomed Pope John's initiatives. But that was not really the point.

Tondini then denounced contemporary scientism, materialism and relativism, a familiar triad of scorn among Italian bishops.[4] Relations between peoples, Tondini warned, were based in fact not on some Utopian fantasy but on hatred and violence. "Being desirous to provide more securely for the salvation of the separated brethren," said the mealy-mouthed Tondini, he invited them to "*return* to the Church of Christ". But these were *hors d'oeuvres.*

Arriving at the meat of his address, Tondini advised that before

1 See the CIA report of 6 June 1963, n.54289, available through the FIOA office. Quoted by Alberto Melloni, "Pope John XXIII: Open Questions for a Biography", *Catholic Historical Review*, January 1986, p. 64.

2 Hebblethwaite, *John XXIII*, pp. 280–81.

3 Giancarlo Zizola, *Quale Papa?* p. 161.

4 See Giovanni Miccoli, "*Sul ruolo di Roncalli nella Chiesa Italiana*", in *Papa Giovanni*, p. 195. The only Italian cardinal who understood him was Montini.

continuing the Council the new pope would be well advised to "let the questions mature for some time" – no doubt until the Greek Kalends, that is, still the never-never. Tondini's partisanship was counter-productive. Pawley reported the comment of a cardinal, "not yet walled up":

> Such a speech would probably have the effect, if it had any at all, of encouraging the "left" and perhaps even moving to the left some of the waverers in the centre who would thus have a gratuitous demonstration of what they might be in for if they had a pope of the right. The Secretariat for Unity say we are to disregard it.[1]

Not for the first time the Curial conservatives had shot themselves in the foot. In attacking Pope John, they were getting at Montini. But they lacked both conviction and a plausible alternative candidate.

Though the CIA spies suggested Siri as the alternative, he was king-maker rather than king. By now the leading conservative runner was Cardinal Ildebrando Antoniutti, Prefect of the Congregation of Religious. He was the candidate of the "blunt-spoken, tempestuous" Siri and of "the witty but reactionary, half-blind" Ottaviani.[2] Even though Antoniutti could not hope to beat Montini in a straight contest, he might at least deny him the two-thirds plus one needed to be elected pope.[3] For the Hispanophiles Montini had blotted his copybook simply by appealing in 1962 for mercy for a young Spaniard condemned to death.[4]

The first votes in the morning of 23 June 1963 suggested this conservative manoeuvre was proving fairly successful. Montini got roughly thirty votes, while Antoniutti hovered around twenty. Lercaro also had about twenty votes.[5] The remaining ten or so were scattered indiscriminately, though the curial dark horse Cardinal Francesco Roberti got enough votes to suggest that he might be a "compromise candidate" should Antoniutti, as seemed likely, falter.

Yet these first two ballots also demonstrated the weakness of the pro-Johannine forces in the conclave: they wanted to continue the Council in the spirit of Pope John, but that conviction did not of itself point to any particular candidate. Assuming that the next pope would be Italian, a case could be made for saying that Lercaro was closer in

1 Report 75, p. 2.

2 The adjectives are borrowed from Andrew M. Greeley, *The Making of the Popes 1978*, p. 260.

3 Zizola, *Quale Papa?* p. 165.

4 Xavier Rynne, *The Second Session*, p. 10.

5 Zizola, *Quale Papa?* p. 163. The author admits that this is an informed guess.

outlook and pastoral experience to John XXIII than was Montini.

Lercaro was a leader in liturgical reform. He was a herald of the "Church of the poor". At the first session of the Council he had proposed that a Synod of Bishops should be set up to co-ordinate the work of the Roman Curia, including the Holy Office.[1] From the point of view of the Roman Curia, this amounted to a lethal cocktail. Lercaro was well to the left of Montini. A Lercaro papacy would be totally unpredictable. He might suddenly decide to give away the Vatican Museums to UNESCO or perpetrate other such follies. There was a rumour that Pope John would have invited the ecumenical Patriarch Athenagoras to stay at Castelgandolfo for the second session of the Council. That was the sort of gesture Lercaro would indulge in.

Suenens urged the Lercaro supporters to shift their votes to Montini. The case for Montini was that all his life had been a preparation for the papacy. Besides he had the balance that Lercaro notoriously lacked. Though a "reformer", he knew enough about the ways of the Curia to understand that he would have to move slowly and gradually. Against him was his reputation for indecisiveness, but that could be explained by the fact that he had lived for so long in the shadow of Pius XII when all subordinate initiative was discouraged. His Milan ministry showed that he could exercise independent leadership and was not merely a permanent second-in-command.

The third ballot, on the evening of 20 June, was as inconclusive as the first two. Then something untoward and dramatic happened: it impressed itself so powerfully on the minds of the participants that, eventually, conclave secrecy was broken.

The unexpected intervention came from Cardinal Gustavo Testa, a Bergamesque whom Pope John had made a cardinal in 1959. He was put in charge of the Congregation for Oriental Churches (where Tisserant had reigned since 1936). Testa, seated between Cardinals Carlo Confalonieri (whose first conclave had been in 1922) and Alberto Di Jorio (Paul Marcinkus' predecessor) lost his temper. Testa told his neighbours, in a voice loud enough to be heard by others, that they should stop their squalid manoeuvring and think of the good of the Church. "Siri hit the ceiling,"[2] says one writer, which would, if true, have endangered Michelangelo's masterpiece. Testa had broken the rules: no discussion was allowed in the Sistine Chapel. After Testa's intervention, the fourth ballot went ahead in the accustomed "religious silence".

What did Testa really say? There is of course no transcript of his remarks, but sources agree they were a plea to stop plotting against

1 René Laurentin, in *Modernité*, p. 592.

2 Greeley, p. 260.

Montini, to remember that in conscience they were supposed to vote for the best man for the office, and that the immense capital of good will built up by Pope John should not be frittered away for partisan reasons.

This impromptu and technically improper statement carried all the more weight – *c'est le cas de le dire* – in that only three days before Testa had confided his doubts about Montini to Msgr Dell'Acqua, substitute and confidant of Pope John. He was worried about what he saw as Montini's inconsistency and lack of steadfastness. Dell'Acqua tried to persuade him that Pope John hoped that Montini would succeed him, and that he was the right man for the difficult period on which the Church was entering. "I'll back him," Testa said, "out of respect for Dell'Acqua, not because I am convinced."[1]

The effect of Testa's mixture of appeal and invective could not be precisely measured: it would have put some off Montini, while striking the consciences of other. When the votes of the fourth ballot were counted it was found that Montini had picked up a few more votes. But he was still some way off the fifty-four plus one he needed.

On the evening of 20 June it was hot inside the sealed up, walled off Apostolic Palace. A merciful breeze brought some sort of relief as night fell. Cardinal Franz König of Vienna met Montini in the Galleria del Lapidario and found him looking worried and sad. König tried to console him. Montini replied: "That's all very well, but I still hope I won't be elected. Sometimes the votes peak, and then get stuck. I hope that will happen to me." He sighed, and then added: "Just now I'm in darkness and cannot see anything clearly."[2] His secretary, Don Pasquale Macchi, says he spent the whole night in prayer.

This evidence counts against the tale that Montini agreed that evening to keep on the eighty-two-year-old Cardinal Amleto Cicognani as his Secretary of State. He did keep him on; but it does not follow that this was part of a deal – which Montini would have regarded as mild simony. Greeley adds this intriguing item: "Cardinal Leo Suenens of Brussels, one of Paul VI's great supporters in the conclave and the man responsible for persuading the Lercaro supporters to switch their votes to Montini, was apparently considered for Secretary of State but was rejected because of the opposition of Siri."[3]

Pawley offers an explanation of the dynamics of the conservative opposition, which he got from Cardinal Augustine Bea afterwards:

1 Zizola, *Quale Papa?* pp. 163–65.

2 Peter Hebblethwaite, *The Year of Three Popes*, p. 74.

3 Andrew M. Greeley, *The Making of the Popes 1978*, p. 262.

> Concerning the conclave he [Bea] confirmed . . . that the "right" hadn't really a candidate who stood a chance. Cardinal Micara, one of the Curia cardinals, therefore suggested that the "right" should own themselves defeated and support the "left" which they meekly did. He was supported by Cardinals Testa, Cento and Confalonieri.[1]

A similar motive would have brought round Ottaviani, by now resigned to a Montini pontificate. A cardinal always feels more at ease with a pope he has elected than with one he has opposed. Besides, they had been good friends in the 1930s. Siri, characteristically, did not accept this argument and advocated dumping the now hopeless Antoniutti in favour of Roberti.[2]

Montini had wanted the cardinals to sleep on their decision. Next morning, after another indecisive ballot, Montini finally got the majority he needed – but did not want – on the sixth ballot: fifty-seven. He had just two more votes than the minimum needed for validity. It was a near thing. Testa said afterwards: "Hair-raising (*orripilanti*) things happened at this conclave – I will have to ask the Pope's permission to speak about them."[3] If he ever asked for that permission, he never received it.

How did Montini feel about his election? He did not regard it as a "victory". Here are two clues to his feelings. As Lercaro knelt before him, he said: "So that is the way life goes, your eminence, you should really be sitting here now."[4] No doubt that partially explains why Paul VI later compensated Lercaro by putting him in charge of liturgical reform; yet he came to regret it.

The other clue about his feelings came nine years later. On the anniversary of his election, Paul VI read out to a general audience a page written on the day he became pope. It is as frank as anything which appears in Pope John's *Journal of a Soul*:

> Perhaps the Lord has called me to this service not because I have any aptitude for it, nor so that I can govern the Church in its present difficulties, but so that I may suffer something and thus that it may be clear that it is the Lord, and no one else, who guides and saves it.[5]

1 Report 78, 1 July 1963.

2 Zizola, *Quale Papa?* p. 167.

3 Ibid.

4 Ibid. p. 170. The remark is also quoted by Greeley, op. cit. p. 262. Perhaps the source was Zizola, but he is nowhere named in Greeley's work.

5 *Insegnamenti*, 1972, p. 662.

This was neither a pious façade nor an expression of conventional humility. There have been popes who have positively rejoiced in their election. "Since we are now pope," said Pio Nono, "let us at least enjoy our pontificate."

Montini was not among them. Having worked alongside Pius XI and Pius XII, he knew only too well "the burden of duties, cares (*bisogni*) and difficulties that the Keys of Peter bring with them", and he believed that he did not possess "the preparation needed for so formidable an office".[1] In that case, one is tempted to ask, who has and who else was better prepared?

He knew exactly what was involved in being pope. Coping with Milan had made him ill. Government of the universal Church was a qualitatively different task, and an awesome responsibility. He knew that, in human terms, his Petrine ministry was bound to "fail" because of the inevitable gap between intentions and achievements: an apparently "successful" pontificate would no doubt be a suspect pontificate. But that is true of most ministries in the Church. Between the aim and its realization falls the shadow of the cross. Paul VI was acutely conscious of this shadow.

He consoled himself with the words that St Leo the Great had used on each anniversary of his election: *Dabit virtutem, qui contulit dignitatem* (He who confers the office also gives the strength to fulfil it).[2] This was the familiar "grace of state" doctrine. But the neo-Paul VI also admitted that after the white smoke he felt dizzy (*vertigo*) at the immensity of the task.

He also knew that from now on he would risk being cut off from "friends and dear ones and above all from the people one exists to serve". The higher one climbs up the hierarchical ladder, he sadly notes, the greater can be the distance between "the one who is chosen and the community".[3] Loneliness as well as uneasiness affects the one who wears the tiara or triple crown.

Some of these misgivings came out publicly. When asked the ritual question, Do you accept? he replied in Latin with his episcopal motto: "*Ita, in nomine Domini*" (Yes, in the name of the Lord). But he added immediately: "Here I am, crucified with Christ."[4]

What did his choice of name mean? He could not be Pius XIII; he did not think of a double-barrelled name, John-Pius. A passage from the

1 Ibid.

2 *Sermo* II, *Patrologium Latinum*, 54, p. 143. Quoted in *Insegnamenti*, 1972, p. 663.

3 *Insegnamenti*, 1972, p. 633.

4 Max Bergerre, *Six papes et un journaliste*, p. 104.

memorandum addressed to Paul III in 1537 would not have escaped his attention:

> You have taken the name of Paul. We hope you will imitate his charity. He was chosen as an instrument to carry Christ's name to the heathen; you, we hope, have been chosen . . . to heal our sickness, to unite Christ's flock again in one fold, and to avert from our heads the already threatening wrath and vengeance of God.[1]

His own explanation was that he wanted to reach out to the modern Gentiles.

At supper he refused the place of honour offered him by the papal master of ceremonies, Msgr Enrico Dante. Having thanked everyone, he set off for the papal apartments accompanied by Cardinal Carlo Confalonieri. There was the usual element of farce. The new Pope and the Cardinal Dean had difficulty in finding the light switches.[2]

It remains to ask how far the conclave conditioned the pontificate that was to follow. The fact that some twenty-two to twenty-five cardinals declined to vote for Montini, even when his election was assured, remained a worrying handicap. They were mostly Italian, and mostly in the Curia. Their refusal to vote for him meant that they were not prepared to yield an inch. Nor were they imbued with the parliamentary virtue by which the minority accepts defeat with good grace. On the contrary, these incorrigibles or intransigents regarded Montini's election as a temporary setback, and lived to fight another day.

They were particularly incensed by the way Suenens tactlessly appeared on the balcony alongside Paul as though he were the kingmaker. If Suenens wanted to become the first non-Italian Secretary of State since Merry del Val, he was due for disappointment. Paul VI did not have that freedom of action or choice.

The persistence of opposition, finally, shaped the most difficult and urgent problem that faced him on his election: the continuation of the Council and curial reform. He would have to find some way of winning the Curia over to the Council while at the same time reassuring it that orthodoxy would not thereby collapse. That involved the velvet glove, combining *la manière douce* with *la main forte*.

Pope John had been able to out-flank or by-pass the Curia. Pope Paul, now sixty-seven, embarked upon a far longer pontificate and

1 Ludwig von Pastor, *History of the Popes*, vol. 11, p. 169. Here after José Gonzalez Faus, *Where the Spirit Breathes*, Orbis, New York 1989, p. 40.

2 Max Bergerre, p. 105.

needed a more radical plan for the reform of the Curia and clearer vision of what the Council should do.

Canon Bernard Pawley took a bottle of champagne along to the Secretariat for Christian Unity, and they toasted *him* because of the "thrilling time he spent with Montini in Milan in 1956". Moved and very happy, he issued a warning and a prediction:

> Nobody should suppose that Paul VI or any other Pope can undo the tangled skein of 400 years separation in a generation. But his election is certainly further confirmation that it is worth our while pursuing the path we have begun, and that there is real ground to hope and pray for the eventual reunion of Christendom.[1]

Back in London, the *Tablet* already had its "scoop", a letter from Montini on "Pius XII and the Jews". It was proudly introduced with the following note:

> The letter that follows reached us on Friday, 21 June an hour after the author had been elected to the papacy, and this tribute to the memory of his predecessor, Pope Pius XII, which we are privileged to print, is one of the last actions of Pope Paul VI as Cardinal Montini, Archbishop of Milan.[2]

That his last act should be to praise Pius XII whose "frail and gentle exterior and . . . sustained refinement and moderation of his language concealed – if they did not, rather, reveal – a noble and virile character capable of taking very firm decisions and of adopting, fearlessly, positions that entailed considerable risk" was surely significant. Pius XII was his model of how to be Pope, not John XXIII.[3]

1 *Rome Report* 76, 21 June 1963.

2 *Tablet*, 29 June 1963, pp. 714–15.

3 Woodruff very nearly did not get his scoop. *L'Osservatore Romano* naturally wanted to publish the Italian version of what was now a papal letter. Woodruff agreed on condition due acknowledgement was made to the *Tablet*.

21

Pope John's Heritage: The Council

> Rarely did a pontificate begin in such discouraging conditions. Never did the keys of St Peter seem so heavy. A predecessor whose death was an apotheosis. He had long enough to set the mighty machine of the Council in motion, but not long enough to give it direction . . . other than the ambivalent term *aggiornamento*. Four and a half years of a *magisterium* exercised empirically, with a tug on the rudder correcting – if need be – yesterday's impulse or excess. An exceptional grace of improvisation, serenity and confidence in the help of Holy Spirit in every situation.
>
> (Anon.)

This cold-waterish yet *nuancé* judgement[1] defined the problem Pope John left his successor, any successor. Pope John was not unaware of its dimensions. He once remarked to Cardinal Gabriel-Marie Garrone: "The Council is like a big ship. I got it out to sea, but someone else will have to manoeuvre it into port."

Between 21 June when he was elected, and 29 September when the second session of the Council began, Paul VI had a hundred days to get the ship on course. His main task was to coax the Roman Curia in the direction of the Council. Some of them were feeling bruised and resentful at the way they had been pushed aside at the first session. Personal projects – the things he had often thought in if-I-were-pope fantasies in his twenty-nine years in the Curia – would have to wait.

He started taking notes for his first programmatic encyclical: he knew it would be on dialogue, and wanted to cast it in a friendly, conversational tone. But that would have to wait too. While the Council

1 The quotation is found in Philippe Levillain, *La mécanique politique de Vatican II*, p. 290, where it is credited to "*documents privés*". Since on p. 30 Levillain tells us that Père Henri de Lubac "kindly opened his archives", and since the passage recalls his characteristic style, it is reasonable to guess that he is being quoted here.

was in session he would have to learn how to be Supreme Pontiff – how absurd and inappropriate this Roman imperial language began to seem – in a context of collegiality. No pope had ever had to do that before.

His most urgent task was to state clearly that the Council would be continued and completed. In his very first message, broadcast to the whole world or at least those parts of it that understood Latin, on Saturday, 22 June, the new Pope Paul VI gave an unhesitating "yes" to the Second Vatican Council. Indeed, he declared that his *entire* pontificate would be devoted to the Council.

He did not have to say that. He might have said, as some conservatives proposed, that it be spread out over a number of years, rather like the Council of Trent, thus diluting its impact, allowing boredom to set in and the Curia to reassert its power. Paul banished all such thoughts: for him the Council would not just be an episode after which the waters would close in and the event be forgotten: it was the *raison d'être*, the defining feature, of his pontificate. Robert Rouquette divined that Paul VI already had up his sleeve some form of permanent collaboration between the pope and the episcopal college, "either by calling successive councils or creating institutions to keep Rome and Christendom in touch".[1] That was shrewd in that it adumbrated the Synod; but it jumped the gun.

With Pope John the Italian text of a speech expressed what he really wanted to say. Paul was a better Latinist, but even so he preferred to write his post-election address in Italian, handing the pages to the translators as he finished each one.[2] It was subjected to minute, microscopic analysis. This would be his fate from now on. He couldn't just teach as he had done all his life: his words expressed the *magisterium*. Yet was not this a distinction without a difference? Was not teaching a continuum, from the mother teaching her child to pray, as Giuditta had taught him, to Henri de Lubac and other great theologians, and so on to his own office? Questions for another day.

On this happy day, the feast of the Sacred Heart of Jesus, he presented his office of ruling the Lord's flock (*regendi dominici gregis officium*) as St Augustine saw it: that is, as an *officium amoris* (a ministry of love).[3] Rouquette claims the Italian translators (for having been translated into Latin, it had to be translated back into Italian) assumed it

1 Robert Rouquette, *Vatican II, La Fin d'une Chrétienté*, I, p. 331. *Mon cher maître*, though wrong about a whole series of councils, got the principle of the synod right.

2 Ibid. p. 331 fn. 3.

3 *Insegnamenti*, p. 3. The Augustine quotation is from *In Johannem*, 123, 5, a commentary on John's Gospel, ch. 21. Cardinal Montini's last sermon before the conclave was on John 21:18 (see epigraph, p. 318).

was *pascendi dominici gregis*, and thus an allusion to St Pius X's 1907 encyclical *Pascendi Gregis* which banned everything in sight. Decidedly, *mon cher maitre* could at times be over-elaborate.

But there was one nuance that mattered and was important for the future. In dealing with ecumenism Paul talked about *recompositio* of unity and the *redintegranda christianorum conjunctio* (the reintegration of all Christians in unity). In using this vocabulary Paul VI was trying to avoid any hint of an ecumenism of "return" to the bosom of the Roman Church. Pope John had not always managed to avoid this language which Dr Geoffrey Fisher, for one, found deeply offensive and, being Fisher, he told him so. Their exchange is worth recording.

Pope John quoted as the most natural thing in the world his encyclical *Ad Petri Cathedram* which looked forward to the time when "our separated brethren would return to the Church".

"Not return, your holiness."

John, puzzled: "Not return? Why not?"

"None of us can go backwards, we are all running on a parallel course, but we are looking forward until in God's good time our two courses come and meet."[1]

Paul had his Milan experience of Anglicans to make such a lesson superfluous. Aldo Moro had popularized the enigmatic phrase "parallel convergence", and in ecumenical contexts Paul always talked of "convergence towards Christ". In *redintegratio* he had stumbled upon a key word which the Council needed so badly that it provided the title of the decree on ecumenism, *Unitatis Redintegratio*.

Precision of language now became an obligation upon him. He was used to it, and knew the theory whether in literature – wasn't it the task of the poet, according to Stephane Mallarmé, to *purifier la langue de la tribu*? – or in theology (*Semper formaliter loquitur Divus Thomas*, as the scholastics said: the Angelic Doctor (as St Thomas Aquinas was known) always speaks with precision. When he spoke, his was the voice of the *magisterium*. The literary comparison is not far-fetched: Paul told Guitton that being Pope was rather like being a writer.

In private, though, he could relax and talk without "committing the

1 Edward Carpenter, *Archbishop Fisher: His Life and Times*. Gives two accounts of the meeting seen from the Anglican side, the first dictated by Fisher to John Satterthwaite twenty minutes after the event, the other recollected by Fisher in his taped autobiography. In the latter version Pope John says, "Return? Why not return?" to which Fisher replies: "None of us can go backwards, we are each now running on a parallel course, but we are looking forward until in God's good time our two courses come – approximately – and meet". After a pause, John is said to have replied: "You are right". p. 737.

magisterium". One of his first audiences was for the little group of Observers who were still in town, among them Bernard Pawley. They were informed at 10.30 p.m. that the new pope wished to see them next day at noon:

> His Holiness received us in the library most cordially. He spoke especially warmly to the Bp of Ripon and to me as "old friends". He spoke of our meetings at Milan and of his being our guest at American Church House. We were all very moved by this occasion, not least the Pope himself. He said he had pledged himself to work for Christian unity, and we should find him true to his word.
>
> As the Russian Observers were present, we made no speech in return (I will explain this in private), but made it abundantly evident that we were very pleased at his election and that we would pray and work for the unity we all desired.[1]

The mysterious Russians were Bishop Kotlianov and Archpriest Vitali Borovoi. Pawley had Foreign Office advice from London that Borovoi was a KGB agent.

One should define a little more closely what that meant. All Soviet citizens, whether bishops or ballerinas, were allowed to go abroad on condition that they reported back on their return. Metropolitan Nikodim of Leningrad was also widely believed to be a KGB "plant" and it is true that he became bishop at the surprisingly young age of thirty-two.[2] Nikodim was writing a study of Pope John XXIII's pontificate, and although that had propaganda potential ("progressive" Pope versus stick-in-the-mud Polish Bishops) it was also an indication of genuine interest in the changes taking place in the Catholic Church. Paul welcomed Nikodim on that basis.

In fact his *first* serious ecumenical meeting was with Nikodim. Every time he lists his meetings with other Christians he invariably puts Nikodim at the top of his list.[3] At their first meeting Paul said:

1 Bernard Pawley, *Rome Report*, 78, 1 July 1963. John Moorman was the Bishop of Ripon; also present were Frere André of Taizé and the Rector of the American Episcopal Church in Rome; and the two Russians.

2 I once asked Nikodim whether, when he became a monk at the age of sixteen, he ever thought that within sixteen years he would be Metropolitan of Leningrad. He solemnly replied, through an interpreter, "Many thoughts pass through the head of a boy of sixteen." He was surprisingly insulting about his priests who were, he said, drunken, lazy good-for-nothings. "That proves he's a genuine bishop," said a Russian Orthodox friend.

3 For example in his address to the Secretariat for Christian Unity, 28 April 1967, *Insegnamenti*, 1967, p. 191. Next came a Methodist bishop, Corson, and Pasteur Marc Boegner of the Reformed Tradition (and member of the Academie Française).

> During the many years we have been out of touch, we have not had any true understanding of each other. So you might think that if I stretch out my hand in friendship, it is about to strike you. But be assured that I really do want to take your hand, not to strike you.[1]

Even if he was a KGB man. It is not difficult to imagine what the Ukrainian Catholic Major Archbishop, Josef Slipyi, rescued from his Siberian labour camp in February, 1963, would think about this touching scene. Slipyi privately denounced the new Pope for "clasping the blood-stained hands of the murderers of the Greek Catholic Church". In fact, Slipyi personally got on well with Nikodim.

Pawley was unaware of such eddies. But he had secured a very important advantage for the Anglican Communion: on the strength of their previous acquaintance in Milan in 1956 Pawley would have easy access to Paul, through Don Pasquale Macchi, his private secretary in Rome as in Milan. He had another advantage no other observer had: he was now permanently living in Rome with his wife, Margaret, and their two children; and they could hold glittering receptions on American Church premises at the corner of via Napoli and via Nazionale. His aim was to gain recognition for the originality of the Anglican Communion, which was distinct from both Protestants and the Orthodox.

Paul, meanwhile, had moved swiftly to ensure the continuity of the Council. The rescript declaring that the Council would continue came only six days after his election. Not only that, but Cardinal Paolo Marella, Archpriest of St Peter's Basilica, and Pericle Felici, his deputy and Secretary of the Council, already knew the date for the resumption of the Council – 29 September 1963 – by the evening of 28 June, a week after his election.[2] Nothing Hamlet-like there.

Yet in Rome one can have wonderful ideas and still be smothered by tradition and protocol. Paul's solemn coronation on 30 June, feast of Sts Peter and Paul, was at odds with the spirit of the Council. He looked uncomfortable up there on the *sedia gestatoria* (or palanquin). He was escorted by a host of hangers on who loved dressing up, colourful prelates, gentleman of honour, the Swiss Guard, the Noble Palatine Guard, the Roman aristocracy, domestics bearing ostrich feathers and Franciscans reminding him, unnecessarily, of mortality. This was the papal court, the pontifical establishment, the black nobility.

Paul VI dealt with them sensitively. He did not create sudden

1 Archbishop Pierre Duprey recalled these words, "not without emotion", when Catholic–Orthodox relations reached a low point in November 1991, ADISTA, 28–30 November 1991.

2 *Problemi Ecclesiologici*, pp. 59–60.

mass-unemployment among families that had performed ceremonial duties since the Middle Ages, but he eased the courtiers out gradually. Then in 1970 he formally abolished the Guards and the papal court. From Leo XIII onwards, when the popes thought of themselves as "prisoners of the Vatican", the court existed as a proof of residual sovereignty. Only a sovereign can have a court; now there was no more need for it.[1]

Already unhappy atop his palanquin, Paul wore the tiara with an air of resigned embarrassment. He didn't know it, but he was the last pope to be crowned.[2] The tiara, a triple crown of Asiatic origin, symbolized royal power. Bismark, on hearing it represented authority over heaven, hell and earth, remarked that he would leave the first two realms to the Pope, provided he could look after the third. Paul would sell his tiara.[3]

On the personal level, which was where he had to live and work, Montini from the outset recreated in the Vatican the office atmosphere he had enjoyed in Milan. Don Pasquale Macchi, author of a thesis on Georges Bernanos, headed his team. "He liked those around him", said Milanese journalist Ernesto Pisoni, "to work in depth (*profondità*) and quiet without undue haste or sudden impulses".[4] This atmosphere of studious calm contrasted with the hurly-burly of news agencies and newspaper offices as well as with the headquarters of the majority and minority of the Council Fathers.

Against all precedent, Msgr Loris F. Capovilla, Pope John's private secretary in Venice and at the Vatican, stayed on so that he could complete the work of editing the *Journal of a Soul* and other writings of the late Pope. This was unheard of: once "their" pope died, secretaries were never seen again. By keeping Capovilla on even in a secondary capacity, he stressed continuity with Pope John and had a good witness to his intentions.[5] Paul created a good working atmosphere around himself.

Calmness reigned beneath the immemorial cedars of the summer

1 Andrea Riccardi, "*Da Giovanni XXIII a Paolo VI*", in *Chiesa e Papato nel mondo contemporaneo*, eds Riccardi and Giuseppe Alberigo, p. 226.

2 John Paul I simply "inaugurated his pastoral ministry" without the *sedia gestatoria*. But it was back again within two weeks: the fans said they couldn't see him.

3 Pope John Paul II offered a characteristically spiritual interpretation of the discarded headgear: "Perhaps it signified the fact that the triple mission of Christ as priest, prophet and king continues in the Church. But everyone in the People of God shares in this threefold mission." Perhaps? Perhaps not. See Peter Hebblethwaite, *The Year of Three Popes*, p. 193.

4 *Corriere della Sera*, 14 September 1963.

5 Two years later, on 26 June 1967, Capovilla became Archbishop of Chieti-Vasto, lasting only four years. From 1971 until he retired to Sotto il Monte, Pope John's birthplace, he was Guardian of the shrine of Our Lady of Loreto.

residence at Castelgandolfo. On 5 August 1963 Paul penned a private note which shows he had few illusions about being Pope:

> The post is unique. It brings great solitude. I was solitary before, but now my solitariness becomes complete and awesome. Hence the dizziness, the vertigo. Like a statue on a plinth – that is how I live now. Jesus was also alone on the cross. We hear that he expressed his desolation by crying out, *Eloi, Eloi.* My solitude will grow. I need have no fears: I should not seek outside help to absolve me from duty; my duty is to plan [*volere*], decide, assume every responsibility for guiding others, even when it seems illogical and perhaps absurd. And to suffer alone. The consolation of confiding in others will be rare and discreet: the depths of the spirit remain within me. Me and God. The colloquy with God must be full and endless (*pieno e incommensurabile*).[1]

This is the most dispassionate, lucid and telling text about the papal primacy ever penned.

But from the outside Paul VI had another, more pressing problem: he was not John XXIII. He was well aware of the difficulties of succeeding a pope who had been so greatly loved. Another unpublished text, probably written that same summer at Castelgandolfo, shows that he had pondered this question. Consisting of four tightly written pages, with many crossings out and corrections, it takes us straight to the heart of Paul VI.[2] It could be called, with slight irreverence, "Follow that if you can."

Paul says first that it would be "naive and vain . . . to claim to be, I do not say his equal, but even to be like him. Let us honour him as a great, good, unique figure." Pope John was a one-off, once-for-all pope, and they don't make them like that any more.

But then Montini asserts that he is in complete continuity with Pope John: "This is proved by the way I am continuing his programme, and

1 Don Pasquale Macchi in *Notiziario* 1, p. 53. This was the text of a homily given in the Milan Duomo on 23 September 1979. Pope Paul's secretary unveiled this much of the inner life of Montini – and then fell silent for ever. Someone in whom Paul did confide, on a regular basis but in special circumstances, was his confessor, Fr Paolo Dezza SJ, who was delivered by limousine to the Vatican every Friday evening at seven o'clock. The only thing Dezza ever revealed about this experience was that Paul VI was "a man of great joy". But these are areas where we cannot, and ought not, to delve. Greatly to his astonishment, Padre Dezza (ordained in 1928) became Cardinal Dezza on 29 June 1991, six months before his ninetieth birthday.

2 This document was first published in *Notiziario*, 13, pp. 15–16, 1986. I translated and commented on it in "From John XXIII to Paul VI", a contribution to the *Festschrift* for Ludwig Kaufmann SJ's seventieth birthday. He died in June 1991.

keeping various people in their offices (who has been removed? etc.). If anything the criticism that I lack initiatives of my own would be nearer the mark, etc." This sounds like the first draft for an abandoned address on his venerable predecessor.

But Pope John left behind another source of embarrassment: the reputation of being a "liberal". It was widely believed that had he lived on, his kind-heartedness and sheer goodness would have led him to endorse the entire liberal agenda from the ordination of married men to contraception and – who knows? – gay marriages and abortion. This was a wish-fulfilment fantasy. But how could Paul convince the world press, which made Pope John its hero, of that?

Perhaps it was impossible. The private note goes sadly on: "Serious harm is done to the memory of Pope John when people assign him attitudes that were not his. That he was good, yes; that he was indifferent, no. How firmly he stuck to [traditional] doctrine, how much he feared dangers etc."[1] Indeed, Paul later told Guitton: "Pope John was much more conservative than me, much more traditional."[2]

But the problem remained. *Because* Paul VI could never fulfil the expectations aroused by this mythical Pope John, the real achievements of his reign would remain unappreciated until after his death. And this he knew as the private note shows:

> Pope John was not weak, was not a compromiser, was not indulgent towards erroneous opinions or towards the so-called fatality of history etc. . . . His dialogue was not goodness leading to cowardly surrender. As far as understanding the modern world and drawing close to it go, I think I am on the same lines as Pope John.

Actually he thinks he is rather better at it than good Pope John.

This is introduced with the remark that "I don't want to brag", but then qualified by saying that "in the field of work, of culture, of human and diplomatic relations, perhaps our life is characterized more clearly than anything else by the love of our own time, and our own world." This may be why he abandoned this draft. He didn't want to boast. And the pontifical plural – proof that this was the draft of a non-delivered speech – made it sound rather odd and self-centred – pope-centred, if you will.

There were also private, almost intimate ruminations as what had happened gradually sank in. But there were three public and practical things Paul could do right away without waiting for the Council.

He strengthened the Holy See's representation in international

1 *Notiziario*, 13, p. 16.

2 Jean Guitton, *Paul VI secret*, p. 104.

organizations, and created new links where none previously existed. So the Vatican "Observer" at the European seat of UNO in Geneva saw his competence extended to the BIT (*Bureau Internationale du Travail*). Msgr Alberto Giovanetti's office at the United Nations in New York was given enhanced status, and the first feelers about a possible papal visit were delicately put out. The first permanent observer of UNESCO in Paris was Angelo Roncalli, the future Pope John XXIII, and Montini signed the letter confirming this appointment.[1] Even now, as he embarked on his papacy, he assigned Giovanni Benelli, one of the brightest stars in the Secretariat of State to UNESCO. All these were indications that under Paul VI the Vatican intended to play a role in international affairs.

The *Ostpolitik*, the complex web of relations with the Communist states of Eastern Europe, was an aspect of this diplomatic activity.[2] Here Paul could build on the great achievements of Pope John XXIII, who had mediated in the Cuban missile crisis, liberated the Ukrainian Metropolitan Josef Slipyi from his Siberian labour camp, and created a new atmosphere with his encylical *Pacem in Terris*, universally described as his last will and testament. The critics said Pope John was naive and that *Pacem in Terris* had lost the Christian Democrats a million votes in Italy. What Paul would have to say on this topic in his first encyclical was eagerly awaited.

A role in international affairs and the *Ostpolitik* were not novelties for the papacy, though Paul got the lumbering machine of Vatican diplomacy working at a brisker tempo and with a clearer sense of its purpose. His attitude to art was more personal. Those hours spent on aesthetics now bore fruit.

Paul was concerned not just with religious art, *art sacré*, which brought dignity and a sense of mystery to worship. He wanted to promote modern religious art *tout court*, as a valid expression of the dramas and struggles of modern people. This was the speciality of Don Pasquale Macchi who charmed or flattered innumerable artists into parting with their works for the Vatican collection of modern art to be opened in 1973.

Paul continued to jot down notes on aesthetic questions. He was delighted by this passage in *Gaudium et Spes*: "Every effort should be made to make artists feel that they are understood by the Church in their artistic work and to encourage them, while enjoying ordered freedom (*ordinata libertate fruentes*) to enter into happier relations with the

1 Andre Dupuy, *La Diplomatie du Saint-Siège*, p. 49. It was signed by Pius XII, the future John XXIII, and the future Paul VI.

2 Achille Silvestrini, "*L'Ostpolitik de Paul VI*", in *Notiziario* 22, pp. 70–83.

Christian community."[1] In this he led by example. The same principles applied in the sciences as well, but in science he was more dependent on others and the Pontifical Academy. These were various attempts to bridge the gap between *faith* and *culture* that was for Paul the gravest weakness of the contemporary Church.

I have allowed this little peep into the future to show that all aspects of Paul's life found their fulfilment in the Council, not so much as a point of arrival as a point of departure. On the more technical questions that immediately faced him he prepared himself for the second session with his usual thoroughness. His unpublished notes refer to an article by Gérard Philips, the Louvain professor now secretary of the Theological Commission, which greatly struck him: "The true theologian will have in some sense (*de quelque manière*) the soul of a father and a pastor."[2] The Philips article distinguished two currents in contemporary theology, thus redefining and refining the conflicts of the first session. By naming the beasts, he hoped to exorcise them.

Philips distinguished between those preoccupied with the immutability of doctrine and those concerned with spreading it in an accessible language adapted to those who were to receive it. Michael Novak, freshly arrived in Rome, turned this into a contrast between non-historical orthodoxy and an orthodoxy which allowed for and required development.[3] This was much better than the American boo!-hurrah! contrast between "liberals" and "conservatives" and its French equivalent, the "*intégristes*" and the "*progressistes*".

Paul certainly did not think in these terms. He made a note of Philips' quotation from Thomas Aquinas: "*Fides terminatur non ad enutiabile sed ad rem*" (Faith comes to rest not in words but in the reality of the thing).[4] Paul's constant aim was to keep this spiritual and theological perspective before the Council. Religious language, like religious art, evokes more than it states. None of the disputes could touch the horizon of mystery towards which faith tends without ever reaching.

Paul knew that organizational changes were also needed. Before his election he had complained about the absence of direction. He thought there should be some kind of "brains trust" to direct the Coun-

1 *Gaudium et Spes*, 62. Paul copied out this and other relevant texts in his notebooks. See Pier Virgilio Begni Redona, "*Note sull'arte*", in *Notiziario*, 22, p. 23.

2 *Notiziario*, 13, p. 26. The article was in the March 1963 *Nouvelle Revue Theologique*.

3 Michael Novak, *The Open Church*, Darton, Longman and Todd, London 1964.

4 *Summa Theologica*, I–II, art. 1, a 2, ad 2.

cil's work.[1] Cardinals Leon-Joseph Suenens, Giacomo Lercaro and his guru, Don Giuseppe Dossetti, all had early audiences on organizational problems and corresponded with Carlo Colombo, Montini's theologian from Milan. All agreed that the *regolamento* was unsatisfactory. Lercaro proposed a plan.[2]

Paul told Suenens that he was unhappy about the organization. "I want to change the way the Council is run," he said.[3] The old system of "presidents" had failed, the Extraordinary Affairs Commission on which they sat was dissolved, while the new Co-ordinating Commission merely fiddled with procedural matters such as voting and other minor canonical details.

"I would like to appoint two legates," he told Suenens, "making you one and Cardinal Pietro Agagianian the other."

This was clearly a balancing act, with the radical Suenens weighing in against the Armenian-born adopted Roman Agagianian.[4] Paul had not yet finished: "If there is a third legate, I would like him to be Cardinal Döpfner."

Curial canon lawyers pointed out that the pope could send "legates" to represent him only when he was absent. The classic case was the Council of Chalcedon in 451 where there were five "legates" armed with Leo the Great's *Tomos*, who ran the Council so successfully that in the end the cry went up: "Peter has spoken through Leo!" But it would be absurd in 1963 for Paul to send a "legate" to his own diocese or to a meeting in St Peter's.

So the "legates" were transmuted into "moderators" (*moderatores*) and Suenens discovered there was a "fourth man", Cardinal Giacomo Lercaro, only when he opened his newspaper while holidaying in Scotland.

Lercaro phoned him in Scotland: "The role of the moderators is being changed. It is being cut down to a bare minimum. Get to Rome

1 Suenens in *Montini arcivescovo*, p. 186. Like most Latin speakers, Suenens calls this body a "brain trust", an expression unknown to the English language. The original "brains trust" was a radio programme during the war when five bright minds answered listener's questions. Since there was nothing else to do in the black-out, it was a great success, and made Professor C. E. M. ("It all depends on what you mean by . . .) Joad and Fr Agnellus Andrew OFM household names.

2 Giuseppe Alberigo, Louvain-la-Neuve, 24 October 1989, MS p. 13.

3 Ibid.

4 Rumour said that Agagianian could not become pope in the 1958 conclave because he could be pressurized through his sister, still alive in Soviet Armenia. But he was a serious rival, and Pope John later revealed that their two names "went up and down like two chickpeas in boiling water". Loris F. Capovilla, *Vent'Anni*, p. 25. By 1963 Agagianian was "more Roman than the Romans".

quickly and tell the Pope that he should respect the basic idea we discussed."

"I can't ask for that," said Suenens, "it is up to the Pope to take on his responsibilities."[1]

Behind this power-struggle lay the main problem of the second session: how to get the Roman Curia and the Council working together. The first session had left the more conservative members of the Curia feeling out-gunned, out-voted and humiliated. So Paul had both to restore their morale and draw them along in the direction of reform and renewal. At the same time he had to reassure the Council majority that he understood their impatience with the Curia, was busily reforming it and took seriously their desire for collegiality.

This was the aim of the two speeches made in late September 1963: on 21 September he addressed the Roman Curia, and on 29 September he opened the second session of the Council. Taken together they were policy statements as important as Pope John's 11 October 1963 address at the start of the Council to which they repeatedly refer.

In many ways the address to the Curia was more original. Not only had Pope John never worked in the Roman Curia, he dreaded the thought of ending up there after his tour of duty in France. But to reform the Curia it was necessary to know it. Montini, the insider with thirty years experience, knew it backwards. There he had found, he said, "wonderful superiors and teachers, excellent colleagues, co-workers and unforgettable friends."[2] Of course he had had some enemies too, but this was no time to carp: magnanimity is the first quality a new ruler needs.

The meeting with the Curia took place in the little used "hall of benedictions" which gives on to the central *loggia* of St Peter's Square. Some sought symbolic meaning in the fact that they were "over" the *aula* in which the Council was being held.[3] Paul VI strode in punctually at the appointed hour of 10 a.m.

Some distinguished prelates, used to the Roman habit of starting late, were caught out and had to make their way to the front while the Pope, standing, waited for them to sidle shamefacedly in. He said that since the talk would be rather long, the rest of the day would be a holiday. Applause. Further, Roman rents had gone up that summer by about 30 per cent, so their salaries would be increased to take this into account.

1 *Montini arcivescovo* p. 196. It should be said again that none of this was known until September 1983, when the last surviving "moderator" revealed it at the Paul VI Institute.

2 *Insegnamenti*, 1963, p. 143. The address was in Italian. There is a handy translation in Xavier Rynne, *The Second Session*, pp. 338–46. I have not used it.

3 For example, Andrea Riccardi in *Chiesa et Papato*, p. 226.

Even more vigorous applause and happy murmurs. Then he sat down and began the speech of his life.

The Curia, he said, had grasped the extraordinary importance of the Council and its worldwide dimensions "more fully than any other section of the Church and public opinion". However, this recognition sometimes took the form of "astonishment and apprehension at the sudden summoning of the Council and about the gravity of the problems it would raise". The Curia, in other words, cared intensely about the Council. It was a double-edged compliment. Readers of *Il Borghese*, the Rome satirical weekly, thought Pope John had been raving mad.

The Curia made no sense, he went on, except as the organ of "immediate adherence and of absolute obedience" to the Pope. The Curia is not an autonomous body: its *raison d'être* is to serve the Pope and to share in his ministry, subordinately. This had been his own practice for thirty years. But it was also part of his own practice to associate input and output. So in his job-description of the Curia he combines active and passive, the executive and the creative:

> Its functions are most delicate: it has to watch over or echo divine truths, while transforming them into a language capable of dialogue with human minds. Its functions are vast: it embraces the whole world. Its functions are noble: it must hear and interpret the voice of the Pope and at the same time not let him miss any useful, objective information, any filial and well thought out advice.[1]

Here he was trying to reconcile the Holy Office's concern for orthodoxy (symbolized by Ottaviani) with the new Curia's concern for dialogue (symbolized by Bea). Paul VI held on firmly to both ends of the chain. He wanted the Curia to listen as well as speak, to learn as well as teach.

Already Bea's Secretariat could chalk up one small but significant success thanks to the new pope (popes are "new" for about six months). On 25 June 1963 Paul seized the ecumenical initiative by "announcing his election" to the heads of the Orthodox Churches – they had read about it in the papers, but Paul was acting for history. He backed this up with a personal, handwritten letter to the Ecumenical Patriarch, Athenagoras, dated 20 September 1963. This was published in the bulletin of the Patriarchate, *Apostolos Andreas*, under the heading "The Two Sister Churches". This was the first step towards the goal of the ecumenical movement for it implied equality: the Churches could not

1 *Insegnamenti*, 1962, p. 146.

be "sisters" so long as Innocent III's claim that Rome was "Mother and Teacher" (*Mater et Magistra*) of all Churches was upheld.[1]

This was just the sort of lesson the "old" Curia needed to learn from history: so far the "new" Curia consisted solely in the Secretariat for Christian Unity. Besides learning from history, the Curia needed to learn from its critics. They were numerous. Never had the prestige of the Curia been so low as in 1963. As this second session began, over 100 Council fathers signed a petition demanding the reform of the Holy Office. Over 500 signed another urging a Synod of bishops to take over some of the Curia's functions.

There was no lack of fraternal criticism, the *fraterna correctio* of monasticism. Paul said it was a helpful feature of Church life: "It impels to vigilance, recalls to observance, invites to reform, stimulates to perfection."

So the Curia should be glad of fraternal correction. "Rome has no need to defend itself by being deaf to suggestions that come from honest voices, especially when they are the voices of friends and brothers. It will reply to the often groundless charges that are made, without replying in kind and without polemics."

Paul VI defended the Roman Curia – on condition that it set about its reform. The pope vs bishops quarrel over "conciliarism" in the fifteenth century was laid to rest: today the papacy takes the initiative of reform, and the bishops respond to it with enthusiasm. St Bernard would no longer need to write pages of searing invective nor would the sixteenth-century reformers have been so devastating.

The Curia was given a qualified blessing. It could not do what Paul wanted if it represented a conservative faction in the Church or a narrow ecclesiology. For many of his hearers it was a tough lesson, requiring conversion or *metanoia*. But as *La Nazione*, the Florentine daily, remarked, Paul had disarmed the critics so that "the more intelligent of the curialists were satisfied".

Paul's most radical practical proposal was slipped in almost as an aside: should not diocesan bishops be involved, on certain questions and in ways to be decided, in the deliberations of the Roman Curia?[2] This sounded ominously like some form of power-sharing.

Paul returned to this theme eight days later in his opening speech to

1 Yves Congar, *Diversity and Communion*, SCM Press, London 1984, pp. 87–89, gives the history of the question. He copied out and sent to Paul VI a text written in 1136 by Nicetas of Nicomedia to Anselm of Havelbeurg: "So, dearest brother, it is true that the Roman Church, to which we do not refuse the primacy among its sisters, and to which we accord the place of honour as president of the general council. . ."

2 Gian Piero Milano, in *Les Réformes Institutionelles*, p. 32.

the Council. The interrupted first Vatican Council had been resumed, and attention now turned to the status of *bishops* in the Church:

> For us personally it will provide doctrinal and pastoral standards by which our apostolic office, endowed though it is with the fullness and sufficiency of power, may receive more help and support, in ways yet to be determined, from a more effective and responsible collaboration with our beloved brothers in the episcopate.[1]

It was no more than a hint, but it suggested that the renewal of the Church must involve the renewal of the Petrine office, and that only some form of collegiality, of which the Council itself was the prime exemplar, would meet that need.

But there were other features of this opening address on 29 September 1963, Paul's first contact with the Council as pope, that were more disquieting.

1 *Insegnamenti*, 1963, p. 174.

22

Vatican II Roughly on Course

> What kind of man is Pope Paul VI? He is slight with a prominent nose and balding head. He has large, clear grey-blue eyes, under black bushy brows. His look is intense, reflective, sensitive. His mind seems to be working constantly, criticizing its own reflections. He moves swiftly, like a man of action, but with a guarded gentleness.
>
> (MICHAEL NOVAK, *The Open Church*, p. 29)

Novak was wrong about the eyes. They were grey-green. Blue eyes are rare in Italy. But otherwise the portrait is well drawn. The comparisons with Pope John continued. "It is not that Paul's heart burns less warmly," Novak went on, "it is only that his style, abilities and habits have made him a very different man from John."[1]

The difference appeared in the day-to-day running of the Council. Paul VI had a "hands-off" approach compared with his predecessor. John XXIII followed the proceedings on television, turning up the volume when someone interesting appeared, phoning the Secretary-General, Pericle Felici, whenever a thought occurred to him. Paul VI, by contrast, preferred to work in a pool of calm, receiving daily *written* reports on the most important events from his private secretary, Msgr Pasquale Macchi.[2]

There was a great contrast too, between Pope John's inaugural address to the Council (*Gaudet Mater Ecclesia*) the previous year and Paul's address this 29 September 1963, at the start of the second session. Pope John had poured into his speech all the wisdom acquired through painful experience: history as the teacher of life, the medicine of mercy preferable to the rod of severity, liberty in non-essentials, unity in essen-

1 Michael Novak, *The Open Church*, pp. 29–30.

2 Henri Denis, *Eglise, qu'as-tu fait de ton Concile*, p. 127. Philippe Levillain opined: "One can say that the absence of the Papacy at Trent was inspired by Machiavelli, at Vatican I by the Jesuits, and in the first session of Vatican II was possible thanks to television", *La Mécanique politique de Vatican II*, p. 297. Had he succumbed to a *belle formule*?

tials, charity at all times. "That speech still echoes in our minds," Paul now said, "and to the Church and the world it seemed like a prophetic utterance."[1]

Perhaps he thought he could not compete. In any event Paul seemed to have put his life experience into his address to the Curia, letting his opening address take the form of a dry, technical, cerebral exercise. Again, while John's speech opened its arms to embrace the whole world, Paul focussed almost entirely on "collegiality". This was, of course, the burning question, and it could not be eluded. Yet theologians had complicated it beyond belief ("Was there a double subject of authority?" enquired Karl Rahner) and it did not make the heart beat faster, even episcopal hearts.

Moreover the constant stress – harping would not be too strong a word – on papal primacy seemed unduly defensive: "Here, around him who is last in time and merit, but identified with the first apostle in authority and mission, the successor of Peter, you are gathered. Venerable brethren, you too are apostles descended from the apostolic college and are its authentic successors."[2]

It was as though Paul feared an attack on papal primacy, some undermining of Vatican I, obscure threats to the office which was important in itself, not because he occupied it. Yet he seeemed obsessed with the Petrine office, as though it filled his whole horizon.

Then, in a characteristic Pauline swoop, he said that was precisely what he was *not* doing:

> The Lord is our witness . . . when we declare to you that in our mind there is no intention of human predominance, no jealousy of exclusive power, but only the desire and the will to carry out the divine mandate which makes us the supreme Shepherd of you and among you, Brothers, and which requires of you . . . fidelity, loyalty, collaboration. This same mandate confers on you that which pleases him most to give – his veneration, his esteem, his trust.[3]

There were lots of undercurrents there. A partial explanation for the apparent hard-line quality of this opening address is that it was intended to complement his first encyclical. But *Ecclesiam Suam* was not yet ready.

What need is there of letters, he asked rhetorically, if I can speak to you directly: "Let this present address be a prelude not only to the

1 *Insegnamenti*, 1963, p. 168; Rynne, 2, p. 359.

2 *Insegnamenti*, 1963, pp. 166–67; Rynne, 2, p. 348.

3 *Insegnamenti*, 1963, p. 167; Rynne, 3, p. 348.

Council, but also to our pontificate. Let the living word take the place of the encyclical letter which, please God, we hope to address to you once these laborious days [*operosis hisce diebus transactis*] are over."[1]

But *Ecclesiam Suam*, when it came, recognized that for some Christians the papal office, in its claim to the primacy of honour and jurisdiction, was an "obstacle" to Christian unity.[2] No hint of that here. Alluding to the apse of the basilica of St Paul's-without-the-Walls, he said:

> We recognize ourselves in the figure of our predecessor, Honorius III, who is represented in the splendid mosaic in the apse of the basilica of St Paul as a humble worshipper, tiny and prostrate, kissing the feet of a Christ of gigantic dimensions, who as a kingly teacher dominates and blesses the people gathered in the basilica which symbolizes the Church.[3]

Of course, he did not intend to remind the Observers that Pope Honorius III (1216–1227) devoted his energies to the fourth and fifth crusades and that he rashly crowned Peter of Courtenay as *Latin* Emperor of Constantinople, thus ensuring him a sticky end. But neither Orthodox nor Protestants were too happy with mediaeval popes.

Belatedly Paul held out an olive branch by evoking the "authentic riches of truth and spirituality possessed by our separated brothers", and going on generously:

> If we are in any way to blame for our prolonged separation, we humbly beg God's forgiveness and ask pardon too of our brethren who feel themselves to have been injured by us. For our part we willingly forgive the injuries which the Catholic Church has suffered, and forget the grief endured during the long series of dissensions and separations.[4]

Gregory Baum OSA, a consultor of the Secretariat for Christian Unity, snorted: "*If* we have done you any wrong . . . He dares to say *if*." Anglican John Moorman, Bishop of Ripon, saw it differently: "Nothing can have been more courageous than this. No wonder that the Pope's voice trembled, for he must have known that while greatly encouraging

1 *Insegnamenti*, 1963, pp. 167–8; Rynne, 2, p. 349.

2 *Ecclesiam Suam*, No. 110. This "prepared" his famous remark to the Secretariat for Christian Unity on 28 April 1967: "The Pope, as we all well know, is probably (*sans doute*) the greatest obstacle in the path of ecumenism." *Insegnamenti*, 1967, p. 193. In conceding that others had such objections or doubts, Paul did not mean that he shared them.

3 *Insegnamenti*, 1963, p. 171; Rynne, 2, p. 352.

4 *Insegnamenti*, 1963, pp. 178–79; Rynne, 2, p. 358.

the Observers, he was deeply offending many of his own friends."[1]

That was the view of most of the Observers. They met Paul on 17 October 1963 and said they found his remarks on ecumenism "realistic and sober". This was the judgement of Danish Professor Skydsgaard who gave the usual address of homage. He was clearly "in the know" about the "Tantur project", as he sketched out its theological basis:

> Let me point out a fact which seems to me extremely important: I am thinking of the role played by salvation-history (*Heilsgeschichte*) in the Old as well as in the New Testament. The more we advance in understanding the secret and paradoxical history of the People of God, the more we begin also truly to understand the Church of Jesus Christ in its mystery, in its historical existence and in its unity.
>
> May your holiness allow me to express again our lively hope that light from such a concrete and historical theology, nourished by the Bible and the Fathers of the Church, may shine more and more on the work of the Council.[2]

Later in the session Oscar Cullmann gave a lecture at the Church of St Louis des Français on "Salvation-history in the New Testament".[3] It was a concerted move to make the study of "salvation-history" the common task of theologians of all the Churches. This was the idea behind Tantur, a house in the Holy Land jointly owned to be used by theologians. This was Paul's project.

Paul's hands-off approach did not mean that he was any less involved in the Council. But he was more interested in its long-term consequences than in the day-to-day slugging match that so delighted the groundlings of the media. They could afford to forget their headlines a week later: he would have to live with and implement what was decided here.

There was also a difference of approach on the key question of collegiality. Though it is difficult to say exactly what Pope John would have thought or done had he lived longer, he had called the Council so the bishops could help him perform his Petrine function better. He liked to quote Suenens: "It takes many to be intelligent." He saw himself presiding over the assembly of charity, no doubt about that, but he was the Bishop of Rome and as such on a par with the other bishops. Paul's starting-point, on the other hand, was papal primacy, and he saw "col-

1 John Moorman, *Vatican Observed: An Anglican Impression of Vatican II*, p. 68.

2 *Insegnamenti*, 1963, p. 235.

3 Xavier Rynne, *The Second Session*, p. 272. It was held there, said rumour, because Archbishop Dino Staffa would not let any of the large halls of the Roman Universities be used by a "heretic". Staffa denied this.

legiality" as a means towards its realization. It made a difference whether one started "from below", as Pope John appeared to do, or started "from above", as Paul surely did.

One could either set primacy in the context of collegiality, or set collegiality in the context of primacy. Different consequences followed. So it was always a simplification to say that the debate was about whether one was "for" or "against" collegiality.

Much more important, immediately, was who was running the Council. Battle was soon joined between the ten "Presidents" appointed by Pope John and the four "Moderators" chosen by the Council Secretariat. Cardinal Eugène Tisserant represented the "old guard" and claimed the true inheritance of Pope John. In his scheme the "Moderators" were no more than chairmen whose sole job was to call up speakers and ring the bell after ten minutes. At one point Amleto Cicognani, Cardinal Secretary of State, decided that the "Moderators" should not even be allowed to speak in the *aula*, since this would impair their objectivity.

It would also gag them. Maybe that was the idea. So Cardinals Suenens, Döpfner and Lercaro replied in unison: "We don't really want this presidential role, and gladly leave it to someone else, provided we recover our right to speak." In fact they did not heed the ban, the heavens did not fall in, and they saw the Pope weekly. That ought to have resolved the management problems. Yet Paul, according to Suenens, was quite unable to delegate the slightest parcel of his authority.

Poor Pietro Agagianian, the sole Curial representative among the team of Moderators, was out on a limb. The others got on so well that they were known as the "three synoptics". They had a back-up team headed by Lercaro's right-hand man, Don Giuseppe Dossetti. After a career in Christian Democratic politics that made him mayor of Bologna and secretary of the party until November 1952, when he resigned to become a priest, Dossetti was skilled in the art of mastering an agenda and handling committees. Felici at the Secretariat of the Council and Ottaviani at the Theological Commission naturally resented this unexpected cuckoo in the nest, but could do nothing yet awhile.

The "three synoptics" meantime were confident Paul was on their side, especially in liturgical matters. Cardinal Arcadio Larraona, head of the Liturgical Commission, had systematically shut Cardinal Giacomo Lercaro out of its affairs as long as Pope John reigned. Now, under Paul VI, Lercaro twice addressed the Council in the name of the Liturgical Commission, on 8 October and 18 November. It was assumed he was speaking for Paul.

Moreover, the Pope was concerned not just with getting the liturgical constitution through the Council but with implementing it as soon as possible, and considered Lercaro the man to do that. Thus on 4 October 1963 he asked Lercaro to draw up a list of reforms that could be introduced the moment the constitution was promulgated. He did not want to wait for the post-conciliar body that canon law required. Paul's first idea was to have a *leggestralcio* or emergency law that could take effect immediately. Lercaro brought the Vincentian radical Fr Annibale Bugnini out of exile to set up a small commission of eight who met at San Gregorio (the church on the hill from which Gregory the Great despatched Augustine to Canterbury) on 18–19 October.

They soon found the idea of a *leggestralcio* unworkable: liturgical change could not be improvised. Much deeper historical studies were needed, on, for instance, concelebration, and the process of change had to be thought through as a whole, not dealt with in piecemeal fashion.[1] Paul's mind was already racing ahead to the *dopoconcilio* (the post-conciliar period).

But the immediate tussle for the control of the Council in the second session lay between the Secretariat and the Moderators. The Moderators had to "invent a role", discover how far they could go.[2] They soon discovered that they could not go very far. To resolve the impasse on *De Ecclesia* Dossetti proposed on 14 October 1963 that four questions be put on:

1 the sacramentality of the episcopal order;
2 their incorporation by right in the college of bishops;
3 the supreme power of the college in union with the Pope;
4 the restoration of the diaconate for married men.[3]

They were printed by order of Lercaro.

The next day, Tuesday, 15 October at 11.45, Suenens announced that the discussion on *De Ecclesia* was closed, and that the four questions would be put to the Fathers tomorrow. But on the morrow, 16 October, Agagianian told the baffled bishops that the vote had been delayed and therefore they would not even receive the four questions. In military parlance: order; counter-order; disorder.

What had happened overnight? Paul VI, alerted by Msgr Felici, was made aware of the four questions, and although they were already

1 Aimé Martimort, "*Le Role de Paul VI dans la réforme Liturgique*", in the eponymous book, p. 62.

2 Claude Troisfontaines, "*A propos de quelques interventions de Paul VI dans l'élaboration de 'Lumen Gentium'* ", *in Problemi ecclesiologici*, Istituto Paolo VI, Brescia 1989, p. 99.

3 Ibid. p. 135.

printed, had them "destroyed".[1] But a copy had already found its way to Raniero a Valle, editor of *Avvenire d'Italia*, the Bologna paper closely linked with Lercaro and Dossetti.

Thus Agagianian announced that the questions would not be distributed on the very morning they appeared in the press. This made him look rather foolish. Paul VI intervened to remove Dossetti from his self-invented office. He did so allegedly at the request of Felici, thus confirming that the real battle was between the Council Secretariat and the Moderators.[2]

But what did this episode really say about Paul VI's attitude to the substantive question? Suenens remains our best source for an answer. Paul VI, he says, was not opposed to the principle of a straw or indicative vote to get the feel of the assembly – the proof is that he accepted it two weeks later. The objection was to the unauthorized or "tainted" source from which the four questions came.

Paul was afraid that the "progressives" were just as capable of machinations as the "right" had been during the first session. Suenens admitted that "it was one of the gravest decisions of my life" and that he deeply embarrassed Paul VI.[3] Dossetti departed like a sacrificed lamb (admittedly not too far away), and yet his four questions set the agenda for the rest of the second session.

For they were the right, crucial questions. A second expanded version was drafted on 19 October by Msgr Gérard Philips, Albert Prigeon and Charles Moeller, all Louvain men staying at the Belgian College, and on Paul's orders presented to an extraordinary "summit meeting" on Wednesday, 23 October, just a week after Agagianian's stalling statement.[4]

This summit was decisive for the whole course of the Council; and it was the result of a *papal* initiative to resolve an impasse. Second, like most of the really important events at the Council, it took place off-stage and in private while in the *aula* of St Peter's speeches were being made on the laity. This does not mean that "interventions" in the *aula* were of no consequence. On the eve of the decisive "summit" meeting, Cardinal Suenens made the most influential speech of the Council so far. The conservatives thought he was exploiting his position as Moderator to hi-jack it.

The laity was under discussion. Suenens began by refuting Cardinal

1 Ibid. quoting Virgilio Carbone, who was part of Felici's team and subsequently helped edit the Council documents.

2 Ibid.

3 Quoted in Claude Troisfontaines, ibid. p. 101.

4 Ibid. p. 136.

Ruffini's view that the *schema* gave too much emphasis to the charisms [*charismata*] or special gifts of the Holy Spirit. Ruffini, like conservatives generally, wanted to stress the claims of official office-holders in the Church – the hierarchy – over against the unpredictable laity. This gave Suenens his opening. Charisms exist in the Church today as they always have done. Far from being minor, peripheral and dispensable gifts, charisms belong to the very essence of the Church for "the Holy Spirit is given to the whole Church, not just to its pastors". The Church was a "pneumatic" reality, founded not only on the Apostles but on the Prophets. It was quite wrong to think of the charisms of the early Church as something out of the ordinary; St Paul mentions such gifts as teaching, the discernment of spirits, and – Suenens looked up – administration. They should heed St Paul's warning not to "stifle the Spirit".

Suenens concluded that the draft should bring out the charismatic as well as the ministerial nature of the Church, stress the role of "prophets" as those who inspire people to live the Gospel, explain the interlocking role of pastors and charismatics in a more constructive manner, and proclaim St Paul's doctrine on the freedom of the children of God.[1] It was heady stuff. Suenens had still not finished. *Since* charisms undoubtedly existed in the Church today, they should be represented at the Council. So the number of lay auditors should be increased and women should be included in their number for "unless I am mistaken, women make up one half of the world's population".

This was one of the most effective speeches made at the Council. It shaped the content of paragraph 12 of *Lumen Gentium*. It had a profound, though delayed-action effect on Paul VI's language and thinking. It set in motion the ideas which made acceptable the Catholic "Renewal" or charismatic movement of the 1970s. Finally, if it did not exactly put "women" on the agenda, it reminded the Council that they existed. Women had hitherto been "invisible" or a joke.

When Josefa Theresia Münch asked Bishop Kampe whether women would be invited to the Council, he replied amid merry laughter, "Perhaps to the Third Vatican Council!"[2] *Il Borghese*, a sensation-mongering Roman weekly that combined pornography with right-wing Catholicism, poured scorn on "The Feminism of his Eminence" and conjured up another "Pope Joan", the horrors of Boccaccio's *Decameron*, and Lysistrata's *Parliament of Women*. But chuckling over feminism didn't

1 Rynne, 2, pp. 216–17; ASCV, 22 October 1963.

2 *The Catholic Citizen, Journal of St Joan's International Alliance*, 1991, No. 1, p. 24. In February 1954 Dr Münch had informed Pius XII of her desire to be ordained priest. She received a negative postcard from Msgr Montini enclosing a picture of Pius XII, another of the Assumption, and the text of the prayer for the Marian Year.

make it go away. Not for the last time, Suenens had struck a responsive chord.

Back in St Peter's the principle of the questions on collegiality was put to the vote. It was accepted only by a small majority and much confusion reigned. New York's Cardinal Spellman got it back to front (that is, intending to vote against, he voted in favour) while Tisserant pedantically raised points of Latinity (should they say *utrum*? or *an*? for the questions).[1] To add to the confusion, the sudden proposal to have a debate for and against whether the Blessed Virgin Mary should be included in *De Ecclesia* or be treated separately distracted the most attentive mind.

Yet this decision was acted on with astonishing rapidity, the debate on the BVM taking place the next day, 24 October. In the event Cardinal Franz König of Vienna, who argued for inclusion, easily defeated Cardinal Rufino Santos of Manila who had only pious gush to offer. It was an unequal contest. A theological and ecumenical point was at stake: was Mary, the Mother of Jesus, "in the Church", in which case she belonged in *de Ecclesia*, or, somehow, outside and above it, in which case she would merit separate treatment?

At the 23 October summit meeting a similar pro and con debate, in the style of a mediaeval disputation, was envisaged as the solution to the collegiality issue. The Council Fathers would have been asked to choose between a Suenens and a Siri formulation of the questions. Siri, however, was "difficult", insisting that he alone should pose a single question, without alternatives, and that it should present collegiality purely as a concession made by the pope in extremely limited circumstances.[2] This manifestly unfair scheme was rejected on 25 October. So it was back to the Philips version of the questions.

Paul VI approved this procedure only at the last moment. Over lunch a week later, Suenens told him: "In this matter you made me undergo all fourteen Stations of the Cross."

"Yes," Paul replied, "you went through all the Stations of the Cross . . . But I wanted this to be the responsibility of the Moderators, without committing myself personally."

Claude Troisfontaines, who reports this story, says it shows that Paul VI had "not yet made up his mind on the issues, and that he held his final judgement in reserve".[3]

None of this was known at the time. What all the books report is

1 Claude Troisfontaines, "*Quelques interventions . . .*", in *Problemi ecclesiologici*, p. 136.

2 Ibid. p. 137.

3 Ibid. pp. 101–2.

that "collegiality" was accepted in principle by large majorities on 30 October 1963. Here are the five "propositions" in summary:

1 Episcopal consecration is the highest degree of the sacrament of order (*placet* 2, 132; *non placet* 34).

2 Every legitimately consecrated bishop in communion with the bishops and the Roman Pontiff, head and principle of unity, is a member of the episcopal college (*placet* 2,049; *non placet* 104).

3 The body of college of Bishops succeeds the college of the Apostles . . . and together with its head the Roman Pontiff and never without this head (whose right of primacy over all pastors and faithful remains secure and entire) enjoys plenary and supreme authority over the universal Church (*placet* 1,808; *non placet* 336).

4 The said authority belongs to the college of bishops by divine right (*placet* 1,717; *non placet* 408).

5 The diaconate should be restored as a distinct and permanent grade of the ministry (*placet* 1,588; *non placet* 525).

Commentators agree that this was the moment at which the log-jam was broken. For Bishop John J. Wright of Pittsburgh, known as the "egg-head bishop", it was the turning-point.[1] "It was the day the Council attained its majority," wrote Henri de Lubac.[2]

But the procedural impasse was resolved only because the questions were "steered" in a particular direction. The formula was: "Does it please the fathers that the text should be written in such a way that . . . ?" To tell the truth, this was the idea of Dossetti and Yves-Marie Congar OP. Felici and Ottaviani opposed it on the grounds that such a vote was not foreseen by the rules of the Council.

Paul VI accepted that the (now) five propositions should be presented "not on his own responsibility, but in the name of Cardinal Suenens and the Moderators". Msgr Albert Prignon, then rector of the Belgian College in Rome, explains: "In this way Paul VI withheld any judgement on the substantial question . . . But the majority in the Council had been clearly established."[3]

The flags and banners were out at the Belgian College, and there was general rejoicing among the majority. It is not certain that Paul rejoiced equally. Prignon points out that from now on Felici was granted

1 Xavier Rynne, *The Second Session*, p. 170.

2 Philippe Levillain, *La mécanique politique*, p. 296. Once again I am assuming that his *Documents privés* were de Lubac's notes.

3 Prignon, unpublished paper, "*Evêques et théologiens belges au concile Vatican II*", given at Louvain-la-Neuve, p. 20.

the right to attend the meetings of the Moderators and never again were they allowed to take such an initiative. They were reduced to being amiable figureheads. Power abhors a vacuum, so it drifted imperceptibly towards the Council secretariat.

Not so imperceptibly, said some critics: the Council secretariat was working according to a plan to which Cicognani, Secretary of State, Felici, just mentioned, and Marella were privy. It is a question of semantics at what point a co-ordinated plan becomes a plot; and in general conspiracy theories are to be avoided unless nothing else can explain the facts.

This was the situation. In 1962 a draft *schema* on Ecumenism (*De Oecumenismo*) prepared by the Oriental Churches Congregation had been rejected. On 18 November 1963 a new draft prepared by the Secretariat for Christian Unity was laid before the Council. It had three chapters:

1 The Principles of Catholic Ecumenism.

2 The Practice of Ecumenism.

3 Christians separated from the Catholic Church including a) the Eastern Churches and b) Christian Communities arising from the sixteenth century onwards.

To this were added chapters 4 and 5 dealing with religious liberty and the position of the Jewish people in salvation-history. These additional chapters were not voted on in this session even though a vote had been promised. The denouement of this affair came in the week between 27 November and 4 December when the Council came to an end. This was the *settimana nera* or black week of the second session.

So there was a count-down in effect to 3 December when a commemoration of the ending of Trent had already been arranged. 4 December was set aside for Pope Paul's speech.

Throughout the session the majority took it for granted that there would be a vote on religious liberty and the Jews before the *end of the session*. It was not expected to be a definitive vote, but rather what Cardinal Léon-Joseph Suenens called a *vote d'orientation* and the Anglo-Saxons a "straw" poll designed to "test the wind" and ascertain the mind (*mens*) of the assembly. The question for the majority was not "Will there be a vote on these two burning issues?" but "*When* will there be a vote on them?"

As late as 27 November Cardinals Joseph Ritter of St Louis and Albert Meyer of Chicago approached the day's Moderator, Cardinal Pietro Agagianian, and courteously enquired whether there would be a vote. "Why, *of course* there is going to be a vote," replied the wily

Armenian.[1] Suspicions were aroused, however, that same day. Paul let it be known that he was about to grant to the bishops on 3 December some forty powers (or faculties). This was considered a "sweetener" to make them forget the vote on the Jews and religious liberty; but what could this "concession" mean if bishops already possessed such powers by virtue of their consecration?

The very next day, 28 November, Cardinals Ritter and Meyer, this time accompanied by Spellman, sought out Paul to protest at the delay, which looked like an abandonment. Yet they were reluctant "to push the Pope to do anything", as one of them put it.[2] Meyer was depressed, furious, silent.[3] Paul had told him to "open his heart freely". He had done so, to no avail: any attempt to change things now would be "an affront to the Holy Father".[4] The only conclusion one could draw was that Paul, at the very least, was not behaving even-handedly, not acting as an independent umpire or referee. As late as 1 December Suenens met the Canadian bishops and still fondly believed that a vote was possible.[5]

At 7.30 the next morning Bea's phone rang. He was due to speak in the *aula*. Cicognani now dictated to him what to say. He was to impress on the Council the idea that the *only* reason for the delay in coming to a vote on the two chapters on Jews and religious liberty was pressure of time. There was no human factor, merely the inexorable working out of the mighty machine that was the Council. No machinations, just the machine, as Serafian remarked.[6] Bea did what was needed, without perjuring himself, ascribing the non-vote to insurmountable time-tabling difficulties. He started praising Pope John, only to find he was mouthing and gesticulating into thin air, for the Moderator for the day, Agagianian, cut off the microphone.

From the tomb, then, Pope John still loomed menacingly for the conservatives. Did Paul accept that view? Did he still feel threatened? It seems that he did: the evidence is that he now appeared to fall under the spell of Felici of the Synod Secretariat and Marella, the sinister figure behind him, letting them take on great responsibility for the Council.

1 "Michael Serafian", *The Pilgrim*, p. 210. This was the *nom de guerre* prudently adopted by Malachy Martin, soon to be an ex-Jesuit.

2 Ibid. Internal evidence suggests this remark came from Ritter; Spellman was tight as a clam, and Meyer *did* want to put pressure on Paul; only Ritter maintained contact with the Secretariat for Christian Unity, which is where "Serafian" was at the time.

3 Ibid. p. 210.

4 Ibid. p. 211.

5 Ibid. p. 210.

6 Ibid.

These highly emotional events distracted attention from the business realities: the second session was actually going to conclude with two documents tucked under its belt, the constitution on the liturgy, *Sacrosanctum Concilium*, and the decree on the mass media (social communications in Vaticanese), *Inter Mirifica. Sacrosanctum Concilium* was of immense importance, and it got a good press.

Inter Mirifica, on the other hand, was by common consent the feeblest of the conciliar documents by a long chalk. Even John Carmel Heenan, Archbishop of Westminster, no friend of the media, considered it "not of conciliar calibre". All this had been pointed out by a group of journalists before the vote. They produced a one-page memo on the topic. They declared that for ever and a day this *schema* would be cited as "a classic example of the way Vatican II proved incapable of facing the world around it". Four *periti* signed including John Courtney Murray SJ and Bernhard Häring CSSR. A group of bishops produced a similar statement and tried to distribute it in St Peter's Square.

An exciting skirmish resulted. Archbishop Pericle Felici, Secretary of the Council, tried to seize the petition from Joseph Reuss, auxiliary Bishop of Mainz, on the grounds that he was "conducting an unauthorized demonstration". Reuss refused to surrender his precious text, Felici lunged towards it, and Reuss warded him off; but then in disgust flung the paper down saying something disobliging in German that Felici, perhaps fortunately, did not catch. St Peter's Square is Vatican territory, and only the right sort of demonstrations are allowed. The Franciscan Fr Carlo Balic was allowed to distribute mariological tracts in the square at will.

Pressure groups were not equal, the playing-field was clearly not even and the umpire or referee (Paul saw himself in this role) rarely blew the whistle. Bishop Edward Mason, who bore the heat and burden of the day as Vicar Apostolic of El Obeid in the Sudan, got up a petition signed by 300 members of the *Coetus Internationalis Patrum*. These were the right-wing intransigents, among whom Archbishops Marcel Lefebvre and Dino Staffa were prominent, who opposed everything new. Mason, an Italian Sacred Heart Father despite his Anglo-Saxon name, alleged that the right to follow one's conscience involved the right to embrace any kind of error including atheistic Marxism. Thus Bea's position on religious liberty was presented as tantamount to blessing Marxist atheism. Absurd as it was, this theory was widely believed, for "error has no rights" and cannot be put on the same footing as "truth". Down that path lay no future. Yet Paul hesitated, knowing that his predecessors up to St Pius X at least would have made this same objection. He had to work his way through that.

One way Paul could influence the Council was through "inspiring" (that is prompting) articles in *L'Osservatore Romano*. Having done this under difficult circumstances in the pontificate of Pius XII, there was no reason why he should not do it now he was Pope. On 25 November 1963 the Vatican daily carried an article by Cardinal Franz König of Vienna. He argued that one aspect of the Council was being entirely overlooked: the Church should not just meet and dialogue with believers, admirable though this was and well though Cardinal Bea's Secretariat coped, but with non-believers. How were non-believers to be reached? Since no problem is allowed to exist in the mind of the Roman Curia unless there is a specialized body to deal with it, one can say that with König's *L'Osservatore Romano* article the idea of a Secretariat for non-believers was carefully planted.

Stephen Leven, auxiliary bishop of San Antonio, Texas, could not equal König in scholarship. But on 27 November 1963 he said something that badly needed saying:

> Why not put an end, once and for all, to the scandal of our mutual recriminations? Every day it becomes clearer that we have a real need of dialogue not merely with the Protestants but among ourselves assembled in the Council . . . Some Fathers speak as though the only text in the whole Bible were, "Thou art Peter and upon this rock I will build my church" (Matthew 16:18). And they dare to preach at us as though we were against Peter and his successors, or as though we wished to weaken the faith of believers or to promote indifferentism.[1]

"Indifferentism": a technical term referring to the idea that "one religion is as good as another" or "there are many paths up the same mountain". Which path you happen to choose is a matter of indifference.

The auxiliary Bishop of San Antonio, Texas was struggling with the question to which König's Secretariat would have to give an answer: How is it possible to combine firmness with openness, certainty and clarity of faith with tolerance of others?

One of the problems of the session was that Paul did not show his hand and offered no help on such questions. His views were not known on another question important for bishops: should they have a statutory age for retirement? The draft text proposed sixty-five, which, if taken seriously, would have meant instant dismissal for a majority of Council Fathers including Paul VI, who was by now sixty-six. On 11 November 1963, Albert Conrad de Vito OFM, Bishop of Lucknow, complained like a true pukka sahib that insisting on a retirement age for bishops

1 ASCV, II, VI, pp. 64–65.

would be "just as outrageous as attempting to change the course of the moon".[1]

Next day, 12 November, Suenens delivered another of his thundering speeches that set the agenda even if they did not settle the question. The argument against the resignation case was based on paternity – fathers never resign, and once a father, always a father. Suenens, whose own father died when he was three, pointed out in normal families sons gradually took over responsibility from their fathers who were happy to put their feet up in their sunset years.

The other argument against episcopal resignation was that the bishop is "married indissolubly to his diocese". But in that case, said Suenens, many of us here have been divorced – by translation or promotion – two or three times over.[2]

Suenens sounded a practical pastoral note. The bishop, as the centre of discernment in the diocese, needs to be constantly alert to new needs and aware of the charisms that may surprise him. Old men can sometimes do that – witness Pope John XXIII – but ordinary psychology applies in the sacramental order as well. If judges and professors know when it is time to go, then bishops should do likewise. Besides, added Suenens, a bishop sometimes has to ask a parish priest to retire on grounds of age. He cannot do that if he is not prepared to set an example. Suenens was fifty-nine at the time, Paul sixty-six. Was Suenens dropping a hint to the Pope?

If so, had he "lost favour" with Paul, to use a vocabulary from seventeenth-century courts? Should the favour of the prince matter so much?

No one knew what Paul really thought. This was a general problem about this session. The *periti* or experts were not much wiser than anyone else.[3] Their status was ill-defined, their backgrounds haphazard, their authority nil. Some were rule-minded canonists, others were world-famous theologians who had influenced the thinking of many bishops. Often they were more honoured abroad than at home: the Bavarian Karl Rahner was present at the Council as the guest of Cardinal König of Vienna; French Dominican Yves-Marie Congar was invited by the Belgian bishops; the Belgian Charles Moeller was present thanks to Cardinal Paul-Emile Léger of Montreal. But since there were 359 *periti*,

1 Ibid. II, IV, p. 722.

2 Ibid. II, V, p. 10.

3 See Karl Heinz Neufeld, "In the Service of the Council", for Henri de Lubac's ninetieth birthday, in René Latourelle, ed., *Vatican II Assessments and Perspectives*, 1988, p. 79.

212 from the diocesan clergy and 147 religious, it was quite impossible to generalize about them.[1]

Yet all 359 *periti* were theoretically on the same level, and were seen as mere "consultants" of the Roman Curia. Each commission was presided over by a cardinal, and its experts were asked merely "to confirm, extend or reinforce what was already known and familiar".[2] Yet there were evident distinctions between them in scholarship and talent. There was bound to be a clash between the curial court-theologians and the creative spirits from elsewhere. Where did Paul VI stand?

On 30 November 1963 Paul gave the *periti* a special audience, designed to show his esteem for their work. But his speech – if there was a speech – was never published.[3] When the same courtesy was extended to the bishops' secretaries and chauffeurs, the theologians felt put in their place. True, in his very personal first encyclical *Ecclesiam Suam* (1964), Paul would directly address the *periti* and freely admit that the *magisterium* needed their work. Later still he went out of his way to name individual theologians whom he knew were under attack in Rome. Both De Lubac and Congar, so recently outcasts, received honourable mentions. But that did not happen in 1963.

So the impression remained that somehow theologians were mistrusted. They were suspected of leaking conciliar information and forming lobbies. A document from the Co-ordinating Commission dated 28 December 1963 said "they are requested not to form pressure groups, or to give interviews, or to present publicly private ideas concerning the Council". Further, "they are not to criticize the Council, and not to pass on to outsiders any information concerning the work of the commissions".[4] These injunctions were stamped: "With the authority of the Holy Father."

This was, of course, the conservative position: the more open the Council was, the more it would feel the pressure of public opinion. Paul VI agreed with that. But it proved very difficult to enforce the ban on interviews (on or off the record); and in any case many *periti* kept diaries, so that we have some more insight into the work of the Commissions than was possible at the time.

But if the "collegiality" so painfully hammered out were to have any

1 Giovanni Caprile SJ, *Il Concilio Vaticano II, il Primo Periodo*, p. 402.

2 Karl Heinz Neufeld, op. cit. p. 79. They were all priests, and therefore all male, and their numbers grew with each session. Laypeople including women were admitted as *auditores* – they were to listen and not be heard.

3 Ibid. p. 85.

4 Ibid.

real meaning, there would have to be an instrument to express it when no Council was in session. This was the germ of the idea of the "Synod of Bishops". In his *Vota* for Vatican II (not revealed until much later) Cardinal Bernard Alfrink, Archbishop of Utrecht, recommended a "legislative council" to help the Pope, on the model of the permanent synods of the Eastern Churches.[1]

On 6 November 1963 Maximos VI Saigh, Melchite Patriarch of Antioch, became the chief advocate of the synod at the Council. Speaking as usual in French on the grounds that he was not a "Latin" but an Oriental Christian, Maximos said: "A small group of bishops, representing the whole college, would have the task of helping the Pope in the general government of the whole Church. This group could form the real 'sacred college' of the universal Church. It could include the principal bishops of the Church." He went on to enumerate them, beginning with the Oriental Patriarchs. In Maximos' mind, some members of the Synod would have to reside permanently in Rome, in order to act as "the supreme, executive and decision-making council of the Church". "All the Roman Congregations," he added, "should be subordinate to it."[2]

Maximos' "model" of the Synod, prompted by Eastern experience, represented the most radical proposal for the new body. Paul was trapped in a dilemma. On the one hand he realized the political difficulty of subordinating the Roman Congregations to the Synod. Yet on the other hand he wanted somehow to involve the world's bishops in the government of the Church. He had admitted as much in his address at the opening of this session.[3] In November 1963 over 500 bishops presented a memorandum urging him to flesh out this proposal, but there was hardly any conciliar debate about the shape of this future body, and Paul VI kept the *modi et rationes* very close to his chest.

On one question at least Paul had good reasons for secrecy. While the Council were discussing the question of the Jews, Paul was planning a pilgrimage to the Holy Land that would need the approval of Arab governments. In November he sent Msgr Jacques Martin of the Secretariat of State and Don Pasquale Macchi to the Middle East to make

1 See Jan Grootaers, "*Une restauration de la théologique de l'épiscopat: la contribution du Cardinal Alfrink à la préparation de Vatican II*", in *Glaube im Prozess, Für Karl Rahner*, pp. 803–4.

2 René Laurentin, *Bilan de la Deuxième Session*, Seuil 1964, p. 118.

3 "For us personally it [the discussion] will provide doctrinal and practical considerations by which our apostolic office, though endowed by Christ with fullness and sufficiency of power, may receive more help and support *in ways yet to be determined* from a more effective and responsible collaboration with our beloved and venerable brothers in the episcopate." *Insegnamenti*, 1963, p. 175; Rynne, 2, p. 355.

the arrangements for the visit. "The secret was easy to keep," said Martin, "because no one in the world imagined that a pope would go to the Holy Land."[1]

It was indeed a bold and imaginative project. The immediate question was how it would affect the Council's draft text on the Jews absolving them from "deicide". This was by no means a straightforward matter. Muslim states would interpret a decree along such lines as favouring Jewish political aspirations. Once the thesis of Jewish "deicide" was abandoned, as it had to be, Muslims would conclude that the favour shown to the Zionist movement in Christian countries was based on Christian doctrine. "So much the worst for Christian teaching," say the Arabs. That is why Arab Christians find it necessary to assert their Arab nationalism, with equal if not extra vigour.

So Paul had good reasons for not showing his hand in the dispute which, if allowed to develop, would have set Cardinal Augustin Bea and the Secretariat against the Arab bishops and Oriental Patriarchs.

Yet if he kept his counsel on some important matters, towards the end of the second session it was possible to believe (as certainly Ottaviani believed) that Paul had fallen under the spell of Suenens. He was the star of the Council. His speeches on charisms, on the restoration of the diaconate, and the age of retirement had all proved extremely effective.

Moreover Paul chose him to deliver the panegyric of Pope John, which in effect contributed to his myth and seemed to bind his successor to liberal policies that he might find questionable. Again Suenens had successfully persuaded Paul to accept that lay "auditors" should be admitted to the Council, adroitly proposing the name of the Pope's old friend, Jean Guitton, as the first of them. Suenens chalked up another victory when a layman, the English former YCW leader, Pat Keegan, actually addressed the Council. Suenens was also battling for *women* to be admitted as "auditors", to the Curia a disturbing and revolutionary step.

Last, but far from least, Suenens had dissuaded Paul from ending the session with the solemn declaration that the bones of St Peter in the crypt were authentic. The announcement in the final speech that Paul VI would go to the Holy Land in January 1964 – dramatic because it came as a total surprise – made a much better impression on the observers.

The return to biblical sources was the principle of renewal. It was something in which all Christians could rejoice and share. Even so he

1 Jacques Martin, "Les voyages de Paul VI", in *Modernité*, p. 318.

gave it a "Petrine" twist saying he would see "that blessed land from which Peter set forth and to which none of his successors has returned". But one could not object to that truism.

But at last the Council had something to show for its labours. The constitution on the divine liturgy, *Sacrosanctum Concilium*, and the decree on the mass media, *Inter Mirifica*, were both solemnly proclaimed. Each document was signed "*Ego Paulus, Catholicae Ecclesiae episcopus*" (I, Paul, Bishop of the Catholic Church) followed by all the remaining Council Fathers.

This had great ecumenical significance. Paul did not sign as Roman Pontiff or Supreme Pastor but as a Catholic bishop. He was a bishop among bishops, admittedly the presiding bishop, but on the same level as his brothers. It was an archetypal collegial act, adumbrating what *Lumen Gentium* would say in more solemn language: "The Chair of Peter presides over the whole assembly of charity, and protects legitimate differences."[1]

Moreover the final voting on *Sacrosanctum Concilium* revealed an impressive unanimity: 2147 voted *placet* (in favour) while there were only a derisory four votes against. The 4 December 1963 promulgation was important for its content as well as its manner. Whatever Paul had thought in the past, he now justified giving the first place to the liturgy: "We may see in this the recognition of a right order of values and duties: God in the first place; prayer our first duty, the liturgy the first school of spirituality."[2]

Annibale Bugnini, chief architect of the document, recalled that it was exactly 400 years since the Council of Trent, on 4 December 1563, despairing of ever getting round to liturgical reform, had entrusted it to the Holy See. "What was marginal at Trent," said Bugnini, "became the number one problem at Vatican I," adding redundantly, "divine Providence has played a part in securing this priority."[3]

Against this it may be argued that if *Sacrosanctum Concilium* had been debated after *Gaudium et Spes* it would have been more "world-oriented" and would not have presented the liturgy as "the summit towards which the activity of the Church is directed, and the fountain from which all her power flows".[4]

1 *Lumen Gentium*, 13.

2 *Insegnamenti*, 1963, p. 375. A year before he had argued that the liturgy was the wrong place to begin, on the grounds that *actio sequitur esse*, the worship of the Church, depended on the nature of the Church.

3 Annibale Bugnini, *The Reform of the Liturgy 1948–1975*, tr. Matthew J. O'Connell, p. 37.

4 *Sacrosanctum Concilium*, 10. It also recognizes, however, that "the liturgy does not exhaust the entire activity of the Church" (9).

Yet starting with the liturgy made a great impact on the Catholic world. First, it affected everyone soon, if not immediately. It was the most obvious instance of "change", and the first public indication that the Council would make a difference in the lives of ordinary people. Second, to have liturgy in the vernacular empowered episcopal conferences and gave them something to do. Third, by the same token it reduced the curial role to one of supervision and revision. Fourth, the news about the liturgy was conveyed through the press, not by pastoral letters, and so, despite the totally inadequate decree *Inter Mirifica*, the media already played a crucial role.

Paul VI was wisely silent about *Inter Mirifica*, which has been apologized for ever since. The true conciliar document on communications, *Gaudium et Spes*, was yet to be written. The only practical consequence of *Inter Mirifica* was that in obedience to it Paul VI set up the Pontifical Commission for the Means of Social Communications.[1] Its first not very exacting task was to produce something better than *Inter Mirifica*.

After two years work the Council was capable of concluding *something*: that was the main point. Reaching a conclusion on the nature of the Church would prove more difficult. Though resolved in principle, collegiality had not yet been formulated in a satisfactory manner. Paul, however, summed up the position in a way the majority found, for the time being, adequate: "The episcopacy is not an institution independent of, or separated from, or still less antagonistic to, the Supreme Pontificate of Peter, but with Peter and under him (*cum Petro et sub Petro*) it strives for the common good. The co-ordinated hierarchy will thus be strengthened but not undermined."[2]

There remained so much to do on such difficult questions as revelation, religious liberty, the correct place of mariology (he slipped in the title "Mother of the Church" without anyone realizing the implications), not to mention the vast area of "dialogue with the modern world" with which Paul was so passionately concerned.

It seemed, therefore, optimistic of Paul to imagine that one more session in 1964 would be enough to bring the Council to a close. He knew that the Commissions were the key to the speeding up of the process:

> We hope that the competent commissions . . . will prepare for the future conciliar session, *in accordance with the mind of the*

1 *Motu proprio In Fructibus Multis* (2 April 1964). The cumbersome title came about because of a desire to avoid the term "mass media". The Church does not address "the masses" but people.

2 *Insegnamenti*, pp. 377–78.

> *Fathers, as expressed in the general congregations*, proposals profoundly studied, accurately formulated, suitably shortened and abbreviated so that the discussions, which we want to remain always free, may be rendered shorter and swifter.[1]

The italicized passage was a last-minute afterthought of Paul VI's added to the manuscript.[2] This was an attempt to reassure the Council Fathers that the Commissions were their servants and not their masters.

Then he made what seemed like a mistake. He declared Our Lady "Mother of the Church". He may have thought this was obvious or that he was reassuring the right-wing, yet again, while also, for once, pleasing Cardinal Suenens.[3] This title, "Mother of the Church", had been considered and rejected by the Theological Commission, repeatedly and unanimously, on the grounds that it appeared to place Mary *outside* the Church. Since the whole thrust of conciliar mariology was to include her *within* the Church, as indeed the first or leading disciple and the "type" of the Church, in St Ambrose's expression, Paul was in opposition with expert theological opinion.

The Observers were puzzled; some were shaken. Even Jean Guitton, normally so *bien-pensant*, admitted Paul had behaved "like a host who suddenly shocks his guests".[4] René Laurentin, an expert in mariology, quoted Paul's observation on 11 October 1963, to the effect that "Mary is both the mother and the daughter of the Church". This is the law of complex analogy, announced Laurentin: to most people it sounded like Zen surrealism. Laurentin tied himself in knots explaining that the Theological Commission rejected the title "Mother of the Church", not because it was wrong but because it was fatally prone to misunderstanding.[5]

The question remains: why did Paul do it? Why did he risk rebuff over a question on which he was not asked to pronounce and on which silence would have been no disgrace?

Sometimes the simplest answers are best. Paul used the title "Mary, Mother of the Church" because he believed in it. He was using his

1 Ibid. p. 377.

2 Giuseppe Colombo, *I discorsi di Paolo VI in apertura e chiusura dei periodi conciliari*, MSS, Rome, September 1989, p. 3.

3 Henri Denis, *Eglise, qu'as tu fait de ton Concile?* p. 68, remarks that Suenens loved the title "Mary, Mother of the Church" because he was devoted to the Legion of Mary.

4 René Laurentin, *Bilan du Concile*, p. 160.

5 Peter Hebblethwaite, "The Mariology of Three Popes", *The Way*, Supplement 51, Autumn 1984, pp. 61–62.

"charism of discernment". Four years later, in October 1967, he announced his intention of building a church in Rome "at a place chosen for reasons of pastoral need, dedicated to Our Lady, Mother of the Church, of which she is the first, blessed and privileged child".[1]

1 René Laurentin, *Bilan du Concile*, p 160.

23

From Jerusalem to Rome

> Paul VI took over Pope John's Council, giving it direction by clarifying its goals: the renewal of the Church, the promotion of Christian unity and dialogue with the modern world. He treated the Council with great respect, assuring it the greatest freedom of discussion by not assigning a date for its conclusion and not seeking to anticipate its results by his decisions.
>
> (*L'Avvenire d'Italia*, 24 June 1964)

Paul VI was never so popular as in the first nine months of 1964. The idea of making his first journey outside Italy a pilgrimage to the Holy Land was the best kept secret in a city which is as leaky as a Gruyère cheese. It was also a master-stroke which dramatized the goals of the Council and caught the imagination of the world. It was a return to the sources, the *retour aux sources*, which was the basis for the biblical, patristic and liturgical movements which flowed into the Council. St Peter had gone from the Holy Land to Rome; Paul would go from Rome to the Holy Land and establish a permanent link between Jerusalem, the city of peace, and Rome. That, at any rate, was his first intention.

Even more urgently, by going to the Holy Land he sought to focus the attention on Christ, crucified and risen, as the agent and content of Christian revelation. Paul would proclaim the Beatitudes, the kernel of Christian faith, as close as possible to the place where they were first pronounced. All office in the Church is subordinate to Christ. The pope not so much the "Vicar of Christ" as his servant and disciple. Theologians pointed out that the pope's earlier and more accurate title was "*Vicarius Petri*" (vicar of Peter), where "vicar" is a Roman legal term meaning "heir and successor". St Peter had gone from Jerusalem to Rome to be crucified in the year 66.[1]

1 Margherita Guarducci, *Saint Pierre retrouvé*, argues for AD 66, p. 27. AD 67 had been the previously accepted date. But it had fluctuated. Guarducci discussed these matters with Paul VI: "He was aware of the scholarly disputes and thought he should follow the example of *Pio Nono*, a 67 man, leaving experts to determine a more exact date if they could" (ibid.).

His successor went from Rome to Jerusalem in *anno Domini* 1964, to be jostled by crowds as he came through the Damascene Gate into the Via Dolorosa where the crush-barriers were broken down and he lost his secretary, Don Pasquale Macchi. "Let me through," wailed Macchi to the officer who barred his way, "I'm the Pope's secretary." "And I'm Nikita Khruschev's secretary," replied the officer.[1] Macchi's personal fate mattered less than the fact that he had the text of Paul VI's speech. So he had to get through.

This visit to the Holy Land was Paul's message to the next session of the Council. Spelt out, it said that ecclesiology was founded on the rock of St Peter's faith.

But this goal enveloped a second purpose that was equally important. Paul went to the Holy Land in order to meet Athenagoras II, the Ecumenical Patriarch of Constantinople. Athenagoras had spent enough time in the United States to realize that the Orthodox Churches could no longer remain in haughty isolation. He was in no sense an Orthodox "Pope", and the thirty thousand Orthodox Christians surviving in secularized Islamic Turkey did not count for much compared with the estimated sixty millions who, though tightly controlled by the Soviet Office of Cults, belonged to the Moscow Patriarchate. But he had "convener's rights", and to that extent could represent the whole of Orthodoxy.

Getting the other Orthodox Patriarchs, particularly those of Russia, Greece, Serbia and Bulgaria, to consent to a meeting with the Bishop of Rome was the diplomatic hurdle that had to be overcome. Paul had already had an exchange of correspondence with Athenagoras who congratulated him on his election. Athenagoras had the greatest regard for Pope John XXIII of whom he famously said: "There was a man sent from God, and his name was John . . ."

In his reply Paul made no mention of a possible meeting, but prepared the ground by speaking of his own office in "Greek" terms: Peter was the "chorus-leader (*coryphaeus*) of the Apostles" and brother of Andrew, patron of the Church of Constantinople. Athenagoras caught the hint, enabling the first-ever meeting between a patriarch and a pope since the schism of 1054 to take place in the Church of the Holy Sepulchre in Jerusalem.

But before he could meet Athenagoras, tact combined with charity demanded that he should first exchange courtesy visits with the Greek Orthodox Patriarch of Jerusalem. Benedict had his reservations about the pope, not least of which was the existence of the so-called *Latin* Patriarch of Jerusalem who was traditionally an Italian. Benedict was won over. Tact and charity also required a meeting with Yeghese Derder-

1 Carlo Cremona, *Paolo VI*, p. 210.

ian, *Catholicos* of the non-Chalcedonian Armenian Apostolic Church that had survived massacres and persecution since the year 302. This was not just an afterthought. Paul would meet the *Catholicos* again.

But beyond doubt the decisive and historic meeting was with the Ecumenical Patriarch himself. The Church of the Holy Sepulchre was jam-packed, the heat intolerable. It was an intensely emotional occasion. Paul himself described it to the cardinals on the evening of his return, the feast of the Epiphany, 6 January 1964:

> Athenagoras, the Ecumenical Patriarch of Constantinople, accompanied by about eleven metropolitans, came forward to meet me and wanted to embrace me like a brother. He shook my hand, and held on to it, leading me, hand in hand, into the room where we exchanged a few words. He said: "We should understand each other, we should make peace, we should show the world that we are once more brothers.[1]

A thousand years of history were, if not swept aside, at least consigned to the God of mercy and forgiveness. Paul tried to tell the cardinals how he felt: "The moment when I was overcome by emotion and tears filled my eyes was during the Mass in the Church of the Holy Sepulchre when I pronounced the words of consecration and adored the sacramental presence of Christ in the place where Christ consummated his sacrifice."

But there was no inter-communion. The pain of division was still felt. Then pope and patriarch said the Our Father together in Greek and in Latin.

It was time for Paul to offer a gift to mark the occasion. After much brooding, Paul decided that a chalice would best signify his desire for fraternal communion. As he departed, Athenagoras pleaded with him: "What should we do, tell me what we should do." It is not often in history that the main protagonist also reports the event. But Paul did not overhear Athenagoras' remark to a bystander: "I ardently hope that Pope Paul VI will one day mix water and wine in this chalice."

The next day was the feast of the Epiphany, which for the Orthodox is the celebration of the incarnation as Christmas is in the West. Paul realized a dream by saying Mass at the altar of the Magi in Bethlehem. From Christ's crib he proclaimed the "new attitudes of mind, new aims, and new standards of conduct" demanded of all Catholics by the Council. But the main message was outward-looking, with every word carefully weighed.

The goal was complete Christian unity:

1 *Insegnamenti*, 1964, pp. 62–63.

> Even on this very special occasion we must say that such a result is not to be attained at the expense of the truths of faith. We cannot be false to Christ's inheritance: it is not ours, but his; we are no more than its stewards, teachers, interpreters. Yet we declare once again that we are ready to consider every reasonable means by which mutual understanding, respect and charity may be fostered . . .
>
> The door of the fold is open. We wait, all of us, with sincere hearts. Our desire is strong and patient. There is room for all. Our affection anticipates the step to be taken; it can be taken with honour and mutual joy. We shall not call for gestures that are not the fruit of free conviction, that are not the fruit of the Spirit of the Lord, who blows when and where he wills.[1]

Then he went up from Bethlehem to Jerusalem for his second meeting with the Ecumenical Patriarch.

It was Athenagoras' turn to offer a gift in exchange for Paul's chalice. The Holy Synod of Constantinople, not just Athenagoras himself, decided on a pectoral chain, called *encolpion* in Greek, worn by bishops as the symbol of their apostolic succession and governance of the Church. Paul had not been warned in advance. He hesitated, and then put it on with the help of Athenagoras.

"Now we are going to read the Gospel of St John, chapter 17," he announced in French, "the prayer of Christ for Christian unity." Verse by verse, Paul read it in Latin while Athenagoras responded antiphonally in Greek. Paul was so overcome he lost his place more than once.[2]

There was a third meeting with Athenagoras in the streets of Jerusalem after Paul had met the Anglican Archbishop of Jerusalem, Angus Campbell MacInnes, and Lutheran representatives. It would take a long time to unpack the full significance of this richly tapestried symbolic event. What, for example, did it mean for the Holy See's relations with the state of Israel and the conciliar declaration on the Jews that the second session had left suspended? The answers would come in time.

There were already implications for the wider reach of ecumenism. Paul VI went back to the sources of Christian unity in the Holy Land. But he was also groping for the mysterious key to the unity of Judaism and Islam and Christianity. He knew it was somehow tied up with the city of Jerusalem, the city of peace, sacred to all three religions. More profound still was his conviction that the *reason why* Jerusalem was

1 Ibid. pp. 30–1. The "invitation to fraternity, peace and union" from Bethlehem was delivered in French.

2 The beginning of the reading can be heard on the Vatican Radio cassette, *Ricordi di Paolo VI*.

sacred to all monotheists was that it was associated with Abraham, "our Father in Faith". In Jerusalem he used the phrase "the three Abrahamic religions" that he borrowed from the French Islamic scholar Louis Massignon.[1]

Paul had another historical memory at the back of his mind. The last pope who planned to go to the Holy Land was Innocent III who wanted to carry out a decision of the Fourth Lateran Council by leading a Crusade against the "Saracens". Paul went to Jerusalem not as commander-in-chief but on foot. Paul went as a humble pilgrim, risking the buffeting of the crowds in the Via Dolorosa. That had another consequence: future journeys would need better forward planning, and Msgr Paul Marcinkus from Cicero, Illinois, of the Secretariat of State, was put in charge of their planning and security.

But the immediate meaning of the visit was already clear: it inaugurated Paul's pontificate and constituted his programme. It made the aims of the pontificate and the aims of the Council coincide.

During the visit to the Holy Land there were secret meetings that prepared Paul's next visit. Sargent Shriver, President Lyndon B. Johnson's special assistant, invariably described as "a devout Roman Catholic", met the Apostolic Delegate to the region, Msgr Lino Zanini, who arranged a private audience with Paul. The Pope had only one question: "How would the President view a papal visit to the United Nations?" Back in Washington a receptive Johnson quickly saw the political capital to be gained from such a visit and put Jack Valenti, an old Texan crony, in charge of negotiating in complete confidence what was envisaged as a crowded single-day visit.[2]

This would be another lived parable and message to the Council: by going to the Holy Land Paul declared that the Church could renew itself only by a return to its origins; by going to the United Nations he would say that this renewal involved a dialogue with the whole world – *Lumen Gentium* followed by *Gaudium et Spes*.

None of this was realized as Paul flew from Amman to Ciampino airport, returning to Rome along the historic Appian Way where St Peter, heading in the opposite direction, had his vision of Christ saying

Abraham "our father in the faith"

1 As recently as 1961 Cardinal Montini sprang to the defence of his friend Massignon on this very phrase which the Holy Office considered "perilous and scandalous", Giulio Basetti-Sani OFM, *Louis Massignon (1883–1962)*, Alinea, Florence 1985, p. 79. Albert Hourani discusses related questions in *Islam in European Thought*, Cambridge University Press 1991. Massignon learned to pray in the school of Mansur al-Hallaj, the Sufi mystic executed in Baghdad in 922, p. 125.

2 Roy Domenico, "The Vatican, the US and Vietnam in the Johnson Years", a paper delivered 13 October 1991 at the conference on Vatican Diplomacy in the Nineteenth and Twentieth Century, University of New Brunswick, Canada.

"*Quo vadis*?" (Where are you going?) Legend said he then returned to his martyrdom. Paul's return "along the Appian Way and through the heart of the city was a veritable Roman triumph, the like of which Rome had seldom seen".[1]

On his return there was an exchange of correspondence which warned of more prosaic dangers to come. Cardinal Albert G. Meyer of Chicago pleaded "as strongly as words permit me" that chapters 4 and 5 of the schema on Ecumenism, dealing with the Jews and religious liberty, should be retained. Meyer, usually thought of as rather dry and cerebral, addressed the Pope with great freedom because when they last met on 28 November 1963 Paul had encouraged him to "open up my heart *cum omni fiducia* (with all confidence)":

> Your holiness, the question of religious liberty is THE NUMBER ONE AND MOST IMPORTANT QUESTION in the whole schema on Ecumenism . . . If these two chapters are rejected, I fear very much for the cause of the whole ecumenical movement, and indeed for the acceptance of anything else which comes out of the Council. I am convinced that our Catholics generally, in the United States, feel very strongly about this matter. They are expecting these two chapters to be acted upon, and acted upon favourably . . . If the Bishops of the United States return home from a third session of the Council without these two chapters, the cause of the Catholic Church in the United States, I am afraid, will suffer greatly.[2]

Paul courteously replied in his own hand within a week. But all he said was that he would place Meyer's remarks before the competent Commissions. He did not reveal his own thoughts on the matter or give Meyer any hint of encouragement.

This was a typical instance of the way Paul's insistence on the proper channels looked like elusiveness. Meyer was not asking for the moon: in seeking to place the two chapters on the agenda of the third session he was presupposing there would be such a session. But that no longer seemed sure.

Worse was to come. In January 1964 Paul was called "Janus-faced" because of confusion over the setting up of the body to oversee liturgical reforms. On 13 January a letter from the Secretariat of State announced that Pope Paul VI was creating a *Consilium ad exequendam*

1 Xavier Rynne, *The Second Session*, p. 319.

2 Unpublished letter dated 24 January 1964, with the Pope's reply 1 February 1964. Thanks to Fr Steven M. Avella of St Francis Seminary, Milwaukee, for making them available to me.

Constitutionem de sacra liturgia (an advisory body for carrying out the Constitution on the liturgy). There was no need to wait for the end of the Council to begin the implementation of *Sacrosanctum Consilium*. The reform of the liturgy began here and now.

The Curia was shocked to discover Cardinal Giacomo Lercaro was named president of the *Consilium*, with Vincentian Fr Annibale Bugnini as secretary (in Roman terms the secretary organized the work of the department). They were to be "balanced" not to say "supervised" by two curial cardinals, Paolo Giobbe, prefect of the Congregation of Rites (as it was still called) and Arcadio Larraona, whom we know.[1] At eighty-four Giobbe's contribution was slight, while Larraona, a sprightly seventy-six, represented the defeated minority kept alert only by *odium theologicum*. Lercaro was his *bête noire*.

Then on 29 January *L'Osservatore Romano* published the *motu proprio*, *Sacram Liturgiam*, which announced the setting up of the *Consilium* and laid down guidelines for the immediate implementation of some conciliar decisions. Article IX called into question the right of episcopal conferences to oversee their own liturgical translations. Cisalpine indignation flared up, Pericle Felici was blamed for another "dirty trick". Certainly the Secretary of the Council had tried to pull a fast one and been rumbled: one can infer that from the fact that the protests forced him to back down, and the text in *Acta Apostolicae Sedis* gives the amended version.[2]

After that mishap, the *Consilium* moved swiftly. On 3 March 1964 Lercaro and Bugnini had proposed the names of thirty-six cardinal members, and four priests, Dom Benno Gut OSB, Ferdinando Antonelli, secretary of the Congregation of Rites, Paul's friend Fr Giulio Bevilacqua, and Msgr Luigi Valentini who promptly died. Bugnini set about the huge task of organizing consultors representing not only different parts of the world but also different disciplines – exegesis, patristics, pastoral theology, the history of the liturgy and music, not to mention the sociology and psychology of ritual. In the end there were 130 consultors and sixty counsellors taking part in forty working groups, called *coetus*, toiling simultaneously on different aspects of the reform.

"Paul VI repeatedly expressed his admiration for the way Padre Bugnini managed and led the *Consilium*," says Aimé Martimort. But at the same time it was also "the start of a long series of troubles".[3] They have been chronicled in Bugnini's own immense tome. Quite apart from the frantic pace that had to be maintained and the midnight oil that had

1 Aimé Georges Martimort, "*Le rôle de Paul VI dans la réforme liturgique*", p. 62.

2 Ibid. p. 63, where the two texts can be compared.

3 Ibid. pp. 63; 62.

to be burned, liturgical reform was expensive. APSA (the administration of the Patrimony of the Holy See) devoutly hoped that it wouldn't take longer than four years or they would be ruined.[1]

A fierce debate raged over another matter involving finance. How much longer would the Council last? An article in *L'Osservatore Romano* of 11 March 1964, by Msgr Fausto Vaillanc, head of the press office, seemed to imply that the next session would be the last and that the Council would be all over by 20 November 1964. Jean Villot, the new Archbishop of Lyons, thought this crazy tempo would end in tears.[2]

The optimists still pinning their hopes on Paul VI were more consoled by his actions than his words. The choice of the Redemptorist Bernhard Häring to give the first Lenten retreat of his pontificate sent a signal to the Curia. He had been silenced in the 1950s. His theme, the Holy Spirit as Paraclete, comforter, was deliberately chosen as a way of getting beyond the arid moralism still prevalent in the manuals. Paul VI told him: "I have brought you here not only for the good of our souls but also to help the whole Roman Curia open itself to the great event that is the Council. For that you will need frankness and plain-speaking."[3]

Häring did his best to oblige. When he argued that the sacraments, as the signs of the living presence of God in the midst of the community, should be in the vernacular, he heard grumblings in the sacristy. "You shouldn't talk in this way in the Vatican; if you go on like that the Pope will soon tweak your ear."[4] Cardinal Bacci, top Latinist, said jocosely in his hearing: "Pray for me, father, for I am a great sinner."[5]

Far from tweaking Häring's ear, Paul gave him every mark of confidence and asked for two memos: a study on priest-workers, and another on St Alphonsus' teaching on the "ends" or goals of marriage. Häring reported that the patron saint of moralists held that the first aim of intercourse was to strengthen the indissoluble bond of the partners through mutual self-giving; although procreation was the intrinsic end (*finis intrinsecus*), this was an accidental rather than an absolute aim, since one could not possibly desire a child from every act of intercourse.[6]

Häring had been present at the February meeting in Zürich at which the main lines of schema 17, the future *Gaudium et Spes*, were set down. The president of the sub-commission, Emilio Guano, Bishop of Livorno, an old FUCI friend of Montini, had an openness to the workings of God

1 Ibid. p. 63.

2 Antoine Wenger, *Le Cardinal Villot*, p. 47. Villot had succeeded Cardinal Pierre Gerlier.

3 Bernhard Häring, *Fede Storia Morale*, Interviews with Gianni Lichieri, pp. 74–76.

4 Ibid. p. 74.

5 Ibid.

6 Ibid.

in history that had come to be called, following Pope John in *Pacem in Terris*, "the signs of the times". This provided the *method* of schema 17. But the difficulty lay in moving from a general description of the "modern world" in which the Holy Spirit was at work to the treatment of more specific problems. In Zürich Häring was entrusted with the drafting of what were then four "annexes" on the family, culture, politics and peace.[1]

Thanks to the Zürich meeting, one could say that the Council was on course. Although the inward-looking, introspective documents on the nature of the Church and its worship remained to be considered, a distinctly new note was sounded: the time had come to move from "the Church in itself" to "the Church in relation to the modern world".

But Paul VI was already looking forward not merely to the next session of the Council but beyond it to the *dopoconcilio* (the handy Italian word for the post-conciliar period). He realized better than the "liberals" that the Council was not just a matter of striking attitudes, however admirable, and voting texts, however theologically deep.

Institutions would be needed to embody, promote and oversee its implementation. With this in mind on Whitsunday, 17 May 1964 – Pope Paul reserved his most important announcements concerning the Council, the "new Pentecost" for this day – he announced the setting up of a new Secretariat, modelled on the Secretariat for Christian Unity which had already proved its usefulness.

Like Cardinal Bea's Secretariat, the new Secretariat for Non-Christian Religions embodied the idea that the Church had to listen in order to learn, and learn in order to teach. They were institutions for dialogue, and so expressed the very essence of Paul's pontificate. Logically, he should have extended his listening range by a Secretariat devoted to non-believers, the outermost circle he imagined in *Ecclesiam Suam* on which he was working. But that was a more controversial idea. It would have to wait.

Paul removed any aspect of risk or controversy from the Secretariat for Non-Christian Religions by naming the Cardinal Paolo Marella as its first president. This pleased the curial conservatives who knew Marella was "one of them". Nothing much was expected to happen, except the occasional group of visiting bonzes or monks in saffron robes to bring a dash of colour to the Vatican corridors. Marella had spent his war in Japan and so had some experience of Shintoism and Buddhism.

1 Ibid. p. 67. For a history of the Zürich text see Philippe Delhaye, "*Le Schéma de Zürich*", in *L'Eglise dans le monde de ce temps*, vol. I, pp. 227–49. These were the "appendices" which Cardinal John Carmel Heenan of Westminster famously attacked: "*Timeo peritos, adnexa ferentes.*"

Unfortunately Marella knew little about Islam, which was the most urgent priority: the fate of the ten million Arab Christians of the Middle East depended on overcoming the legacy of the Crusades. To make Islam a partner in dialogue would be one of the chief aims of the Secretariat. Its immediate task, however, would be to contribute to the Council *schema* on Non-Christian Religions. Paul was expected to take a more generous view on the virtues of non-Christian religions than was found in Propaganda Fide, the missionary congregation, which regarded non-Christians as raw material for conversion.

A decisive point in the conciliar preparations was reached at the meeting of the co-ordinating commission on 26 June 1964: the text was sufficiently advanced to be sent out to the Council Fathers for discussion. Paul took a week to think it over and approved the document on 3 July.[1]

For the first time the theme of dialogue or openness to the world began to move from the shadows of discussion in the conciliar commissions into the light of conciliar debate. Comments were invited by the following 1 October, by which time the third session of the Council would have assembled. The document got a new name. The overall reduction in the number of proposed texts moved it down from schema 17 to schema 13. Providence excluding luck, only superstitious journalists joked about unlucky numbers.

Paul VI's contribution at this stage can best be seen in the light of the questions and problems that poured in. Some, mostly conservatives, said that the Council had no business speaking about historically contingent matters at all since they were evanescent and dogmatically ungraspable. The counter-argument was that unless the Council spoke to the aspirations of contemporary people, especially the poor, its impact would be muted or even nullified. Others argued that the whole document was "too European" anyway.

Within the mixed commission Emilio Guano, Bishop of Livorno and president of the Commission for the Apostolate of the Laity, was commonly and rightly regarded as the Pope's man. But he was gravely ill and often absent. That made his appearances all the more significant. He assured the Council on 4 October 1964 that hunger, peace, atheism and other such themes would be dealt with but in 1965. The birth-control problem would soon be solved by the "Pontifical Commission for the Study of Population, Family and Birth", to give its full, quaint title for the last time.[2] But that is to anticipate.

1 Georges Cottier OP, "*Interventions de Paul VI dans l'élaboration de* 'Gaudium et Spes' ", in *Paolo VI e il rapporto Chiesa-Mondo al Concilio*, Istituto Paolo VI, Brescia 1991, p. 18.

2 Ibid. pp. 19–20. Père Cottier advises historians to search among the archives of Livorno for Guano's notes on his papal audiences.

At his general audience at Castelgandolfo on 5 August 1964 Paul said he was "going to share a confidence as though this were what is called a press conference". But it was a most peculiar press conference since no one else was allowed to speak. Paul's "revelation" was: "We have finally finished writing our first encyclical letter."[1] That was literally true. He did write it himself. The complete manuscript exists. It is the most *personal* encyclical ever written, an expression of his temperament and convictions. *Ecclesiam Suam* appeared the next day, 6 August 1964, the feast of the Transfiguration.

The best summary of it is provided in his own words at the "press conference":

> But what in the end is this encyclical about? In it we say what we think the Church of today should do to be faithful to its vocation and fit for its mission. So we are talking about the method the Church should follow in order to walk in the way of the Lord. Perhaps we could sub-title it: the ways of the Church.
>
> Three ways are proposed. The first is spiritual: it concerns the awareness the Church should have and should cultivate of itself. The second way is moral: it looks at the practical, ascetical and canonical renewal the Church needs to be in conformity with its self-awareness, to be pure, holy, strong and authentic. The third way is apostolic: we have used for this the vogue-word "dialogue" which refers to the art or style that must inspire the Church's ministry to the dissonant, voluble, complex concert that is the contemporary world.[2]

Awareness, renewal, dialogue: these were the chapter headings and the slogans of the pontificate.

Ecclesiam Suam, however, was read in the light of the Council. In saying that dialogue with the modern world was the way to solve the problems that arose, he was already half-way to sketching the agenda for *Gaudium et Spes*:

> We have no intention here of dealing with all the serious and pressing problems affecting humanity no less than the Church at this present time: such questions as peace among nations and among social classes, the advance of new nations towards independence and civilization, the current of modern thought over against Christian culture, the difficulties experienced by

1 *Insegnamenti*, 1964, p. 472.

2 Ibid. p. 473. This passage may throw light on the enigmatic remark of Pope John Paul II at his inauguration Mass: "Man is the way of the Church."

> so many nations and by the Church in those parts of the world where the rights of free citizens and of human beings are being denied, the moral problems concerning the population explosion, and so on.[1]

The fact that he was *not* going to deal with such questions left the Council free to deal with them. Paul VI's contribution here was a shift from a world-denying to a world-affirming attitude.

Moreover the method of dialogue involves listening before speaking, listening with love, persistence and reverence.[2] Whatever right-wing critics might say, this approach implied neither weakness nor surrender to the world. The "world" as such is neither good nor bad. It is ambivalent. Many theological articles showed that there was "the world" that God so loved and "the world" to which the Christian should not be conformed. But there is only one world, in the order of nature transformed by grace, and we are all in it.

The Curia was watching hawk-eyed for what he would say about Communism. He was more *nuancé* than John, and contradicts him on one point: while John had said that the Church today preferred to use the medicine of mercy rather than condemnations, Paul repeats the "condemnation" of "ideological systems which deny God and oppress the Church . . . and among them especially atheistic Communism". He condemned it as "a blind dogma which degrades and makes human life sad in so far as it strives to extinguish the light of God".

So the conditions for a dialogue with Communist political regimes were not given. Dialogue needs common ground and common recognition of truth. Hence dialogue with them was "difficult, though not impossible". However, he said he "did not despair that one day they might begin a different and positive kind of dialogue with the Church". He alluded to the Chestertonian idea of Marxism as "a Christian idea gone mad". But for the time being he was reduced to "complaints and lamentations".[3] This was the basis of Paul's *Ostpolitik*. In his dealings with Communism it was a case of *spes contra spem* (hope against hope). It was a policy of patience, designed for the long haul.

Reassured on Communism, the curial conservatives wanted to know more about the dialogue with other Christians. Would it prove a sell-out? How much more holding hands with Greeks would there be? Interest centred on the brief passage in *Ecclesiam Suam* in which Paul reflected on his own office. Papal primacy of honour and jurisdiction,

1 *Ecclesiam Suam*, 15.

2 Ibid. 69.

3 Achille Silvestrini, "*L'Ostpolitik de Paul VI*", in *Notiziario*, 20, p. 71.

he conceded, seemed to many fellow Christians to be an "obstacle" to Christian unity that should be done away with. Paul replied: "We beg our separated brothers to consider the groundlessness of this opinion. Take away the Sovereign Pontiff and the Catholic Church would no longer be Catholic. Moreover, without the supreme, effective and authoritative pastoral office of Peter the unity of Christ's Church would collapse."[1]

Read in kindly fashion, that was no more than a simple restatement of Vatican I. Self-evidently no pope could be expected to saw off the branch on which he was sitting.

At the same time ecumenists consoled themselves with the thought that a pope who understood why some considered the papacy itself the "obstacle" would exercise the office in a different way. The style could change if the substance could not. The method of dialogue recommended by *Ecclesiam Suam* and the familiar conversational tone Paul adopted were novel. Yet the passage also suggested that he was still wondering about how to harmonize collegiality with the primacy.

Paul had remarked to Père Emile Gabel during the second session: "History is moving too quickly for us: the institutions don't give enough time for theological reflection to mature: collegiality is an example."[2] That scruple gave the conservatives their opportunity.

Another example of the acceleration of history was provided by the Jesuits, with 36,000 far and away the largest religious family in the Church. Their General, Johann Baptist Janssens, died on 5 October 1964, on the eve of the third session of the Council. Janssens had already decided that a General Congregation, the thirty-first in Jesuit history, would be needed to assimilate the teaching of Vatican II. The Canadian, John L. Swain, Vicar of the Society as Janssens' health declined, planned to call a Congregation for Easter 1964.[3] Go ahead if you must, Paul said rather mysteriously, but I will say nothing until the Council is over.

The death of Janssens meant that the Jesuits now had no option: constitutionally they had to hold a Congregation to elect his successor. This could not be done swiftly since so many prominent Jesuits likely to be elected by their peers were already pre-empted as Council *periti*; and, in any case, time had to be allowed for meetings on the local level ("provincial congregations") in the build-up to the 31st General Congregation now fixed for May 1965. What was true of the Jesuits held for all religious orders and indeed for the Church generally: the Council was a time of rethinking and renewal.

1 *Ecclesiam Suam*, 110.

2 Antoine Wenger, *Le Cardinal Villot*, p. 41.

3 Pedro Miguel Lamet, *Arrupe*, p. 261.

But – and this was probably what Paul's cryptic remark meant – no binding decisions were to be taken before the end of the Council. Everything, therefore, was in a state of suspended animation, and everyone lived in the state Roger Schutz, Prior of Taizé, called *le dynamique du provisoire*. Conservative critics said this led to chaos and confusion.

But as Paul saw it, the state of indeterminacy would not last much longer. Robert Rouquette SJ had never shared in the media hype and hysteria about Pope John XXIII, and was not sure he could have concluded the Council he so boldly called. Paul, he judged, was much more capable of steering the ship of the Council into safe waters.

After a year as pope, Paul could feel reasonably content with his ministry. The memory of Pope John was fading. With the pilgrimage to the Holy Land he had given an evangelical and ecumenical direction to his pontificate. With *Ecclesiam Suam* he had proposed a methodology for the Council. Moreover a confident Paul seemed to combine the doctrinal firmness required by the "conservatives" with the "openness" to the modern world demanded by the "liberals". Was it too much to hope that he would reconcile them so that the third session and the Council itself could end before Christmas 1964 with a kiss of peace all round? That was Paul's aim and ambition.

24

Conservatives Counter-attack

> The good captain of the ship, to save the boat rocking too much, has put in a little weight on the other side, to comfort them, and to keep the balance.
>
> (BERNARD PAWLEY, letter to Dr Michael Ramsey, Archbishop of Canterbury, 21 November 1964)

The third session of the Council began with a solemn farewell to St Andrew's head. Stolen by the Crusaders, the relic of St Peter's brother was going home to the Orthodox diocese of Patras. Andrew was the patron of the Church of Constantinople as Peter was of Rome, so Pope Paul's imaginative gesture was the basis for future good relations between the two brother patriarchs. Brother patriarchs entailed sister churches.

The third Pan-Orthodox Conference, meeting on the island of Rhodes in November, received news of St Andrew's restitution with great enthusiasm and most of them made the pilgrimage to Patras to see it.[1] Unimpressed, the curial conservatives gave the impression they would have preferred the head of Paul VI on a platter.

The pressure began on the eve of the third session. On 13 September 1964 Paul VI received a "personal and private note" which greatly perturbed him, as it was intended to. It was an outright attack on collegiality as found in Chapter 3 of *Lumen Gentium*:

> *From a doctrinal point of view it contains*:
>
> a) novel opinions and doctrines;
>
> b) these are not only uncertain, but are not even probable, or solidly probable;
>
> c) they are often vague and lacking in clarity as to their real meaning and real aims.
>
> *As far as their arguments go, these are*:

1 Stepjan Schmidt SJ, *Augustin Cardinal Bea: Spiritual Profile*, p. 142.

a) very feeble and fallacious, as much from a historical as a doctrinal point of view; the proof is that the drafters of the last version simply excluded the Biblical Commission's answers to your Holiness' questions about the validity of the scriptural proofs for what is said here;

b) the arguments are also strangely nonchalant about fundamental principles, even those from previous Councils or solemn definitions;

c) so much so that one detects an indubitable and verifiable bias, coming from non-doctrinal forces, whose aims and methods are not beyond reproach.[1]

With lots more in the same vein.

This diatribe came from Cardinal Arcadio Larraona, canonist and notorious champion of Opus Dei. That he should be leading the campaign against collegiality was not in the least surprising: Opus Dei was unpopular with bishops because it tried to escape their authority by appealing directly to that of the pope.

However, this eve-of-session letter was not just an Opus Dei plot. It was signed by about twenty cardinals, a few bishops and twelve major superiors.[2] Among the cardinals was Paolo Marella to whom Paul had entrusted the fledgling Secretariat for Non-Christian Religions. Among the religious was Marcel Lefebvre, former Archbishop of Dakar, Senegal, by now General of the Holy Ghost Fathers.[3]

That some heads of religious orders like the Master of the Dominicans, Aniceto Fernandez, or the French Benedictine superior, Dom Jean Prou, should feel threatened by collegiality was not surprising either; for in varying degrees they were "exempt" from diocesan control, and like Opus Dei were able to go to the pope over the heads of the bishops.

This puts the debate in juridico-political terms. The key *theological* question was whether there was, willed by Christ, a definite *constitution*

1 Italics in the original. Hand delivered on the evening of 13 September 1964. This document was first published by Archbishop Marcel Lefebvre in *J'accuse le Concile*, pp. 55–56, who wrongly dates it 18 October 1964. A better version, with full discussion, is found in Paolo VI, *Discorsi e documenti sul concilio 1963–1965*, ed. Antonio Rimoldi, Istituto Paolo VI, Brescia 1986, pp. 340–46.

2 The complete list is given by Giovanni Caprile, "*Contributo alla storia della 'Nota explicativa praevia'* ", in *Paolo VI e il problemi ecclesiologici*, pp. 602–3. Cardinals Francis J. MacIntyre of Los Angeles, Rufinus Santos of Manila and Jaime Câmara of Rio de Janeiro, were the only non-curial signatories among the cardinals.

3 *L'Osservatore Romano*, 19 September 1982, p. 7. Also in *Discorsi e documenti sul concilio*, p. 353. The letter was signed by Cardinals Ruffini and Pizzardo. Though he agreed with its content, Ottaviani thought signing incompatible with his office as President of the Theological Commission. It was not signed by Karol Wojtyla, Archbishop of Kraków.

for the Church. This was the question that preyed on the mind of Paul VI with his keen sense of precedent. Was the Church essentially monarchical or essentially collegial?

Various models loomed out of history, none of them definitive. The minority at Vatican II opted for the strong monarchical view of Innocent III (1198–1216) following St Bonaventure. They held that the pope possessed the *plenitudo potestatis*, the fullness of power, while the powers of bishops and priests were *derived* solely from him "as the light of the moon from the sun". This sleight-of-hand (which made bishops merely reflective) was achieved by distinguishing between the power of orders and that of jurisdiction. *Of course* bishops had the sacramental power of *orders*, but it was unavailing until the pope granted them the authority of *jurisdiction*, of which he enjoyed a delegatory monopoly. In this way bishops became little more than "vicars of the pope", rubber-stamping his decisions, echoing his voice, applauding his speeches.[1] Larraona and the minority maintained that Vatican I took this position.

Yet long before the thirteenth century when Innocent and Bonaventure had made this ruinous distinction, the tradition was simply that bishops possessed authority in virtue of the sacrament of holy orders or episcopal ordination. They did not need anything else. This tradition was revived on 30 October 1963, in the second session.

Larraona, Lefebvre and the recalcitrant minority set up Vatican I against Vatican II, refused to accept the verdict of Vatican II, and continually played on Paul's anxieties and scruples. They were mistaken in their belief that he could be pushed off collegiality. Paul VI loyally accepted the decisive vote of the previous session, and did not see it as a threat to his primatial authority.

Now, by a *primatial* act, he strengthened the *conciliar* commissions. The new names were significant and provided a better overall "balance": Abbot Christopher Butler joined Karl Rahner and Cardinal Alfredo Ottaviani on the Theological Commission; Dom Helder Câmara was shunted to Laity and Mass Media; Cardinal William Conway of Armagh went to Clergy. The Secretariat for Christian Unity, always the engine of progress in the Council, was strengthened by the addition of Maxim Hermaniuk, Ukrainian Metropolitan of Winnipeg, John W. Gran of Norway and Charles H. Helmsing of Kansas City-St Joseph.[2]

Yet the right-wing attack visibly rattled Paul who went down to St Peter's the next morning with this heavy burden on his shoulders. It should have been a joyous occasion. He used the new rite of concelebra-

1 See Brian Tierney, "Pope and Bishops: An Historical Survey", in *America*, 5 March 1988, pp. 230–7.

2 *Acta Synodalia*, III, vol. III, part I, p. 20.

tion for the first time, being flanked by twenty-five Council Fathers of nineteen different nationalities. Pope John had said Mass, almost invisibly, on ground level, on a movable altar on wheels, while the steps of the high altar were just about big enough to hold the papal throne.

But now, in 1964, everything was reordered and, above all, recentred: Christ and his sacrifice were at the heart of the Church; pope and bishops stood elbow to elbow in collegial equality; and the participation of the people, never easy in the vast basilica, was more lively than ever before. With this renewed rite Paul VI dramatized the truth that the Church was collegial, ecumenical and Christocentric. *Lex orandi, lex credendi* (As we pray, so we believe).

But on this morning of 14 September 1964 there was a contrast between collegiality made visible and the speech in which Paul struggled to hold it in balance with his own primacy:

> The Council must embark upon a series of difficult theological debates. It must determine the nature and mission of pastors (bishops) in the Church. It must discuss, and with the help of the Holy Spirit, determine the *constitutional* prerogatives of the episcopal order. It must show the homogeneous nature of the *constitutional* idea of the Church in its different Eastern and Western forms. It must make clear both for the faithful of the Catholic Church and for the separated brethren the true notion of the hierarchy which "the Holy Spirit has appointed as bishops to rule the Church of God" (Acts 20:28).[1]

Paul then turned to the question of whether Vatican I had finally *limited* the constitutional powers of the bishops.

Its vigorous assertion of papal primacy might incline one to think so. However, Paul goes on, "the doctrine of primacy remained to be filled out, so as to explain the mind of Christ on his whole Church, and especially on the nature and function of the successors of the apostles, that is, of the episcopate".[2]

Vatican I was interrupted by war before it could get round to the bishops. It did not limit their powers because it did not speak of them. It followed that Vatican II could release them, and so "complete" the unfinished business of Vatican I. But this meant returning to a much earlier, more collegial model of the Church.

To this end Paul was able to use a quotation from St Gregory the

1 *Insegnamenti*, 1964, p. 540. In the original it was a single sentence that I have broken down into six. My italics to stress that the constitutional question was what really worried Paul.

2 Ibid. 1964, pp. 539–40.

Great, already exploited by Vatican I, to show that the papal office "asserted, confirmed, and vindicated" the authority of the bishops.[1] True, Pius IX boosted episcopal authority not for its own sake but against the threat of state control; but this put the pope on the same side as the bishops.

The quotation from St Gregory the Great was significant. Gregory, pope in the last years of the sixth century – he confidently expected the end of the world in 600 – had heard that the Bishop of Constantinople, Rome's rival at the Eastern end of the Mediterranean, was now styling himself "universal patriarch". Gregory wrote rebuking him. Then, when the Bishop of Alexandria in Egypt flatteringly applied this title to Gregory himself, this ex-Roman senator got angry: "You have addressed me by the proud title of Universal Pope. I beg you not to do this again . . . I do not consider anything an honour to me by which my brother bishops lose the honour due to them . . . My honour is the united strength of my brothers."[2]

Paul quoted this in his address to the third session of the Council. But he omitted the first two sentences. Why? Because he knew that what St Gregory the Great disclaimed towards the end of the sixth century had been energetically claimed by St Gregory VII in his *Dictatus Papae* in 1071: "The Roman Pontiff is alone rightly to be called Universal Pontiff . . . He can be judged by no one . . . He alone can depose and reinstate bishops."[3]

Paul's problem was summed up in the question: which Gregory should he follow? Pius XII, whom he venerated, laid the emphasis on Gregory VII's centralizing policies that formed the basis of the "Gregorian" reforms in the eleventh century; yet the example of John XXIII's spirituality and self-denying ordinance suggested that Gregory the Great was right to see the papal ministry strengthened rather than weakened by being set in the context of the universal episcopate.

The solution lay in looking at office in terms of *ministry* as gift-for-others rather than *power* over others. Following the Swiss Protestant theologian Oscar Cullmann, Paul gathered the scriptural evidence for an equality of dignity but difference of role among all the successors of the Apostles. St Peter addresses his brothers as "elders", claiming only to be a "fellow elder" (I Peter, 5:1). From St Paul he borrows the term

1 Vatican I, *Pastor Aeternus*, in J. Neuner and J. Dupuis, *The Christian Faith*, No. 827. See also Alberic Stacpoole OSB, "The Institutionalization of the Church in the Middle Ages", in *Ampleforth Journal*, Autumn 1968, pp. 337–52.

2 *Patrologium Latinum*, vol. 77, col. 933. Half-quoted *Insegnamenti*, 1964, p. 542.

3 See Brian Tierney, "Pope and Bishops: An Historical Survey", p. 232.

"my fellow partners in tribulations and consolations" (II Corinthians, 4:7). Paul summed up:

> We are in duty bound to recognize the apostles as teachers, rulers and sanctifiers of the Christian people, "stewards of the mysteries of God" (I Cor. 3, 1), witnesses to the Gospel, ministers of the New Testament and, in some sense, the very reflection of the glory of the Lord (II Cor. 3, 6–18).[1]

This was very edifying, no doubt, but it cut little ice with the minority for whom tradition, not scripture, was "the norm of truth". They heard rumours of his dinner with Professor Oscar Cullmann and Henri de Lubac SJ, and drew sinister conclusions.

Another feature of Paul's opening speech at the third session disedified the right-wing without consoling those for whom it was intended. No women had attended the first or second sessions in any official capacity. Paul was determined to put that right. So he hailed the newcomers: "We are delighted to welcome among the *auditrices* (listeners) our beloved daughters in Christ, the first women in history to participate in a conciliar assembly."[2]

Alas, there were no women actually present to receive this accolade. A bureaucratic blunder meant that the history-making few arrived only after the session was well under way.[3]

However, "non-Catholic" women got in for ceremonial occasions as clergy wives. They were not invited to the opening of the first session, but were present at its close – placed far away in the middle distance, without books or kneelers. "Thereafter," explained Margaret Pawley, wife of Bernard, director of the Anglican Centre, "we moved further forward – as in grandmother's footsteps – and were progressively given kneelers and books."[4] Her husband was meanwhile writing voluminous reports on the Council for the Archbishops of Canterbury and York, as we shall see.

The Dutch electrical firm Philips installed facilities for simultaneous translation, free of charge, on 21 October. Cardinal Gustavo Testa, responsible for the technical arrangements but who had never otherwise set foot in the *aula*, was delighted by this business coup. They did a test. Felici was less pleased. He believed that the translation could be picked

1 *Insegnamenti*, II, 1964, p. 542. Paul VI acknowledged his debt to Oscar Cullmann, whose *Peter in the New Testament* rescued Peter from polemics. He dined, discreetly, at about this time with Cullmann and Henri de Lubac SJ.

2 Rynne, *The Third Session*, p. 294.

3 See Francine Cardman, "Women and Laity since Vatican II", in *Vatican II, Open Questions and New Horizons*, Michael Glazier, Wilmington, Delaware 1984, p. 120.

4 Alberic Stacpoole, Introd. to *The Council by those who were there*, p 14.

up outside St Peter's, thus breaking conciliar secrecy and giving journalists a field day. Another consequence was that with simultaneous translation coming over the loudspeakers in the bars, the *aula* would soon have been empty. The experiment was judged a failure. Vatican II was probably the last Council to be conducted in Latin.[1]

Larraona disdained footling questions about technical details and women. Proper priests didn't have wives and soared above such matters. His letter lay accusingly on Paul's desk. He wanted the pernicious doctrine of collegiality abandoned. The question was not "ripe", said Larraona, so it should be referred to a competent mixed commission; this would exclude all members of the existing Theological Commission (who were thus declared "incompetent"). No date should be fixed for the fourth session, to allow time for this putative body thoroughly to explore the meaning of "collegiality". The Holy Father should suspend the Council and set up this new mixed commission.

Matters should no longer be decided by vote. No more voting: it gave a false impression of democracy and led the media to speak of "majorities" and "minorities" where a papal fiat would do. There follows the most perfidious and mealy-mouthed part of Larraona's entire letter:

> To avoid anything untoward which might impede the exercise of the Holy Father's freedom in a decision of such importance, it seems to us opportune and even necessary that the decision should be taken by the Holy Father himself, without asking the views of the Council still less having any votes. Such an act of authority – yearned for by many – would not only be a practical reaffirmation of papal primacy, but would also favour the re-establishment of the balance needed to get ahead . . .

The Larraona/Lefebvre plan was that Paul should restore papal authority by disavowing at a stroke the work of the Theology Commission and the majority verdict of the Council Fathers. They claimed that this rejection of the Council would enhance papal authority. In fact it would have been an act of pontifical hara-kiri.

By now Paul was sure collegiality did not threaten papal primacy. It was a *faux problème*. If the Church is truly a communion (*koinonia*) of Churches, there can be no opposition between primatial and episcopal responsibility; and the Bishop of Rome enjoys both. So this is not a game of roundabouts-and-swings in which what one gains another must lose.

Yet the ever scrupulous Paul was worried. He stayed up late at night

1 Henri Denis, *Eglise, qu'as-tu fait de ton Concile*, p. 69.

ploughing through John of St Thomas, Cardinal Louis Billot, Piolanti and other authors who had, sometimes unwittingly, laid the foundations for collegiality. Msgr Angelo Dell'Acqua, substitute, told Caprile: "He spent so many nights with his books, making sure he studied collegiality thoroughly."[1] What is extraordinary is that he never delegated this study to experts.

So study he did, with Msgr Carlo Colombo at his elbow. He left no theological stone unturned. He drafted a memo replying to the Larraona letter a week after he received it. This translation is slightly expanded to make it intelligible:

> 21-IX-64. On the Secret Note [of Larraona]
>
> 1) *Quadam amaritudine affectus sum* (I am afflicted by some bitterness): by the timing: on the eve of the Council; by the number of the signatories: it looks like a manoeuvre; by what it hints at: the ruination of the Council etc.; by its arguments, intransigently opposed, and not always well-founded.
>
> 2) Summary of proposals (see notes).
>
> 3) *Quid faciendum*? (What to do?) (see proposals).
>
> 4) Reasons of convenience: the Council should end well; profit from good dispositions; stress advantages: *collaboration is not a limit to authority but a help; "communion" in charity and truth.*
>
> 5) Pray; think; try to persuade in serenity.
>
> These documents are not based on sound reasoning (and have caused me grievous suffering); but I will have to give them an answer that is calm, serene and very kind (*risposta calma, serena e molto buona*).[2]

This note, anguished yet firm, was written on the eve of the vote on Chapter 3 of *Lumen Gentium* on "The Hierarchical Nature of the Church, with Special Reference to the Episcopate", the most crucial vote of the third session.

It went the way of Paul VI and the majority. The highest negative vote was 328 against a steady 1907.[3] The crisis passed. Paul felt much better. He minuted:

> After the vote of 22-IX-64.
>
> *Deo Gratias*. Our assent: both on grounds of personal convic-

1 Paolo VI, Discorsi e documenti sul concilio, p. 351.

2 This "note" was first published by Giovanni Caprile SJ in *L'Osservatore Romano*, 19 September 1982, in an article called "*Paolo VI e il Concilio*". My italics.

3 See Rynne, *Third Session*, p. 23, for the details.

tion, and the judgement of the Council. We have abstained, and also we have done what was possible and in the line of duty in the preparation of the draft (see our intervention towards the end of the first session, and subsequently *multifariam* – in various ways). Some expressions can be improved.
But we are satisfied because:
this is not a new doctrine, except for the good that it allows us to foresee;
it is not *immatura*, as yet unready: the "yes" vote is attributable to Vatican I, to the two previous sessions, to the really deep studies of the Theological Commission, to the general development of theological studies in the Church, to the Church's self-awareness, to ecumenism.
It is not contrary to the primacy (reaffirmed at least 20 times) . . .

The Church is both monarchical and hierarchical; *having collaborators is not a limitation*; what would happen if this doctrine were not approved? (feudalism, ecclesiastical irresponsibility etc.).
Instead: *solidarity*, *charity*, *unity*; *intrinsic and constitutional bonds with the primacy*; overcoming of Gallicanism and nationalism (cf. local episcopal conferences), and fears of papal aggression; obedience derived from within; authority without jealousy or exclusiveness (*non rapinam arbitratus est* – he did not think it plunder).[1]

The living Church: one single heart etc.; co-ordinated and articulated in a single college of charity (cf. Patriarchs etc.); honours and dignifies all living elements in the Church; invitation to separated brethren. Firmness in jurisdictional unity, respect towards what is of divine law, free and fruitful application of canon law.[2]

These rather scrappy notes, jotted down late at night on 22 September 1964, take us right to the heart of Paul VI. They are like points for meditation. They show that Paul was personally convinced before God of the doctrine on collegiality found in Chapter 3 of *Lumen Gentium*.

His reading of Henri de Lubac's *Meditation on the Church* confirmed many of the ideas that were to find their way into the document on the

1 The reference is to the christological hymn in Philippians 2:6–11, which speaks of the Christ's emptying out leading to glory, from *kenosis* to *doxa*. Paul is saying Christ will not stand on dignity but take the form of a slave or servant.

2 Caprile, "*Paolo VI e il Concilio*", pp. 351–52.

Church. De Lubac developed the patristic idea of Mary as the "type of the Church", placing her therefore clearly *within* the Church. He also presented the Church as "mystery" and "sacrament" rather than the juridical reality favoured by the Roman school for whom the Church was a "perfect society", the "bulwark" (*Il Baluardo* – title of Ottaviani's collected speeches) against the infiltrations of the modern world. For Ottaviani modern ideas were not just erroneous: they were an insidious poison undermining it from within. In so far as Montini favoured dialogue with the modern world on the French model, he too had become contaminated.

But he still had to do something about the intransigent minority. They had not given up. The next battle was over the *modi* or amendments. A record number of 4800 *modi* were submitted on Chapter 3 of *Lumen Gentium* of which 3600 were on collegiality.[1] Many of them were repetitious. In the end the Theological Commission accepted 242 for consideration. The minority cried foul and there were accusations of vote-rigging. On 20 October Paul directed that a representative of the minority should be present when votes were being counted, optimistically explaining that this indicated "no lack of confidence" in the system, "but rather a desire to make the minds of all the Council Fathers more serene and trustful".[2] At the same time and in the same eirenic spirit Paul replied to Larraona's eve-of-session letter.

He began by rejecting charges of manipulation by the Theological Commission. The fact that Cardinal Ottaviani, Pro-Prefect of the Holy Office, and Msgr Parente, Holy Office assessor, accepted the chapter should reassure Larraona. Nor could one seriously maintain that the majority were merely victims of "all manner of psychological pressures" or that the doctrine of collegiality had been "imposed by certain groups who have exploited psychological and non-theological factors".

There follows a more personal passage which takes the form of an appeal:

> We see in your serious suggestions and considerations a noble concern for doctrinal orthodoxy and an anxious solicitude for our personal weakness in the duties of our apostolic charge . . . We ask you to believe that *we are following closely the final stages of the editing of the text to remove anything that is not in conformity with sound doctrine and to make whatever changes seem justified.* Yet we do not hide from you that perhaps there will be new problems for the life of the Church; it

1 Rynne, *The Third Session*, p. 53.

2 *Discorsi e Documenti sul Concilio*, p. 352.

> will be the task of the one who has the function of leadership at the top to see that these problems find solutions in harmony with the basic tradition and higher interests of the Church . . .[1]

This is a French translation, done in the Secretariat of State, of his original Italian version of 18 October 1964. Perhaps that accounts for its pompous stiffness.[2] It contains two important statements: first about the pope's right to make changes in conciliar texts; second about his fear that collegiality would indeed bring new problems in the future.

One of the "new problems" was already troubling the faithful and threatening to divide them. On 23 October 1964 Archbishop Pericle Felici, Secretary of the Council, announced that the question of artificial birth-control would be removed from the competence of the Council since there already existed a special commission to deal with it. Though some Council Fathers were no doubt relieved to be rid of this question, which was not "ripe", many wondered why they were not allowed at least to debate it, especially since in *Gaudium et Spes* (still in 1964 known as schema 13) they would lay down the basic principles on "responsible parenthood" that might help resolve the problem. It looked as though Pope Paul, while assenting to collegiality in theory, was reluctant to trust it in practice.

Sensing this, Cardinal Léon-Joseph Suenens made another dramatic intervention, this time on birth-control. He wondered whether the emphasis on "increase and multiply" had not obscured the other text in Genesis, "they will be two in one flesh". He questioned whether moral theology took sufficient account of scientific progress which can help determine "what is according to nature". He solemnly warned: "I beg of you, my brother bishops, let us avoid a new 'Galileo affair'. One is enough for the Church." He drew an analogy with the "social doctrine" of the Church that had been regularly updated from Leo XIII's *Rerum Novarum* to Pope John's *Mater et Magistra*. "The truth – natural and supernatural – will set you free," he concluded.[3]

A few days later, while speaking on another topic, Suenens issued a "clarification" which left his original statement largely intact.[4] Everyone supposed Paul had ticked him off. Could *science* be the source of *moral*

1 Ibid. pp. 347–49. The full text of this letter was first published, not without errors, in Archbishop Marcel Lefebvre's pamphlet, *J'accuse le Concile*, 1975.

2 *Discorsi e Messagi*, p. 339. Could the translator have been Msgr (now Cardinal) Paul Poupard?

3 ASCV, 3, 6, p. 58.

4 Xavier Rynne suggests that Cardinal Suenens' "purpose may have been merely to dissipate an impression that he was presuming to dictate to the Pope", *The Third Session*, pp. 161–62.

norms? That had never been Church teaching. In any case, it was difficult to see the link between anovulent pills and the revolution of the planets around the sun. Not everything that *can* be done by science *may* be done. The tensions between Suenens and Paul began to intensify from this point onwards.

Another papal initiative misfired on Saturday, 24 October 1964. This was a great day in Paul's life and, he believed, in European history. He went to Monte Cassino to consecrate the rebuilt abbey church devastated in 1944. This was where he had made so many retreats. He spoke eloquently of the *beata pacis visio* (the blessed vision of peace) that was part of St Benedict's charism.

From Monte Cassino Paul VI solemnly proclaimed St Benedict "patron of Europe". Europe had got along without a patron for many centuries, so the meaning of the gesture was unclear. Poles felt that Benedict was the patron of *Western* Europe, and that SS Cyril and Methodius, the two Greek monks from Thessalonika who evangelized the Balkans and Eastern Europe in the ninth century, deserved equal honour.[1]

Moreover he was silent as the tomb on one of the projects dearest to the heart of the majority: the proposal to beatify John XXIII by acclamation. Fifty thousand priests and people from John's home diocese of Bergamo signed a petition for his canonization. Msgr Luigi Betazzi, one of Cardinal Lercaro's auxiliaries in Bologna, proposed Pope John be canonized by acclamation, as in the Middle Ages.[2] With the Council in session it was juridically possible. The bandwagon rolled on. Bishop Bogdan Beize, auxiliary of Lodz in Poland, said that "beatifying Pope John would make a great impression on modern culture". Dom Helder Câmara, from Olinda-Recife, Brazil, suggested that Pope John's canonization as "the prophet of new structures, God's friend and the friend of all people" would be a fitting way to end the Council on a high note.

The ringleaders in this campaign were Cardinal Léon-Joseph Suenens and Giacomo Lercaro. They circulated a document which said that "from Pope John the world has learned that it is not so alienated from

1 I deduce this from the fact that one of the first acts of Pope John Paul II was to declare SS Cyril and Methodius co-equal patrons of Europe with Benedict. He explained this as follows: "Benedict embraces the mainly Western and Central culture of Europe, which is more logical and rational, while Cyril and Methodius highlight ancient Greek culture and the Eastern tradition which is more mystical and intuitive", 6 November 1981. It may also be that so many Polish troops perished in the assault on Monte Cassino that the place had sinister memories for them.

2 See Giuseppe Alberigo, ed., *Papa Giovanni*, p. 231. Fn. 108 on p. 243 gives further details.

the Church after all, nor is the Church alienated from the world". The pastoral renewal of the Church depended on it. The hopes for dialogue with other Christians, other religions and with "all men and women of good will" depended on it.[1]

This put yet more pressure on Paul VI, as it was meant to. He resisted it because he rejected the implied contrast with Pius XII, whom he continued to revere. He could not allow a battle of the symbols with Pius XII taking on John XXIII. He stressed the continuity between his two predecessors, and their esteem for each other. It was not a matter of either/or but of both/and. He fell silent on this issue until the very last day of the Council a year later, and thus put a damper on a lot of hopes.

It is difficult to know which episode showed him most out of touch: making Benedict patron of Europe was fine, if you knew where the easternmost frontier of Europe was; otherwise, wasn't he fiddling while married couples burned?

With supernatural optimism Paul bounced back, and conceived a great plan for Friday, 6 November. Paul intended to stage an historic event – the first time a pope had actually presided at a working session of a Council since Trent. He sat not on the throne but at the Presidents' table as though to dramatize the link between the pope and the Council. He was the Bishop of Rome among his brother bishops.

Much thought was given to the timing of his appearance. The discussion on Schema 13 was underway, but it was deemed too controversial. The "Propositions" on missionary work seemed a safer bet. Canonizing the twenty-two Uganda martyrs on 18 October, Paul said: "You want the Pope to be a missionary; very well – he is a missionary, a word which means an apostle, a witness, a pastor on the road".[2] He made the same point in announcing his journey to India after the session.

So it made sense for him to introduce the debate on missionary activity. Before he could begin his address, the students of the Ethiopian College, who had provided the choir for the Mass, enthusiastically continued to beat drums, clash cymbals and rattle castanets while frantic secretaries vainly waved their arms at them. Paul seemed to enjoy the humour of the situation.[3]

But it did not last. Paul began his ten-minute speech, declaring the

1 Kenneth L. Woodward, *Making Saints*, Simon and Schuster, New York 1990, p. 289. The quotations in the previous paragraph are on p. 287.

2 *Insegnamenti*, 1964, p. 591. He publicly regretted that he could not also canonize the Anglican martyrs along with the Catholics.

3 "I don't know what's going on up there," said Thomas ("Tommy") d'Esterre Roberts, former Archbishop of Bombay, "but I *think* they are getting ready to boil a cardinal."

Propositions "praiseworthy" and hoping that with a little polishing here and there they would "meet with your approval".[1] This was, however, a faulty appreciation. Bishop Donal Lamont "shuddered in disbelief" as he heard the Pope commend these "thirteen lifeless propositions culled from some worm-cankered textbook on missiology".[2] That these dry bones would never live was the judgement of the vast majority of missionary bishops, a formidable battle-hardened group including 296 from Africa, 93 from the Philippines, Japan and Indonesia, and 84 from India. Hardly represented at Vatican I, at Vatican II they did not wish to be patronized or fobbed off with an unworthy text.

Lamont wondered how Pope Paul, whom everyone knew was a good listener in private, "had formed this strange idea about the Propositions, so much at variance with the opinions of the Bishops in the front-line".

He didn't have to wait long for an answer, for the next speaker was Cardinal Gregory Peter Agagianian, Prefect of Propaganda and *ipso facto* President of the conciliar commission on the missions, who officially presented the Propositions which came from his Congregation: there was a traditional tension between Propaganda, which financed and controlled the missions, and the bishops in the field. Paul had backed the wrong horse.

Agagianian seemed merely sycophantic as he thanked the Pope for his presence and support, reminding them that Paul VI would soon show his practical concern for the work of the missions by visiting India. That enabled Paul to leave St Peter's to moderately sustained applause.

But three days later, by 1601 votes to 311,[3] the Propositions were sent back for complete revision. This left the Pope looking rather foolish. He had listened to Agagianian instead of the 800 missionary bishops.

But he also failed to reassure the minority. They needed something more. It was precisely now that the idea of the *Nota Praevia* was born. Never, in the history of human footnotes, has so much been written by so many about so few words. This was a footnote to Chapter 3 of *Lumen Gentium* explaining that papal primacy remained unchanged.[4] It was designed to "win over" the intransigent minority, to be their "pound of flesh" and give them sufficient grounds for voting *placet*. After the Council Paul said there should be no victors and vanquished, only *des convaincus, pas de vaincus*.

1 *Insegnamenti*, 1964, p. 630.

2 Donal Lamont O. Carm, "*Ad Gentes*: A Missionary Bishop remembers", in *Vatican II by those who were There*, ed. Alberic Stacpoole OSB, p. 276.

3 Rynne, *The Third Session*, p. 200.

4 Walter Abbott SJ, *The Documents of Vatican II*, pp. 97–101; or Austin Flannery OP, *Vatican II: The Conciliar and Post-conciliar Documents*, I, pp. 423–26.

November 1964 was Paul's cruellest month. Even well-meaning gestures turned to farce. On 13 November Paul VI laid his tiara on the altar of St Peter's as a symbolic gift to the world's poor. Fine. But then it was learned that the nobly discarded tiara was to be sold on the open market by Cardinal Francis J. Spellman. Shouldn't the bishops join the pope in despoiling themselves of some of their trappings? Tommy Roberts proposed passing round a basket and collecting episcopal rings.[1] But that smacked of dangerous enthusiasm.

Many wondered[2] why Paul should pay so much heed to a doomed minority of mostly curial conservatives. This is where the *Nota Praevia* made its first appearance at a meeting of the Doctrinal Commission on 6 November 1964. Msgr Gérard Philips, its Secretary, proposed *Addenda* of an unspecified nature designed to "accommodate" the refused *modi*. Philips was manifestly acting under orders from above. On 10 November Msgr Carlo Colombo presented his own "introductory note" which, despite his insistence and after lengthy discussions, was thrown out.

Was Colombo the emissary of Pope Paul, his Trojan horse within the Commission? It became harder to deny the evidence that he was, when, in the next stage, Philips' *Addenda* were rewritten so thoroughly that they no longer even pretended to be a *reply* to the rejected *modi* and simply reproduced their content.

On 16 November, Monday of the last week of this session, soon to be known as the "black week" (*la settimana nera*), Msgr Pericle Felici presented the *Nota Praevia* to the Council, and did so with great relish. At the final vote on 19 November he insisted that "the votes today and tomorrow must be understood in the light of the *Nota*, which forms part of the *Act* of the Council". The joy unconfined of the minority gave the game away. The majority was baffled.[3]

What had at first been presented merely as an explanatory footnote to Chapter 3 of *Lumen Gentium* was now magically transmuted into the key to the entire document. This was putting the cart before the horse with a vengeance.

But the chief source of unhappiness and embarrassment in this last

1 Rynne, *The Third Session*, p. 272.

2 A good example is ibid. pp. 273–74. After saying that Pope Paul incessantly refers to his own office, he goes on: "It is as if he were tortured by the thought that the world might forget who the Pope really is, at a time when the world has never known better. Since it is part of the strategy of the minority to accuse the majority of disloyalty to the Holy Father, Paul's constant harping has caused *the majority to think that he does share these misgivings*, at least to a certain extent." (My italics.)

3 For this section see Jan Grootaers, *Primauté et Collégialité, Le Dossier de Gérard Philips sur la Nota Explicativa Praevia*, pp. 36–38.

week were the papally-imposed eleventh-hour amendments to the decree on ecumenism. Far from being "approved by the Secretariat for Christian Unity", as Felici blithely assured the Council, the Secretariat regarded them as a set-back to the entire ecumenical project. As newcomers to the ecumenical field Catholics could not afford to make mistakes. Yet within the Secretariat there were degrees of disapproval. Gustave Thils remembers going through the forty or so *modi* with Cardinal Augustin Bea, retaining only those which did the least ecumenical damage.[1] Pierre Duprey tells a slightly different story.[2]

There was no reason in principle why Paul VI should not make suggestions for the improvement of conciliar texts. As the "President" of the Council, even though he acted through delegates, he was entitled to make whatever proposals he thought fit. He was, after all, "inside" the Council, not hovering somewhere above it. That was one of the implications of collegiality. But then, he should have made them at the appropriate stage, not at the last minute, *after* they had been voted on and approved.

Moreover Duprey soon discovered that eight out of the nineteen amendments proposed by Paul VI corresponded, literally and exactly, to *modi* proposed by the minority which had been fully considered by the Secretariat and explicitly rejected by them in the *expensio modorum*. Duprey surmised that the defeated minority had "got at" Paul privately and persuaded him to accept their views.

Next morning, Monday, 16 November, Duprey was summoned to the Vatican by Msgr Angelo Dell'Acqua who wanted to talk about a matter unconnected with the Council. On his desk sat three bulky files concerning the documents on ecumenism, religious liberty and non-Christian religions (which included Jews). Dell'Acqua said each one of them gave rise to "difficulties" which would mean delaying a vote until the next session. To this Duprey, his beard shaking in outrage, "reacted". He meant he was angry.

The two declarations on ecumenism and religious liberty, though closely linked, were in fact separable documents. It would be, he averred, a "catastrophe" if the decree on ecumenism were not voted on the following Friday.

"If we promulgate the document on the Catholic Oriental Churches but *not* the decree on Ecumenism," Duprey pointed out, "all our dealings with the Orthodox Churches will be put in jeopardy, and the

1 Conversation at Louvain-la-Neuve, where the Thils archives are housed, 1 October 1988.

2 Pierre Duprey gave his account of these events for the first time at a Paul VI conference held in Brescia in September 1986. I am using the text distributed there.

Council will lose all credibility in their eyes." Dell'Acqua looked embarrassed, but would not budge from his brief.

Duprey hastened to the Council and reported this conversation to Msgr Jan Willebrands, vice-president of the Secretariat. He too had received a summons to see Dell'Acqua at 12.30 that same day. They met Cardinal Augustin Bea in the coffee bar known as bar-jonah, and considered whether the time had not come for a direct approach to Pope Paul. The wily Bea said no: first find out what Dell'Acqua has to say.

Willebrands arrived punctually at 12.30 in Dell'Acqua's office where he learned that there had been no decision to postpone the ecumenism text. But there were still "certain difficulties" about it. Religious liberty and Non-Christian Religions would be voted on in principle now, and promulgated in the next and final session. There were only four days to go before the solemn promulgation session fixed for Saturday, 21 November.

Willebrands took notes about the "difficulties", the Secretariat for Christian Unity pondered them that afternoon, and by 6.30 p.m. Willebrands was back in Dell'Acqua's office with their official replies. Dell'Acqua, who had some experience of the Orthodox as Pope John XXIII's secretary in Istanbul, thanked him and promised to pass on his remarks to the Pope. He said he had always supported the work of the Secretariat, and would continue to do so now. Willebrands grimly replied that "he did not see how the work of the Secretariat could continue if the decree on ecumenism were suppressed".[1]

The papal amendments were accepted as the price that had to be paid for the promulgation of the document. In practice they were not too objectionable. Some involved qualifying terms such as *fere* (almost), *etiam* (also), *frequentius* (more often than not), *non raro* (not uncommonly), that were more irritating than insulting. That Protestants should be said to "seek" God in the Bible rather than "find" him there (*inquirunt* instead of *inveniunt*) was only worrying if one failed to remember Blaise Pascal ("You would not seek me if you had not already found me"). The other amendments could be given a similarly benevolent exegesis. So the whole exercise looked like a show of strength, mere arm-wrestling to prove a point, an arbitrary assertion of last-ditch papal authority, even in areas where it didn't much matter.

None of this was known at the time. So when on Friday, 20 November, the penultimate day of the session, Cardinal Eugène Tisserant announced that Religious Liberty could not be voted on in this session since so many Fathers wished to amend it, there was consternation.[2] Congar described the pandemonium:

1 Ibid. W.F., Pierre, p. 21.

2 René Laurentin, *Bilan du Troisième Session*, p. 275.

> Among the vast majority of the Council Fathers there was astonishment and sadness (*stupeur et tristesse*). Straight away after the announcement little knots of people gathered round Cardinals Meyer and Ritter. Here and there, up and down the basilica, five or six petitions were being addressed to the Pope urging that a vote should be taken after all (*malgré tout*) on this question.[1]

One of the sidelined Presidents of the Council, Albert Meyer, Archbishop of Chicago, and Joseph Ritter of St Louis were appealed to because religious liberty had become the "American issue" at the Council.

The petitions Congar refers to were headed: "*Instanter! Instantius! Instantissime!*"[2] That same night Meyer and Ritter pleaded with Paul VI to allow a vote. They got no satisfaction, and had nothing to say at the airport when they got home.

The minority had every reason to feel satisfied as the session ended. They numbered some 200–300 fathers, and were organized in a *Coetus Patrum Internationalis* (an international group of Council Fathers), a deliberately vague name. They held a package of views that went together. Opponents of collegiality also opposed the restoration of the diaconate, religious liberty, because "Error has no rights", to any form of ecumenism, to any openness to Jews and those of other religious traditions, and to the entire project of Schema 13 (the future *Gaudium et Spes*) on the relationship of Church and world. On all these questions Paul VI accepted the majority view but "respected" the minority.

Yet the session ought to have ended in triumph. There were massive majorities all round:

Lumen Gentium	2151 placet; 5 non placet
Unitatis Redintegratio	2148 placet; 11 non placet
Orientalium Ecclesiarum	2148 placet; 39 non placet

These were epoch-making documents and should have been the occasion for much tossing of mitres into the air. Yet the gloomy mood persisted and when Paul VI was carried into the basilica of St Peter's on the *sedia gestatoria* on 21 November 1964 observers said he looked "stony-faced and glum".[3] The applause was perfunctory and came not from bishops but mostly from visitors.

1 Yves Congar, *Troisième Session*, Cerf, Paris, 1965, pp. 121–22.

2 Laurence Sheehan, *A Blessing of Years*, p. 183.

3 Rynne, *The Third Session*, p. 267. Such judgements are notoriously subjective. René Laurentin, for example, says nothing about the ending of the session, except to discuss the significance of the novel title of Mary as "Mother of the Church". See *Bilan de la Troisième Session*, pp. 244–46.

Why was the atmosphere this 21 November so grim? A whole set of factors converged. They all involved, or appeared to involve, Pope Paul. One now saw the disadvantage of his hands-off, fingertip approach to the Council. It seemed almost as though Paul set himself above the Council and did not fully respect its freedom.

The last straw was the proclamation of Our Lady as Mother of the Church, *Mater Ecclesiae*. Paul said it was coming at his Wednesday audience on 18 November. If the official account is to be believed, the pilgrims present in St Peter's applauded like mad and broke spontaneously into the *Salve regina* ("Hail, Holy Queen").[1] But most of them assumed he was referring to the Saturday evening service planned for Santa Maria Maggiore which was not a "conciliar" event. He was due to concelebrate with twenty-two bishops from famous Marian shrines. In that context it might just have passed off unnoticed as a devotional exercise for the Roman populace.

But it had quite a different meaning when solemnly proclaimed before the observers at the final gathering of this third session. Paul presented it as the crowning achievement (*fastigium*) of the session and the completion of the constitution on the Church.[2] The observers were not amused. They felt, said the *bien-pensant* Jean Guitton, "shocked by their host". A great volley of applause lasting over a minute greeted the news. It was embarrassing because it came so obviously from the minority.[3] One observer remarked that no one applauded Christ or the Holy Spirit.

The reason for the minority's rejoicing was that Paul had taken up a title, *Mater Ecclesiae*, that the Theological Commission had deliberately rejected on the following grounds:

> The title *Mater Ecclesiae* is sometimes found in ecclesiastical authors, but very rarely, and it cannot be called traditional. In any case, it is completed by the addition of titles like *Daughter* and *Sister* of the Church. It is therefore clear that it is a metaphor. From the ecumenical point of view this title is certainly not recommended, even though it is theologically admissible. The Commission thought it better to put it another way.

The fundamental objection to Mother of the Church was that it seemed to place Mary outside the Church, over and above it.

Paul's laudable motive was once again to give comfort to the minority who believed that the inclusion of Mary in the constitution on the

1 *Insegnamenti*, pp. 662, 664.

2 Ibid. p. 676.

3 René Laurentin, *Bilan de la troisième session*, p. 281.

Church, instead of having a separate document devoted to her, somehow "insulted" the Madonna. Laurentin, having thought about it for more than twenty years, explains Paul's motive thus: he needed to "compensate for Mary's integration in the Church by giving her a glorious title that showed her *superiority* over the Church."[1]

He may be right, but it is hard to see any necessity in such a move. It looked like a sop thrown to the minority, yet another hostage to fortune. Lefebvre and Larraona could plausibly claim that Paul VI disagreed with the Theological Commission about *Lumen Gentium.*

So Paul VI got a bad press. He could explain that away by conspiracy theories. More distressing was the news that Henri de Lubac, whom he so esteemed, on his return to France would say nothing about what had happened. His garrulous colleague, Jean Daniélou, more than made up for his silence.

Paul VI felt under attack from the majority at the Council. He thought this unfair, but could not reply officially. Unofficially he could put his case through intermediaries like Fr Daniel Pézeril, *curé* of St-Jacques-du-Haut-Pas in Paris (the man who heard novelist Georges Bernanos' final confession in 1949). Pézeril reported him as saying:

> I am perhaps slow. But I know what I want . . . The declaration on religious liberty has been held over (*reportée*) out of respect for the rights of the minority. That is the only motive: respect for them. I could not simply ignore them. But in substance, nothing has changed. Religious freedom remains intact.[2]

However there were so many concessions to the minority – which showed not the slightest sign of gratitude – that once again he seemed to be their secret ally. His accommodations alienated the majority without convincing the minority. Thus he had the worst of both worlds.

Various theories were evolved to defend Paul VI and explain his attitude. One could contrast the overheated atmosphere in St Peter's, in which few could see beyond their noses or next vote, with Pope Paul's far-sighted lucidity. The battle of religious liberty was not lost, merely postponed. As usual the man with direct access to the Pope, Giovanni Caprile of *Civiltà Cattolica*, stated the papal case: Paul VI did not want the minority to feel crushed as they stumbled to defeat in vote after vote. He wanted *pas de vaincus, mais des convaincus.*

Perhaps the best explanation of Paul's position came from an out-

1 Giovanni Battista Montini, *Sulla Madonna, discorsi e scritti 1955–1963*, ed. René Laurentin, p. 10.

2 Quoted in *Modernité*, p. 267. Pézeril's article appeared in *Le Monde* where Henri Fesquet assiduously promoted the idea that Paul VI was "above all else the referee".

sider, Canon Bernard Pawley, the Archbishop of Canterbury's "representative" in Rome. On 21 November 1964 he wrote a personal letter to his archbishop, Michael Ramsey, describing the mood after Paul's speech at the closing session:

> I have just returned from St Peter's and have not had time to sort it out. All the Observers, absolutely *all*, are very disappointed, our friends in the Secretariat are puzzled and annoyed, but all the "old gang" in the Vatican are exultant.
>
> My interpretation (subject to later thought and consultation with others) is as follows. The Council as a whole has been a severe disappointment to the old guard Roman Catholics who have run the Church here for centuries. The Pope has "let them down" by agreeing to collegiality, to ecumenism (can you think what a bitter pill this is?) and to the severe blow dealt to the BVM in *de Ecclesia*.
>
> There is no doubt that he has been appealed to on all sides to modify these decrees and has refused. So the good captain of the ship, to save the boat rocking too much, has put a little weight on the other side, to comfort them and to keep the balance. And I suppose we don't mind her being called Mother of the Church, do we, now that we know officially (*ex cathedra*) this morning that she has a *subordinatum munus*. All is not lost. Am I right?[1]

He was.

Willebrands and the whole staff of the Secretariat for Christian Unity were present on 26 November for a farewell dinner to Bernard and Margaret Pawley. Willebrands made a little speech praising the Anglicans for "sincerely trying to understand what was going on in the RC Church and to evaluate it pragmatically."[2]

There was an implicit contrast here between the Anglicans, with their famed "good humour", and what Pawley calls "the rather unself-critical dogmatic reactions of e.g. the Lutherans". But on the evidence of this farewell dinner the Lutherans were not entirely unself-critical, for among their observers a "great debate" was raging about whether there was such a thing as a "Lutheran Church *überhaubpt* [at all]". Dr Edmund Schlink, Professor of Dogmatics at Heidelberg, himself a Lutheran, thought there was not: the World Lutheran Federation had no executive

1 Bernard Pawley, Canterbury Cathedral Archives. Letter dated 21 November 1964. The best Pawley material is contained in his twice-weekly accounts of what is going on. They are numbered. Henceforward: *Rome Reports*.

2 Bernard Pawley, *Rome Reports*, No. 167, 30 December 1964.

authority, there was no universally accepted statement of belief, no uniform pattern of ministry or church order (in Sweden they were an Episcopal state Church).

A rumour shot round the table, started by Cardinal Bea's secretary for the last nine years and future biographer, Stjepan Schmidt SJ: since his remark that "One Galileo case is enough" Cardinal Suenens had fallen out of favour with Paul VI, who was ominously "seeing more" of Cardinals Roberti and Browne. That could be serious.

He made his farewell personally to Cardinal Bea on 27 November. The cardinal, friendly as ever, said he would welcome Pawley's successor, Canon John Findlow. He offered a positive reading of the third session and said it would be remembered for the two great documents, On the Church, and On Ecumenism. The acceptance of the document on the Jews was, Cardinal Bea thought, very important because

1) it had been done uphill against constant attrition;

2) not even the political pressure from the Middle East had been enough to stop it;

3) it formed a healthy rejoinder to the influence of such things as the Rudolf Hochhut play, *Der Stellverterter* (*The Representative*);

4) it had been rescued from its improper place at the tail-end of the decree on Ecumenism.[1]

Bea insisted that Findlow must be particularly vigilant to follow up the implementation of the decree on Ecumenism, since there would be those who while praising it would try to torpedo its application.

Finally, Pawley's "farewell" audience throws new light on the "black week" and on Paul's attitude to Anglicans:

> I had a final audience with the Pope on 28 November. This was very remarkable because he invited me to bring all the family, which I did, having warned him that I would not be responsible for what Felicity (aged three) and Matthew (aged two) might say or do. He replied that he was quite used to his great-nephews and nieces, some of whom had made havoc in the Vatican Palace a few weeks previously. In the event nothing disastrous happened, and the whole thing was a success. The children were slightly more impressed, naturally, with the Swiss Guards than with the clergyman in a white cassock.
>
> I had an audience alone first. His Holiness enquired about the Archbishop of Canterbury's health and plans . . . I was

1 Ibid. p. 1. In the US *The Representative* was called *The Deputy*.

able to explain our hopes about the future of the Church in Nigeria. The Pope asked how these new "united" churches would stand in relation to Canterbury. Did I think this would be the general pattern of reunion schemes in other parts of the world? He hoped that the Archbishop's visit to Rome would not be long delayed. I thought it might happen in 1965 if a date could be found free of the Council and of the Archbishop's journeys.

The Pope was complimentary about my mission and regretted it had ended . . . I thanked him and said I could have wished to have had answers for some questions in the last week of the Council.

He smiled and said, "There were difficulties, but all is well now." I said it was not always easy objectively to report what was really going on. He smiled again and asked what I had reported about the last days. I told him. His face went serious and he said "*bene, bene*" with some emphasis. "I think Anglicans often understand what is going on among us better than anyone else. They have a hierarchy, they believe in the Church. I have clear principles on which I act in times of difficulty. I must act in faith. I must show that I understand the aspirations of the two sides when they disagree, that I love them personally, that I respect their institutions and ways of thinking. As captain of the ship I have to keep her on a steady course . . . So you bring all along with you. I am not going to act in a hurry. We have made great strides, but we have made them together" (meaning that the new documents, through not being rushed, had had an almost unanimous vote). "It is better for me to go ahead slowly and carry everyone with me than to hurry along and cause dissension. Especially when I speak in public I must show that I love all my sheep, like a good shepherd."

. . . This interview was one of the most satisfactory I have had, offering immediate opportunities for exchange at quite a deep level, without wasting time on courtesies. It was a return to the old Milan days.[1]

So within five weeks of the *settimana nera*, just at the time when people were reading articles about how awful it had been, Paul himself was over the hump and not at all in the state of confused and acute distress painted by the media.

Even the shambles on religious liberty now disclosed a positive

1 Bernard Pawley, Diary for 28 December 1964, Canterbury Archives.

aspect. John Courtney Murray SJ and Abbot Christopher Butler OSB both held that the delay, though a short-term disappointment, would lead to an overall improvement in the text.

As for the decree on ecumenism, *Unitatis Redintegratio*, it already had an effect where it mattered most to Paul VI: among the Orthodox Churches gathered in Rhodes. The section on "The Special Position of the Eastern Churches" (14–18) was acceptable to them, especially when it quoted the Acts of the Apostles: "In order to restore communion and unity or preserve them, one must 'impose no burden beyond what is necessary' (Acts 15:28)." True Florence and earlier Councils had said that before. Everyone agreed that the mistake of Florence had been to reach an agreement at the summit that could not be communicated down below. Now that there were exiled Orthodox Churches in many parts of the world, it should be possible to "have friendly collaboration in a spirit of love, without quarrelsome rivalry".[1] But it was St Andrew's head that did it.

Then it was time to go to India.

1 *Unitatis Redintegratio*, 18.

25

A Missionary Pope Makes A Fresh Start

> There has never been anything like it within living memory, and there will never be anything like it for decades to come. Long after the children who made their first Holy Communion that day at the Cooperage have grown to maturity and many of the priests who were ordained that evening on the Oval will have come to the evening of their days, the memory of the day the Holy Father came to India will be recounted, not without the tears that can only result from a strongly felt experience.
>
> (MSGR BENNY D'AGUIAR, "Indian Triumph", *The Examiner*, Bombay, 12 December 1964)

That Paul's second choice for a "pilgrimage", after the Holy Land, should be to the sub-continent where the mass of the population are deeply religious and Christians are only a tiny minority was imaginative and striking. India had a population of 500 million of whom 2.4 million were Christian and only 1.2 million Catholic. Here we had "Paul" the apostle of the Gentiles, consciously breaking new ground and entering into dialogue with world religions.

He revealed he would be going to India in dramatic fashion on 18 October 1964 during the canonization of the Uganda Martyrs:

> This is the second time we have had occasion to announce that we are about to undertake a journey abroad, something that hitherto has been outside the ordinary scope of the apostolic ministry of the Roman Pontiffs. But we think that like the first journey to the Holy Land, this journey to the gates of the immense continent of Asia, which is like the new world of our age, is not foreign to the nature, still less to the mandate, implicit in the apostolic ministry.[1]

1 *Insegnamenti*, 1964, pp. 590–91.

"Thunderous applause" greeted this news, although it was delivered in Latin.

The timing of the announcement was skilful. The canonization of the Uganda Martyrs enabled him to speak of Africa as a *vera patria Christi*, truly a land of Christ. Again, in Uganda young Anglicans had been massacred along with Catholics, and in Africa as in India, denominational differences imported from European Reformation quarrels seemed remote, irrelevant or even shocking. Finally the wholly inadequate draft on missions, dismissed as "dry bones" by Bishop Donal Lamont, was faltering. By going to India and "becoming a missionary" even if only for three days, Paul hoped to lift that debate out of the morass into which it was bogged down.

The visit to India had a history. Cardinal Valerian Gracias, who succeeded Thomas d'Esterre Roberts SJ when he resigned as Archbishop of Bombay in 1946, had invited Pope John XXIII to the Eucharistic Congress. John said that he was too old to travel and, anyway, would be dead by 1964.[1] Gracias had raised the matter with Paul VI immediately after his election in June 1963. There was no instant answer. The Holy Land was Paul's top priority. "Let's see how that visit goes," he told Gracias, "and then we'll think about India."

Gracias was in Rome for the third session of the Council. On 30 September 1964 at 8.30 in the evening he was told "the Pope wishes to speak with you very urgently". When Gracias arrived in the papal apartments Paul embraced him warmly and then said, in Italian, "If it please the Lord, I will come to India." He insisted on a number of conditions: utter simplicity after the manner of Mahatma Ghandi; it must be a spiritual pilgrimage in the Indian tradition; and he would want to meet and be with the poor, irrespective of class and creed. Gracias seemed a little disappointed that Paul would not be riding on an elephant, the Indian equivalent of the *sedia gestatoria*, but he understood that such pomp and splendour did not become the "servant Church".

One of the lessons learned from the chaos of the Holy Land was that such visits had to be meticulously prepared if the Pope were not to put himself unnecessarily at risk. Paul chose as his impresario Paul Casimir Marcinkus, the tough American football-player from Cicero, Illinois, famed as Al Capone's home town. This delighted the press, and was completely irrelevant. Paul had known Marcinkus since 1952 when he came to the Secretariat of State recommended by the Gregorian theology faculty, who thought him bright.

1 "Pope Paul's Visit to India", a memoir by Msgr Benny Aguiar, editor for many years of *The Examiner*, Bombay, specially written for this book.

Back in Rome after diplomatic experience in Bolivia and Canada, he became well-known as a "fixer". His huge Chevrolet ferried visitors, clerical or lay, to the catacombs or the golf course. He also coached Paul VI in English, which perhaps was a mistake.[1] Marcinkus, soon dubbed the "gorilla", was never in fact a papal bodyguard. His main work was forward-planning, going over the ground in advance, stop-watch in hand.[2]

Paul arrived at Bombay's Santa Cruz airport at 5 p.m. on Wednesday, 2 December. Framed in the door of the aeroplane, Paul joined his hands as in prayer and uttered the word *Namaste*! which is used both as greeting and farewell. It means: "I bow to you." From the outset Paul "bowed to India" and India took him to its heart.

Everyone had a story of his kindness and thoughtfulness. How he knelt to give communion to the orphans who were too small to receive otherwise. One of the orphans, Anthony Mascarenhas, read an address of welcome in which he said some of them had no father, others no mother and some, like himself, had no one in the world at all. Paul embraced him and wept. The children stole the show.

Throughout Paul showed himself to be sensitive to the Indian religious tradition. In his meeting with non-Christian religious leaders, a gathering unique in the history of Bombay, he paid tribute to "this land of ancient culture, the cradle of great religions", and made an eloquent plea for better understanding. He found the spirit of Advent expressed in words first uttered long before Christ: "From the unreal, lead me to the real; from darkness, lead me to light; from death, lead me to immortality."[3] After the speeches he met Appa Sahib Patwardhan, an associate of Mahatma Ghandi and a member of the Shanti Sena, who devoted his life to the service of the Harijans (or outcasts).

On Thursday, 3 December, feast of St Francis Xavier, over three hundred thousand people attended Paul's Mass at which he ordained

1 John Cornwell, *Thief in the Night: The Death of Pope John Paul I*, p. 40. Not the least merit of this admirable book is that the author, instead of resorting to the press clippings, gave Marcinkus a chance to explain himself at length.

2 Marcinkus held the post until 1982 when the Italian government sought to arrest him for his alleged participation in the crash of the Banco Ambrosiano. His place was taken by Fr Roberto Tucci SJ, head of Vatican Radio, who proved that in this post diplomatic skills were more important than toughness. Marcinkus had notched up ten papal trips. I was with him in Zaïre in 1981. As we waited in the dawn light for President Mobutu and the Pope to arrive, a storm raged, making the red carpet sodden and flooding the Congo river down which tree trunks and dead elephants floated. Marcinkus tried to jump down on to the launch that would take us across the river. He slipped and uttered an unepiscopal remark. "We're not gonna have any more of these crazy papal trips," he said. Which, in his case, turned out to be true.

3 *Insegnamenti*, 1964, p. 693.

bishops from all five continents, explaining: "We have chosen them from the five parts of the world so that it may be clear that we are obedient to the love of Christ, that immense love, pouring forth upon all peoples, upon all men of the earth.[1]

"Your authority," he told the new bishops, "derives from this, that you can call every man you meet your friend; and if he responds to you you will call him brother and son."[2] In this Christian context he quoted the Upanishads: "Truth alone triumphs, not falsehood. The divine path to liberation has been laid with truth, which the seers who have overcome desire tread, and wherein also is that supreme treasure to be gained by truth."[3]

Many non-Christians were present including India's Prime Minister Lal Bahadur Shastri. His presence was controversial, but he answered critics by saying that the Eucharistic Congress was "a test for the image of India which tolerates all religions and cultures". Tolerance, said Shastri, is the very essence of Hinduism.

However, from the point of view of the future mission of the Church in India, it was important to stress that Christianity put down roots in India only a few decades after Christ, being evangelized, according to legend, by St Thomas the Apostle. To make the point that Christianity was indigenous in India Paul became the first pope to preside at a Mass in the Syro-Malankara Rite[4] on 4 December. *The Times of India* confirmed the same idea from another angle: "As the late Mr Nehru never tired of pointing out, Christianity is as Indian as any of the other religions with which this country is associated, and it has contributed greatly to the building up of a cultural inheritance, distinguished by a unique fusion of tolerance and spiritual fervour."

At the Syro-Malankara Mass, cripples, the sick and the lame lay strewn around the foot of the altar, and Paul came down and blessed them. They were a reminder of another fact of Indian life: poverty.

Paul had thought about this too. Just before the Eucharistic Congress the Food and Agriculture Organization (FAO), whose headquarters is in Rome, held a seminar in Bombay on "Food and Health". This meant that FAO's Director-General, Dr B. R. Sen, was conveniently on hand to deliver a stirring address to the Eucharistic Congress on "Freedom

1 Ibid. p. 701.

2 Ibid. p. 702. This and the last quotation show how blithely unaware people were about the use of "inclusive" language.

3 Ibid.

4 These are a group of Christians who entered into communion with the Bishop of Rome in 1930. Their metropolitan see is at Trivandrum. Paul also met His Holiness Mar Basilios I, Catholicos of the ancient Syrian Orthodox Church of Malabar in south-west India.

from Hunger – the Challenge of the Century". This not only prevented the Eucharistic Congress from sailing off into the stratosphere of spirituality but it prepared Paul's appeal at the Press Club. It was very simple, very brief, and just what exhausted journalists needed:

> We entrust to you our special message to the world. Would that the nations could cease the armaments race, and devote their energies and resources instead to the fraternal assistance of the developing countries! Would that every nation thinking "thoughts of peace and not of affliction" and war, would contribute even part of its expenditure for arms to a great world fund for the relief of the many problems of nutrition, clothing, shelter and medical care which afflict so many peoples.[1]

India, a leading member of the Non-Aligned Movement, was the right place from which to issue this appeal. It anticipated the "peace dividend" which only became feasible when the "Cold War" was over. It was also Paul's way of booking a ticket to the United Nations.

What did the visit mean? *America* magazine summed up:

> Here is the real significance of the papal visit to Bombay. It was not a personal triumph of Pope Paul. Nor was it a shock treatment designed to focus the attention of the Church on pet theories of coping with India's population explosion. Rather we would like to think it created in Asia a hitherto unappreciated image of the Church: that of the compassionate Vicar of Christ – a Christ born poor – more at home in the slums of Bombay than in the magnificence of the papal court.[2]

The *Guardian* in Britain put it more succinctly. The reason why Paul was given "a greater reception than any previous visitor to India" was that "he had the advantage of being a holy man in a country which loves holy men". He also had "three other advantages – dignity, charm, and an unerring sense of priorities. For him it was a question of visiting orphanages rather than Maharajah's Palaces."[3] In this case the secular press was more perceptive than the Jesuits.

On the eve of the papal visit, 25–28 November, St Pius X College, Goregaon, Bombay hosted a theological conference on "Christian Revelation and Non-Christian Religions". Traditionally, Eucharistic Congresses had a theological component. The statistics of India and the

1 *Insegnamenti*, 1964, p. 716.

2 *America*, 16–26 December 1964. It was the Christmas number.

3 A final thanks to Msgr Benny d'Aguiar from whom all these quotations derive. Paul also gave his white Lincoln convertible to Mother Teresa of Calcutta, who was not yet the cult-figure she later became. It was auctioned for 100,000 rupees.

recently approved conciliar texts led them to look once again at the maxim "No salvation outside the Church". The conference marked a stage in the maturity of Indian Catholic theology, though too many of the theologians were seminary professors and expatriates. Hans Küng was among the guest speakers, provocatively retranslating Boniface VIII's bull *Unam Sanctam* as "No salvation outside the *papal* Church."[1]

Lumen Gentium, voted on less than a month before (21 November 1964), gave the principle of the solution to this problem:

> Nor is God remote from those who in shadows and images seek the unknown God, since he gives to all men life and breath and all things (cf. Acts 17:25–28), and since the Saviour wills all men to be saved (cf. 1 Tim 2:4). Those who through no fault of their own do not know the Gospel of Christ or his Church, but who nevertheless seek God with sincere hearts . . . those too may achieve salvation.[2]

This passage was filled out a week later by *Nostra Aetate* on Non-Christian Religions. Cardinal Augustin Bea pointed to its originality and importance when he introduced the text to the Council:

> It concerns those – more than a thousand million people – who have either not yet come to the knowledge of Christ and of his work of redemption, or do not acknowledge them. Nevertheless they can be saved if they obey the voice of their conscience. Yet it is the very grave duty of the Church to enter into dialogue with them on this matter.[3]

This was enough for Paul VI, who needed a *practical* theology to enable him to reach out to other-believers and non-believers. The assumption was that grace is at work in them; and all grace is the grace of Christ. In that spirit he had founded the Secretariat for Non-Christian Religions.

But the theologians meeting at St Pius X College, Goregaon, Bombay on 25–28 November needed something more than practical solutions.

1 Hans Küng, "The World Religions in God's Plan of Salvation", in *Christian Revelation and World Religions*, ed. Joseph Neuner, Burns and Oates, London 1967, p. 32. It is worth noting that three other contributors, all Jesuits, were Council *periti*: the Belgians Piet Fransen and Joseph Masson and the Austrian Joseph Neuner, professor at Poona, since 1938. The fifth was Raymond Panikkar, a scholar of Indian religion on the rebound from Opus Dei.

2 *Lumen Gentium*, 16.

3 Joseph Neuner, op. cit. p. 7. One might ask why Cardinal Paolo Marella, President of the Secretariat for Non-Christian Religions, did not present this decree. The technical answer is that *Nostra Aetate* grew out of a concern for the Christian relationship with the Jews, which belonged to the Secretariat for Christian Unity. But Marella, who had missed the journey to India, did not show much concern for the salvific value of non-Christian religions.

Unfortunately an inaccurate account of their "conclusions" appeared in *Le Monde*, was broadcast round the world and attacked by Fr Jean Daniélou SJ. They were taken to be saying that recognizing the positive value of non-Christian religions made missionary endeavour superfluous. Others concluded that the missionary's main task would not be so much to baptize and proclaim the Gospel as to enable others to realize the riches of their own traditions. Either way the missionary was disarmed. Yet these alarmist views were partly the product of right-wing fantasies. An example was Bishop Jean Gay of Basse-Terre, Guadalupe,[1] a Holy Ghost Father and ally of his General, Archbishop Marcel Lefebvre.

If that debate was one unintended by-product of his visit to India, Paul deliberately used it to "plant" the idea that the money saved from disarmament should be used to start a fund to feed the hungry. This gave him a chance to wangle – no other word is appropriate – the visit to the United Nations he so ardently desired.

He had already squared President Lyndon B. Johnson. Now he needed U Thant, Secretary-General of the United Nations, which he saw as the modern world in miniature. Msgr Alberto Giovannetti, one of the few Vatican diplomats to have written a novel,[2] was set to work. He handed over an autograph copy of Paul's disarmament appeal to U Thant, Secretary-General. An accompanying letter added that the response to the Pope's Bombay appeal had been so great that there was hope that "the words of His Holiness would find a generous response on the part of governments". U Thant was invited to make use of it, "so that the expectations of so many may not be deceived".

U Thant replied on 20 January 1965, in a letter of great warmth which showed that Paul would not only be made welcome at the UN but would be received with eagerness. The UN was in its twentieth year; it had gone through many tensions and strains, and its future was not assured in a bi-polar world of superpower rivalry. So U Thant was grateful to have the support of the Catholic Church for disarmament and the fight against hunger, two of the principal goals of the UN.[3] The prospect of the visit lent an added urgency to the conciliar statement on religious liberty. Paul could not go to New York without it being accepted in principle. He insisted its coming as early as possible on the agenda of the final session. No one yet knew why.

Giovannetti was left to take diplomatic soundings and work out the details. The first plan was for Paul to go to San Francisco in June for

1 See Rynne, *The Fourth Session*, p. 140.

2 *Requiem for a Spy*.

3 U Thant's letter, in French, is in *Insegnamenti*, 1965, p. 544.

the twentieth anniversary celebrations. But that left too little time for planning, and trouble flared up in the Dominican Republic where the Papal Nuncio was trying to mediate; he sent a message instead, read out by Archbishop Martin J. O'Connor on 26 June 1965. Giovannetti was in Rome from 7 July to fix the final details. Opposition in the Roman Curia based on the principle they-come-to-us, we-don't-go-to-them had to be circumvented. Protocol was a tangle. Was the Pope to be received as a head of state or as the head of the Church? U Thant cut through that undergrowth: he intended to receive him as Pope Paul VI.

Meanwhile the Bishop of Rome and Primate of the West had to carry on with the ordinary business of the Church. There were bishops to be appointed at the rate of about three a week. Though this was delegated to the Congregation of Bishops (still called Consistorial Congregation), Paul took an interest in the major sees.

The Chicago succession was watched with particular interest. Cardinal Albert Meyer, a genuine scripture scholar, the intellectual leader of the US bishops, much loved and esteemed, died in April 1964 leaving a gap that was difficult to fill. A long *vacatio sedis* (that is, the gap between the death of a bishop and his replacement) was evidence of indecision and argument behind the scenes. Chicago had to wait sixteen months until August 1965, which suggested a titanic battle.

Moreover the "resolution" of the crisis aroused astonishment, mirth and incredulity in varying degrees. Chicago mourned the death of Meyer in 1964, but it was a Church lifted by the hope that his successor would be a fully "conciliar" bishop. It got in John Patrick Cody, then Archbishop of New Orleans, an uninspiring bureaucrat. As Bishop of Kansas City, Missouri he had gilded the dome of his cathedral.[1] He was welcomed in Democrat Mayor Daley's Irish-dominated city by a brass band. As Charles Dahm put it:

> The Vatican Council . . . had by its teaching endorsed not only the innovations of the Council in Chicago but also greater co-operation between clergy and laity in decision-making. As Fr John Egan said: "We were full of goodwill, anxious to co-operate, had a generous spirit, and a burning hope that we could build on the traditions we had established."[2]

This good will was squandered. Cody failed utterly, producing "a demoralized and atomized clergy". The phrase comes from Fr Andrew

1 "And what was his *other* great achievement?" enquired satirically the *National Catholic Reporter*, the newly-founded paper of liberal Catholicism edited by Bob Hoyt.

2 Charles Dahm OP, *Power and Authority in the Catholic Church: Cardinal Cody in Chicago*, University of Notre Dame Press 1981, pp. 4–5.

Greeley who, in his kinder moments, called Cody a "madcap tyrant" and a "clinical sociopath".[1] Chicago suffered much from Cody, who survived into the next pontificate, pursued by Federal justice officials.

Why did Paul make such an obviously dud appointment? The answer is that Cardinal Francis J. Spellman was still dictating episcopal appointments in the United States, and the other would-be power-broker, Cardinal James Francis McIntyre of Los Angeles,[2] was subservient to him. Besides, Egidio Vagnozzi, the Apostolic Delegate, wanted to see his old Roman classmate, Cody, installed in Chicago, the largest and most vigorous diocese in the United States. For once, the interests of Spellman and Vagnozzi coincided. One had to wait for the appointment of the Belgian delegate, Jean Jadot, before US episcopal nominees began to reflect the policies of the Council.

Yet Paul VI had already learned one lesson of great importance from the US bishops. They needed a statement on religious liberty, and even the conservative Spellman had brought in the Jesuit John Courtney Murray to make this case. Cardinal Meyer had astonished the Council by the brash vigour of his defence of religious liberty. "Unless the Council enacts this or a similar declaration," he said, "nothing else it does will make much difference."[3] On which Cardinal Lawrence Shehan remarked: "Those acquainted with Meyer's retiring disposition and his distaste for mere rhetoric realized that he would have been the last person in the world to have used such words except as a result of long reflection and deep conviction."[4]

Clergy and laity were proud of their archbishop and were full of drive and initiative. Cody, by contrast, did not appear to have any convictions at all, except about his own authority.

All this time Paul was thinking about the final session of the Council. That involved pondering the lessons of the "black week" at the end of the third session. Paul defended himself through intermediaries.

As usual Giovanni Caprile had the inside story. One day, when the story was told of the heroic efforts Paul made to bring these decrees home to port, we would all be lost in admiration at "his humble, con-

1 Ronald D. Pasquariello, *Conversations with Andrew Greeley*, Quinlan Press, Boston 1989, p. 176. This judgement was not a matter of hindsight.

2 Cardinal Spellman had said: "There is an axis in the Middle West working against me . . . so I thought I would make my own axis." John Tracy Ellis, *Catholic Bishops*, Michael Glazier, Wilmington, Delaware 1984, pp. 98–99. McIntyre, Ellis remarks, "was prone to angry outbursts on matters on which he was less than well informed", ibid. p. 97.

3 Lawrence Shehan, *A Blessing of Years: The Memoirs of Lawrence Cardinal Shehan*, pp. 196–97.

4 Ibid. p. 197.

stant and laborious attempt to find what the Holy Spirit wants for the Church".[1] An interview in *Le Monde* by Daniel Pézeril explained that the sole reason for the holding over of the text on religious liberty was "the need to respect the rights of the minority, as guaranteed by the Council regulations. To have ignored them would have been a dangerous precedent. Besides, it is not generally known that the case was put to the Adminstrative Tribunal of the Council, presided over by Cardinal [Francesco] Roberti."[2]

Why, if it was so important, had this fact not been mentioned earlier? Indeed it was not fully revealed until September 1989, when Vincenzo Carbone disclosed that he himself, as under-secretary of the Council, had met Cardinal Roberti late on 18 November 1964 to arrange for a meeting of the Tribunal for resolving disputes on 20 November. The Tribunal upheld the judgement of the minority: "The text is substantially different and therefore cannot be voted upon until it has been discussed again."[3] The defence of Paul VI in the black week was that he had acted conscientiously and responsibly.

Yet he was attacked for acting arbitrarily. *Le Journal de Genève* alleged the delay in the vote on religious liberty was "a psychological error, a partisan act and proof of papal absolutism".[4] The Observers – or some of them – had been among his sharpest critics, so much so that Cardinal Paolo Marella and Pericle Felici appear to have decided that there was no point in their returning for the final session. Msgr Willebrands pointed out the elementary fact that the Observers were invited to *the Council* as a whole, not to individual sessions. Grootaers thinks a "catastrophe was narrowly averted". But it is difficult to take this proposal seriously, except as a revelation of the anti-ecumenical mind of Marella and Felici.[5]

So the document on religious liberty was *different* and *new*. From 18 to 25 February it was worked through again by a commission of experts which included two Americans, John Courtney Murray and Paulist Thom Stransky. Pietro Pavan, who had drafted *Pacem in Terris* for Pope John, was the only Italian. Yves Congar was present and Wille-

1 Giovanni Caprile, "*Aspetti positivi della terza sessione*", *Civiltà Cattolica*, 20 February 1965. A popular version appeared in the different language editions of *L'Osservatore Romano* as "Positive Aspects of the Third Session".

2 *Le Monde*, 27 February 1965.

3 Vincenzo Carbone, "*Il ruolo di Paolo VI nell'evoluzione e nella redazione della dichiarazione Dignitatis Humanae*", in *Paulo VI et il rapporto Chiesa-Mondo*, p. 152.

4 Ibid.

5 Jan Grootaers, "*L'opinion publique en Belgique et aux Pays-Bas*", in *Paulo VI e i probleme ecclesiologici al Concilio*, p. 447. This story is based on what Marella said to Villot who reported it to Antoine Wenger.

brands presided. Their brief was to incorporate the emendations suggested by Council Fathers up to 15 February, wrote Cardinal Bea in a covering letter to Paul that accompanied their text.[1] The Secretariat for Christian Unity, made ultra-cautious by the experience of dirty tricks, played everything by the book. On 18 April 1964 Willebrands sent Cardinal Alfredo Ottaviani at the Holy Office thirty copies as requested, insisting that they should remain secret.[2]

On 6 May at 5.45 Paul had a long conversation with Pericle Felici at Carlo Colombo which ranged over the whole question. Later that night Paul wrote a five-page memo summarizing with great skill the state of the question. Here are the last three pages. They suggest that this was *the first time* that Paul had begun to think seriously about this question:

> *Religious Liberty*
> Can be understood as freedom from external compulsion; freedom *from*; *nemo cogatur* [let no one be compelled];
> or as the ability (juridical or *de facto*) to profess a given religion; freedom *for*; *nemo impediatur* [let no one be prevented] within certain limits of public order, of respect for others, of public morality etc.
> – it can refer to groups, associations, communities, or to the Church *vis-à-vis* the State, as when the Church claims religious freedom for itself;
> or it can refer to the State, which should concede and safeguard religious liberty – whether in pluralist fashion, in which the same measure applies to all religions; or on a preferential manner to the particular religion of a given people as a whole, or to a nation (history, popular awareness etc.).
>
> *Religious Liberty*
> – can be studied in its historical manifestations, whether in the Old Testament or among various peoples, or in the life and documents of the Church;
> – and it must be studied, above all, in the thought of Christ, in the Gospel and the New Testament in general whether from the point of view of *nemo cogatur* (see the parable of the wheat and the cockle, or Luke 9:55, *Nescitis cuius spiritus estis* [you know not of whose spirit you are] or John 18:11 *mitte gladium tuam in vaginam* [Put your sword in its scabbard]; or from the point of view of *nemo impediatur* in relation to the freedom

1 Ibid. p. 153.
2 Ibid. p. 154.

> to preach and bear witness to religious truth (cf. martyrs, witnesses).
>
> It can be further studied
> – as the freedom of the act of faith, in the individual person; this is the fundamental aspect which leads to consideration for the rights of the individual conscience;
> – as freedom for the authority of the Church to frame its own laws.[1]

Though these are only headings, they show that Paul was perfectly capable of going to the heart of a complex matter and bringing *evangelical* criteria to bear upon it. That is what distinguishes him from the "conservative minority" who stress *institutional* criteria, that is, the rights of the Church.

But he was not yet out of the wood. On 8 May he minuted: "Please arrange a short audience for Father John Courtney Murray (Columbus Hotel)." Murray, known to him since the 1950s, had written an article on the question for *Aggiornamento Sociali*, a Jesuit publication in Milan that had greater freedom than *Civiltà Cattolica*, not being censored by the Secretariat of State.[2] But what led to Paul's invitation was a letter he received from the American Jesuit that 8 May 1965:

> Your Holiness
> . . . I think the text has been considerably improved. The doctrinal line is very solid; the human and civil right to religious freedom is based, *not* on freedom of conscience (which is dangerous), but on the dignity of the person and on the principles of social order which flow from the dignity of the person. Hence the argument moves entirely in the objective order; the charge of subjectivity cannot legitimately be made.
>
> The method is also sound. The question of religious freedom, as a problem in the civil order, is clearly distinguished from other questions which are of the theological order – in particular freedom and order within the Church.
>
> The concept of religious freedom as a "right" in the sense of immunity from coercion (not as an empowerment) is clearly maintained. This is most important.
>
> The section on scripture and revelation has again been put at the end. This is good and necessary, even though some French bishops will not like it.

1 Vincenzo Carbone, "*Il ruolo de Paolo VI*", pp. 155–56.

2 John Courtney Murray, "*La Libertà religiosa, materia di dibattito conciliare*", in *Aggiornamenti Sociali*, April 1965, pp. 303–10.

The doctrine does exhibit a development of doctrine – but *eodem sensu eademque sententia* [with the same sense and meaning]. The roots of the doctrine are in Leo XIII – in his doctrine on the two orders of human life, and in his emphasis on the freedom of the Church as the cardinal principle governing the relations of the Church to the temporal order. The more proximate roots are in Pius XII, in his doctrine on the human person as *subiectum et finis* [the subject and goal] of the whole social order (by which he transcended the more ethical doctrine of Leo XIII, derived from Aristotle ultimately, on the society-state).

Finally the immediate roots of the doctrine are in *Pacem in Terris* and its doctrine of freedom as the cardinal social virtue, along with justice, truth and love. The line of development is clear, the schema simply presents a more explicit *enucleatio doctrinae* [encapsulating of doctrine]. The development, I think, is not only valid but necessary for today.

Please accept again my profound gratitude for your great kindness to me. I shall help in every possible way according to your wishes. (I shall also get in touch with Cardinal [Michael] Browne.)

Ad pedes provolutus Sanctitatis Vestrae, servus in Christus [Prostrate at the feet of Your Holiness, your servant in Christ],

John Courtney Murray SJ.[1]

After a few rumblings from Ottaviani, concerning "fairly fundamental reservations", by 28 May Felici conveyed to him Paul's approval for the printing of the *textus re-emendatus* on 28 May 1965.

It was substantially the same text, in content and structure, as that on which no vote was taken on 17 December 1964. There were two "novelties" or "developments". First the concept of "toleration of error" gave way to a definition of religious liberty as *immunity from coercion*. Second, the starting-point for thinking about religious liberty was the ontological nature of the human person, rather than anything else. Cardinal Giuseppe Siri huffed and puffed,[2] but otherwise the text came through unscathed to the final session of the Council.

The final version of schema 13 presented even more intractable and wide-ranging problems. Canon Pierre Haubtmann, Rector of the Institut Catholique in Paris, presided over the final drafting of the document.

1 Vincenzo Carbone, "*Il ruolo de Paolo VI*", pp. 156–57.

2 He wrote to Paul as late as 5 September 1965, well beyond the deadline. Siri still believed in pulling rank.

He kept a diary of two crucial papal audiences. Made available only in 1989, they cast new light on Paul's commitment to what would become *Gaudium et Spes*.[1]

Presented with the final programme of the work of the commission on 16 February 1965, Paul exclaimed, "But it's a whole encyclopaedia." He was afraid that too ambitious an agenda at this late stage would lead to inevitable disappointment. He thought that sometimes people have unreasonable expectations of the Church. It should provide principles rather than solutions, direction rather than directives, leaving priests and laity free but not free-floating. Therefore its teaching should include messages to "workers, intellectuals, those who suffer, doctors and maybe four or five other groups to whom an appeal would be echoed by the press". Haubtmann noted this down dutifully if a little dubiously.

The idea of messages bore fruit not in *Gaudium et Spes* itself so much as in the seven messages released to the world on the final day of the Council, 8 December 1965. They were conceived as a translation of *Gaudium et Spes* into accessible if not popular language.[2]

Much depended on who would work on the final draft. Paul VI was happy with the names put to him, and knew most of them personally. Jean Daniélou and Gérard Philips were obvious choices. Of Roberto Tucci, editor of the Rome Jesuit fortnightly *Civiltà Cattolica*, he remarked: "There's a wise man of great value."[3] He agreed with Haubtmann about the weaknesses of much theological work: "Yes, all too often we don't know how to answer the questions of the modern world . . . We just don't know." He also agreed that one of the main aims of schema 13 was to break down the popular view which contrasted Church and world as two antagonistic forces.

Then Haubtmann raised a strategic question of great importance especially in the light of the disasters of the third session (though he was too tactful to allude to them). If a tricky (Vaticanese: "delicate") matter cropped up, would there be a chance to refer it to the Holy Father? Paul replied: "But of course, that is what I want. I don't want to have to intervene in the last session when it's too late (*après coup*) but in good time. You will really be doing me a service by keeping me well-informed. You really must do this."[4]

But how was this desirable result to be achieved? Through Msgr Emilio Guano, Bishop of Livorno, his old friend from FUCI days, Msgr

1 Georges Cottier OP, "*Les Interventions de Paul VI dans l'élaboration de* 'Gaudium et Spes' ", in *Paolo VI e il rapporto Chiesa-Mondo al Concilio*, 1991.

2 Ibid. p. 24.

3 Ibid. p. 25.

4 Ibid.

Pericle Felici, Secretary of the Council, and Msgr Carlo Colombo. "We'll meet beforehand," Paul said, 'before the text is sent out to the Council Fathers."[1]

Georges Cottier wonders whether such working meetings actually occurred. But at least the chain of command was unveiled. By the time the third session began Guano was replaced by Msgr Garrone, Archbishop of Toulouse since 1956. He had even better access. Paul's door would be open "whenever the good of schema 13 demanded it". Paul promised Haubtmann that schema 13 would come second on the agenda of the fourth session of the Council, immediately after religious liberty. He could not explain that at the time. But he needed religious liberty in the bag before he went to the UN.

In a second audience on 20 May 1965 Paul and Haubtmann discussed whether the *French* text, which had a certain swing (or *élan*) to it and had in fact been the working basis of the discussion, could be considered "official" or at least equal to the rather clumsy Latin version on offer. It suggested limp paraphrases for modern terms like "sport", "couple" and – rather surprisingly – "responsibility".[2]

Paul's judgement was that the Latin text should precede the French version and other translations. "One has to deal carefully with people's susceptibilities," said Paul, "they can be often very powerful. We don't want anyone to say this is a French text." His image of the French was of a quarrelsome people: of two French intellectuals one was likely to be on the train to Rome to denounce the other. Haubtmann did not have a high opinion of Jean Guitton, who told this story, and added that Msgr Pericle Felici was now "better disposed" towards the text. The natural conclusion was that the Secretary of the Council, though improving slightly, was still lacking in enthusiasm for it.[3]

Haubtmann's notes on this 20 May 1965 audience contain two postscripts. In the first he insisted that schema 13 should be designated a "*pastoral* constitution". Attempts were being made to devalue it even within the co-ordinating commission itself. The contrast between a *dogmatic* constitution such as *Lumen Gentium*, approved by the third session, and a *pastoral* constitution such as was envisaged for schema 13, did not entail a difference of authority so much as a difference of address. The danger was that those for whom "pastoral" meant something less serious than dogmatic, would seek to drop the whole of the second part and simply hand over this material to Paul VI who could quarry it for

1 Ibid. p. 16.

2 Philippe Delhaye, "*Le Schéma de Zurich*", in *L'Eglise dans le monde de ce temps*, vol. I, p. 228 fn. 5.

3 Cottier, "*Les Interventions . . .*", in *Chiesa Mondo*, p. 24.

future encyclicals.[1] No idle threat, this was a dagger at the very heart of the pastoral constitution.

Haubtmann's second postscript simply notes that he had heeded Paul VI's request, conveyed through his usual intermediaries, Emilio Guano and Carlo Colombo, that the text should stress Redemption as much as Creation. This opened up the optimism-pessimism debate that occupied much of the fourth session. But the really important fact to emerge from Haubtmann's notes is that Paul VI was committed to *Gaudium et Spes* as conceived by its authors, and remained firmly opposed to any attempts to whittle it down.

While the optimism-pessimism debate was, if not exactly raging, at least filling space in the secular press, 218 Jesuit delegates were gathering at Borgo Santo Spiritu 5, just round the corner from the Vatican.[2] Their sole task, formally speaking, was to elect a new General. They were not invited to reinvent the wheel or the Company of Jesus.

At the start of the Congregation, before they were locked up incommunicado, Paul VI addressed them in friendly fashion, yet his speech disconcerted the Jesuits because it was so backward-looking. With the long generalate of John-Baptist Janssens at last over and the Council in session, the Jesuits expected this 31st General Congregation to be devoted to renewal and *aggiornamento.*

Yet for Paul – it seemed – all Jesuit glories lay in the past, before the suppression by Clement XIV in 1773. He laid great stress on the fourth vow (after poverty, chastity and obedience) of obedience to the Pope, which only the professed take. In the name of this fourth vow he appealed to the Jesuits to undertake a new task: that of obstructing atheism (*ut atheismo obsistant*).[3] This was variously interpreted. It was not so much a call to a crusade against atheism as a matter of getting in its way, heading it off, obstructing its growth and hopefully halting it in its tracks.

Atheism was, of course, a major concern of the schema 13 drafting committee, which included a number of Jesuits.[4] On 9 April 1965 it was announced, without any previous warning, *motu proprio*, that Paul had founded a Secretariat for Non-believers. Its purpose was "to *study* atheism and unbelief". Its first President was Cardinal Franz König,

1 Robert Tucci SJ, "*Introduction historique et doctrinale à la Constitution Pastorale*", in *L'Eglise dans le monde de ce temps*, II, p. 101.

2 Pedro Miguel Lamet, *Arrupe, una explosión en la Iglesia*, Ediciones Temas de Hoy, Madrid 1989, p. 264.

3 *Insegnamenti*, 1965, p. 265.

4 Apart from Roberto Tucci, it included Jean Daniélou, Otto Semmelroth, Piet Smulders and Alois Grillmeier.

Archbishop of Vienna, who accepted on condition that he would not have to reside in Rome. König naturally asked: What precisely are we supposed to do? "*Usus docebit* (You will find out from experience)," Paul replied.[1] So König stayed in Vienna as archbishop leaving the work in the capable hands of the Salesian Vincent Miano.

There were no fanfares for the Secretariat for Non-believers as there had been for the Secretariat for Non-Christian Religions the previous year. The reasons for this reticence were plain. If the curial conservatives could just about drag themselves to the point of recognizing some positive values in non-Christian religions, recognizing anything positive in atheism and unbelief would pose a much sterner test of nerves. For under "atheism" they saw "atheistic Communism". For the three hundred or so who belonged to the *Coetus Internationalis* the only test of schema 13 that mattered was whether it would condemn "atheistic Communism".

Which pope would the Council follow? Pius XI who condemned it in *Divini Redemptoris* in 1937[2] or Pope John XXIII who in *Pacem in Terris* only two years ago distinguished between the error – always to be rejected – and the person who errs – always to be respected?

Pope John's words could be considered no more than a variant on St Augustine's advice to "hate the sin but love the sinner". More politically damaging was his recognition that whatever Communist "philosophy" might say, its "programmes" could contain "just and commendable elements" with which Christians could be comfortable. Paul knew that the curial conservatives could not be shifted in their belief that the benevolent language used by Pope John in his "last will and testament" had lost the Christian Democrats in Italy a million votes in the 28 April 1963 election.[3]

That may be why Paul allowed König to stay in Vienna: this would show that the Secretariat for Non-believers was an international rather than an Italian concern. The Curia drew the short-term conclusion that a body without its head in Rome could not expect to be taken seriously since *les absents ont toujours tort*: there was no one to argue its corner.

In fact König proved that it was possible to run a Vatican office without actually being in Rome. His minuscule Secretariat had an impor-

1 Peter Hebblethwaite, *The Council Fathers and Atheism*, p. 41.

2 *Divini Hominis*, 54: "Communism is intrinsically wrong, and no one who would save Christian civilization may collaborate with it in any way whatsoever."

3 This was impossible to prove. In any case the sight of Pope John hob-nobbing with Khrushchev's son-in-law, Alexis Adjubei, probably struck the imagination more vividly. Ordinary Italians thought: If the Pope can be friendly with Communists, why shouldn't we? This caused Cardinal Ottaviani at the Holy Office to hit the roof. See Peter Hebblethwaite, *John XXIII, Pope of the Council*, pp. 481–84.

tance out of all proportion to its size: by its very existence it showed that the Church had something to learn from atheists and those who opposed her. This was of decisive importance in the development of schema 13, the future *Gaudium et Spes*.[1]

The Jesuits played a key role in helping the fledgling Secretariat for Non-believers take wing.[2] The election for the new Jesuit General was on 22 May 1965. The 220 delegates began praying in the chapel at 6.35 a.m. and by 11.40, at the third ballot, they elected Pedro Arrupe, Basque, former Provincial in Japan, the twenty-ninth *praepositis generalis Societatis Jesu.* Soon known in the Jesuit Curia as Don Pedro, he was shocked to find they lacked the most elementary means of communication (telex at that date) that he had already installed in Japan.

Paul VI was the first to be informed of Arrupe's election. He arranged a lengthy audience for the first free date in his diary: noon, 31 May 1965. Paul VI said: "You speak Spanish, and I'll reply in Italian, and in that way we'll understand each other."[3] In fact they spoke French:

> *Paul*: I know that the Society is at my disposal; I can count on thirty-six thousand soldiers under my orders.
> *Arrupe*: That is precisely what I was going to say to your Holiness: I want to place the whole Society under your command. You can ask what you will, because obeying you is an essential part of our Institute.
> *Paul*: Yes, I want to use the Society, but not abuse it. You understand this will involve some sacrifices.
> *Arrupe*: Which? We are ready to carry them out.
> *Paul*: I'll tell you once the Council is over.
> *Arrupe*: As for the struggle against atheism, I accept what you said on the day of the audience with the fathers of our General Congregation. Has your Holiness anything more precise to ask of us?
> *Paul*: Yes, I have more to say. I will tell you after the Council.

1 Peter Hebblethwaite, *The Council Fathers and Atheism*.

2 If I may allow some personal memories to intrude here, Provincials sometimes off-loaded their trouble-makers on to the Roman Curia. One early member of the Secretariat was a Californian Jesuit who pulled a revolver on his superior to bend the poor man to his will – successfully. The gun was empty. A Lebanese Jesuit travelled the world for the next decade claiming to have been charged by the Holy Father with the mission of devising a new name for the Secretariat, since "Non-believers" seemed so negative and uncomplimentary. His patient work bore fruit in 1988 when the humble Cinderella of the Secretariat was transmuted into the Council for Dialogue with Non-believers.

3 Pedro Miguel Lamet, *Arrupe*, p. 272.

Arrupe: Anything else?

Paul: Yes, the Society should commit itself to forming lay-people so they can do what the Council asks of them. This is absolutely necessary, and without it there will be dangers. But I'm completely confident about the work of the Society.[1]

Arrupe emerged happy and smiling.

It was good to have the Jesuits on his side. But Paul had to think about others who did not always agree with him. At Pentecost, 6 June 1965, Archbishop Marcel Lefebvre released a thunderous document about the "Trojan horses" which, he believed, had successfully infiltrated the Church.

The modern world had entered the citadel of Catholicism, said the Superior General of the Holy Ghost Fathers (as he then was), through the pernicious doctrine of collegiality; but happily the worst effects of collegiality had been averted thanks to the *nota praevia* which he described as "a truly celestial message which eliminates juridical collegiality". The traditional doctrine of the Church had been thus, at the last gasp, saved. It remained to do battle against religious liberty, which threatened to overturn the sound Catholic doctrine that error has no rights. If Lefebvre had known about Paul VI's meetings with John Courtney Murray or Canon Pierre Haubtmann, he would undoubtedly have sniffed out yet another Trojan Horse.

There was no particular reason why Paul VI should have paid any attention at this date to Archbishop Marcel Lefebvre. He was not as notorious as he later became. But Paul already knew that Lefebvre, far from being alone, was the tip of a considerable iceberg. How big it was could be deduced perhaps from the 430 Council Fathers who had signed the petition calling for a condemnation of Communism.[2] If it was a minority, it was a sizeable one, with allies within the Roman Curia.

There was work for Cardinal Franz König this summer. On 12 July 1965 Cardinal Jöszef Mindszenty celebrated the fiftieth anniversary of his priestly ordination. The Hungarian Primate, appointed on 2 August 1945, was given a life sentence on trumped up charges in 1949. He had known three days of freedom in the "counter-revolution" of 1956, since when he had been immured in the US Embassy in Budapest. König, who had the use of an Austrian diplomatic passport, went not as an emissary of the Vatican but as the Archbishop of Vienna visiting a

1 Ibid.

2 Giuseppe Colombo, p. 38.

brother bishop.[1] König brought Mindszenty Paul's gift of a gold chalice and a "cordial letter".[2]

This was not König's first visit to Mindszenty. He first went to Budapest in 1962 at Pope John's request. When he tried to explain just how difficult it was to get to the Hungarian capital, John simply said, "All you have to do is go to the station, buy a ticket to Budapest, and set off." In the end, that is what he did.

Mindszenty greeted him with "*Quid desiderat Summus Pontifex*?" (What does the Supreme Pontiff want?) The pontiff wanted to invite him to the Council. But then, as on subsequent meetings, it soon became evidence to König that Mindszenty had not the slightest interest in the Council, could not see the point of it, and intended to stay put in Budapest as a conscientious thorn in the side of the Hungarian government.[3]

By his fiftieth anniversary celebrations of 12 July 1965 Mindszenty had reason to feel suspicious. For on 15 September 1964 Archbishop Agostino Casaroli had signed an agreement with the Hungarian Ministry of Cults giving the Pope the right to name bishops but with government approval, and on catechism for children under eleven years.[4] Mindszenty, out of touch with his own Church, was excluded from this deal.

Mindszenty was now under pressure from all sides. The United States administration wanted better relations with the Hungarian government and asked the Holy See to remove this awkward cuckoo in the embassy nest. The Holy See needed him out just as much as the Americans because he was an obstacle to *détente* and "dialogue". But Paul wanted Mindszenty to leave freely. Pope John had tried to sweeten exile with the promise of a curial career. Paul realized this would make this obstinate old man, haunted by a sense of injustice, even more resolved to remain where he was. So long as he stayed he was a symbolic figure, to be exploited by the 430 Council Fathers seeking an explicit condemnation of Communism. So Mindszenty played a part in the Council, and may be said to have contributed to *Gaudium et Spes*.

Throughout the summer of 1965, mostly spent at Castelgandolfo, Paul VI jotted down notes on the general theme of "concluding the Council". Intended to help towards speeches he had to make, they some-

1 Franz König, *Where is the Church heading?* Interview by Gianni Licheri, St Paul Publications, Slough 1986, p. 68. Eng. tr. of *Chiesa dove via?* Borla, Rome 1985.

2 Jöszef Mindszenty, *Memoirs*, Weidenfeld and Nicolson, London 1974, p. 117. The original German title was *Errinerungen*. The "cordial letter" described by Mindszenty is not in *Insegnamenti*.

3 König, op. cit. p. 69.

4 Achille Silvestrini, "*L'Ostpolitik de Paul VI*", in *Notiziario*, 20, p. 73.

times reflected his reading and the way his mind was working. I will summarize them briefly.

He had read the book of Yves Congar and Pierre Dupuy on *L'Episcopat et l'Eglise Universelle*; Robert Rouquette in *Etudes* "especially on the reform of canon law"; von Pastor's *History of the Popes*, volume IV, on "Adrian VI and the Catholic responsibility for the heretical reaction of the Reformers"; and St Thomas Aquinas in the *Summa Theologica* on the "passions", notably his discussion on whether "union is the effect of love" and whether "love is a passion". He wondered whether he should follow up the idea of Msgr André Baron and be present at all the sessions, "not however presiding, and not intervening except on special occasions". None of these considerations had any effect on the speeches of the final session.

Nor did his attempts to draw up a balance-sheet (or *bilan*) of its achievements. "The council must come to an end," he noted, "it began spontaneously and it must end spontaneously. Much has been done, but much remains to be done." He made notes on particular questions:

> About the Jews: all antipathy and oppression (*vessazione*) on grounds of religion [or race] must stop. Sympathy for their religious election, of which Christianity is the heir and guardian, also for their promises and hopes. Not too much looking backwards so as not to be balked in offering them loyal friendship.

On ecumenism generally he recalls Pope John's principle: the Church's house has been rebuilt. So what he has to say essentially to the separated brothers is: "This is your home" (*Ecco la vostra casa*).

But Lefebvre's attacks had made him nervous and anxious again. In a note for his farewell speech he stresses the dangers of "laxist and progressist tendencies etc." and is inclined to warn bishops to be "vigilant and to be teachers". When bishops are exhorted to be teachers this is invariably a reminder that they should lead their flock in faith, not follow them. He distinguished the three psychological moments of the Council thus: "1) enthusiasm; 2) the critical phase; 3) the promise (fidelity to the truth, unity, acceptance, paligenesis? etc.)." I have no idea what he meant by the last cryptic phrase.

Yet, although Paul VI hoped the Council would end as spontaneously as it had begun, there was still much hard work to be done to achieve the desired result.

26

The Council Vindicated and Triumphant

Certainly the Council has been a great event. It is such a new beginning in the life of the Church that it will force everyone to speed up.

(CARLO CARRETTO, *Letters to Dolcidia*, HarperCollins 1991, p. 147)

You have to run twice as fast as you possibly can in order to remain where you are.

(LEWIS CARROLL, *Alice in Wonderland*, quoted by Bishop Christopher Butler OSB)

The fourth and final period of Vatican II began on 14 September 1965, the feast of the Exaltation of the Holy Cross, and ended on 8 December, the feast of the Immaculate Conception, one of the two Marian dogmas not accepted by Protestants or the Orthodox. It had its own very special character. No more postponements or deferrals. Few grand speeches in the *aula*. Blocks of solid voting with nothing much to do, while, off-stage and invisible, the Council commissions hammered the documents into acceptable final shape. Pressure groups made their appearance. It was the last-chance tidying up session.[1]

Paul VI inaugurated it in a new more fraternal style, entering St Peter's on foot – instead of on the *sedia gestatoria*, wearing a simple cope instead of the heavy papal dalmatic, a mitre rather than the tiara, and carrying a crozier designed by himself. No one could think of any

1 It was also the moment when the author enters the story, arriving in Rome to report the Council for *The Month*, the British Jesuit magazine. So from now on some first-hand impressions will come from my own observations. It helped to be part of the team described by Robert Rouquette SJ: "Every evening a small group of editors of reviews met, late into the night, in the hospitable Roman house of *Civiltà Cattolica* whose serenity we disturbed. With the aid of a *peritus* or a bishop, we pooled information, passionately discussed the events of the day, we reported on meetings we had had, and compared our reactions. It was an incomparable observation post." *Vatican II, la fin d'une Chrétienté*, I, Cerf 1968, p. 12.

good reason why popes should not carry a crozier. Paul joined the collegial ranks of the bishops, enthroning the book of the Gospels himself as a symbol of its primacy. His address was on the need for charity all round.

Even more than the bishops, Paul was thinking ahead to the post-conciliar period that would soon be upon them. "Post-conciliar" or *dopoconcilio* is not just a chronological marker: it indicates the spirit of an historical period. Thus the Church after the sixteenth century Council of Trent was the *Tridentine* Church, just as after Vatican I it was the monarchically centralized Church that lasted till the 1960s. So what happened in the two months before Christmas 1965 would shape the life of the post-conciliar Church . . . until the next Council.

With so much hanging upon it, the final session got off to a bad start. On its eve Paul VI issued an encyclical, *Mysterium Fidei*, which denounced dangerous errors in Eucharistic theology. Some theologians – mostly Dutch or Flemish – had taken to talking about "transfinalization" or "transignification" (meaning that the bread and wine changed their *purpose* or their *meaning*). These terms, noted the encyclical, fell short of the "transubstantiation" defined by Trent. True: but that observation left the problems raised by Aristotelian metaphysics intact, and anyway Trent said merely that transubstantiation "aptly expresses" the mystery, not that it exhausts it.[1]

Enough of *Mysterium Fidei*. It has an *ad hoc* feel.[2] It does not bear Paul's personal stamp. It was the work of Augustinian Fr Agostino Trapè. It made little impact and sank without trace.

Its main result was to put some *periti*, notably the Canadian Augustinian Gregory Baum, in a bad mood. When a Council, the living embodiment of collegiality, is in session, why was the Pope going it alone? Perhaps he was reminding the Council that collegiality did not

1 The matter is discussed by Edward Schillebeeckx OP in *The Eucharist*, Sheed and Ward, London 1968. The following reflection on *orthodoxy* is poignant: "Orthodoxy, the true orientation towards the reality of faith, is essential to faith, for the good reason that a Christian does not believe what he pleases, but what God postulates in Christ as reality of salvation and thus defines as the mystery of faith. Of course man, listening in faith and therefore also interpreting in faith, is himself in history, and his interpretation of what he hears is consequently also coloured by his situation. And this never gives the individual the right to call a fellow-Christian "unorthodox". How can I judge another's orthodoxy when I myself can have no human or critical certainty about my own orthodoxy and can only firmly *hope* for this by virtue of God's grace?" The Holy Office, on the verge of reform, would have trouble with this notion of hoping for orthodoxy.

2 *Ad hominem* might be more accurate. An unverifiable rumour said that it was a response to a lecture given by Edward Schillebeeckx OP at IDOC, via Santa Maria dell'Anima 30, the Dutch information centre, which by the fourth session had an international role. It was the scene of some memorable encounters.

abolish the primacy; it was an application of the *nota praevia*: "As supreme pastor of the Church, the Sovereign Pontiff can always exercise his authority as he chooses, as is demanded by his office itself" (4). Of course he *can*, said Bishop Christopher Butler, but *should* he? But this explanation of *Mysterium Fidei* was essentially frivolous. Paul VI did not engage in such arm-wrestling.

A new character trod upon the international Church stage: feminism – or rather that Catholic version of it prudently called ecclesial feminism. The St Joan's International Alliance, founded by two English suffragettes in 1911, held its General Assembly in Rome on 14 September 1965. It was the first time that feminists from Europe and North America had met. They passed resolutions in favour of the ordination of women to the diaconate and the priesthood, and on access to theological studies. They scored a great coup when Fr Jean Daniélou SJ, who had written articles in favour of the diaconate for women, attended their reception and called for "deeper research" into the matter of priestly ordination for women. This was code for saying that a question should be opened up.

However it was not opened up in the *aula*, and women barely got a look-in even in *Gaudium et Spes*. They are mentioned in the company of the starving and labourers as a group who "claim for themselves an equity with men before the law and in fact".[1] The argument for feminine invisibility was that, of course, women were intended every time *homo* and *homines* were used. Archbishop Paul J. Hallinan of Atlanta, Georgia submitted a written intervention in October which showed the ease with which women's concerns could have been attended to. He criticized the dismayingly negative way married women were classed in the liturgy as "neither virgins nor martyrs" (*nec virgines nes martyres*).[2] None of his suggestions were heeded, with the result that from the feminist point of view, *Gaudium et Spes* represents a missed opportunity.

It was as though theologians of the Roman school could not bring themselves to say the simple things about the equality of women and men because to concede it would deprive them of their sole argument against women's ordination. In *L'Osservatore Romano* Gino Concetti OFM piled up anti-feminist quotations from the Fathers and insisted that respect for the very order of creation and salvation demanded the

1 *Gaudium et Spes*, 9. This is a feeble echo of *Pacem in Terris* 40–41 where Pope John speaks of three positive "signs of the times" in the modern world: the ending of colonialism, the "improvement in the economic and social condition of working men", and women's "increasing awareness of their dignity".

2 Archbishop Paul Hallinan, in *Acta Concilii Vaticani II – Periodus IV*, pp. 754–58. This contribution deserves to be better known.

exclusion of women from ordination. Above all, it should not be explained by the cultural conditions prevailing at the time of Christ.[1] It was "ontological" – in the very nature of things. *L'Osservatore Romano* does not have a letters page, so that was, unsatisfactorily, that. Women were not taken seriously.

But these were noises off. During the summer Paul VI had taken the decision to make the post-conciliar Church less monarchical and more collegial. In his opening address he announced

> the setting up, in accordance with the wishes of the Council, of an episcopal synod of bishops to be chosen for the greater part by the episcopal conferences and approved by us, which will be convened, according to the needs of the Church, by the Roman pontiff, for consultation and collaboration when for the general good of the Church this will seem most opportune to us.

He added that the Synod would be of great use to the Roman Curia in its day-to-day work. The Curia need not feel threatened. He promised further details "as soon as possible".[2] Applause.

There was even more vigorous applause for his announcement – kept to the end – that he would be going to the United Nations in New York (*Consilium Nationum Unitarum in sua Neo-Eboracensi sede*) as a witness to peace. It was the first anyone had heard of this visit. Another well-kept secret.

The details about the Synod were released the next day. Manifestly, the *motu proprio*, *Apostolica Sollicitudo*, setting it up was already written. Pericle Felici, the Council Secretary, read it out in the Pope's presence, while Cardinal Paolo Marella expounded its meaning.[3] It was the old Felici–Marella double-act again. They had obviously worked on the draft.

Apostolica Sollicitudo[4] thus fulfilled Paul VI's immediate aim of starting the final session with a concession (as he saw it) to the progressive majority, crestfallen by the "black week" at the end of the previous session.

1 Gertrud Heinzelmann, "The Beginnings of Ecclesial Feminism", in *The Catholic Citizen* (Journal of St Joan's Alliance), 1991, No. 1, pp. 15–17. Dr Heinzelmann is the author of *Wir schweigen nicht laenger*.

2 *Insegnamenti*, 1965, p. 470.

3 ASCV, vol. IV, pars I, p. 65.

4 AAS 57 (1965), pp. 775–80. Trs. in Walter Abbott, *The Documents of Vatican II*, pp. 720–24. The Code of Canon law, canons 342–48, codifies and to some extent supersedes it. *Christus Dominus*, no. 5, also refers to the Synod of Bishops.

It had some excellent features. It was established on a permanent basis ("by its nature perpetual"): so it would be difficult to suppress. The vast majority of its members – all but 15 per cent – were to be *elected* by episcopal conferences. Three types of synod were envisaged: ordinary, extraordinary and special, corresponding to different needs.

But whichever type of synod is envisaged, the "sovereign will of the pope" appears with the utmost clarity. The Pope calls the Synod when and as he chooses, confirms its membership, determines its agenda, appoints its president and secretary, decides how its results are to be communicated, settles where it will be held and presides over it through his delegate. In short, it would be "immediately subject to the Roman Pontiff" (article 3).

Nevertheless, as envisaged by *Apostolica Sollicitudo*, the Synod was not a completely toothless and spineless creation. Though not a decision-making body, there was the hope that it might become one some day: "By its very nature the task of the Synod is to inform and give advice. It may also have deliberative power, when such power is conferred upon it by the Sovereign Pontiff." Further, its elective system guaranteed a relative autonomy, and its purposes could not be ensured without some freedom of speech.

Paul VI in *Apostolica Sollicitudo* produced a diplomatic compromise designed to satisfy the bishops at the Council without offending the Roman Curia too much. "The Synod," he remarked wistfully, "like all human institutions, can be still more perfected with the passage of time." In effect Paul VI said: "You may have your synod, but on my terms, and perhaps the infant will grow up in time."

The burning issue of religious liberty was not a question on which compromise was possible. It was touch-and-go right up to the last minute. If the pragmatic Americans sought urgent action, the French wanted a sweeping theological statement, while the "Spaniards" worried about their Concordat which forbade Protestant "proselytism". Cardinal Siri declared that "error" could have no rights since God, at best, could only "tolerate" it. Back in the real world, Josef Beran, Archbishop of Prague, talked about the execution of Jan Hus at the Council of Constance in 1411 as "the hidden trauma of the Czech Church". The right-wing group, the *coetus internationalis Patrum*, used every procedural device, fair and foul, to impede it.

The crunch came on 20 September 1965. A meeting of the Central Co-ordinating Commission, the Moderators and the General Secretariat, considered three options:

1 an indicative vote on the declaration in principle, according to a formula proposed by Cardinal Bea;[1]

2 a vote only on certain key points;

3 no vote at all.

It was a stormy meeting. The "conservatives" said Bea's question was too obscure, the "progressives" thought the second solution highly dangerous, and that if there were no vote at all it was difficult to see how this could be the final session of the Council. Patience was wearing thin. Spellman emerged angry.

The one thing the Commission agreed on was that they would accept the Pope's decision. Late on 20 September, Msgr Angelo Dell'Acqua summoned Cicognani, Tisserant, Agagianian and Felici for a meeting in his study next morning at 9 o'clock.[2] This was cutting it fine. The Council was already in St Peter's, where the Eucharist was being celebrated. After that they would move towards the sixty-second speech on religious liberty. At the meeting in his study Paul, after listening to everyone, decided that there should be a vote, using the wording suggested by the Commission the previous day; second, he decided that "*bravi teologi o comunque esperti* [decent theologians or other experts]" should take part in the work of revision. He included John Courtney Murray in his list.

Paul had taken a stand. There was nothing Hamlet-like about his crisp, clear, even peremptory intervention. Someone noticed that Tisserant (Council president for the day), Agagianian (one of the *moderatores*), and Felici (Secretary of the Council) arrived very late for Mass. Agagianian asked, on a standing/sitting vote, whether they were ready to close the debate. Massive exhausted approval. Felici, even more like a headmaster than usual, then invited the Council fathers to take out their pens (or biros) and copy down to his dictation a question: Do you accept this draft as the basis for the definitive text? The result of this vote, the first of the final sesssion, was 1997 *placet* against 220 *non placet*, with a solitary null vote. Felici superfluously congratulated the Pope for *Mysterium Fidei*, for the *moto proprio* on the Synod, and for going to New York. More applause.

This was one of the most decisive "interventions" of Paul in the

1 Bea's formula: "Does it please the Fathers, while firmly maintaining revealed doctrine on the one true religion for all, that it should be declared there exists a natural right to religious liberty, founded on the dignity of the human person and to be recognized in civil law, according to the doctrine expounded in the *schema* which will be further improved according to the observations of the Fathers? Long-winded, perhaps, but not obscure.

2 Vincenzo Carbone, "Il ruolo di Paolo VI", in *Rapporto Chiesa-Mondo*, p. 162.

work of the Council. It was not just that he needed this vote in order to go to the United Nations, though that was true. The difference between Paul at the third and the fourth session was that he had by now personally studied the question in greater depth.

The visit to the United Nations and the United States was remarkable in many ways, first of all for its length: less than one day. The Alitalia jet left Rome at 4.30 a.m., raced the sun across the Atlantic, landing at Kennedy Airport in the crystal light of a brisk October morning, and departed for Rome after dusk that same day. The date, 4 October, the feast of St Francis of Assisi, the *poverello*, was chosen by Paul for its symbolic potential: Francis, patron of Italy, peace and ecology, the most Christ-like of saints, was loved by all. Francis, moreover, had tried to reach out to Islam and stop the Crusades. Paul was well aware of the thirty-seven Arab nations at the UN and the war that was brewing up between India and Pakistan over Kashmir.

Paul looked about him with delight as he drove in a bubbletop limousine through Harlem and Central Park to St Patrick's Cathedral. He had chosen the long way round. This was his visit to the local Church, the Church in New York. A glittering social occasion, with the Kennedys in the front row, a radiant Jaqueline still among them, it allowed Cardinal Francis J. Spellman to play host to the Pope he'd known since the 1930s. There was a touching moment when Paul offered his arm to support the ageing Spellman. Spellman noticed that sore throats seemed to be afflicting the papal suite: Amleto Cicognani, the Cardinal Secretary of State and sometime Apostolic Delegate in the US, Antonio Samoré and Angelo Dell'Acqua of the Secretariat of State, Egidio Vagnozzi, present Apostolic Delegate to the US, Msgr Pasquale Macchi, Paul's personal secretary, and the new man – six-foot-four ex-football player Msgr Paul Marcinkus.

So much was crammed into this thirty-six hour day, and since he was the first reigning pope to visit the United States everything he did was "historic". Outstanding was the first meeting between Pope and President on US soil, if a hotel room at the Waldorf Towers Hotel may be so earthily described. Johnson had wanted to go to the airport – but then it would have seemed the Pope had come to visit *him*, not the United Nations. It was potentially a most tense encounter because of the Vietnam War. Neither Johnson nor his cabinet colleagues could go anywhere without being shouted down by anti-war demonstrators.

The President wanted to dispel the impression that he was a rabid war-monger. His war was the war on poverty, he claimed. As if to prove the point while Paul VI was *en route* President Johnson spent the morning discussing school desegregation with Chicago's Mayor Richard

Daley, after which he advised his daughter, eighteen-year-old Luci Baines, a Catholic convert, on how to dress for the Pope.

At 12.40 Pope and President began a fifty-minute conversation, in the company of the President's press secretary Bill Moyers, and Marcinkus on hand to help out if need be. "The talk was insubstantial," sniffed one critic, "and was marked by a great deal of mutual admiration."[1] True, sincere though it was, Paul's language could soar away into the stratosphere: "When men of the spirit look to men of public affairs for guidance, it is people like the President who serve the world, not only with ideas but with action." Or perhaps he just meant that while he had no divisions at his command, Johnson presided over a superpower. There were no subtleties in Johnson's unstinting praise of Paul's quest for peace.

For one commentator, Pope and President had a similar approach to comparable problems:

> The Pope's task of completing the *aggiornamento* (updating) of the Church is at least as formidable as the President's desire to turn a rich and powerful nation into a "Great Society". Each man uses a similar technique, that of reassuring opponents and maximizing his "consensus". The Pope worries about being practical, the President worries about being right.[2]

On this occasion President Johnson worried needlessly about introducing his daughter Luci to the Pope. Then he accompanied Paul down to his limousine on Park Avenue, a gesture unforeseen by protocol that was widely taken as evidence of the warmth of their relations.

Then to the United Nations. This was the encounter of the modern Church with the modern world, *Gaudium et Spes* realized. It put an end to the nineteenth-century Syllabus of Errors era in which the Church, as the last of its temporal power faded, condemned democracy and modern civilization, creating a fortress Church with drawbridges pulled up. With *Pacem in Terris* Pope John XXIII had broken out of the fortress and addressed all "men of good will", whether believers or unbelievers. The encyclical had been enthusiastically received at the UN when it was presented by Cardinal Suenens in May 1962. Pope John had earned the respect of the Communist nations, especially Soviet Russia. U Thant, a Buddhist from Burma, Secretary-General of the UN, was well-disposed and believed that religion could be a factor for peace.

1 Roy Domenico, "*The Vatican, the US and Vietnam in the Johnson Years*", a paper delivered 13 October 1991 at the conference on Vatican Diplomacy in the Nineteenth and Twentieth Century, University of New Brunswick, Canada. pp. 15–16.

2 John K. Jessup, "Pope Paul's Magnificent Risk", in *Life*, 15 October 1965, p. 56A.

In this setting Paul VI delivered the speech of his life, a thirty-minute address for which thirty years in Vatican diplomacy had prepared him. He was cordial, discreet, human and radical in the sense of going to the deepest roots of the institution.

He first established his "title" for being there at all. He did not claim any authority over the UN. He was not some mediaeval pope asserting his power to ban kings and depose emperors. From the tribune of the United Nations he presented the Church as an "expert in humanity".[1] The Church had a right to speak in virtue of its centuries-long experience of building community and discerning where the true progress of humanity lay. So the aims of the Church and the aims of UN overlapped.

At Kennedy Airport he had made this explicit:

> We are happy to note the natural sympathy existing between these two universalities, and to bear to your terrestrial city of peace the greetings and good wishes of our spiritual city of peace. One is a peace which rises from the earth, the other a peace which descends from heaven, and their meeting is most marvellous: justice and peace have kissed one another. May God grant that this be for mankind's good.[2]

Before the UN Paul was too discreet to appeal to God directly. But this passage expressed his underlying theological idea, which was close to Karl Rahner's thesis: the implicit "christology from below" made up of human hopes and aspirations is met and fulfilled beyond expectations by the "christology from on high" that Christians call Revelation. This also provided the ground-base of *Gaudium et Spes*.

In the UN speech this rich idea was implicit. Paul spoke in the name of the millions who had perished in the wars of the twentieth century, of those who painfully survived and of today's young people "who legitimately dream of a better human race". He spoke in the name of "the poor, the disinherited, the suffering, of those who hunger and thirst for justice, for human dignity, for freedom, for progress". He felt, he said, "like a messenger who, after a long journey, finally succeeds in delivering the letter that had been entrusted to him".

There followed a more juridical section on the originality and aims

1 *Insegnamenti*, 1965, pp. 507–16. Tr. in Rynne, *The Fourth Session*, pp. 285–91. No detailed references will be given. I have modified the translation.

2 *Insegnamenti*, 1965, p. 528. This message was delivered in English. Msgr Alberto Giovanetti, then a member of the Holy See's UN delegation with observer status, once told me that the main UN speech was delivered in French because the Pope's English rendering of the word "peace" gave rise to misunderstanding and merriment. But he got away with it at Kennedy. Giovanetti was on surer ground when he said that Paul had difficulty in understanding what "hawks" and "doves" were. He heard "orks and duffs".

of the UN, which made a distinctive contribution to international thought. It raised the sights of the UN which had so often become the scene for angry displays of petulance. The UN was not yet the instrument of international peace-making its founders intended; yet it provided the basis for a new world order in a world that modern communications and jet-travel had united as never before. He did not use the phrase "new world order" (with or without capitals) but that is what he meant in speaking of "an orderly and stable system of international life".

Obviously the UN did not *create* nation-states or what he preferred to call "sovereign national communities"; but it recognized and legitimated them. This was a crucial step towards political maturity: for most people in history had lived under empires and this was still true at the start of the twentieth century. The UN's repudiation of "imperialism" and "colonialism" was the obverse of its granting of "equal citizenship in the international community". So far, of course, the equality was more *de jure* than *de facto*. "You are not equal," said Paul, "but here you make yourselves equal." For some – he meant the superpowers – this would imply a self-denying ordinance:

> For several among you, this may require an act of high virtue. Let me say this to you as the representative of a religion that believes salvation is achieved through the humility of its divine Founder. Men cannot be brothers if they are not humble. It is pride, no matter how legitimate it may seem, that provokes tension and struggles for prestige, domination, colonialism, egoism. Pride disrupts brotherhood.

This was a way of stating "the secular meaning of the Gospel", a phrase which Harvey Cox popularized at the time.

It was the basis for the most famous phrase of the speech: "*Jamais plus la guerre! Jamais plus la guerre!*" (Never again war!)[1] He set it alongside John F. Kennedy's remark four years before: "Mankind must put an end to war, or war will put an end to mankind."

The march of humanity – here he spiked the guns of the colonels – must be towards peace. That would require the UN to develop a systematic pedagogy of peace. It had four elements:

1. "Relations between states should be governed by reason, justice, law, and negotiation – not by war, fear, violence or deceit."
2. This could not be done without disarmament: "If you wish to be brothers, let the arms fall from your hands. You cannot love while holding offensive weapons."

1 Ibid. p. 511.

3 The money saved from renouncing expensive weapons – what was later called the "peace dividend" – should be devoted to aid for the developing nations and solving the problems of hunger and famine.
4 Yet people had deeper desires than not starving. The UN proclaimed "fundamental human rights and duties, human dignity and freedom – above all religious liberty."

With that simple phrase, Paul sent a message to the Council. Human dignity, *dignitas humana*, would provide the key concept (and the opening words) of the decree on religious liberty. Only religious freedom is consonant with human dignity.

The same principle governed "respect for human life", and here he broached the most "controversial" theme of his address:

> You deal here with human life, and human life is sacred; no one should dare assault (*attenter*) it. Respect for life, in regard to the great problem of natality, should find here in your assembly its highest affirmation and its most reasoned defence. Your task is so to improve food production that there will be enough for all the tables of mankind, and not press for an artificial control of births, which would be irrational, so as to cut down the number of guests at the banquet of life.[1]

Some were shocked at this contemptuous dismissal of the population-problem. But Paul wanted to make sure that attack on poverty did not become an attack on the poor; and it was "controversial" only for those who expected change in the Church's teaching: in 1965 *Casti Connubii* was still officially valid, even though the Pontifical Commission was sitting. But the passage contained the key concept, *humana vita*, and, once again, the first words of the document that would eventually enshrine this position for good or ill.

Paul VI concluded with two discreet allusions to scripture. Isaiah 2:4 on beating swords into ploughshares could appeal to Jews and Muslims as well as Christians. Finally he said he did not want to disguise his faith in the God in whom he believed,

> that unknown God of whom St Paul spoke in the Areopagus or market-place to the Athenians. Unknown to them, though without realizing it they sought him; and he was close to them, as happens to many in our time. To us, in any event, and to all who accept the ineffable revelation that Christ has given us, he is the living God, the Father of all.

He had found the right balance between grandeur and simplicity, rhet-

1 *Insegnamenti*, 1965, p. 514.

oric and sincerity. He made an historic event a moving and human event.

Perhaps he should have gone home then. But at eight o'clock New York time, 3 a.m. on his internal clock, he was saying Mass in the Yankee Stadium. As this was an all-American occasion, I will leave its description to *Life* magazine:

> As he drove slowly around the field, as the wind fluttered his embroidered vestments, while he stood at the altar under the gold-colored canopy, applause drew huge circles of sound around him and the explosion of flashbulbs in the crowd of 90 thousand was a constant celebratory barrage of winking fireworks.
>
> He said Mass with great dignity in a baseball field, and when it was over he blew his nose against the cold. As the Pope circles the cinder track around the playing field, standing up in the open limousine to bestow blessings, a delirium sweeps over the crowd. There are cries of *Viva il Papa!* wave upon wave of foot-stomping, and cheers match any evoked here by a Ruthean home run.[1]

And what did he say? "God bless America," he cried, "God bless you all."

At ten o'clock – now 5 a.m. on his internal clock – he wearily visited the Vatican exhibit at the World Fair: Michelangelo's *Pietà*. Then it was the night flight home.

The visit was a tremendous success. Schoolchildren had a holiday. The streets of New York were jammed with thousands of families who applauded the Pope whenever he appeared. He responded with a wave that could also have been a blessing. Thousands of papal flags fluttered. Catholics felt proud of their pope, and had a lump in their throats.

But what did it all mean? Some said that if Pope John's key word was *aggiornamento*, Paul's motto was *avvicinamento*, coming closer to people. He had found a new way to address all people of good will. The Italian press was ecstatic, claiming variously that in the 119 members of the United Nations the entire world acclaimed the Pope and that a new era in Vatican diplomacy had begun. Certainly from now on there could be no doubt that Paul VI was, in the jargon of international politics, a "transnational actor", and more and more nations sought to get themselves accredited to the Vatican.

The friendly welcome from the United Nations, from President Johnson and from the people of New York, made the visit a public relations

1 *Life*, 15 October, 1965, Loudon Wainwright was one of the writers. "Ruthean" refers to "Babe" Ruth, a legendary New York baseball player.

triumph. Considered as a way of making known the Church's positions on controversial issues of war and peace, population and resources, and perhaps convincing some, the visit was a success in the eyes of the world.[1]

But its most important immediate function in the life of the Church was gently to steer the fourth session of the Council on the relations of the Church and the world, the Church and politics. Back in Rome a jet-lagged Paul was applauded all the way up the aisle of St Peter's towards the end of the morning session.[2]

By a remarkable piece of timing that was certainly no coincidence, the Council began discussing the final chapter of *Gaudium et Spes*, on war and peace, on 5 October, the very day Paul returned from the UN. The debates went on for three days.

There was much here that could embarrass the US government, and consequently US bishops like Cardinal Spellman who still enjoyed the title of military ordinary or chief chaplain. In paragraph 98–101 the draft raised questions about the horrors of modern warfare, conventional versus atomic weapons, war crimes, just and unjust wars, the "balance of terror" and MAD (Mutually Assured Destruction), the morality of *possessing* nuclear weapons as distinct from their use, the danger of escalation in warfare, the right to conscientious objection and the need to "humanize" war by respecting "the rules of humanity". The draft called for international action to avoid war, stressing in particular the need for a "public authority wielding effective power at the world level".

After the papal visit to the UN there was only one candidate for this role. In the 1930s the Holy See had been suspicious of the League of Nations, seeing it not only as ineffectual but as a rival. Now all that was changed. The chapter in *Gaudium et Spes* on "Building up the International Community" (83–90) committed the Church to working with the United Nations and its agencies. No other Church or religion has done that.

Paul's next intervention was to forbid a conciliar debate on clerical celibacy. The ban was conveyed in a letter to Cardinal Eugène Tisserant dated 10 October 1965 and read out in the Council the next day. It said: "It is not opportune to debate publicly this topic which requires

1 Roy Domenico, Upsala College, NY, "The Vatican, the US and Vietnam in the Johnson Years", a paper delivered 13 October 1991 at Kingsclear Conference, University of New Brunswick, Canada.

2 This was the first time I set eyes on Pope Paul VI. I was seated next to Barbara Wall, novelist (as Barbara Lucas) and member of Pax Christi. To fill in the time of waiting we indulged in cardinal-spotting. Barbara, godmother to my wife, remarked on how handsome the African cardinals were.

the greatest prudence, and is so important. Our intention is not only to preserve this ancient law as far as possible, but to strengthen its observance."[1]

Again there was no Hamlet-like hesitation about Paul's negatives.

Msgr Paul Poupard, then working in the Secretariat of State, tried to explain this decision, much criticized as "arbitrary". Bishops had written "beseeching the Pope to remove this question from the Council agenda". Poupard explains:

> Their motive was the fear of allowing the public appearance of divisions which would have serious consequences for priests, who were not all that solid (*souvent fragiles*); and also the fear that, in view of the pressure from the mass media, their interventions on this subject would not be free.[2]

That sounds fine: celibacy was removed from the Council's competence at its own request. Paul merely "responded" to a conciliar initiative.

But this edifying interpretation does not hold water. Poupard omits to say who these anonymous bishops were. They included the *Coetus Internationalis Patrum*, shadowy figures like Msgr Dino Staffa and Archbishop Marcel Lefebvre who felt the Council had done enough damage already. So Paul had made yet another concession to the minority.

That the requests came from this source is evident from the two arguments adduced in its favour. If avoiding public disagreements was the norm, the Council would never have discussed any new question at all. Again the judgement that priestly celibacy was so fragile that it would be put in jeopardy by the mere fact of discussing the ordination of married men revealed an astonishing lack of confidence in priests. The upshot was that Paul conceived an encyclical on the subject. Thus a papal monologue on clerical celibacy replaced the dialogue that never was. And celibacy joined contraception as the second topic subtracted from the Council's agenda.

Artificial contraception, however, could not be entirely ignored in *Gaudium et Spes*' treatment of marriage. Indeed the Council Fathers were liberated by Paul's decision to remote it from their competence. They could present the case for a positive, post-manichaean view of responsible sexuality and marriage as a community of love; and thus, without saying so in so many words, prepare the ground for change.

The Pope's worries came out (or so it was believed) in a speech by Cardinal Giovanni Colombo, his successor in Milan. Colombo, while

1 ASCV, 4, 1, p. 40.
2 *Modernité* p. 292.

claiming to accept "without any problem the schema's fully human and personalist approach", warned about separating "love" or "mutual comfort" from "the possibility of procreation". He wanted no equivocation on this point.[1]

Thus two "ends" of marriage were conjoined: making love and making babies were two aspects of the very *meaning* of sexual intercourse. That is so close to *Humanae Vitae* that one wonders whether the Bishop of Rome was not speaking here through the successor of St Ambrose and St Charles Borromeo, Giovanni Colombo.

His namesake, Carlo Colombo, who was even closer to Paul, issued warnings as late as 19 November that the draft chapter on marriage, though beautiful and uplifting, failed to tell priests what to say in the confessional.

If these warning signals had been read more carefully, the "papal bombshell" that burst on 24 November would have been less of a shock. The Mixed Commission engaged on the final revision of schema 13 met at 4.30 in the afternoon with Cardinal Alfredo Ottaviani in the chair. Time was pressing. Further revisions could go only in the direction the Council had already voted on. They had to be ready by 29 November to allow time for the chapter by chapter vote on *Gaudium et Spes* on 2 December and the final, global vote on 6 December. Tight deadlines, requiring much midnight oil.

All this action was taking place out of sight of the two thousand bishops of the Council, and *a fortiori* of the journalists. In the privacy of the Mixed Commission, its secretary, Fr Sebastian Tromp SJ, read out a letter from the Cardinal Secretary of State:

> I announce to you that the August Pontiff desires that, in virtue of the office and authority which are yours, you inform the Commission . . . that there are certain points which must of necessity be corrected . . . concerning the section which treats of "promoting the dignity of marriage and the family".

It then demanded explicit mention of *Casti Connubii* and Pius XII's address to midwives. It went on:

> Secondly, it is absolutely necessary that the methods and instruments used to make conception ineffectual – that is to say, the contraceptive methods which are dealt with in the encyclical *Casti Connubii* – be openly rejected; for in this matter admitting doubts, keeping silent or insinuating that such opinions

1 ASCV, 5, 3, p. 34.

> may perhaps be admitted, can bring about the gravest dangers in public opinion.[1]

Four *modi* or amendments accompanied the polysyllabic pomp of the letter showing how these dangers might be averted. The main one would list *artes anticonceptionales* (birth-control techniques) along with polygamy, divorce, free love and other *deformationes* which plagued marriage.

Consternation! It was like the *nota praevia* again. The section on marriage had already been approved by the Council by 2052 to 91 votes. Was this the dirty tricks department at work? Was the letter genuine? Even if it was, did Paul really intend to *impose* these amendments without discussion or was he *proposing* them for last-minute consideration? Were they designed to pre-empt the decision of the special commission? Did it mean winding up the papal commission and declaring that birth-control was no longer an "open question"? That would have been a great victory for the minority, who naturally drew that conclusion. Cardinal Michael Browne, the Irish Dominican, exclaimed, *Christus ipse locutus est* (Christ himself has spoken).

That was not strictly true. Between 17 and 21 November the sub-commission dealing with marriage considered the final forty amendments. The chief spokesmen for the "minority" hardline position were Fr Ermenegildo Lio OFM, author of the rejected pre-conciliar *De Castitate* draft, and Fr John Ford SJ. Carlo Colombo was also present, trailing a certain aura of authority as "the Pope's theologian". No doubt he played a part in this story. But it was Ford who saw Paul and told him bluntly that "the silence of the Council on *Casti Connubii* would in effect be its repudiation".[2]

That explains the papal *modi*. Stylistic grounds and the fact that Fr Ford chose to publish it on the eve of *Humanae Vitae*, suggest that he was the author of the letter and Fr Lio drafter of the *modi* which bear an uncanny resemblance to his rejected *De Castitate*.

The puzzled Mixed Commission met again on 25 November to consider what to do. They were in the pilgrim's refectory in the Santa Maria palazzo, without heat or microphones. The acoustics were as bad as the tempers. To Cardinal Paul-Emile Léger it was evident that the *modi* pre-empted the decision of the birth-control commission, depriving it of any function or meaning. The alarmed lay auditors wrote a letter to Paul

1 Published for the first time by John C. Ford SJ and J. J. Lynch, "Contraception: a Matter of Practical Doubt", *The Homiletic and Pastoral Review*, April 1968, p. 563.

2 Philippe Delhaye, "Dignité du mariage et de la familie", in *L'Eglise dans le monde de ce temps*, vol. II, p. 418: "*Le P. Ford fut reçu alors par le Saint-Père et fit valoir que le silence du Concile sur* Casti Connubii *passerait pour un désaveu.*"

warning him of the effect on public opinion of a simple reaffirmation of *Casti Connubii.* Ramon Sugranyes de Franch set off with Cardinal Maurice Roy to deliver their letter to the Pope. They reached the Secretariat of State – a cardinal cannot be denied entry – and handed the letter to Msgr Angelo Dell'Acqua who promised it would be on the Pope's desk in ten minutes.[1]

Tempers improved by the afternoon session partly because Cardinal Ottaviani found a heated room with better acoustics for their meeting. The Pope replied by letter that "in sending the amendments he had not wished to impose a definitive formulation, still less to settle the question of artificial contraception that was still being studied. So the Commission was free to express in the most appropriate way the positions he had taken."[2]

It would have been better for everyone's nerves had he said that twenty-four hours earlier. So now he was taken at his word, and they judged the *modi* on their merits. "Contraceptive arts" became "illicit practices against human generation", which was tautological.[3] *Casti Connubii* would be cited, but in a footnote and flanked by Paul's address to the cardinals describing the origin of the Pontifical Commission and its purpose.[4] On the "ends of marriage" they finessed and stopped short of giving priority either to love or procreation. And they included a reference to conjugal chastity.

As the final session drew to a close Paul had a series of meetings with bishops from different countries. *Christus Dominus*, which they had massively approved on 28 October, gave the Episcopal Conference (which acquired the dignity of capital letters) the green light:

> An Episcopal Conference is a kind of council in which the bishops of a given nation or territory jointly exercise their pastoral office by way of promoting that greater good which the Church offers mankind, especially through forms and programmes of the apostolate that are fittingly adapted to the circumstances of the age.[5]

1 Georges Cottier OP, "*Interventions de Paul VI*", in *Paolo VI e il rapporto Chiesa-Mondo*, pp. 28–29. Sugranyes concluded that Paul VI was definitely *not* the source of the original amendments. Later in the conference Cottier tried to withdraw this suggestion, p. 178, which had been "gravely deformed by news agency reports".

2 Antoine Wenger, *Vatican II: la quatrième session*, pp. 188–89. In papal style the Pope speaks of himself in the third person singular.

3 *Gaudium et Spes*, 47.

4 Walter Abbott, ed., *Documents of Vatican II*, p. 256 fn. 172. Msgr Charles Moeller explains: "Normally, conciliar texts have footnote references only to biblical, patristic, scholastic or pontifical sources . . . That is why this unique footnote is famous." Quoted in Georges Cottier, op. cit. p. 28.

5 *Christus Dominus*, 38, 2.

This was a radical change. Under St Pius X the Holy See had been suspicious of assemblies of bishops, so much so that in France it was said "there are bishops but no episcopacy".

Now in 1965 centralization gave way to a certain autonomy, a limited autocephaly. The Episcopal Conference became the way the local Church, rediscovered in *Lumen Gentium*, expressed itself. The Episcopal Conference could also be seen as collegiality in action.

In these farewell meetings towards the end of the Council Paul exhorted the episcopal conferences to commit themselves to conciliar renewal, and in particular to be generous in sending *Fidei Donum* priests to what was beginning to be known as the Third World (a scheme in which Eastern Europe was the "second world" coming after the developed and industrialized G7 nations). Paul urged English and Welsh, Scottish and Irish bishops to send volunteers to Africa,[1] while French, Spanish and US bishops were to cope with the immense needs of Latin America. These exchanges would illustrate the unity of the Church and of planet earth or "spaceship earth" as it was called – the whole world having been excited by the view of the earth from the moon.

But the Polish bishops posed more sublunary problems. On 13 November 1965 Paul received thirty-eight of them. He could hardly believe his ears when in fluent Italian Cardinal Stefan Wyszyński addressed him thus:

> We are aware that it will be very difficult, but not impossible, to put the decisions of the Council into effect in our situation. Therefore we ask the Holy Father for one favour: complete trust in the episcopate and the Church of our country. Our request may appear very presumptuous, but it is difficult to judge our situation from afar. *Everything that occurs in our Church must be assessed from the standpoint of our experience* . . . If one thing is painful to us, it is above all the lack of understanding among our brothers in Christ.[2]

Paul, taken aback, coolly replied that no doubt the Council would be implemented "energetically and willingly" in Poland as elsewhere. He resented the suggestion that only a Pole can understand Poland. As he surveyed the Polish bishops before him, he wondered whether the Archbishop of Kraków, Karol Wojtyla, the only serious intellectual in the group, might fulfil the task his Primate deemed so difficult.

1 Thomas Holland, *For Better and for Worse*, p. 291. Within six months of this appeal, fifty priests were on their way.

2 Hansjakob Stehle, *Eastern Politics of the Vatican 1917–1979*, pp. 341–42. My italics. The principle stated by Wyszyński, if true, must apply to all other Churches as well.

Yet Wyszyński, the heroic confessor of the faith, had earned the right to speak for Poland. He believed that if in Poland there was the "Church of silence", which couldn't speak, in Rome he found the "Church of the deaf", which couldn't listen. Wyszyński did not think the Church was in need of reform. So he was unhappy with the Council. He was alarmed by its apparent lack of enthusiasm for popular devotions, for the mass processions and pilgrimages that were the staple of Polish piety. He was disconcerted by its understated mariology. He detested liturgical change, believing its effects would be unsettling. He thought the new-fangled "kiss of peace" would turn the church into a salon. As for "ecumenism", it was irrelevant in Poland, there being no interlocutors. In Poland religious liberty was something the Church claimed, not something it conceded to others. Above all, *Gaudium et Spes*' eagerness to "learn from the world" combined with its lack of any direct condemnation of Communism would, Wyszyński believed, sow confusion in his well-disciplined ranks.

In short, whichever way you looked at it, the Council had made life difficult for the Polish bishops. What the laity might think was another matter into which Wyszyński did not enquire. What made all this particularly disappointing for Paul was that he set his heart on a visit to Czestochowa, Poland's holiest shrine, for May 1966 to celebrate the millennium of Christianity in Poland. Msgr Achille Silvestrini, then in the Secretariat of State, worked on the planning for the Polish visit which, after the Holy Land, India and the United Nations would have "admirably completed the series of conciliar visits, inspired by the great texts of Vatican II".[1] Paul VI wanted very much to go to Poland, a Catholic country repressed since 1939, to dramatize the changed new situation of dialogue.

Rebuffed by the Poles, Paul found consolation in a Memo from Msgr Roger Etchegaray, Secretary of the French Episcopal Conference.[2] Dated 4 November 1965, the feast of St Charles Borromeo, it took as its starting point *Christus Dominus*, 38: "Contacts between episcopal conferences of different nations should be encouraged in order to promote and safeguard their higher good." Etchegaray was not, or not at the moment, proposing a European equivalent to CELAM, the Council of Latin American bishops set up in 1955, which had already proved its worth at the Council. He simply listed the exchanges already occurring in Europe that called for pastoral action: the migration of workers from the south to the north, the forty-five million holidaymakers who every

1 Achille Silvestrini, "*L'Ostpolitik de Paul VI*", in *Notiziario*, 20, p. 76.

2 Text in *I Vescovi d'Europa e la Nuova Evangelizzazione*, Preface, Cardinal Carlo Maria Martini, Introd. Hervé Legarnd OP, pp. 39–43.

year set off, usually in the opposite direction; the development of political and economic institutions which were creating a European "space" with recognizable characteristics.

The response to Etchegaray's "simple note" was encouraging. On 18 November 1965 the Presidents of thirteen Episcopal Conferences met and agreed to set up a committee to examine what forms their post-conciliar co-operation should take. This was the germ of the CCEE (Council of European Bishops' Conferences).

But Latin America received the lion's share of Paul's attention. The tenth anniversary of the foundation of CELAM fell in 1965. On 23 November 1965, in the Clementine Hall, Paul VI delivered a substantial "pastoral exhortation" to the Latin American bishops on the need for pastoral planning *on the continental level.* He had invited the president and vice-president of CELAM, Manuel Larrain, Bishop of Talpa, Chile, and Dom Helder Câmara, to contribute to the draft. So he knew the mood among the Latin Americans and sensed the gulf between the "progressive" Chile and Brazil represented by Larrain and Câmara and the benighted colonial conservatism of arch-traditionalist bishops like Sigaud who equated modest proposals of land reform with "atheistic Communism". Paul tried to coax them along, together.

The continent – the sleeping giant – was waking up. By the year 2000, Paul said, it would top 500 million and count more than half the world's Catholics.[1] Yet the gap between rich and poor was widening. Catholics had to become sensitive to justice, otherwise "the social messianism" of Marxism would prove attractive and promote "violent revolution".[2]

The Cuban revolution which brought Fidel Castro to power on 1 January 1959 was a watershed in Latin American history. Cuba had emerged from Spanish colonialism in 1898 only to fall under the domination of the United States. So Marxism apart, Cuba was seen as the place where "socialism" delivered the final knock-out blow to Yankee imperialism. Already there were rumblings of revolution among Latin American students in Louvain. The "remedy", Paul thought, was not sterile anti-Communism but that integration of faith and life that *Gaudium et Spes* recommends: "The Christian who neglects his temporal duties neglects his duties towards his neighbour and towards God, jeopardizing his eternal salvation."[3]

1 *Insegnamenti*, 1965, p. 655.

2 Ibid. pp. 656–57.

3 *Gaudium et Spes*, 43. The whole of Chapter IV, Part I was devoted to denouncing a false "dualism" that would lead Christians to shirk action for justice on the pretext of other worldly spirituality. Such "dualism" became the favourite target for liberation theologians.

Larrain and Helder Câmara stressed other aspects relevant to Latin America. Helder Câmara went about saying "Development is the number one problem of the Council" (by which he did not mean the development of doctrine). Larrain reminded Paul VI that "every year more people die of hunger and disease in the Third World than perished in the four years of the Second World War".[1] The conciliar debates on ecumenism and collegiality did not engage Latin Americans very deeply. Larrain warned Paul: "What we have experienced here in Rome is impressive, but unless we are attentive to our own signs of the times in Latin America, the Council will just pass us by."[2]

But there were two texts, voted on in this final session, which were decisive for the future of Latin America. The magnificent opening chord of *Gaudium et Spes* on the way the Church shared in the joys and hopes, the griefs and the anxieties of humanity, added "especially those who are poor or in any way afflicted" (*pauperum praesertim et quorumvis afflictorum*). From this slim launching-pad, the "option for the poor" could take off.

The second decisive text for Latin America was from *Ad Gentes* on missionary activity. To bear witness to the Gospel could lead "to the shedding of blood". Martyrdom was, in Tertullian's words, "the seed of the Church".[3]

Paul drew a number of conclusions from his meeting with the Latin Americans. First CELAM would have to organize an assembly that would act as "the Council for Latin America", and he would like to be present. Next he would stay in touch through CAL, the Pontifical Commission on Latin America, one of whose most influential members was Pedro Arrupe, the new General of the Society of Jesus.[4] Third, *Gaudium et Spes*, so radiant with paschal optimism about the Church's impact on the world, was weak on economic analysis and had not dispensed with further developments of papal "social doctrine". So the way was prepared for *Populorum Progressio* in 1967 and the CELAM conference at Medellin in 1968. The fourth conclusion was that new policies would require new bishops.

These meetings with the bishops from all over the world were an *au revoir*. He would see them again. But he said *adieu*, goodbye,

1 Gustavo Gutierrez, "*Le rapport entre l'Eglise et les pauvres, vu d'Amérique Latine*", in *La Réception de Vatican II*, ed. Giuseppe Alberigo and Jean-Pierre Jossua, p. 245.

2 Ibid.

3 *Ad Gentes* 24 and 25. Quoted by Guttierrez, op. cit. p. 255.

4 CAL was founded on 19 April 1958 as a Roman body to liaise with CELAM, co-ordinating and controlling its work. Sometimes it controlled more than it co-ordinated, but it was a necessary link in the chain of communion.

to the ecumenical observers on Saturday, 4 December at St Paul's-without-the-Walls. Paul VI orchestrated this meeting so that the great adventure of Council ended where Pope John XXIII announced it. If St Peter represents order and stability among the settled flock, St Paul indicates missionary outreach and the expansion of catholicity. So St Paul's was the right place.

No pope had ever taken part in an ecumenical service before. Pope John may have wanted to but did not because the decree On Ecumenism which made it possible did not exist. Paul experienced the round of prayers, psalms, lessons from scripture, intercessions, and hymns that became commonplace in churches throughout the world. The readers represented the three main Christian traditions: Sulpician Father Pierre Michalon, successor of Abbé Paul Couturier, who had dreamed of this day; Dr Albert Outler, an American Methodist, and the Archimandrite of Rome, Maximos Aghiogorgoussis, who read the Beatitudes according to St Matthew in Greek.

All of which was very touching. But old habits die hard and the day was very nearly wrecked by excessive papolatry. When Tom Stransky and John Long of the Secretariat for Christian Unity arrived at St Paul's to check the preparations they found that the monks had erected a papal throne of such mediaeval magnificence that it would have isolated Paul above everyone else. The abbot had to be persuaded that this was contrary to Paul's wishes. He reluctantly produced a straight-backed moderately ornamental chair and put it on ground-level.

Other difficulties were not due to misunderstandings but to Felici's ill-will and general surliness. The announcement of the meeting was made at the last minute, the *periti* (experts) were pointedly not invited, there was no time to bind a copy of the service booklet in buckram as tradition demanded. The last was a blessing in disguise: instead of a volume embossed with the papal arms, Paul had the flimsy little pamphlet to which Christians all the world over soon became accustomed.

Paul had intended to use this occasion to announce the lifting of the anathemas with Constantinople. Last-minute hitches meant he had to wait three more days, until 7 December. So in his address before the final prayer he drew up a simple *bilan* or balance-sheet of ecumenism. It was very positive.

"We would like to have you always with us," said Paul, and sounded convincing:

> We can first of all note an increased awareness of the problem [of ecumenism], a problem which concerns and binds us [*nous concerne et oblige*] all. We can add another fruit, still more precious: the hope that the problem – not today, certainly,

> but tomorrow – can be solved slowly, gradually, honestly and generously. That is a great thing!
>
> And this shows that other fruits have ripened too. We have come to know you a little better . . . Through you we have come into contact with Christian communities which live, pray and act in the name of Christ, with systems of doctrine and religious mentalities and – let us say it without fear – with Christian treasures of great value . . .
>
> We have recognized certain failings and common sentiments that were not good. For these we have asked pardon of God and of you. We have discovered their unchristian roots and have decided, for our part, to do what we can to transform them into sentiments worthy of the school of Christ. One proposes to give up polemics based on insulting prejudices, and not let vain prestige come into play. One tries rather to bear in mind the exhortation of the Apostle at whose tomb we are praying this evening, to avoid "quarrelling, jealousy, anger, selfishness, slander, gossip, conceit, and disorder".

The farewell to the observers ended with a parable, taken from "one of the great Eastern thinkers of modern times", Vladimir Soloviev. It has an autobiographical feel, which is no doubt why Paul remembered it.

A Russian intellectual (Paul calls him a "philosopher") was staying in a monastery to receive spiritual direction from a holy old monk. Their spiritual conversation went on so late into the night that the philosopher could not grope his way to the cell assigned to him. So, unwilling to disturb any of the monks, he paced up and own throughout the night, absorbed in thought:

> The night was long and drear, but at last it was over and with the first light of dawn the tired philosopher easily recognized the door to his own cell that he had passed time and time again throughout the night. He concluded: that is often the way with seekers after the truth. Awake, they pass it by without seeing it, until a ray of light from the divine Wisdom (Sophia) makes its disclosure as easy as it is consoling.
>
> The truth is near, beloved brethren. May this ray of divine light enable us to recognize the blessed door. This is our hope. And now let us pray together at the tomb of St Paul.

It was magnificent. Some of the observers, and many of the bystanders, were close to tears. This address was as important as the decree On Ecumenism for the entire ecumenical movement. For it represented the clear commitment of the Pope to implement it fully and without mental reservations. It involved a move from theology to action.

And it was really new. From the seat (*sedes*) that had issued mostly anathematas and denunciations since Hildebrand in the eleventh century came words of love. By the tomb of St Paul the schism of 1054 and the even more grievous conflict of the Reformation seemed, if not to fade away, then at least to be relativized.

Yet there were some dry eyes. Paul was criticized for quoting Soloviev who was received into communion with the Catholic Church by Fr Nicholas Tolstoy in 1896, four years before his death at the age of forty-seven.[1] But Soloviev's "conversion" did not involve a repudiation of the Russian Orthodox Church. It was a vision of all the Churches, under pressure from the anti-Christ, being brought together under the pope "just before the curtain is rung down on life in this world".[2] But one could not say that in Soloviev's parable the "door" was the Catholic Church. Paul VI counted himself among the seekers after truth, he prayed that "the divine light would enable *us* to recognize the blessed door".

Paul reserved another surprise for his final address to the Council. The proposal to canonize Pope John XXIII by acclamation, overleaping the usual channels, was on record. Dom Helder Câmara hoped it would bring down the final curtain on the Council and be the ultimate commitment to its implementation and spirit. But Paul VI's final curtain was a wet blanket: he devised the "diplomatic solution" of starting the processes of John XXIII and Pius XII simultaneously. The Franciscans got John and the Jesuits Pius.[3] The effect was to frustrate the majority who, while respecting Pius XII, had no particular desire to see him canonized. Nothing much happened.[4]

But the "good news" on this 7 December was the common declaration "lifting the anathemas" of 1054 signed by Paul and the ecumenical

1 Donald Attwater, Preface to Vladimir Soloviev, *God, Man and the Church*, Clarke, Cambridge 1957, p. ix.

2 Frederick C. Copleston, *Russian Religious Philosophy: Selected Aspects*, p. 53.

3 Kenneth L. Woodward, *Making Saints*, New York, Simon and Schuster 1990, pp. 295–96, has a plausible explanation for this attribution. The Franciscan postulator general, Fr Antonio Cairoli, was in charge of the cause of Cardinal Andreas Ferrari, one of Montini's predecessors in Milan. So it was "natural" that he should look after John XXIII, who had Ferrari as his spiritual director. Pius XII had put Jesuits in key positions, so it was "natural" they should look after his cause. Besides, the Jesuit postulator's father had also been a friend of Giorgio Montini.

4 It was on this topic – I think – that Cardinal Léon-Joseph Suenens said to me at the *L'età di Roncalli* conference in Bologna in 1984: "The trouble with Paul VI was that he thought there was a diplomatic solution to everything. He imagined he could split the difference. It can't be done."

Patriarch Athenagoras. Since the schism between Orthodox and Catholc, East and West, was a process rather than an event, it cannot be precisely dated: 1054 was a symbolic date; but by the same token, so was 7 December 1965. Cardinal Augustin Bea read out at this final session of the Council the *tomos* which was simultaneously being read in the patriarchal church in Constantinople. It said:

> Among the obstacles which exist on the way towards the development of brotherly relations of confidence and esteem [between the Churches], we find the remembrance of the decisions, acts and painful incidents which led in AD 1054 to the sentence of excommunication published against Patriarch Michael Cerullarios and two other persons by the legates of the Roman see, headed by Cardinal Humbert; the legates were then subjected to a similar sentence issued by the Synod of Constantinople . . . We must recognize today that the sentences were directed at particular persons and not at the Churches, and did not aim to break ecclesiastical communion between the sees of Rome and Constantinople.[1]

In short, 1054 had been an accident, much ado about nothing very much, frozen into permanent schism only by later "non-theological" events like the sacking of Constantinople by the Crusaders in 1204.[2]

So the dispute with Cerullarios was not really about papal primacy. Anyway Humbert had exceeded his authority. The lifting of the excommunications paved the way for Paul's historic visit to Constantinople in 1967. In Church language, to call something "symbolic" is to enhance its importance, not diminish it.

The Council was over. Its last act was to issue "messages" to rulers, intellectuals, women(!), the poor, sick and suffering, workers, and young people. These were "delivered" in St Peter's Square on a sunlit 8 December, the feast of the Immaculate Conception, and "received" by appropriate people. Jacques Maritain got the message to intellectuals. "We'll only know what the Council really means," said Gregory Baum as we left the square, "in twenty years time."

1 *Insegnamenti*, 1965, p. 735. See John Meyendorff, "Rome and Orthodoxy: Authority or Truth?" in *A Pope for All Christians*, ed. Peter J. McCord, SPCK, London; Paulist 1976, for an Orthodox view.

2 Humbert of Silva Candida's ham-fisted document condemned "the supporters of Cerullarios' folly" while praising the orthodoxy of the emperor and citizens of Constantinople. This was a crucial point. The bull described the Emperor and citizens of Constantinople as "very Christian and Orthodox", even though their idea of the Roman primacy "was certainly closer to that of Cerullarios than, shall we say, to Vatican I". See Joseph Ratzinger, *Tablet*, 9 November 1991, p. 1379.

Paul was alone again. The Council and his visit to the UN had empowered him. Before the year was out he appealed for a Christmas truce in Vietnam and, though the tone of voice was rather grating, showed he could communicate with ordinary people in words of direct eloquence:

> Dear children, the word which comes to our lips for this weekly greeting is the hope of a good Christmas: a good Christmas for the city of Rome; a good Christmas for the whole Church, for the whole world.
>
> But we must tell you that our mind is full of sadness because of the many divisions and struggles and antagonisms which disturb humanity and in various places give rise to conflicts between peoples. Among them is Vietnam, a country which is very dear to us and which has its own place in civilization. The war in Vietnam is becoming more serious and more bloody. The number of combatants grows, as does the number of victims, the piteous mass of refugees, and the danger of wider conflagrations.
>
> Where is peace? Where is the human and Christian Christmas? We have heard of negotiations to resolve the conflict mentioned. We know of certain proposals for a truce at least for the blessed day of Christmas. And we know of many statesmen of good will who are seeking to resolve the difficult situation. But we also know that millions of hearts tremble, suffer, and wait for the return of peace . . .
>
> Unite, dear children, in a prayer of hope: that Mary, with Christ, the centre of Christmas, may show herself as Mother and Queen of Peace, *Regina Pacis*.[1]

There was a Christmas truce in Vietnam, a little glimpse of *gaudium et spes*.

1 *Insegnamenti*, 1965, p. 1155. The phrase about "those seeking to resolve the conflict" was a veiled reference to Giorgio La Pira, Christian Democrat and former mayor of Florence, who had seen Ho Chi Minh in Hanoi in November 1965 and come back with what he thought was a peace plan. Mario Primicerio, a Florentine professor of mathematics, who accompanied La Pira to North Vietnam, said that La Pira "frequently exchanged views on international matters with Paul and Angelo Dell'Acqua". See Roy Domenico, "The Vatican, the US and Vietnam in the Johnson Years", a paper delivered 13 October 1991 at Kingsclear Conference, University of New Brunswick, Canada.

27

Moved, Anxious, Happy

A Pope lives from crisis to crisis, from moment to moment. He goes, like the Hebrews in the desert, from manna to manna. And he has not much time to look back on the road he has travelled, or forward to the way that lies ahead.

(JEAN GUITTON, *Dialogues avec Paul VI*)

With the Council over, the pontificate of Paul VI could begin to take shape. He had more plans for travel. After three symbolic journeys – to the Holy Land, to India and to the United Nations – the next journey would be a foray into a Communist country. Poland was celebrating its millennium, the baptism of its first ruler Miesko in 966. He knew Poland from his 1923 stay. He would expect a tumultuous reception at Czestochowa. But all this depended upon the *agrément* of the Polish government. Feelers were put out.

The ending of the Council changed the mood in the Roman Curia. Some were glad it was all over, and felt that the waters would now flow in again and cover over this four-year-long aberration. Now that the foreigners (*questa gente da fuori*) had gone home, order would be restored and the Council would be safely neutralized. Cardinal Alfredo Ottaviani, still in place at the Holy Office, took this view: "You go home, but we remain."

Instead of removing Cardinal Alfredo Ottaviani, the baker's son from Trastevere who had been kind to him in the 1930s, Paul tried to "balance" him by appointing Msgr Charles Moeller, the Belgian polymath and author of a remarkable four-volume work, *Le Salut dans la Littérature Contemporaine* (Salvation in Contemporary Literature), as under-secretary of the Congregation.

Moeller, however, could make little impression on an organism that had its own routine. The Holy Office continued to act on denunciations and listen to those for whom the Council might just as well never have happened. For example *La Gente*, the Opus Dei paper in Mexico, attacked Sergio Mendez Arceo, Bishop of Cuernavaca, for his defence of Freud and Marx at the Council, his laxist views on Protestants, Jews and Freemasons, and above all for harbouring "that strange, devious and slippery personage, crawling with indefinable nationalities, who is called, or claims to be called, Ivan Illich".[1] Illich was sent a silly questionnaire.

The last paragraph contains an anachronism. The Holy Office no longer existed. With a motu proprio, *Integrae Servandae*, issued on the crowded last-but-one day of the Council, Paul changed its name to the Congregation for the Doctrine of Faith (CDF). But since the address remained the same, via del Sant'Uffizio, and the same melancholy fountain continued to plash in the forbidding building to the left of St Peter's, few noticed the difference. Yet it was a very important reform. Quoting 1 John 4:18 ("perfect love casts out fear") Paul said that "today the defence of faith is better provided for by encouraging good theology".

So the new name, Congregation for the Doctrine of Faith, was intended to accentuate the positive and to encourage rather than repress. It was to hold study sessions on disputed questions: though this plan was never realized, the idea of the International Theological Commission was not unrelated to it. In the last resort the Congregation still had the role of "fraternally correcting errors", but that was not its main task. Ottaviani blandly announced that he had yielded:

> The procedure has been changed . . . The accused has a greater chance to defend himself, to express his own opinion and have it discussed. We have returned to the procedure envisaged by Benedict XIV. We have to admit that in the course of centuries the Holy Office had departed from that procedure and substituted an authoritarian approach. It was unfortunate that this happened.[3]

"Unfortunate" was an understatement. Since Benedict reigned from 1740 to 1756 one can say it had taken an unconscionably long time to implement the procedure so wisely "envisaged" in the age of Enlightenment.

The trouble with Paul's reform of the Holy Office was that it had to be implemented by the very people who had all along resisted it. "It was," said Charles Moeller, who represented token change, "like asking the Mafia to reform the Mafia." It was easier to abolish the Index of Forbidden Books.

All over the "free world" the Council documents were being trans-

1 Francine du Plessix Gray, *Divine Disobedience*, p. 269.

2 In 1992 it was changed to via Paolo VI.

3 Interview in *La Gente*, an Italian weekly, 13 April 1966.

lated, studied and commented upon. Paul welcomed the comprehensive multi-volume *Commentary on the Documents of Vatican II*, edited by Herbert Vorgrimler. Books were written exploiting the new "insights" of Vatican II. In Eastern Europe, however, there was silence. Poland was intent on its millennium celebrations, and little was known about the Council texts until Archbishop Karol Wojtyla published *Sources of Renewal* in 1972.[1] Even then he stressed what the Council reaffirmed rather than any new emphases.

Paul knew that the Council documents could not of themselves effect change. The Council had to be applied and translated into practical terms. Each conciliar text needed to be complemented by a commentary or directory which turned it into practical guidelines for action. For example the "Norms for the implementation of the decree *Perfectae Caritatis*, on the appropriate renewal of religious life", appeared on 6 August 1966. Given that there were over a million religious women at this date, *Ecclesiae Sanctae* was an immensely important document. Religious life was to be renewed in the light of three criteria: fidelity to the Gospel; the charism or special grace of the founder; the needs of the modern world. The principle that "all the members of an institute must be involved in the renewal of that institute", though it did not mean democracy, certainly involved much consultation so that general chapters would be responsive to the stirrings of new life. The Jesuit 31st General Congregation, having elected Pedro Arrupe in 1965, was due to resume its second session on 20 August 1966, just in time to consider the implications of *Ecclesiae Sanctae*.

The drafting of these implementation documents was not entrusted to the Curia which, left to itself, would simply revert to type. Paul had promised that the local Churches would be involved as well. He had to solve an administrative problem with theological dimensions, or a theological problem with managerial dimensions; both were true. St Paul thought there was a "charism" of administration. He needed it now.

But Poland began to grip his mind. The Polish bishops had prepared for 1966, the celebration of a thousand years of Christianity in Poland, with a "novena of years", in which the icon of Our Lady of Czestochowa would be carried from the Tatras Mountains to the Baltic.[2] The millennium was to be crowned in May 1966 with a great celebration at Czestochowa presided over by Paul, and with representatives of all the world's

1 Karol Wojtyla, *U Podstaw Odnowy*, Polish Theological Association, Kraków, 1972, tr. P. S. Falla, *Sources of Renewal*, 1980.

2 Achille Silvestrini, "*L'Ostpolitik de Paul VI*", *Notiziario*, 20, p. 76. This was the first time details of the planning for the Polish journey were disclosed.

Churches present.[1] Paul very much wanted to go, both to encourage the Church in Poland and to show that a new sort of relationship with the Communist regimes was possible.

But there had always been a problem with Wyszyński. Like other East European bishops, he was not enamoured of the Council and thought it would make life difficult at home by encouraging progressives like the *Znak* group and the "clubs of Catholic intellectuals". He did not like laymen like Tadeusz Mazowiecki taking an independent line on political questions. The situation of the Polish Church was unique in the Eastern bloc: there were the full complement of seventy freely appointed bishops, priests in abundance, no restrictions on religious orders and the sense of embodying the culture and history of the nation.

In dealing with the regime Wyszyński believed this could be achieved more by tough confrontation than by diplomatic negotiations, which he despised. He held that what he called "thunderstorms" – gigantic Church–State rows – "cleared the air". Paul and the Secretariat of State urged him to be more accommodating. They feared that his aggressive guerrilla tactics, though effective in the short-term, would weary Polish Catholics who were not all capable of following their Primate's heroic lead. Then they might turn against the Church, and succumb to the secularization that happened in industrial societies even without the help of Communism.

At the end of 1965 the Polish bishops – in effect Wyszyński – released a statement about their reconciliation with the German bishops. This praiseworthy initiative, however, was done without any consultation either with the Polish government or the Vatican. The Polish government was very angry and refused Wyszyński a visa for Rome in January 1966. It also meant that the plans for a papal visit to Czestochowa for the millennium celebrations of Christianity in Poland had to be scrapped. Hansjakob Stehle noted:

> Wyszyński was less unhappy about this than most Catholic Poles. He alone – vested with the office of papal legate – now dominated the millennium celebrations, and the demonstrations of strength by millions of Poles; he alone won this new trial of strength, and he alone concluded the next informal and provisional truce.[2]

1 Ibid.

2 Hansjakob Stehle, *Die Ostpolitik des Vaticans*, Piper, Munich 1975, p. 379. ET *Eastern Politics of the Vatican 1917–1979*, p. 344.

It was splendidly heroic, but it made the Vatican scared.

At this point Paul had the idea of making Karol Wojtyla, Archbishop of Krakow, the second Polish cardinal in the hope that he might counterbalance the Primate. He had made some good, if obscure, speeches at the Council; he was the leading thinker among the Polish hierarchy; he was becoming well known in Rome thanks to his presence on various committees, though he was an irregular attender and tended to miss important meetings. He could always plead visa problems. Or he may have preferred to stay at home for the millennium. Paul made him a cardinal the following year.

On 4 October 1966, the feast of St Francis of Assissi and first anniversary of his visit to the UN, Paul issued *Christi Matrem*, the least well-known of his encyclicals. He had hoped to promote the feast of St Francis as a day of peace. He certainly sounded convinced. He desperately wanted to do his utmost for world peace. "Those in whose hands rests the safety of the human race," he wrote, "must examine their own consciences . . . [and] come together for sincere negotiations."[1] He sent Archbishop Sergio Pignedoli, his former auxiliary in Milan, now apostolic delegate in Canada, to Vietnam to urge the Bishops to compromise.

Such sentiments seemed feebly defeatist to certain sections of the United States Church. A glance at the diocesan press, which reflected episcopal views, illustrated the clash of opinion. The "hawks" were symbolized by the Los Angeles *Tidings* (strong on the "domino" theory and the "Better dead than Red" argument) and the *Guardian* of Little Rock, Arkansas, which saw the war as a "crusade" against "the forces of evil at work on all sides, threatening the destruction of civilization."[2] The "doves" included the *Catholic Voice* of Oakland, California, which urged the cessation of bombing and withdrawal from South Vietnam, while the *St Louis Review* pointed out that the war rendered the United States increasingly friendless in a hostile and violent world.

Pignedoli's mission to Vietnam and Hanoi failed. For ever after he was reluctant to discuss it at all. When he did, he stressed its pastoral rather than diplomatic nature. But since the Vietnamese bishops were clearly unwilling to listen and regarded Pignedoli as a meddler in their affairs, he failed on the pastoral level too. Hanoi pronounced his efforts

1 Roy Domenico, "The Vatican, the US and Vietnam in the Johnson Years", p. 18.

2 John G. Deedy, jr, "The Catholic Press and Vietnam", in *American Catholics and Vietnam*, p. 122. The Catholic Press reflected the views of the hawkish Fr Patrick O'Connor, who covered the war in Vietnam for NC News Service, the bishops' official news agency. Most diocesan papers ran his column. Only newly founded *National Catholic Reporter* had its own correspondent, the young Michael Novak (p. 127).

"pathetic".[1] There was no question, however, of Paul VI blaming Pignedoli for this. He knew he had given him an impossibly difficult mission. Perhaps someone more independent of the Holy See like Giorgio La Pira, the visionary mayor of Florence, might succeed where Pignedoli had drawn a blank.

No formal link between La Pira and Pope Paul existed. But Paul knew about the journey and frequently discussed international affairs with him.[2] La Pira claimed to act "in the spirit of the Church" and that his actions "always had the Pope's seal". Paul announced, meanwhile, that he had heard rumours of impending peace initiatives and praised "those who loyally act to solve the menacing conflict". This no way meant that La Pira was a Vatican emissary. Acting on his own, he possessed the virtue of deniability.

This was just as well, for the US media guyed La Pira, presenting him condescendingly as a Dom Camillo character, a bumbling, bungling amateur out of his depth in the tough world of international diplomacy. To some extent these same criticisms were carried over to Paul VI. Like La Pira he was well-intentioned, well-informed and claimed the high moral ground: but what business did he really have to qualify for superpower negotiations. There was the suspicion, moreover, that the Holy See, though firm enough on Communism in Europe, was inclined to be softer on it in Asia.

This was not President Johnson's view. He received Msgr Paul Marcinkus at the ranch: Marcinkus brought a letter from Paul urging a ceasefire and an end to the bombing. "LBJ," writes Joseph A Califano, jr, his top aide in domestic policy, "wanted the Holy Father to help nudge the Vietnamese to the negotiating table."[3]

When travel plans are thwarted, you can compensate by being a good host. In 1966 the world came to Paul VI. The visit that made history was that of Michael Ramsey, Archbishop of Canterbury, on 23–24 March 1966. On 2 December 1960 Dr Geoffrey Fisher became the first Archbishop of Canterbury since the Reformation to visit a pope. The last visit of *any* archbishop of Canterbury was that of Arundel in 1397.[4]

Compared with the Ramsey visit, the Fisher visit of 1960 had been a hole-and-corner affair and treated like a guilty secret. No photographs

1 Roy Domenico, op. cit. p. 18.

2 Ibid. p. 20, citing Mario Primicerio, a Florentine mathematics professor.

3 Joseph A. Califano, "The President and the Pope: LBJ, Paul VI and the Vietnam War", *America*, 12 October 1991, pp. 237–39. This article is an extended version of a section of *The Triumph and Tragedy of Lyndon Johnson – the White House Years*, Simon and Schuster 1991.

4 Owen Chadwick, *Anglican Initiatives in Unity*, p. 103.

allowed. No public words were exchanged. The *Daily Mail* published a cartoon with the heading: "The picture we could not take." "Behind those famous walls," one frustrated TV commentator was reduced to saying, "history is being made." Even so, Dr Fisher spent sixty-seven minutes with Pope John – very long by the standards of a papal audience; and as late as September 1966 the Lambeth Palace staff felt astonishingly that Ramsey was "less enthusiastic about relations with Rome than his predecessor".[1]

Though there was only five years between the visits it seemed more like five hundred years to Colonel Robert Hornby, the Archbishop's press secretary on both occasions. If the formidable walls did not come tumbling down, the gates were wide open. While Fisher had been received in the Pope's private library, Ramsey was welcomed in the awesome and humbling setting of the Sistine Chapel. "By your coming," said Pope Paul, "you rebuild a bridge, a bridge which for centuries has lain fallen between the Church of Rome and Canterbury." The image was an ancient one, and one of the Pope's titles, *Pontifex*, means precisely "bridge-builder". This was completed by the image of a house with an ever-open door: "As you cross our threshold, we want you especially to feel that you are not entering the house of strangers, but that this is your home, where you have a right to be."

That is the translation in the notes on the conversation between Pope and Archbishop written by Owen Chadwick. They go on:

> They were not naïve: Ramsey talked of the goal as a good way ahead, Paul VI talked of the bridge they were building as still rickety (*nondum satis firma*) and under construction. Ramsey pleaded that they should join in persuading the nations to disarm and to modify their insistence on national sovereignty.
>
> In the late afternoon they met again, for a private talk in the Pope's study, with only two helpers, John Findlow[2] and Msgr Willebrands.
>
> Characteristically Ramsey did not begin the agenda with Church politics, or with the friction between the Churches, or with ecumenical ideals, but with spirituality. He evidently

1 Owen Chadwick, *Michael Ramsey: A Life*, p. 314. Chadwick's explanation of this paradox is that the Evangelical Fisher was "a cheery man of common sense" who believed that "the difficulties between the Churches would be blown away if people were sensible instead of bigots", while the Anglo-Catholic Ramsey resented the way English Roman Catholics "proselytised" (as he saw it) among devout Anglicans.

2 Canon John Findlow replaced Bernard Pawley as Archbishops' representative in 1965. His wife, Irina, a Russian Orthodox Christian, wrote a moving *Memoir* after his premature death. Pawley felt that Ramsey was loath to "do anything" about Rome.

wondered whether the right way forward was through a growing unity in prayer. He raised the possibility that there might be joint retreats. He went on to say that on occasion lay people valued common worship (*communicatio in sacris*).

Pope Paul answered this with a sentence that no Pope before him would have spoken: "This is a sign from God, since the People of God expressed the Spirit of God."

They talked of the possibility of common forms of prayer, and a common translation of the Lord's Prayer and the Creeds. The Pope said that he already had people looking into these possibilities. Later in the conversation he returned to this theme. The two Churches venerated certain saints in common – he mentioned St Augustine of Canterbury, the Venerable Bede and Edward the Confessor. He said that he had visited Durham and Canterbury and mentioned St Anselm.[1] Ramsey reminded him how the tomb of Edward the Confessor in Westminster Abbey was still a place of pilgrimage for Roman Catholics.

Only then, after the question of common worship, did Ramsey turn to theology. Did there not need to be a joint commission of theologians? The Pope accepted the plan and they discussed how to start it. The Pope even suggested a name for the Roman Catholic side in the commission – the French Oratorian, Louis Bouyer. Ramsey said that he knew Fr Bouyer well. He "has written one of the best books on Newman".

This set the Pope off into a digression on the importance of Cardinal Newman's thought for our time. "I would like to honour him by publishing his works and spreading his thought."

What did the Pope mean? The doctrine of faith was not widely taught in Newman's form. The idea of the development of doctrine was vastly influential in reconciling Catholics with modern historical studies but the precise formulation by Newman was superseded. The *Idea of a University* is still a book which every minister of education should be forced to read before he takes office. The noble sermons of the early days at St Mary's in Oxford can still help the preacher – the sense of solitude before God, the moral response to the Christian vision, the feeling of the little child before God, and so much more. The historian would have liked Ramsey to have asked Paul

1 Owen Chadwick remarks: "Paul VI was learned in the study of St Anselm of Canterbury, and felt devotion towards that archbishop." *Anglican Initiatives in Christian Unity*, p. 104.

what he was thinking about. But he did not. Characteristically Ramsey said, "In my view it is Newman's spirituality that is particularly important."

Then Ramsey asked about Anglican Orders. Since Leo XIII's bull *Apostolicae Curae* of 1896 it was official Roman Catholic doctrine that the ordination of Anglican ministers was invalid and therefore their sacraments were null.

A year before, in March 1965, the Pope summoned John Findlow to a private audience. He told Findlow the matter was being studied again. "It is unlikely," he said, "that there can be any changes made in the decree of Pope Leo XIII. But it is always possible that the question can be put in a new light. It could be expressed in terms more pleasing to those whom it concerns . . . The winter, in which everything is cold, and which itself is often destructive, has now ended and we are at the beginning of spring and waiting for everything to burst into leaf and blossom."

This was a new kind of utterance for a pope, in that March 1966. Therefore Ramsey could raise the subject. The Pope said: "This is a question which gives rise both to suffering and to hope. It is necessary to study it in the broader context of the priesthood, the sacraments, the episcopate and the sacraments in general. An historical study led to a negative conclusion by Pope Leo XIII. I am ready to reopen the study of this question in a broader theological context."

So far all was harmony. Ramsey then raised the points where he was unhappy: the rebaptism of converts; the rigidity over mixed marriages. The Pope gave away little. He said that he would write to Archbishop Heenan that there should be no apparent minimizing of Anglican baptisms. He said that the joint commission which was now called ARCIC (Anglican/Roman Catholic International Commission) would be able to treat of marriage; and that meanwhile canonists would work on the problem. But he insisted that the Church needed to be strict over the form of marriage. He drew Ramsey's attention to the "openness" of the documents of the Second Vatican Council.

The meeting hardly resolved Ramsey's particular difficulties. The Pope conceded what to him must have been weighty, that the gulf over Anglican Orders might be less unbridgeable than was supposed. But this would be more important to Ramsey as a sign of charity than as a real con-

> cession: for Archbishops of Canterbury were by tradition contemptuous of any doctrine that a gulf about Anglican Orders needed to be bridged, and would resent the prospect of a commission of canonists weighing up what to them needed no weighing. The fact that in his extreme old age Pope Leo XIII acted unwisely and erroneously made a problem for the Church of Rome, not for the Church of England. The meeting gave the all-clear to ARCIC: a decision which in the event proved to be more fertile and far-reaching than anyone predicted.
>
> This meeting had another and hidden consequence. Ramsey formed more than a respect, he formed an affection for Pope Paul. No doubt personal affections weigh as feathers in the scale of ecclesiastical politics. But if we pause and consider when in history an Archbishop of Canterbury was on such terms with a pope – certainly not with Fisher and John XXIII, though both were outstanding men – we conclude that this was another new stage in the history of the Churches since the Reformation.
>
> Ramsey's personality and appearance made a big impression on the Roman people. They thought he looked like Pope John XXIII.[1]

The Romans also tended to confuse him with *Dottore* Sir Alf Ramsay, manager of the England World Cup squad, then preparing for victory in 1966 ("Gis' a smile, Sir Alf"). This did the Archbishop's reputation a power of good.

The day after the solemn meeting in the Sistine Chapel, the Bishop of Rome and the Archbishop of Canterbury prayed together in St Paul's-without-the-Walls. They came in side by side and sat, on the same level, close to each other. There were scripture readings, Psalms, Anglican hymns and a Common Declaration which entrusted to the God of mercy "all that in the past has been contrary to the precept of charity".

They made their own St Paul's words: "Forgetting those things which are behind, and reaching forth unto those things which are before, I press towards the mark for the sake of the high calling of God in Christ Jesus" (Philippians 3:13–14).

The carefully crafted Common Declaration had a phrase about bas-

1 Owen Chadwick kindly provided me with this hitherto unpublished document. It is based on the minute of the "private meeting" but "worked up" into more usable form. It presents the "Anglican" side of the meeting, at a time when Ramsey was still smarting from what he considered Cardinal Heenan's scandalous attempt to pre-empt the question of mixed marriages. The memorandum appears, in a more edited format, in *Michael Ramsey: A Life*, pp. 320–22.

ing the future dialogue on "the Gospels and the ancient common tradition". Many thought this was a typical "Anglican" insertion, designed to bolster their claim to continuity with the Saxon Church, but Ramsey later explained this was not so: "Those were Pope Paul VI's own words, which he thought to be right."[1]

Besides setting up ARCIC, the meeting also blessed the establishment of the Anglican Centre in Rome. It was not, as many supposed, a *pensione* run by the Anglican Church, nor did it minister to Anglicans in Rome, who were already provided for, nor was it an embassy, since embassies are to states.

It was something new – a permanent representation of the worldwide Anglican Communion in Rome, to be equipped with a first-rate library and thus permit Roman Catholics to study Anglican theology directly. "The Anglican student," said Dr Ramsey, opening the Centre, "is often a debtor to writers within the Roman Catholic Church: this Centre is an attempt to repay that debt by making available the resources of Anglican learning to any who will come and enjoy them."[2]

Next morning, 24 March 1966 Pope and Primate came together at the basilica of St Paul's-without-the-Walls.

Gift time: as ever the gifts exchanged on such an occasion were significant. Dr Ramsey gave Pope Paul a pectoral cross which he wore at the general audience and at the St Paul's service. Wherever he went, Archbishop Ramsey wore the ring the Pope gave him on leaving the basilica. In a private meeting with the students of the Venerable English College, where his party lodged, he was asked: "Do you think the English RC bishops are all they ought to be?" Ramsey raised his famous eyebrows ever so slightly. "They are all I *expect* them to be," he said, breaking into a chortle, Ha-ha-ha, hee-hee-hee.

As he prepared to leave the English College, cradle of so many martyrs, the students gathered in the courtyard gave him three rousing cheers: Hip-hip-hip hurrah! In response he threw his Canterbury cap high in the air.[3] And caught it as it came down. Bravo!

Extravagant hopes and cynical cold water were both out of place in judging the significance of this meeting. Paul struck the right note of cautious optimism the previous Sunday: "It is not yet a visit of perfect

1 Dale Coleman, ed., *Michael Ramsey, the Anglican Spirit*, p. 71. The book consists of notes taken during Dr Ramsey's lectures at Nashotah House, a US Episcopalian seminary in 1979.

2 *Newsletter* of the Friends of the Anglican Centre in Rome, Spring 1989, p. 3. Henceforward *Newsletter*.

3 This paragraph is based on first-hand memories of participants. The Italian press showed great and unsatisfied curiosity concerning the whereabouts of Mrs Ramsey. She was left at home.

union, but it is a visit of friendship and a beginning of union. Therefore we are moved, anxious, happy."[1]

The difference between the apologetic Fisher visit of 1960 and the Ramsey spectacular of 1966 can be attributed to the Council. It also marked the advance of the Secretariat for Christian Unity from a barely tolerated cuckoo-in-the-nest to an equal if not superior agency to the Holy Office.

Cardinal Bea had written an article on the significance of the Fisher visit in which he had not taken part; six months after the Ramsey visit, when the Anglican Centre, having been opened by the Archbishop of Canterbury in March, became fully operational, Willebrands uttered these carefully crafted words that he had certainly cleared with Paul VI:

> I think that the Bishop of Ripon [Dr John Moorman] in his speech this morning [at a papal audience] in saying that we shall find here in this Anglican Centre a means of exchanging and knowing our different traditions, said nothing other than what the Pope and the Archbishop of Canterbury already said when they spoke of *our common traditions*; indeed we have common traditions as well as traditions which have become divergent and which now separate us.
>
> I think that the Council's decree On Ecumenism which speaks of *Fratres disjuncti* (not joined) rather than *Fratres separati* (cut off) wished to bring out a nuance. "Cut off" means a break which goes to the root; "not joined" means there is a failure, a lack of full communion, but there remains communion on the basis of faith, baptism, of prayer and the Bible. There is a great deal that we all have in common. But let us remember, there are also traditions which separate us.

This is a sketch for the idea of "partial" or "imperfect communion" which was Paul VI's most personal and important contribution to ecumenism.

It posited a spectrum ranged from "full communion" to "non-communion", but allowed for many intermediate stages. All one could say in 1966 was that the Orthodox Churches were very near to full communion, while the Anglican Communion was distinctly closer to it than more "Protestant" Churches.

1 *Insegnamenti*, 1966, p. 945. This remark was made on 20 March, before the visit. Paul said he looked forward to two important visits in the coming week: before Dr Ramsey arrived he was due to make a state visit to Giuseppe Saragat, President of the Italian Republic. It was the feast of St Benedict, patron of Europe, and Paul also had a long conversation with the Prime Minister, Aldo Moro. Ibid. pp. 122–26.

Willebrands explained on 6 October 1966 how he saw the role of the Anglican Centre:

> I think that this Centre which is the immediate fruit of the visit of his Grace the Archbishop of Canterbury will contribute by research, by studies, by conversation to the dialogue which will be developed in the immediate future. It will contribute by personal contact, thought and prayer.[1]

If from now on the Anglican–Roman Catholic dialogue is not pursued in much detail here, that does not mean that it was not important. It was a fundamental dimension of Paul VI's pontificate.

No sooner had the Archbishop of Canterbury gone home than the "birth-control commission" met for two sessions, one in May and the longest, last and most fateful one in June. Anglicans were involved to the extent that *Casti Connubii* was written against the 1930 Lambeth Conference. But there is no hint in Owen Chadwick's account that it was discussed.

The final session of the commission was as important for its method as much as for its eventual decision. One of the married couples, Patricia and Patrick Crowley of the Christian Family Movement in Chicago, had five children and had used the calendar rhythm method with moderate success. The Crowleys' originality was to bring empirical evidence to bear on the discussion. While the theologians worked things out from first principles, they surveyed 3000 devout Catholic couples from eighteen countries, asking them whether the rhythm method, which all had tried, worked in practice and whether it helped or hurt the marital relationship.[2] This really was to open a Pandora's box of problems; yet theirs was the experience that counted.

The Crowleys summed up the evidence in this way:

> *Does rhythm have a bad psychological effect?* Almost without exception, the responses were, yes, it does.
> *Does rhythm serve any useful purpose at all?* A few say it may be useful for developing discipline. Nobody says that it fosters married love.
> *Does it contribute to married unity?* No. That is the inescapable conclusion of the reports we have received. In marriage a husband and wife pledge themselves to become one in mind, heart and affection. They are no longer two, but one flesh.

1 *Newsletter*, p. 5.

2 John Kotre, *Simple Gifts: The Lives of Pat and Patty Crowley*, Andrews and McMeel, Kansas City 1979. A popular book, but very revealing about the work of the Commission.

> Some wonder whether God would have us cultivate such unity by using what seems to them such an unnatural system . . . Instead of love rhythm tends to substitute tension, dissatisfaction, frustration and disunity.
> *Is rhythm unnatural?* Yes – that's the conclusion of these reports. Over and over, directly and indirectly, men and women – and perhaps especially women, voice the conviction that the physical and psychological implications of rhythm are not understood by the male Church.[1]

Clearly the rhythm method did not have the tonic effects on the marriage relationship attributed to it by celibate thinkers. Did this evidence reach the desk of Paul VI? The Crowleys certainly urged the commission secretary, Henri de Riedmatten OP, to lay it before the Pope, but we cannot be sure that it ever got there.

On the other hand, a book by Karol Wojtyla, Archbishop of Kraków, is credited with having some influence on Paul VI. His *Milosc I Odpowiedznalnosc* (Love and Responsibility) had been published in Polish by the Catholic University of Lublin in 1960.[2] A French translation with an enthusiastic preface by Père Henri de Lubac SJ appeared in 1965, just in time to affect the thinking if not of the Commission, then of those who "received" its report on 28 June 1966. The Polish archbishop had the merit of being franker about what he called "sexology" than most moral theologians. He was actually prepared to discuss the nature of the female orgasm ("the curve of arousal of the woman is slower than that in man") and *coitus interruptus*.[3]

Curiously, though by now a full member of the Commission, Archbishop Wojtyla failed to turn up for its decisive final meetings. Why? Out of solidarity with Wyszyński – he explained – who, in this millennium year, had been refused a visa to travel to Rome. Should he have

1 Ibid. pp. 98–99.

2 The Catholic University of Lublin (KUL) was the only independent university between the river Elbe that divided West from East Germany and the Pacific. *Love and Responsibility* was based on lectures given at Lublin in 1958–59, as the author explains in his new preface to the English tr. (Collins 1981) published when he was pope.

3 *Love and Responsibility*, tr. H. T. Willetts, Collins 1981, pp. 272, 282. Twenty-five years later the Polish archbishop, now Pope John Paul II, claimed that his book had been based on "experience" which showed that artificial contraception was degrading to women. In his 1980 preface to *Love and Responsibility* he produced a hymn to experience that has never before been uttered by a theologian, still less a Pope: "This work is open to every echo of experience, from whatever quarter it comes, and it is at the same time a standing appeal to all to let experience, their own experience, make itself heard . . . Experience does not have to be afraid of experience. Truth can only gain from such confrontation." Ibid. p. 10.

let Polish considerations prevail over the needs of the universal Church? However this puzzle is resolved, the result was that Archbishop Wojtyla missed all the key debates and the decisive votes.

Thus he was absent in late May 1966 when the Crowleys reported *their* experience; and he also missed the two scripture scholars who told the Commission that the Bible had nothing to say about birth-control. Onan's sin was not "withdrawal" but the refusal to continue his brother's line. On 3 June 1966 there was a rare moment of unanimity: all agreed that it was opportune to speak up without delay. Votes were taken by the theologians and bishops on these questions:

1 Is contraception intrinsically evil? – No.
2 Is *Casti Connubii* irreformable? – No.
3 Is the Church in a state of doubt? – Yes.
4 Could the Church change its position? – Yes.

On 28 June the co-President of the Commission, Cardinal Julius Döpfner, and its secretary Henri de Riedmatten OP were able to present to Paul the final report which concluded that the Catholic position on artificial contraception "could not be sustained by reasoned argument".[1] Döpfner had an audience arranged for 4 July, which gave the Pope time to read the report. Döpfner realized that Paul had already been "got at" by Cardinal Alfredo Ottaviani who had turned Fr John Ford SJ's 23 May paper on the consequences for papal authority of abandoning *Casti Connubii* into the Commission's "minority report".

This it could not be, for the Episcopal Commission had agreed to submit just one report as its own work. The Ford document was just one of the many papers that were prepared putting the case for and against in the strongest possible way: it was the traditional scholastic way of testing the truth of a proposition. Fr Ford's paper was not about contraception at all, but about authority:

> The Church could not have erred through so many centuries, even through one century, by imposing under serious obligation very grave burdens in the name of Jesus Christ, if Jesus Christ did not actually impose these burdens . . . Therefore one must very cautiously enquire whether the change which is proposed would not bring with it an undermining of the teaching and the moral authority of the hierarchy.[2]

1 John Marshall, letter to the *Independent*, 16 September 1987. Professor Marshall, a neurologist, was the only English member of the Commission, although the Australian economist, Colin Clark, taught in Oxford.

2 John Kotre, *Simple Gifts*, p. 100.

Döpfner felt that Paul's concern for his own authority caused him to wobble on the central question.

Yet the commission had answered the Ford objection, pointing out that the tradition leading up to *Casti Connubii* was not of apostolic origin, was not infallible, and was not an expression of universal faith. The injunction to be "two in one flesh" was as binding as that to "increase and multiply".

NB

Cardinal Döpfner wrote to Bishop Joseph Reuss, his leading expert on the question, on 8 July: "May God grant that everything go for the best and that we do not muff this great opportunity. Unfortunately, during my last audience, I got the impression that the Holy Father is very uncertain and hesitant in the whole matter."

De Riedmatten went on television, but gave nothing away. "Now begins the period of *decision*," he said, and this belonged to the Holy Father whose verdict would "not be sensational".[1]

What would happen next? Bernhard Häring, one of the few Commission members on the spot in Rome, naturally tried to find out. What he learned alarmed him. The Papal Commission having reported, there was nothing further for it to do. From now on its ex-members were not consulted and were just as much in the dark as anyone else – though the membership of the now lapsed Commission still lent them a spurious authority in the eyes of outsiders.

Cardinal John Heenan felt particularly miffed by this treatment, since much of his authority at home derived from his supposed "inside knowledge" and he fully expected change. But the Commission members were cast down, as it were, from riches to rags overnight. By 29 June 1966 they were returned to the ranks.

The whole question of birth-control reverted to Cardinal Alfredo Ottaviani and Archbishop Pietro Parente at the Holy Office. From their point of view it should never have been taken out of their hands in the first place: the whole experiment in consultation and letting non-professional theologians into the debate had already inflicted untold damage on the Church. For Ottaviani and Parente the issue provided a test-case on the superiority of an encyclical to the Council. No matter what the chapter on marriage of *Gaudium et Spes* said, and even though it "pointed" clearly in the direction of "responsible parenthood", the Holy Office could (and did) reply that "*Gaudium et Spes* is only a pastoral text, while *Casti Connubii* is the milk of pure doctrine."

What of Paul? At this point we can speak of "Hamletism". Paul was simply torn apart. Fr Ermenegeldo Lio OFM said that Paul VI "was

1 Robert Kaiser, *The Politics of Sex and Religion*, Leaven Press, Kansas City 1985, p. 178.

favourably impressed by the report, and was attracted by its conclusions". However, "two meetings with Cardinal Ottaviani and Lio himself" were enough to persuade him of his mistake.[1] But Ottaviani had the greatest hold over him because he was an old friend from the 1930s, permanently resident in Rome, and played on Paul's fears of undermining papal authority. By comparison Suenens and Häring were latecomers in his life; in any case, Suenens' visits were rare and Häring was denied access.

Quietly, in total secrecy, Ottaviani set about reversing the majority report. There was to be no nonsense about balancing different tendencies. Of the ex-members of the Papal Commission now retained as consultors, the three Jesuits Zalba, Ford and de Lestapis and the Redemptorist Visser stood four-square on *Casti Connubii*. To them was added the Franciscan Lio. "They only obey the Pope," said a commentator, "when the Pope obeys them." The fund of experience gathered by the Papal Commission was set aside. So the scene was set for the final stages of the production of *Humanae Vitae*. The buck stopped with Paul VI.

This was what he had dreaded. For the next two years he agonized over a question for which he was not well-equipped. Forty years after he had written so eloquently on marriage to his brother Lodovico, the question Paul inherited from Pope John XXIII's Commission was different. He was not asked about married love in general but about the "pill" which inhibited ovulation and therefore acted as an artificial contraceptive.

The question had been complicated by Pius XII's casuistic acceptance in the 1950s of the "safe period". It was a version of the does-the-end-justify-the-means debate. If it were legitimate to avoid conception by "natural" methods, then it became more difficult to condemn those who achieved the same result by other means. The next step was to say that there is a radical indeed absolute difference between "natural" (approved) and "artificial" (condemned) methods. But determining what is "natural" and what is "artificial" is not easy, and it is not self-evident that the use of a thermometer is more "natural" than the use of a piece of rubber. So many "cultural" factors intervene between the state of "pure nature" (which never existed) and "civilization" (which is the product of human decisions).

Jean Guitton arrived at Castelgandolfo for his annual conversation on 8 September 1966. His account of Paul's thinking on the question of contraception is essential reading. It shows that Paul's "studies" at this

1 Häring, *Fede Storia Morale*, p. 79.

date were almost exclusively "scientific" and concerned the unpredictable side-effects of "the pill". Paul says:

> One should not say the Church is in a state of doubt or is not sure of itself. The Church is well-informed on all the latest data about contraception. Maybe something has changed? In that case, let's see what science has discovered that our ancestors didn't know. Let's see if something should change in the law. Put questions to the scientists. But having listened to them, let's listen to the voice of conscience and the law. These must make demands, raise the level. Any attenuation of the law would have the effect of calling morality into question and showing the fallibility of the Church which then, like the Jewish synagogue, would have imposed too heavy a yoke on people. Then the Church before John XXIII would appear as a "Judaeo-Catholic" Church, a Church of an impracticable Law, from which I, a second Paul, had freed it.
>
> Theology would then become the servant of science, *ancilla scientiae*, science's handmaid, subject to change with each new scientific discovery so that tomorrow, for example, we would have to admit procreation without a father: the whole moral edifice would collapse, and with it the edifice of the faith. For certainty would then come not from revelation but from the latest scientific discovery. Who is to say that another scientific discovery will come along that will subvert the discovery that gave us the pill, showing for example that the pill may produce monsters in the next generation?[1]

This discourse under the cedars of Castelgandolfo does not suggest that Paul had assimilated the report of his now defunct Pontifical Commission, or even that he had read it very carefully.

That may be unfair. What seems to have happened is that he read it from the point of view of "traditional Catholic moral theology" as represented by Fr John Ford and Cardinal Alfredo Ottaviani. It had its own style and jargon. For example: though the Papal Commission said a "state of doubt" existed in the Church, Paul denies this. The same term is being used in two completely different senses: for the Pontifical Commission it meant that people were actually having difficulties with this doctrine, were suffering under it or ignoring or flouting it. For Paul the "state of doubt" referred to the *magisterium*. It had not yet changed.

1 Jean Guitton, *Paul VI secret*, pp. 81–82. Whatever one thinks about the "monsters", the allusion to test-tube conceptions, long before they had happened, shows far-sightedness.

Therefore, until *Casti Connubii* was replaced, it was still valid and operative.

The emphasis on the scientific data is also typical of the traditional moralists. The Crowley family introduced what were essentially *psychological* considerations about the "safe-period": these were notoriously "subjective" and unprovable. In any case the use of the safe-period itself was "not traditional", dating back to Pope Pius XII's address to the midwives in 1951, so that the Crowley evidence against it was no knock-out blow against the traditional position which favoured abstention.

Objective scientific evidence counted for more than unverifiable experience. Yet the scientific evidence itself was not *the source* of moral norms, only the necessary factual basis for them. Not everything that was scientifically possible was morally acceptable. This was not well understood in the Church in 1966.

Thinking such thoughts in September 1966, Paul VI opted for a holding operation to gain time for yet more thought. Giacomo Perico SJ, well known for his studies of medical morals and a member of the now defunct Commission, published an "inspired" article called "Why the Pope doesn't Speak". Summing up the difficulties inherent in the question, Perico thought it was perfectly reasonable for the Pope to "make a personal study of the *scientific data* and the relevant theological and moral considerations involved", and to subject them to a "fresh examination".[1]

No sooner had Perico explained Paul's silence than he broke it. Addressing a congress of obstetricians and gynaecologists on 29 September 1966, he stressed three points:

1 The Council and *Gaudium et Spes* have not substantially changed the doctrine of the Church.

2 The work of the Pontifical Commission requires still further study.

3 The norms hitherto taught remained in force for the time being, and should be generously and faithfully obeyed. For it is wrong to say that the Church is "in a state of doubt".[2]

This address to the gynaecologists, intended to reassure, in fact made matters worse.

For if the Church's teaching were not in doubt, what had been the point of the Pontifical Commission? In any case the doubt in the mind of many of the faithful was a real and not a pretend-doubt. Paul's denial that doubt existed led Charles Davis, editor of the *Clergy Review*, to

1 Jan Grootaers, "*La Rédaction de l'encyclique* 'Humanae Vitae' ", *Modernité*, pp. 386–87.

2 Ibid. p. 386.

leave the Catholic Church, banging the door and saying: "The papal statement was dishonest – it was a diplomatic lie, covering over an awkward but plain fact."[1]

Asked whether he thought the Church was "in a state of doubt", Cardinal Suenens replied that it was not. Asked why not, he lamely replied, "because the Pope says we are not". He was more candid in assessment of Paul VI's attitude:

> As a theologian, the Pope is rather conservative. On the birth-control question, the Pope hasn't developed. But I must say in his defence that he is concerned about people. He thinks we are living in a dangerous time because the people are not prepared for change. I think the Pope would announce the tentative judgements of his Commission but for one thing: there is such a great risk of abuse.[2]

Suenens' eyes glazed over as he made this remark, as well they might.

Besides the not-in-a-state-of-doubt address, Paul made another speech that same September on the relationship of theologians and the *magisterium*. He shook off his doubts and rose to the event. The occasion was a Congress in the Domus Mariae to study, or rather to celebrate, the theology of Vatican II. All the great names were there – Karl Rahner ("The multiple presence of Christ in the Church"), Edward Schillebeeckx ("The Church as sacrament"), Yves Congar ("Catholicity as the foundation of the Church's dialogue with the world"). There were ten themes and seventy-four papers.

It was extraordinary to hear John Courtney Murray SJ and Bishop John J. Wright expounding religious liberty as the necessary condition for ecumenical dialogue as though this had been controversial a very long time ago. Equally astonishing was the arrival of Karl Barth, now very aged, who tottered up the aisle to immense applause sustained by his equally fragile wife. Invited to the Council by the Secretariat for Christian Unity as a "personal observer" (a new category), Barth responded with a slim volume, *Ad Limina Apostolorum*, in which he commented generously though not uncritically on the conciliar texts.[3] He said that if Hans Küng's interpretation of his doctrine of "justification" was right, then the entire Reformation reposed upon a mistake.

But this was a mere episode in the most important post-conciliar

1 Charles Davis, *A Question of Conscience*, p. 93.

2 Robert Kaiser, *The Politics of Sex and Religion*, p. 127.

3 Karl Barth, *Ad Limina Apostolorum*. For Paul VI, who remembered Barth's attack on the Roman Catholic Church in Amsterdam at the foundation of the WCC in 1948, this was proof of a remarkable transformation.

congress ever. The theologians who had been under a cloud in the 1950s, and had then emerged as *periti* at the Council, now came to savour their Roman triumph. Very often they drew attention to ideas or themes which they had themselves "planted" in the conciliar texts. So, for example, Schillebeeckx pointed out that the best expression of the Church as sacrament was to be found in the decree on Missions, *Ad Gentes*, which declares that "Missionary activity is nothing else and nothing less than a manifestation or epiphany of God's will, and the fulfilment of that will in the world and in history."[1]

Yves-Marie Congar confirmed this approach with another quotation from this most "pneumatological" of the Council documents: "Missionary activity wells up from the Church's innermost nature, and spreads abroad her saving faith. It perfects her Catholic unity by expanding it. It is sustained by her apostolicity. It gives expression to the collegial awareness of her hierarchy."[2]

Taken together, the two ideas of "catholicity" and "Church as sacrament" opened up the question of "anonymous Christians" which Karl Rahner would soon develop.

These ideas caused alarm in the Curia. But this was not the Curia's day. True, Paul formally thanked Cardinal Giuseppe Pizzardo, Prefect of the Congregation for Catholic Universities, for organizing it – but the main work had been done by Fr Edouard Dhanis SJ of the Gregorian University. And Archbishop Dino Staffa, Secretary of the same Congregation, used his sermon to denounce "transignification" as the greatest theological danger facing the Church. But his was a lonely voice.

How would Paul react? His address on Saturday, 1 October 1966 was the most substantial treatment he ever gave to the relationship between the *magisterium* and theologians. Much of it was familiar. The *magisterium* and theology are both subject to the word of God, to divine revelation. Paul alluded to but did not quote the passage in the dogmatic constitution, *Dei Verbum*, which says that "the *magisterium* is not above the word of God, but serves it, teaching only what is handed on".[3] Indeed his reminder that Vatican I taught that the *magisterium* was "proximate and universal norm of the indefectable truth of revelation"[4] could be considered a qualification, though not a retraction, of *Dei Verbum*. A reference to the 1950 encyclical *Humani Generis*, which had silenced many of the theologians he was addressing, seemed unhappy. But no doubt it was designed to comfort Cardinal Pizzardo.

1 *Ad Gentes*, 9.

2 Ibid. 6.

3 *Dei Verbum*, 10.

4 *Insegnamenti*, 1966, p. 451.

It also provided a solid base on which to build his most original and constructive remarks. Theologians, he said, have a double responsibility, towards the *magisterium* and towards the People of God. They are the intermediaries between the faithful and the teaching authority of pope and bishops. Their service to the *magisterium* and to the faithful is to articulate and render "reasonable" Catholic faith. They communicate upwards and downwards: the theologian is a go-between.

> Theologians are, as it were, mediators between the faith of the Church and the *magisterium*. They are attentive to the living faith of Christian communities, their truth, their accents, their problems, the initiatives that the Holy Spirit arouses in the People of God – *quid Spiritus dicat ecclesiis* (what the Spirit is saying to the Churches).[1]

This was novel. For pre-conciliar theology had spoken as though the *magisterium* (the *ecclesia docens*) plucked its teaching from mid-air, while the faithful (the *ecclesia discens*) had only to receive it passively.

Instead of opposition between the *magisterium* and theologians which had prevailed in the past, Paul proposed "communion" in a common task:

> For it is theology that shapes the understanding and the minds of pastors . . . and without theology the *magisterium* would lack the essential instruments on which to compose the symphony which should pervade the whole community so that it learns to live and think according to the mind of Jesus Christ.[2]

No pope had spoken in this way before. It remained to find a way of giving practical, administrative expression to this healthy way of stating the relationship between theologians and the *magisterium*.

There was much gossip in the bars of the Congress about a recent visit Paul had paid to the tomb of St Celestine V near Agnani. Celestine was famous as the last pope to have resigned – in 1294. Was Paul dropping a hint? Were the battles with Ottaviani and Pizzardo proving too tough for him? Was he considering the prospect of resignation, if not now, then at some future date if ever he came to feel unequal to the task?

He used his homily at the tomb of Celestine V to show how the difficulties of the papacy were proof of divine guidance. It was an old theme of apologetics. Celestine's papacy was astonishing, brief and dis-

1 Ibid. pp. 452–3. I have translated *theologia* as theologians to make the remarks less abstract.

2 Ibid. p. 453.

astrous. Elected at the age of eighty, after an interregnum of twenty-six months, at a time when the college of cardinals numbered only twelve, he threw in the towel after a few months. His successor repudiated the little he had done, and clapped him in prison. "Terrible times," sighed Paul and then: "St Celestine, after a few months, understood that he was being deceived by those who surrounded him."[1] Did he sometimes feel that way himself? He went on to quote Dante, while admitting that the words may not have been about Celestine, but about those who "resign not out of *viltà* but heroic virtue". To resign could be, he concluded, a duty.

He did not sound in the mood for resignation when he addressed the Jesuits on 3 December 1966, the feast of St Francis Xavier, as they concluded the 31st General Congregation. "Certain rumours have reached our ears," he said, "concerning your Society, that have caused us great pain." He did not say precisely what they were or where they came from. Pedro Arrupe knew precisely where they came from. In August a group of Spanish Jesuits, meeting for a conference on the *Spiritual Exercises* at Loyola, birthplace of St Ignatius, denounced Arrupe as unfaithful to Ignatius and the traditions of the Society. Their report had gone directly to Paul. Arrupe thought he should be the link with the pope, not these self-appointed censors. Paul said the "black clouds" had been dissipated. But it was a warning of troubles to come.

At Christmas 1966 Cardinal Francis J. Spellman went to Vietnam to console the US troops. Spellman was not some lone ranger: he had the support of the vast majority of the US bishops. At their 1966 annual meeting they had won national headlines by declaring their support for what opponents considered their country's "military interventions in the internal affairs of Vietnam".[2] Asked in Saigon what he thought about the US involvement in Vietnam, Spellman replied that he "fully supported everything it does". He then paraphrased a nineteenth-century naval hero: "My country may it always be right. Right or wrong, my country."[3]

The problem for Paul was not just that the US bishops were "conservative" in their attitude to Vatican II: it was that the Vietnam War revealed that they shared in the sense of national mission enshrined in the Declaration of Independence and the Constitution, and confused America with the Promised Land. This attitude then combined with the fear of the Communist threat to make the *Pax Americana* the supreme good.

1 Ibid. p. 1079.

2 Thomas E. Quigley, ed., *American Catholics and Vietnam*, p. 109.

3 Ibid. p. 110.

Spellman and, to the extent that he was representative, the US bishops were in contradiction with Paul's speech to the United Nations, with *Gaudium et Spes* to which he was committed, and to the *Ostpolitik* which, since Pope John's *Pacem in Terris*, was discriminating in its approach to Communist leaders, and encouraged "dialogue" (the Catholic word for "negotiations") with them. The US bishops ignored the exhortation of *Gaudium et Spes*: "It is our clear duty . . . to strain every muscle as we work for the time when all war can be completely outlawed by international consent."

Paul had three responses, more or less long-term. First he must find a new type of bishop for the US, less like top executives who can read a financial statement, more enabling pastors with enough theology to know what implementing the Council meant: but he had to wait till 1973 to appoint Jean Jadot Apostolic Delegate in Washington. Second, he brought an American Bishop, John J. Wright of Pittsburgh, to Rome to be Prefect of the Congregation of the Clergy. This not only helped "internationalize" the Curia but gave him a direct line to the US bishops. Wright was called "the egg-head bishop" because he was known to read books. Third, Paul could show that peace was his top priority by launching his World Peace Day project at the earliest opportunity. He celebrated the first World Peace Day on 1 January 1968.[1]

It mattered enormously to Paul that the United Nations approved of his plan. Every year World Peace Day would be a continuation of his visit in October 1965. It would remind the world that peace, while it has to be sought through disarmament and negotiation, must also be *prayed for*. True peace, the right ordering of relationships between nations, was a gift of grace. *Dona nobis pacem*. He saw no reason why Communists should make off with all the noblest feelings:

> There are sometimes people of great breadth of mind, impatient with the mediocrity and self-seeking which infects so much of modern society. They readily make use of sentiments and language found in our Gospel referring to the brotherhood of man, mutual aid, human compassion. Shall we not one day be able to lead them back to the Christian sources of these moral values?[2]

That is what he was doing with World Peace Day: as an "expert in humanity" he was trying to articulate the deep human aspiration to peace, and root it in Christian ground.

1 *Insegnamenti*, 1968.

2 *Ecclesiam Suam*, 104.

28

Against the Euphoria of the Age

> The impression Pope Paul gave . . . is of a man who is on top of his job, well-informed of the realities of his time, relaxed in his estimate of the currents in contemporary Catholicism, capable of wry bursts of humour directed sometimes at himself, purposeful but without illusions of easy solutions, informal in manner but never far from the secret emotions that surround his solitary decisions.
>
> (Frank Duff SJ, summarizing Paul VI's interview with Alberto Cavallari, in HUGH MORLEY OFM, *The Pope and the Press*, p. 68)

There was one evident gap in the "new Curia". Where were the laity? Declared "the people of God" by the Council, with a radical equality in grace before the Lord, they nevertheless had no place in the decision-making processes of the Church. To remedy that Paul VI published the motu proprio *Catholicam Christi Ecclesiam* on the feast of the Epiphany 1967. This set up a *Concilium de Laicis* (*about* the laity). Some had expected a Council *pro Laicis* (*for* and made up *of* the laity) but that was not what Paul understood himself to be committed to by his "superior" the Council.

The decree on the Lay Apostolate invited the Pope to found a "secretariat to promote and serve the apostolate of lay people", and located it *apud Sanctam Sedem* (in the whereabouts of the Holy See). This deliberately vague expression was meant to ensure that the new body would not be trapped in a curial straitjacket from the outset.

Paul's diplomatic solution was the *Consilium de Laicis*, which he described as his "listening-post to the world". So the laity were for him the voice of the world in the Church. But working out what that meant was not, as Derek Worlock remarks, plain sailing: there were choppy seas, reefs, tempests, tantrums before the haven of 1971 when the provisional became definitive.[1]

Their originality was that they were all laypeople. The Australian Rosemary Goldie (of COPECIAL which dealt with liaison with UN and other international bodies) and the Polish-Swiss Mieczyslaw de Habicht (of International Catholic Organizations) became joint under-secretaries; but for curial reasons Msgr Achille Glorieux had the title of "secretary" (in Roman terms the man-in-charge). Their first task was to sort out overlapping competencies. As executive secretary of COPECIAL Rosemary Goldie was already heavily involved in the preparations for the next (last and third) world congress on the Lay Apostolate due at the end of October 1967. The Justice and Peace Commission was set up at the same time, and Cardinal Maurice Roy was President of both.

Away from Rome, of course, the laity were passionately interested in what Paul was going to say about birth-control. He left them clutching thin air. But he issued two encyclicals in 1967 as if to prove that Vatican Council for all its richness had not made the papal *magisterium* redundant.

He timed them with care. *Populorum Progressio*, his first and only social encyclical, appeared on Easter Sunday, and made a good impression on the laity. *Sacerdotalis Coelibatus*' reassertion of mandatory celibacy for the ordained ministers in the Western Church, which appeared on his feast day, St John the Baptist (24 June 1967), though of less immediate concern to the laity, made an impact on those who worried about the emotional lives of their priests.

Both were, as the press loves to say, "controversial" – *Populorum Progressio* because it was, according to the *Wall Street Journal*, "souped-up Marxism", and *Sacerdotalis Coelibatus* because it dashed hopes that the Catholic Church would soon have married priests.

Paul's two 1967 encyclicals confirmed the cliché judgement that he was "progressive" on social matters but "conservative" in theological questions – a common Roman position. But it was the encyclical that did not appear, on birth-control, that caused Paul the most anxiety and

1 Derek Worlock, "Toil in the Lord: the Laity at Vatican II", in *Vatican II by those who were There*, ed. Alberic Stacpoole OSB, p. 247. Archbishop Worlock shared his memories, often hilarious, of the sessions. The first Council, made up entirely of lay people, refused to take the curial oath of secrecy demanded of them on various grounds; for some North Americans the whole idea of secrecy was unacceptable; others felt that they were still answerable to the organizations that had nominated them. The Curia was baffled by such attitudes. Thanks to Archbishop Worlock, letter to the author, 18 March 1992, for this whole section.

gave rise to apprehension and debate as the moment of decision, which was not prescribed in advance, drew near throughout the year. "How easy it is to study, to study," Paul said in an interview with *Corriere della Sera*, "how hard it is to decide."

However Paul was not writing his encyclicals in a vacuum, and the Church in Italy was in a state of turmoil. The conflicts disclosed by the Council were carried over into the dioceses as its implementation began in earnest. Conservatives like Cardinal Giuseppe Siri in Genoa continued to believe and act as though John XXIII had been out of his mind; progressives like Cardinal Giacomo Lercaro were sure Siri was out of his mind. There were any number of national variations on the same theme which may be summed up in the words of Lord Macauley: "Those behind cried 'Forward', while those before cried 'Back'."

In Italy matters came to a head at the April meeting of CEI, the Italian episcopal conference. Paul had shown his confidence in Cardinal Giacomo Lercaro, his rival in the conclave, by putting him in charge of the reform of the liturgy, where sensitive nerve-ends were most easily jangled. He renewed his confidence in August 1966 when Lercaro, who would be seventy-five in October, tendered his resignation as Archbishop of Bologna. Paul refused it, saying he needed him still.

Lercaro divided his ministry as Archbishop of Bologna into a pre- and post-conciliar phase. After fourteen years as a conventional bishop, now he would make a "fresh start". Vatican II had liberated and emboldened him for the second stage in which he aspired to be "a herald of the Gospel, in its simplest form and without mediations, for all the people of Bologna".[1] Did all the people include Communists, who were in power in Bologna? It was hard to deny it. Lercaro underplayed the Church as institution and wanted to be "just a servant of the Gospel 'without any gloss' as St Francis would have said". Disinterested and disarmed, Lercaro claimed his ambition was to "disappear, as it were, before the Gospel". This "prophetic" view of the nature of the Church reflected the ideas of Giuseppe Dossetti.

Bologna also irritated other dioceses, not by making a hero out of Pope John XXIII – nearly everyone except Cardinal Siri in Genoa was doing that – but by claiming to have a monopoly of research into his works, special access to his deeper intentions, and by believing that they were "implementing Vatican II" better than anyone else because they

1 Sandro Magister, *La politica Vaticana e l'Italia*, p. 348.

understood his mind better.[1] Also included in the progressive package was indignation at the actions of the US in Vietnam.

Paul VI had started his own "peace offensive" in Vietnam. He set Archbishop Sergio Pignedoli, Apostolic Delegate in Canada, the task of exploring the possibilities of a negotiated peace. Pignedoli visited Hanoi, North Vietnam, and contrary to the Vatican's usual diplomatic practice, his mission was given as much publicity as possible.

Pignedoli took to Hanoi the message that Pope Paul and the Holy See would "collaborate without limits" to assist the quest for peace. Part of Pignedoli's task was to try to promote peace by wooing the Vietnamese bishops away from their anti-Communism and support for the Thieu government. He would be back again the following year to preside over an extraordinary meeting of the Vietnam bishops with the same aim. Pignedoli, a genial man who card-indexed everyone he had ever met (and remembered them), was becoming Paul's roving trouble-shooter.

His services would have been useful at the Italian bishops' meeting in April 1967 where there was an outright attack on Lercaro and his diocese. Neither he nor Bologna was named, but that was unnecessary. Cardinal Giovanni Urbani, Archbishop of Naples, weighed in against "reviews and cultural centres of the so-called *avant-garde*" which had gone too far too fast.

This shaft was aimed at the Documentation Centre, founded by Don Giuseppe Dossetti, and the reviews – *Testimonianze* (formerly in Florence under the aegis of Giorgio La Pira) and *Il Regno*, edited by the Dehonian Fathers. Bologna also had the daily paper *L'Avvenire d'Italia*, edited by Raniero La Valle.[2] No other diocese in Italy was such a laboratory of reform. None had such an array of quality publications.

What upset Lercaro in April 1967 was that the attacks on the Bologna experiment came not from the usual quarters but from bishops "close to" Paul VI. Carlo Colombo, by now dean of the Milan theology faculty, denounced the "new breed" of irresponsible theologians said to be wrecking the Church. Bishop Franco Costa, chaplain to Catholic Action (ACI) and as such in charge of "restructuring" the Catholic press,

1 On 23 February 1965 Cardinal Giacomo Lercaro gave a lecture to the Luigi Sturzo Institute as part of a series called "Italian Catholics from the 19th century to Today". Lercaro's contribution, *Linee per una ricerca su Giovanni XXIII*, was subsequently recognized, in Bologna at least, as the starting point for the serious historical and academic study of Pope John. However it contributed to the myth of Pope John in that it set up a contrast between "*il programma conciliare di papa Giovanni e i risultati effetivi gia raggiunti dal Concilio*" (Pope John's programme for the Council and what the Council has already achieved). In Giacomo Lercaro, *Giovanni XXIII, Linee per una ricerca storica*, Storia e Letteratura, Rome 1965, p. 32.

2 Sandro Magister, *La politica Vaticana e l'Italia*, pp. 346–47.

ousted La Valle from *L'Avvenire d'Italia* on 1 August 1967. The paper went into a decline from which it never recovered. Reeling under these blows, Lercaro tried to persuade Paul VI to make Don Dossetti his coadjutor with right of succession. He overestimated his influence.

Paul did his reputation a world of good with *Populorum Progressio*. The impulse to writing it within fifteen months of the promulgation of *Gaudium et Spes* came from the visit to India. Agostino Casaroli says that he started a dossier on "human development" immediately on his return.[1] By calling "development the new name for peace" and insisting that in the long run the North–South divide would prove more menacing than the East–West conflict, Paul VI was prophetic and ensured that he would have the support of those who cared about the "Third World".[2] Previous social encyclicals, including *Mater et Magistra* of Pope John XXIII, had been written from a predominantly "European" point of view, with North Americans included as honorary Europeans. With *Populorum Progressio* the Church became truly Catholic, universal and planetary.

Populorum Progressio was better understood in France than elsewhere, no doubt because it reflected the thinking of Louis Lebret OP, editor of *Economie et Humanisme*, to which Paul had subscribed since it began. Paul had summoned him to the Council as a *peritus*, and used him on UN missions. After his death in July 1966 Paul said that *Populorum Progressio* would be a "tribute to the memory of Père Lebret".[3]

François Perroux, professor at the Collège de France, called it "one of the greatest texts of human history", a profound and original synthesis of the Ten Commandments, the Gospel teaching and the Declaration on Human Rights.[4] This novel synthesis issues in the Four Commandments the modern world needs:

Feed the hungry.

Care for the health of all people and all peoples.

Educate humanity.

Free the enslaved.

1 Cardinal Agostino Casaroli, sermon in Brescia cathedral, 24 September 1984, MS, p. 14.

2 A term introduced at about this time. It implied a First World (Europe and North America) and a Second World (the Soviet bloc). But "Third" did not involve invidious grading or inferiority. It translated *tiers* not *troisième*. So it meant the outsiders, the marginal, those not invited to the banquet of life.

3 Murray Millard, in *Theology*, January 1986, p. 47.

4 François Perroux, "*L'encyclique de la Résurrection*", in *L'Eglise dans le monde de ce temps*, 3, pp. 202–3.

The encyclical develops the promise of Paul's UN speech. It is addressed to all men and women. It provides them with a vision of a *common human culture* for "spaceship earth", which nevertheless respects cultural, ethnic and national diversities.

However, Michael Novak, plumper and older than when last seen, declared that *Populorum Progressio* is naïve, "lacks humility", wavers in tone between "pessimism and Utopian hope", uses a logic that is merely "abstract" and a language that is "highly enflamed", and that it "lashes out against unrestrained liberalism", describing it as a "woeful system".[1] A great deal of this can be considered projection. If one asks why Paul VI should set out to subvert "sound Catholic social doctrine", Novak's answer is that Paul brought together to write it "intellectuals who specialized in Third World development . . . Louis Lebret, Barbara Ward and George(s) Jarlot".[2] In other words there was a conspiracy.

Now Jarlot, a crusty old Norman, professor at the Gregorian, could never be accused of modishness. Barbara Ward (later Lady Jackson) was in the same tradition of Christian humanism as Lebret. Her main contention reflected in *Populorum Progressio* was that just as progressive taxation in the developed world had gradually led to distributive justice, thereby reducing the gap between rich and poor, an analogous process would have to take place on the international level. The world would become an integrated, tolerable place, only through cultivating a sense of interdependence and solidarity. *Populorum Progressio* uses the word solidarity, which was not invented in Poland in the 1970s.[3]

In summarizing the way *Populorum Progresssio* was ahead of its time, Barbara Ward incidentally explains why the right-wing did not like it. Paul had seen destitution and hunger in India. In the encyclical he "cried out against the euphoria of the age", rejecting the "trickle down" theory of development which leaves it all to market forces.[4] What most distressed his North American critics was the following passage:

> We must repeat once more that the superfluous wealth of rich countries should be placed at the benefit of poor nations. The

1 Michael Novak, *The Development of Catholic Social Thought*, Harper and Row, New York 1984, pp. 134, 140.

2 Ibid. p. 239 fn. 42.

3 Barbara Ward and René Dubos, *Only One Earth: The Care and Maintenance of a Small Planet*, André Deutsch 1972. It would be truer to say that *Solidarnosc* derives from Catholic Social Doctrine rather than contributes to it.

4 Barbara Ward, "Looking Back on *Populorum Progressio*", in Charles E. Curran and Richard A. McCormick SJ, eds, *Official Catholic Social Teaching, Moral Theology*, 5, Paulist, New York 1986, p. 131. This article originally appeared in *Doctrine and Life*, the review of the Irish Dominicans.

> rule which up to now held good for the benefit of those nearest to us, must today be applied to all the needy of the world. Besides, the rich world will be the first to benefit as a result. Otherwise their continued greed will certainly call down on them the judgement of God and the wrath of the poor, with consequences no one can foretell.[1]

The free marketeers called this naïve, empirically false, and exciting (a marvellously give-away phrase) "the envy of the poor".

Yet Paul was the better prophet. He pointed out that if in a market (a good tool, but a bad master) the inequality between the bargainers is too great, then every single deal will make the rich richer and the poor poorer. With *Populorum Progressio* behind him Paul could look the Latin Americans and Africans in the eye, and think of going there. He was on their side.

Paul could have enjoyed the praise and popularity his second encyclical brought him. But then on 13 May 1967, he made a quick dash there-and-back to Fátima in Portugal on the fiftieth anniversary of the alleged appearance of Our Lady. This disconcerting visit interrupted the series of journeys to places of symbolic importance for Christian life. But with Czestochowa and Poland closed to him, perhaps there was a case for visiting another European Marian shrine.

Yet Portugal for Poland was not a fair exchange: not only was the devotion at Fátima modern, unhealthy, dubious theologically, and politically right-wing, but he would have to meet Antonio Salazar, a Catholic authoritarian leader who had led Portugal into an almost uninterrupted series of colonial wars in its African territories of Angola and Mozambique. A report warned him of the dangers in advance. The result was a curious, curt, half-hearted visit, officially in response to "an invitation of the Portuguese bishops", in which he spent his time explaining that he was not doing what he appeared to be doing.

Thus he met Salazar, an economics professor before assuming the role of saviour of the nation, in hole-and-corner fashion without photo-opportunities. While commemorating the fiftieth anniversary of the appearances at Fátima and the twenty-fifth anniversary of Pius XII's consecration of the world to the Immaculate Heart of Mary – an act apparently requested by the Lady herself – he played down these aspects in a meeting with the separated brethren, and based his remarks on scripture: "Blessed are you among women, and blessed is the fruit of thy womb."[2]

1 *Populorum Progressio*, 59.

2 *Insegnamenti*, 1967, p. 242.

Though he prayed for "lands where religious freedom is not allowed, and where the negation of God is presented as if it were the truth of the modern age and the liberation of their peoples", that was as close as he came to the "Blue Army" crusades directed towards "the conversion of Russia". And he said nothing at all about the mysterious "fourth secret of Fátima" which is reputed to be locked in his drawer in the Vatican. A commentary on Vatican Radio, not unprompted, summed up what his visit had achieved:

> Paul VI purified devotion to Our Lady at Fátima. He swept away the atmosphere of secrecy, of political and social exploitation, of false mystery, of whisperings and gossip. In his discourses the Pope made no mention of the mysterious Fátima that intellectuals [*sic*] had exploited to put forward their own ideas under the cover of Our Lady.[1]

So that made it a very *radical* visit. What he chiefly remembered was the huge crowd of two million, stretching out towards the horizon, who filled the immense plain and reminded him of Armageddon.

One good reason for giving a shame-faced character to the Portugal visit was that only a week later Paul had to meet the Justice and Peace Commission for the first time. Its Secretary was Msgr Joseph Gremillion, and among the consultors were Barbara Ward and Margot Pompe. The new Commission was set up in direct response to the speech at the Council by James Norris, then President of the International Committee on Migration, on 5 November 1965. The gap between rich and poor nations could only be closed if "in each country groups of people of good will are firmly organized, well-informed and courageous, and prepared to consider poverty in the world as one of the great central concerns of our time". As a direct result of this intervention, and some shrewd lobbying, a request for such a body was included in *Gaudium et Spes*, 90.

Paul compared the Justice and Peace Commission to a weathercock placed on the gable of a church "as a symbol of watchfulness". Its brief would be "to keep the eye of the Church alert, her heart open, and her hand outstretched for the work of love she is called upon to do".[2] The existence of local Justice and Peace Commissions was a novelty of great importance. It placed greater responsibility on local Churches, stimulated them to discern the "signs of the times" in their own country, greatly increasing lay participation and providing Paul and the Curia

1 Peter Hebblethwaite, *The Runaway Church*, pp. 90–91. I suspect the "intellectuals" were right-wing Italians.

2 *Insegnamenti*, 1967, p. 171.

with an alternative source of information about national situations. The Rome bureau had both to stimulate and co-ordinate. Msgr Benelli indulgently called it "the *enfant terrible* of the Roman Curia". This was a polite way of saying it could be awkward.

In the wings of this meeting all the talk was about the leaked report of the Birth-Control Commission. If editors could be muzzled in Italy, this was not so elsewhere in the Catholic world. Under the very nose of the Pope was IDOC, originally the Dutch information centre, now with an international mission but the same address, via Santa Maria dell'Anima 30, overlooking the Piazza Navona. Its director, Leo Alting von Geusau, then a priest of the Groningen diocese in the Netherlands, somehow "acquired" a copy of the final report of the Pontifical Commission.

He had no scruples about publishing it: but where? His first thought was *Le Monde*, but Henri Fesquet was unenthusiastic, being unwilling to upset the Pope. Gary McEoin, the Irish-American freelance writer, chanced to pass through Rome. His judgement was that *Le Monde* would not publish it in full but would reduce it to a mere "news story", thus doing more harm than good. He would arrange for publication of the full text in the *National Catholic Reporter*, Kansas City, the exciting new paper founded by Bob Hoyt and friends in 1964. Far from rushing into print, Hoyt waited from 2 February to April, checking the authenticity of the document with Commission members and moral theologians. They pronounced it genuine. Hoyt, sure this was "the biggest story of the year, of the decade", nevertheless called for a vote in the newsroom before going ahead with publication on 16 April 1977. In London the *Tablet* followed suit on 22 April 1967.[1]

Publication of the final report of the Birth-Control Commission wrecked Paul VI's carefully laid plans. It meant he could no longer make up his mind in secret, without the world knowing the evidence on which his final judgement was based. He was really angry, and wondered who had blown the gaff. He ordered Cicogani to write to the episcopal members of the Commission: "The Supreme Pastor has grieved most heavily over the publication of these documents (*Supremus Pastor vehementer doluit . . . quod textus documentorum editi sunt*). The reports, scattered so imprudently, and the inept conjectures spread abroad, have hardly helped bring a correct solution."

"The reports were supposed to remain secret," he wailed, impo-

1 This paragraph is based on an interview with Gary McEoin in the offices of the *National Catholic Reporter* on 22 October 1991. He gave whatever dollars he earned to a black South African who was working his way through medical school. For more on this remarkable man, see Gary McEoin, *Memoirs and Memories*, Twenty-Third Publications, Mystic, Conn. 1986.

tently. "They tried to force my hand by publishing this report," he told Jean Guitton, "but I won't give way. I'll wait."[1]

To make matters worse, what no one knew was that by 17 June 1967 a version of the encyclical based on a draft by Gustave Martelet SJ *already existed*. Prepared within the Congregation for the Doctrine of the Faith, with Carlo Colombo acting as secretary, the fifteen-page text took an uncompromising stand on three principles:

1 the necessity to safeguard the continuity of the *magisterium* and therefore the impossibility of rejecting *Casti Connubii*;
2 any relaxation of teaching on this matter would encourage hedonism and the "permissive society";
3 to accept contraception as "normal" would open the door to nations abusively imposing family planning policies on unwilling people.[2]

This was considered hardline and unyielding, especially in view of the leaking of the report. The same authors (Carlo Colombo, Gustave Martelet) were set to work again, but with additional experts making a total of twelve.

The main difference at this intermediate stage was that *pastoral* considerations, totally neglected in the first take-it-or-leave-it draft, began to be taken into account. In other words: how would such a doctrine be received? An article by Giacomo Perico SJ in *Civiltà Cattolica*, usually a reliable barometer of papal thinking, while affirming continuity with *Casti Connubii*, avoided direct judgement on the morality of artificial contraception and described cases in which the anovulent pill might be prescribed (for example to regularize periods). But that approach was judged too pragmatic and too casuistical. For the final stage two groups of experts were set up, one co-ordinated by Agostino Casaroli in the Secretariat of State (concerned more with government population policies), and the other managed by Cardinal Alfredo Ottaviani at the Congregation for the Doctrine of the Faith until his resignation in November 1967.[3]

Before Paul VI could recover from the shock of the leaked report a new front was opened up. The battle for Bologna was disclosed as no more than an episode in the battle for Europe. On 10–23 July seven cardinals and sixty-eight bishops met at Noordwijkerhout in the Netherlands for the very first symposium of European bishops. Their eminently practical theme was "Post-conciliar *Diocesan* Structures". In effect the

1 Jean Guitton, *Paul VI secret*, p. 94.

2 Jan Grootaers, "*Quelques données concernant la rédaction de l'encyclique Humanae Vitae*", in *Paul VI et la Modernité*, p. 387.

3 Jan Grootaers, "*Humanae Vitae*", in *Dictionnaire d'histoire et de géographie ecclésiastiques*, Letourzey, Paris 1992, col. 540–41.

Council would be vain unless it came home on the local level in priestly councils and diocesan synods.

Paul VI welcomed the meeting, which included some bishops from Eastern Europe, as corresponding to "the growing experience of interdependence of the European countries". He listed what by now were the three standard topics: emigration, tourism and mass media. The letter went on: "Pastors solicitous for the good of souls face common problems demanding harmonious solutions. It is therefore with great joy that his Holiness welcomes this active awareness (*prise de conscience*) of pastoral solidarity, which is in line with the collegiality highlighted by the recent Council."[1]

It sounded as though the Holy Father was genuinely pleased about the Noordwijkerhout meeting.

No doubt he was. But he was also worried. This could be seen in the despatch of Msgr Carlo Colombo to read a lecture on the *doctrinal* aspects of collaboration between Churches. It is not unfair to say that Colombo's contribution was eclipsed by the truly magisterial opening keynote lecture from Cardinal Bernard Alfrink, Archbishop of Utrecht and host for the meeting. His theme was "The Relationship between Local Church and Universal Church". Alfrink had waited for this moment for a long time.

The seven Dutch bishops had worked together before and during the Council, aided by the fact that they all lived at the Dutch College and could call on a stream of highly competent theologians including Jan Groot, Edward Schillebeeckx and Piet Smulders. Though only seven, they could count on support from Dutch missionary bishops in Indonesia, South Africa and elsewhere, as well as on certain major superiors. From their pre-conciliar *vota* onwards they had insisted on the importance of the local Church and its relative autonomy theologically, juridically, liturgically, organizationally.[2] These views having been accepted by the Council, the time had come to gather in the harvest.

Alfrink's paper at Noordwijkerhout was an extended commentary on one of the most important texts of *Lumen Gentium*. Though Vatican II did not make the local Church its starting-point, nevertheless he insisted that the universal Church existed only through the local Churches:

> This Church of Christ is truly present in all legitimate local congregations of the faithful which, united with their pastors, are themselves called churches in the New Testament. For in

1 *I Vescovi d'Europa e la nuova Evangellizzazione*, p. 45. Paul's message took the form of a letter from Cardinal Amleto Cicognani, Secretary of State.

2 J. H. Y. A. Jacobs, "*Les 'vota' des évêques néerlandais*", in *Cristianesimo nella storia*, June 1991, p. 324.

> their own locality these are the new people called by God, in the Holy Spirit and in much fullness. In them the faithful are gathered together by the preaching of the Gospel of Christ, and in them the mystery of the Lord's Supper is celebrated "that by the flesh and blood of the Lord's body the whole brotherhood may be gathered together" . . . In these communities, though frequently small and poor, or living far from any other, Christ is present.[1]

From this passage, Alfrink drew the following conclusions. *Item*: the local churches are not just a "part" which gains significance only when added to the "whole", that is, the universal Church; they are uniquely and irreplaceably the Church for and in this place. *Item*: in the New Testament *ecclesia* is plural as well as singular. Paul and Barnabas lay on hands *per singulas ecclesias* (Acts 14:23); Paul asks the Romans to greet Aquila and Priscilla to whom he owes so much as do *cunctae ecclesiae gentium* (Romans 16:3, 4). In the Apocalypse John writes to the "seven churches that are in Asia (Revelation 1:4). These are all local realizations of the one Church. New Testament usage does not speak of "the church of Corinth" but rather of the "church that is at Corinth" – indicating that there is only one Church.

Far from being disinterested exegesis, this was Alfrink laying the basis for the autonomy of the Dutch Church. He was defending the "Pastoral Council" which had met for the first time the previous year. He was defending the *New Catechism* popularly known as the "Dutch Catechism". It sold over a quarter of a million copies in its first year; an English translation came out in September 1967 and made the fortune of its publishers. Dutch theologians, before the Council regarded as arch-conservative, now replaced the French as the intellectual vanguard of the Church.

But the Dutch had also replaced the French as the principal target of right-wing criticism. A Commission of Cardinals examined the *New Catechism*, and indicated in ten points what was wrong with it.[2] It was held to be particularly weak on the Virgin Birth and on "the personal existence of angels and devils" affirmed by the Fourth Lateran Council. Subsequently the book was allowed to appear only if flanked by a hefty sixty-page *Supplement*[3] incorporating the points made by the Com-

1 *Lumen Gentium*, 26. This passage was inserted as a result of an intervention by Dr E. Schick, auxiliary Bishop of Fulda, West Germany. It can be read in *Council Speeches of Vatican II*, ed. Yves Congar, Hans Küng and Dan O'Hanlon, pp. 27–40.

2 *Acta Apostolicae Sedis*, 60, 1968, pp. 685–91. Dated 15 October 1968.

3 Edouard Dhanis SJ and Jan Visser CSSR, *The Supplement to a New Catechism*, Search Press 1969.

mission of Cardinals. But what was novel was that the revision of the book was done by its original authors.

Edouard Dhanis SJ and Jan Visser CSSR, whose names appear on the cover, explain this method of composition and pay special tribute to Msgr Herman Fortmann of Utrecht who, alas, died on 3 May 1968 and so was unable to take part. This co-operation between the censors and the censored was novel, and an improvement on past practice.

In September Paul sent Antonio Poma, already Archbishop of Mantua, to Bologna as coadjutor with right of succession.[1] Why? Lercaro had set up ten mixed commissions (that is, of clergy, religious and laity) examining matters such as the place of women in the Church or the role of the laity in the appointment of parish priests and bishops. He dreamed of organizing a vast "pastoral council" in his diocese to implement Vatican II. It would have been a model for the whole Church. It would have involved the participation of all and the "co-responsibility" which Cardinal Suenens spoke of but did not, or so it was said, practise. It looked as though Poma had been sent to scotch Lercaro's great plan – "to stop a moving train" was how Lercaro put it.[2]

Paul was ill throughout most of the summer and autumn of 1967. But Giovanni Benelli, the new *sostituto*, kept the paper on the move, the memos circulating and the office ticking over; he did not, at this stage, overstep his brief. With Paul he master-minded *Regimini Ecclesiae Universae*, the long-awaited, long-dreaded apostolic constitution re-shaping the Roman Curia.

The main thrust of this document was to break the power of the baron-cardinals who had held power under Pius XII. Never again could there be a Cardinal Eugène Tisserant holding three distinct offices at once (that was the old meaning of "pluralism"), building up his empire through his unfashionable Congregation (Oriental Churches), and clinging to office until death. Paul VI decreed that Prefects of Roman dicasteries would no longer have "tenure". Their offices would be up for review every five years, be renewable twice only and lapse altogether on the death of the pope; all curialists would have to tender their resignation at seventy-five.

This reflected the difficulties Paul had himself experienced. His pon-

1 Sandro Magister, *La politica Vaticana e l'Italia*, p. 350.

2 In 1992 on the hundredth anniversary of Lercaro's birth, a conference was held on the theme "Giacomo Lercaro and the living tradition of the Bolognese Church". It turned into an argument between those like his successor Cardinal Giacomo Biffi who stressed the pre-conciliar "conservative" Lercaro, and those like Dossetti and Giuseppe Alberigo who preferred the post-conciliar prophet of renewal. ADISTA, 22 February 1992, p. 3.

tificate would have got into its stride so much more effectively if he could have started afresh with his own team. John Paul II should be grateful to Paul VI for enabling him to have such a distinctive pontificate right from the start. The 1967 reform of the Curia enormously strengthened the pope's hand.

Not only that, but the Secretariat of State emerged as the nerve- and brain-centre of the Vatican, and the pope's personal instrument in the governance of the Church. Paul's clear intention was to make the Secretariat of State the hub of the whole enterprise. From now on it would supervise and co-ordinate everything that went on in the Curia. Further to enhance its prestige, he made cardinals Antonio Samorè and Angelo Dell'Acqua the heads of the two sections: previously the Secretariat had only one cardinal, the Secretary of State himself. Next he flanked them by the brightest "young men" (in Vatican terms) he could find, Agostino Casaroli (for relations with states) and Giovanni Benelli (*de omni re scibile, et quovis alio*) as substitute. Never in history had the pope been so institutionally powerful. Never before had the Curia been so well organized.[1]

There was one simple clause in *Regimini Ecclesiae* that brought fresh breezes blowing through the Vatican: "In addition to Latin, it is acceptable to communicate with the Curia in any of the widely known languages." You wouldn't get very far with Irish or Polish. Better to stick to the languages mastered – or used – by Benelli and Casaroli who from the summer of 1967 were the key aides of Paul VI.

Benelli was the personnel manager, the *chef de cabinet*, a bustling, efficient human dynamo who relaxed by driving his Alfa Romeo sportscar at speed. Nothing escaped his eagle eye. Casaroli, as head of the Council for the Public Affairs of the Church, was responsible for dealing with states or governments. So he was in charge of the Vatican diplomatic service which at that time consisted of thirty-six nuncios, thirty-six pro-nuncios, sixteen Apostolic Delegates and one *chargé d'affaires*. Their task was defined by Archbishop Igino Cardinale, former head of protocol, then Apostolic Delegate in London, as "the art and science of fostering good relations between Church and State".

But because the Vatican diplomats could serve many other purposes

1 Sandro Magister swears, on the basis of a non-divulgeable source, that Paul VI had decided to appoint Franco Costa his Secretary of State because of his knowledge of Italian affairs. But with Giovanni Benelli on hand as *sostituto*, Italian affairs were well catered for and, two years later, Paul VI could risk a non-Italian Secretary of State, Jean Villot. See *La politica Vaticana e l'Italia*, p. 380 fn. 80. This is more than likely for it was precisely at this date, 1967, that Paul brought Villot to Rome to head the Congregation for the Clergy in order to groom him for the succession.

besides their ostensible ones, the competencies of Benelli and Casaroli often overlapped. Benelli sometimes trod on Casaroli's toes, though his own toes were safe. For though Casaroli dealt with the renegotiation of the Concordat with Spain (and later with Italy), he specialized in the countries where the Holy See had no diplomatic relations since the post-war period: Eastern Europe with its estimated sixty million Catholics living under Communism.

Ever since Pope John XXIII sent him to Vienna in 1963 for a conference on consular relations Casaroli had been involved in the Vatican's *Ostpolitik* – the term used to describe the complex web of relations with the Communist states. It varied from Poland where a strong church had just triumphantly celebrated its millennium, to the tightly controlled Czechoslovak and Hungarian Churches, to the churches of the Soviet Union that were intensely persecuted in Lithuania and still illegal in the Ukraine.

The purpose of the *Ostpolitik* was to improve the lot of Catholics living under Communism, and to contribute something to peace and *détente* on the wider international scene. It had a pastoral and a world-political objective. It was often misunderstood by exiles from Eastern Europe, and sometimes by the East Europeans themselves.[1] The presupposition of the *Ostpolitik* was that the division of Europe into two antagonistic blocs was artificial, anomalous and would not last for ever. Addressing the participants in a conference devoted to "Western Europe and the Countries of the East", Paul remarked: "You have chosen a fundamental theme on which may depend the *definitive* organization of European society. With you the Holy See is convinced that along this path lies the chance of a *rapprochement* that would be both loyal and deep."[2]

It would be *loyal* because it would not betray the sacrifices of the martyrs that were still going on especially in Lithuania and the Ukraine. Casaroli always quoted this passage to show that Paul sought to overcome the division of Europe into hostile ideological blocs, and did not simply accept the status quo.

That was the first presupposition of the Vatican's *Ostpolitik*. The second presupposition, defined by Casaroli in words borrowed from Winston Churchill, was that "the real boundary between Europe and

1 Poles, Czechs and Slovaks thought of themselves as "Central Europeans", which achieved three aims at a stroke: it pushed "barbarism" and a lack of culture eastwards; it placed Warsaw or Prague at the centre of Europe; and by dividing Europe into three instead of two it offered an alternative to the East–West confrontation.

2 *Insegnamenti*, 1967, p. 201.

Asia is not a chain of mountains or a physical frontier but the set of convictions and ideas we call Western civilization."[1]

The *Ostpolitik*, worries about birth-control, and concern for the autonomy of local Churches led Paul to make Karol Wojtyla a cardinal on 26 June 1967. Yet the Archbishop of Kraków was only one of the twenty-seven new cardinals created this day. The nominations, though they displayed Paul's customary skill in balancing opposing tendencies, made one wonder whether this was the best way to govern the Church. Thus Dino Staffa, secretary of the Congregation of the Clergy, ever conscious of his dignity ("He's a one-man procession"), and Michele Pellegrino with his plain wooden cross represented the extremes thrown up by the Council; but they also cancelled each other out.

With other appointments Paul thanked old Secretariat of State friends like Angelo Dell'Acqua and Pierre Veuillot of Paris, and those like Pericle Felici and John J. Krol of Philadelphia who had served the Council as secretary or under-secretary. Indonesia, a predominantly Muslim country Paul wished to visit, got its first-ever cardinal, Justin Darmojuwono; and Chicago got the fireman's son John J. Cody.

Paul had a gift for his neo-cardinals. On St John the Baptist, his name-day, 24 June 1967, he presented them with his defence of clerical celibacy in *Sacerdotalis Caelibatus*. It severely dented Paul's "liberal" image, especially in the Anglo-Saxon world. It showed that priestly celibacy had never been for him a genuinely "open question". When he withdrew the question from the competence of the Council, his mind was already made up. Some wondered whether the same was not true of artificial birth-control.

Yet everyone knew that clerical celibacy was not a dogmatic or doctrinal question, but a "disciplinary" question that, as Pope John was supposed to have said, "could be changed by a stroke of my pen". The Oriental Churches including those in communion with Rome had a different discipline, "finally established", as Paul admits, "by the Council of Trullo held in the year 692".[2] Unable to dispute the legitimacy of the Oriental tradition, Paul was reduced to explaining lamely the different disciplines by "the different historical background of that most noble part of the Church, a situation which the Holy Spirit has providentially and supernaturally influenced."[3]

1 Agostino Casaroli, "*La Santa Sede e l'Europa*", *Civiltà Cattolica*, 19 February 1972, p. 376. This was the text of a lecture given by Archbishop Casaroli at the Milan Istituto di Studi di Politica Internazionale on 20 January 1972. It shows Casaroli to have thought long and hard about Europe and its future.

2 *Sacerdotalis Caelibatus*, 38.

3 Ibid.

That raised the question: Why should the Holy Spirit act so differently in East and West? But this question is not answered, not even addressed. The most careful and historically accurate paragraph of the encyclical, devoted to the "Western Church", tries desperately to be honest:

> The Church of the West, from the beginning of the fourth century, strengthened, extended and approved this practice by means of various provincial councils and through the Supreme Pontiffs . . . The supreme pastors . . . restored ecclesiastical celibacy in successive eras of history, even when they met opposition from the clergy itself, and when the practices of a decadent society did not favour the heroic demands of virtue.[1]

The idea that the "clergy opposition" was invariably linked with the decadence of society generally does not deal with the problem of the transition from *legitimate* clergy marriage to the imposition of celibacy. In the eleventh century celibacy was opposed as a new-fangled thing, while clerical marriage was the traditional, more "conservative" position.

Paul brushes this aside and with a mighty leap of his seven-league boots reaches the sixteenth century, when "the obligation of celibacy was solemnly sanctioned by the Council of Trent, and finally included in the Code of Canon Law".[2] He makes it sound like the most natural thing in the world. Yet this text grudgingly admits it took fifteen centuries for this "dazzling jewel" to impose itself on the Catholic world.

Sacerdotalis Caelibatus is built on a contradiction or at least a tension. It has to begin from the Council's statement in the decree on the Priestly Ministry that virginity "is not, of course, required by the nature of the priesthood itself. This is clear from the practice of the early Church itself and the traditions of the Eastern Churches."[3] But if celibacy is not *essential* to the priesthood, then the efforts expended here to prove that it is "particularly suited" to the priestly ministry will never amount to the *necessary* link between priesthood and celibacy that the encyclical wishes to assert.

If the link really were necessary, it would admit of no *exceptions*. Yet even apart from the historical example of Oriental Catholics, the "Western Church" has not insisted on celibacy for married convert clergymen. Echoing the practice of Pius XII, Paul says: "A study may

1 Ibid. 36.

2 Ibid.

3 *Presbyterorum Ordinis*, 16.

be allowed[1] of the particular circumstances of married sacred ministers of others Churches . . . and of the possibility of admitting to full priestly functions those who desire to adhere to the fullness of this communion and to continue to exercise the sacred ministry."[2]

That means ordaining convert clergymen. True, this concession is accompanied by the warning that "the circumstances must be such, however, as not to prejudice the existing discipline concerning celibacy".[3]

Despite such precautions, the ordination of convert clergymen clearly means that one sacrament – marriage – cannot for ever be seen as an obstacle (*obex*) to another – orders. Nor did this provision remain a dead letter. The principle was confirmed in 1969 when Paul authorized the ordination of four former Anglican priests who were already married. Moreover they were treated just like any of their colleagues and became parish priests in the normal course of events.[4]

The restoration of the permanent diaconate, married or not, also helped to break the tabu of celibacy. For deacons were allowed to be married and were indisputably "clergy" (as contrasted with "laity"). Thanks to these moves by Paul VI, the Western Church acquired in the strict sense a married clergy alongside those graced with the charism of celibacy. The example of the Oriental Churches, the ordination of married convert clergymen and the restoration of the diaconate combined to erode the notion that "clerical celibacy" was an absolutely inviolable norm.

The difficulties of *Sacerdotalis Caelibatus* reflect Catholic confusion on this topic generally, and were not peculiar to Paul. The "tradition" had been toughly resisted and won through only with difficulty. Psychologically, therefore, it was difficult to abandon it. Paul uses the "argument from consistency", maintaining that it was "unthinkable" that the Church should have got this wrong for so many centuries.[5] But that is only true if one believes that the Church must never admit mistakes.

1 This was the hallowed phrase in Paul's pontificate for saying that a question was "open". It hereby entered the realm of what the theological series edited by Karl Rahner called in good mediaeval fashion *Questiones Disputatae* – matters for debate.

2 *Sacerdotalis Caelibatus*, 42.

3 Ibid.

4 The notion that ordained convert clergymen could not be parish priests was a novelty devised in 1986 when Fr Peter Cornwell was about to be ordained. One of the 1969 crop of Australian priests, Fr E. G. Beyer, said that he and all his colleagues had become parish priests. Moreover surveys showed that "not only do Catholics readily accept a married priest as their pastor, they warmly welcome him and his wife and family into their midst" (*Tablet*, 11 October 1986, p. 1978).

5 *Sacerdotalis Caelibatus*, 41.

The alternatives presented by the encyclical are too stark. It is not just celibacy versus truncated human beings. Some are fulfilled and expanded by celibacy; others are not. It is the *absoluteness* of the link between celibacy and the priesthood that was under attack.

Paul knew this only too well. Jesus, he concedes, did not make celibacy a "prerequisite in his choice of the Twelve, nor did the Apostles for those who presided over the first Christian communities".[1] But merely to reply that "Jesus remained throughout his whole life in a state of celibacy, which signified his total dedication to the service of God and men" seems inadequate. Did Jesus ask celibacy of St Peter?

The arguments in favour of a bond between celibacy and the priesthood in fact show its linkage with *religious life*, confirming the suspicion that what happened in the twelfth century was the extension of the monastic ideal to the whole clergy under the leadership of a series of monk-popes, notably Hildebrand, Pope Gregory VII. The theme of the "undivided heart" is introduced to define an ideal of Christian heroism: "Who can doubt the moral and spiritual richness of such a consecrated life, consecrated not to any human ideal no matter how noble, but to Christ and his work to bring about a new form of humanity in all places and for all generations?"[2]

Indeed: yet once again it sounds like a description of religious life, and in any case the "consecrated married" can also live according to this ideal.

Another weak point in the encyclical comes when it sweeps away empirical evidence without any serious consideration of it: "It is simply not possible to believe that the abolition of ecclesiastical celibacy would considerably increase the number of priestly vocations: the contemporary experience of those Churches and ecclesial communities which allow their ministers to marry seems to prove the contrary."[3]

Wishful thinking. Subsequent experience suggested rather that the married couple make a good ministerial team, and that at least some of those professing celibacy in the seminary were homosexuals trying to "sublimate" their personal difficulties.

The most moving part of *Sacerdotalis Caelibatus* is also the most personal:

> The priest by reason of his celibacy is a solitary; that is true, but his solitariness is not emptiness because it is filled with God and the brimming riches of his kingdom . . . At times loneliness

1 Ibid. 5.
2 Ibid. 24.
3 Ibid. 49.

> will weigh heavily on the priest, but not for that reason will he regret having generously chosen it. Christ too in the most tragic hours of his life was alone – abandoned by the very ones he had chosen as witnesses to, and companions of, his life, and whom he had loved unto the end, but he said, "I am not alone, for the Father is with me."[1]

Paul must have felt very alone as he composed and published his encyclical; but not all heart-break in the presbytery could be explained away so easily.

Thus Paul's attempt to settle the question exacerbated it. Priests' groups in Europe and the US demanded to be allowed to marry and claimed this as a "human right". Cardinal Suenens urged the importance of ordaining married men, especially in Africa, lest the Church become a Bible-only Church. This question came up at the 1971 Synod.

So Paul was left with only a few broken shards as a result of this attempt vigorously to assert his authority. The enduring achievement of the letter was a new approach to laicization. Under the headings "Lamentable Defections" and "Celibacy not to Blame"[2] Paul first berates unfaithful priests and says they would not depart "if they knew how much sorrow, dishonour and unrest they bring to the Holy Church of God". But having got that off his chest, he grants that some such *may* have "serious dispositions which give promise of their being able to live as good Christian lay people". To these the Church "sometimes grants a dispensation, *thus letting love conquer sorrow*".[3] Paul was at his most Christian in that simple phrase, which echoed his Christmas Day visits to resigned priests in their poverty.

The new discipline could not come into force in 1967 because Ottaviani was still at the Holy Office. But the encyclical foreshadowed the compassionate legislation of 1971 which made resignation from the priestly ministry and sacramental marriage possible.

Paul always made much of the feast of SS Peter and Paul, 29 June. In Roman rhetoric Peter was the guardian of the flock, the faithful sheepdog who shepherded them well; Paul stood for mission, outreach, adventure, the appeal to those who built an altar "to the unknown God" on the Areopagus. Paul VI's choice of name indicated that he wanted to be Pauline in spirit; but his entourage wanted him to be Petrine. So sometimes he seemed like St Peter masquerading as St Paul. Yet even in

1 Ibid. 58–59.

2 Ibid. 83.

3 Ibid. 88. My italics.

his gravest Petrine solicitude for established Christian communities he kept something of the dash and brio of Paul.

On the feast of SS Peter and Paul 1967 he announced that a "Year of Faith" would begin, solemnly concluding exactly one year later. The purpose of the "Year of Faith" was to celebrate the nineteen-hundredth anniversary of the martyrdom of Peter of Galilee. Some scholars thought he died in AD 67. Others preferred AD 64, the year when Nero, wanting to pin the blame for the fire of 18–19 July 64, organized spectacular games on the other side of the Tiber, just east of the Vatican Hill. But there was a case for 67 and, anyway, in 1964 everyone was distracted by the Council.

What was the point of the Year of Faith? As it turned out, it seemed designed to batten down the hatches of orthodoxy, presumed threatened by reckless theologians and disintegrating Dutchmen. That, at least, was the view Cardinal Ottaviani saw, or rather intuited, from the Holy Office. It is not sure that Paul VI saw it that way. He had ordered a survey of episcopal conferences on the most modern form of atheism, atheistic humanism.[1] That made it sound like a study project for the Secretariat for Non-believers, involving real partners in dialogue and a genuine quest for a truth as yet unknown. Ottaviani soon turned it into a new Syllabus of Errors.

Did Orthodox Christians think there was a crisis of faith? What did they think about the encyclical on celibacy? Did they believe the Catholic Church was seriously committed to ecumenism?

These questions came up because on 15 July 1967 during the consistory at which his old friend Antonio Roberi, now nuncio to Spain, received the red hat, Paul announced that in ten days time he would be visiting Turkey for a meeting with Patriarch Athenagoras. This would be an historic event, like their Jerusalem meeting: no pope had been to Constantinople since Pope Constantine I (708–715).

By linking the Year of Faith with the visit to the sites of the ancient ecumenical Councils, recognized by all Christians, Paul was showing how fundamental were faith and the memory of the sources to ecumenism. One had to go back to go forward. By going to Turkey he would be recalling "the important ecumenical councils held there, and also in Ephesus the pious memory of the Madonna". It would be, he said, a splendid opening to the Year of Faith.[2] Western theologians who failed to recognize this aspect complained that the Year of Faith spelt the death of theology. "One could close down all theological institutes," said one theologian, "and just buy the gramophone record from Rome."

1 René Laurentin, *Le Premier Synode, Bilan et Perspectives*, pp. 99–100.
2 *Insegnamenti*, p. 379.

The Ecumenical Patriarch is a beleaguered figure in modern Turkey, with his flock reduced to a few thousand and no influence outside the Phanar, his "Vatican". So by going at all Paul was boosting his importance. Paul tactfully showed his appreciation of Turkey by returning the Turkish standard captured at the battle of Lepanto which had been kept in Rome since 1571.

At the end of their meeting in the Patriarchal Church of St George, Paul handed Athenagoras an official brief, *Anno ineunte*, which broke new ground in describing Rome and Constantinople as "sister Churches". This went further than the Council's decree on ecumenism which prudently said, not that the Orthodox Churches were sister Churches of Rome, but that "they *regard each other* as sister Churches",[1] a very different matter. For Rome to declare its sisterhood with the Orthodox was to step down from the pedestal of *Mater et Magistra* (Mother and Teacher). Used by the Orthodox *vis-à-vis* Rome, "sister Church" was a claim; used by Rome of the Orthodox Church, it was a concession. In *Anno ineunte* Paul said:

> We have lived this life of sister churches for centuries, celebrating together the ecumenical councils which defended the deposit of faith against any alteration. Now after a long period of division and mutual incomprehension, the Lord has allowed us to recover ourselves as sister churches, despite the obstacles that faced us.[2]

The basis for this mutual recognition is the sacramental presence of Christ in each Church.

Once the two Churches regarded each other as sister Churches, one had to ask: what more is required for full communion? Basing himself on the patristic tradition, Paul gave his answer:

> To rediscover unity in diversity and faithfulness can only be the work of the Holy Spirit. If unity of faith is required for full communion, diversity of usage is no obstacle to it. On the contrary, did not Irenaeus, "whose name suited him because he was a peacemaker both by name and in deed" (Eusebius, *Ecclesiastical History*, V, 24, 18) say that "the difference of customs confirms the agreement of faith"? As for Augustine, the great doctor of the African Church, he saw the diversity of customs as one of the reasons for the beauty of the Church.[3]

1 *Unitatis Reintegratio*, 17.

2 See Yves-Marie Congar, *Diversity and Communion*, pp. 88–91, for commentary.

3 Ibid. pp. 32–33.

So why remain divided? The usual rationalizations – the *Filioque* was the most notorious example – were wheeled up to justify a breach of communion only because the two Churches were already divided.

But once they had gone their separate ways a different "culture" grew up on both sides, involving spirituality, the style of authority, the way of relating to the world, which could be as hard to reconcile as theological differences. But there remained the intractable problem of dogmas defined by the Roman Catholic Church after 1054, notably the Immaculate Conception (1854) and the Assumption (1950).

Paul was in Turkey at the end of July 1967. From 26 to 28 October he welcomed the Ecumenical Patriarch, Athenagoras II, in the Vatican. This was a double-first: no reigning Ecumenical Patriarch had ever been to Rome, and his visit coincided with the last week of the first-ever meeting of the Roman Synod, an idea borrowed from the Greeks (*syn-odos*).

In fact the Athenagoras visit overshadowed the Synod which tried to cram five topics into four weeks. The Synod was a success as a "trial run", claimed Cardinal William Conway of Armagh; but Melchite Archbishop Neofito Edelby judged it was only "five per cent a true Synod".[1] By comparison, the visit of the Ecumenical Patriarch marked a fresh stage in ecumenical relations, a breakthrough, "a luminous point where the lights of all the great ecumenical events of the last years *converged*". This was the view of Cardinal Augustin Bea, himself now a frail old patriarch of eighty-six who, it seemed, a puff of wind might blow away. "Convergence" became a favourite word of Paul's. He liked to define ecumenism as "convergence towards Christ".

Athenagoras lodged in the Torre San Giovanni, at the top of the Vatican hill that Pope John XXIII had reordered. He did not arrive empty-handed. Before setting off he had visited the autocephalous Churches of Romania, Bulgaria and Serbia. His meeting with the Russian Orthodox Patriarch was cancelled at the last minute: par for the course. Athenagoras' contacts, however, were enough to give the encounter a pan-Orthodox flavour. They allowed Paul to note with joy that plans for the Pan-Orthodox Synod, first mooted in 1961, were forging ahead and revealed a remarkable "convergence" (that word again!) with Vatican II.[2]

Even more remarkable was the service in St Peter's, attended by Athenagoras' Synod and the Roman Synod. They were asymmetrical:

1 Peter Hebblethwaite, *Understanding the Synod*, p. 110. Should you need to know more about the first Synod, this book may be recommended.

2 Augustin Bea SJ, "Pope and Cardinal", in *The Month*, March 1967, pp. 49–52. The same commentary appeared in other SJ publications like *Civiltà Cattolica*.

twelve Orthodox compared with 220 Catholics. A special rite was devised which included a long prayer of thanksgiving, like a canon except that the words of consecration were omitted. This came as close as possible to a Eucharist while marking "the pain of division". It was in fact a "dry Mass", such as future ordinands said in seminaries. It ended with the Our Father and the kiss of peace. Cardinals and Archimandrites fell over and upon each other. Among Athenagoras' suite was Metropolitan Meliton, his chief theologian who would dangerously remark, "Paul VI has made the papacy out of date."[1]

The quarrel between East and West seemed to drift away into the distant dome of St Peter's. Paul insisted on no title other than the "primacy of charity" of which St Irenaeus spoke. Athenagoras saw in Paul's actions a spirit of humility akin to that which led Jesus "to wash the feet of his disciples". Paul quoted his patron: "Be eager to give one another precedence" (Romans 12:10). Rules for the future: no poaching, nobbling or nibbling; work together for justice and peace; and "common action on the pastoral, social and intellectual level" accompanied by proper respect for the loyalties fostered by either Church. That was Paul VI speaking; but it could have been Athenagoras, so close were they.

This was very edifying and remarkable because a surprise: it would not have been predicted ten or even five years before. Yet it raised an awkward problem that Paul had himself evoked in *Ecclesiam Suam*: if dialogue with other Christians and other-believers was so desirable, then it was *a fortiori* necessary within the Catholic Church. "How greatly we desire," he wrote, "that this dialogue with our own children may be conducted with the fullness of faith, with charity and with dynamic holiness."[2] But this does not mean, he added darkly, "that the virtue of obedience is no longer operative".[3]

Considering his role in previous congresses, Paul might have been expected to take a great interest in the World Congress of the Laity which overlapped with the Synod. But the decade that had elapsed between the last congress and this one, the theology of the laity and the way they saw themselves, had totally changed. One could not simultaneously say that the gifts or charisms of the Holy Spirit were showered equally upon all members of the People of God, before distinctions of office were introduced, *and* sit them down in neat

1 Yves-Marie Congar, *Unity and Diversity*, p. 88. Meliton was *praising* him.

2 *Ecclesiam Suam*, 113. I have eliminated the capital letters for "We" and "Our children".

3 Ibid.

: Pope receives the apostolic brief officially ouncing the end of the Second Vatican Council. presented by Archbishop Pericle Felici.

sident Lyndon B Johnson accompanied Paul to his ousine outside the Waldorf Astoria on October 4, 5; behind Paul can be descried Archbishop Paul imir Marcinkus, papal bodyguard and financier.

Graham Greene was received in private audience on July 15, 1965.

Paul's visit in 1966 to the tomb of St Celestine V, the first pope to resign, aroused speculation that he would retire himself: in fact, the question of resignation arose only in the last two years of his life. It was rejected.

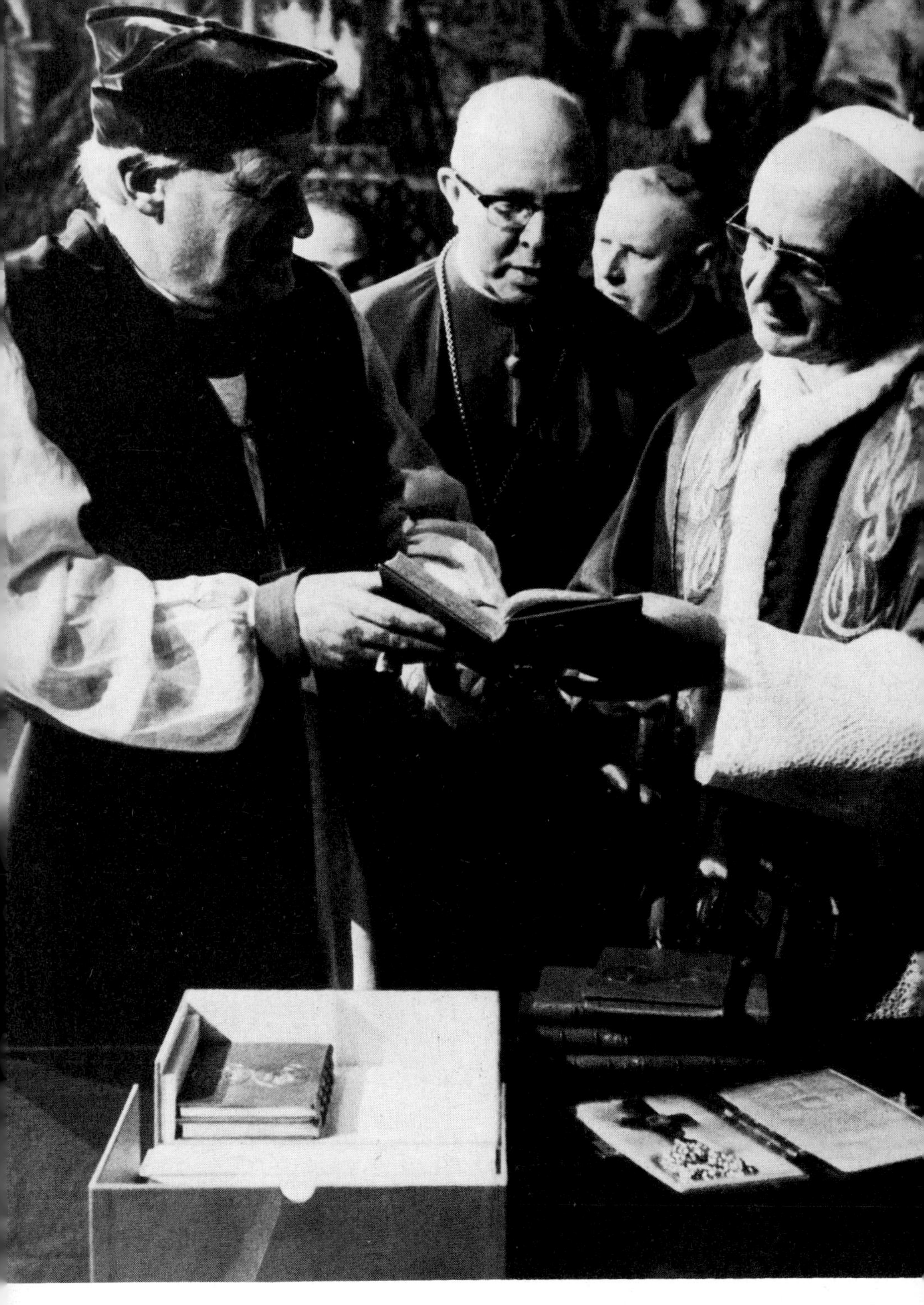

Paul meets Dr Michael Ramsay, Archbishop of Canterbury, in March 1966, and declares "this is your home, this is where you have a right to be." Archbishop Jan Willebrands hovers.

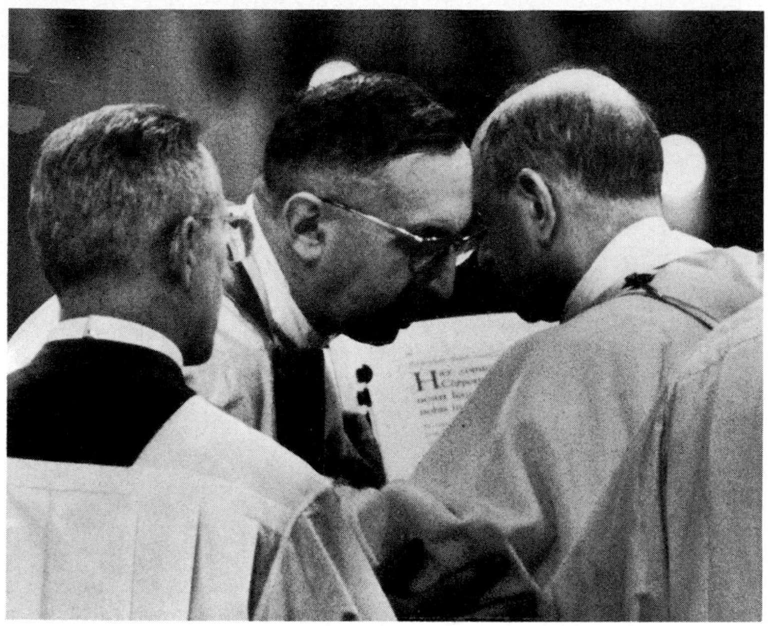

Homage at the 1967 Synod by Cardinal Jean Villot, soon to be his Secretary of State, with special responsibility to co-ordinate local Churches.

Paul and Athenagoras, Ecumenical Patriarch, in St Peter's, October 1967; Metropolitan Meliton later commented, "Paul VI has made the papacy out of date."

Back from Saigon, President Lyndon B Johnson drops in by helicopter on December 23, 1967. Usually presented as a tense, angry encounter; in fact a convalescent Paul helps Johnson find a way to peace.

Archbishop Sergio Pignedoli, Paul's trouble-shooter is briefed for his peace mission to Vietnam.

Assassination attempt in Manila, the Philippines, in 1970 by the mad Bolivian painter, Benjamin Mendoza y Amor. His explanation: "I acted alone to save humanity from superstition."

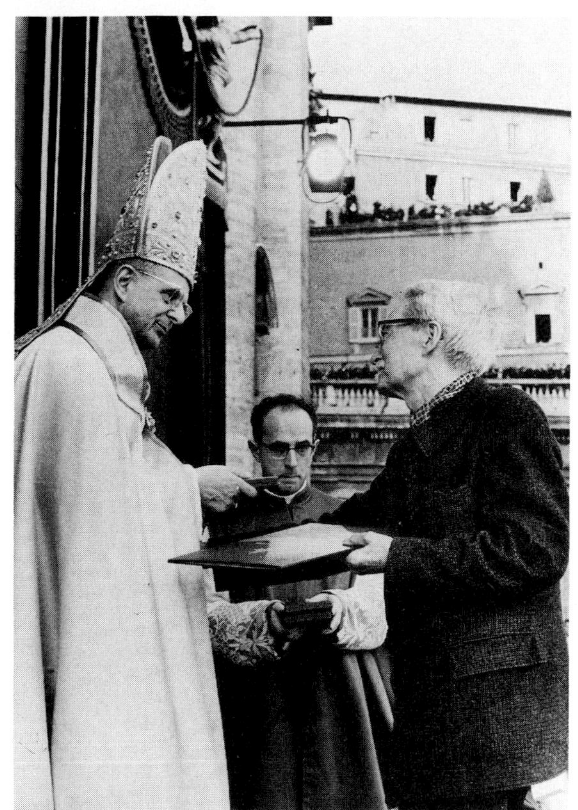

Left: Paul with Jacques Maritain, his master in the 1930's, now in decline.

Below: Paul concelebrates Mass at the 1971 Synod with Cardinal Joszef Mindszenty, rescued from the US Embassy in Budapest where he had been immured since the revolution of 1956. Mindszenty was not grateful, and attacked Paul in his autobiography.

Left: A late portrait of an exhausted Paul.

Below: Paul meets President Anwar Sadat of Egypt, this balancing the visit of Mrs Golda Meir.

ıl comforts Rosaria Moro, sister of the murdered Aldo Moro, at the funeral in John Lateran where Paul upbraided God for letting this happen: Moro's wife ł children refused to attend as a protest against government inaction.

ıl with Cardinal Albino Luciani, Patriarch of Venice, who succeeded him efly on August 26 1978, and took the name John Paul I.

The body of Paul VI lies in state in St Peter's. "His coffin was surmounted", wrote Yves Congar, "not by the tiara that he had given away, not even by a mitre or a stole, but by the open book of the Gospels, its pages riffled by the light breeze."

rows to listen to clerics telling them how to run their families and their work.

The 2500 delegates, though carefully screened, were no longer as docile as they used to be. The Pope's speech was criticized as negative in tone and depressing, made up of attacks on secularization and warnings not to infringe on the authority of the hierarchy. The suspicion grew that any moves at the congress towards establishing a more permanent lay organization – some sort of "senate" alongside the Synod – were doomed. The *New York Times* noted the difference:

> "When Pope Pius addressed us in 1957," said one participant, "it was the major event of the Congress. Hours were spent in discussion and exegesis of every page. This year, Pope Paul's speech passed unnoticed. In so far as it was discussed at all, in private groups, it was to point out how far behind the congress it was."
>
> There was even discussion in one large group of mixed nationality, of sending a deputation to the Pontiff to express disappointment with his admonitory tone. This project was abandoned out of concern for the Pope's current ill-health.[1]

That was kind of them.

He needed to save his energies for Athenagoras. So he was spared the immediate impact of the "resolutions" of the Congress demanding "representative structures to be established at different levels of the Church" (or democracy under another name). These were responsible men and women – somehow Dorothy Day was there – so they distinguished between "decision-taking", which they agreed should be the prerogative of the bishops, and "decision-making", to which they should be allowed to contribute.[2] And birth-control?

On this they were very "responsible". They warned against the geopolitical intervention by the superpowers – by which they meant that the International Monetary Fund (IMF) and the World Bank should not make aid dependent on the use of contraception to achieve population control. Then they recalled:

> the very clear feeling among Christian lay people that there is need for a clear stand by the *teaching authorities* of the Church which would focus on fundamental moral and spiritual values, while leaving the choice of scientific means for achieving responsible parenthood to parents acting with their Christian

1 Robert C. Doty, "The Laity jolts the Church", *New York Times*, 22 October 1967.

2 Jean-Guy Vaillancourt, *Papal Power: A Study of Vatican Control over Lay Catholic Elites*, pp. 120–23.

faith and on the basis of medical and scientific consultation.[1]

This text was approved shortly after midnight, in a rowdy session that lasted till 2.15 a.m., with sixty-seven *placet*, twenty-one *non placet* and ten abstentions. A Lebanese stormed out crying heresy.

What *L'Osservatore Romano* chastely described as "the malaise from which the Holy Father had been suffering for weeks" finally laid him low, and he was unable to deliver his address at the end of the Synod on 29 October, feast of Christ the King. It was read for him by Msgr Amleto Tondini, an unhappy choice, for this was the man who had slandered Pope John in his *de eligendo pontifice* address at the conclave of 1963.[2] Brother Benildo, a Christian Brother, was canonized.

Paul had needed an operation for an enlarged prostate for several months, but because of the Synod and the meeting with Athenagoras he begged his doctors to delay. This meant, however, that throughout this period he had to wear a catheter, which was burdensome and distressing for so fastidious a man.[3]

There had been debate about whether he should become the first pope to go to the Gemelli hospital, but Dr Pietro Valdoni, the leading Italian urologist who did the operation, realized the commercial possibilities of being known as "the-doctor-who-operated-on-the-Pope-inside-the-Vatican". He was aided by the Pope's personal physician, Dr Mario Fontana, who, with the Rome rumour-mill speculating wildly, explained that there was "nothing to be alarmed about, mere routine in men of a certain age".[4] But he did not say what it was.

Just to be sure he saw a friendly face when he came round, Paul called up the doctor-poet Ugo Piazzi, first met in 1925 wearing baggy zouave trousers and a disconcerting black shirt.[5] Piazzi told Jean Guitton that "certain Roman prelates are saying the Pope has not been operated upon, that the wound has merely healed over, that the Pope is inoperable and is already condemned to death".[6] The sheer heartlessness of the Curia comes out in that unfounded gossip. There were already those who wished him dead.

1 Ibid. p. 123.

2 See chapter 20 above, p. 325.

3 Carlo Cremona, who otherwise is the first to speak plainly of the operation, gets the date wrong (putting it on 4 November 1968, which would have put it after *Humanae Vitae*), and observing that the catheter "was hard to reconcile with onerous papal pontifical tasks", *Paolo VI*, p. 255.

4 Benny Lai, *Les Secrets du Vatican*, pp. 186–87.

5 *Notiziario*, 11, p. 38.

6 Jean Guitton, *Paul VI secret*, pp. 97–98.

29

Vietnam and Contraception

> Paul VI was secretive. He was simultaneously – and paradoxically – indecisive and authoritarian. When he had taken a decision, it was quite impossible to get him to modify it in any way whatsoever.
>
> (JEAN GUITTON, *Paul VI secret*, p. 11)

Paul had just recovered from his prostate operation. On waking up from the anaesthetic he was allowed to make six and a half rounds of his library – "just long enough to say the rosary". Dr Ugo Piazzi stayed to supervise his convalescence and cheer him up. Towards midnight Paul would hear Piazzi, a poet as well as a doctor, typing away and say, "Come and read me your poem before I go to sleep." He thought the Psalms were poetry and specially liked the music of *In pace in idipsum dormiam et requiescam* (I will rest and go to sleep in peace).[1] But convalescence could take up to about three months.

Paul got up from his sick-bed in time for an eve-of-Christmas visit from President Lyndon B. Johnson who dropped in – literally, by helicopter – on 23 December. This impromptu arrival is said to have "angered" Paul. Johnson was back from Saigon on a whirlwind round-the-world-in-seven-days trip, and landing in the Vatican Gardens was the best way to beat Roman traffic. Pope and President met for the second time in Paul's private library and had "a lengthy and intense talk about the search for peace in Vietnam".[2]

Most accounts present this meeting as fraught and tense. Apart from descending from the skies, Johnson is also deemed to have caused offence by using a pocket-knife to prise open his gift to the pontiff – a plastic

1 Jean Guitton, *Paul VI secret*, p. 97. Paul gathered the medical team together and gave them each a watch inscribed with the date of the operation: Feast of St Andrew 1967.

2 Wilton Wynn, *Keepers of the Keys; John XIII, Paul VI and John Paul II, Three who Changed the Church*, Random House, New York 1988, p. 177.

bust of himself.[1] Neither action seems particularly heinous, and both might be considered instances of "Texan" heartiness.

The *New York Times* said there was an ill-starred clash of visions which contrasted "the Pontiff's world-oriented, humanitarian concerns and the President's national-military-political approach". In *Time* Wilton Wynn alleged that Paul, angered by the massive, indiscriminate bombing of Hanoi on 13 and 14 December, "slammed his hand on to his desk and shouted at Johnson".[2] The Vatican press office issued the usual denials.

There is new light on this meeting from one of Johnson's aides, Joseph A. Califano.[3] Johnson agreed with Paul in wanting to get Hanoi to the conference table; the question was whether more or less bombing would bring them there. Johnson eventually came round to Paul's view, and on 31 March 1968 announced a pause in the bombing and declared that he would not stand for another term as President. By removing the issue from the election campaign Johnson hoped to win credibility in his efforts for peace and get the North Vietnamese to the negotiating table.

So it was fitting that Paul had already decided to launch World Peace Day on 1 January 1968 with a special "message" that became an annual fixture. It was the logical consequence of *Populorum Progressio* and the new Justice and Peace Commission designed to implement it. Paul saw no reason why Communists should purloin the vocabulary of peace (so that "peace-loving" was applied to those who were armed to the teeth), and wanted to rescue this language for humanity. In so doing he created a sort of "secular feast", a day for those who, whatever their beliefs, could accept Christian "values".[4] He was behaving as "an expert in humanity", voicing humanity's aspirations; and he was trying to realize what he had hinted at in *Ecclesiam Suam*: "Could we not one day bring back Marxist ideas to their Christian origins?"[5]

The main threat to peace as 1968 began appeared to come from Vietnam. Neither Paul nor anyone else imagined what a dramatic year it would be. Dates are not magical, yet there is something special and odd about years which end in eight: 1688 the "glorious revolution"

1 Roy Domenico, "The Vatican, the US and Vietnam in the Johnson Years", a paper delivered 13 October 1991 at "The Holy See in the Modern Age" conference, University of New Brunswick, Canada, p. 23.

2 In *Keepers of the Keys*, Wynn offers a milder version of this story: "The papal gesture [in offering his palace for pre-talks] went for naught. It was no wonder that the frustrated Paul VI slapped his desk when he met Johnson", pp. 196–97.

3 Joseph A. Califano, "The President and the Pope: LBJ, Paul VI and the Vietnam War", *America*, 12 October 1991, pp. 239–40.

4 "World Communications Day", some time in the spring, never had the same appeal.

5 *Ecclesiam Suam*, 104.

in England; 1788 the French revolution; 1848 the year of revolutions throughout Europe; 1948 the Communist takeover or the spurious revolution. What would 1968 bring?

Where were his friends now? Aldo Moro had been Prime Minister since 1965. Vittorio Veronese, former Director-General of UNESCO, was still sorting out the confusion of the Third World Congress on the Lay Apostolate, at which he presided, before proceeding to steer Catholic Action in the direction of the "spiritual option". Giuseppe Lazzati was Rector of the Catholic University of Milan, his predecessor, Ezio Francheschini, having taken early retirement, exhausted by coping with the student unrest which, in Milan, anticipated 1968.[1]

But Paul was losing his friends among the cardinals who had made the Council. Léon-Joseph Suenens knew about the preparations for *Humanae Vitae* and tried to block them. In Montreal Paul-Emile Léger resigned and went off to a leper colony, thus "exchanging the scarlet of a cardinal for the plain white soutane of the missionary priest".[2] There was not much Paul could do about Léger except wave him goodbye, which he did.[3]

But Paul ought to have done something to stop the wilder and wilder attacks on Cardinal Giacomo Lercaro, Archbishop of Bologna, architect of the liturgical reform and president of the *Consilium*. Cardinal Antonio Bacci wrote an adultory preface to a book by Tito Casini, a would-be Catholic intellectual, which described Lercaro as "the most formidable threat, after Martin Luther, to the unity and integrity of the Church". Lercaro allegedly ran the liturgical *Consilium* like Adolf Hitler. He is compared to a termite – or white ant – gnawing away at the very vitals of the Church.[4] Lercaro was distressed and angry that Paul, though protesting against "the unjust and irreverent attack" on him and on the *Consilium*,[5] did nothing about Bacci.

1 Also in the Catholic University Don Luigi Giussani was gathering the disciples who would emerge from the year rebaptized as *Comunione e Liberazione* (taking one word – *koinonia* – from the Council and the other – liberation – from current political vocabulary). Paul had been his bishop. They did not get on, since Giussani was trying to do what FUCI was supposed to do.

2 Michael Higgins, "Symbol of Catholic Canada", Obituary of Cardinal Léger, *Guardian*, 15 November 1991. Léger died on 13 November 1991.

3 *Insegnamenti*, 1967, pp. 1042–43.

4 Tito Casini, *La Tunica Stracciata*, Florence 1967.

5 *Insegnamenti*, 1967, p. 167. Paul added: "This publication, as is obvious, cannot have our approval; it does not edify anyone, and it does not commend the cause that it seeks to promote, that is, the use of Latin in the liturgy; this is a question that needs addressing, but it cannot be resolved in a way that goes counter to the great principle of the Council: the intelligibility of liturgical prayer on the level of the people."

But worse was to come, Lercaro opened his *L'Osservatore Romano* for 12–13 February 1968 and was astonished to read that the Holy Father had "kindly accepted his resignation for reasons of advanced age and bad health". A letter from Cardinal Amleto Cicognani thanked him for this "spontaneous decision". Paul VI was still half-convalescing. Perhaps that excused the brutality of this statement, false in every particular. Lercaro was not ill, and he had not resigned. He was sacked.[1]

Lercaro could not understand why Paul, who had for so long trusted him to oversee liturgical reform, should not make any effort to defend him *and his work*. For behind minor figures like Bacci and Casini was Archbishop Marcel Lefebvre who found evidence of Protestant heresy at every turn: the "new Mass" was not a sacrifice but a meal, and so on – it soon became a rigmarole.[2] The unexplained sacking of Lercaro meant that Paul began 1968, the most fraught year of his pontificate, with an act performed in his name that was unjust and unwise.

There has been much speculation about the "real reason" for Lercaro's dismissal. He was said to be "too friendly" with the Communists who ran the Bologna city council. He opposed the Vietnam war too passionately. His ten mixed commissions discussed everything from the place of women in the Church and society to the election of bishops. He made the "local Church" the starting-point of his thinking just as much as Cardinal Bernard Alfrink did in the Netherlands.[3]

No doubt these factors played a part. Fr Annibale Bugnini had worked closely with Lercaro as secretary of the *Consilium* for four years. In his huge history of liturgical reform he relegates the Lercaro "resignation" to a brief footnote.[4] But he adds the significant detail: on the very day the Pope "accepted Cardinal Lercaro's resignation" Cardinal Arcadio Larraona was sacked as Prefect of the Congregation of Rites, and one man, the Benedictine Abbot Benno Gut, *replaced them both*. So one reason for Lercaro's dismissal may have been the need to call a halt to sparring matches and demarcation disputes between the two departments. Lercaro wrote to thank all those who had worked with him, remarking, "I am sure that the secretariat of the *Consilium*

1 See Giuseppe Dossetti, "*Memoria di Giacomo Lercaro*", in *Chiese Italiane et Concilio*, ed. Giuseppe Alberigo, Marietti, Turin 1988, p. 310. Dossetti points out that Lercaro, seventy-five on 25 July 1967, had tendered his resignation on 15 August, as he was bound to do, *but it was not accepted*.

2 Lefebvre was somewhat shocked when his order, the Holy Ghost Fathers, failed to re-elect him General. But he was now liberated for his freelance sniping.

3 These suggestions were raised at a conference called "Giacomo Lercaro and the Living Tradition of the Bologna Church" held in Bologna, 7–8 February 1992, on the hundredth anniversary of his birth.

4 Annibale Bugnini, *The Reform of the Liturgy*, p. 80.

will continue at the same pace and in the same spirit on the road still to be travelled in implementing fully the directives and dictates of the conciliar constitution."[1]

Lercaro's confidence in the future of the liturgy was justified. But he was not to know that at the time. And in any case he had not been given this or any other explanation.

The Lercaro affair did not go away, despite an audience on 23 March. He wrote to Paul on Easter Sunday 1967:

> Beatissimo Padre
> I cannot let this Easter Sunday go by, for those fortunate enough to believe in Christ a day of resurrection and commitment to embark on a new way of life, without opening my mind and my heart to you, with that frankness and loyalty that should always govern the filial relation of a bishop to the Supreme Pastor and Father.
>
> I want to tell you in all sincerity that in the affair of which I am still at the centre, even after the audience you gave me on 21 March, the procedure was illegitimate and the result undeserved.
>
> I still feel the burden of a defamatory publication to which men who hold high office in the Curia lent a hand.
>
> But, having said that, Holy Father, with equal frankness let me tell you that I love you filially and cannot continue to live like this, feeling I have a thorn in my heart preventing me being in communion, not just of faith and charity, that have never been in doubt, but of total and filial devotion to you without gray areas or bitterness.[2]

Paul did not, perhaps could not, answer this letter. The "thorn" (*spina*) remained between them.

But "out there in the world" lurked a whole thorn-bush of difficulties. This epochal, astonishing and disturbing year turned out to be anything but peaceful in Europe and America. There were student protests and "direct action" in most developed countries. In France a student-led revolt nearly toppled the de Gaulle regime, while at Kent State University in the United States National Guards shot protesting students dead. In Czechoslovakia Alexander Dubček promoted what he called "socialism with a human face", which brought hope – until its

1 Ibid.

2 Published in 1988 for the first time in Giuseppe Dossetti, "*Memoria*", in *Chiese Italiane*, p. 312. Dossetti, in other words, "kept these things in his heart" for twenty years, and only then broke silence.

savage repression by the tanks of the Warsaw Pact, the only time that Alliance creaked into action. And there was Paul's own contribution: *Humanae Vitae*.

Yet in some ways 1968 was a generational conflict in which Paul's heart was on the side of the young. De Gaulle saw 1968 as "a revolt against the consumer society, against the technological society, whether Communist in the East or capitalist in the West". The Prague "spring" declared in effect the bankruptcy of Marxism, and there were rumours of an underground religious revival in Russia itself. In the United States the crescendo of indignation against the Vietnam war forced Lyndon B. Johnson to try to negotiate.

Paul was sympathetic to all these developments. Yet his repudiation of the consumer society, support for the liberalizing movement in Czechoslovakia and opposition to the war in Vietnam counted for little and were barely noticed. One could see birth-control as an aspect of the consumer society – the pill trivializing sexual intercourse without responsibility or commitment. Paul took the final step towards *Humanae Vitae* this spring 1968. By the previous autumn he was already persuaded that the old norms should be maintained on grounds of consistency; what was new was that this conviction could be bolstered by an appeal to "natural law".

Cardinal Suenens, in a letter dated 19 March 1968, urged Paul not to act alone but in conjunction with the episcopal conferences. He argued that since the final meeting of the Commission in June 1966 collegiality had not been respected, and that married lay people had been deliberately excluded from the final stages of a document on which they were bound to be better informed than clerics should be. Consequently, not just a "credibility gap" but a "credibility chasm" would be opened up that would affect the Church most grievously.

To save the pontificate from disaster Suenens proposed that birth-control and the ordination of married men should be put on the agenda of the next Synod.[1] Intended as a way of getting Paul VI off the hook, it was a psychologically inept point to make precisely at the moment Paul had made his mind up.[2]

Paul was also under pressure from Cardinal Franz König, another "star" of the Council. His Secretariat for Non-believers had by now drafted its Directory, the set of guidelines for talking with unbelievers.

1 Antoine Wenger, *Le Cardinal Villot*, p. 83.

2 Roberto Tucci SJ assured me at the time that Suenens' intervention was doomed. It was as though, he said, a scrupulous man, after long agonizing, finally decides to go to Naples rather than Milan. The uninvited guest who told him he really ought to have gone to Milan would get short shrift.

Paul did not intervene directly – he had other things on his mind – but Giovanni Benelli, the newly arrived *sostituto*, "took great interest in our work".[1] He could say that again.

Benelli represented the traditional Secretariat of State view that saw the world in political terms. He feared, says König, "that our document veered too much to the left, giving substance to the charge of an alliance between the Church and left-wing elements. It was also feared that these political forces might use the new Secretariat as a means for exploiting the Church."[2]

What König does not say is that this fear arose because of the Secretariat's semi-official involvement in the dialogues of the *Paulusgesellschaft* founded and directed by Dr Erich Kellner, a German priest of vast, windy, uncritical enthusiasms.

In 1967, the previous year, Karl Rahner and Johann Baptist Metz had journeyed to Marienbad (in Czech Marianské Lazné), the spa town with crumbling hotels, to "dialogue" with Marxist theoreticians. A Czech remarked that if he was an "anonymous Christian" then Rahner must be an "anonymous Marxist". Nothing untoward happened, except that it became clear that Czech intellectuals sat very loosely towards Marxism and had in fact relativized it even as they "revised" it. They prepared the Prague spring of 1968 and gave *Last Year in Marienbad* – title of a modishly successful film by Alain Renais – a fresh resonance. So the work of König's Secretariat was having some positive effects.

But, as usual, the Curia always looked for the *Italian* impact of such encounters and feared lost votes for the Christian Democrats. This was misguided. The Communist Party was becoming more and more conservative in Italy and elsewhere. In Paris, where students engaged in pitched battles with the police pigs, the Communist Party was on the side of "law and order", fearing an insurrection it did not lead, and one in which "workers" surrendered their role as "the engine of history" to students.

Unknown to the world and unknown to almost everyone until now, Paul VI was engaged upon the most important diplomatic initiative of his pontificate. The Christmas meeting with President Johnson began to bear fruit. In late April 1968, a Saturday, Johnson instructed Joseph A. Califano, jr to contact Archbishop Luigi Raimondi, Apostolic Delegate in Washington, and get him to put the following plan to Pope Paul VI: the Pope should offer the Vatican as a neutral ground where both parties

1 Franz König, *Where is the Church heading?* Interviewed by Gianni Licheri, Foreword by Cardinal Basil Hume OSB, St Paul Publications, Slough, p. 61.

2 Ibid. pp. 61–62.

could hold, if not the first phase of negotiations, then at least "talks about talks" concerning when and where to meet.

Paul responded positively via Raimundi on 27 April 1968. He wondered only if the offer would be better made secretly or publicly "immediately after being assured that his intervention – naturally to be made on his own initiative – is desirable". He also wanted to know whether he should extend an invitation to the South Vietnamese government as well, "if that is not considered an obstacle to the pre-negotiation".

As soon as President Johnson read Raimundi's memo, he called his Secretary of State, Dean Rusk, and then said to Califano:

> Call Raimundi right now and tell him: One, as far as we are concerned, the sooner the Pope makes an announcement of his intention the better. Two, there's no need to give any advance notice of his announcement, but we'd appreciate it if possible. Three, it's unnecessary to invite the South Vietnamese since the NLF [National Liberation Front, the organization of the Viet Cong insurgents in the South] isn't being invited and we're keeping the South Vietnamese occupied anyway. All we're talking about now is a meeting to set a site and date for substantive talks.[1]

Johnson took the papal intervention very seriously. He urged Califano to keep on calling Raimundi until he got the Pope's answer.

Ever the hustler, President Johnson maintained the pressure the next day, Sunday, while out sailing on the Potomac in the yach *Sequoia*. Califano must get hold of Raimundi immediately:

> Tell him that the sooner he makes the invitation the better, the more lives that may be saved, and tell him we think it important that the Pope make it a public invitation without any prior notice [to the North Vietnamese]. If the Pope wants to be a peacemaker, doing it publicly and without prior notice will strengthen his hand and put more pressure on the North Vietnamese.[2]

Califano helped Raimundi draft the cable conveying this information, and offered to stay until the answer came in. In Washington it was 9.30 p.m. Raimundi pointed out that it was 3 a.m. in Rome and that there would be no one there.

1 Joseph A. Califano, "The President and the Pope: L.B.J., Paul VI and the Vietnam War", *America*, 12 October 1991.

2 Ibid. p. 239.

Such leisurely Roman ways shocked the Americans. Johnson called Califano at 11.22 p.m. – all these calls were routinely logged – and told him to pick up the reply first thing next morning, 29 April. The reply came the next day, Tuesday. Raimundi reported: "For grave serious reasons, the Holy Father has decided to issue the invitation privately through diplomatic channels. The Holy Father thought the parties might be able to meet secretly without anyone knowing about the meeting, and this would relieve external pressures on them."

The same message was being delivered to Hanoi at the same time through "European channels", by which was meant the Italian Foreign Ministry. Johnson said: "This is a beautiful message. I would like a few hours before I respond."

This episode illustrates Montini at his diplomatic best. He preferred a private invitation so that neither side could claim a propaganda advantage. He was concerned with bringing the parties together, not with gaining prestige for the papacy. It worked. At 1 a.m. on 3 May, just forty-eight hours after the papal message to Hanoi, Walt Rostow woke President Johnson with the news that "Hanoi has suggested we meet in Paris . . . on 10 May or a few days later."[1] This was Paul VI's contribution to international politics. And it has never been recognized.

He might have wished that birth-control was susceptible of a similar "diplomatic" solution. It was not. Political matters – he did not need to learn this from Maritain – involved compromise and the "art of the possible". The morality of contraception, as he had come to see it, involved absolutes on which he could not yield. The key lay in the age-old debate about the "ends" or goals of marriage. Once the *unitive* meaning of sexual intercourse was separated from its *procreative* meaning, then there was no case to be made against buggery, bestiality or indeed any kind of sexual gratification.

His Catholic opponents – the members of the defunct Pontifical Commission – insisted that they were only talking about the responsible use of artificial birth-control within a stable marriage that had already proved its openness to procreation by producing splendid children. Fine. But there was no known way of limiting contraception to such admirable families. Inevitably there would be other, less responsible users of birth-control who simply saw it in a way of having sex without having children. For men it was an instrument of seduction, a "Casanova's charter"

1 Ibid. This whole episode, hitherto totally unknown, is comparable to Pope John XXIII's intervention in the Cuban missile crisis of October 1962. Nikita Khruschev told Norman Cousins, "What the Pope has done for peace will go down in history." See Peter Hebblethwaite, *John XXIII, Pope of the Council*, pp. 444–46, for this story. It provided the impulse for Pope John to write *Pacem in Terris* as his "last will and testament". Yet US historians have ignored it.

as it was called. The contraceptive society encouraged the "permissive society" about which people began to worry at precisely this time. There was no fear of pregnancy to lead anyone to say "no".

At the same time everyone kept saying that the Pope must come off the fence, make up his mind, and put an end to the state of doubt he alleged did not exist.

As Paul was poised for the publication of *Humanae Vitae* there occurred a farce that seemed at the time inseparable from Vatican events. It proved that the Congregation for the Doctrine of the Faith, despite its change of name, still had a lot to learn, and that its new Prefect, the genial Yugoslav Cardinal Seper, was not yet in command of his ship. Msgr Ivan Illich, forty-one, a naturalized American of mixed Spanish, German Croatian and Jewish origins, was summoned to Rome to be interrogated.

After working with Puerto Ricans in New York (he said Puerto Ricans didn't go to Mass there because it started on time) Illich founded what became the Center for Intercultural Documentation (CIDOC) at Cuernavaca, Mexico. Supported by Cardinals Spellman and Cushing, aided by the Jesuit Fordham University and addressed at its opening session by Dom Helder Câmara, CIDOC helped prepare missionaries, lay and clerical, for Latin America. There were crash courses in Spanish and an invitation into the "culture of poverty". Helder Câmara called it a school of "de-Yankeefication".

Illich was not told in advance why he had been summoned to Rome. On arrival at the Holy Office (the old name remained in popular use) he found that he had to answer questions in four broad areas: dangerous doctrinal opinions, erroneous ideas against the Church, bizarre conceptions on the priesthood and subversive interpretations of the liturgy. The truth began to dawn on Illich. The Mexican Opus Dei paper, *La Gente*, ran a campaign against his bishop, Sergio Mendez Arceo, famous for declaring at the Council that "one Galileo affair is enough" and recommending dialogue with Marx and Freud.[1]

Before the interrogation, and in fluent Serbo-Croat, Illich discussed the weather with Cardinal Seper who seemed "very kind, very correct, most humane, rather apologetic, behaving like a man caught up in a

1 Bishop Mendez Arceo addressed the Council on 28 September 1965, during the debate on *Gaudium et Spes*. MEXICAN BISHOP ENDORSES FREUD was the *New York Times* headline. Mendez Arceo made life difficult for himself by bringing along Belgian Benedictine Grégoire Lemercier as his *peritus*. Lemercier having been psychoanalysed to deal with the inevitable problem of celibacy – he explained – his monks followed suit with the result that thirty out of fifty of them returned to "the world". The remaining twenty worked better than the thirty misfits, they argued. This was treacherous ground.

transaction which embarrassed him profoundly".[1] Illich was led into the bowels of the Holy Office. He politely introduced himself and enquired with whom he had the honour to be speaking. We are your judges, the two *monsignori* explained, our names are irrelevant. Eventually they admitted to being Msgr Giuseppe Casoria, a specialist in non-consummated marriages, and Msgr Sergio de Magistris.

Illich was happy to take an oath declaring he would tell the truth. But he refused to swear another committing him never to divulge the secrets of his interrogation. He argued that it was contrary to the *Integrae Servandae*, Paul's 1965 decree reforming the Holy Office, which said the proceedings of the Congregation should be a matter of public record. That was the maddening thing about Illich. One could never get the last word.

The judges waved papers in consternation, cried *Mamma mia*! and *Bisogna appellare al Santo Padre*. Illich would have been quite happy to appeal to the Holy Father. At last after consulting Seper they agreed to Illich's request to see a *written* list of questions so that he could prepare his defence. It was brought round to him that afternoon. It enquired after his thoughts on limbo, how he distinguished between "shepherds and sheep", what he thought about "peaceful co-existence", and whether it was true that he heard women's confessions without a grille. The high point of absurdity was reached in the following question: "What would you answer to those who say that you are petulant, adventurous, imprudent, fanatical and hypnotizing, a rebel to all authority except that of the Bishop of Cuernavaca, Mexico?"

Illich's reply was that he was going home rather than continue with this travesty of justice. Before leaving he saw Seper again, who embraced him warmly. Illich judged his feelings were "somewhere between perplexity and incredulity, exasperation and humorous annoyance". Seper's farewell words were "*Hajite, hajite, nemojete se vratiti*" (Get going, get going, and don't come back). Those were the last words of Dostoevsky's *Grand Inquisitor*.[2] Heads rolled after this episode. De Magistris and Casoria retired. The Congregation had made itself ridiculous on the eve of *Humanae Vitae*.

On 20 July, with the encyclical completed and translated and only a week to go, Paul VI sought the cool of Castelgandolfo and the company of his carp while he awaited the world's reaction. The next day the *Féderation Nationale des Patros* of Belgium came out to Castelgandolfo to greet him on their national feast day. He urged them to build a world

1 Francine du Plessix Gray, *Divine Disobedience: Profiles in Catholic Radicalism*, p. 234. This is the source for the Illich story.

2 Gray, *Divine Disobedience*, p. 240.

of greater peace, justice and fraternity. He congratulated them on the harmony that existed – so he had been assured – between the Flemings and Walloons.

The Belgians can have had no inkling of what Paul really meant when he exhorted them, many from Suenens' diocese of Malines-Brussels, to "trust their bishops":

> In this work [of justice and peace] be docile towards those who have been placed in the People of God as judges and teachers of the faith. I refer to your bishops who, besides inviting you to play your role of "co-responsibility" in the Church, have the task of guiding and giving you a sense of direction, and helping you to decipher the "signs of the times" in the light of Tradition.[1]

This was a shrewdly calculated appeal, perhaps too subtle for his audience. For if Belgian youth gathered at Castelgandolfo listened carefully to Cardinal Suenens, they would have learned that the "co-responsibility in the Church" they had been promised had been cavalierly set aside in the production of *Humanae Vitae*. To be quoted by the Pope is usually a mark of approval: in this case it was a shot across the bows.

At the eleventh hour Rome was awash with rumours about an imminent statement on birth-control. The Vatican Press Office continued to deny them. Msgr Fausto Vaillanc, his credibility already battered, went on insisting that such rumours were "absolutely false" until Monday, 29 July when *Humanae Vitae* appeared. He was then obliged to eat his words. Perhaps Paul, already on holiday at Castelgandolfo, reckoned that with everyone away from home his encyclical would not attract too much media comment. He could hardly have been more wrong.

He failed to understand that by 1968 the thirty-second television sound-bite was a more effective form of communication than lengthy articles in *L'Osservatore Romano* or the dailies. The Italian national TV cmpany, RAI, had done more for the unification of Italy than the *Risorgimento*, causing accents and dialects to disappear. At his Wednesday audience he announced that the bones found in the crypt of St Peter's were authentically those of the first Pope[2] – dramatic news in other circumstances. But ignored now.

1 *Insegnamenti*, VI, 1968, p. 321.

2 Margherita Guarducci, *Saint Pierre retrouvé*, p. 5. *Insegnamenti*, 1968, pp. 279–82. Paul VI had originally planned to make this announcement on All Saints Day 1964 but Cardinal Suenens dissuaded him. In 1968 it also concluded the "Year of Faith" though no one seemed to pay much attention to the fact.

Humanae Vitae was reduced to a single banner headline: POPE BANS PILL. Yet it could have been presented very differently. "The defence of human life must begin at the very origin of human existence," says Paul at the outset. This could have opened the way to the "consistent ethic" or "seamless garment" approach to morality later developed by Cardinal Joseph Bernardin of Chicago: if one is opposed to abortion one must be equally opposed to indiscriminate bombing and nuclear weaponry. For most people recognize some distinction between preventing life and taking life.

Humanae Vitae casts glances in this direction. It defends human rights as it denounces governments who seek to *impose* birth-control, so claiming "the power to intervene in the most personal and intimate responsibility of husband and wife".[1] This was already happening in China where women pregnant with a second child were carted off in a blanket and forcibly aborted. In opposing compulsory abortion Paul was defending human rights and defending the Third World against a neo-colonial imposition. But no matter what he did or said, it came out as POPE BANS PILL.

The plan of *Humanae Vitae* is of great simplicity. Chapter 1 admits that procreation (and therefore contraception) appears in a new context. Chapter 2 argues that Church has the duty to recall the traditional principles (drafted by Ermenegeldo Lio OFM, and Fr Luigi Ciappi OP). Chapter 3 adds important pastoral directives (often attributed to Gustave Martelet SJ) which modify the harshness of the doctrine.

Martelet always maintained he had nothing to do with the writing of *Humanae Vitae* – meaning, Grootaers thinks – with the decisive chapter 2. But Martelet presented the encyclical to the press with his customary exuberance, and Paul often quoted his commentaries on it as the best and most authoritative. But Paul himself had modified the final text, making the following changes: he cut out any reference to "mortal sin"; he always refused to qualify the encyclical as "infallible"; and he inserted a passage on "compassion for sinners":

> It is an outstanding manifestation of charity . . . to omit nothing from Christ's saving doctrine, yet this must always be accompanied by tolerance and charity. For when he came, not to judge but to save the world, was he not severe towards sin, but patient and abounding in mercy towards all sinners?
>
> Husbands and wives therefore, when deeply distressed by reason of the difficulties of their life, must find stamped in the

1 *Humanae Vitae*, 17.

> heart and voice of their priest the likeness of the voice and love of our Redeemer.[1]

That was traditional too. Trent said the priest in the confessional must be *potius medicus quam iudex* – more like a doctor or healer than a judge.

But quite astonishing was the next sentence: "We hold it as certain that while the Holy Spirit of God is present to the *Magisterium* in proclaiming sound doctrine, he also illumines from within the hearts of the faithful and invites their assent."[2]

"Invites their assent?" That is not the tone of the insensitive, authoritarian bully who is sometimes said to be the author of *Humanae Vitae*. The Spirit without speaks to the Spirit within the married couple.

But this almost mystical approach to the question was not followed up by crusader spirits who merely wanted to know whether priests or laypeople said "yes" or "no" to *Humanae Vitae*. After all this was 1968 when all authority figures were being called into question. So dissenting priests were "suspended" (that is, could not say Mass or preach) while dissenting laypeople shopped around for sympathetic confessors, and sometimes "left the Church".

The papal diplomatic corps was ordered by the Secretariat of State to produce evidence of spontaneous adhesion of groups or prominent individuals. *L'Osservatore Romano* excelled itself, printing these and other instances of enthusiastic support from all over the world and never once admitting that there was a breath of criticism. This could not deceive a pope who had written only seven years before:

> *L'Osservatore Romano* does not only give news; it puts thoughts in your head. It is not enough for it to relate the facts as they happen, it has to say what should have happened, or should not. It does not simply converse with its readers: it comments, editorializes, argues, polemicizes.[3]

Nothing had changed since he made that judgement on the centenary of the paper.

At the first Wednesday audience after *Humanae Vitae*, on 31 July, the feast of St Ignatius, he naturally talked of his encyclical. This was,

1 Ibid. no. 29. The end of the paragraph urges married couples "to approach more often with great faith the sacraments of the Eucharist and Penance. Nor must they ever despair because of their weakness." It would seem that "refusing absolution" and similar high-handed methods are not what is intended here.

2 Ibid.

3 Cardinal Giovanni Battista Montini, "*Le difficoltà dell' 'Osservatore Romano'* ", *Notiziario*, 17, p. 18. The article was written for the centenary number of the Vatican paper, 1 July 1961.

as it were, his own editorial on the subject. The encyclical, he said, referring to a book by Gustave Martelet SJ,[1] was positive not negative. He claimed to have used "personalist" criteria and above all to have acted with "responsibility".[2]

He admitted to feeling overwhelmed by the mass of documents he had to study:

> How often we have had the feeling of being submerged in a sea of documents, and humanly overwhelmed at the human inadequacy of our poor self; yet still obliged by apostolic duty to pronounce upon the question. How often we have trembled before the dilemma of giving in to contemporary opinion or making a judgement that would be ill-received by modern society, or might be thought an arbitrary imposition on married couples.[3]

Yet in his engaging simplicity Paul did not realize how counterproductive this tone of pathos could sound. Those overwhelmed by the demands of bringing up children were not impressed by someone who was overwhelmed merely by paper.

He expected opposition, but he attributed it simply to "the climate of expectation which had given rise among Catholics and in public opinion in general, to the idea of making things easier by concessions and liberalizing the moral and matrimonial doctrine of the Church.[4]

Paul's position was that he expected to be criticized and misunderstood by the secular media, and by those in the Church suffering from what Hans Urs von Balthasar, the Swiss theologian, called "anti-Roman prejudice". Von Balthasar saw opposition to *Humanae Vitae* as part of the general surge of criticism and protest that marked 1968. But from cardinals and bishops Paul VI expected loyalty to the hilt. Hence his

1 Gustave Martelet, *Amour conjugal et renouveau conciliaire.*

2 *Insegnamenti*, 1968, p. 870.

3 *Insegnamenti*, 1968, p. 871. See John Mahoney, *The Making of Moral Theology*, p. 269. Mahoney's judgement inspires confidence since Paul VI appointed him to the International Theological Commission on 1 August 1974. He was specially brought in to strengthen the moral theology section; but when his mandate came up for renewal in 1979 it was not renewed by Pope John Paul II. Some *bons mots* had done the rounds, notably: "It takes remarkable perversity to devise a version of the Gospel that makes its main point opposition to artificial birth-control and the refusal to ordain women." So he moved from the Jesuit-run Heythrop College, University of London, to the "Anglican" King's College, which appeared safer.

4 Quoted in "The Timelessness of *Humanae Vitae*", Msgr Diogini Tettamanzi, in *Briefing*, London, 10 June 1988, pp. 256–59. I have been unable to find this quotation in *Insegnamenti*.

pain when this manifestly did not happen. It was too early yet to talk about the "reception" or "non-reception" of *Humanae Vitae*.

The most urgent matter on his desk that summer at Castelgandolfo was the new *Ordo Missae* – the Order of Mass according to the Latin rite. On 18 May 1968 he had authorized Fr Annibale Bugnini, still Secretary of the *Consilium* despite Cardinal Lercaro's sacking, to send the latest draft to the cardinals who were heads of Roman dicasteries. Their comments, in the main positive, were in by 15 August.[1]

To gain extra cover for a decision which would have such momentous consequences for Christian worship for the foreseeable future, he also invited Bishop Carlo Colombo – of course – and Carlo Mazianza, the Oratorian friend from the 1920s whom he had named Bishop of Crema, a suffragan of Milan, in December 1963, to assess the comments of the cardinals. Carlo Colombo's view was that it was difficult to judge a text "cold":

> A liturgical text yields up its true value only after prolonged experience of it . . . Older people will have more difficulty in coming to terms with a new liturgy that is not always adapted to their sensibilities. We will have, therefore, to see whether the young can adapt more easily, and will find in it the spiritual nourishment their elders found in the old *Ordo*.[2]

Bishop Carlo Manziana took more seriously objections of some of the curial cardinals. Three issues aroused their mistrust: *unjustified* changes (were they really necessary?); *excessive* participation of the laity (should they say words hitherto reserved to the priest?); greater *freedom of choice* (would it not lead to chaos and confusion?). Manziana summarized these objections and went on:

> My answer to all of them would be that long centuries of *liturgical immobility* have given us an exaggerated concept of changelessness and formulas without alternative as desirable. This is a view that was certainly foreign to the early liturgy. In any case if territorial conferences are worried that *ad libitum* formulas will generate confusion, they can determine the selection more narrowly.[3]

1 Annibale Bugnini, *The Reform of the Liturgy*, p. 372.

2 Ibid. p. 473. Translation slightly modified.

3 Ibid. p. 374. Manziana says "territorial conferences" rather than "episcopal conferences" because, for example, the German-speaking world includes not only Germans but Austrians and Swiss as well. There was no point in their duplicating the work. ICEL (International Committee on English in the Liturgy) performed this function for the English-speaking world.

Paul finally approved the new *Ordo* on Wednesday, 6 November 1968, when between 7 p.m. and 8.30 he prayed it through for the hundredth time with Fr Annibale Bugnini and penned the simple words: "I give the New Order of the Mass my approval in the Lord, Paul VI, Pope."[1]

We have jumped ahead to complete what possibly was the most important decision of Paul's pontificate: the new Mass. Was it more important, even, than *Humanae Vitae*? That case could be made.

In any event the timing of Paul's journey to Bogotà and Medellín, Colombia in late August 1968 had nothing to do with *Humanae Vitae*. It was fixed in advance by the Eucharistic Congress and the second CELAM conference. Yet in practice *Humanae Vitae* was better supported by Latin Americans than in Europe and the United States. This was because the IMF and the World Bank often insisted on family planning as a condition of loans and aid. So they could complain that birth-control was imperialist and neo-colonialist. Helder Câmara said it was "a matter too delicate to be resolved from without". Did that mean that it must be decided by the loving couple within Christian marriage? No: Helder Câmara's "within" refers to the Church's *magisterium*.[2] He had objections to family planning programmes being imposed by Europe or North America.

The journey to Medellín had been announced at the Wednesday audience on 8 May 1968 in the last stages of his preparation of *Humanae Vitae*. This first-ever papal visit to Latin America would be his way of endorsing the Council in that continent. The CELAM meeting was seen as "the new Pentecost" for Latin America. It was consoling for him to go to a place where he was hailed as the author of *Populorum Progressio* rather than reviled for *Humanae Vitae*. In Latin America the "conservatives" were those embarrassingly allied with military regimes who had no concept of "social justice". The prophetic figures like Helder Câmara were on his side.

So it was safe to go and kiss the ground of Colombia. The visit lasted two days, Thursday to Friday, 22–23 August.[3] This enabled him to conclude the Eucharistic Congress in Bogotà and inaugurate the CELAM meeting in Medellín. Bogotà was a more populist occasion with the ordination of 200 priests and *deacons* that made a statement about

1 Ibid. p. 383. All of which proves – as Fr Annibale Bugnini intended – that far from being an impulsive improvisation plucked out of thin Protestant air, as Archbishop Marcel Lefebvre alleged, the New Order of the Mass was carefully thought about and prayed over. Trouble came from cardinals who were *not* heads of Roman dicasteries and consequently were not consulted. One such was Cardinal Antonio Bacci, Latinist, who made mischief on a grand scale.

2 See Alistair Kee, *Marx and the Failure of Liberation Theology*, p. 156.

3 *Insegnamenti*, 1968, pp. 345ff.

ministry in Latin America. Paul preached a simple homily stuffed with biblical quotations.

Medellín was the great turning-point in the modern history of Latin America. Its impact was "enormous but uneven". In Europe and North America urbanization and industrialization had happened long ago; in Africa and Asia Christian faith was too weak to be an agent of social transformation; in Latin America the process of social change and the renewal of Vatican II coincided.[1] A more immediate reason for the success of Medellín was that Paul VI showed his trust in the Latin Americans by going against the Roman habit of diplomatic caution which says one never enters a meeting without knowing its outcome.

Paul's visit came at the *start* of the meeting to mark the fact that they were free men, able to confer and conclude among themselves. He did not pretend he knew how Latin America should live its "new Pentecost". He also made clear through his legate, Cardinal Antonio Samorè, that they could publish their conclusions at the end of the conference even before he had looked at them. Juridically this required a special papal indult. He provided one dated 6 September 1968.[2] It meant they did not have to be always looking over their shoulder.

Psychologically this was a most important step: to be trusted is to be empowered. This was too much for some conservatives, who waited on orders from the centre; but it was a tonic for the majority who wanted to do for their continent what *Gaudium et Spes* describes as the duty of theologians and pastors to "scrutinize the signs of the times, interpreting them in the light of the Gospel".[3]

The main achievement of Medellín was to re-express the Christian concept of "salvation" in terms of liberation, *liberación* not only from individual sins and peccadilloes but from the sinful built-in structures of society. This was legitimate and pastorally necessary. Salvation had always carried with it hidden metaphors such as "bringing health". But now the dominant image was that of redemption or liberation from captivity.

It had a lot to commend it in Latin America where the much-trumpeted "decade of development" was proving a disappointment. At

1 Segundo Galilea, "*Example d'une réception 'sélective' et créative du Concile: l'Amérique Latine aux conférences de Medellín et de Puebla*", in *La Réception de Vatican II*, ed. Giuseppe Alberigo and Jean-Pierre Jossua, Cerf, Paris 1985, p. 87.

2 Francisco Pimento-Pintel is the source, quoting the Bishop of Itaguai, Rio de Janeiro, Vital Wilderink, a Dutch-born Carmelite.

3 *Gaudium et Spes*, 4 and 44.

Medellín "liberation" took over when "development" faltered.[1] Yet it would be absurd to imagine that the Latin American bishops "invented" liberation theology at Medellín. Rather they gathered up available theological insights and stimulated new ones. They put into words what was "in the air". The theology that emerged as a result of Medellín was uneven in quality, sometimes frenetic in tone, but it was the expression of new-found vitality and hope and Paul could respond to that. The clumsy old giant that was Latin America was waking up with a pride in the continent that was no longer dependent on Europe. "We have faith in God, in man, and in the values and future of our continent," they declared.

The Latin American bishops sought to be in continuity with *Populorum Progressio*. Yet they clearly ranged beyond it. They appreciated his point about the way an unequal starting-line made a mockery of "free trade" (58); but they had swept well beyond his ringing statement that "development is the new name for peace", and many found that what he said on the possibility of a "just revolution" pussy-footing and ambivalent.[2] But the Latin American bishops were not united. Though there was a majority for change, there were pockets of resistance everywhere, and Colombia would fight liberation theology to the death.

Paul could affect the issue by episcopal appointments, particularly in Brazil, which as the largest and richest in resources was the key. The Franciscan Bishops Paolo Evaristo Arns (named to São Paolo in 1970) and Aloisio Lorscheider (promoted to Fortaleza in 1973) emerged as leaders in a Church that would take seriously the option for the poor.

The founder and first Secretary-General of CELAM, Helder Câmara, already Archbishop of Olinda-Recife since 1964, embodied the "spirit of Medellín" and became a conscientious thorn in the flesh of the Brazilian military government. They regarded his lecture tours abroad as subversive. Helder Câmara was the "prophetic figure" who denounced injustice

1 This was a most important shift. In 1969 SODEPAX – the short-lived joint commission between the Vatican and the World Council of Churches – produced an in-house report optimistically called *In Search of a Theology of Development*. A young Peruvian Indian theologian, Gustavo Gutierrez, explained to them how after Medellín "development" was unviable and that it had already been replaced by "liberation". This was the starting point for his 1971 book, *Teologia de la liberacion, Perspectivas*, Lima, Peru 1971.

2 "We know, however, that a revolutionary uprising – save where there is manifest, long-standing tyranny, which would do great damage to fundamental personal rights and dangerous harm to the common good of the country – produces new injustices, throws more elements out of balance and brings on new disasters. A real evil should not be fought at the cost of greater misery" (*Populorum Progressio*, 31). Conservatives in Latin America could appeal to the main clause, "progressives" to the inserted clause, which did no more than recall the classic doctrine on the conditions for overthrowing a tyrant.

come what may. But he also had a Gandhi-like abhorrence of violence. Faced with "institutionalized disorder" he would be *Violent for Peace*, to quote the title of one of his books.[1]

If Helder Câmara was already a legend at Medellín, the key man in organizational terms was Argentinian Eduardo Pironio. A *peritus* at Vatican II, an auxiliary bishop from 1964, he organized the conference and became Secretary-General of CELAM for the crucial period 1968–72.

Paul VI's Latin America policy was not limited to the application of Medellín, important though that was. It was set in a wider world context. The deadlock that resulted from superpower interference had to be broken. For in Latin America the US and the USSR were in self-conscious competition, and the martyred continent paid the price of this rivalry. Soviet diplomats spent their time discrediting US imperialism; US officials were more concerned with the supposed Marxist or Communist threats in the region than with the interests of the countries themselves.[2]

Medellín offered a way out of this impasse, a "third way" that rejected both unrestricted capitalism and Soviet-style Communism. That the Latin American sense of identity should come from a meeting of bishops rather than from, say, the Organization of American States (OAS) was a matter of great political and ecclesiastical importance. In short Paul enabled the Latin American Church to act as the tribune of the continent.[3] For the first time in history he empowered the local Church.

Back from Latin America he began a detailed study of the final proposals for the "new order of the Mass". Msgr Bugnini says he gave this study the highest priority, reading through the text many times and praying over it. He annotated the text in red and blue pencil, glossing thirty-four out of the hundred and four paragraphs. But he did not impose his views on the *Consilium*. "I ask you to take account of these observations," said his covering memo, "exercising a free and carefully weighed judgement."[4]

1 Alistair Kee, *Marx and the Failure of Liberation Theology*, p. 155, remarks: "His [Helder Câmara's] worldwide reputation is based on his criticisms of capitalism, socialism and materialism, his denunciations of the powerful rulers of Brazil, and of the even more powerful directors of multi-national companies, his unmasking of greed and indifference. *Indeed, what has he not criticized with perception and courage, except the papacy, the Church and its theology.*" My italics. For Kee this is a matter of surprise. Helder Câmara would be surprised at his surprise.

2 See Cole Blasier, *The Giants' Quarrel*, Pittsburg University Press, 1983, p. xiv.

3 See Peter Hebblethwaite, "The Vatican's Latin American Policy", in *Church and Politics in Latin America*, ed. Dermot Keogh, Macmillan, London 1990, pp. 49–64.

4 Annibale Bugnini, *The Reform of the Liturgy*, p. 377.

If we take a few examples of Paul VI's suggestions for the final *Consilium* meeting, 8–17 October 1968, it will soon become clear that his views were always respected if not always accepted, and that he had a direct influence on the shape of the liturgy as we know it today:

Sign of the Cross. The Consilium proposed that it should be said *aloud* only if there was no opening hymn. Paul insisted that Mass should always begin with the sign of the cross, after or before the hymn. *Accepted.*

Kyrie, Christe eleison. Paul asked why the traditional nine invocations were not retained. He accepted the explanation that six made an antiphonal priest/people dialogue easier.

Liturgy of the Word. Paul proposed ending the Scripture readings with "The Word of God" or "The Word of the Lord" to which the response is *Deo Gratias.* He also proposed that "Praise to you, O Christ" be reserved for after the Gospel. *Accepted.*

Eucharistic Prayers. "I agree with the scriptural addition 'which will be given up for you'. I agree to transferring the words 'Mystery of Faith' to the end, after the consecration of the chalice ('Do this in memory of me'). 'Through him, with him and in him': would it not be better to read 'Through Christ and with Christ and in Christ'? The result in the vernacular would be clearer and more dignified." *Not accepted.*[1]

Paul was meticulous and thorough in applying the conciliar criteria of clarity and comprehensibility.[2] He applied them rigorously but not mechanically, for liturgy speaks to the heart as well as the mind and gestures can sustain and fill out the words.

Yet 1968 will remain the year of *Humanae Vitae.* By Christmas the first pastoral letters commenting on it had appeared. They spanned the whole gamut from enthusiastic endorsement to finessing about a "conflict of duties" and the "lesser evil", both set in a context of conscience. The possibility of both "dissenting from *Humanae Vitae*" and remaining in the Church was soon established. Paul abandoned the reproachful tone when an English bishop pointed out to him that only *good* Catholics protested about *Humanae Vitae,* the others did what they liked anyway.

The rejoicing of the curial conservatives should have been a warning to him. The *De Castitate* of Fr Ermenegildo Lio OFM, rejected by the Council, had eventually prevailed. Lio wrote articles in which he pointed

1 Ibid.

2 *Sacrosanctum Concilium,* 34.

out that his *De Castitate* can be considered as a dress-rehearsal or sketch for *Humanae Vitae*. The bridge between the two documents was neatly provided by the last-minute papal amendments to *Gaudium et Spes*, as Cardinal Pericle Felici remarked in *L'Osservatore Romano* (October 1968). This crowing over victory emphasized the Pope's ability to act *on his own* as the *Nota praevia* had foreseen.[1] Paul's attempt to exercise authority non-collegially weakened his primatial authority.

Paul recognized this by never publishing another encyclical, though of course other documents flowed from his pen. Don Pasquale Macchi gives the reason why: "He did not want to provoke . . . He did not want an encyclical, a solemn form of the teaching *magisterium*, to be treated as though it were merely a matter of opinion even by bishops."[2]

But he could not just leave it at that. In December 1968, just six months after *Humanae Vitae*, he announced that an Extraordinary Synod would be held starting on 11 October 1969 to explore the relationship between primacy and collegiality.

1 For this paragraph see Jan Grootaers, "Humanae Vitae", in *Dictionnaire d'histoire et de géographie ecclésiastiques*.

2 Carlo Cremona, *Paolo VI*, p. 230. Since this is important, here is the Italian: "*Non voleva provocare . . . Non voleva che una enciclica, documento solenne, fosse ogetto di opinabilità anche da parte dei vescovi.*"

30

Cardinal Suenens and the Council's Logic

> The press has to have hot quotes and sharp points of view. Real news is bad news. Since the press lives on advertising, and all advertising is good news, it takes a lot of bad news to sell all the good news. Even the good news of the Gospel can be sold only by hellfire. Vatican II made a bad mistake in this, as in other matters.
>
> (Marshall McLuhan to the Canadian Prime Minister, Pierre Elliott Trudeau, 24 January 1969, *Letters of Marshall McLuhan*, Oxford University Press, Toronto, p. 362)

If Paul VI had been able to eavesdrop on this exchange between two Catholic intellectuals in Canada – the land that gave us Bernard Lonergan SJ, the wonder theologian of the age – he would have had good reason to feel miffed that McLuhan had not even tried to understand the Council. Many other middle-aged "converts" felt the same: Evelyn Waugh, Julien Green and Jacques Maritain all tended to whinge.

In Maritain's case, whinge is too weak a word to describe *le Paysan de la Garonne* in which he reverted to the anti-Modern attitudes of *Trois réformateurs* of 1928. Though he had translated the work in his youth, Montini had long overcome its Maurrasian account of European intellectual history which saw contemporary unbelief as the product of the Reformation, rationalism and romanticism. Giuseppe Lazzati met Maritain again in 1967 and was shocked at his sad decline.[1]

McLuhan, the expert on the media, watched the Council flounder in its treatment of this subject. He complained that the Church today no more understood the implications of the electronic media than the sixteenth-century Church had grasped the Gutenberg revolution. McLuhan could have worked on the instruction designed to implement the

1 In 1961, Raissa having died, Maritain went to live with the Little Brothers of Jesus (Charles de Foucauld Brothers) near Toulouse; in 1970 he finally joined them for the last three years of his life, dying at ninety-one.

decree *Inter Mirifica*, but he did not. *Communio et Progressio* was famously better than the text it "implemented", but that was no great achievement, and anyway in 1969 it was still in the pipeline from which it did not emerge until January 1971.

There was an unpleasant note of I-told-you-so about McLuhan's remarks perhaps based on the feeling that he should have been consulted earlier. Paul VI had a good grasp of the workings of the press: he had once written devastatingly of *L'Osservatore Romano* that "not content with relating what happened, it had also to explain what *should have* happened";[1] and he regularly discussed media matters with Assumptionist Father Antoine Wenger, editor of *La Croix*, which he preferred to *Le Monde* for its reporting of religious affairs.[2] But he had less understanding of television and the importance of the "sound-bite" – the brief extract from the speech that the media could use. Indeed the superficiality of this kind of communication was repugnant to someone whose key word was *approfondir*.[3]

Cardinal Léon-Joseph Suenens was a natural publicist, skilled in all levels of the media. Cardinal Heenan of Westminster complained that he was always playing to the gallery, and the invisible audience he would reach through the media seemed more important to him than those he was immediately addressing.[4] Suenens had successfully planted the idea that *Humanae Vitae* was a non-collegial or even an anti-collegial act. This was potentially very damaging for the Church's unity.

Paul VI responded in December 1968, just six months after *Humanae Vitae*, by announcing that an Extraordinary Synod would be held, starting on 11 October 1969, to explore the relationship between primacy and collegiality.

Apart from that, the pontificate seemed to be drifting. Cardinal Jean Villot, Prefect of the Congregation for the Clergy, wrote privately on 16 February 1969:

> Nothing new here in Rome for the time being. It seems that Paul VI thought seriously about holding a consistory, but the general opinion is that it will not be before the end of the year. Why? No one knows. Some appointments were just not ready

1 *Notiziario*, 17, p. 18. His comments appeared in 1961, in the centenary number of *L'Osservatore Romano*.

2 Antoine Wenger, "*Cinq Audiences de Paul VI*", in *Notiziario*, 18, p. 77.

3 Jean Guitton, *Paul VI secret*, p. 24: "Quant à la vision de Paul VI, je crois pouvoir la résumer d'un mot qu'il prononçait avec un application lente, détachant les syllabes: AP-PRO-FON-DIR." Pope John XXIII's key-word was *rajeunir* (rejuvenate).

4 Heenan, no stranger to the gallery, knew what he was talking about. The *Times Literary Supplement* headlined a review of his autobiography: "Were you there, when they televised my Lord?"

> – Toledo, recently named; the succession of Cardinal Bea who could be replaced by Pedro Arrupe, General of the Jesuits, or perhaps by Pellegrino whose government of the diocese of Turin leaves much to be desired.
>
> Though no one has talked to me about it, I am struck by the physical decrepitude of Cardinal Cicognani during the last two months. It will create problems in the end, not patent of any easy answer; for one can't see a diplomat taking over the post at a time when the Holy See has to present a more pastoral aspect.[1]

Four weeks later Villot knew that he himself would be replacing the decrepit Cardinal Secretary of State, though it was not officially announced until 28 April at the consistory Villot thought unlikely. Indeed most of the Villot's predictions were off the mark. If the head of a Roman dicastery, soon to be Cardinal Secretary of State, could be so wrong, what hope was there for outside commentators.

Villot had to overcome self-doubt to take the post. He admitted that Agostino Casaroli would have been a better choice – "He had diplomacy in his veins" – but his expertise on Eastern Europe and China would still be available to whoever was Secretary of State.[2] In any case Msgr Giovanni Benelli, the industrious and dynamic substitute, dealt with "ordinary affairs" just as Montini had for Pius XII. No one knew where "ordinary affairs" stopped, and in Cicognani's dotage – he was eighty-six in February 1969 – Benelli as the personal manager of the Vatican was already the effective head of its diplomatic service. Even after Villot's appointment, Benelli continued to receive ambassadors to the Holy See on Thursdays and Saturdays.[3]

In theory this arrangement left Villot with a more pastoral and ecclesial role. He would be responsible for dealings with episcopal conferences. He would oversee the practical realization of "collegiality". He would be in position before the autumn Synod to consider this question.

1 Antoine Wenger, *Le Cardinal Villot*, p. 88. The letter was to Msgr Charles Duquaire in Lyons, Villot's confidant. Duquaire was the champion and protector of Paul Touvier, the ex-*Milice* officer condemned to death *in absentia* after the war for complicity in killing Jews. This damaged the Church so much that it forced a full-scale historical enquiry: René Rémond, ed., *et al.*, *Paul Touvier et l'Eglise*, Fayard, Paris 1992. Duquaire continued campaigning for a pardon for Touvier after he joined Villot in Rome. Villot does not seem to have realized how dangerous this was not just for himself but for Paul VI.

2 Ibid., *Le Cardinal Villot*, p. 93.

3 Ibid. "Contrary to what has often been written, Benelli was friendly with Villot and had encouraged the Pope to appoint him. As counsellor in the Paris nunciature and later observer at UNESCO, he saw Villot frequently in Lyons." We shall see how long this idyllic relationship lasted.

Above all an obviously "pastoral" Secretary of State would answer the objection of those who shared the Suenens' judgement that, in the era of collegiality, the Vatican diplomatic service was an anachronism and an anomaly. The motu proprio *Sollicitudo Omnium Ecclesiarum* was in preparation. To Benelli's mind it would put a stop to "wilful indifference and misunderstanding" about papal nuncios, dissipate "widespread ignorance" on this topic, and prove that papal representatives were "an irreplaceable instrument for the realization of the supreme pastoral activity of Peter's successor, the Bishop of Rome".[1]

But as Secretary of State Villot was not much help on the main non-theological worry that added to Paul VI's burdens in 1969. The Pope was neither knowledgeable nor much interested in international finance. Although the Council had spoken of "the Church of the poor", through the IOR (Institute of Religious Works) the Vatican was heavily involved in the world of international high finance, and was going to get more and more involved with the arrival of Archbishop Paul Marcinkus as its energetic new-broom President. His plan seemed eminently sensible: IOR investments should be removed from Italian companies, fatally prone to scandals, and placed with international companies which were believed to be less hazardous.

In the spring of 1969 there was a highly secret meeting in the Vatican between the Pope and a Sicilian banker called Michele Sindona. The deal they discussed was the Vatican £150 million in the conglomerate *Società Generale Immobiliare*. Its President was Count Enrico Galeazzi, former Governor of Vatican City. It financed the Rome Hilton, many other hotels in Italy, the Pam-Am building on the Champs Elysées (opened by Maurice Chevalier in 1968), the Montreal Stock Exchange, and most notoriously the Watergate complex in Washington, DC.

Paul wanted quite simply to dispose of it. To sell it off. The deal was that Sindona would take some of the shares, sell the rest, and thus would raise capital for the Vatican's good works while ridding it of an embarrassing albatross. But Paul had in fact backed a crook. The story did not break till 1975, but financial anxieties beset Paul VI from now until the end of his pontificate in 1978.

Paul tried desperately to get a grip on things by making the consistory of Monday, 28 April 1969 the most spectacular consistory ever seen: thirty-five cardinals at one fell swoop, though one remained unan-

1 These expressions were used by Cardinal Giovanni Benelli in his preface to Mario Oliveri, *The Representatives: The Real Nature and Function of Papal Legates*, Van Durren, Gerrards Cross 1980, p. 12. Benelli can claim paternity of this work, since when he was *sostituto* Msgr Oliveri had acted as his secretary.

nounced *in pectore*.[1] The Secretariat for Christian Unity got a new President in the rotund shape of Johannes (known as Jan) Willebrands. A veteran of the hide-and-seek dialogues of the 1950s, he had been with Cardinal Augustin Bea from the foundation of the Secretariat for Christian Unity in 1960. It was a choice of continuity plus energy. The notion that Don Pedro Arrupe or Cardinal Michele Pellegrino might have been kicked upstairs, floated by Villot in February, was exposed as a fantasy.

The "traditional" Jesuit cardinal turned out to be not Arrupe but the patristic scholar Jean Daniélou. This was a "surprise" (that is, his name had not been mentioned in the pre-match speculations); but it was a double surprise for Paul VI had wanted Henri de Lubac as his learned Jesuit cardinal. But de Lubac declined (though later, under John Paul II and at eighty-seven, he was prevailed upon to accept, largely as a gesture).

De Lubac, it was learned, refused to be ordained bishop as a condition for being created cardinal: he considered it an abuse of the sacramental office of bishop. His younger Jesuit colleague, Daniélou, had no such scruples and there was an unseemly demonstration at his episcopal ordination in Notre Dame, Paris, as leaflets fluttered down from the clerestory complaining "Paul VI, you only make your friends bishops!"

The college of cardinals now had a wholly unprecedented 133 members. It had been truly internationalized in ways Paul had only dreamed of in the post-war 1940s. The Chinese, the Koreans, the Zaïreans, the Guatemalans were all able to claim their "first-ever" cardinals. By creating so many cardinals, said commentators, Paul VI had set up the conclave that would elect his successor.

He also tried to make the consistory worthwhile. It was not just an occasion for rejoicing and junketing (though Cardinal John J. Carberry's friends did both, and he played the mouth-organ to entertain them on the flight over). Paul chose this occasion to make important announcements.

This time there were three: the new *ordo missae* was announced along with the new Calendar of the Roman Church. The title of the *motu proprio* dealing with these matters, *Mysterii Paschali*, was chosen to show that the whole purpose of liturgical reform was to bring out the absolute centrality of the whole Paschal mystery, cross and resurrection, in Christian life.

The second announcement was not unlinked with the first: he had

1 *Insegnamenti*, 1969, p. 241. Among them were four Americans, Dearden (Detroit), Cooke (New York), Carberry (St Louis) and Wright (Pittsburgh), who succeeded Villot as Prefect of the Congregation for the Clergy. Flahiff (Winnipeg, Canada) would become the women's advocate in the Synod of 1971, while Höffner (Cologne) would lead the German reaction. The cardinal *in petto* was an East European.

decided to divide up the Congregation of Rites into two new dicasteries, the Congregation for Divine Worship, which would be exclusively dedicated to "animating and supervising the 'Church at prayer' (*ecclesia orans*)"; and the Congregation for the Causes of Saints, which would be responsible for everything to do with beatifications and canonizations. This was a sensible division of labour, since Worship required pastoral skills while Saints needed competence in assessing historical data. That is not to say that some were not upset: empire-builders always deplore the break-up of their fiefdoms.

The same thought also applied to the third announcement made on this memorable day. Paul said that, according to the *votum* or desire of the 1967 Synod, he was setting up an International Theological Commission (ITC) of thirty members. They would come from various parts of the world and continue the healthy experience of the Council. On the crucial question – their relationship with the Congregation for the Doctrine of the Faith (CDF) – Paul restricted himself to the remark that the new body would take its place "alongside" those theologians whom the CDF already used as consultors, who were to be thanked for their admirable work (*illis Theologiae cultoribus, quorum consilium Congregatio pro Doctrinae Fidei utitur . . . haec nova se adiunget Commissio*).[1] The only reason, he explained, why there had been so much delay in setting up the ITC was the need to consult with so many people.

That was true. But it was not the whole truth. The CDF under Ottaviani would never have accepted the ITC because its very existence cast doubt on its own theological competence. The "reformed" CDF, now in charge of the Croatian Franjo Seper, accepted the new body because the Holy Father wanted it. It then proceeded to try to neutralize it. But this was not immediately apparent. Anyway the appointment of the Louvain scholar and "renaissance man", Msgr Charles Moeller, as Secretary of the CDF, was a good sign.

But further trouble was brewing in Belgium. Cardinal Léon-Joseph Suenens had an unhappy meeting with Pope Paul early in March. The Pope handed him a letter criticizing his authoritarian ways in Belgium: he spoke in the name of the conference, said his critics, but the only person he consulted was his theologian Gustave Thils. Suenens, much mortified, not only defended himself but counter-attacked, accusing the Nuncio of spying on him. Paul heard him out and said merely: "Yes, pray for me; because of my weaknesses, the Church is badly governed."[2]

Far from being mollified by this kid-glove treatment, Suenens went public with his criticisms and displayed the media skills he could always

1 Ibid. p. 255.

2 Antoine Wenger, *Le Cardinal Villot*, p. 108.

call on. It was as though he regarded the forthcoming Synod as a showdown, collegiality's last hurrah. He determined to get public opinion on his side. The Suenens interview in *Informations Catholiques Internationales* (15 May 1969) was dramatic.

Popes had been criticized by cardinals before, but only between consenting adults and in private. Now thanks to media-hype, Suenens' critique of current papal policies resounded through the whole world. It boiled down to one simple proposition: Paul VI was frustrating the collegiality defined by the Council because of his exaggerated concept of the papal office.

Graver still – from Paul's point of view – was that Suenens, far from being a lonely individual of eccentric views, emerged as the spokesman for a great many people in the Church. A whole galaxy of theologians including Karl Rahner and Hans Küng cheered Suenens on. Bishop Christopher Butler OSB called the interview "one of the most important contributions to the contemporary discussion of the Church", adding: "His frankness and prudence should prove a rallying-point for all those who share his position 'at the extreme-centre' of the post-conciliar Church."[1]

To Paul this body-blow was deeply disturbing. Continually harassed by the remaining conservatives in the Curia, he imagined that he occupied the middle-ground and stood at the "extreme-centre" now clamorously claimed by Suenens. Moreover, to have a cardinal acting as an alternative "rallying-point" seemed to throw down an intolerable challenge to papal authority itself.

According to conventional Vatican wisdom (frequently disregarded in practice) the pope is like the British royal family: he "cannot reply" to charges made against him. This conveniently exempts him from the ordinary learning process to which most public figures are subject. It is a handicap masquerading as an advantage. So Paul at first did not reply because his lips were sealed.

In his stead the three French cardinals of the Curia, Eugène Tisserant, Jean Villot and Gabriel-Marie Garrone fired off "private" letters of indignant disapproval to Suenens, varying only in their degree of rudeness. They were soon "made known" to the press if not actually "published". Were their eminences acting off their own bat?

Tisserant the ancient orientalist and incorrigible individualist, famous for criticizing John XXIII at his elegant dinner-table, quite possibly was. He pronounced the Suenens interview "disrespectful, defamatory and even slanderous."[2] Tisserant, a choleric old cavalryman now

1 Elizabeth Hamilton, *Cardinal Suenens: A Portrait*, 1975, pp. 151–52.

2 Hamilton, p. 142.

side-tracked, may have felt that coming to the aid of the beleaguered Pope was more fun than spinning epigrams about how badly the Church was faring since his retirement. However, Paul VI must have authorized Garrone and Villot, both top curial officials, to reply. They represented French urbanity faced by Belgian crudity.

But then on 23 June, the feast of his patron John the Baptist, Paul replied himself and in milder fashion than the trio of cardinals. There were an astonishing forty Roman cardinals present at this event most of whom expected him to rebuke Suenens. But he was meekness itself. He thanked Tisserant, who had given the address of homage, for combining his "habitual courtesy with realistic authority".[1] Then he went on:

> It is not easy to hold a post of responsibility in the Church today. It is not easy to rule a diocese, and we well understand the conditions in which our brothers in the episcopate have to exercise their mission.
>
> We cannot be insensitive to certain criticisms, not all of them accurate or well-founded, not always considerate (*riguardose*) and opportune, that have been directed from various places against this Apostolic See, known more vulnerably as the Roman Curia.
>
> It would be easy and perhaps is a duty to put right certain judgements contained in these complicated and clamorous objections; but we think that the people of God, informed of the truth of the matter and illumined by hope, can easily do this for itself.[2]

This confidence in the wisdom of the People of God was misplaced. Both Paul VI and Suenens had in mind John Henry Newman's axiom, "Truth defends itself and falsehood refutes itself". That suggests a kind of *moratorium* on discussion while the truth sorts itself out.

But real life did not permit such delay, and the result was the clash and din of controversy. Yet Paul's refusal to condemn Suenens does him credit. Tisserant would have booted him out forthwith. Hurt though he was, Paul claimed to understand why Suenens had done it: "We well understand the conditions under which our brothers in the episcopate exercise their mission." Translate: they were under intense pressures

1 *Insegnamenti*, VII, p. 447. Is there a trace of irony here?

2 Ibid. p. 449. One can imagine how Pius XI would have thundered away at the impertinence – he once made Angelo Roncalli kneel for half an hour in his presence as a punishment for an alleged lapse. Pius XII's aides would have stressed how ill it made him.

from priests, laypeople and, increasingly, women to reform the Church and do it quickly.

Paul said he would take the objections into account. He even declared himself ready to "modify existing juridical positions, when it seems reasonable to do so, desirous as we are to renew canon law for the better service of the Church . . . and welcoming aspirations towards a legitimate pluralism in unity".[1]

Had Suenens transgressed that invisible boundary? Or was there something in his criticisms? Paul seemed to concede that he would take aboard the criticisms "with humble and sincere objectivity, ready to consider the plausible reasons for such clashes".[2] The truth is that Suenens' stab in the back – that is how it appeared to Tisserant and others – was a terrible distraction from Paul's mission in these months.

On 10 June 1969 he had visited – another first – the World Council of Churches in Geneva. Following his usual practice, Paul began by "introducing himself" to the assembled bureaucrats – as many women as men – "Our name is Peter!"[3] This disconcerted Protestant souls unused to the papal plural who thought his name was Paul. He then confused them utterly by saying that "the name Paul we have chosen suggests the direction we have wished to give to our pastoral ministry". Dr Eugene Carson Blake in his report on the papal visit stressed this last sentence "as a counterweight to the Petrine claims of the rest of the paragraph".[4]

In July he became the first pope ever to visit Africa. In his usual style he announced it in advance on 17 March 1969: he would go to Kampala, capital of Uganda, for three days from 31 July to 2 August. His immediate motive was to visit the shrine of the Twenty-Two Martyrs he had canonized during the third session of the Council. An altar had been built on an island at Namugongo 30 kilometres from Kampala. There were Anglican Martyrs too, though they had a separate shrine. They were young men, some of them were boys and some catechumens, all murdered by the Kabanga, as the local king was known.

Paul had prepared this visit to Africa in depth, as was his habit. At Vatican II the 311 bishops from Africa formed only 8 per cent of the total; and of them only sixty were genuinely African. One effect of the

1 Ibid. 1969, p. 449.

2 Ibid.

3 This was the form of speech adopted by Gregory VII and the Popes who followed him, in their quarrels with the Emperor over investiture. But that, from the point of view of the WCC, made it worse.

4 Edward J. Yarnold SJ, *They are in Earnest: Christian Unity in the Statements of Paul VI, John Paul I, John Paul II*, p. 85.

Council was that the bishops became aware of their "African" identity and learned to work together in AMECEA (Association of Member Episcopal Conferences in East Africa). In 1967 Paul published *Africae Terrarum* which urged further collaboration and tried to apply *Populorum Progressio* to the African situation. This bore fruit in 1969 when the regional conferences came together in SECAM (the Symposium of Episcopal Conferences of Africa and Madagascar). That provided the second motive for going to Africa.

Paul was greeted on his arrival at Entebbe Airport at 3.02 p.m. by President Milton Obote who had deposed the Kabanga in 1967. Presidents from neighbouring countries including Julius Nyrere of Tanzania, the only Catholic among them, were in attendance, making the point that this was a visit to Africa and not just to Uganda. Besides the usual clutch of cardinals Paul brought with him a layman, Giuseppe Amichia of the Justice and Peace Commission, which was beginning to play an important role in monitoring human rights in East Africa, though in Uganda it was destined to be annihilated when General Idi Amin wrecked the country. The papal visit was a brief gleam of hope before the storm.

Compared with subsequent papal visits, Paul's African safari was a leisurely stroll rather than a hectic marathon. He concentrated on one major speech a day. On the evening of his arrival he addressed SECAM – all the bishops of Africa. He saluted them with the words of St Paul, "All the Churches of Christ greet you" (Romans 16:16), an interesting example of how Paul could exploit positively the local Church theology developed by Cardinal Bernard Alfrink. It was a novelty for the Churches of Africa to be treated as equals – or even to think of themselves as such. Yet that was what he had come to say:

> We have no other desire than to foster what you already are: Christians and Africans. Hence we wish our presence among you to have the significance of a recognition of your maturity, and of a desire to show you how that communion which unites us does not suffocate, but rather nourishes the originality of your personal, ecclesial and even civil personality.[1]

The time had come, he said, for Africans to become "missionaries to yourselves". This did not make redundant help from "collaborators coming from other Churches", a delicate defence of expatriates, but it

1 *Insegnamenti*, 1969, p. 527. Those are the words the Pope pronounced in English. The quaintness of the style is due to his translators, not to me. But I have eliminated capital letters in such expressions as "Hence We wish Our Presence".

said unmistakably that the Church was "well and truly planted in this blessed soil".[1]

But if this well and truly planted Church were to be more than a mere transplant from Europe or elsewhere, a further step had to be taken. Paul took it cautiously. The Churches of Africa must be *Catholic*, that is, must hold on firmly to the faith of which "the martyrs were the champions and the missionaries the scrupulous teachers". The next passage was particularly important, and not just for Africa:

> You know that the Church is particularly tenacious, we may even say conservative, in this regard. To make sure that the message of revealed doctrine cannot be altered, the Church has even set down her treasure of truth in certain concepts and verbal formulas. Even when these formulas are difficult, at times, she obliges us to preserve them textually. We are not the inventors of faith, we are its custodians.[2]

That is the only instance of Paul using the word "conservative".

The danger he was warning against was hasty syncretism, quick fixes and instant syntheses with African religion. But once reassured on this point, he went on:

> the expression, that is, the language and mode of manifesting the faith may be manifold; hence it may be original, suited to the tongue, the style, the character, the genius, and the culture of the one who professes the one Faith. From this point of view, a certain pluralism is not only legitimate, it is desirable. An adaptation of the Christian life in the fields of pastoral, ritual, didactic and spiritual activities is not only possible, it is even favoured by the Church. The liturgical renewal is a living example of this. *And in this sense you may, and indeed must, have an African Christianity.*[3]

The last sentence has been much quoted. Indeed it is almost the sole memory that endures of Paul's journey to Africa. The context suggests that it is less liberating than it sounds in isolation.

Next morning Paul ordained twelve bishops, among whom was the youthful Emmanuel Milingo, Archbishop of Lusaka, Zambia, who was just thirty-nine.

At sundown the same day he addressed the Ugandan Parliament in

1 Ibid. p. 528, a reference to *Ad Gentes* 6.

2 Ibid. pp. 529–30. Once again these are Paul's own words in English.

3 Ibid. p. 530. Once again the translation feels as though it were done by an inexperienced computer armed with a nineteenth-century dictionary.

the presence of President Milton Obote and the four neighbouring heads of state. The interesting thing here was not so much what Paul said as how he was regarded by Milton Obote. The Ugandan President milked the occasion for all it was worth, but at the same time he illustrated how far the Pope had become a "transnational actor" on the international stage. The papal visit to Uganda was "a source of inspiration", said Obote:

> Your presence here is a public recognition of Africa as a rapidly evolving continent fully resolved to play its part – spiritual and temporal – in the concert of nations. You have drawn attention to the numerous and difficult problems of Africa and the world. This vast continent is afflicted by enormous problems: illiteracy, poverty, ignorance and disease, racial struggles and the injustices that accompany them, that so often issue in the loss of human life and destruction . . . Here in Uganda your decision to visit the shrine of the Martyrs at Namungongo is seen as a clear and positive sign which proves to the people of Uganda and the whole world that religion should bring people together rather than drive them apart.[1]

This rings true. The Pope noticed the distress of Africa. He was the voice of those who had no voice. Most of the news from Africa in the Western-dominated media – and in Uganda this would soon be tragically verified – was of disaster, catastrophe or tragedy. Paul's visit disinterestedly put them on the map. No mean achievement.

Yet for Paul, getting outside Europe in an ecumenical context in which his international role was assured and internal Catholic quarrels were cut down to size, was not really an option. He was so soon back at his desk, where they piled up before him. Significantly Benelli, though an old Africa hand, had not gone with him to Kampala. *Lavoro*, too much *lavoro*.

Paul's hope of rallying support and regaining the initiative now lay with the Synod already announced and with the reform of the diplomatic service of the Holy See. This was a two-prong reply to critics like Suenens. *Sollicitudo Omnium Ecclesiarum* tried to explain how the exercise of the primacy meshed in with episcopal authority without destroying it. Papal representatives were not spies on the local Churches nor just the long arm of the Vatican in their midst. The Extraordinary Synod would explore the relationship between primacy and collegiality from another angle. To some extent Paul was accepting the Suenens agenda, confident that he would gain the consensus.

1 President Milton Obote's address is given in indirect speech in ibid. pp. 512–13.

But there was a weakness in the Synod plan. The first in 1967 had been an "ordinary" synod, with its members *elected* by the episcopal conferences. At the 1969 Synod only *presidents* of episcopal conferences would be present. Suenens was disgruntled: although presidents of episcopal conferences could be elected by their peers, not all were, and the effect of this move was to make the 1969 Synod less representative, distinctly less "co-responsible" than its predecessor.

Suenens, informed of the Synod through the newspapers, remained sceptical. He hoped it would be an open and honest assembly but feared it would be curially manipulated. He said that bishops needed solid information: "It is true that we bishops have a grace of discernment – that is our charism; but we also need information."[1]

This was double-edged once again. The Bishop of Rome had the charism of discernment too, and he might even be said to possess it "pre-eminently"; but that in no way dispensed him from first searching out the facts. One basic fact was that *Humanae Vitae* had not been well "received" in the developed world, and that this non-reception could not be explained away by ill-will or anti-clerical hostility to the Church. This was what Suenens tried, and failed, to get across to him.

It was the *style* of papal authority that was under attack, not papal authority itself, Suenens claimed: "Neither at the Council nor since has the primacy of the Successor of Peter ever been questioned. The central issue at the Council was to clarify papal primacy as defined by Vatican I, and to show that it is at the heart of the collegiality emphasized by Vatican II."[2] Suenens was seeking a "balance" between primacy and collegiality. This was not a roundabout-and-swings tussle in which one gained what the other forfeited.

Paul, in principle, did not disagree. "Episcopal conferences," he frankly declared, "are an improved structure in the Catholic Church, novel by what they have to do, by their canonical and ethnic character, and by the way they realize decentralization."[3] That was fine as a theory for the forthcoming Synod. But it skated elegantly round Suenens' key question: why were the episcopal conferences not consulted before *Humanae Vitae*? That was the question which the debate on primacy and collegiality had to face. Paul hoped the Synod would confirm his own "courage" in making up his own mind and displaying "leadership" qualities. He would not be disappointed.

1 "Cardinal who stands at the extreme-centre" interview with Peter Hebblethwaite, *Catholic Herald*, 24 January 1969. The interview took place at the Belgian Embassy in Belgrave Square, London.

2 Ibid.

3 *Insegnamenti*, 1969, p. 547.

But before the Extraordinary Synod assembled, Suenens did it again. He went to Chur in Switzerland where a hundred or so priests held their parallel meeting while the bishops conferred on their own. They had been impelled by the student revolts of 1968 to *prendre la parole* (to speak out).[1] Suenens conveyed the impression that he was on their side. He told this wild-eyed gathering that although he might not endorse all their views, in the words of St Augustine, "for you I am a bishop, with you I am a fellow Christian". Such was the prevailing ignorance that this familiar quotation, so often used by Paul (and quoted in *Lumen Gentium*, 32), struck the Chur priests with the force of an original thought.

What Chur showed was that Suenens intended to continue acting as the rallying-point for dissidence or, as Norman St John-Stevas put it on his behalf, as the focus of "the loyal opposition".[2] The failure to understand this concept was said to be one of Paul's greatest weaknesses: but the point was not that he failed to understand it – it was that he thought it incompatible with the *koinonia* which was central to his ecclesiology. But Suenens was now on the campaign trail and being deliberately provocative.

That was the meaning of his presence among the dissident priests at Chur. Yet even the sagacious Christopher Butler regarded Suenens' speech as the high point of the otherwise rather platitudinous Chur meeting. Suenens talked about the flexibility of the idea of Christian priesthood throughout history, invited those present to consider the basic functions of the priest, the challenge presented to the whole People of God (and not only to the hierarchy), and to reflect upon the future role of the priest in a renewed Church.[3] They assumed, perhaps understandably, that he was telling them to abandon celibacy. He was not quite there yet. But that was the next frontier, to be traversed at the 1971 Synod.

Paul reflected on the difference between Belgians and the Dutch. The Belgians were a "Catholic nation", while in the Netherlands Catholics were a minority though creeping up towards the 50 per cent mark. Yet Flemish Suenens was displaying a tenacity of purpose – called "obstinacy" if you didn't like it – that brought him very close to his brothers in the Netherlands who were on the verge of claiming a virtual autonomy for their episcopal conference.

1 The late Michel de Certeau SJ became famous for a single *mot*: "*En 1789 les Français ont pris la Bastille; en 1968 les Français ont pris la parole.*"

2 Norman St John-Stevas, *The Agonising Choice: Birth Control, Religion and the Law.* It was dedicated to Hans Küng and Bishop Christopher Butler.

3 Elizabeth Hamilton, *Cardinal Suenens*, p. 150.

Yet Suenens posed the subtler threat. The Dutch muscled in with drums beating, trumpets blaring, extras cheering and journalists celebrating. However outrageous he might sound, Suenens bore in mind "the art of the possible" and left himself possible escape-routes (*échappatoires*). Whatever he did, he made sure he had the media on his side. The Vatican found this very unfair. But no one knew what to do about it.

While these alarums were going on there was an important and wholly unexpected event on the diplomatic front. In late March 1969 the Hungarian Ambassador to Italy, acting on behalf of the Warsaw Pact, drew the Holy See's attention to the Pact's "Appeal to all European countries" approved on 17 March 1969 (feast of St Patrick, though it is doubtful if Budapest realized this). It proposed a "pan-European" conference to discuss "security and peaceful co-operation". It invited the Holy See to take part. This was its first invitation to an international conference since the Congress of Vienna in 1815.

It was flattering but was it serious? Was it a trap? The Warsaw Pact had made similar proposals before: they had been dismissed by the West as propaganda. But in May the Finnish government offered to host the proposed meeting in Helsinki, and it came a step closer. Paul and Agostino Casaroli pondered this unprecedented invitation. Other minuscule states of Europe, possessing none the less the essential attribute of sovereignty, were invited (San Marino, Monaco and Liechtenstein). But beyond that "juridical" reason, Paul saw in the invitation a recognition of the Holy See as a "moral force" that could contribute towards peace and security in Europe.

Casaroli was authorized to answer the invitation on 10 October 1969. He stressed the unique character of the Holy See, which, though physically in Europe, had a more than European responsibility. Further hesitation came from article 24 of the Lateran Treaty of 1929 which committed the Holy See "to remain extraneous to all temporal disputes between states and to international conferences held for such objects". Should it be excluded from the proposed conference on those grounds? No, because there was a qualifying clause ". . . unless the contending parties make concordant appeal to its mission of peace".[1] That was happening in this case, so the last objections were dismissed as an overscrupulous quibble.

In the course of the next four years Casaroli was more and more involved in "preparing for Helsinki". This diplomatic task gave him a

1 Text in Eugene Cardinale, *The Holy See and the International Order*, p. 326. Casaroli explains what happened in "*La Santa Sede e l'Europa*", *Civiltà Cattolica*, 19 February 1972, p. 380.

convenient and legitimate excuse for travelling around Eastern Europe and thus contributed to the *Ostpolitik* (the attempt to improve relations with Communist governments).

This was important for future political developments. But for the inner life of the Church, Paul's address to the first plenary session of the International Theological Commission on Monday, 6 October 1969 was of more immediate interest. The thirty theologians – all male and all priests – had been meeting at the Domus Mariae and discussing what their brief was. Paul talked about the "charism" of theologians in the light of Ephesians 4:12 ("some are teachers . . . for the equipment of the saints, for the work of ministry, for the building up of the body of Christ").

It was important that the special grace or "charism" of theologians should be recognized: it meant that they could no longer be regarded simply as the conveyor-belt of the *magisterium*. But by the same token the Petrine "charism" had also to be acknowledged, for it was "essential for the government, stability, peace and unity of the Church".[1] To reject the Petrine ministry was to "weaken the apostolic strength of the Church". Far from favouring ecumenism, it would on the contrary lead to the dispersal of the flock of Christ.

None of the thirty theologians thus addressed, it may safely be supposed, had the slightest intention of undermining the Petrine ministry. Paul's insistence on it could seem neurotic at times, and this was one of them. But in the oscillating balance of his style he straight away conceded that the charism of the Petrine ministry did not dispense him from calling upon the study of theology, and therefore that he *needed* theologians, and depended on them: "Not only can we not prescind from theological reflection, but we consider it to be a vital, intrinsic and necessary part of the ecclesiastical magisterium."[2]

This may seem obvious to fellow Christians. But Paul was touching here on a crucial problem which the ITC was intended to resolve: the *magisterium*, the Church's central teaching authority, had been dependent for years on the theologians of the Roman universities, who tended to palm off their own partisan views as the voice of the *magisterium* itself.

Paul quoted the French Dominican, Marie-Dominique Chenu, in an important article, *Les théologiens et le Collège Episcopal: autonomie et service*.[3] Theologians serve the Church not only through their deeper

1 *Insegnamenti*, 1969, p. 653.

2 Ibid.

3 Ibid. It should not be forgotten that Chenu's book on le Saulchoir had been severely censured in 1942.

study of doctrine, but by their openness to other disciplines which can pave the way towards a "more exact, more complete and more comprehensible" presentation of faith. They live and work in frontier regions. That requires freedom. Paul was anxious from this first meeting to dispel the impression that the theologians of the ITC were merely court-theologians who had surrendered their academic freedom:

> It is our intention to respect that freedom of expression and research that theology needs for its development, and that we know many of you hold dear. On this point we would like to dispel the fear that the service asked of you should in any way restrict your legitimate researches and their logical formulations.[1]

Karl Rahner was among his hearers. He who had suffered so much under Pius XII recognized that Paul was breaking new ground on the relationship between theologians and the *magisterium*.

Paul came as close as possible to saying that the papacy needed the theologians just as much as the theologians needed the papacy. Let us not quarrel, he said, about whether authority or theology has the "primacy": "In the area of divine truth, there is only one primacy, that of revealed truth and of faith, to which both theologians and the ecclesiastical *magisterium* give assent each in their own way (*unanima consensione, licet ratione diversa*)."[2]

The trouble was that this splendid theoretical statement came so soon after *Humanae Vitae*. That encyclical could not be lifted bodily into the realm of "revealed truth and faith" which had the absolute primacy. The Bishop of Rome had singularly exercised his primacy. And that was that.

As the ITC met, the Extraordinary Synod was assembling. It was already being presented in the press as a settling of accounts after *Humanae Vitae*.[3] Three questions were on the agenda:

1 A doctrinal approach to collegial unity and ecclesial hierarchy.
2 Improvement of the relationship between episcopal conferences and the Holy See.
3 Improvement of the relations between episcopal conferences.

The central question was how the relationship between what was then called the "centre" and the "periphery" should be understood so that

1 Ibid. p. 654.
2 Ibid. p. 651.
3 See Jan Grootaers, *De Vatican II à Jean Paul II, le grand tournant de l'Eglise catholique*, pp. 25–29.

greater autonomy for episcopal conferences could be achieved without infringing upon the pope's freedom of action. Cardinal Edouardo Pironio from Argentina provided the theological key to the problem:

> The community of the bishops with the Pope should not be understood as though the Pope was the only centre of unity, while bishops represented merely diversity. The college of bishops, united with the Pope, is itself a principle of unity. The bishop represents the particular church in which the universal Church dwells. The Roman Pontiff is the defender of legitimate diversity to the extent that he favours the cultural diversity of the Churches and prevents the absorption of particular Churches.

Pironio was Secretary-General of CELAM. Paul VI had been to Medellín the previous year to open their historic conference.

For the first time the Synod broke up into nine language-based discussion groups (*circuli minores*). This meant less emphasis on the big speech in the *aula* (sometimes addressed to the gallery) and improved the level of communication. There was surprising unanimity. Differences between "progressives" and "conservatives" faded.

The 1969 Synod made it clear that the bishops *wanted* to collaborate with the pope in all matters of importance, above all in the preparation of pontifical documents and decrees, in order to strengthen the Church's unity and discipline. It was a tacit, if unemphatic, restatement of the point made by Suenens. One cannot prove cause and effect but it is a fact that Paul VI issued no more encyclicals in the remaining nine years of his pontificate.

But alongside the relationship between the pope and the world's bishops, and as a condition of its efficacity, was the relationship between episcopal conferences themselves. This was something that Jean Villot, the new Cardinal Secretary of State, intended to work on. As the first non-Italian Secretary of State since Merry del Val under Pius X, he would stress his ecclesial role, leaving the politics and diplomacy to Benelli who was more than eager to take them over. Villot's role would be to keep episcopal conferences in touch, co-ordinating their activities and forestalling where possible unilateral declarations.

The other newcomer to the Curia, Cardinal John J. Wright, who had replaced Villot at the Congregation for the Clergy, warned the Synod that centrifugal forces were threatening to rend the Church asunder and that episcopal conferences could become the instrument of "*nationalismus immoderatus*" (unbridled nationalism). Wright did not mention any names. This could be considered a piece of conservative bluster from the first North American to be Prefect of the Clergy Congregation. But it evoked a real danger and made a theological point that Henri de Lubac developed in an important book.[1]

The practical value of episcopal conferences was not in doubt, said de Lubac, and the great contribution made by CELAM was beyond question. But distinctions have to be made, corresponding to the three chapters of *Christus Dominus*. Bishops can be seen in relation to the universal Church, and only when they are acting as members of the College of Bishops as a whole can they perform a truly *collegial* act. In his own diocese (the particular Church) the bishop is the leader, teacher and witness of faith – and he cannot shuffle off this task to any commission or conference. Paul reminded bishops that their duty to preach was "a matter of personal responsibility and absolutely inalienable".[2]

Acts of episcopal conferences are *collective* rather than collegial. They cannot be a substitute either for the individual accountability of the bishop in his diocese (the buck stops there) and the collegial activity of bishops in a general council. But it was becoming fashionable to speak of the episcopal conference as the manifestation of the *local Church*, acting as intermediary between the particular (or diocesan) Church and the universal Church.

The other main lesson of the 1969 Extraordinary Synod was that the practice of collegiality could not stand still. Collegiality was not an "achieved state" so much as a "dynamic process" like riding a bicycle: the synod would fall over if it stopped moving forward. The Extraordinary Synod of 1969 reformed the Synod itself as an institution. By 130 votes out of 145 the Fathers accepted the Suenens proposal for a more effective secretariat, controlled by a board representing the episcopal conferences, with power to choose the topics for future Synods. This was a more important concession than it might seem.

A more radical version of this proposal was the "Poma-plan", so named after Cardinal Antonio Poma, President of the Italian Episcopal Conference, a man known to be close to Paul VI. This would have made the Synod Secretariat a body truly representative of the episcopal conferences. It would consist of twenty elected members and be permanently responsible for the liaison between the pope and the episcopal conferences. It would meet several times a year and be responsible for planning the forthcoming Synod.

Paul met this suggestion half way. On 23 March 1970 the Synod Council was set up, consisting of fifteen members, twelve elected by the Synod (three per continent) and three named by the pope. It would meet twice a year, usually in spring and autumn, and have the task of

1 Henri de Lubac SJ, *Les Eglises particulières dans l'Eglise universelle*, 1971.
2 Ibid. p. 95.

preparing the next Synod.[1] It never had the broader function, envisaged by Poma, which was closer to the original idea of Alfrink and Maximos.

However this achievement came too late and was too minor to affect a series of measures which seemed to suggest that collegiality was in abeyance. The encyclicals *Sacerdotalis Coelibatus* (1967) and *Humanae Vitae* (1968) had been prepared without collegial consultation. The question was not whether Paul VI *could* issue such documents but whether he *should*. The mildest thing Suenens could find to say about them was that they would have carried more weight and had more credibility if they had been preceded by widespread consultation, a pre-reception process.

Third World bishops objected to not being consulted about *Sollicitudo Omnium Ecclesiarum*. They felt even more strongly than Suenens that the papal diplomatic service, even as reformed by this document, still left episcopal conferences under the Congregation for the Evangelization of Peoples (the old *Propaganda Fide*) subordinate to the Vatican representative. At the very least they were financially dependent, and therefore under humiliating pressure to conform.[2]

The Christmas festivities were spoilt for Paul VI by the news from Holland. It was evident that the harmony apparently reached at the extraordinary Synod existed largely on paper. Paul VI now faced a greater challenge than ever on the question of clerical celibacy. It came not from disgruntled or deranged individuals but from a united episcopal conference, which moreover claimed to speak in the name of European priests generally. The Dutch were as emboldened by Chur as Paul was depressed by it.

On Sunday, 21 December 1969 he launched a new "tradition" – the blessings of the statues of the infant Jesus (*Gesù bambino*) destined for the cribs of Rome. He would need the prayers of children as he prepared to confront the Netherlands Province of the Church in the most decisive primatial act of his pontificate.

1 This is enshrined in the Code of Canon Law, canon 348.

2 These complaints were not publicly expressed until the 1974 Synod on Evangelization. Bishop James D. Sangu was particularly insistent on the need for "equal partnership" between the "young Churches" of Africa and the "old Churches" of Europe. See Jan Grootaers, *De Vatican II à Jean-Paul II*, p. 82.

31

Dykes, Rainforests and the Outback

> There is no better defence of the Papacy than to unveil its inmost being. If weakness is shown up, you can reckon on a more friendly judgement through historical understanding than if, as often until now, it is all kept secret and men are left to suspect what they will.
>
> (G. H. Pertz, 1824, quoted in OWEN CHADWICK, *Catholicism and History*, p. 23)

There was one Dutchman at least with whom Paul VI seemed content: Johannes (Jan) Willebrands, created a Cardinal on 28 April 1969, now President of the Secretariat for Christian Unity in succession to Cardinal Augustin Bea. Though utterly loyal to Bea, Willebrands at sixty-one had more energy and less caution than the patriarch. The tempo quickened. Texts that had been log-jammed were now rapidly completed: *Matrimonia Mixta*, the *motu proprio* on mixed marriages (31 March 1970); documents on Ecumenism in Higher Education; and *Dans ces derniers temps* (7 January 1970). This last was directed against what was called "wild-cat intercommunion" in English or "*oecumenisme sauvage*" in French. Liberated Catholics were doing much as they pleased, happy to thumb their nose at the Vatican.

Intercommunion, however, was never just a matter of friendliness or being hospitable: it raised questions about the validity of priestly ministry and the importance of apostolic succession. It involved a *de facto* recognition of orders. As President of the Secretariat for Christian Unity, Willebrands did what Paul asked of him with flair and imagination. In the on-going clash with the Congregation for the Doctrine of Faith (CDF), Willebrands outwitted the inexperienced Cardinal Franjo Seper.

Paul's priorities were these. The "dialogue of charity" with the Orthodox came first because it was the first rent in the seamless robe of Christ's Church. We were already in "imperfect communion" with them, to use Paul's expression. Equally ancient were the Coptic Church in Egypt and the Armenian Apostolic Church which survived partly in the Soviet Union, partly in exile. Then came the theological bilateral dialogues already engaged with the Anglicans (the Anglican–Roman Catholic International Commission or ARCIC), with the Lutherans, with the Reformed tradition and with the Methodists.

It was a formidable agenda. Willebrands was eager to push ahead. He preached in Great St Mary's, Cambridge during the Octave of Prayer for Christian unity in 1970. He seemed to be contemplating a "Uniate" solution for the Anglican communion when he spoke of it as a *typos* of a Church found "where there is a long coherent tradition, commanding men's love and loyalty, creating and sustaining an harmonious whole of complementary elements, each of which strengthens and supports the other".[1] It was not exactly a local or particular Church as defined by Vatican II, nor was it primarily a diocese or a national Church (though it might coincide with one): it was a *typos*. When liturgy went into the vernacular theologians began to talk Greek.

Paul had never been particularly happy about the Dutch Pastoral Council; but he had put up with its first four sessions in 1968 and 1969, consoled by the thought that at least the Nuncio, Msgr Angelo Felici, was vigilant and active. But now Felici was threatening to stay away from the fifth session, due in January 1970, on religious life and priestly ministry, for he thought he knew exactly what would happen. Proposals to abolish the mandatory link between celibacy and the priesthood would vie with claims that "ex-priests" should be restored to the ministry forthwith. He did not wish to be associated with so flagrant a repudiation of Paul's encyclical *Sacerdotalis Coelibatus*.

So apprehensive about this meeting was Paul that he addressed a private letter, dated Christmas Eve 1969, to the seven Dutch bishops asking how he could help them avert this catastrophe. This revealed a misunderstanding of the Dutch bishops that, but for its tragic consequences, would have been touching. "It is very evident," he wrote, "that it is not the bishops that created these difficulties: they found them on their path and had to face up to them."[2] He felt sure they would act responsibly – that is, agree with his encyclical. In fact he misjudged their mood.

His offer to "reinforce their authority" was another misunderstanding. The most recent polls in Holland showed that 88 per cent of the Catholic population had every confidence in their bishops and their ability to solve the problems of their Church. The only way Paul could have reinforced episcopal authority *in the Netherlands* was by trusting the bishops. But the Dutch bishops had a different view of how their

1 *Tablet*, 24 January 1970.

2 Pierre Brachin, "*Paul VI et l'Eglise des Pays-Bas*", in *Paul VI et la Modernité dans l'Eglise*, p. 771.

authority should be exercised: they consciously entrusted themselves to a process the exact outcome of which could not be prescribed in advance. There were no "answers at the back of the book".

The Dutch Synod, meeting as usual at Noordwijkerhout, concluded with a four-point resolution:

1 That the obligation of celibacy should not be imposed on priests in the future.
2 That in certain conditions married priests or those about to marry should keep their posts or, if ousted, be restored to them.
3 That married men should be ordained as priests.
4 That celibacy should no longer be considered a necessary condition of the priestly ministry.

A rather menacing note added that once all these points were accepted the bishops should at once move to the implementation of point 3, which seemed to present the least difficulty; but that in the meantime they should put points 1 and 2 into effect without too much delay.[1] These resolutions were almost unanimous. The bishops, however, abstained.

That was only a small crumb of comfort for Paul VI. If he thought the Dutch bishops were going to disown the Pastoral Council he was soon disabused. Two weeks after the meeting they issued a communiqué which declared:

> The Bishops think that, for their community, it would be good that alongside priests living out their celibacy in complete freedom, one could admit in the Latin Church married priests, in the sense that married men could be ordained priests and that, in particular cases, priests who had married could be reintegrated into the priestly ministry, under certain conditions.[2]

This was much less absolute and aggressive than the resolutions of the Pastoral Council. It was relatively diplomatic. It sought to complement celibate priests rather than to replace them. The Dutch bishops were talking only about the Netherlands. And married priests were to be reintegrated into the pastoral ministry on a case-by-case basis and under strict conditions.

But it was nevertheless a terrible blow for Paul. In his speech to the college of Cardinals on 15 December 1969 he had spoken of defecting priests as his "crown of thorns", adding that although he would not judge such "unhappy hearts" in the internal forum, from the outside he was sure that "such desertions cause so much bitterness and scandal in

1 Ibid. p. 772.
2 Ibid.

the People of God".[1] The fact that the laid-back Dutch looked on such "changes of ministry" within the church so undramatically seemed to Paul further proof that secularization had bitten deep. Now the crown of thorns was pressed more tightly home.

Yet at this stage his reply to the Dutch was characteristically indirect. He seized the occasion of the Angelus on Sunday, 1 February to declare that "it was impossible to abandon celibacy or call it into question".[2] Yes, celibacy was difficult and demanding, he conceded, "but that is precisely what makes it attractive to young and ardent souls".[3] In his traditional address to Rome preachers at the start of Lent he developed the idea, claiming that "celibacy, spiritually transfigured and transfigurating, is the best incentive to recruiting new vocations to the priesthood".[4]

The decision that priests should publicly renew their vows (strictly, promise) of celibacy on Maundy Thursday was taken at this time and in this atmosphere. But these ideas and this measure merely illustrated the gulf that now yawned between Holland and Rome. They were acting out a different ecclesiology based on different premises.

But still Paul did not rebuke the Dutch bishops. His effective reply to the Dutch Pastoral Council took the form of a letter to Cardinal Jean Villot. This might seem a curious way of behaving: why address a letter to someone he saw every day? A letter to the Cardinal Secretary of State was a transparent and indeed a traditional device: it was a way of letting episcopal conferences round the world know the pope's mind. It would leave the Dutch bishops in no doubt about where he stood, but without coming down on them too heavily.

However, the situation was even odder than it seems. The letter to Cardinal Villot was written by Cardinal Villot himself. Paul had asked him to draft a reply to the Dutch bishops after consulting the heads of Roman Congregations.[5]

Paul was able to accept Villot's draft as his own. Yes indeed, declarations coming from Holland had caused uncertainty and perplexity among many in the Church, especially priests and those preparing for the priesthood. Villot knew how hard he had tried to prevent this happening: this was a reference to his still secret letters and no doubt also an answer to his curial critics who blamed him for "doing nothing",

1 *Insegnamenti*, 1969, p. 799.
2 Ibid. 1970, p. 95.
3 Ibid. p. 96.
4 Ibid. p. 123.
5 Antoine Wenger, *Le Cardinal Villot*, p. 110.

leaving him to understand that they would have acted decisively.[1] Willebrands exercised a steadying influence. Precipitate action might lead to schism.

Point by point Paul/Villot replied to the Dutch Synod:

1) The link between celibacy and the priesthood in the Latin Church must remain. To abolish or underestimate its value would be temerarious, because celibacy was "the sign consecrated by tradition of total dedication to the love of Christ". Celibacy had evangelical and missionary motives, and was required for complete availability in the service of the risen Christ.

2) There could be no question of reintegrating laicized priests in the pastoral ministry. Paul pointed to the more liberal legislation he had introduced for those who sought dispensations from their vows and promises.[2] But such "paternal understanding" in individual cases did not prevent him "deploring an attitude so little in conformity with what the Church expects of those who are definitely consecrated to the Lord's exclusive service".[3] In other words he was prepared to be compassionate, even if it broke his heart, but he was not going to pretend that the marriage of a priest changed nothing.

3) On the ordination of married men Villot suggested a concession which Paul VI at first found disturbing and unacceptable:

> In a situation where there is an extreme shortage (*estrema carenza*) of priests . . . and confined to regions which are in similar situations: would it not perhaps be possible to envisage the eventual priestly ordination of older men (*di età gia avanzata*) who have already given proof in their lives of an exemplary family and professional life?[4]

Villot had in mind countries like Indonesia where there was a risk that the expatriate priests, who made up almost the entire clergy, might be expelled. Paul frowned. Villot would rather withdraw than face papal disapproval. "Holy Father," he said, "act as if this text never existed: though it expresses more than just my personal opinion, it is only a project." Off he went to produce another draft.[5]

1 *Insegnamenti*, 1970, p. 99.

2 The new "Norms for Laicization" were already being applied, though they were not published until 13 January 1971. They were abrogated and made "more strict" by Pope Paul II in *Per litteras ad universos*, 14 October 1980.

3 *Insegnamenti*, 1970, p. 101.

4 Ibid. p. 102.

5 Wenger, *Le Cardinal Villot*, p. 120.

But then Paul, now truly Hamlet-like, changed his mind again and included Villot's proposal in the final version of the letter. But his reluctance comes strongly through. This tightly qualified and highly tentative suggestion is hedged about with further doubts. Could the ordination of married men *really* be limited to places where there was "an extreme shortage" of priests? Would not people be tempted to resort to it as a solution to the current lack of vocations? Would it not prove, as the curialists always argued, "the thin end of the wedge" that, hammered home, would bring down the whole edifice of clerical celibacy?

Yet the idea of ordained mature married men had been planted in Paul's mind. It had great importance for the future and bore fruit in the 1971 Synod. But it said nothing about the situation in the Netherlands where "an extreme shortage" of priests did not yet exist. In considering this "eventuality" Villot/Paul was responding to requests coming from Third World countries such as Brazil and Indonesia, not to browbeating from the Netherlands. Yet Paul still maintained that he wanted to "seek with the Dutch Bishops a means of solving *their* problems, bearing in mind the good of the whole Church".[1] The Dutch bishops thought that *he* had problems.

Armed with the letter he had drafted, Villot flew to Holland and had a clandestine meeting with Cardinal Bernard Alfrink in Utrecht on 7–8 March. So secret was it that *Le Monde* reported it the next day. The six-foot-four Villot was hard to disguise. The Vatican Press Office was indignant on Paul's behalf at the unfairness of this monstrous intrusion on privacy. But they should have learned by now that in media-conscious Holland one could no longer get away with the confidential meetings Paul, as an old diplomat, preferred. The feeling of being pressurized by public opinion was enhanced when Cardinal Léon-Joseph Suenens muscled in with an interview in – inevitably – *Le Monde*.[2]

Suenens asserted that clerical celibacy as such was not the issue. Personally he was in favour of it. As with *Humanae Vitae* in 1968, the real question was whether the pope acting alone had the right to say that this topic or any other should not be discussed. This time Suenens blamed Pope Paul personally:

1 *Insegnamenti*, 1970, p. 103.

2 Though Henri Fesquet, religious affairs writer of *Le Monde*, was on his side, Paul remained slightly mistrustful of *Le Monde*. "It has some good things," he told Antoine Wenger, "but it only sees the 'phenomenal' aspect of the Council, the quarrels and disputes, and not the work of the Holy Spirit that the eyes of faith alone can discern." "*Cinq audiences de Paul VI au Père Antoine Wenger, rédacteur en chef de la Croix*", *Notiziario*, 18, p. 77.

> The deadlock (*impasse*) – and deadlock there is – arises from the fact that the Pope did not allow the subject to be discussed by the Fathers of the Council. And this ban has been upheld in clear and repeated statements – thus excluding any collegial intervention, exactly as happened over birth-control. So with public examination and discussion blocked by authority, bishops cannot even swop thoughts on this subject among themselves or with the Pope.[1]

For Suenens the fact that the pope *could* reserve certain questions to himself did not mean that he *should* regard this as normal procedure. This was a very widespread theological opinion.

So the charge was that Paul VI was ignoring collegiality, acting as solitary papal monarch, behaving as though he were some sort of Atlas carrying the entire burden of the Church on his shoulders. This meant, Suenens plunged on, that bishops were torn between conflicting choices: the appearance of disloyalty to Rome or a shirking of their responsibilities at home. They lost either credit with the pope or credibility with their people.

The Suenens interview was deliberately timed to coincide with the first-ever meeting of the Synod Council, the fifteen representative bishops who were to act as a kind of "board of management" of the Synod. Their most important task was to set the agenda for the next Synod, due in autumn 1971.

Paul addressed them on 15 May 1970. In a passionate speech he replied to the Suenens interview, claiming that the very existence of the Synod, an institution he had created, proved his commitment to the Council and to collegiality. He denied that he was the prisoner of any particular theological school (he meant "the Roman school"). He declared that the "dynamism of the Council" (a phrase much used by Suenens) was developing for the good of the Church.

He drew comfort from some remarks of Cardinal François Marty, Archbishop of Paris, who had recently spoken of his "conciliar tenacity" and described the Petrine vocation as that of "bringing together the apostolic college" (*rassembleur du collège apostolique*). Since he only spoke well of people, Marty could be named but not Suenens:

> This is in sharp contrast to what has recently been said to our amazement and sorrow (*con Nostro doloroso stupore*) – and said in a way which, in our opinion, does not seem in keeping

1 Elizabeth Hamilton, *Cardinal Suenens: A Portrait*, p. 153.

> either with the fraternal style required for collegiality or the gravity of problems which, as everyone is aware, are being studied by responsible and competent persons.[1]

It was a very defensive speech from a rattled and anxious man.

Yet Paul's rebuke to Suenens was characteristically mild. It contrasted with the abuse heaped upon him by Cardinal Valerian Gracias of Bombay. In his address of homage to Paul VI at the first meeting of the Synod Secretariat he sought to curry favour by quoting Mahatma Gandhi's remark that "what has kept Catholicism fresh is celibacy". There is no room in the Church, he added, for "inane dialogue or false concepts of co-responsibility".[2] This was fatuous and unhelpful, and the man who resigned to make way for him, Archbishop "Tommy" Roberts, wondered whether he had done the right thing.

The truth was that Paul's apologia failed to answer Suenens' main point: the question of celibacy should be collegially discussed. Where were these "responsible and competent persons" who were said to be studying the problem? They did not exist.

Unless, of course, celibacy could be put on the agenda of the 1971 Synod. It was at this first meeting of the Synod Council that the idea that the 1971 Synod should be devoted to the priestly ministry was conceived. The quotation about married priests from the 2 February letter to Cardinal Villot could be included in the working-paper. The priesthood would then be set alongside an outward-looking theme, Justice in the World, as the Extraordinary Synod of 1969 had urged.[3] It would no longer be possible to say that Paul VI had systematically dodged collegial discussion of the question of the ordination of married men.

But while this might just about pacify Suenens it did not meet the requirements of his Dutch neighbour, Alfrink. Alfrink's relations with the Nuncio, Angelo Felici, had gone from bad to worse. In the first six months of 1970 they did not see each other at all. They finally met at a reception on 28 June, when three reasons for celebration combined: it was the feast of Sts Peter and Paul; the golden jubilee of Paul's ordination; and – more ominously – the hundredth anniversary of the conclusion of Vatican I in a thunderstorm in 1870.

The result of the meeting was that Alfrink was invited to Rome but

1 *Insegnamenti*, 1970, p. 498. The Marty quotations came from his diocesan bulletin, *L'Eglise de Paris*, 1 May 1970.

2 Elizabeth Hamilton, *Cardinal Suenens*, p. 155.

3 See René Laurentin, *Nouveaux Ministères et fin du clergé*, p. 157. The 1969 Synod passed two resolutions, one urging episcopal conferences to encourage initiatives in promoting justice, and the second on the idea of setting up a fund for progress. Msgr Giovanni Benelli had many discussions with Cardinal Terence Cooke, Archbishop of New York, on the second project, but they came to nothing. Ibid. p. 155.

only to discuss "how to implement the principles clearly stated in the 2 February letter". Arriving on 8 July he met Villot and Msgr Giovanni Benelli who "prepared" him for his two meetings with Paul VI on 10 and 14 July. At his Wednesday audience Paul had spoken of pastoral authority as "a duty, a burden, a debt and a ministry towards others". He insisted that the Church leader must lead his flock, not follow it.[1]

This was a clear message to Alfrink: he had the wrong view of authority. Yet in his two meetings with Paul he felt he was not being taken very seriously; his audience was slotted in between more important events like the liberation of James Edward Walsh, the Maryknoll bishop, from his Chinese gaol, and the state visit of West German Chancellor Willy Brandt. Alfrink returned home empty-handed, somewhat chastened, now more than ever sure that even the ordination of married men was a long-term prospect. He no longer knew how Holland could be provided with future priests. He summed up the results of his Roman visit in a bleak communiqué:

> The Bishops will seek to provide the priests Holland needs in the years to come . . . The Pope maintains that the reasons for keeping the traditional link between celibacy and priesthood in the Latin Church are still valid. This for him is a conviction of conscience in which he is supported by the majority of bishops, even though he realizes that other bishops take a different view. The ordination of married men can be examined collegially at the 1971 Synod.[2]

In August Alfrink showed his obedience by declaring that a married priest who celebrated the Eucharist "put himself outside the Church". He was left with the slender thread of hope represented by the 1971 Synod.

This preoccupation with the "cockpit of Europe" – as the Low Countries were known in the seventeenth century – reflects the media coverage at the time. But it distorts the pontificate. Paul was pope of the universal Church. He faced many other problems of life-and-death urgency, notably in Latin America where the populist and democratic forces released by Medellín collided with military dictatorships.

In Brazil the military seized power in 1964 and set out to wreck trade unions, student movements, left-wing groups and other civic institutions. The presidency of General Garrastazu Medici (1969–74) was a time when the "institutionalized violence" denounced by Emmanuel Mounier was particularly brutal. In the name of the "national security state", any

1 *Insegnamenti*, 1970, p. 699.

2 René Laurentin, *Nouveaux ministères et fin du clergé*, p. 271.

political opponent could be dubbed a Marxist and made to "disappear". There were over 500 *depaparacidos* in Brazil in 1970 (a small number compared with the 10,000 in Argentina). The Dominican Frei Betto appealed from his prison cell:

> The Church is the only hope for us prisoners because it is the only Brazilian institution not under the control of the military. Its mission is to defend and promote human dignity. The time has come for the Bishops to say, before it is too late: "Put an end to the tortures and injustices perpetrated by this regime."[1]

But the Brazilian bishops were divided. Cardinal Angelo Rossi, Archbishop of São Paolo since 1966, vacillated and tried to reconcile the unreconcilable. A close friend of the President, he appeared at military functions alongside him, suggesting that the Church blessed the regime. To the prisoners in gaol this was hollow mockery if not blasphemy. It could not be allowed to go on.

Paul "intervened" in October 1970 through Cardinal Maurice Roy, President of the International Justice and Peace Commission. Roy denounced the use of torture in Brazil, his article was published in *L'Osservatore Romano* and backed up by a resolute editorial on 19–20 October 1970. Rossi was summoned to Rome along with bishop Ivo Lorscheiter, named by the Brazilian bishops as the man responsible for dealing with the prisoners. At his Wednesday audience on 21 October Paul declared that "torture, that is to say cruel and inhuman methods by which the police extract confessions from the lips of prisoners, is to be explicitly condemned".[2] Though he did not name "the great country", the allusion to Brazil was transparent. This was the time when Henry Kissinger was predicting that wherever Brazil went with its vast population and rich natural resources, the rest of Latin America would follow.

Even as Paul was speaking Cardinal Rossi, back home in São Paolo, was assuring the press that the Pope knew perfectly well there was no religious persecution in Brazil and "appreciated President Garrastazu Medici's efforts to lead Brazil along the path of development, while

1 Peter Hebblethwaite, *The Runaway Church*, p. 183.

2 *Insegnamenti*, 1970, p. 1052. Knowing that he would be accused of "interfering in politics" Paul took the precaution of going back to Pope Boniface VIII's controversial claim that *ratione peccati*, that is, seen in their transcendental relationship to God, all things were subject to "the keys of Peter". This is the famous Bull *Unam Sanctam* of 1302 which declares that "submission to the Roman Pontiff is necessary for salvation" (see *The Christian Faith*, ed. J. Neuner and J. Dupuis, pp. 217–18). Of course Paul was not trying to breathe new life into a doctrine definitively slain by Vatican II, merely trying to justify his universal moral concern. After some disaster in a Pacific island, he joked, headlines asked: "What does the Pope say about this?"

trying to stem the tide of subversion and ward off the intense campaign of lies so unjustly directed against Brazil".[1] Next day Cardinal Rossi received a telegram informing him that he was urgently needed in Rome as Prefect of the Congregation for the Evangelization of Peoples (formerly Propaganda). Having crossed the wires, Rossi had tripped up over them.

This decisive and rapid action by Paul was an indication of the strength the *sostituto*, Msgr Giovanni Benelli, brought him. Pope and *sostituto* were at one on this: though the Vatican diplomatic service was improving, the Justice and Peace Commission provided an alternative and often more accurate source of news because it involved competent lay experts and was unhampered by traditions of caution. Justice and Peace could take the risk of prophecy.

The Rossi episode also illustrated another aspect of the International Justice and Peace Commission (IJPC). Modern communications – the telex was just coming in – meant that its President, Cardinal Maurice Roy, did not have to leave Quebec, where he was Archbishop, to be effective. With a good team in Rome, and the crucial support of Msgr Benelli, the IJPC was already at work preparing the 1971 Synod on Justice as well as the eightieth anniversary of the 1891 encyclical *Rerum Novarum*.

But the IJPC was of little help in Paul's efforts to bring the Vietnam War to an end. Throughout 1970 the United States and the Soviet Union vied with each other in winning the support of the Holy See. The US feared a condemnation that the Soviets desired. On 2 March the new President, Richard Nixon, flew to Rome specially to see the Pope, who had been unavailable on retreat during an earlier first visit. Rumours – routinely denied in Washington – hinted that Nixon was about to establish some kind of formal diplomatic relations with the Vatican. Yet Nixon reinstated the office of personal representative to the Holy See and Henry Cabot Lodge presented his credentials on 4 July 1970.

Lodge, Nixon's running mate in the 1960 election and former ambassador to Vietnam, was clearly appointed with Vietnam in mind. His presence did not prevent a reportedly acrimonious meeting between Paul and Nixon in September. When in November Andrei Gromyko, the Soviet Foreign Minister for decades, had an eighty-minute audience with Paul, the Rome right-wing paper *Il Tempo* chided the Pope for showing more warmth to Gromyko than he had done to Nixon.[2]

Paul kept the Vatican policy in his own hands. The influence of

1 Peter Hebblethwaite, *The Runaway Church*, p. 184.

2 Gerard P. Fogarty SJ, "Nixon and Paul VI", a paper given at the conference on The Vatican and World Affairs, New Brunswick, October 1991.

Benelli was strongest in Italian politics. This was the traditional sphere of activity of the "substitute", but the fact that the Secretary of State was French and "not expected to understand" still further enhanced the role of the *sostituto*. Audiences now tended to be with Paul and Benelli. On 11 February 1970, Emilio Gabaglio, head of ACLI the Catholic trades union movement, saw them both, and came away optimistic, but only because "he didn't really understand what was being said to him".[1]

If he had listened more carefully, he would have understood that Paul was very displeased with the way ACLI was not only no longer supporting the Christian Democrats "collaterally", as the phrase was, but was increasingly veering towards the extreme left. ACLI was subjected to a veritable inquisition. Paul – or more likely Benelli – simply by-passed CEI, the Italian Bishops' conference, and ordered Cardinal Antonio Poma, its President, to write a letter deploring the way ACLI was exploiting the idea of "the autonomy of the secular" to engage in "coalitions and experiments involving a language, a system and a commitment derived from sources incompatible with the Christian vision".[2] That was on 2 March 1970. By the end of the year ACLI was virtually excommunicated, and all chaplains were withdrawn from it.[3]

In March ACLI had been supporting Aldo Moro in his attempts to solve the latest government crisis. Moro was under intense pressure from Benelli on the question of divorce. The Vatican wanted to prevent divorce becoming the object of a referendum. Two alternatives were suggested in an "inspired" article by Fr Bartolomeo Sorge in *Civiltà Cattolica*: either insert divorce into the framework of the re-negotiation of the 1929 Concordat (which all agreed was necessary); or introduce a clause restricting divorce to those married civilly or in non-Catholic churches. Either way the embarrassment of a referendum on divorce might be avoided.

Disciplinary measures flowed thick and fast from the Vatican in this month. Villot had quashed the Dutch on celibacy; an "apostolic visitor" was investigating the Archbishop of Ravenna, Salvatore Baldassari; *Il Regno* lost its *imprimatur*; and the Association of Italian Moral Theologians meeting at Padua on 31 March to 3 April was censured. On 3 March Paul refused to grant an audience to Aldo Moro on the divorce issue, indicating that "while being opposed to divorce on principle, he left the responsibility in temporal matters to the conscience of poli-

1 Sandro Magister, *La Politica Vaticana*, p. 433, quoting Domenico Rosati, *La Questione politica delle ACLI*, Naples, 1975.

2 Magister, *Politica Vaticana*, pp. 393–94.

3 It was not until 7 December 1991 that harmony and chaplains were restored with a Mass in the Paul VI hall.

ticians".[1] Moro abandoned the attempt to form a government and handed on the poisoned baton to Amintore Fanfani, rumoured to be "very close" to Benelli, who denied it.

Benelli may have been the expert on Italian and international affairs but he lacked Paul's ecumenical passion. In the Secretariat for Christian Unity jolly tales were told to illustrate his ecumenical ignorance. He confused Calvinists with Lutherans, for example.

So he was kept well out of the way when it came to the canonization of forty English and Welsh martyrs. This was a topic about which Cardinal Augustin Bea was as angry as such a mild man could be. For he had given solemn assurances to Canterbury that the "cause", after hanging fire for many decades, would not be pursued in the era of ecumenism. Bea's opposition to the cause impelled the English bishops to work even harder to promote it, until his death in 1969 removed him from the scene. Cardinal John Carmel Heenan was wont to patronize Bea as ignorant of the English situation ("Like most foreigners he had a picture of the typical Anglican which applied only to High Churchmen") and of the language ("His English was scarcely intelligible").[2]

Willebrands took exactly the same line as Bea on this question: to rekindle memories of the bitterness and hatred of the sixteenth century would surely set back ecumenism, for canonization was a particularly Catholic way of celebrating exclusively Catholic heroes. Anglicans, having no part in it, could only clench their teeth and go on about triumphalism and repentance.

In the event the canonization of the Forty Martyrs appeared as a rather tranquil oasis in this turbulent year. An estimated 10,000 English and Welsh pilgrims made their way to Rome; 500 of them could claim some kinship with the martyrs. Their mood was summed up by a stout lady from Liverpool who remarked, "At least it means we'll meet some saints in heaven who speak English." The guest list at the reception given by the British minister to the Holy See, Desmond Crawley, read like a page torn from Debrett.

In St Peter's the fluty tones of the Westminster Cathedral Choir replaced the *molto vibrato* of Msgr Domenico Bartolucci's Sistine choir, singing William Byrd's Five-Part Mass. Queen Elizabeth I was intrigued by Byrd's capacity for survival for he combined traits she thought irreconcilable, being "a stiff Papist and a loyal subject". Ralph Vaughan Williams' hymn *For All the Saints* swirled round the baroque altars. And for the first time ever there was a reading *in Welsh*.

1 Magister, *La Politica Vaticana*, p. 394.

2 John Carmel Heenan, *A Crown of Thorns*, pp. 325, 329.

Everything now depended on Paul's homily. The meaning of canonization is not univocal or given in advance. It declares that these saints contributed something to on-going salvation history. Paul submitted his text to Willebrands and the Secretariat for Christian Unity who proposed seventeen amendments. But on Saturday, 24 October 1970, the night before the canonization, Paul added in his own hand the following passage, which surprised even Paolo Molinari SJ and James Walsh SJ, postulators of the cause, who had drafted it:

> May the blood of these martyrs be able to heal the great wound inflicted on God's Church by reason of the separation of the Anglican Church from the Catholic Church . . . Their devotion to their country gives us the assurance that on that day when – God willing – the unity of faith and life is restored, no offence will be inflicted on the honour and integrity of a great country such as England. There will be no seeking to lessen the legitimate prestige and usage proper to the Anglican Church when the Roman Catholic Church – this humble "servant of the servants of God" – is able to embrace firmly her ever-beloved sister in the one authentic communion of the family of Christ: a communion of origin and faith, a communion of priesthood and rule, a communion of saints in the freedom and love of the spirit of Jesus.[1]

This saved the day. What had looked like a threat to ecumenism actually advanced it. The Church of Rome and the Church of Canterbury were "sister Churches".

Then the theologians began to discuss this generous statement. Yves Congar argued that "sister Church" here does not have the same meaning it did in the context of Catholic-Orthodox relations. The Anglican Communion does not make a claim to apostolicity independently of Rome, as the Orthodox Churches do; nor did Rome recognize the ministry and Eucharist of the Anglicans as it did those of the Orthodox. So "sister Church" here referred to some future event that was "somewhere over the rainbow, way up high". Of course Paul's words represented ecumenical progress in so far as they implied acceptance of Dom Lambert Beauduin's formula in the Malines Conversations – "*l'Eglise Anglicane unie mais non absorbée*".[2]

However, Edward J. Yarnold SJ, who as a founder member of ARCIC was well placed to know, thought Congar mistaken:

1 *Insegnamenti*, 1970, p. 1067.

2 Yves Congar, *Diversity and Communion*, p. 92.

> I cannot agree that Paul VI was only looking forward to the time when the Anglican Communion would *become* a sister. Do you call one who is not yet your sister your "ever-beloved sister"? Moreover *the explanations the Pope gave in private* indicated that he regarded the Anglican Communion as already a sister. This was such a revolutionary thing to say that neither he nor his successors as far as I know have repeated it.[1]

They have, but in grudging fashion.

Apart from this canonization, the most important international event in Rome in the autumn of 1970 was the first-ever World Congress of Secular Institutes. Ninety-two secular institutes from twenty-seven nations were represented, among them a reluctant Opus Dei. The key question was: what, in the end, is a "secular institute"? The Council had attempted a definition in its decree on religious life:

> Secular institutes are not religious communities, but they carry with them into the world the profession of the evangelical counsels which is genuine and complete, and recognized as such by the Church. This profession confers a consecration on men and women, laity and clergy, who live in the world . . . These institutes should preserve their proper and special character, a secular one, so that they may everywhere measure up successfully to that apostolate which they were designed to exercise which is both in the world and, in a sense, of the world.[2]

Paul addressed them on 26 September 1970.

Rather than rehearse yet again the canonical aspects of their special vocation he preferred to dwell on "the psychological and spiritual aspects of your special dedication to the following of Christ".[3] They were different, first of all because they were in the world. "Alpinists of the Spirit", he grandly called them because of the special difficulty of being "in the world, not of the world but for the world".[4]

1 Edward Yarnold, review of Congar's *Diversity and Communion* in *New Blackfriars*, December 1985, p. 536. On the papal plane to Africa in 1980 I asked Pope John Paul II whether he would refer to the Anglican Communion as a "sister Church" when he met Dr Robert Runcie, Archbishop of Canterbury, in Accra, Ghana. He replied in halting English: "Reread *Lumen Gentium*. There you will find that we are all brothers and sisters." I thought he had misunderstood my question, but he turned back and added: "Sister Church is only an analogy." When a philosopher says that something is "only an analogy" you may be fairly sure he means it has little value. Msgr William Purdie, then of the Secretariat for Christian Unity, said to me in 1978: "Sister Church, eh? That's fine. But you try treating them as a sister Church and see what happens."

2 *Perfectae Caritatis*, 11.

3 *Insegnamenti*, 1970, p. 935.

4 Ibid. p. 939.

Their second original feature was that they were laypeople (even though they might count priests among their members) living at the grass-roots "who from direct experience may have a better knowledge of the Church's needs on earth, and perhaps also can better discern its weaknesses".[1] They were a sign of vitality. He compared the Church to an age-old olive tree, its gnarled and twisted shape suggesting old age, and yet in the springtime it pushed out fresh shoots. This was a childhood memory from Concesio. The olive tree can be blasted by winter storms and look utterly devastated. But it renews itself from within.

Paul very much wanted this conference to succeed, and put Giuseppe Lazzati, Rector of the Sacred Heart University in Milan, himself a member of a secular institute, in charge of it. Difficulties came not from ill-will as much as from the ambivalence of the "secular institutes" themselves, and uncertainty about their role and identity.

Some were "secular institutes" in name only, and were so organized that it was hard to distinguish them from "religious institutes". Others had successfully avoided features of religious life such as living in community and having superiors, but it was hard to distinguish them from lay Christians committed to a life according to the Gospels. So "secular institutes", being neither fish nor fowl, tended to drift either upwards towards religious life or downwards towards lay movements.

It was precisely at this moment that Don Luigi Giussani's movement, *Comunione e Liberazione*, began to take off. Giusani abandoned his first movement, *Gioventú Studentesca* (Student Youth), in 1965 when it (in his view) committed the cardinal sin of joining official Catholic Action. He started again in 1969 with *Comunione e Liberazione*, which neatly mopped up the aspirations of 1968 students for authenticity and a simpler, anti-consumerist life-style, which had been – Giussani urged – betrayed by the left. At the heart of the movement was an Association, *Memores Domini*, living a community life but working "in the world" and sharing their income. Giussani, however, had no intention of founding a secular institute. He was content to gather round him people of talent like the philosopher Rocco Buttiglione and political activist Roberto Formigoni, both of whom became well known in the next-but-one pontificate. But in 1970 Communion and Liberation (CL) was no more than a gleam on the distant horizon.

Opus Dei, which sang *Te Deums* on being pronounced the first "secular institute" in 1950, now sulked in its corner having lost its claim to distinctiveness. The Founder, the Blessed Msgr Josemaria Escrivá de Balanguer, was still alive. He devoted his remaining years to trying to change Opus Dei's juridical status. His argument varied bewilderingly.

1 Ibid.

Sometimes he said that "secular institutes" were not secular enough for his organization. Sometimes he claimed to have "anticipated" the Council by his emphasis on holiness in the secular world. What he was looking for was autonomy, independence. At this stage he thought it could be best secured by turning Opus Dei into a *prelatura nullius* along the lines of the *Mission de France* which dealt with priest-workers or rather "priests-at-work" (not *prêtres ouvriers* but *prêtres au travail*). But this would have been a canonical monstrosity since the *Mission de France* was for a given country, for a precise purpose and with special training. Opus Dei, on the other hand, worked "universally", seemed intent on promoting its own institution, and kept the nature of its formation programmes a closely guarded secret.[1]

Those were the general grounds on which Paul mistrusted Escrivá and Opus Dei. There was another reason. In the Madrid Nunciature, 1962–65 Giovanni Benelli deplored Opus Dei's secrecy and subordination to Franco. Opus Dei's justification for secrecy was that it permitted the "Christian penetration of the secular world". Agostino Gemelli had tried that in the Italian context. It invariably ended in tears, as the "occult manipulators" of power were eventually unmasked to the scandal of the Church.

On 21 November 1970, just before departing for the Far East, Paul took a decision which set older members of the College of Cardinals against him. Pomp and dress had already been simplified: no longer did two acolytes walk backwards before them as they visited the Hotel Columbus. The distinction of three ranks – cardinal priests, bishops and deacons – was in effect abolished and their names appeared alphabetically in the *Annuario Pontificio*. That, at a pinch, could be borne. But now they learned from the *motu proprio Ingravescentem Aetatem* that on reaching eighty they would no longer be eligible to take part in the conclave.

This compromise annoyed just about everyone, "progressives" because it left intact the non-scriptural, non-traditional college of cardinals, while cardinals on the verge of eighty seethed and raged. They went on TV and publicly criticized the pope. Cardinal Eugène Tisserant, cavalry officer in the First World War, conducted his last hurrah! on television. He had not been consulted, the Pope was trying to please everyone by getting rid of the old and indulging in a sort of moral euthanasia. Tisserant, solid as a rock, said he was looking forward to his hundredth birthday in 1984.

The many-jowelled Cardinal Alfredo Ottaviani was not such a natu-

1 Giancarlo Rocca, "*L'Opus Dei*", *appunti e documenti per una storia*, Rome 1985, p. 98.

ral television performer as the bearded Tisserant, but he managed to splutter that he found Paul's decision "absolutely unheard of, arbitrary, revolutionary . . . in contempt of a centuries-old tradition".[1] Both Tisserant and Ottaviani drew the inference that Paul VI would have to retire if he reached the age of eighty. If being eighty made you incapable of electing a pope, they said, it must surely disqualify you from being one. Paul was seventy-two when he took this decision, fast approaching seventy-five, the year at which diocesan bishops had to tender their resignation. Why should the Bishop of Rome be an exception, asked Tisserant?

Cardinal Villot, sixty-five, scotched such stories. He told Fr Antoine Wenger, editor of *La Croix*:

> You may write without fear of contradiction that Paul VI will not resign at eighty, if God grants him so much time. A Pope is not elected for a limited period; a father cannot cease to be a father. If his state of health no longer allowed him to govern the Church, we would be there to tell him.[2]

Paul Poupard added that Paul VI wanted to canvass "all possible views" before he made up his mind, and that he came to the conclusion that "a pope can only resign if he feels in conscience unable to fulfil his mission, not because he is seventy, seventy-five or eighty".[3]

Electing a pope was often the only thing a cardinal had to look forward to in retirement. Cardinal Tisserant, still feeling deprived, did not live to be a hundred as he had predicted, but died some fifteen months later, on 21 February 1972, amid stories of frank and uninhibited diaries hidden in a trunk in the Pyrenees.

It was with relief that Paul embarked on his longest journey both in time and distance. He set off for Asia on 26 November 1970, with stopovers in Tehran and Karachi, sixteen speeches in the Philippines, four in American Samoa, fourteen in Australia, five in Jakarta, Indonesia, a mere two in Hong Kong, and three in Sri Lanka, inevitably the "pearl of the Indian Ocean". He was back home by 5 December. This ten days on the road prefigured without remotely competing with the marathons that his successor-but-one would take in his Polish stride.

There was no mystery about why he wanted to go to Asia: it was his last unvisited continent. He explained the strategic meaning of his pilgrimage in a broadcast for Radio Veritas, Manila, the Philippines in

1 René Laurentin, "*Paul VI et l'après-concile*", in *Paul VI et la Modernité*, pp. 577–78.

2 Ibid. p. 670.

3 Ibid. p. 672.

which he addressed "all the peoples of Asia". Its opening greeting in English ran: "To you, the countless millions of men and women, our brothers and sisters who live in Asia, this cross-roads of cultures ancient and modern, and in a special manner to those among you who are our own children in Christ – the blessing of God, abiding peace and fraternity."[1]

The "countless millions" of Asia were not just a figure of speech. Asia made up 60 per cent of the world's population, and it was estimated that by the year 2000 the population of Asia would be equal to that of the world in 1970.[2] So in some sense the "future" would be made in Asia.

Yet except in the Philippines and Australia the Christian presence was pitiably small. So Paul made the visit to the Philippines the pivot of his pilgrimage. In the broadcast from Radio Veritas he said:

> It is our duty to say a word about the presence and action of the Catholic Church in your midst. We do so all the more willingly from the land of the Philippines, in which for centuries the Catholic Church has been fully at home.
>
> The Church feels at home not only here but in all your nations. What she has to bring to you also, that is, the message of Christ, is not imposed upon its hearers but rather proclaimed in open and friendly words. It is offered for your instruction and meditation, and it is not such as in any way to cancel out or lessen the cultural and spiritual values that constitute your priceless heritage.[3]

This breathed the spirit of *Ecclesiam Suam* and applied its principles of dialogue to the peoples of Asia.

But the traffic was not entirely one-way. Paul called upon the peoples of Asia for help in combating the "materialism" to which a Western "model of growth" so frequently led: "With your traditional spiritual outlook, your sense of discipline and morality, and the integrity of your family life, you must be able to counter materialism and even help Western civilization to overcome the very dangers that progress brings in its wake."[4]

This was the age of the guru. India had taught Paul that non-Christians would respond to his presence, given a chance. But within

1 *Insegnamenti*, 1970, p. 1245.

2 These statistics come from *L'Engagement Chrétien devant la Fait Européen*, ed. André Schafter, for the OIC (*Organisations Catholiques Internationales*), September 1977, p. 59. Roger Etchegaray, president of CCEE, was the source.

3 *Insegnamenti*, 1970, p. 1249.

4 Ibid. p. 1248.

this general context he had a number of special messages which touched on all the major problems of the late twentieth century.

He addressed China through the medium of a brief visit to Hong Kong on 4 December 1970. He arrived at 1.20 p.m. and left at 3.45. This gave him time to say Mass at the Happy Valley racecourse. It was in Chinese, and most of the 247,000 Hong Kong Catholics seemed to have turned out. Paul preached in English and found words of eloquent simplicity to conclude. What is the Church? And what does it have to offer the East?

> The Church is the unifying effect of the love of Christ for us. It can itself be considered a living sign, a sacrament of unity and of love. To love is her mission. While we are saying these simple and sublime words we have around us – we can almost feel it – all the Chinese people wherever they may be.
>
> There comes to this far eastern land, for the first time in history, the humble apostle of Christ . . . And what does he say? Why does he come? To sum it up in one word: love. Christ is a teacher, a shepherd, and a loving Redeemer for China also. The Church cannot leave unspoken this good word: love, which will be for ever.[1]

This was 1970. China was still suffering from the effects of the cultural revolution. Chairman Mao was still presiding emperor-like over his teeming millions. The "cult of personality" had not yet been exposed as a fraud.

Yet Paul had issued an invitation to China on which his successors could build once the Chinese monolith began to disintegrate. He had diplomatic foresight. As he left Hong Kong, he quoted a Chinese saying: "All men are brothers."[2] Did he imply that this maxim could not be realized except in Christ? He left that hanging in the air.

But every change of policy leaves behind casualties so it was important that Paul should meet a delegation from Formosa (now known as Taiwan) whose anti-Communism was visceral, systematic and comprehensible. The Taiwanese thought they were the true China and saw contacts with mainland China as treachery. Paul did not enter into the merits of the case. He wisely confined himself to remarking that he had come to Asia as "the bearer of an essentially spiritual message" and was happy to greet his dear brother Cardinal Yü Pin.[3]

As for the Philippines itself, there was a notable contrast between

1 Ibid. p. 1388.
2 Ibid. p. 1391.
3 Ibid. p. 1203.

the official speech in English addressed to President Ferdinand Marcos ("We have been informed of the lofty and upright *intentions* that have inspired and still inspire the policies of your government")[1] and the spontaneous remarks made in Italian, translated into Tagalog, when he visited the shanty-town of Tondo. Brief and no doubt superficial as it was, this encounter enabled him to set out a preferential option for the poor. He asked what it meant to say that the Church loved the poor, and replied:

> It means that the Church recognizes your dignity as human persons and sons of God; your equality with all other people; the preference that is due to you because you have many needs, so that you may have fulfilled lives and well-being, material as well as spiritual.
>
> I feel I must proclaim, here more than anywhere else, "the rights of man" for you and for all the poor people of the world.[2]

The liberation theologians of Latin America took note of this speech. They believed the Kennedy-prompted "decade of development" was a flop. The prosperity of the few had failed to "trickle down". Out of the ruins of the theology of development, they thought that what was now needed was a "theology of liberation".

Such thinking would influence *Octogesima Adveniens*, still in draft and of uncertain status – would it be an encyclical? – and the Synod of 1971 on "Justice in the World".

The Asian visit had a missionary dimension. In the cathedral of Sydney, New South Wales, Paul ordained the first native of Papua New Guinea (not yet so called) to become a bishop, Louis Vergeke. This said something about the missionary nature of the Church: "To forget it or to carry it out carelessly would be, on our part, a betrayal of the Master."[3] And it said something about the *Asian* vocation of Australia, no longer able to regard itself as a chunk of Europe set in the South Pacific.

The ostensible purpose of the visit to Australia was to mark the two hundredth anniversary of the arrival of Captain James Cook in Botany Bay. On 1 December 1970 Paul celebrated an open-air Mass on Randwick Racecourse – bookmakers' stands had been tactfully removed by

1 Ibid. p. 1197.

2 Ibid. p. 1263. Pope John Paul II visited Tondo ten years later in 1980 and little had changed.

3 Ibid. p. 1361. Later Dr Donald Coggan, Archbishop of Canterbury, would hear about the pain of Catholic bishops in New Guinea as they felt obliged to refuse intercommunion with him.

fork-lift trucks. The most remarkable feature of his homily was its emphasis on the aboriginal peoples. "Australia was already inhabited at the time," that is, in 1770, "and we are pleased to greet the representatives of those inhabitants."[1] Paul was not, of course, the cause of the changed Australian attitudes towards the aboriginal people and Chinese and Vietnamese refugees, but he gave them a powerful stimulus.

The ecumenical service in Sydney Town Hall next day was organized by a prominent Jew, Asher Joel (later knighted). This was the most advanced ecumenical service Paul had taken part in so far, and it made a sharp contrast with the fiasco in Geneva the previous year (when the Secretariat of State – that is, Benelli – would not let him enter the WCC chapel). The Anglican Archbishop of Sydney, Marcus C. Loane, boycotted the meeting. Sydney was notoriously the most "Protestant" diocese of Australia, perhaps anywhere, and Loane was – as far as could be discovered – protesting against papal primacy. His absence was denounced as uncivilized in a thunderous editorial in the *Sydney Morning Herald*, written by its proprietor, Sir Warwick Fairfax. At the service itself Paul was nobly tolerant. "History cannot be written off overnight," he said, "and the honest hesitations of sensitive consciences always demand our respect and our understanding."[2] The way of ecumenism is the way of the cross.

The visit, finally, was an instance of "travelling collegiality" in so far as Paul took part in the final meeting of the Oceanic Bishops' assembly in Manila. He heard pleas for a change in Australia's immigration policy from the Bishop of Tonga, and suggestions on the need to ordain married men from other missionary bishops, especially the Indonesians who felt vulnerable in a Muslim nation. "No one," he told them, "can speak to an Asian better than another Asian." And he assured them that the Vatican diplomatic service was on their side.

But it was not all sweetness and light. Along the route to Manila cathedral demonstrators waved placards proclaiming "Santos retire" and "Explain the unexplained wealth of the Church". Cardinal Rufino J. Santos, archbishop since 1953, was very close to President Ferdinand Marcos and reputed to be a millionaire.[3] The entire visit to Asia was, however, overshadowed by an assassination attempt.

There had been a bomb scare in Karachi on the way east. Now, at Manila Airport, a Bolivian known locally as "the mad painter", Ben-

1 Ibid. p. 1322.

2 Ibid. p. 1337. The editors think the ecumenical meeting took place in "Tower Hall". Thanks to Father Edmund Campion for material on the Australia visit.

3 He was removed, or ousted, towards the end of 1973, though only sixty-five at the time. He was succeeded by a man ominously called Sin.

jamin Mendoza y Amor, donned clerical dress and got close enough to Paul to draw a *kris* (a foot-long double-edged knife) and have a stab at him. Early versions of the story claimed improbably that Mendoza had been felled by a karate chop from President Marcos; later everyone repeated that Paul Marcinkus had "saved the Pope's life". The truth was more prosaic: Don Pasquale Macchi pushed Mendoza away and into the arms of Bishop Anthony Galvin of Singapore, a six-foot ex-rugby-playing Yorkshireman and Mill Hill Father, who swiftly overpowered him. Mendoza's explanation was: "I acted alone to save humanity from superstition." Paul, shaken but unhurt, forgave him there and then. It was time to go home. An absurd story alleged that Benelli had framed the murder attempt to win sympathy for the beleaguered Pope. It really was time to go home.

32

Mindszenty and Married Men

> I should like to say that there have always been two ways of looking at reform, two movements of the mind in relation to the world it has to evangelize. The first movement is from the world to the Church, from the periphery to the centre. The second goes from the Church to the world, from the centre to the periphery. These two ways are like the two movements of breathing, in-out, in-out.
>
> (Paul VI, in *The Pope Speaks: Dialogues of Paul VI* with Jean Guitton, p. 177)

The Synod scheduled for the autumn of 1971 had two themes: the priestly ministry and justice in the world. The existence of the Synod as institution gave a forward-looking quality to the thinking of the Church and organized the energies of theologians and others towards a common end. One could not yet say that it engaged the interest and prayers of the ordinary laity. Secrecy still reigned. But it was patchy. On "priestly ministry", the inward-looking topic, it was maintained, while no one could prevent the laity discussing so outward-looking and comprehensive a theme as "justice in the world" that was the stuff of their everyday life.

The two themes reflected the distinction between *ecclesia ad intra* and the *ecclesia ad extra* Suenens used to articulate the planning of the Council. They also reflected the double action of breathing in and breathing out, teaching the world and learning from it.

But to the European priests who belonged to the *Echanges et Dialogue* group this was entirely the wrong way to set up the question. Priestly ministry was at the service of the world, and priests, they maintained, should have the "right" to work at ordinary jobs and the "right" to marry. So the two themes of priesthood and justice neatly dovetailed. They saw the Synod as a last chance if not to get their way, at least to put their questions on the agenda of the universal Church. These rumblings combined with dissent from *Humanae Vitae*, often dealt with by heavy-handed suspensions, to make the clergy restless, unhappy and rebellious.

Some priests went ahead and married with the approval of their communities. In San Francisco a married priest was excommunicated but his parish voted by 604 to 38 to keep him. Crisis-talk was in the air. "Is the Church only the hierarchy?" asked priests from the Dominican Republic, complaining that their bishops had endorsed *Sacerdotalis Coelibatus* without consulting them.[1]

No pope in modern history had to cope with such dissidence. One of the difficulties in dealing with it lay in a lack of real knowledge about its extent and depth. Only the Dutch had used opinion-polls to discover the state of mind of priests. The Italian bishops ordered a survey of Italian priests to which 25,000 (out of a total of 43,000) replied, a good market response. It was not published, but Archbishop Clemente Gaddi of Bergamo reported on it to his fellow-bishops. A very small "conservative" group thought all would be well if only priests rediscovered the spiritual and ascetical attitudes of the past. The more numerous "radicals" at the other extreme wanted the priest to be immersed in the world, pooh-poohing *Lumen Gentium*'s statement that there is a distinction of essence and not merely of degree between the common priesthood of all the faithful and the ministerial priesthood.[2] That was indeed the crucial question, and Cardinal Joseph Höffner of Cologne, already chosen as *relator* for the part of the Synod devoted to priestly ministry, duly noted it.

Behind him loomed the figure of Hans Urs von Balthasar, the Swiss theologian who had hitherto been content to develop his personal theology without seeking any role in the universal Church – he had not been a *peritus* at the Council – and would be important for the future of the pontificate. Associated with Höffner and von Balthasar were Henri de Lubac SJ, Joseph Ratzinger and Cardinal Karol Wojtyla who were planning a new multi-language theological review to be called *Communio*, designed to offset the subversive Dutch-financed *Concilium*.

That was still to come. Archbishop Gadda continued his report with the remark that the vast majority of Italian priests were moderates who were "unprepared for the new situation in the Church and in the world, and so must adapt to them". It was the *aggiornamento* solution.

But even the "moderates" were not absolutist or hard-line on celibacy:

> All appreciate the theological, ascetical and pastoral value of celibacy. Some emphasize that this value would be increased if

1 René Laurentin, *Nouveaux ministères et fin du clergé*, lists the groups of priests, country by country, who wanted an end to mandatory celibacy: they were all in Western Europe, Canada and the United States (pp. 238–39).

2 *Lumen Gentium*, 10.

> one's choice of a state of life were free. Others wonder whether, in certain cases and for pastoral reasons, the ordination of married men should be considered. In general, the problem of celibacy does not arise in a *dramatic* fashion. It is raised either in order to strengthen celibacy by a free choice or to modify the law of celibacy in particularly demanding situations.[1]

The conclusion was too bland. There were some "defections" of well-known priests, rarely without pain on both sides, hardly ever without publicity.[2]

The critical urgency of this question lent an air of dreamlike unreality to one of Paul's pet projects. He first mentioned it on 20 November 1965 as he briefed the Commission for the Revision of the Code of Canon Law. Given that the 1917 Code would need a complete overhaul in the light of Vatican II, should one not seize this opportunity to provide a "constitution" for the Church? Thus was born the idea of a *Lex Ecclesiae Fundamentalis* (LEF) as a kind of basic constitution for the Church.

This sounded like a dry canonical affair. Yet at issue was the central problem of his pontificate: how far can one organize the Holy Spirit? Put like that, of course, the question is absurd. But it translates a deep and fundamental question about Christian life: what is the relationship between law and grace, between Church order and charismatic spontaneity, between institution and Spirit?[3]

This project was entrusted to a small commission (called *Coetus Consultorum Specialis*) headed by Cardinal Pericle Felici and Msgr Willi Onclin of Louvain. Members included Alvarez del Portillo, second-in-command of Opus Dei, Gregorian Jesuits like William Bertrams and Raymond Bidagor, Bishop Carlo Colombo as Paul's eyes and ears, and Ignatius Ziadé, Maronite Bishop of Beirut representing the Oriental Churches who have a strong sense of the Holy Spirit animating the Church.

However there was no discussion about it because everything took

1 "The Italian Ferment", in *Herder Correspondence*, June 1970, pp. 184–87. This, sadly, was the last number of the English-language edition of *Herder Korrespondenz* that had been edited with provocative zest by Robert Nowell. From July 1970 it was taken over by the *Month*, the Jesuit magazine of which I was editor.

2 Statistics are hard to come by. Between 1963 and 1983 the Vatican statistical service records 46,302 dispensations for priests to marry. "But for every priest who gets a dispensation," writes ex-Dominican David Rice, "there was another who was refused or never bothered to ask." *Shattered Vows*, p. 24.

3 See Peter Hebblethwaite, "*Lex Ecclesiae Fundamentalis*", in *Month*, October 1971, pp. 99–103.

place in secret. Only bishops were able to read Onclin's explanation of what the proposed "constitution" was for:

> What is required is that the image of the Church (*imago ecclesiae*), namely its nature and structure, should be set down as distinctly as possible, so that it may appear to all what the Church is, what its structure is, how it is divinely instituted, endowed, and on what fundamental truths it is based.[1]

Whatever else it may have been, this was clearly a *theological* task. Some canon lawyers concluded that the LEF was merely a *preface* to the new Code of Canon Law. But no one could think it trivial in the light of Onclin's next remark: "Since a fundamental *law* is required, on which all other laws in the Church will depend, it is necessary to maintain the character proper to the juridical order, so that what is contrary to its juridical character may be avoided."[2] The language was obscure, opaque even, canonical fiddling while the house prepared to burn, but it said clearly that the LEF would not only be juridically binding but would have supreme normative force (*valor*) as Onclin explained:

> Laws promulgated by the supreme authority of the Church are to be understood according to the prescriptions of the LEF, unless the contrary is expressly stated, and things which derogate from it are to be interpreted strictly; laws promulgated by inferior ecclesiastical authority contrary to the LEF lack all power.[3]

This dispelled any notion that the LEF was a kind of innocuous prelude before the real legislative work could get under way.

In March 1971 bishops received the draft of the LEF with Onclin's commentary and a covering letter from Felici urging them to say by 1 September 1971 whether they judged it "opportune that a *Lex Ecclesiae Fundamentalis* be devised for the universal Church as a sort of juridical and theological foundation for the new canon law", and what they thought of the draft.

Puzzled bishops consulted canonists and theologians with the inevitable consequence that the black-out on the work of the commission could no longer be maintained, and the draft was published in the Bologna-based magazine, *Il Regno*.[4] Leaking confidential documents

1 *Textus Emendatus*, Vatican Press, pp. 119–20. It was, of course, *sub secreto*.

2 Ibid. p. 120.

3 Ibid. p. 123.

4 *Il Regno*, 15 March 1971.

was regarded as very bad form: the entire editorial team of *Il Regno* was sacked.

Yet what was there to hide? Why should the LEF be kept under wraps? Flushed out by all this publicity, Msgr Onclin was prevailed upon to give a press conference in which he adopted a notably different tone: "He recalled that the draft text was only a working paper which will probably be modified in conformity with the wishes of the bishops. These, in their turn, may consult priests and laymen, and the result will therefore be a truly Church-wide consultation."[1]

Humbug. If a truly Church-wide consultation had been intended from the outset the text would have had to be disseminated and therefore discussed as widely as possible.

Now the cat was out of the bag the project was subjected to such a barrage of incredulity and criticism that the poor creature, whose chances of survival had always been slight, was doomed. Onclin's attempt to reply to objections revealed its weaknesses. The first objection was that since the Church had got on perfectly well without a constitution for nigh on 2000 years, why was one needed now? "It is part of the evolutionary processes of society," said Onclin who pointed out that France did not have a constitution until after the Revolution and Italy until after the Second World War. But that only proved that constitutions emerged out of turmoil and did not explain why the Church needed to follow secular models. The point of *Lumen Gentium* was that they did not apply, and that the Church was better understood in terms of New Testament "images" – the People of God, the Body of Christ, the Bride of Christ, the Lord's vineyard and so on – than in terms of civil society.

Karl Rahner then joined in the debate: the very nature of the Church makes the task of constitution-framing impossible, since the Church is always developing in response to the promptings of the Holy Spirit who could never be *part* of its constitution, and yet without the Holy Spirit the Church would simply "cease to be itself": "As the great theologians of the Middle Ages used to say (St Thomas, *Summa Theologica*, I.IIae.q.106.ad 1) what principally constitutes the Church is the Holy Spirit in men's hearts, and all the rest (hierarchy, papacy, Eucharist, sacraments) are at the service of this inner transformation."[2]

Onclin had no answer to that. Rahner, still a member of the International Theological Commission, irritatingly tended to have the last word as well as the last-but-one-word. Other German theologians rallied round Rahner. Walter Kasper, in a formidable article, argued that the

1 Peter Nichols in *The Times*, 6 July 1971.

2 *Sacramentum Mundi*, vol. I, Herder, p. 319.

LEF was an instrument in a policy of "restoration" that would undo all the achievements of the Council.[1] That was the end of it.

The lesson for Paul was twofold. In the post-conciliar Church it was no longer possible for special committees to work on texts in secret. The point had been lucidly made in *Communio et Progressio*, the instruction designed to implement the feeble conciliar decree on the mass-media. It contained a plea for open government:

> The spiritual riches which are an essential attribute of the Church demand that the news she gives out of her intentions as well as her works be distinguished by integrity, truth and openness.
>
> When ecclesiastical authorities are unwilling to give information or are unable to do so, then rumour is unloosed and rumour is not a bearer of truth but carries dangerous half-truths. Secrecy should therefore be restricted to matters involving the good name of individuals or that touch on the rights of people whether singly or collectively.[2]

It was difficult to ignore this document, which had been issued on 29 January 1971. Paul recognized that the Church henceforward would have to be judged by the criteria it had officially propounded in his name.

So Paul cast about him for another way to state the relationship between Spirit and institution. He began to show a growing concern for pneumatology and the Holy Spirit. His interest in the charismatic renewal took off from this demonstration of the impossibility of cramming everything within juridical categories. None of this meant that canon law could be dispensed with. On the contrary, it was the best way to entrench the spirit of Vatican II, provided it had built into it the principles of subsidiarity and co-responsibility. Cardinal Jean Daniélou reminded readers of *Le Monde* that canon law was a means not an end. It followed that "the law may be criticized when it does not achieve its object or when it leads away from it. It also means that the law should be revised according to new situations."[3]

1 Walter Kasper, "*Ein Grundgesetz der Kirche, ein Grundgesetz der Restauration?*" in *Kein Grundgesetz der Kirche ohne Zustimmung der Christen*, pp. 18–43.

2 *Communio et Progressio*, 121. The text is given in Austin Flannery OP, *Vatican Council II, The Conciliar and Post-Conciliar Documents*, I, pp. 293–349. Though this edition does not say so, Patrick O'Donovan of the *Observer* worked on this translation, which stands out for its vigour and freedom from gobbledegook. O'Donovan was one of the finest journalists of his time, as can be seen in Patrick O'Donovan, *A Journalist's Odyssey*, 1985. I owe him an immense, incalculable debt.

3 Jean Daniélou, *Le Monde*, 31 July 1971.

The European bishops illustrated this point in March 1971 when at Paul's request they gave themselves a structure known as CCEE (*Consilium Conferentiarum Episcopalium Europae*). The Presidents of the European Episcopal Conferences had been meeting on a more or less regular basis since the end of the Council in 1965. From now on they would meet more formally, and "without having any juridical power whatsoever CCEE would act as an organ of service, co-ordination and collaboration between the episcopal conferences". They were not, or not at this stage, trying to be a European CELAM. CELAM was defined more ambitiously as "the sign and instrument of collegiality, and the organ of contact, collaboration and service of the Latin American Episcopal Conferences".[1] The difference between CELAM and CCEE was that the pope is a "European bishop" and therefore a member of this organism in a way he is not of CELAM.

So CCEE was more immediately *cum Petro et sub Petro* (with Peter and under Peter). Yet it was not utterly spineless. At this 1971 meeting the European bishops elected Roger Etchegaray, Archbishop of Marseilles, as their president and Msgr Bodeslaw Kominek, Apostolic Administrator of Wroclaw (formerly Breslau) as vice-president. Though often attacked for being too pro-western, the CCEE elections showed sensitivity towards an eastern Europe still cut off by the "iron curtain", porous though it was becoming.

In his address to the European bishops on 25 March 1971 Paul struggled to keep Spirit and institution in balance. He first defined the Church as "the communion of all those who are reborn in Christ and animated by his spirit of charity". On this level, there had to be space for all, whether priest, religious or layperson. On the other hand Paul denounced "the vain opinion of those who want a merely charismatic Church".[2] In a veiled reference to the National Pastoral Council of the Netherlands Church, he said that "political models" were not to be the norm of Church order, and that the principle of "subsidiarity" should not be exploited to "subvert the nature of the Church".[3]

There was a certain ambivalence here. The question of the competence of the local Church had not been clearly defined. Paul was sure that a decision on married priests, for example, could not be taken by a local Church but involved the universal Church. No one episcopal conference could go it alone: the convoy would have to move at the

1 These definitions are taken from the "Historical Notes" in the *Annuario Pontificio*, 1991, Vatican Press, pp. 1672–73.

2 *Insegnamenti*, 1971, p. 222.

3 Ibid.

speed of the slowest ship. The creation of the CCEE strengthened his hand in this respect.

The CCEE plan had been entrusted to Cardinals William Conway of Armagh and Joseph Höffner of Cologne, two street-wise, tough-minded conservatives. That suggested that one of its "co-ordinating" functions would be to lock the Dutch Church more tightly into the European Church. This was Höffner's year. The richest diocese in the world – thanks to the West German system of *Kirchensteuer* (Church-tax) – became the most influential diocese in the world.

Friday, 14 May 1971 was the eightieth anniversary of Leo XIII's *Rerum Novarum* which had often been used as an occasion to push "Catholic social teaching" forward. Cardinal Maurice Roy at Justice and Peace produced a draft text for an encyclical "up-dating" Catholic social teaching on the assumption that new questions had arisen since *Populorum Progressio* although it was only four years old.

After much agonizing Paul decided that *Octogesima Adveniens* would not be an encyclical but rather a "letter to Cardinal Maurice Roy". Few noticed this nuance, and it is often misdescribed as an encyclical. But, as we have seen, after the treatment meted out to *Sacerdotalis Coelibatus* and still more *Humanae Vitae*, dismissed by one commentator as "the private theological opinions of the Bishop of Rome", Paul preferred to commit himself less definitively.

Paradoxically *Octogesima Adveniens* gained in authority by being less authoritative. It breathed a different spirit, and was like moving into another world, where a different set of values operated. They derived not from Europe but from Latin America. The visit to Medellín had not been in vain. Though the notion that a few days in another country is enough to learn much about it, the learning curve depends not on length of time so much as on talent.[1]

The most novel feature of *Octogesima Adveniens* was its modesty. It completely transformed the idea of "Catholic social doctrine", which had come to mean in effect "*papal* social doctrine". Yet here was Paul or his ghost-writer declaring from the outset that "in view of the varied situations in the world, it is difficult to give one teaching to cover them all or to offer a solution which has universal value. *This is not our intention or even our mission.*"[2] Yet that had undoubtedly been his

1 This was a point that the novelist Graham Greene frequently made. A novel does not depend on the experience of the novelist but on his talent. Thus one glance through the window of the Guards Regiment in London would enable a lady novelist *of talent* to write a superb novel.

2 *Octogesima Adveniens*, 4. My italics. Needless to say, Pope John Paul II was of a different mind, and did not accept this abdication of authority.

intention when he wrote *Populorum Progressio* in 1967. What had changed was the perception of the complexity of situations.

So *Populorum Progressio* was on the right lines. The next development in Catholic social doctrine would consist not in repeating but in applying it. The task of discerning the "signs of the times" was no less urgent, but it was now entrusted to "the Christian communities" scattered throughout the world. Their task is to diagnose their own situations in the critical light of the Gospel. The result would evidently be a "pluralism of options".[1]

The other original feature of *Octogesima Adveniens* is that it is the first document in Catholic social teaching to be discriminating about "socialism". From Leo XIII, who had caricatured "socialism" as the state abolition of all private property, to John XXIII who borrowed Teilhard de Chardin's term "socialization" to gesture in the direction of "social democracy", socialism had been treated negatively. Paul's letter to Cardinal Roy has a long section on "the historical development of socialisms" – the plural is important.[2] It distinguishes four aspects of socialism:

1 continual struggle against domination and exploitation;
2 the exercise of political power in a single-party state;
3 an ideology based on historical materialism and the denial of transcendence;
4 a scientific approach to social and political realities.[3]

It is clear that "socialism" is here used as a euphemism for "Marxism" and that the authors of *Octogesima Adveniens* had Latin America in view.

Liberation theologians in general, and the Christians for Socialism Movement in Chile in particular, felt vindicated by these distinctions. For their claim was that "Marxism" was not a slippery slope such that if you used the *analysis* you found yourself inevitably sliding to the bottom of the hill lumbered with *dialectical materialism*. They thought it was possible to be discerning in their Marxism, usually accepting the scientific analysis and the struggle against exploitation while rejecting the one-party state and the denial of transcendence. To Poles and other East Europeans with actual experience of Marxism, this all sounded like a recipe for insanity.

However one should not forget that *Octogesima Adveniens* began by renouncing the claim to "cover all situations". In any case it invites

1 Ibid. 50.
2 Ibid. 30ff.
3 Ibid. 33.

Catholics to exercise the keenest critical discernment when presented with any vision of political Utopia, whether in the shape of a collectivist ideology or a liberal ideology.[1] The tradition of crying a plague on both ideological houses was retained.

In one important respect *Octogesima Adveniens* anticipated the Synod six months later. It drew attention to the gap between the proclamation of human rights and their actual exercise:

> In fact, human rights are still all too often disregarded, if not mocked, or else they receive only formal recognition. In many cases legislation still does not keep up with real situations . . . If, beyond legal rules, there is really no deeper feeling of respect for and service to others, then even equality before the law can serve as an alibi for flagrant discrimination, continued exploitation and actual contempt.[2]

This was addressed to the world, though it could be applied to the Church. For there were not two sorts of justice: one for outside the Church and another within it.

This was a far-reachng principle. One needs to recall another: the notion of approval *ad experimentum*. Almost everything that was happening in the post-conciliar Church – parish pastoral councils, senates of priests, diocesan synods, episcopal conferences, right up to the Roman Synod itself – was still at the experimental stage. They were in place but still needed juridical embedding. Hans Küng said in *Infallible?* that if the canon lawyers of the "progressives" had articulated the theology of "collegiality" with the same skill that the Roman canonists had defended papal primacy, then the whole course of Church history would have been changed.

But they had imprudently left canon law in the hands of conservatives like Cardinal Felici. The draft of the *Lex Ecclesiae Fundamentalis* canonized the theology of the *Nota praevia* and the papal monarchy, so much so that it disdains all post-conciliar structures. For example: "It is not the function of law to clarify the idea of collegiality. Besides, collegiality, in the strict sense . . . is found only when the college of bishops acts as a whole."[3] All these questions, it was confidently hoped, would be dealt with if not resolved by the Synod in the coming fall.

One question was apparently resolved. On 23 June 1971 Cardinal

1 Ibid. 35.

2 Ibid. 23. This is an implicit critique of "the bourgeois revolutions" of the nineteenth century. The right to free speech, free assembly, free press and so on, only makes sense if all the people are on a roughly comparable level. Leonardo Boff OFM constantly made this point, recognizing its Marxist source.

3 Msgr Willi Onclin's *Relatio*, quoted in *Month*, October 1971, p. 101.

Franz König informed his brother cardinal, Jöszef Mindszenty, still unable to leave the US Embassy in Budapest, that he would shortly be receiving some Roman visitors. They were Msgr Jöszef Zágon, Rector of the Hungarian College in Rome, and Msgr Giovanni Cheli. Cheli had been involved with Agostino Casaroli in the second agreement with the Hungarian government of 23 September 1969 on the nomination of four bishops and four apostolic administrators.[1] Cheli presented a suspicious Mindszenty with the new breviary, as a personal gift from Pope Paul, conveyed the good wishes of Cardinal Jean Villot, Secretary of State, and then departed, leaving the two Hungarians alone.

Their negotiations dragged on for three days. Zágon put Paul's view that Mindszenty's illness made it necessary for him to leave. Were he to die in the US Embassy there would be grave political complications. Zágon concluded:

> Therefore the Holy Father has arrived at a solution that will place Your Eminence's sacrifice in a new light, so that your moral importance will be seen in the eyes of the whole world to have increased. You will have lost none of your well-earned credit, and will be able to serve as an example for the whole Church. The Holy Father wishes to do everything he can to bring this about.[2]

Zágon shrewdly added that there would be little chance of Mindszenty publishing his memoirs, on which he was known to be working, unless he went abroad where he could have a most useful ministry among the Hungarian diaspora.

Mindszenty, realizing that he would have to go, offered himself as a bargaining chip. The Communists should not be allowed to exploit his departure for propaganda purposes, and in exchange for going quietly there should be some further government concessions – freedom of religious instruction and the banning of the "peace priests". Zágon saw little prospect of progress on either question.

Paul laid down four conditions for Mindszenty's departure:

1) He would retain the title of Archbishop of Esztergom and Primate of Hungary, while leaving the work to be done by an apostolic administrator appointed by Rome.

2) He would leave the country "quietly" and not publish pastoral letters or issue statements about his departure. Zágon suggested he summed

1 Achille Silvestrini, "*L'Ostpolitik de Paul VI*", *Notiziario*, 20, p. 73.

2 Jöszef Mindszenty, *Memoirs*, p. 232.

up his reasons for leaving in a letter the Vatican press office would distribute.

3) Once abroad he would make no statements that "might disturb the relations between the Holy See and the Hungarian government or might be offensive to the Hungarian government or the People's Republic".

4) He would keep his memoirs secret, and will all his manuscripts to the Holy See, which would publish them "at an appropriate time".

Mindszenty fought hardest over conditions 3 and 4. He "declared unequivocally" (his own phrase) that he could not let the Hungarian government, which was causing the destruction of the Hungarian Church and the nation, decide what he should or should not say. He thought the Holy See should be the sole judge of whether his demand for complete rehabilitation was well-founded or not. Zágon glanced through the manuscript of the memoirs, and opined they could well be published in his lifetime. He promised that the Holy See would pay to have them typed.

Zágon drew up a minute of their discussions but Mindszenty refused to sign. He objected to the concluding sentence which said he was able to go abroad as a free man under no restrictions "exception for conditions 1–4". He demanded more time to think about the whole affair. He wrote a letter to Paul VI rejecting the charge that he was "the greatest obstacle to normal relations between Church and State". A letter to President Richard Nixon received an instant reply – he was, after all, in a US Embassy: it recommended that Mindszenty should "bow to his fate". He realized that from now on he would be an unwanted guest in the Embassy. The game was up.

Paul's letter arrived soon after President Nixon's. He noted that the Cardinal was now prepared to leave the US Embassy, said that his personal envoy would be in Budapest for four days from 14 July, and invited him to be in Rome at least in time for the opening of the Synod in September.

Cheli and Zágon arranged the practical details: the Vatican diplomatic passport, the despatch of the precious manuscript by diplomatic courier to the US Embassy in Vienna, the two cars to Vienna airport and the arrival in Rome on 29 September 1971. The timing was dramatic: the eve of the Synod. Mindszenty describes what happened:

> Pope Paul VI awaited me at the Torre San Giovanni, where I was given princely quarters. He embraced me, took his pectoral cross and hung it round my neck, offered me his arm, and led me into the building. He rode up in the lift with me and showed me through the whole of the splendid apartment that had been

> placed at my disposal. Patriarch Athenagoras had stayed there before me. Later, too, the Pope gave me almost daily signs of benevolence.[1]

There were even more favours to come.

It is difficult to imagine what more Paul VI could have done to honour Mindszenty. At the opening Mass of the Synod Mindszenty concelebrated at his right hand, and heard the following panegyric:

> Among us today is our Venerable Brother, Cardinal Jöszef Mindszenty, Archbishop of Esztergom, who has just recently come to Rome after many years of enforced absence. He is a guest whom we have awaited with longing, who is concelebrating with us as a glorious symbol of the living unity between the Hungarian Church and this Apostolic See, a unity that has existed for a thousand years.
>
> But he is also a symbol of the spiritual bond with those brothers who are prevented from maintaining normal relations with us. He is a symbol of unshakeable strength rooted in faith and selfless devotion to Christ. He has proved this first of all by his tireless activity, then by prayer and long suffering. Let us praise the Lord and together say a reverent *Ave* to this exiled and highly honoured Archbishop.[2]

No other bishop was ever praised in such extravagant terms in the pontificate of Paul VI. Cardinal Josef Slipyi, head of the Ukrainian Catholic Church, had been welcomed in comparable fashion when Pope John XXIII extricated him from a Soviet Labour camp in February 1963. And Slipyi duly reappeared at the 1971 Synod, denouncing the injustice done to the Ukrainian Church by the Russian Orthodox Church, quivering with indignation, his stove-pipe hat bobbing back and forth.

But it was unlikely that the dramatic arrival of Mindszenty and Paul's extravagant words about him would lead the Synod to reduce "injustice" to the sufferings of what was still called "the Church of silence". The beatification of the Polish Conventional Franciscan, Maximilian Kolbe, on 17 October came in the middle of the Synod. Kolbe had offered himself in exchange for a married layman condemned to death in Auschwitz. His life was a clear illustration of the priest as "a man for others". And he was Polish: at the concelebration Paul had Cardinals Wyszińśki and Wojtyla on either side.

Yet these heroic confessors of the faith were ceding ground to the

1 *Memoirs*, p. 237.

2 *Insegnamenti*, 1971, pp. 840–41.

Latin Americans who, after Medellín in 1968, were feeling confident that they had something to contribute.

The 1971 Synod was the first to take place in the custom-built auditorium above Pier Luigi Nervi's new audience hall. It was the first Synod to involve lay experts like Barbara Ward and to consult laypeople in advance through the national Justice and Peace Commissions. This showed how a Synod could healthily "conscientize" the whole Church.

And it was the first Synod to have available a full-scale report from the new International Theological Commission. *The Priestly Ministry* is a scholarly and profound treatise.[1] It was the work of a sub-committee that included Hans Urs von Balthasar and Bishop Carlo Colombo, presided over by Fr Marie-Joseph Le Gouillou OP. Few had heard of the report at the time, and fewer still had read it. But it was in the hands of Cardinal Joseph Höffner, the *relator*, who extracted ten "theses" from its conclusion and imposed them on the Synod as its final "propositions" to the Pope. There was a circularity in this procedure, as the Synod was steered towards its pre-ordained conclusion. The most important thesis/proposition was directed against Hans Küng's book, *The Church*:[2]

> Though one must acknowledge a certain development in the structures of the early Church, one cannot maintain that some Churches – the Pauline ones – had a purely charismatic constitution, in contrast with the ministerial constitution of the other Churches. For the primitive Churches there is no opposition but rather complementarity between the freedom of the Spirit in dispensing his gifts and the existence of a ministerial structure.[3]

Demonstrating that the Church could not live by charisms alone was one of the main activities in 1971.

The distinctive voice of Latin America made itself felt in the discussion on priestly ministry. It was a question of theological method. The Höffner/von Balthasar line had merits but did not allow much room for creative response. Bishop Santos Ascarza from Chile distinguished two approaches:

> The first starts from Scripture and the priesthood of Christ in order to determine the purpose, scope and means of the priestly ministry once and for all (*semel pro semper*), and then to draw

1 Michael Sharkey, ed., *International Theological Commission, Texts and Documents 1969–1985*, pp. 1–87.

2 Hans Küng, *The Church*, tr. Ray and Rosaleen Ockenden, 1967.

3 Michael Sharkey, ed., *Texts and Documents*, p. 87. The ITC Report is dated Rome, 10 October 1971, which says something about its *ad hoc* nature.

> conclusions appropriate for our time. It is clear but abstract.
>
> The other way starts from the signs of the times, the crisis in the priesthood, and the conditions in which the apostolate is developing, and then discerns what Christ is asking of us today.[1]

The Latin Americans lost that round, at least in the 1971 Synod.

But they did better on *Justice in the World*, the Synod's final document. It insisted that "action on behalf of justice and participation in the transformation of the world fully appear to us as a *constitutive* dimension of the preaching of the Gospel".[2] It was not therefore an optional extra or something you tacked on when you had put across the "spiritual" message of the Gospel: the social teaching was essential to it. This was the launch-pad of "liberation theology" and much else besides.

But did this talk of justice apply to the internal life of the Church? Some said there were no "human rights" in the Church, since they were voluntarily forfeited along the *via crucis*, the way of the cross. But that could be an alibi for all manner of crimes. So the Synod stated the following principle: "While the Church is bound to give witness to justice, she recognizes that anyone who ventures to speak about justice must first be just in their eyes."[3] This was then applied to the Church's own life-style (the Church should not be "an island of wealth in an ocean of poverty") and judicial procedures (the accused "had the right to know their accusers and also the right to a proper defence").

Though banal enough in secular terms, such statements were novel from this source. They influenced many religious orders in the next decade. But they posed a problem for Paul VI. Such documents were clearly addressed to the whole Church if not the whole world. But was it the business of the Synod to be writing documents at all? It did not fulfil its function "to inform and give advice" to the Pope by making such pronouncements. On the last day Synod President Cardinal Léon-Etienne Duval warned that "the Synod of Bishops cannot and ought not to be thought of as a mini-council (*veluti parvum concilium*)", and he recommended for next time a "simplified procedure" and concentration

1 Peter Hebblethwaite, "The Synod on Priests", *Month*, December 1971, p. 165.

2 Austin Flannery OP, ed., *More Documents of Vatican II*, vol. 2, p. 696. In *The Christian Faith in the Doctrinal Documents of the Church*, eds J. Neuner and J. Dupuis, Collins 1983, no. 2159, the word "transmission" replaces "transformation" in this text, thus making nonsense of it.

3 Flannery, p. 703.

on a more manageable topic.[1] This was seen as an inspired rebuke.

Thus, paradoxically, the Synod that had produced the best document so far ended in unhappiness. A good statement on justice was cancelled out by a set of theses on priestly ministry. Cardinal George Bernard Flahiff, Archbishop of Winnipeg, who always wore a lumberjack's check shirt when not at the Synod, had not the faintest idea what would happen to his suggestion that a mixed commission to study in depth the question of women's ministries in the Church should be established.

The mood of gloom was compounded by the feeling that the Synod's views on the ordination of married men had been misrepresented. In the debate on priestly ministry there had been urgent pleas, especially but not exclusively from the younger Churches, that they be allowed to ordain suitable married men where otherwise the Eucharist, to which all the baptized had a right, could not be assured. To resolve this question the Synod was invited to consider two propositions:

Formula A: Excepting always the right of the Supreme Pontiff, the priestly ordination of married men is not permitted, even in particular cases.

Formula B: It belongs solely to the Supreme Pontiff, in particular cases, by reason of the needs and the good of the universal Church, to allow the priestly ordination of married men who are of mature age and proven life.[2]

The Synod was asked to vote for one or other of those propositions: A got 107 votes; B got 87.

Those who voted for the ordination of married men admitted defeat, but pointed out that it was not by the two-thirds majority required by a Council (not that they were a Council). They could also claim that they had a majority of *elected* members. What was galling was that their honestly given advice was swept aside as though it had never existed. In his closing speech Paul said: "From your discussions it emerges that the bishops of the entire Catholic world want to keep integrally this absolute gift by which the priest consecrates himself to God; a not

1 Peter Hebblethwaite, "The Future of the Synod", *Month*, January 1972, p. 4. Note also in the same issue John Harriott's "The Difficulty of Justice", which lists ten reasons why the final Synod document was an advance on *Gaudium et Spes*, *Populorum Progressio*, and *Octogesima Adveniens*.

2 Flannery, *More Post-Conciliar Documents*, vol. 2, pp. 689–90. Flannery gives the whole document called "The Ministerial Priesthood", pp. 672–94, but curiously attributes it here and in the index to 30 November 1967. "Priestly Ministry", the original theme of the Synod, was changed to the ugly and pleonastic "Ministerial Priesthood" at the request of Cardinal Karol Wojtyla, who was anxious to preserve the "essential distinction" between the ordained priesthood and other forms of ministry.

negligible part of this gift – in the Latin Church – is consecrated celibacy."[1]

He said not a word about the ordination of married men. This raised the question: if the Synod of Bishops cannot put a question on the Church's agenda, who can?

Yet the deliberations of the 1971 Synod were "received" by Paul in his own time and at his own pace. He put teams to work on "lay ministries" and the "minor orders" which would throw light by contrast on the priestly ministry. He would set up the commission on women's ministries Cardinal Flahiff had asked for as soon as he found the right people to be on it. And he confided in Franciscan Archbishop Paolo Evaristo Arns whom he had appointed to São Paolo, Brazil in 1970. Nineteen years later Arns recalled:

> At the 1971 Synod we had the chance to vote on the possibility of ordaining married men. Paul VI gave us that opportunity. It is a pity that the majority of the bishops, especially the Europeans, voted against. Paul VI told me personally that if this measure had been accepted, then he would have carried it out. Nineteen years have gone by, and now the climate has completely changed.[2]

This conditional approval from what Paul surely regarded as a grave departure from tradition is striking. Did Arns mishear him? Or did it no longer matter once the vote had gone against?

What is rather strange in the entire debate is that no one seems to have seriously consulted the experience of the Oriental Churches who have a married clergy. True, Cardinal Slipyi reversed the familiar cliché by relating how a celibate priest had cracked up under interrogation while the married priest, who happened to be his brother, held out heroically, sustained by the love of his equally heroic family.

The Oriental Churches were used to being ignored. The Ukrainians felt this most keenly. Because, officially, they "did not exist" in the Western Ukraine, having been abolished and forcibly incorporated into the Moscow Patriarchate in 1946, their ghostly existence continued only in the diaspora. In practice this meant largely Canada, the United States and Australia. But Ukrainian priests in the diaspora were not allowed to marry, said the Congregation for the Oriental Churches, because . . .

1 *Insegnamenti*, 1971, p. 873.

2 Interview in *Il Regno-attualità*, 14/90.
At the Colloquium of the Paul VI Institute held at Brescia 25 to 27 September 1992, it was revealed that Paul VI was the undisclosed author of Formula B. "Why didn't they accept Formula B?" he asked plaintively.

Because what? The reasoning tended to peter out at this point. The evident fear was that Latin priests might decide to emulate the Ukrainians or join them in order to marry. So wherever there were overlapping jurisdictions, as happened, for example, in Cardinal Flahiff's diocese of Winnipeg, the "Oriental tradition" the Council had solemnly sworn to respect was put in cold storage. Slipyi did not give in so easily. He ordained married priests in Rome intended to be "missionaries" in the Ukraine, as he had every right to, but then, since they could not actually go to the L'viv (to give it its Ukrainian name) for the time being, they might as well be usefully employed in Canada.

The main point, however, was that Slipyi, like Mindszenty, set out to create the maximum embarrassment for Paul, and succeeded. They called into question both Agostino Casaroli's *Ostpolitik* and Jan Willebrands' cultivation of good relations with the Russian Orthodox Church. By placing the Ukrainian question under the heading of "Justice in the World" and presenting, quite rightly, their suppression in 1946 as "the most dishonourable act perpetrated by the Russian Orthodox Church in modern times",[1] Slipyi put its fate on the agenda of the Church where it stayed, a ticking time-bomb, until it emerged from underground in 1990, five million strong.

1 Michael Bourdeaux, *Tablet*, 13 March 1971, p. 264. Michael Bourdeaux, an Anglican priest, founded Keston College, Kent, the best and sometimes sole source of news about East European dissidents. After the collapse of Communism, he migrated to Oxford as Director of Keston Research.

33

No Resignation at Seventy-Five

> Those who have to take important decisions that affect the lives of their fellow men are not left to do so unaided. They do not themselves go out to ask questions and get answers . . . They must not be tempted with anything that is not essential for them to know. The skill lies in the exclusion of the irrelevant.
>
> (PATRICK DEVLIN, *Easing the Passage: The Trial of Doctor John Bodkin*, Bodley Head 1985, p. 57)

Paul VI certainly did not "go out to ask questions and get answers". He was more dependent on subordinates even than the high court judge envisaged by Lord Devlin. The world and its rumours came to him at second- or third-hand. They reached him as a jumble of press cuttings in which alarming theological opinions were marked by zealous nuncios with blue pencil. However, private audiences were one way in which he could stay at first-hand in touch with the modern world. I will give three examples of audiences, with a French Jesuit, with a North American neurologist, and with a once powerful Italian cardinal.

He did not often get the chance to meet those who had been denounced. Bruno Ribes, the editor of *Etudes* in Paris, was summoned to Rome to be rebuked for his adventurous liberal ideas. *Etudes* and the Swiss Jesuit fortnightly *Orientierung* received more *monita* (warnings) from Roman Congregations than all other European reviews combined. (The Netherlands had been given up as a hopeless case, and anyway nobody read Dutch.) The usual form was a letter from the Cardinal Secretary of State saying that a given article had "offended against truth and the Holy See" – as though the two terms were synonymous and interchangeable.

On this occasion *Etudes* had published an article distinguishing between "human life and humanized life".[1] This simply meant that fully humanized life presupposes acceptance and recognition by society, while

1 "*Encore l'avortement*", *Etudes*, January 1973, p. 71.

the foetus possesses "human life", its basis and condition. The article was certainly not "advocating abortion" but this was what it was accused of. Paul delivered his prepared lecture, the set piece he always had to hand for any meeting (called in Vaticanese the *scaletta*). Ribes listened patiently, nodding at appropriate moments. Then he said, "Holy Father, do you have the slightest idea where these accusations come from?" The Holy Father had not.

Ribes then outlined the links between the right-wing movements in France, including that of Archbishop Marcel Lefebvre and the abbé Georges de Nantes, and the armaments industries which financed them. Paul asked for a two-page memo on the subject. As Ribes took his leave, Paul said: "You realize why I had to have my say, but in the end the essential thing is *aimez l'Eglise, aimez l'Eglise, et faîtes ce que vous voulez*."[1]

Professor Robert J. White is a neurologist from the United States. Starting in 1968 there was much discussion on what came to be known as "the Harvard Criteria for Irreversible Coma". In fact "irreversible coma" turned out to be a less appropriate term than "brain-death", and White gave seminars at the Jesuit Curia on its medical implications. This led to an invitation to discuss these matters with Paul in a series of three or four audiences which began early in the 1970s. Msgr Justin Rigali, a Californian at the Secretariat of State, acted as interpreter. White found Paul well-briefed and very incisive in his questions. White says:

> He had clearly read or had been educated regarding this very important subject. The second thing that struck me was his continued interest in my research, which had concentrated on brain isolation and transplantation in the experimental animal, as well as techniques literally to freeze brain substance. Again I was amazed at his knowledge of my work.[2]

White found Paul "a happy person, in spite of his infirmities, who laughed and smiled a lot throughout our discussions". Paul insisted on his bringing his wife, and provided rosaries for their ten children (to stop them falling all over the place, he counted them out into an envelope and put a rubber band round it).

An audience with the conservative Cardinal Giuseppe Siri of Genoa illustrates another facet of Paul's character: he knew what he wanted –

1 "Love the Church, love the Church, and do as you will" is a reminiscence of St Augustine's *Ama, et fac quod vis*. Neither is an invitation to anarchy. The anecdote comes directly from Bruno Ribes. I have placed it a little earlier than it actually was.

2 Robert J. White, letter to the author, 6 March 1992. Professor White is director of Neurological Surgery at Case Western Reserve University, Cleveland, Ohio.

until someone came along to contradict him. Siri still commanded a certain respect in the Curia if not elsewhere as the unsuccessful dauphin of Pius XII, and he still thought himself *papabile* at the two conclaves of 1978. But his outspoken hostility to Pope John XXIII ("It will take a century to recover from his pontificate") and opposition to the Council were well-publicized.[1] Siri wanted his financial backing for the theological review he had founded, *Renovatio*. Paul jibbed a little: "I don't want *Renovatio* to become just an anti-*Concilium* tract, or to be thought of in that way. That's why I have arranged that our theologian, Carlo Colombo, should be a member of the board; and we will try to help you financially."[2]

So Paul may have subsidized *Renovatio*. How many more reviews were helped in this way? Did *Communio*, founded by Henri de Lubac and Hans Urs von Balthasar after the 1971 Synod, seek financial aid? It certainly had good anti-*Concilium* credentials.

But *Renovatio* proved a disappointment to Paul. It did not even try to aim at the "balance" he thought so crucial. Its title began to sound merely ironical, since it was opposed to all innovations of any kind. In particular it was dead set against one plan he was considering: the conclave to elect his successor would take the form of an Extraordinary Synod, and would therefore include those bishops who were elected presidents of their episcopal conferences.

Though simple this proposal was very radical: it would break the monopoly of the college of cardinals, and it would have given fuller expression to Paul's sense that while bishops are "of divine right" in the Church (such that the Church cannot be the Church willed by Christ without them), cardinals are a dispensable invention of the eleventh century. The Council had brought out the importance of the college of *bishops*; that meant that the college of *cardinals* could be eclipsed and eventually abolished. A common theological opinion was that after Vatican II "it was an anomaly, if not a scandal, that the episcopal college existing by divine right had so very little part in the government of the Church, while the college of cardinals enjoyed all the power, privileges, precedence and tenure".[3]

Siri reports a conversation lasting an hour and a half on the conclave theme:

1 It is only fair to add that Cardinal Siri came to have a grudging admiration for Pope John, and testified to this before the beatification tribunal. What had changed his mind was that every home in Genoa, including those of Communists, had its picture of Pope John.

2 Benny Lai, *Les secrets du Vatican*, p. 171.

3 René Laurentin, "*Paul VI et l'après-concile*", in *Modernité*, p. 577. See also Karl Rahner, "The Episcopal Office", in *Theological Investigations*, 6, pp. 313ff.

> It was like a game of ping-pong; he listened to my arguments and countered with his own dialectic. I held back till the end one last objection: it was a mistake to put on the same level cardinals who are named by the pope and bishops who are appointed in a different way. Cardinals are answerable to no one, while bishops have to account for their decisions. So they can be easily "conditioned". This term alarmed Paul VI. "Very well," he said, "it will be the sacred college and it alone that will elect the pope." Then I took his hand, kissed his ring, and fled. If I had gone on any more, he would have flung an ash-tray at my head.[1]

A large pinch of salt should be applied to this story. Siri typically overestimates his influence. The idea that cardinals are more genuinely independent than bishops is true only if the bishops desperately want to become cardinals, and are thus paralysed by caution.

But Paul did not make up his mind after a single meeting with Siri. He listened to the *altera pars*, which in this case meant Cardinal Léon-Joseph Suenens, the severest critic of the college of cardinals and the most determined that the next conclave should take the form of an Extraordinary Synod. Suenens had always underplayed the office of cardinal. It was Suenens too, who, having got accepted the idea that residential bishops should resign at seventy-five, indicated that the college of cardinals was top-heavy with ancients making the Church a veritable gerontocracy.

But there was also a theological argument involved. It was summarized by Antoine Wenger:

> In his interview Cardinal Suenens again raised the question of the election of the Pope. He places this problem, commendably, within the realm of theology. He quotes in this context the idea of Bishop Christopher Butler OSB, which is that on the death of the pope, authority in the Church devolves upon the college of bishops as such. The cardinals' privilege of electing the pope is then justified only by reason of some sort of implicit delegation of this right by the world college of bishops. Cardinal Suenens wonders whether the papal election should not belong to the presidents of episcopal conferences, since they are the collegial group, rather than the College of Cardinals – which merely forms an advisory council for the pope.[2]

1 Benny Lai, *Les secrets du Vatican*, p. 172.

2 Quoted in Roger Aubert, "Church Institutions: A Critical Interpretation", in *The Suenens Dossier*, ed. José de Broucker, p. 173.

After much agonizing Paul split the difference (or thought he had): in the end, only cardinals were admitted to the conclave (victory for Siri); but cardinals over eighty years old were excluded from it (semi-victory for Suenens).

In January 1972 Msgr Giovanni Benelli went on a quick trip to Jerusalem. His immediate aim was to resolve the legal difficulties surrounding the *Centre Notre Dame*, built by the Assumptionists in 1885 to accommodate French pilgrims. It was badly damaged during the 1948 war when it was used as a bunker and frontier-post in no man's land. The Assumptionists tried to sell it, and the building was due to be donated to the Hebrew University. The Holy See – or at any rate Benelli – disapproved of this deal which had been embarked upon without prior approval from Rome. The law had been called in. Benelli went to conclude an out-of-court settlement by which the Israeli government rescinded the sale of Notre Dame and sold it back to the Holy See.[1]

This illustrates Benelli's preference for acting behind the scenes. It also illustrates a constant feature of Vatican policy towards Israel. Arab Christians and Arabs generally were increasingly worried as the properties of non-Jewish owners were taken over one by one. So Notre Dame was a symbol of fidelity, proof positive that the Holy See was not abandoning the Arab Christians to extinction. The same motive explains the persistence with which Paul supported Bethlehem University, entrusted to the Christian Brothers, and Tantur, the ecumenical centre he had founded.

Another traveller was Suenens. Though he continued to be the bogey-cardinal of the conservatives, their stereotype was out of date: for a "new" or at least recycled Suenens was emerging. In March 1972 he went on a lecture tour of the United States and deepened his first-hand experience of the Charismatic Renewal movement. His biographer tells this edifying story:

> When he was in Philadelphia in March 1972 some nuns arrived from New Jersey to tell him what the Holy Spirit was bringing to pass in their prayer house at Convent Station. Because they had braved a terrific blizzard to come, he felt bound to receive them and to listen to what they had to say. This was his first real contact with persons involved in the Charismatic Renewal.[2]

1 George E. Irani, *The Papacy and the Middle East: The Role of the Holy See in the Arab-Israeli Conflict 1962–1984*, Notre Dame Press 1986, pp. 93–94.

2 Elisabeth Hamilton, *Cardinal Suenens: A Portrait*, p. 190.

Oh happy blizzard, *felix culpa*. After that Cardinal Suenens so to speak never looked back or up. Unlike his predecessor, the "new" Suenens was no longer interested in the external reform of Church structures, or in advocating the ordination of married men as he had done at the Synod only five months before.

Paul did not personally experience the full force of the transformed Suenens until 1973. Meanwhile he had a report on Jesuit Fr Walter Burghardt's introduction to Suenens when he gave the John Courtney Murray lecture at the Church of St Paul the Apostle in New York:

> He is *not* the person some imagine him to be; he is *not* an enemy of Pope Paul; he is *not* turning the Church into a democracy . . . He is a cardinal indeed, but he has transformed the meaning of the word from "prince of the Church" to "servant of man".[1]

That there were many in the audience who would be disappointed by these denials was significant; that it marked Cardinal Suenens' abandonment of the "liberal" or "progressive" camp was even more significant.

The elections for the Synod Council in 1971 – an innovation designed to make the Synod more responsible – marked a generation change. The first three names out of the hat were all presidents of their episcopal conferences and none was a cardinal: Joseph Bernardin, United States; Aloisio Lorscheider, Brazil; and Roger Etchegaray, France. Karol Wojtyla was the only *cardinal* to be elected but he was exceptionally young at fifty-one and didn't look much like a curial cardinal.

Yet Cardinal Wojtyla behaved like one at the first meeting of the Synod Council, which met on 29 February to 3 March 1972. They had "long and lively discussion" on how to implement the resolutions of the previous Synod. Wojtyla insisted that it belonged to the Holy Father alone to draw the conclusions of the Synod (thus foreshadowing his own practice). No one disagreed, but the whole point in *electing* the Synod Council – themselves – was to enhance the responsibility and dignity of the Synod. It was not to be a mere rubber-stamp for papal decisions.

That question could be deferred. Their immediate task was to select the topic for the 1974 Synod which would be the *third* ordinary Synod. The lesson of 1967 was that five topics were totally unmanageable; that of 1971 was that even two themes were one too many. "He who controls the agenda controls the meeting" is a Roman saying; and Paul – even though he retained the last word – had handed over considerable power by inviting them to make suggestions. Karol Wojtyla exploited this to

1 Ibid. pp. 187–88. Burghardt was editor of *Theological Studies* for many years, and was by common consent the finest preacher in the United States.

the full. His survey of possible themes was intended to show their interconnectedness. It did that, but it also disclosed his anxieties:

> Thus catechesis could be linked with the problem of vocations; the working out of *Lex Ecclesiae Fundamentalis* would have been a continuation of the Synod of 1967; there were links between the problem of democracy in the Church and the *Magisterium*; the condition of women in the Church, marriage and morality were all interrelated matters. The problem of the *Magisterium* had already emerged with the utmost clarity apropos of *Humanae Vitae*, which also illustrated the influence of theologians on the decisions of episcopal conferences.[1]

This was barbed language, and these were marked cards. The last remark, for example, suggested that those episcopal conferences that introduced nuances of conscience into the interpretation of *Humanae Vitae* were pushed into it by aberrant theologians. This was as unjust as it was fanciful. Anyway, it did not help Paul to make up his mind what to do about the next Synod.

For Paul was entering a period of dark night, of depression, of deep agonizing over his stewardship. Was he a good pope or a bad pope? The answer was far from self-evident to him. He knew by heart the passage in George Bernanos' novel, *Le Journal d'un Curé de Campagne*, in which the Curé de Torcy, an old *Action Française* monarchist, says that every Christian finds his own special place in the mysteries of the life of Christ. His secretary, Don Pasquale Macchi, had written a thesis on "evil in Bernanos".

Where did Paul place himself in the life of Christ? He said the rosary every day: he identified with the first "sorrowful mystery" – the Agony in the Garden; and on his walks in the Vatican Gardens he often paused to meditate at the shrine of St Peter *ad vincula* (in chains). Sometimes he had been found weeping there. Nothing wrong with that: the old Missal had a special Mass "for the gift of tears". The text he had used for his eve-of-conclave sermon in San Carlo now struck him with full force: "Truly, truly, I say to you . . . when you are old, you will stretch out your hands, and another will gird you and carry you where you do not wish to go."[2] *When you are old*: he was old now.

But Paul's tears and lamentations at this date, 1972, were not over his sins but over the state of the Church. He marked the ninth anniversary of his election on 29 June 1972, the feast of Sts Peter and Paul, the

1 Giovanni Caprile SJ, *Karol Wojtyla e il Sinodo dei Vescovi*, p. 125.

2 John 21:18.

feast *par excellence* of the Roman Church. The traditional theme – valid theologically as much as rhetorically – was that Peter represented the pastor of a stable, settled community, while Paul launched forth adventurously into the places where "unknown gods" might be found. That was why he had chosen the name Paul.

Yet he inaugurated his tenth year as pope by appearing a cautious, nervous, anxious, alarmed Peter with Paul nowhere in evidence. By some extraordinary fluke – just conceivably – his sermon in St Peter's does not appear to have been recorded. *L'Osservatore Romano* and its satellites provide only a summary (*un resoconto*) of what he actually said.[1] The crucial phrase, in quotes, was that "through some crack in the temple of God, the smoke of Satan has entered".[2] That was the sound-bite that made the headlines.

The paraphrase explained Satan's fumigation thus: in the Church we find doubt, uncertainty, problems, restlessness, disquiet, dissatisfaction, polarization (*il confronto*). Nothing new there. The novelty was, Paul went on, that "any jumped-up prophet who wrote in the papers or any movement that appealed to him was believed", while the authentic voice of the *Magisterium* was ignored. Modern sciences, physical and human, he maintained, end up by teaching "I don't know, we don't know, we can't know."[3] This was not entirely fanciful, as French philosophers such as Jacques Derrida were busily "deconstructing" the universe and pointing to the unreliability of concepts such as "substance" or, still more worringly, "the human". One of them, Louis Althusser, was committed to a mental hospital after strangling his wife. That could be considered a proof *e contrario*.

But Paul's words were unlikely to be read by French post-structuralists. On the other hand they were avidly reported by the Italian press for whom "the devil" is a mediaeval joke. Cartoonists refurbished their stock of clichés, producing cloven hoofs, long sinuous tails, ugly contorted faces and terrifying implements of torture. For the cartoonists Paul VI was definitely not a modern man.

Whatever he was, Paul still had to make his mind up about the next Synod. Much depended on it. The Synod could stretch him, extend his range, get him off the devil. Unfortunately the second meeting of the Synod Council, 24–27 October 1972, was just as inconclusive as the first one in the spring. The rival merits of five themes were debated at length:

1 *Insegnamenti*, 1972, pp. 703–9.

2 Ibid. p. 707.

3 Ibid. p. 708.

1 Marriage and the Family.
2 Evangelization.
3 Faith and the *Magisterium*.
4 The Local Church.
5 Youth.

To this list were added Laypeople in the Church and Religious Life. Religious Life was insisted upon by Cardinal Karol Wojtyla because, he maintained, it was in a state of serious crisis marked by "defections, lack of vocations, weaknesses in the observance of the vows", the remedy for which was "greater insertion in the life of the Church and a re-examination of the concept of exemption".[1]

But Marriage and the Family looked the most likely topic at this stage. The Laity Council meeting in September took it for granted that this was already decided upon. Archbishop Derek Worlock of Liverpool noted the wry faces of Europeans and North Americans at this suggestion, while people from the Third World were enthusiastic.

By chance Worlock had an *ad limina* meeting with Paul in October 1972. It followed the usual pattern. Paul asked some questions about the quinquennial reports on his diocese, noted his good relationship with the Anglican bishop, ex-England cricketer, David Sheppard, thanked him for the work he was doing, and then ended, as he usually did: "One more question – is there anything I can do *for you*?" Archbishop Worlock takes up the story:

> I said there was something that concerned me, the subject of the next Synod. Pope Paul said: "We've carried out a consultation and nearly all the bishops in the world want Family Life." I had more courage on the spur of the moment than I might otherwise have had, and I said there was one bishop at least who didn't want it. I said: "I don't think it is the right subject." "Why?" "I fear it might lead to a resumption of all the arguments and pain and distress [that surrounded *Humanae Vitae*] in 1968, and quite frankly, I don't think we're ready for that." I shall never forget the look on his face; it was almost as if I'd struck him.[2]

One wonders why no one had put this obvious argument to Paul VI before October 1972. The reasoning was clear. 1974 was only six years

1 Ibid. pp. 126–27. It was often said that Cardinal Wojtyla had a problem with the Jesuits of Kraków who would not join in his theological *consortium*. If so, they suffered for it in 1981–82. He certainly thinks in decades: the 1994 Synod was due to be on Religious Life.

2 Interview with Archbishop Derek Worlock, 4 March 1988.

after *Humanae Vitae*. To hold a Synod on Christian marriage would have been to reopen the old wounds just as they were beginning to heal. Attempts to brow-beat "dissident" theologians into acquiescence had failed, as they were bound to since *Humane Vitae* was never put forward as "infallible". The pastoral letters that interpreted it could not be explained away as a result of bishops surrendering to the improper influence of theologians – as Cardinal Wojtyla's comments implied. Bishops, as pastors close to their people, knew that married couples had as much difficulty in understanding the teaching of *Humanae Vitae* as obeying it. The concentration, almost obsession, on birth-control was preventing other equally important aspects of the Christian doctrine on marriage from being brought out. It was better not to stir up this hornet's nest.

Giovanni Benelli grasped the point at once. He saw Worlock at a meeting on the afternoon of the *ad limina* visit. Worlock continues:

> He said: "You are quite right." I didn't want to give anything away, so I said Mmm . . . "Ah," he said in a stage whisper, "*Humanae Vitae*." Then later we discussed what could be put in its place. "I think we ought to start looking at the world. Ever since the Council we've been looking inwards at priests and collegiality. Couldn't we look outwards at the work the Church is engaged in such as evangelization – not just in mission territories but in our own countries?" "Yes," he said, "the mission to the world . . ."

It could be put in terms of Cardinal Suenens' distinction, back in 1962, between *ecclesia ad intra* and *ecclesia ad extra*. It was high time to look outwards.

But for Benelli and Pope Paul there was another, clinching consideration. Until 1970 there had been no divorce in Italy. Then the Baslini–Fortuna law was passed by a small majority in Parliament. Catholic groups asked for a referendum, which was their constitutional right. The referendum should have taken place in 1972 but the Christian Democrats hesitated, unsure of the outcome. But campaigning for and against divorce had already started.[1] Therefore one could not hold a Synod on Christian Marriage without appearing to be calling upon the whole Church to come to the aid of the Pope on an Italian political question. No doubt these various factors converged, and perhaps there were others. But the fact is that after October 1972 there was no more talk of Christian Marriage as the theme of the 1974 Synod.

Paul's choice of Evangelization as the theme of the 1974 Synod was

1 Giuseppe de Rosa SJ, "Learning the Hard Way", *Month*, August 1974, p. 669.

one of the most fateful of his pontificate. If he had opted for Christian Marriage his whole pontificate would have gone down in history as the birth-control pontificate. Evangelization gave him a chance to look up and break out of this narrow mould.

At his 23 March 1973 address to the Synod Secretariat Paul showed himself well aware of these implications. He set the theme of Evangelization in the context of *Ad Gentes* and *Gaudium et Spes*, the two most outward-looking Council documents. His announcement came at the end of their meeting, as though to say that his mind was finally made up and there would be no further discussion. Cardinal Karol Wojtyla, who had clearly wanted a showdown on *Humanae Vitae*, was consoled for his disappointment by being given the task of *relator* and presenting a position-paper at the Evangelization Synod.

But none of this meant that *Humanae Vitae* faded from the scene. As a question for married Catholics it was resolved by the primacy of conscience. John Henry Newman's famous toast was much quoted: "I drink to the Pope, but to conscience first." In vain did careful scholars explain that Newman did not mean what he appeared to mean. The Holy See, for its part, concentrated on the "public policy" aspect and used discreet lobbying and private interventions to influence governments.

Yet Paul produced a surprise during the summer vacation. Two apostolic letters came out on 15 August 1972. *Ministeria Quaedam* reformed the so-called "minor orders". It abolished five of them, and the two that remained, lector and acolyte, were given back to the laity from whom they had been removed (as the document explicitly remarks).[1]

Ad Pascendum completed *Ministeria Quaedam* by fixing the norms for the diaconate which the Council had restored as a permanent state in the Church: hitherto it had been a mere stepping-stone, often a meaninglessly brief one, on the way to priestly ordination. Now the diaconate was an office in its own right. Paul, says Aimé Martimort, was "deeply worried by the abolition of minor orders, which he saw as steps towards the priesthood".[2] But that was in 1966; by 1972 he allowed himself to be persuaded.

The 1971 Synod had not been in vain. Its debate on ministry, and even up to a point the theses of Hans Urs von Balthasar, showed that in the Church there was one mission but many ministries. It followed that the distinction between clergy and laity could no longer be that the former had "ministries" while the latter did not. Hitherto the tonsure –

1 Austin Flannery OP, *Post-Conciliar Documents*, 1, p. 427.

2 *Paul VI et la Réforme Liturgique*, p. 71.

shaving off the hair at the crown of the head – had been the point of entry into the clerical state. Now the tonsure was abolished, and the diaconate became the way in to the clerical state. It followed that from now on the Latin Church had a "married clergy" in the shape of married deacons.

Paul's second innovation was to state firmly that the offices of acolyte and reader were "lay *ministries*". Previously the laity's mission was invariably described in terms of "the apostolate", while "ministry" and "minister" were reserved for the clergy. Here was new language indeed: "*Ministries may be committed to lay Christians*. They are no longer to be regarded as reserved to candidates for the sacrament of orders."[1] That was the most "revolutionary" utterance of Paul; and he reasserted it with some vigour in *Evangelii Nuntiandi* of 1975.

But while the extension of ministries to laypeople was welcomed by "progressives" they were less enamoured of the hardening of the distinction between cleric and layman. There could be no doubt about it, for while deacons and priests were *ordained* for the ministry, lay ministers were merely *installed*. Paul insisted on some distinction and set up his friend Msgr Emilio Guano to argue for it in the *Consilium*.[2]

However, *Ministeria Quaedam* was novel in that it invited episcopal conferences to show "creativity" in setting up new ministries:

> There is nothing to prevent episcopal conferences from requesting the establishment of other offices from the Holy See, over and above those that are common to the whole Church, if they decide that this is necessary or helpful for reasons peculiar to their own territories. Examples of such offices are those of exorcist, porter and catechist.[3]

"Catechists" were often "installed" especially in Africa; "porters" were transmuted into "ministers of hospitality" especially in North America; there was no great proliferation of exorcists. But the principle counted for more than the detailed examples given. The freedom to experiment led to the *makumbi* of Zaïre and "the ministry explosion" of the 1980s.

But in one important respect *Ministeria Quaedam* looked backward rather than forward. That maleness should be required for the diaconate was at least a defensible position as long as the clerical state was exclu-

1 Flannery, *Post-conciliar Documents*, 1, p. 429.

2 Aimé Martimort, "*Paul et la Liturgie*", p. 71. In Guano-speak the lay ministers were *instituted* rather than *installed*. The Congregation for Divine Worship produced a *Ritus institutionis* which ought to have settled the question.

3 Flannery, *Post-conciliar Documents*, 1, p. 429.

sively male. What was indefensible and illogical was that the offices of acolyte and lector should also remain a male preserve. These offices were being given back to the laity; but they were given back only to the male half of the laity. In the next decade this distinction proved unworkable.

The chief practical development everyone noticed was in "extraordinary" ministers of the Eucharist where priests were in short supply; this was quickly extended to women, regarded as desirable in itself, and soon the *extraordinary* became *ordinary*.

Not for the first or last time, Paul had done a good thing, and then spoilt it in mid-course. Why? His compromises were always a balance between what he could bring himself to assent to and the pressures to left and right to which he was subjected. On *Ministeria Quaedam* he had wrestled with his conscience. An indication was that the press conference to present the document was given by Fr Paolo Dezza SJ who had no link with the Congregation for the Sacraments or the *Consilium* but was Paul's confessor. Every Friday punctually at 7.45 p.m. a Vatican Mercedes arrived at the Jesuit Curia to collect Dezza.

There are obvious limits to what a papal confessor can say, but Fr Dezza's testimony has a special value:

> It is truly consoling to see how, after the incomprehension of so many during Paul VI's lifetime, since his death there has been an ever-growing esteem and admiration for him. I met Paul VI before he became Pope, but they were fleeting encounters.[1]
>
> However the meetings I had with him as Pope were much more frequent, and I believe I can say that if he was not a saint when he was elected Pope, he became one during his pontificate. I was able to witness not only with what energy and dedication he toiled for Christ and the Church, but also and above all how much he suffered for Christ and the Church.
>
> Given his natural temperament, his sufferings brought him deep inner pain, but I always admired not only his deep inner patience and resignation, but also his constant abandonment to divine providence.
>
> In particular I was edified by his attitude towards those who were the cause of so much of his suffering. No anger, but evangelical pardon and love. I will never forget the answer he

1 Fr Dezza, eighty-eight at the time of this interview, had been Rector of the Gregorian during the war. Though half blind and unable to read he had a phenomenal memory for Scripture, the Constitutions of the Society of Jesus, and what Jesuits were doing in higher education throughout the world. Pope John Paul II made him a cardinal in June 1991. The old boy was as pleased as punch.

> told me to give to Msgr Marcel Lefebvre at a delicate moment in that conflict which caused him so much pain: "Tell Msgr Lefebvre of all my affliction, but also of all my affection."[1]

It is fair to add that this statement was evoked in response to the Argentinian bishops who, apparently having nothing better to do, petitioned the Holy Father to consider the beatification of Paul VI. Fine by me, said Pope John Paul II.

I am not caricaturing the Argentinian bishops. Their Primate, Cardinal Raul Francisco Primatesta, explained why they had taken up this cause: "Someone had to be the first, and perhaps the Lord was thinking: since the Bishops don't have much to do, at least let them do something good."

Not a bad principle.

1 *Thirty Days*, February 1989, p. 17.

34

The Ten-Year Itch

> The ten years of Paul VI's pontificate have been an uninterrupted attempt to open up a dialogue with the modern world. But in this attempt he has failed.
>
> (VITTORIO GORRESIO, quoted in *Modernité*, pp. 217–18)

And that was one of the kinder assessments on the tenth anniversary of his election. The trouble was he had talked of the devil. Literally. He said he could see "smoke from Satan rising up within the Church . . ." In Italian secular culture the devil is a comic figure, so that one reference permitted him to be mocked as mediaeval and obscurantist. The right-wing and those close to Archbishop Marcel Lefebvre thought he was at last coming to his senses after all this nonsense about the Council. The "devil" they saw belching smoke into the Church looked remarkably like Hans Küng. Carlo Falconi, a knowledgeable resigned priest, neither mocked nor enthused but suggested that Paul VI had heard the first rumblings suggesting cracks in the fabric of a Church that might well disintegrate.[1]

That was a melodramatic way of putting it. As he faced the multitude of problems that came across his desk, day after day, Paul VI could be forgiven for thinking that being pope was like being a juggler. He had to keep at least ten plates spinning round all the time. Now persecution in China, now torture in Brazil. Now the fight against the Smith regime in Rhodesia (later Zimbabwe), supported by the local Justice and Peace Commission, now the overthrow of President Salvatore Allende in Chile. These are only examples. Paul felt he had to consider so many dossiers personally.

But international problems could up to a point be delegated. Theological questions and the preparation of documents on homosexuality and women's ordination, for example, could not be delegated without dereliction of duty. That did not mean he was not open to advice. On

1 Luigi Accatoli, "*La figura di Paolo VI nell'opinione publico italiana*", in *Modernité*, p. 218.

3 May 1973 Paul announced the setting up of a Study Commission on Women and Society. He was responding to a proposal of the 1971 Synod which urged "a mixed commission of men and women, religious and laypeople, of differing backgrounds and competence" to foster "women's share of responsibility and participation in the community life of society and likewise of the Church".[1] Its President was Enrico Bartoletti and its secretary Dr Rosemary Goldie. Its brief did not formally include women's ordination – though it was impossible to avoid it altogether. Meeting them for the first time, Paul said:

> Your chief purpose will be to gather, verify, interpret, revise, sharpen the ideas that have been expressed on the role of women in modern society . . . That is already enough to give you some idea of the work of observation, research and reflection that is entrusted to you with the aid of theologians and experts.[2]

In practice its main function was to sensitize Paul to women's issues and help him make an enlightened contribution to the International Women's Year fixed by the United Nations for 1975.

The Congregation for the Doctrine of Faith, headed by Cardinal Franjo Seper, did not like this new cuckoo in the nest and feared it would end in tears, as did the birth-control Commission. Despite the "reforms" there was still tension between the CDF, whose main concern was with orthodoxy, and the Secretariat for Christian Unity headed by Cardinal Jan Willebrands, whose main concern was for ecumenical dialogue. Paul needed them both, and the primatial art consisted in holding the two emphases together in dialectical tension and exploiting what was valid in both approaches.

Easier said than done. Besides, there was another "institutional" problem that centred on the role of Giovanni Benelli as *sostituto*. He combined the roles of *chef de cabinet*, office manager, personnel officer of the Roman Curia and the Vatican diplomatic service (he hired and fired). He was the hour-glass connecting Paul VI and the world. He controlled access. If he did not "control" Paul himself he helped determine how the Pope spent his time by briefing him, arranging meetings, making proposals, and organizing the work of the Curia.[3]

1 Rosemary Goldie, *The Church and the International Women's Year, 1975*, p. 11.

2 *Insegnamenti*, 1973, pp. 1113–14. The four verbs were *recueillir, vérifier, interpréter, reviser* and *mettre au point*. There was much dispute afterwards about what they meant and whether they had been fulfilled.

3 A confession and a revelation. On 11 and 18 March 1973 I published two articles in the *Observer* on the role of Archbishop Giovanni Benelli. Part one was titled (not by me) "The Most Powerful Man in the Church". The article purported to show that Benelli, who had not taken part in the Council, was the power behind the throne

Paul had been *sostituto* himself under Pius XII; but Pius had wanted "executants, not collaborators", and he had no influence on the Pope's thinking or policies. Now he was Pope himself he was dependent on Benelli, and increasingly so. Hence Benelli's many nicknames: "the Berlin Wall" (nothing got past him), Your Efficiency (instead of "Your Excellency") and "His Omnipotence".[1]

This aroused resentment. Benelli was constantly with the Pope and could drop in on his meals. Cardinal Jean Villot, although Secretary of State and the man to whom Benelli was technically the "substitute" or deputy, saw far less of Paul and thought this wrong. From his retirement the ancient Amleto Cicognani, Villot's predecessor, grasped what was happening and wrote memos criticizing Benelli's "highly personal" way of conceiving his role, and suggesting that he would not have allowed himself to be pushed around in this way.

Villot also had policy disagreements with his *sostituto* being "more liberal" on Italian questions on which Benelli thought the French incompetent. As part of his duties Villot read the proofs and met the editor of *Civiltà Catholica* once a fortnight. This gave him an education in Italian subtleties. He got on well with Roberto Tucci SJ and when Tucci became head of Vatican Radio in 1973, with his successor, Fr Bartolomeo Sorge SJ.

But resentment against Benelli was widespread. This was partly the result of the reform of the Curia, which gave the Secretariat of State a "co-ordinating" function. Sometimes "co-ordination" tipped over into

if not the evil genius. Decent ecumenists, committed Justice and Peace people, and all men and women of good will, I implied, were bound to find Benelli a nasty piece of work who should be removed forthwith – for the good of the Church. The effect of this article was astonishing. It was said to be an Arrupe-inspired plot to undermine Benelli: in fact Don Pedro Arrupe did not know of my articles in advance, and telegraphed the Provincial, Bernard Hall, to stop the second article – an evident impossibility. Italian Vatican experts such as Giancarlo Zizola claimed that I had been set up by the reactionary right-wing in the Curia for whom Benelli was a menacing reformer. The tyres of his car – he loved driving very fast – were slashed in the Vatican car park because he had insisted that only those genuinely employed by the Vatican – and not their cousins and aunts – had the right to buy duty-free goods in the Vatican supermarket. *The Times*, then edited by William Rees-Mogg, denounced me in an editorial for naïvety. Every world leader, it said, needed a tough guy as *chef de cabinet*, whose function was to keep out undesirables. President Richard J. Nixon had Bob Haldeman who was just as unpopular, and just as necessary, as Benelli. When Haldeman went to prison, I felt vindicated. As for Benelli himself, I was told that he had my articles xeroxed and distributed round the Secretariat of State. "At last," he is supposed to have exclaimed, "someone has understood how important I am around here!" Jean Tillard OP said these articles prevented Benelli from becoming pope in the second conclave of 1978. He soon died of a broken heart. Oh dear!

1 Giancarlo Zizola, "*Il mio amico Onnipotente*", *Panorama*, 15 November 1982, p. 92.

"control". Prefects of Roman Congregations were made to feel that their work was being judged not by the Pope but by Benelli. This was not necessarily so, but Benelli did nothing to dispel this view.

Yet the *sostituto* was no substitute-pope, and Paul still had to determine where the priorities lay. In tackling intractable political questions he displayed lucidity, responsibility and patience. These qualities were needed where there was no give and take, no movement and little progress.

The visit of the Israeli Prime Minister Golda Meir to the Holy See on 15 January 1973 was the first papal audience with a "Zionist" since Theodore Herzl met St Pius X in 1904.[1] There had been "informal talks" since 1967 when the former Governor of Jerusalem, Chaim Herzog, had an audience with Paul as did Foreign Minister Abbas Eban in 1969. But the visit of the Prime Minister was in principle a huge step forward, a moment of history.

The audience had been arranged two weeks earlier. Golda Meir was coming to Rome and the Israeli ambassador to the Quirinale, Amiel Najar, enquired whether she might have a private audience with the Holy Father. The reply came from Giovanni Benelli, by now regarded as an authority on the Middle East: "If you request an audience with the Pope, there will be a positive response."[2] This curious form of words was chosen to avoid giving the impression that the Pope had *invited* her.

Mrs Meir knew full well that since the creation of the state of Israel in 1948 the Holy See advocated the "internationalization" of Jerusalem, this "thrice holy" city, so that Jews, Christians and Muslims might have guaranteed access to their holy places. This proposal might have had some pertinence when Jerusalem was a city divided between Jordan and Israel; but the Israel view was that after the Six Day War it no longer made sense. Golda Meir insisted that no one had the right to ask the Jewish people to surrender any parcel of Jerusalem and that "we are ready to declare Jerusalem inaccessible even if that means placing an insurmountable obstacle in the path of peace".[3] The unstoppable force met the immovable obstacle, and the Palestinians were trapped in between.

Paul was seventy-five, just a few months older than Mrs Meir. They went into the meeting with different, indeed contrary, aims. Golda Meir wanted diplomatic recognition from the Holy See. Intent on the "civiliz-

1 André Dupuy, *La Diplomatie du Saint-Siège*, p. 106.

2 Muriel Spark, "When Israel went to the Vatican", *Tablet*, 24 March 1973, pp. 277–78. The novelist, author of *The Prime of Miss Jean Brodie* and *The Mandelbaum Gate*, had just taken up residence in Italy.

3 Ibid. p. 115.

ation of love", Paul was trying to "help the Palestinians". He thought the Israelis, having survived the *shoah* or Holocaust, ought to treat the Palestinians with compassion rather than harshness and inhumanity. This roused Golda Meir to anger: "Your Holiness, do you know the first memory of my life? The pogrom of Kiev! When we were merciful and meek and didn't have a country, then they took us to the gas chambers."[1]

The joint communiqué about the visit, agreed in advance, naturally made no mention of these heated remarks. At her press conference, mainly concerned with Italian matters, Meir confined herself to saying, "I'm very happy that the Pope found it possible to receive me, and very happy that the audience took place."

She said this because after her audience with Paul, Frederico Alessandrini, Vatican press officer, stressed that Golda Meir had *not* been invited by the Pope but had invited herself, that she was *not* the object of any preferential or exclusive treatment, that the audience was *not* the fruit of previous agreement (that is, there was *no* plot), and finally that it "neither signifies nor implies any change in relations".[2] The Israelis regarded this as a Borgia-style stab in the back. The Vatican's left hand didn't know what its right hand was doing.

The simplest explanation was that on the night of 14 January the Arab states put pressure on the Secretariat of State to make a counter-statement cutting the audience down to size. Alessandrini was acting for Benelli. Paul, who had already given Golda Meir a silver dove, suitably inscribed, now sent a messenger racing across town with a Bible handsomely bound with his coat of arms and a copy of the catalogue of the Vatican Library. It was, wrote Muriel Spark, "a moment of history surrounded by historic misunderstandings, informed by the atavistic echo of ancestral voices". It fulfilled what an American prelate called "Murphy's Law": everything that can possibly go wrong will go wrong.[3]

Paul VI tried to get round the intellectual and diplomatic impasse by founding a Commission for *Religious* Relations with Judaism within the Secretariat for Christian Unity, but this was not a distinction the Israelis appreciated.[4]

1 Interview in the Hebrew paper, *Maarviv*, on her return to Jerusalem. Quoted in ibid. p. 278.

2 Ibid.

3 Ibid. Spark quotes the Israeli Ambassador, Amiel Najar: "Our form of Machiavellianism is to speak the truth. It takes everyone by surprise."

4 The Commission came to birth on 22 October 1974. It consisted for the most part of members of the Secretariat for Christian Unity wearing different hats, and was headed by Msgr Pietro Rossano. It had some success among European and US Jews who were prepared to make the distinction between Judaism as a religion and Israel as a political reality found in *Nostra Aetate* 4. It stressed the special bond that links

Contraception to most people in the West seemed like a question of individual morality, of importance to couples only. Paul on the contrary saw it as a public policy issue. He was concerned not only that governments would forcibly impose birth-control on unwilling couples but that the IMF and the World Bank would make it a necessary condition of their aid programmes. Thus throughout 1973 Paul gave much thought to the Holy See's participation in the UN Conference on Population Problems to be held in Bucharest on 19–30 August the following year.

Preparations began in January 1973 with the setting up of a new organism, the Committee for the Family. Its purpose was to "bring out, safeguard and promote, the spiritual, moral and social realities of the family". In short it would undertake "concerted action" to "defend the family", deemed under attack from hedonists, abortionists, feminists and gays (the word was coming in as those it indicated were coming out). It is fair to say that the Committee for the Family was, so to speak, more Villot's baby than Paul's.[1] It also served the purpose of giving a more universal setting to the campaign against divorce in Italy, which Paul and Villot on the whole thought more prudent to leave to the Italian bishops (CEI).

Though distinct from the Council of the Laity, the Committee for the Family had symbiotic links so intimate that for the crucial first twelve months Cardinal Maurice Roy, Archbishop of Quebec, was President of both. Paul instinctively knew that Canada was the place where the laymen and women were taken most seriously.

However there were Canadians and Canadians. With Roy away in Quebec, Sulpician Edouard Gagnon, formerly bishop of St Paul, Alberta and now head of the small Canadian College in Rome, was the effective head of the Committee for the Family. Gagnon, a timid man, uneasy with women and with an excessive reverence for authority, submitted to Villot's co-ordinating efforts. He took no initiatives and was content to be a faithful bureaucrat.[2]

Gagnon was notorious for believing that *Humanae Vitae* should have been an infallible definition and for acting as though it were. It was not surprising that the Committee for the Family should reflect this view. Its composition was rigged to achieve this end (24 French and Italians out of 38 members; a predominance of lawyers, canon and civil;

the two peoples of the Bible. The fact that it was responsible for *religious relations* marked it off from the Secretariat of State, alone competent in political matters. See Donald Nicholl, "*Nostra Aetate*", in *Modern Catholicism; Vatican II and After*, ed. Adrian Hastings, p. 128.

1 See Michael J. Walsh, "The Holy See's Population Problem", *Month*, July 1974, p. 634.

2 Paul Lakeland, "Distinguishing the Scribes", *Month*, June 1974, pp. 597–99.

no population experts). Its real aim was to ensure that only the members of the official Vatican delegation would be heard at the Bucharest meeting. Fr Henri de Riedmatten said that the views of other Catholics present should be ignored.[1]

Yet the CICO (Conference of International Catholic Organizations) had set up its own working party on population questions and could call on experts like Mill Hill Father Arthur J. McCormack and Canon Joseph Moerman of the International Catholic Child Bureau. Their work was not wanted, their publications were published in semi-*samizdat* form.[2]

On 21 February 1973 Cardinal Suenens had an audience with Paul VI that changed the life of both of them. Suenens, the star of the Council, the darling of the liberals, the proponent of an "alternative logic" of the Council, was no more. He was now a man repentant, transformed, and inclined to disown his past. He claimed continuity, however: his episcopal motto was *In Spiritu Sancto*, he had made the decisive speech at the Council on charisms, so pneumatology or the doctrine of the Holy Spirit was not exactly new to him. What was new was that in the late 1960s Suenens had tended to contrast charism and institution, Spirit and office, now he saw them as complementary. This was music to Paul's ears. What happened at their meeting? "I had a long audience with the Holy Father and I spoke to him for over half an hour about the Charismatic Renewal. I shared with him my discoveries in that field. I know he appreciated what I shared with him and listened very sympathetically."[3]

So sympathetically that he charged Suenens with the mission of "accompanying" the Charismatic Renewal movement. Negatively, this would prevent the Renewal movement going the way of Protestant sects. Positively, Suenens half persuaded him that just as the biblical and lit-

1 John F. X. Harriott, "Bitter Pills in Bucharest", *Month*, November 1974, pp. 755–59. Harriott's hero was Bishop Peter Kwasi Sarpong of Kumasi, Ghana. "Development is the ability to cope with one's problems," he said, "and in that sense no country in the world today can be called developed."

2 See Joseph Moerman and Michael Ingram OP, eds, *The Population Problem: A Challenge to the People of our Time*, Search Press 1975. The fog of controversy surrounded this volume. Originally published in French, the English translation was done without permission of Canon Moerman, and a whole new section entitled "Special Ethical and Religious Considerations" was added. In a letter to the *Tablet*, 17 January 1976, Ingrams contended that the Vatican had objected to the book in a secret memo sent to hierarchies in 1973 and leaked to *The Times* in 1974. The memo did not say the book opposed or was contrary to Catholic teaching; it said that it offered a different line from the strict interpretation of the Secretariat of State, and as such should not be published as coming from a Catholic international organization. It did not object to the private circulation of the work. To Ingrams and other British Catholics this seemed an intolerable, inadmissible procedure.

3 Edward D. O'Connor, *Pope Paul and the Spirit*, Ave Maria Press, Indiana 1978, p. 36.

urgical "movements" of the 1950s had flowed into the life of the Church at Vatican II in such a way that they were now no longer separable, even so the Charismatic Renewal would run through the whole Church and cease to be visible.[1]

What was the effect of the new Suenens on Paul? He had always been aware of the pneumatological aspect of faith so strongly asserted by the Orthodox Churches. Yet hitherto when he spoke of charisms he tended to stress their risky nature:

> As a result of human frailty, charisms may at times be confused with one's own disordered ideas and inclinations. Hence one must judge and discern charisms in order to check their authenticity, and to correlate them with the criteria derived from the teachings of Christ and with the order that should be observed in the ecclesial community. Such an office pertains to the sacred hierarchy, which is itself established by a singular charism.[2]

Charisms are all right but they must be kept in their place and held on a tight rein. But that was in 1971.

Now on 21 February 1973, just two days after his meeting with Suenens, Paul took a more positive line on charisms. True, modern man was losing his religious sense, yet here and there were "strange and consoling signs" of people discovering God in the most adverse circumstances. He cited the conversion of the ex-Communist André Frossard, whose book, *Dieu existe: Je l'ai rencontré*, was a best-seller. He went on:

> This is the charismatic sphere, about which so much is said today. "The Spirit blows where he wills." We will certainly not suppress [his breath] remembering the words of St Paul, "Do not quench the Spirit" (1 Thess. 5:19). However, we must at the same time recall the following words of the same Apostle: "Test everything; hold fast what is good" (v. 21).[3]

That is still cautious but he is beginning to tilt towards acceptance. He then asked what, for him, the universal pastor, were the crucial questions: "Does the Spirit breathe only outside the usual framework of the canonical structure? Has the "Church of the Spirit" left the institutional Church? Is it only in spontaneous groups, as they are called, that we will find the charisms of the real, original, Pentecostal spirituality?"

1 Léon-Joseph Suenens, *A New Pentecost?* 1975.

2 O'Connor, *Pope Paul and the Spirit*, p. 33.

3 Ibid. p. 36.

It was a conclusion he was reluctant to accept. But the influence of the new Suenens grew.

Suenens had lost none of his old skills in handling the media, though his new style puzzled most reporters. Suenens arranged for the next International Conference on Catholic Renewal to take place in Rome in 1975. Hitherto it had always convened at Notre Dame, Indiana, where Kevin Ranaghan had been a theology professor. Notre Dame, though not exactly a ghetto, was cut off from the world. Suenens also arranged for it to be back to back with the International Mariological and Marian Conferences also due in 1975. He thus established a correlation between Mary and the Holy Spirit that Paul liked and soon adopted.[1]

While Paul was discovering the Spirit, one of the most significant ecumenical events in the pontificate took place on 5–10 May 1973. The visit to Rome of his holiness Amba Shenouda III, Pope of Alexandria and Patriarch of the Church (of the Preaching) of St Mark was a step towards healing the breach between the Coptic Church and Rome that had existed for over sixteen centuries. Shenouda III's remote predecessor, Dioscorus, was condemned by the Council of Chalcedon in 451, after which the Egyptian (Coptic) Church became formally Monophysite and increasingly isolated from the rest of the Christian world.

Its isolation was intensified after the Muslim Arab invasion of 642. Though it enjoyed long periods of relative calm, persecution was savage under the Caliph el Hakim (996–1021) who destroyed over 3000 churches and induced many Copts to apostatize. Religious freedom really only came when the British replaced the Turks as occupiers after the battle of Tel-el-Kebir in 1881. Muslims and Coptic Christians were held to be equal before the law and even put out a joint flag which included both the cross and the crescent. Islam in Egypt possessed a relaxed quality that came from being a very ancient civilization.

Paul VI and the Secretariat for Christian Unity had been steadily building up the relationship with the Coptic Church which began when it accepted Pope John XXIII's invitation to send "observers" to Vatican II. Two of them were among the bishops accompanying Shenouda in 1973.[2] In 1968 Paul VI had returned the relics of St Mark to Cairo where the new cathedral of St Mark was inaugurated in June 1968.[3] This gesture improved the atmosphere, a pilgrimage of Copts visited Rome in 1969, and a Vatican delegation was present at the enthronement of Patriarch Shenouda III.

Meanwhile the theological dialogue had advanced to the point at

1 Ibid. p. 45.

2 *Insegnamenti*, p. 413.

3 Ibid. p. 416.

which a common declaration could be signed expressing the faith of the first three ecumenical councils. It mattered enormously that St Athanasius, Bishop of Alexandria, was a figure revered both in Egypt and in the universal Church. Present at the Council of Nicaea in 325, he became the hammer of the Arians, challenging successive emperors and spending forty years in exile including a period in Rome where he was welcomed by Pope Julius I. He was the original "pillar of the church" (a Coptic title). Said Paul VI: "He professed his faith in the divinity of Christ before the powerful and those in error, so much so that the Oriental liturgy describes him as 'the pillar of true faith', while the Catholic Church counts him among its doctors."[1]

Besides Athanasius, St Cyril of Alexandria also belonged to the universal Church. And Paul concluded the principles of religious life taught by St Anthony in the desert influenced the whole Christian world.

There was every reason to believe at this date that the first post-Vatican II realization of unity would be with the Coptic Church with its six million members. Pope Shenouda III, who had been lodged in the Torre San Giovanni (that Pope John had restored for his own use), was delighted with his welcome.

But there were reasons for disquiet, little clouds that could build up into blacker ones. The Common Declaration said nothing about the papal primacy but spared a thought for "the suffering and homeless Palestinian people". Another strange silence concerned the *Catholic* Coptic Church which came into being in 1741 when the Coptic Bishop of Jerusalem became a Catholic. By 1973 it numbered some 200,000 and its leader, Patriarch Sidarouss, felt squeezed out of these negotiations. There was a political dimension too. President Anwar Sadat, who succeeded Nasser in 1970, in July 1972 threw out his Soviet advisers and turned for finance to Saudi Arabia and other oil-rich Gulf States.[2]

Coptic Christians always had a tradition of patriotism, claiming indeed to be the "original" Egyptians, and in the October 1973 war against Israel "texts from the Koran and the Gospels were cited side by side", while Muslim and Christian names were inscribed on the pyramid containing the tomb of Egypt's Unknown Soldier, which proclaims: "None can fix the rank or religion of this dear symbol: he is no more than an Egyptian soldier."[3] He was also more likely than not to be a

1 Ibid. p. 408.

2 Paul Johnson, *A History of the Modern World from 1917 to the 1980s*, pp. 667–68.

3 William Soliman Kilada, "Christian–Muslim Relations in Egypt", in *The Vatican, Islam and the Middle East*, ed. Kail C. Ellis, Syracuse University Press 1987, pp. 258–59. Copts claim to represent the uniquely Egyptian sensibility. The names of the months used by the Egyptian *fellah* are those used in ancient Egypt and correspond to

defeated soldier. The Israelis won yet another victory in October 1973. Paul denounced this war more fiercely than ever before as "irrational", and thought he saw one more "the lamentable symptoms" which presaged the war of 1939.[1]

A less onerous decision was whether to call a Holy Year in 1975 as tradition demanded. It began in 1300 and in recent times had been held every twenty-five years. Paul remembered the Holy Years of 1925 and 1950, considered how much water had flowed under Tiber bridges in the intervening years, thought how much the Church had changed, and wondered whether to go ahead. "We have asked ourselves," he agonized on 9 May 1973, "if such a tradition should be maintained at a time which is so different from times gone by".[2]

1950 had been a triumphalistic celebration of post-war freedom to travel. But one could press the tradition for some theological content. The "jubilee" was based on the Jewish idea of setting aside a "year of special public observance, with abstention from work, a return to the original distribution of land, the cancellation of debt and the freeing of Hebrew slaves". There were plenty of slaves who needed freeing. Land redistribution was a matter of justice in Brazil, for example. Cancelling debts of Third World countries – technically called "rescheduling" – was implied by *Populorum Progressio*. So why not reanimate the tradition and give it contemporary relevance?

There was the usual Paul VI scruple. He knew some of the Dutch and North Americans would resent it as another Rome-centred and Pope-centred exercise that was anomalous in the post-conciliar collegial Church. The Holy Year was an act of the monarchical papacy, not of the new, post-conciliar, consultative, collegial, Petrine-ministry papacy. However Suenens was no longer raising this objection. On the contrary he was telling Paul to use this opportunity to the full, and make the Holy Year a charismatic and Marian year.

That settled it. Paul made his decision in May 1973 and explained that it would start in the local Churches before moving to Rome. He essayed a bold metaphor:

> The fact that the Holy Year unfolds its sails in the individual local Churches precisely on the blessed day of Pentecost is not without significance. It is in order that believing mankind may

the calendar of the Coptic Church. One of the rivers of Paradise is Gihon (Genesis 2:13), the name of the Nile in Coptic liturgical prayers. On the other hand the liturgical text is written in two columns with Coptic already the Arabic which is in everyday use.

1 Jacques Dupuy, *La diplomatie du Saint-Siège*, pp. 118–19.

2 *Insegnamenti*, 1973, p. 450.

> be carried in a single direction, and with harmonious emulation, towards the new goal of Christian history, its eschatological "harbour", by a new current or movement that will be truly "pneumatic", that is, "charismatic".[1]

"Charismatic" has lost its power to do harm. It no longer needs qualification. Suenens won another battle. The theme of the Holy Year would be Reconciliation all round.

Paul put the Flemish aristocrat, seventy-one-year-old Cardinal Maximilien de Furstenberg, in charge of the planning. Organizing a Holy Year is rather like mobilizing an army with a count-down to Holy Year Day. Furstenberg caught the prevailing charismatic breeze and claimed that the idea of Holy Year 1975 was prompted by the Holy Spirit. He added, with no sense of irony: "Of course, even granting the primacy of the Holy Spirit, we need a certain amount of organization and a co-ordination to serve the Spirit and meet the needs of the Church community." The Holy Spirit is commended for having got the show on the road; but then the organization men took over.[2] The Holy Year was on its way. It would be interestingly different.

Important as all these questions were, they were not so close to his heart as the "truce with artists" he proclaimed in the Sistine Chapel on 23 June 1973. Two hundred and fifty artists, if we are to believe Don Pasquale Macchi, volunteered to sent works which were intended to answer the question: Is there a valid modern religious art as distinct from "sacred art" which belongs in the liturgy? If the Vatican collection does not quite answer this question, perhaps that it is because it is unanswerable. Francis Bacon's *Study for a Pope* was "religious" only in a very extrinsic sense.

Opening the exhibition, Paul remembered his reading from the 1930s. "The modern artist," he said, "seeks within himself the motifs for his work." Moreover modern art is not easily accessible, "the paths leading to immediate comprehension are no longer our paths". But there was a plangent note of repentance about this speech, as though Paul were apologizing for all the incomprehension the Church had visited upon artists:

> We have sought for oleographs and works of little artistic or real value, perhaps because we have not had the means to understand great things, beautiful things . . . We have walked

1 O'Connor, *Pope Paul and the Holy Spirit*, p. 36.

2 The quote and the comment come from Peter Hebblethwaite, *The Runaway Church*, p. 23. The priggish author thought that "the Holy Year of 1975 appeared as something of an anachronism, deliberately cultivated to encourage a faction within the Church", p. 24.

> along crooked paths where art and beauty and the worship of God have been badly served . . . Shall we make peace again? Here, today? It must be left to you to sing the free and powerful song of which you are capable.[1]

This passage was quoted by Sir John Rothenstein, former director of the Tate Gallery in London, in his review of the exhibition in *The Times*.[2] He was most impressed by Giacomo Manzù's life-size statues of St Ambrose and St Charles Borromeo – "a miraculous fusion of elegance and piety, the work of an agnostic". In fact of a Communist. Sir John thought the Vatican Museum of Modern Art would be deluged with indifferent works, and recommended a "firm hand". That was in June.

On 3–7 July Archbishop Agostino Casaroli attended the Conference on Security and Co-operation in Europe (CSCE). This was the first time the Holy See had taken part in an international conference since the Congress of Vienna in 1815. Paul was delighted at this return to the international scene for which he had worked so hard. He did not exaggerate the contribution the Holy See might make; yet he believed its presence would "underline the pre-eminent place of moral factors" in the arduous enterprise of bringing peace and security to the whole of Europe, East and West.[3]

Paul placed great confidence in the diplomatic skills of Archbishop Agostino Casaroli. He was patient, thorough, steady, witty, capable of mastering any brief that was given him. Casaroli addressed the Helsinki conference on 6 July 1973. At the Angelus two days later Paul rejoiced that it had enabled "the *magisterium* of the Holy See" (an unusual expression) to make its voice heard.[4] But Helsinki still had a long way to go. On Paul's instructions Casaroli worked closely with Aldo Moro, then Italian Prime Minister. He also met Dr Garrett Fitzgerald, Ireland's Foreign Minister.

Getting a hearing for the voice of the *magisterium* was an increasing concern of Paul VI. On the tenth anniversary of his election as pope, 22 June, the world press was generally kind but the Italian press was ruthlessly cruel. Some of the assessments of his ten years as pope read like obituaries. He was considered already dead, a useless obstacle to progress. In the Italian context the anti-divorce campaign, for which he was not directly responsible, led to accusations of obscurantism and

1 *Insegnamenti*, 1973, pp. 648–49.

2 "Modern Art in the Vatican", *The Times*, 18 September 1974. Rothenstein was a Catholic convert, and discussed aesthetic matters with Vincent Turner SJ, for many years senior tutor at Campion Hall, Oxford.

3 *Insegnamenti*, 1973, p. 640.

4 Ibid. p. 712.

mediaevalism from people whose notion of the Middle Ages was sketchy to say the least. He soldiered on, for the most part alone.

Perhaps the Synod, due in 1974, would come to his aid and rescue him from the sense of being assailed on all sides.

35

The Italian Factor

> Montini the intellectual was well known for weighing up indefinitely every aspect of a question before making a decision. He saw all too clearly the infinite complexity of situations, and his mind was too subtle to admit the reduction of people or things to schematic bare bones. His contemplative temperament sometimes gave the impression that he ignored the constraints of reality. It was rather that he saw beyond the immediate day-to-day questions, and tried to force reality to conform to his demands. (ACHILLE SILVESTRINI, *Les Réformes Institutionnelles*, p. 11)

"We think in centuries here" is a claim frequently heard in the Vatican. Certainly centenaries are marked with special fervour and 1974 was the 700th anniversary of the Council of Lyons. This 1274 Council had great importance for East–West or Catholic–Orthodox relations, which had not yet finally hardened into unresolvable opposition. The Council of Lyons simultaneously took a step towards the Orthodox and another away from them: it accepted the "Unionist" profession of faith from the Byzantine Emperor, Michael VIII Palaeologus; but it also solemnly defined the *Filioque*, the clause in the Creed which confesses that the Holy Spirit proceeds "from the Father *and the Son*". The Greeks thought this an illegitimate addition. They had not changed their minds in the twentieth century. Paul VI had already decided to send Cardinal Jan Willebrands to Lyons for the celebrations; but what message would he take?

What Achille Silvestrini calls the "constraints of reality" tightened their grip on Paul in 1974 as the world obstinately failed to conform to his demands. The parlousness of the Vatican's financial situation came home to him. It proved vastly expensive to run the "new Curia", which needed much jet-travel to realize the "consultation" everyone called for in theory but sometimes jibbed at in practice. Archbishop Paul Marcinkus tried to solve the jet travel problem by fixing a deal with Catintours, a Rome travel agent.

All curial dicasteries held plenary sessions in which the participation of diocesan bishops was regarded as symbolically important, if no more. Since the Council the bureaucracy had doubled. Synods were a further expense. A high price was paid for collegiality.

Peter's Pence – the annual collection for the pope's needs – had declined since the Council and was often used as an index of Paul's unpopularity. The investments of APSA (the money received from Italy in 1929 in "compensation" for the loss of the Papal States) failed to cover the shortfall. Paul persisted in the belief that the Istituto per gli Opere di Religione (IOR), popularly but mistakenly called the "Vatican Bank", should bail it out.

Cardinal Di Jorio, a formidable figure who shrouded the affairs of the IOR in impenetrable mystery, refused point-blank. "We are independent," he declared, and Paul had to give in to him. In 1971 Paul had replaced Di Jorio with his protége Paul Casimir Marcinkus who had been at the bank since 1968. Paul made this appointment though knowing that Giovanni Benelli, his right-hand man, considered Marcinkus too "American" – that is, uncultivated and unsophisticated. Cardinal Jean Villot, Secretary of State, was theoretically President of APSA, but knew nothing about the financial dealings of IOR even though he sat on its board. Villot was still trying to understand Vatican finances.

With the international press demanding transparency, the habit of never issuing *démentis* when grotesque statements were made about the vast, unknown wealth of the Vatican, made matters worse. "The Pope," said Villot, "should treat them either with more humour or with more energy. But he merely says things like, 'Yes, there's something in that charge,' or 'Yes, we do lend ourselves to that accusation.' "[1] That intensified the rumours.

There was not much the Pope could do about the IOR. The money invested in it, mostly by religious orders, episcopal conferences or Catholic organizations, did not belong to the Holy See, and therefore could not be diverted to cover the deficit of APSA. Marcinkus at IOR cherished the independence of the IOR as much as Di Jorio had done.

APSA was another matter. The "patrimony of the Holy See" was his direct responsibility. It was, literally, the inheritance of the Papal States. Most of the enterprises APSA owned or invested in were in Italy. Paul now decided that henceforward it should not be the dominant partner in any given firm, and that its investments should be spread around different countries so that it could not be blamed for the

1 Antoine Wenger, *Le Cardinal Villot*, p. 114.

economic problems of any one of them. That meant selling shares and companies. The man brought in to do this was Michele Sindona, a Sicilian self-made banker.

This was a fatal move. Sindona's links with the Mafia and Liceo Gelli's pseudo-masonic lodge, P-2, were unknown at the time (though not unsuspected). In any event Sindona's first act was to acquire *Generale Immobiliare*[1] for himself. The Watergate complex in Washington was financed by it. However if Archbishop Paul Marcinkus is to be believed Sindona worked exclusively on behalf of APSA. Marcinkus claims to have warned him as he went to the United States: "Hey! You operate over there like you operate in Italy, and you'll end up in jail."[2] That was prophetic.

It was soon verified. In 1974 Sindona's luck ran out. His US-based Franklin National Bank collapsed, but before that could be dealt with he was brought back to Italy to answer charges about what Italians vividly call the "crack" of the *Banca Privata Finanzaria*. One collapse could be bad luck; two looked like sheer carelessness. Another Milanese banker and friend of Don Pasquale Macchi, Roberto Calvi, President of the prestigious Banco Ambrosiano of Milan, replaced the imprisoned Sindona as financial adviser to the Vatican. This locked the IOR into the fate of the Banco Ambrosiano of Milan, and thus remotely prepared the tragedy of 1982. And once more Archbishop Marcinkus wriggled to defend himself: "I never did *one* bit of business with Calvi," he said in 1988, adding lamely, "but my office did."[3]

In 1974 Paul came up against the "constraints of reality" in other ways. Was Italy a Catholic country any more? As already mentioned, until 1970 there had been no divorce in Italy, and Italian law backed up canon law. The law permitting divorce was proposed by a Socialist Fortuna and a Liberal Baslini and hastily pushed through Parliament in December 1970. The campaign for and against the Fortuna-Baslini law culminating in the referendum of 12 May 1974 was a revelation: 59.1 per cent voted to keep the existing divorce law, while 40.9 per cent voted for its repeal.

The referendum marked the end of neo-Christendom in post-war Italy and declared that the nation was now quite evidently secularized and pluralistic. This had important consequences for how the Gospel could be handed on in a secularizing world. Paul VI was disconcerted by the result. It gave the theme chosen for the Synod in the autumn – Evangelization in the Modern World – a fresh urgency.

1 Ibid. p. 207.

2 John Cornwell, *A Thief in the Night*, p. 99.

3 Ibid. p. 98.

Yet there was much argument about the meaning of the referendum and the lessons to be drawn from it. Throughout 1972–73 the Vatican had tried to get the law repealed by quiet negotiation, as it had every right to do. For divorce was not an internal matter concerning Italy alone. Article 34 of the 1929 Concordat affirms that the Italian state "wishing to reinvest the institution of marriage, which is the basis of the family, with the dignity conformable to the Catholic traditions of its people, recognizes the sacrament of matrimony performed according to canon law as fully effective in civil law".[1]

The Concordat was still in force in 1974. The Vatican did not want a referendum not because it thought it might lose but because it was a blunt and inappropriate instrument for dealing with such delicate matters, and because it would be bound to revive the clerical versus anti-clerical conflicts characteristic of the nineteenth century. From Milan where he was now Rector of the Catholic University, Giuseppe Lazzati wrote to Paul VI warning him presciently what would happen.

But the anti-divorce enthusiasts now had the bit between their teeth. A national Committee for a Referendum on Divorce (CNRD) was set up by Dr Gabrio Lombardi, younger brother of Padre Riccardo Lombardi, "God's microphone". Within a short time they collected 1,370,134 signatures – a million was enough to demand a referendum as a constitutional right.

But still the Christian Democrats hesitated. A referendum campaign would not stick to divorce: it would range over all Church–State issues, casting them as heartless "mediaeval" obscurantists trying Canute-like to stem the tide of progress, while the Communists and other "lay parties" could pose as the champions of freedom of conscience seeking only to modernize Italy and make it a fully adult member of the European Economic Community.

But the Christian Democrats were not united. Amintore Fanfani, political secretary of the Party, thought that political capital could be made out of a referendum. He believed it would reinforce "the political unity" of Italian Catholics, by which was meant their support for the Christian Democrats. He calculated that it would split the working-class, mainly Communist, vote, since on a Christian "moral issue" even Communists would not want the break-up of the Italian family to which, according to the clergy, divorce inevitably led. "Political unity" would be further reinforced, Fanfani believed, by the fact that the Italian bishops would feel obliged to throw themselves into the referendum

1 Tr. in Hyginus Eugene Cardinale, *The Holy See and the International Order*, p. 338.

campaign in order to "save Italy for God".[1] All these political calculations were wrong.

What did Paul think? Publicly he remained inscrutable, judging it constitutionally improper to intervene in an Italian *political* question. For the question was not "Does Catholic doctrine permit divorce?" The answer to that was evidently no, and anyway it was not a matter to be settled by a vote. The real question was "What makes for *good law* in the Italy of 1974?" Unfortunately in the heat of debate the two questions were bound to be confused. It was often said that Giovanni Benelli, reputed to be "close to Fanfani", was in favour of the referendum and threw all his energies into winning it. But Benelli privately denied this. His only contact with Fanfani in 1973 had been at the wedding of his daughter and the reception afterwards at the Hilton Hotel.[2]

Here is what Benelli said at the time:

> There were great pressures from some parts of Christian Democracy and some of the Bishops to get the Pope, and us, to accept our responsibility and go for the referendum. But Paul VI said from the outset that the responsibility lay with the Italian Bishops and not with us. DC wanted to know just one thing: if they decided to hold a referendum, would the Church support it and what would be the attitude of the Bishops? The presidency of CEI (the Italian Episcopal Conference) met and Casaroli and I went along. I spoke against a referendum and Casaroli did the same. We foresaw the danger of polarization, the mobilization of dissent, perhaps defeat. I suggested another way of reforming the Fortuna–Baslini proposal by using Carrettoni's project. Other members of CEI agreed with us: the whole enterprise was too risky. (Enrico) Bartoletti, secretary of CEI, was of the same mind.
>
> But he couldn't oppose his superior, Cardinal (Antonio) Poma, who said that the pastoral judgement should prevail over the diplomatic judgement, and that the responsibility of the Italian Church prevailed over that of the Holy See, and that the consequences for the Concordat should not be overlooked.

1 Giancarlo Zizola, "L'Eglise Catholique et le divorce en Italie", in *Concilium*, 100, December 1990. Also Giuseppe De Rosa SJ, "Learning the Hard Way: The Divorce Referendum in Italy", *Month*, August 1974, pp. 668–71.

2 Giancarlo Zizola, "*Il mio amico Onnipotente*", in *Panorama*, 15 November 1982, pp. 92–99. This revealed for the first time that Benelli was in the habit of dropping in on Zizola, then the *Vaticanista* of *Il Giorno*, and talking freely about whatever was on his mind.

> CEI therefore decided: it could not fail to make a statement on the principles of marriage if it came to a referendum. But the decision whether or not to hold a referendum belonged solely to DC, because of its political nature. DC, however, could rest assured that if they went for the referendum, they would have the backing of the Bishops they wanted.

What did Paul VI make of all this passing the buck or Pontius Pilate hand-washing?

Personally he could not see why Catholics should refrain from trying to remove a law contrary to the indissolubility of marriage. But he was ready to respect the judgement of the Italian bishops, whatever it might be. He went along to the offices of CEI on 8 May 1974 and said that, as an Italian bishop, he endorsed *their* decision. But it was *not* his decision.

It was only four days before the referendum was due. Paul had good reason for going to the Domus Aurea on the via Aurelia to bless the new headquarters of CEI. Cardinal Antonio Poma, as president of CEI, in his customary address of homage, alluded to the "grave and impending event" of the referendum. "Most people", he claimed, had welcomed the bishops' effort to "illumine the conscience of the faithful". Poma went on: "Unfortunately some have rejected this invitation and consider our intervention misplaced (*abusivo*). This causes us great pain."

He was referring to groups called "Dissenting Catholics" and "Critical Catholics" who thought they formed "base communities" on the Latin American model. They included priests like Don Giovanni Franzoni, former Abbot of St Paul's-without-the-Walls who was suspended ("No doubt milder form of hanging", as *1066 and All That* put it), and Gregorian sociology professor Emil Pin who was charismatically dismissed from the Society of Jesus by Arrupe.

Paul made no mention of such dissidents in his reply. They might just as well not have existed. It almost seemed he might get away without mentioning the referendum at all. He praised the Italian bishops for their growing maturity. He detected promising signs of renewal in the Italian Church. He produced a rhetorical flourish based on St Ignatius of Antioch: "Priests should be in accord with their bishops like the strings of a harp." Then, only then, did he pronounce the one sentence the media were waiting for:

> We cannot at this time remain silent concerning our complete adhesion to the position taken – out of fidelity to the Gospel and the constant *magisterium* of the universal Church – by the Italian Bishops in the present circumstances for the defence and

> religious, moral, civil, social and juridical promotion of the family.[1]

Hardly a ringing clarion-call. Just the twang of a harp. Few understood the reasons for his discretion. Yet this last-minute "intervention" in the national debate was enough to rouse the ire of the "lay" parties without inspiring the masses or mobilizing the anti-divorce campaigners and the Christian Democrats. The *Comunione e Liberazione* movement regarded him henceforward as wet and wimpish, and began to cast about for a more robust successor.

On the eve of the vote he addressed Alcoholics Anonymous, praising Matt Talbot, a celebrated reformed drinker from Dublin. On 12 May, the fateful Sunday, he confined himself to imploring the help of Our Lady.

At his next Wednesday audience Paul looked out over the blushing faces of newly married couples and could not avoid some comment on the devastating referendum result. He chose the mode of pathos:

> Alas, what brings us astonishment and grief is that the due solidarity in supporting the good and right cause of the indissolubility of marriage was lacking in not a few (*non pochi*) priests. We must suppose that these priests acted without being fully aware of the grave consequences of their actions . . . The law of God and of the Church has not changed.[2]

Alas, the incriminated and suspended clerics might reply, it is the Pope who has failed to realize that Italian society has changed. The referendum proved the depth and extent of the change. Looking for scapegoats gets in the way of understanding.

Giuseppe De Rosa SJ offered a first attempt to substitute analysis for lamentation:

> For the Church, the referendum has been a painful trial for all concerned: for the bishops who have found themselves neither followed nor listened to, and have been criticized as "preconciliar" by some Catholics; for the many faithful who have suffered an inner tug-of-war between fidelity to the directives of the episcopate and their own convictions; from the whole Christian community, which has emerged from the trial of the referendum divided and disturbed.[3]

He was too kind to refer to the effect on Pope Paul.

1 Ibid. p. 411.

2 Ibid. pp. 428–29.

3 Giuseppe De Rosa, "Learning the Hard Way", *Month*, August 1974, p. 671.

The sense of an old order passing away was enhanced by the death of an old friend, Aldo Carpi, painter and director of the Brera Academy in Milan, who had survived the Nazi death camp of Gusen.[1] Paul treasured two gifts from Carpi: an oil painting of the boatman encouraging an exhausted pope with a wave of the arm; and the MS of his concentration camp diaries. The painting reversed the usual cliché of the pope as the intrepid helmsman; and the diaries taught him how "goodness can grow more profound in the midst of hatred, cruelty and oppression".[2]

Yet what Archbishop Silvestrini calls the "constraints of reality" tightened their grip on Paul in 1974 as life failed to conform to his wishes. No pope operates in a sociological vacuum, and in 1974 two crises left him perplexed. The right-wing opposition, especially in France, said he had betrayed the Church and thrown away the papal inheritance by abandoning what was called "the Mass of St Pius V" – the Dominican pope who excommunicated Elizabeth I in 1570, shattered the Turks in the battle of Lepanto the following year, and then sanctioned the form of Eucharistic worship that had endured until Paul's Missal of 1969. The opposition was by no means confined to Archbishop Marcel Lefebvre and his followers,[3] but they were its chief representatives.

Yet the material realities could not be ignored. The Calvi scandal did not break until after Paul's death. But Sindona was trouble enough. The IOR was badly burnt. Its total losses were estimated at $200 million, sustained through the Banco di Roma per la Svizzera, owned half and half by Opus Dei and the Banco di Roma. Opus Dei's founder, Msgr Escrivá de Balanguer, believing that one good turn deserved another, chose this moment to press Paul VI to make Opus Dei a "personal prelature". Though happy enough with the status of "secular institute" as long as it was unique in the genre, Opus Dei now sought to improve its status. There were too many secular institutes for comfort. The field was rather too crowded.

According to the official Opus Dei account, "the Holy Father [Paul

1 Paul VI recalled Carpi's *Diario di Gusen* in his address for World Peace Day 1974, remarking that the eighty-year-old painter had died "some months ago" (*Insegnamenti*, XII, 1974, p. 9). He set Carpi alongside Gandhi and Albert Schweitzer as "one of the individuals who changed the world". Carpi taught him "the possibility of love in the midst of hatred, and a sense of justice that transcends merely making claims to become self-giving in the service of others, with patience, humility and sheer goodness".

2 *Insegnamenti*, 1974, p. 9.

3 Yves Congar mentions also the abbé Coache, abbé Barbara, Msgr Ducaud-Bourget (I remember this apple-cheeked eighty-year-old at the conclaves of 1978). There was also a scurrilous publication, *Le Courrier de Rome*, that smelled out heresy in every liturgical change. Yves Congar, *Challenge to the Church, The Case of Archbishop Lefebvre*, ET, preface by George Patrick Dwyer, Archbishop of Birmingham, Collins, 1977, p. 25.

VI] was very happy about the progress of the General Congress, and encouraged our Father to continue it".[1] But this was really a brush-off. Each time the substantive question was raised about the status of Opus Dei in 1976 and 1978, Paul VI always said "the question remained open" (*la questione rimaneva aperta*). This suggested he was unlikely to conclude it. He left that to his successors.[2]

One good reason Paul VI was unwilling to accede to the Opus Dei request was that they had tried to buy influence in the Vatican. Escrivá dangled before Paul's eyes a solution to his financial problems: Opus Dei undertook to take over 30 per cent of the running costs of the Vatican. The scheme came to naught because of disagreements about how the money should be transferred. The Vatican wanted it to come directly to the IOR through the Banco Ambrosiano; Opus Dei preferred to route it through the various banks controlled by Rumasa (the firm of José Maria Ruiz-Mateos, then a member of Opus Dei).[3]

Paul VI, sensitive and scrupulous by nature, was worried by the financial crisis in itself and by a solution which smacked of simony. He had talked about "the Church and the poor" and been critical of capitalism in *Populorum Progressio*, but now he was invited to ally the Church with international capitalism to finance its renewal. It was more than a paradox. It was a terrible cross to bear, made all the more intolerable because he could not speak about it.

An astute witness, Michael Campbell-Johnston, recently arrived in Rome from Latin America as Fr Pedro Arrupe's assistant for social questions, captured the atmosphere of the time:

A survey recently published in Italy has accused the Vatican

1 *Transformazione dell'Opus Dei in Prelatura Personale*, MS, p. 5. This request for the status of personal prelature was sent from Alvarez del Portillo to Cardinal Sebastiano Baggio in his capacity as Prefect of the Congregation of Bishops. Although del Portillo's covering letter is dated 23 April 1979 it refers to a decision of the new Pope, John Paul II, on 15 November 1978 to "resolve urgently the juridical position of Opus Dei". The contrast between Paul VI's foot-dragging and John Paul II's brisk enthusiasm is striking. Opus Dei was finally recognized as a personal prelature, a unique example of the *genre*, with a declaration of the Congregation of Bishops dated 23 August 1982.

2 There is a famous story about Pope Benedict XIV (1740–58) who made an impact on the eighteenth century in the way Pope John XXIII did on the twentieth. A fanatical monk appeared before him claiming that Anti-Christ was born in the Ambruzzi mountains. "And how old is Anti-Christ now?" enquired the Pope. On being told that he was three years old, Benedict sighed and said: "In that case, my successor can see to him." Maurice Andrieux, *Everyday Life in Papal Rome*, p. 36.

3 Michael Walsh, *The Secret World of Opus Dei*, Grafton Books 1989, pp. 147, 155. At one point Ruiz-Mateos owned 245 companies including the chain stores Galerioas Preciados and Sears Roebuck and, in Britain, the Augustus Barnett chain of off licences. Rumasa's enterprises collapsed in 1983. Three years later Opus Dei virtually disowned him. Ibid. pp. 156–67.

> not only of owning more than a quarter of Rome's real estate, but of carrying out a highly profitable tax-free business in land speculation. I suppose any institution is subject to abuses, and the Vatican may be far less venal than most. But the impression is of high level intrigue, jockeying for power, shady deals and unworthy compromises, all fanned by a continuously circulating flow of rumours.

That was how the Vatican's involvement was perceived. There was little Paul could do about it. But Villot was right to say his ambition was to eliminate, or at any rate reduce, the level of shady deals and unworthy compromises. Perhaps it was a task beyond Hercules.

Don Pasquale Macchi, his secretary, provides a glimpse of Paul VI's prayer life at this time to set against the obsession with financial matters that concerned the media more than the Curia. From the French novelist, Georges Bernanos, he drew the idea that the aim of prayer was to learn to say "Our Father", but to say it as if for the first time and then to lose oneself in the experience. "Our Father" was his *mantra* this 18 July 1974.

The celebration of the centenary of Lyons, 1274 raised the fundamental question: what really belongs to the *essence* of the Church? For one must not "impose more than is necessary". Paul's task – better ministry and mission – was to remove needless obstacles to union. In his 5 October letter to Cardinal Willebrands he referred to the 1274 Council of Lyons as "the sixth of the General Synods held in the *Western* World", thus not including it in the series of fully ecumenical Councils. Moreover he admitted that at Lyons "the Greek Church had no chance to express itself freely", and declared that "the unity it envisaged could not be accepted completely by the mind-set [*la mentalité*] of the Oriental Churches".[1]

Paul was here going a stage further than in the brief *Anno Ineunte* in 1967 when he recognized the Orthodox Church as a "sister Church" and Athenagoras as a "brother Patriarch". The implication of his remarks about Lyons appeared to be that Latin dogmas, so solemnly proclaimed and insisted upon in the past, did not have universal relevance, and were not to be imposed as a condition of union. Did this mean that such dogmas were to be regarded as what the Greeks called *theologoumena*, theological positions taken up by theologians without formal ecclesiastical sanction? That would be to go too far, no doubt. But Paul's words indicated an approach which threw new light on papal authority and suggested that it could be limited by some self-denying

1 Alexander Meyendorff in *A Pope for All Christians?* ed. Peter McCord, p. 140.

ordinance. A pope might say: "I do not deny the power of jurisdiction and the charism of infallibility invested in the primatial office, but for the greater good of the whole *oekumene* I do not propose to exercise them."

However the necessity of a primacy became clear during the autumn Synod on Evangelization in the Contemporary World. This theme turned out to be very controversial, since in fact it was an invitation to tackle the question of liberation theology, as the following passage from its preparatory document (*Lineamenta*) made clear:

> There are those who describe evangelization as though it were something only on the spiritual and religious level, meant only to free men from the bonds of sin. Others, however, describe Christ as the new Moses and consider the Gospel is ordered only towards human development, at least in the present moment of human history.

At this point a new actor entered the scene whose importance was not realized at the time: Cardinal Karol Wojtyla. Frustrated in his desire to have a Synod on marriage, he was named *relator* as a sop. The *relator*'s task was to give a position-paper on the theological aspects of evangelization, to draw the conclusions from the debate and to work on the final report.

Cardinal Wojtyla's paper disappointed the Latin Americans. Their report on experiences presented by Cardinal Edouardo Pironio, President of CELAM, was about popular religion, base communities, the liberation movement, new ministries – in short all the exciting developments that had flowed from Medellín in 1968. Wojtyla's paper disappointed the Africans too, who emerged at this 1974 Synod as mature Churches ready to make their contribution to the universal Church: they wanted to discuss colonialism, *apartheid*, Africanization (described by the ugly neologism "indigenization"), political ideologies and "frontier evangelization".

Cardinal Wojtyla's paper was a disappointment because it was supposed to be *in response* to these continent-by-continent reports. But this it could not be, since it had been written in advance with the help of the Kraków theologian, Józef Tischner, during their summer holidays in the Masurian Lakes. So instead of the "signs of the times" approach to evangelization developed by the Latin Americans, Cardinal Wojtyla tried to take the Synod back to the old deductive method in which pastoral experience was of secondary value.

For Wojtyla the starting point of evangelization is Christ's mandate to the Apostles, and it is continued through the mission of bishops and pastors. It consists in "conversion and liberation" by the power of the sacraments, but the "liberation" in view is from sin and Satan, and "conversion" consists in rejecting the "world" and its false values. True, proclaiming the Gospel does have socio-political implications, but these are of their nature *indirect*.

To make matters worse the Wojtyla approach prevailed in the final document, with the effect that the Synod rejected it. The result was *impasse*. But it was not tragic. "The rejection of the final text of the Synod of 1974," wrote Jan Grootaers, "was a sign of the dynamic vigour of the younger Churches."[1] Msgr Jean Guy Rakotondravahatra, Bishop of Ihosy, Madagascar, summed up the reasons for optimism:

> We have had a chance, for the first time ever, to talk about our problems, our desires, our hopes and our eventual disagreements. We have seen that the majority of our colleagues agree with us. The Holy Father has listened to it all. What is the point of reducing the great wealth of our discussions to a few poverty-stricken propositions.[2]

So everything was simply dumped in the papal lap, and Paul was invited to sort it all out. But since "informing the pope" was one of the functions of the Synod, one could not say that collegiality had failed: better honest confusion than hasty papering-over the cracks. To the Pope fell the task of synthesis. He began the dossier that would lead to *Evangelii Nuntiandi*.[3]

After the Synod the Jesuits met on 1 December 1974 for the 32nd General Congregation. There were many signs that Paul was unhappy with the Jesuits. The dark clouds that seemed to have passed over in 1966 had now returned, blacker than ever.

The Jesuit General, Don Pedro Arrupe, wearying of incessant attacks from a group of Spanish Jesuits who wanted to set up a breakaway Society faithful – they alleged – to the true spirit of St Ignatius, had consulted the whole Society whether he should call a General Congregation to clear the air. The answer was overwhelmingly positive, so the Jesuits held a General Congregation that did not have to elect a new Superior, a rare event. The unique 32nd General Congregation would either renew Arrupe's mandate or remove him from office. It was a bold step, characteristic of the man.

It was difficult, indeed impossible, not to like Don Pedro Arrupe. He radiated joy and hope, his eyes alert with the love of Christ. The contrast

1 Jan Grootaers, *De Vatican II à Jean-Paul II*, p. 75.

2 Ibid. p. 76. Bishop Patrick Kalilombe, soon to be expelled from Malawi, was the spokesman for East African Episcopal Conference.

3 His farewell speech was very positive, *Insegnamenti*, 1974, pp. 1002–11.

was great with his predecessor, the austere Belgian John Baptist Janssens, a remote bureaucrat, the unseen relayer of *ukases* on Henri de Lubac and Karl Rahner. Arrupe communicated bans when he had to: he held up, for example, John J. McNeill's book on *The Church and the Homosexual* for as long as he decently could.[1] But bans were not his top priority.

Far from staying in Rome he travelled the world encouraging his thirty thousand brethren to rediscover their Jesuit "charism". Study of the founder's charism, fidelity to the Gospel and response to the needs of the modern world: these were the three criteria proposed by *Perfectae Caritatis* for the renewal of religious life.

The Jesuits were able "to go back in order to go forward" because the study of the original sources in *Monumenta Historica Societatis Jesu* and reviews of spirituality like *Manresa* in Spain, *Christus* in France, and latterly *The Way* in Britain, had dusted off the portrait of Ignatius inherited from the nineteenth century. In his *Autobiography*, now revealed for the first time in its authentic text, Ignatius sought to discern the hand of God in the story of his life and everyday things.

In Arrupe's vision the *Spiritual Exercises* were not a set of hoops you jumped through but a school of prayer and the key to Jesuit identity. They threw light on the *Constitutions*, not vice versa. They forged the unity of the Society of Jesus. Jesuits could not be defined by the work they did. They could be defined by their inner spirit. That is what it looked like from the inside, where Don Pedro, a Basque with an extraordinary physical resemblance to his fellow-Basque, Ignatius, was regarded as a "second founder".

Outsiders did not always grasp this. Where Arrupe saw legitimate liberty or necessary risk, they saw mayhem, politicization, the abandonment of traditional works, the move from big barrack-like institutions to small communities, strange theological novelties, opposition to *Humanae Vitae*, endless consultation replacing obedience, notions like "the third way" (deep asexual friendships with women) or the superior-in-the-community replacing the superior-over-the-community. And Arrupe did nothing!

It was not, of course, true that Arrupe did nothing. But his was an enabling authority which released energies as far as possible. He was radical rather than liberal, going to the essentials. He did not believe,

1 John J. McNeill SJ, *The Church and the Homosexual*, Darton, Longman and Todd 1977. The Preface tells the story. Arrupe's final condition was that O'Neill should "make clear where his manuscript differs from the traditional teaching of the Church", p. x. Agence France-Presse constantly used the O'Neill case to prove that Arrupe was "soft on homosexuals".

for instance, that leaving the Society of Jesus was the end of the world or the end of all ministry.

He charismatically dismissed the Dutch poet Huub Oosterhuis, saying, "You can have an excellent ministry as a layman." Arrupe maintained that there were two sorts of departure from the Society: in some cases there was a personal psychological problem that could only be resolved in this way; but others were a symptom of a malaise, an indication that something was wrong with the way the Jesuit life or the priesthood was being lived. He never used the Roman language of "defections" and stayed friends with those who departed. "Ignatian" spirituality was wider than "Jesuit" spirituality, as thousands of sisters and laypeople had discovered.

Perhaps it was this which Paul found most difficult to stomach about Arrupe. For Paul "defections" were a crown of thorns, each one a new thorn pressed down. Yet apparently he "got on well" with Arrupe, who said of their meetings:

> Paul VI's great concern was that the Society should remain faithful, and it is true that we gave him, from time to time, cause for concern. His solicitude, and even sometimes his anxiety, were not just personal – based on his lifelong links with so many Jesuits – but also *ecclesial*. He told me this more than once: the influence of the Society is immense, and what it does affects religious life as a whole and the entire Church. I felt I was with a father who wanted his son to do better. After the audiences, I felt encouraged, even if he had tweaked my ear. Our relationship was always cordial.[1]

Cordial indeed. But Paul's letter to Arrupe of September 1973 and long address to the 32nd General Congregation on 3 December 1974 could hardly be described as cordial or dismissed as a "tweak on the ear".

They were a massive doom-laden warning that Arrupe's stewardship was on the wrong lines. The letter warned him against "new methods of deliberation and decision-taking that not only undermine the very notion of obedience, but alter the very nature of the Society of Jesus itself".[2] It alleged there had been "hazardous and uncontrolled experimentation alien to the very character of the religious family". It referred to "the fact that over the last few years in several parts of the Society tendencies have arisen of an intellectual and disciplinary nature which,

1 Pedro Arrupe, *Itinéraire d'un jésuite*, interviewed by Jean-Claude Dietsch SJ, p. 131. The book was completed just before Don Pedro had the stroke on 7 August 1981 which paralysed him and obliged him to resign.

2 This was a private letter to the Jesuits. It does not appear in *Insegnamenti*.

if fostered and given support, could lead to serious and possibly irreparable changes in the essential structure of your Society".[1] It was a formidable indictment.

Where did the information on which Paul's letter was based come from? Clearly it was not first-hand, for popes cannot have first-hand experience in such matters. It came from the same Spanish Jesuits as before. They had got at Paul via Cardinal Jean Villot, and they demanded Arrupe's resignation. But there were other sources too. Paul refers in his 3 December 1974 address to "pastors of dioceses" (that is, bishops) as the source of the denunciations. They were never lacking.[2]

One effect of these various interventions was to create a total misunderstanding about what the 32nd General Congregation proposed to do about "grades". This was a question the 31st General Congregation had dodged in 1965–66. St Ignatius conceived of the Society of Jesus as a band of "reformed priests" who had a university education, were outstanding (*insignis*) by their personal gifts and – most important of all – had caught the burning spirit of the *Spiritual Exercises*. After a few years, the numbers of those wanting to join this "company" had grown so that Ignatius decided to accept less talented priests and young men who wanted to become priests or lay brothers. These he termed spiritual and temporal coadjutors. They might eventually "make the grade" and become fully professed. They might not. That was in the sixteenth century.

In the twentieth century the distinction had become a dead letter; no one outside the Society knew or cared whether a given Jesuit was professed or not; a high standard of education was required for *all* candidates for ordination; and since the Council, lay brothers came to be treated as equal participants in the Society's work and ministry. Thus the question before the 32nd General Congregation was whether this two-tier system should be abolished since *Perfectae Caritatis* discouraged making distinctions between members of the same religious family. "Most delegates arrived thinking this would be one of the easy issues of the 32nd General Congregation," wrote Brian Daley SJ, "simply a matter of bringing the law up-to-date with life, a change in technicalities."[3]

1 Thomas Corbishley SJ in "The Pope and the Society", *Month*, April 1974, raises a mild query: is the Pope talking about *tendencies* or more or less disconnected incidents? He also saw the funny side of "the ascetical value of community life", p. 358.

2 *Insegnamenti*, 1974, p. 1183. At a dinner for SJ editors Don Pedro described how bishops assailed him with complaints: here a Jesuit said Mass in a boiler-suit, there a Jesuit was a gun-toting guerrilla. "My instinct," he said, "is always to defend you – but please, please make it easier for me to defend you!"

3 Brian Daley SJ, "Identifying Jesuits: The 32nd General Congregation", *Month*, May 1975, p. 147.

After a long process involving prayer and scholarship, sociology and discernment, the 32nd Congregation voted to abolish grades by 228 votes to 8. Far from implying the abolition of the "fourth vow" of obedience to the pope, it meant, on the contrary, its extension to everyone in the Society.

Nor was this a decision of *Fr Arrupe*. So long as the General Congregation was in session, it was sovereign and he was its servant. Then came the shocks. Arrupe was summoned to the Vatican.[1] He took with him Fr Vincent O'Keefe as *socius*, as was the usual practice. But in the antechamber he was curtly told the Pope wanted to see him alone. Msgr Giovanni Benelli stood alongside a grim, unsmiling, frigid Pope Paul. "Take down what Msgr Benelli dictates to you." That was all he said.

Arrupe already guessed: the Jesuits were to make no changes in the matter of grades. As Arrupe left, his eyes filled with tears. Of course the Jesuits would obey. The fourth vow. But the fourth vow was *circa missiones*, when the Pope wanted *something done*. Not this, which was like being asked to be "as obedient as the stick is in the hands of an old man", a false concept of obedience he had refuted as novice-master. Of course St Ignatius said it would take him only fifteen minutes to accept the suppression of the Society. Of course. Of course.

Don Pedro trudged straight back to Borgo Santo Spirito 5 where the Congregation had moved on to other business. Never had Arrupe looked so *demacrado*, said an eye-witness, so emaciated. He told them what was in the letter he would shortly receive from Pope Paul, transcribed from Benelli's dictation: "Therefore, we repeat again, with due respect for you and the Fathers of the Congregation: 'No innovations may be introduced concerning the fourth vow.'"

They took it, if not like lambs, then at least on the chin.

Brian Daley's account of the affair begins tongue-in-cheek: "The 237 delegates to the Jesuits' 32nd General Congregation spent more than three months in Rome this winter, within easy cross-bow range of the Swiss Guards, trying to identify themselves."[2]

Some enemies were within the camp. *Civiltà Cattolica* had carried an article alleging that the abolition of grades was the first step towards turning the Society into a secular institute composed indiscriminately of priests and laymen and, it was whispered, *laywomen*.

Don Pedro explained how he saw it:

1 What follows comes from Pedro Miguel Lamet, *Arrupe*, p. 350, who is quoting Don Pedro in his last years after the death of Paul VI.

2 Brian Daley SJ, "Identifying Jesuits", p. 146.

> The Holy Father intervened only because we hadn't really understood he wanted us to take into account certain points, especially on the subject of "grades". We had thought – and even voted on the assumption – that this was an open question which the members of the Congregation could discuss freely. But for the Holy Father it was a fundamental point of our Institute which could not be changed in any way whatsoever. When I explained his opinion to the fathers of the Congregation, all accepted it without discussion. For me this was one of the finest examples of total obedience in the Society; and I still have a great admiration for that Congregation.[1]

But the story did not end there.

After the 32nd General Congregation had gone home, bloody but unbowed, a letter from Cardinal Jean Villot, Secretary of State, dated 2 May 1975, "drew attention to certain delicate[2] aspects of the decrees that had just been voted". There was the risk of "confusion between the promotion of justice and political commitment", which Arrupe conceded, was a possibility. But he also said: "If we keep decree 4 on the promotion of justice as an essential dimension of preaching the Gospel, then we must expect to have martyrs." A prediction that was soon fulfilled. The Jesuits went, at the Pope's command, wherever the good of the Church demanded. They went to Latin America and were martyred.[3] Frmo the 1970s there were more martyrs in Latin American right-wing regimes than under Communism in Eastern Europe.

Theologians, however, tended to die in their beds. There were many Jesuits on the International Theological Commission (ITC). On 16 December 1974 Paul VI welcomed ITC to Rome for a study session on "The Origins of the Christian Moral Conscience". The topic was chosen because of the controversies that followed *Humanae Vitae* but also because new questions were cropping up in bioethics that needed scientific and philosophical as much as theological clarification. They had two documents before them: *Nine Theses on Christian Ethics* was contributed by Hans Urs von Balthasar; and Heinz Schürmann from East Germany supplied a note on *The Question of the Obligatory Character of the Value Judgements and Moral Directives in the New Testament*.[4]

1 Pedro Arrupe, *Itinéraire d'un jésuite*, pp. 132–33.

2 The Roman term for "awkward" or "I wish you hadn't said that."

3 One of the lesser-known martyrs is my friend Luis Espinal SJ, a Catalan poet from Manresa – yes, where Ignatius' cave is – who performed the remarkable feat of translating Gerard Manley Hopkins into Spanish. His TV documentaries proved too strong for the Franco regime so he went to Bolivia where he was murdered in 1980 as he returned home. A cross was gouged out on his chest.

4 *Texts and Documents*, pp. 105–28.

Could the mediaeval synthesis based on human nature, which implied that some actions were *actus humani* – truly human acts, in accord with human nature, while others fell short – be sustained? In particular, did the linkage established by *Gaudium et Spes* (51) between sexual intercourse and openness to procreation exclude all other forms of sexual (or what was coming to be called "genital") expression? There were pastoral problems here not only about gays and lesbians but about pre-marital intercourse and masturbation. This anticipated the Congregation for the Doctrine of the Faith's declaration, *Personae Humanae* of 29 December 1975. Paul VI was in a hurry, impelled by "the unrestrained glorification of sex" in the media and advertising as much as "the confusion of minds and the corruption of morals".[1]

To help him shift the emphasis to moral theology, Paul had drastically reshaped the ITC. Of the original thirty only thirteen members remained including the Secretary, Louvain professor Philippe Delhaye. This was partly the natural turn-over after the first members had done their five-year stint. But there was also a certain *malaise* among members of the ITC and, on Paul's side, a desire to take a firmer grip on its work.

The *malaise* of the members of ITC concerned their relationship with the Congregation for the Doctrine of the Faith. Cardinal Franjo Seper as Prefect of the CDF refused to relinquish control over doctrinal matters. Period. The theologians complained that for Seper, and those he employed, "integration" into the work of the CDF was another word for subordination to it. Since recruitment to the CDF was largely a matter of co-opting like-minded volunteers after a copious lunch at the Circolo Santa Marta, the idea that it should positively encourage theological research, once upheld, was now, in practice, abandoned.

Among the absent theologians were Yves-Marie Congar and Karl Rahner, who in pre-conciliar days had been the victims of the Holy Office. Rahner resigned because, he said, the ITC was "stewing in its own juice". With Bavarian frankness, not to say brutality, he explained:

> I would have liked the ITC to be seriously consulted on the questions that concerned the CDF. The Prefect at that time, Cardinal Seper, clearly did not want this. So the ITC ended up by being a theologians' club where intelligent theologians intelligently (impotently) dialogued with one another. I felt I didn't need to go to Rome for that. I could do it just as well with my colleagues in Germany ... I can eat ice-cream in

1 These phrases come from the Declaration on Certain Problems of Sexual Ethics, *Personae Humanae*, ed. Flannery, *More Post-conciliar Documents*, II, p. 486.

> Germany too, excellent though the ice-cream of Rome may be.[1]

Rahner recommended a very good ice-cream shop near the Piazza Navona.

The function of the Commission was to monitor and improve documents prepared by the CDF. The CDF took the opposite view. *Impasse.* Congar agreed with Rahner that there was little point in having an International Theological Commission if in practice it was wholly subordinate to the CDF. There are stories of some "great row" he had with Paul VI in this year 1974 which, however, failed to "clear the air".

The quarrel was not just a demarcation dispute. It laid bare more fundamental questions on the relationship between the papal primacy and collegiality. If the CDF was the expression of the primacy in the theological field, then clearly the ITC would be subject to it. But if the ITC were seen to be enriching the reflection of the CDF, then the picture would change. Paul VI was sympathetic towards the second view, but adopted the first. The ITC later produced a set of *Theses on the Relationship Between the Ecclesiastical Magisterium and Theology.* Karl Lehmann, formerly Karl Rahner's assistant, added a *Commentary* which included the following reflection:

> At one time the dialogue on doubtful matters between the *Magisterium* and theologians was conducted *directly*, between the competent authority and the individual theologian. Today, in cases of conflict, "publicity" often intervenes between the *Magisterium* and theologians. Thus pressure is applied, tactical moves are considered etc., in all of which the "atmosphere" of dialogue is lost. The authenticity is thus reduced.[2]

Lehmann was no doubt thinking of his Swiss colleague, Hans Küng.

But the ITC felt under-used. Its remarks on ministry – or rather, Urs von Balthasar's theses – had some effect on the 1971 Synod. It made a useful contribution to *Mysterium Ecclesiae* in 1973 on the historical conditioning of dogmas. This was a somewhat Rahner-like statement, and represented the high-water mark of his influence.[3] But that was the extent of its influence.[4]

1 Karl Rahner, *I Remember*, p. 84.

2 Michael Sharkey, ed., *Texts and Documents*, p. 143.

3 "The document is conservative, and takes only a hesitant step; nevertheless the principle of the historical conditioning of dogma has now been accepted." Raymond C. Brown, *Crises Facing the Church*, London 1975, p. 116.

4 According to Cardinal François Marty, Archbishop of Paris, "the ITC never managed to service the Synod as had been envisaged at its foundation. It was, ultimately, at the service of the CDF." François Marty, *Chronique vécue de l'Eglise de France*, p. 180.

There were organizational problems. The thirty ITC members lived so far apart that they could not work effectively together. In 1973 Joseph Ratzinger gave the example of the five-man sub-commission on "pluralism" of which he was a member: he was in Bavaria, the Hungarian Jesuit Peter Nemeshegyi was in Japan, Walter Burghardt, another Jesuit, was in the United States, Oratorian Louis Bouyer divided his time between the United States and France; Tomislaw Sagi-Bunic was in Zagreb, Yugoslavia.[1] Apart from an annual meeting, all the work had to be done by correspondence.

Another problem for the ITC lay in the nature of theology itself. Since "theology" is not one discipline but rather a cluster of sub-disciplines, each speciality (say moral theology or New Testament studies) would be only thinly represented in a body of thirty. So their documents could represent a bland, acceptable consensus. Paul tried to meet this problem by stressing the "inter-disciplinary" nature of the ITC.

His address of 16 December 1974 was a rather desperate appeal to the ITC to come to his aid in a time of great vulnerability and need. He reminded the new members that according to statute they were supposed to be marked by "theological knowledge and fidelity towards the Holy See",[2] which suggested that some had been lacking in this fidelity. He set it to study "The Sources of Christian Moral Conscience" because "pragmatic philosophy and moral relativism" causing him great concern, Italy having experienced at first hand "the dramatic problem of abortion".[3]

A long quotation from Alessandro Manzoni's *Osservazioni sulla morale cattolica*, to the effect that although moral ideas could be conceived without religion, they necessarily remained "incomplete and imperfect",[4] puzzled non-Italians without reassuring Italians. Paul gave his pessimism a Euro-dimension when he asked: "If Nietzsche were to be acknowledged as the prophet of the modern world, what would remain of the Gospels, and where would the modern world end?" Paul also wondered aloud about the spiritual vacuum of Europe that led its

1 See Desmond O'Grady, "The Ratzinger Round", *Month*, December 1973, p. 421. In view of his subsequent career it is interesting that at forty-six Ratzinger complained about the Roman bureaucracy: "In the Curia are some who are opposed to the publication of our findings which, they maintain, should merely have consultative value. It seems to me, however, that some publicity is needed to demonstrate that collaboration is actually happening."

2 *Insegnamenti*, 1974, p. 1306.

3 Ibid. p. 1309.

4 Ibid. p. 1308.

youth to seek gurus from the east.[1] It was an aspect of what-to-do-about-the-Beatles? that worried many churchmen at the time.

Paul expected help on this question from the "new" Cardinal Léon-Joseph Suenens. He had assigned Suenens the task of "accompanying" the Charismatic Renewal Movement and thus preventing – Suenens used the term – "a second Reformation". Catholics had subtly transformed classic Pentecostalism for which the experience of "Baptism in the Spirit" was absolutely fundamental. The proof of the experience was *glossolalia* or speaking in tongues.

For Suenens, however, "Baptism in the Spirit" was seen rather as the mature realization of the sacramental graces conferred in infant baptism. He linked *glossolalia*, which strikes the outsider as a rhythmic babble of unintelligible syllables, with the simpler non-discursive forms of prayer used by the mystics. He saw "the gift of tongues" as providing a release from the shyness, inhibitions and defences that often afflict those who try to pray with others. "It helps us," he wrote in *A New Pentecost?* "to cross a threshold and, in so doing, to attain to a new freedom in our surrender to God."[2]

On 16 October 1974, right in the heart of the Synod, Paul praised *A New Pentecost?*:

> It describes and justifies this new expectation of what may really be an historic and providential development in the Church, based on an outpouring of those supernatural graces that are called charisms.
>
> How wonderful it would be if the Lord would pour out again the charisms in increased abundance, in order to make the Church fruitful and beautiful, to enable it to win the attention and astonishment of the secularized world.[3]

"This is the most strongly favourable language ever used by Paul VI," says Edward D. O'Connor, "about the Charismatic Renewal."[4] It would play its part in the Holy Year. Suenens' rehabilitation was complete.

Thus on Christmas Eve Paul, with the three stoutest hammer blows he could muster, unsealed the Holy Door of St Peter's through which pilgrims had to pass to gain the Holy Year indulgence. A shower of unexpected dust tumbled about him. On Christmas Day three cardinals opened three similar "holy doors" in the three major basilicas. Paul was still hesitant about playing his part in this medieval pageant, which

1 Ibid. p. 1307.

2 Léon-Joseph Suenens, *A New Pentecost?* p. 102.

3 *Insegnamenti*, 1974, p. 939.

4 O'Connor, *Pope Paul and the Spirit*, p. 42.

contained so many things Protestants disliked, including indulgences in however modified a form. But he would have to give it ecumenical significance by the words he pronounced.

And it was rather fun. For Dante, who took part in the first Holy Year in 1300, the jostling crowds in the narrow Roman streets were a foretaste of hell.[1] In 1975 the fear was that the traffic would snarl up once and for all, polluting Rome with lead-poisoning, its Roman remains and baroque churches crumbling in the smog.

It depended how many people came. Would the Holy Year of 1975, reluctantly called, be a success? Would it act as a test of Paul VI's popularity, a sort of plebiscite on his pontificate?

1 *Inferno*, 18, 28–33.

36

Women on the Road to Rome

Archbishop Bugnini wrote his great book, *The Reform of the Liturgy*, to prove that liturgical reform had been carried out in an honest and honourable way . . . *cum Petro et sub Petro* [with and under Peter]. He was emphatic on this point: "People must know how much the reform is the work of Paul VI, and how much the work of his humble and faithful followers." Towards the end it consoled him to be able to say: "I have faithfully carried out the will of Paul VI and the Council."

(Gottardo Pasqualetti IMC, Preface to ANNIBALE BUGNINI, *The Reform of the Liturgy 1948–1975*, p. xxi)

1975 was celebrated as a Holy Year, a year of Reconciliation, of the "civilization of love" or *agape*. Peter Nichols said that Paul's personality, so "striking at close quarters . . . is not easily projected". Though he loved crowds he was more natural and more himself the smaller the occasion.[1] The Holy Year brought him the throngs, *bains de foule*, gusto, the Charismatic Renewal, waving arms, enthusiasm and women.

For besides being a Holy Year, 1975 was celebrated by UNO as International Women's Year, and though some found this patronizing Paul was determined to show the Church had a contribution to make on this topic. It was also the tenth anniversary of the ending of Vatican II. The changed attitude to women's questions was the most striking difference between 1965 and 1975. In 1965 they were not taken seriously. Now in 1975 they were everywhere.

Even so it was something of a surprise to find the arch-feminist, Betty Friedan, author of *The Feminist Mystique*, entering the Vatican "where the only skirts are those worn by priests" for a private audience with Pope Paul VI.[2] She refused to wear a veil, symbol of feminist subjection, and got a famous hatter to devise a headpiece that looked

1 Peter Nichols, *The Times*, 4 June 1975.

2 Betty Friedan, "A Visit with Pope Paul", *McCall's*, February 1974, pp. 72–80. As can be seen, Ms Friedan's audience was a little earlier than I have placed it.

like a veil but was actually a hat. Harvey Cox suggested she took as a gift for Paul the feminine symbol "which looks like a cross with the equals sign". Ms Friedan thought that was a good idea. Here is her story:

> I walk close to this awesome symbol of power and I see a man who is quite *human*, and quite old, holding out his hand to me in a sort of half-welcome, half-blessing, with eyes full of the guile and authority one would expect in a man who has risen to the pinnacle of such a powerful political world, staring at me, studying me.
>
> I was told that he would speak first. He motioned to an aide who brought a jewel box, and said in English: "We want to express our gratitude and appreciation for all the good you have done for the women of the world."
>
> "I have brought you a present too," I said, and handed him the chain with the gold-plated symbol of women's equality. "This is the sign of the women's movement – the sign of the female in biology, crossed by the sign of absolute equality. As your Holiness can see, when women are completely equal to men, it becomes a different kind of cross . . ."
>
> The Pope put on his glasses to examine the chain and equality cross. "Is this for me?" And I said that during his papacy he had done more to give women a voice than in the 1900 previous years. And so I hoped the Commission on the Role of Women that he had created would confront the barriers to true equality and participation of women in both society *and* the Church . . .
>
> The Pope said, again, that the Church had always upheld the dignity of women . . . He took my hand in both of his, as if he really meant his concern for women. He seemed much more human, somehow, than I had expected, with a warm and caring expression; he wasn't going through perfunctory motions in meeting with me; he seemed strangely intent, curious, interested in this meeting, which was going on much longer than anyone had given me reason to expect . . . And he held out his arms, as if to bless me, I guess, and I was ushered out.

Paul's present was a bronze medal, with a likeness of himself with the same intent expression she had noticed. As Friedan came out into St Peter's Square, the doves she had seen flying about were gone and it had started to rain.

What precisely had Paul done for women? He had set up the Study

Commission on Women and extended its life by a year to "help him talk sense about women", as one of its members rather unkindly put it. But the Commission was only one fraction of the inter-disciplinary work being done: it replaced the liturgy as the workshop of the Curia. At the Congregation for the Evangelization of Peoples (formerly Propaganda Fide) Fr Joseph Masson SJ was directing a study on *The Role of Women in Evangelization.*[1] This was a *pastoral* commission and it confined itself to women in the *apostolate* rather than *ministry*; but there may have been an element of subterfuge in that.

Then the International Theological Commission did a study of *Women in the Diaconate*, the results of which have never been divulged. The Biblical Commission turned its mind to "Can women be priests?" and by twelve votes to five concluded that "it does not seem that the New Testament alone will permit us to settle in a clear way and once and for all the problem of the possible accession of women to the priesthood".[2] Round the corner Fr Louis Ligier OP was preparing the first draft of *Inter Insigiores*, which said no to the priestly ordination of women in 1976. And Cardinal Edouard Gagnon's Committee on the Family struggled to get a word in edgeways. Never in the history of theology have so many words been uttered by so many on so restricted a theme.

The starting-point for everyone in all these discussions was the Yahvist account of creation in Genesis 2:18–24. Man and woman were created for each other. They have the same nature and equal dignity: *'ish* and *'ishsha* together form the "image of God". Ignace de la Potterie SJ, Professor at the Biblicum, gave many papers on this theme to these various groups. Marie-Josephe Le Guillou OP complemented him with a lecture on "The Novelty of the Evangelical Outlook on Women".[3]

De la Potterie and Le Guillou both see the New Testament as *restoring* that equality and dignity which existed "in the beginning" (Matthew 19:4). In repudiating divorce, says Le Guillou, Christ "cut at the root the principle of male domination over women, appealing to the plan of creation that is restored in the light of his own resurrection."[4] Nobly spoken.

1 Published in Austin Flannery OP, *More Post-conciliar Documents*, 2, pp. 318–30, under the title, *Dans le cadre . . .* which meant "in the context of International Woman's Year and the more general context of the universal movement towards the liberation of women".

2 Biblical Commission Report, *Can Women be Priests?* published (leaked?) in *Origins*, 1 July 1976, pp. 92–96.

3 Ignace de la Potterie, "Woman in Holy Scripture", and Josephe-Marie Le Guillou, "The Novelty of the Evangelical Outlook on Woman", formed part of the study-kit sent to Episcopal Conferences in preparation for International Women's Year. They were published in the Bulletin of the Pontifical Council for the Laity, 1975.

4 Ibid. p. 91.

The trouble was that while the women in the Study Commission were up to a point prepared to listen to lectures by learned Jesuits and Dominicans, they thought the experience of women was also of some value. This was no problem for Archbishop Enrico Bartoletti, who presided over the Commission, still less for Rosemary Goldie who was its effective secretary.[1] But they had to watch their flanks. A piece of bungling got the Commission off to a bad start. When it was announced, Vatican diplomats were sent a confidential memo, soon leaked, explaining that women's ordination was no part of their brief.

The Commission was therefore written off as a waste of time. Although it was obvious that it was incompetent to take such a decision, some of its members "deeply regretted this limitation". They included five women who produced their own minority report complaining about the methods used:

> The most important thing for us was to deal with the fundamentals of the problem and to ascertain, on the basis of life, reality and the human sciences, what men and women are; and then to look for clarification in revelation and listen to the Word of God.
>
> The inductive method used by *Gaudium et Spes* was not accepted by those in charge of the Commission. Moreover it was very difficult to work because a number of disciplines were lacking, and time was always short.[2]

They tried to resign. At first they thought their resignation letter was being ignored. Then on 2 December 1974 Msgr Giovanni Benelli wrote to Msgr Igino Cardinale, who had moved from London to Brussels as Nuncio, indicating that he should explain to Mme Claire Delva, the presumed ringleader, that "the Holy Father, after a careful study of their letter, expressed the hope that the five members would rethink their decision and continue to take part in the work of the Commission which had been extended until January 1976 to help participation in International Women's Year". They came back, a little crestfallen, but complained that they were treated "with suspicion" henceforward.

Was this true? Rosemary Goldie does not think so. The problem lay

1 She used to go to Bartoletti's Mass at CEI most days, which speeded things up. What follows is based on documents supplied by Rosemary Goldie and conversations with her in Rome in June 1991.

2 "*Des Femmes en appellent aux Pasteurs de l'Eglise*", *Pro Mundi Vita*, Brussels, Bulletin 108, 1987/1, pp. 16–17. The signatories were Maria del Pilar Bellosillo, Claire Delva, Marina Lessa, Maria Vittoria Pinheiro, Deborah A. Seymour, and they were joined by Maria Vendrik. Their report was dated 29 December 1975. So they waited twelve years to publish it.

in joining up different specialities, and setting theologians alongside activists. Only one of the women on the Commission was a qualified theologian, Sister Teresa Ann MacLeod OP from Scotland, and she was not a member of the protesting group. Karl Rahner wrote a letter to one of the five in which he says, again and again, that revelation has very little to say about men and women because one never knows how far the statements of the Old and New Testaments are culturally conditioned.[1] All one can safely say is that women are mothers while men are fathers.

Bartoletti, Rosemary Goldie thinks, was an "inspired choice" for this work.[2] Though a monoglot Italian he could enter into opposing positions with great sympathy. A man of equal charity and diplomacy, his aim in the Commission was to make the Church's attitude to women more intelligible and therefore more credible. The minority report of the five laywomen and one sister *did* reach Paul's desk, whatever they may say. Bartoletti's final report for the Pope declares that "it is urgent to give a fully justified answer to the question posed by the non-admission of women to the ordained ministries".[3] As for the non-ordained lay ministries – lector and acolyte – there were no grounds whatsoever for excluding women from them since they depended on baptism, which made one a *laos*-person, a member of the People of God.

And even if we may have to give a negative response to the ordination of women to the priesthood, Bartoletti advised Paul, let it be a motivated response with a solid ecclesiological foundation and not just a disciplinary *niet.* The Commission has been suspect from both sides: "conservatives" saw in it the threat of women's ordination and other unheard of novelties; "liberals" regarded it as a way of saving time and dodging the question. There is a much better case for ordination to the diaconate, Bartoletti thought, mentioning the ecumenical dimension of the question.

This introduced the Anglicans into the discussion. In the United States, Bartoletti reported, two nuns, Sisters Letitia Brennan and Agnes Cunningham, took part in a dialogue with the Anglicans which reached the following conclusion:

1 Karl Rahner, *Lettre à un consulteur da la Commission, Pro Mundi Vita*, 108/1, pp. 23–26.

2 Rosemary Goldie, "*Bartoletti e il ruolo della donna nella Chiesa e nella società*", in *Un Vescovo italiano del Concilio, Enrico Bartoletti, 1916–1976*, p. 222.

3 Enrico Bartoletti, "*Problèmes ouverts et questions posées*", the final dossier of the Commission, just two typed pages. Bartoletti also wrote "*La Question des Femmes et des Ministères Ordonnés*", a seven-page memo presented personally to Paul VI at Castelgandolfo in August 1975. It has never been published or used before. Thanks to Rosemary Goldie for making it available.

> The discussion so far has shown that the traditional reasons for denying priestly ordination to women are not universally acceptable. It has also shown that problems concerning the doctrine of God, the incarnation and redemption are implied at least indirectly in the solution of this question, such that any decision, whether for or against women's ordination, will demand that the Church should explain and develop its essential tradition in a new manner. The Church has to face a problem that demands a new effort of self-understanding in relation to the Gospel.

Bartoletti added that in practice religious women, nuns, did what the ordained deacon is expected to do.

He also dealt with what became known as "the argument from Africa" which tried to relativize the movement for women's ordination by saying it was confined to middle-class women of the developed world. African women did not take part in it. Bartoletti replies that African women take part in very little, but when they do appear at international conferences they are well aware of the problem. Once Africans start thinking about it for themselves, he observes, "the mere argument from 'tradition' against women's ordination will carry very little weight because the Africans will say: this may be a very long history but it is not *our* history."

Bartoletti also included a select bibliography, and recommended that, as an interim measure, the present state of research should be explained and the pastoral reasons for retaining the traditional practice be made known. Finally, on this August day 1975, he said it

> seems necessary that qualified women should be involved in all future research and in the formulation of whatever answer is to be given. For as we have said, more and more women are involved in the study of different theological disciplines. In any case, *their contribution is necessary to find a language adapted to the contemporary mentality.*

That is the final sentence of the Bartoletti memo.

No one, in short, can complain of the quality of the advice given to Paul on women. To picture him as ignorant of the "women's movement" is wholly false. For a man of seventy-seven he showed a remarkable openness and capacity to learn. His language already began to change. In the apostolic exhortation, *Marialis Cultus*, he noted "a certain disaffection for the cult of Mary and a difficulty in taking her as a model for today" because of the changed circumstances. Modern women do not live in the same world as women of the Middle East at the time of

Christ. To this Paul replies that Our Lady is proposed as a model not for her particular life-style but for her *faith*. So Mary is the type of *the disciple*, and as such a model for men as well as women.[1]

Moreover Mary of Nazareth's free assent to the divine plan is a courageous choice, which – he notes with "joyous surprise – was far from being the action of a woman passively submitting to an alienating religiosity, but rather of a woman who did not fear to proclaim the God who exalts the humble and oppressed, and topples the mighty from their thrones".[2]

And there was the Holy Year, which gave shape to Paul's papal ministry. The *sindico* or mayor of Rome welcomed it as a boost to the city's tourist industry, but worried that the Roman traffic might come to a complete stop. But to concentrate on the economic consequences or folklore charm of the Holy Year was to distort it.

The meaning of "holiness" itself had changed between 1950 and 1975, and Rome was no longer a "sacred city" as defined by the Concordat of 1929. Whereas 1950 celebrated a "separated sacred" that took Christians "out of the world" and lodged them in the sacred space of the sanctuary (or the sacristy), for Paul *the sacred was the secular but seen in the light of God's plan*.[3] A leading Italian *Vaticanista* noted this distinction: "The originality of Paul VI's Holy Year was to recognize as 'holy' ordinary time, our common history, in short the 'profane'. This meant new models of holiness. Those who fought for justice and peace, even without episcopal 'mandate', could be seen as saints."[4]

The Council justified this approach. *Lumen Gentium* urged Christians not to keep their faith and hope locked up in the depths of their hearts but to express it continuously "in the framework of secular life".[5] *Gaudium et Spes* added that since the incarnation nothing and no one can be "purely secular" any more.[6]

Yet there was at the same time a tension between this positive approach to worldly realities and the Charismatic Renewal. Cardinal Léon-Joseph Suenens may have been rehabilitated but even he did not know how Paul would receive the thousands of charismatics who poured into Rome for their conference in the week before Pentecost. They met

1 *Marialis Cultus*, 34–36.

2 Ibid. 27.

3 A *retractatio*: in *The Runaway Church*, I presented the Holy Year of 1975 as an instance of the "separated sacred". Writing before the event, I was not to know I would be proved wrong.

4 Giancarlo Zizola, *Nel Basso dei Cieli*, p. 249.

5 *Lumen Gentium*, 35.

6 *Gaudium et Spes*, 22.

to "witness to the Spirit" under an awning on the Appian Way close to the catacombs of St Callistus, somewhat awed by the tombs of the martyrs beneath their feet. They were uncertain how Paul would receive them because they knew he had been under pressure to refuse any official recognition. Dr William Storey of Notre Dame, one of the original leaders of the movement, now denounced it to Jean Villot, Cardinal Secretary of State.[1]

Nothing daunted the charismatics filed into St Peter's on Pentecost Sunday, filled with "a quiet delirium of joy". They "thundered their applause for the man they recognized in the Spirit as the Vicar of Christ . . . who seemed visibly touched by their affection".[2] No doubt he was, though in his homily he avoided the expression Charismatic Renewal and stressed in cold-waterish fashion the need of preparation for the gift of the Spirit by inner silence, prayer and the confession of sins.[3] This cautious tone was justified because the charismatics made up only half of the congregation. But he was not prepared for what happened next:

> At the elevation of the Mass, as he raised first the Host and then the chalice, a gentle melody of prayer in tongues rose through the basilica. This has to have been the first time such a thing ever occurred in St Peter's, but it was so spontaneous, so discreet and so lovely that no one seems to have made any objection. Whether Pope Paul made any comment on it is not known.[4]

The charismatics were not to know that, and they streamed out of the basilica singing and dancing exuberantly as they crossed St Peter's square. Next day, though Paul spoke to them with some warmth, he let Cardinal Suenens say Mass for them.

The charismatics remained perplexed about his attitude to them. The safest conclusion is that he deliberately refrained from passing judgement on the Charismatic Renewal as a whole – he tied himself into linguistic knots to avoid their own preferred self-description – while considering some of its fruits to be signs of the renewing presence of the Spirit in today's world. He stopped short of enthusiasm.

Part of the reason was that most Catholics had a very different experience of the liturgy without waving of arms, swaying and the susurration of tongues. The point of liturgical reform had been not to

1 Edward D. O'Connor, *Pope Paul and the Spirit*, p. 55, quoting *National Catholic Reporter*, 15 August 1975.

2 Ibid. p. 46.

3 *Insegnamenti*, 1975, p. 532.

4 O'Connor, *Pope Paul and the Spirit*, pp. 47–48.

escape into the realm of the "separated sacred" but to be ushered into the "real" world, bringing the fruit of the vine and the work of human hands into Christ's sacrifice. The old form of dismissal banally said *Ite, Missa est* (Go, the Mass is over). "Go in love and peace to love and serve the Lord" sent one out into the "world" with, in principle, the Gospel ringing in one's ears.

Archbishop Marcel Lefebvre's dissidents likewise wanted to immerse the faithful in an alternative cosy world where the French revolution had not yet happened. In the Holy Year – the year of Reconciliation – Paul made a great effort to resolve the Lefebvre problem. Lefebvre began the year aggressively by publishing his "Profession of Faith", yet another critique of Vatican II. Paul had appointed a special commission of cardinals – John J. Wright, Gabriel-Marie Garrone and Arturo Tabera – to follow events in Lefebvre's seminary at Ecône. Acting on their advice the Bishop of Lausanne, Geneva and Fribourg, Pierre Mamie, withdrew official recognition from the seminary. But it made no difference. In a letter dated 5 May 1975 the trio of cardinals told Paul that Lefebvre "appeals to the popes of yesterday against the pope of today".

Paul's response to Lefebvre was carefully graduated. On 29 June 1975 he wrote a personal letter. The date – the feast of Sts Peter and Paul – was chosen with care: it was the twelfth anniversary of his coronation, and also the day when Lefebvre did his valid but illicit ordinations. "*Cher frère*," it begins, "we write to you today in distress", and concludes *In veritate et caritate* (In truth and charity).[1]

Paul asks for a straightforward and public "act of submission, in order to make reparation for the damage your writings, your words and your attitudes have done to the Church and the *Magisterium*". He appeals to Lefebvre's "sense of episcopal responsibility". He makes a concession. Yes, there have been "superficial readings of the Council, individual or group initiatives deriving more from private judgement than adhesion to the tradition of the Church". He suffers from that too, and tries to remedy it "in season and out of season". The key question is: "What does it mean for a member to act alone, independently of the Body to which he belongs?" He deals with the example of St Athanasius, solitary defender of the true faith, whom Lefebvre claimed to emulate:

> Yet Athanasius' defence of the faith was precisely the defence of the Council of Nicaea. The Council was the norm which inspired his fidelity, just as it did that of St Ambrose [of Milan]. How can someone today compare himself with St Athanasius,

1 The letter is not included in *Insegnamenti*, 1975. See "La Condamnation Sauvage", *Itinéraires*, special number, September 1966, pp. 41–45. Most of this space is occupied with footnotes which refute Paul's allegations.

> while daring to combat a Council like Vatican II, which has no less authority and which, in certain respects, is more important than Nicaea?[1]

Paul looks forward, finally, to the day when he can "open his arms to embrace his brother in restored communion". That suggested that communion was already broken.

Paul exposed himself to rebuff yet again, with another personal letter on 8 September 1975. He is still standing there with arms outstretched, waiting for a sign. "Perhaps you think," he tells his "dear brother", that "we don't understand what you are trying to do, or perhaps you think the Pope is misinformed or subject to pressures".[2] Lefebvre must disabuse himself of such notions. "*Priez l'Esprit Saint, cher frère*" (Pray to the Holy Spirit, dear brother) – a reminder that Lefebvre was formed as a Holy Ghost Father. But still there was no reply.

If Lefebvre could not be moved, at least the bureaucracy could be reorganized. On 11 July 1975 Paul promulgated an apostolic constitution aptly called *Constans Nobis Studium* bringing together once again the Congregation for the Discipline of the Sacraments and that for Divine Worship.[3]

At this point, though possibly *post* rather than *propter hoc*, Archbishop Annibale Bugnini, the architect of the whole process of liturgical reform and the object of so many vicious attacks throughout the whole period, was dropped, suddenly, unaccountably, unjustly. The fate of the President of the Liturgical *Consilium*, Cardinal Giacomo Lercaro, in January 1968 now befell Bugnini in July 1975.

Bugnini did not, of course, disappear through a trap-door. Where was he?

> Archbishop Bugnini retired on tiptoe, as it were, to his modest rooms at San Silvestro al Quirinale. His service to the liturgy came to a sudden and dramatic end, without any plausible explanation being given to him. Months of utter silence followed during which no one but a few faithful friends caught so much as a glimpse of him.[4]

Archbishop Bugnini – a Marist, who had been ordained Archbishop only

1 Ibid. p. 45. The commentator concludes from this that Paul VI is prepared to throw Nicaea overboard.

2 *Itinéraires*, 208, p. 50.

3 The two Congregations were divorced again on 5 April 1984, and, astonishingly, remarried four years later by the apostolic constitution *Pastor Bonus* of 28 June 1988.

4 Annibale Bugnini, *The Reform of the Liturgy*, from the preface by Gottardo Pasqualetti, p. xix.

because protocol required it of a Secretary of a Roman Congregation – did not repine and immediately started writing his book, which he did not think of as an apologia for himself so much as for Paul VI.

Fr Gottardo Pasqualetti noted:

> At each revision harsh expressions that still conveyed something of thc author's original bitterness were toned down, and the exposition was made as serene and objective as possible . . .
>
> He had at first trusted to the Holy See to defend his honour as a bishop and a faithful servant of the Church. Then he realized that he could rely on God alone.[1]

By Christmas 1975 Archbishop Bugnini had taken up his new post: Apostolic Delegate in Tehran. With admirable resilience he set about writing another book, on *La Chiesa in Iran*, and was in position to be mocked by the "student" revolutionaries when the Ayatollah Khomenei came to power in 1979.[2]

The sacking of Bugnini, the letters to Lefebvre, the fusion of the two Congregations and the appointment of a colourless Australian, Cardinal James Knox, dragged from Melbourne where he had been a blameless archbishop since 1967[3] to head the new–old combination, were taken to mean that the creative period of liturgical experimentation was now officially over.

That was an understatement. From now on the emphasis would fall on the correct administration of the sacraments rather than the promotion of a vigorous liturgical life. Cardinal Knox would halt local experiments in "inculturation" in India, for example. He showed no understanding of Asian theologians, who soon pointed out the weaknesses of his approach:

> Contrary to the conciliar teaching on liturgy, what happened was often a change of *rite*, and not a change of *life*. And once the new rite lost its novelty, the Church was back to square one. Soon spirituality had to be imported from outside to vivify the liturgy. Charismatic renewal and oriental mysticism invaded the Western Church, reinforcing not only the personal

1 Ibid. p. xx.

2 Archbishop Annibale Bugnini died at his post in Tehran on 3 July 1982. It is a mystery why no one has come to his defence. Perhaps the name Hannibal suggests a joke-figure.

3 Paul had known Knox in the Secretariat of State, 1948–50, and had appointed him to Melbourne after seventeen years as Vatican diplomat in Japan, East and West Africa and finally India.

> but also the traditionally apolitical character of both spirituality and liturgy.[1]

The dialogue with other religions got no help from the Congregation for Divine Worship, and looked instead to the Secretariat for Non-Christian Religions.

Bishop Emmett Carter, then at London, Ontario, and chairman of ICEL (International Committee on English in the Liturgy) had a "Western" form of the same objection. With his customary frankness he wrote to Cardinal James Knox deploring the inadmissible way the Vatican was increasingly taking decisions that had been delegated to episcopal conferences or groups of them. The effectiveness of liturgical reform, he said, had depended in large measure on the decentralizing initiatives of the old liturgical *Consilium*. "I understand the principle of subsidiarity to mean," wrote Carter, "that when a legitimate authority is already in the field, a superior authority does not intervene".[2] The debate about "subsidiarity" had a long history: though addressed in the first place to governments, it also had an application in the inner life of the Church. Or did it?

But Paul raised his eyes to the hills, whence came his salvation, and tried to rise above his manifold difficulties. To cheer himself up as much as the Church, he wrote an apostolic exhortation, *Gaudete in Dominum*, on Christian joy that met with a leaden response. Joy is not the first thing that springs to mind in remembering him. Was he not like Pinocchio, obliged to laugh lest he burst into tears? Yet Montini's joy was deeply Pauline. God's ministers are "always rejoicing" (2 Corinthians 6:10), and even when afflicted St Paul is "overcome with joy" (2 Corinthians 7:4). *Gaudete in Dominum* was intended to mark the Holy Year. It was barely noticed. Yet it proves Montini's consistency, reflecting the themes of his first-ever book in 1930, *The Prayer of the Soul according to St Paul*.[3]

St Paul and his Epistle to the Romans were very much in mind as in June 1975 the new Commission for religious relations with Judaism published its *Notes for Preaching and Teaching*. Though generally admitted to be excellent, its understatements sometimes bordered on the bland. "We must remember how much the balance of relations between

1 Aloysius Pieris SJ, *An Asian Theology of Liberation*, p. 5.

2 Michael W. Higgins and Douglas R. Lettson, *My Father's Business: A Biography of His Eminence G. Emmett Cardinal Carter*, Macmillan of Canada, Toronto 1991, p. 76.

3 Giovanni Battista Montini, *La preghiera dell'anima, le idee di S. Paolo, Colloqui Religiose*, pref. G. B. Scaglia. It has a chapter called "Women and the Apostolate" which, in the language of 1975, would no doubt have been called "Women and Ministry".

Christians and Jews over two thousand years has been negative" hardly does justice to the history of persecution. The hope that "catechesis should help in understanding the meaning for the Jews of the extermination during the years 1939–1945" seems deplorably inadequate when faced with the *shoah* or Holocaust which, anyway, raises a problem for Christians as well as Jews.[1]

So far Paul's thoughts about women had nimbly skirted round the taboo question of priestly ordination. A letter from Dr Donald Coggan, Archbishop of Canterbury, on 9 July 1975 put it inescapably on the papal agenda. Coggan courteously informed the Pope of "the slow but steady consensus of opinion within the Anglican Communion that there are no fundamental objections in principle to the ordination of women to the priesthood".[2] Clearly the Bartoletti memorandum already discussed was designed to help Paul answer this letter. He waited until 30 November 1975 to reply: "Your Grace is of course very well aware of the Catholic Church's position on this subject. She holds that it is not admissible to ordain women to the priesthood, for very fundamental reasons."

These "very fundamental reasons" boiled down to a prevailing male apostolate, the constant practice of the Church, and the "living teaching authority which has consequently held that the exclusion of women from the priesthood is in accordance with God's plan for his Church". This letter anticipated *Inter Insigiores* of October 1976. It was disappointing in view of the promise of the Study Commission still – just about – in existence.

The timing of these exchanges – between July and November 1975 – was influenced by two factors, one external and the other internal. The external factor was that the Anglican Synod in Westminster was due to hold a crucial debate on women's ordination in November; if Dr Coggan cared to use the argument that the Roman Catholic Church would object to Anglicans going it alone, he would be free to do so. In fact he did not, though the Bishop of Chelmsford, Albert John Trillo, produced the papal letter as a trump card. Dr Coggan, a fair-minded man, assured me that he did not resent Pope Paul's letter as an unwarranted interference in Anglican affairs.

But it was Roman Catholic wavering rather than Anglican nibbling that led Paul to act swiftly to halt the drift towards the ordination of women. Just a week before his letter to Dr Coggan, 10–14 November the Anglican/Catholic Working Group for West Europe had been meet-

1 Donald Nicholl, "Other Religions" (*Nostra Aetate*) in *Modern Catholicism, Vatican II and After*, ed. Adrian Hastings, p. 129.

2 *Insegnamenti*, 1976, pp. 662–63. Dr Coggan's letter is given in Italian.

ing in Assisi. Its brief was to consider: "To what extent and in what ways Churches with women priests and Churches without women priests can be reconciled in sacramental fellowship."

French Dominican Hervé Legrand (student and successor of Yves Congar) and English Franciscan Eric Doyle put the Catholic case and concluded that there was no theological objection to women's ordination.[1]

They did not present this as the official Catholic position but as their own considered theological judgement. Their concern was not with women's ordination as such, but rather with its effect on the theology of the ministry on which Catholics and Anglicans had already reached a measure of agreement described by participants as "substantial". The ARCIC statement, *Ministry and Ordination*, was dated September 1973. Its main concern had been to hammer out an agreement on the nature of priestly ministry – not to ask *who* should be admitted to it. Thus ARCIC had never been bothered by the fact that most Anglican priests were married – something formally rejected by the discipline of the Roman Catholic Church.

The feast of the Immaculate Conception, 8 December, was the tenth anniversary of the end of Vatican II. Paul marked the occasion by publishing *Evangelii Nuntiandi*, his last and finest apostolic exhortation.[2] It was also the climax of the Holy Year, which, begun in doubt and perplexity, was ending in something like tranquillity. Had a point of balance, of stasis, been reached after all the upheavals of the last decade?

Evangelii Nuntiandi is a work of discernment and synthesis. The Synod of 1974 left all its unsolved problems in a heap on Paul's desk. His response was a text that is at once synodal and papal and therefore deeply collegial. It was quite different from his encyclicals in which Peter spoke for himself. The encyclicals were solo performances while in *Evangelii Nuntiandi* he acted as "the chorus-leader of the Apostles". The Synod provided the raw experience and many of the insights, while Paul articulated them using his "charism of discernment". It was a new way of relating to the Church, a novel and more effective form of the *magisterium*.

It makes important new statements about, for example, liberation theology (nos. 38–39), basic communities (no. 58), and above all on

> the close links between evangelization and human advancement, that is, development and liberation. There is a link in

1 Eric Doyle OFM, "The Ordination of Women in the Roman Catholic Church", in Monica Furlong, ed., *Feminine in the Church*, p. 36.

2 *Insegnamenti*, 1975, pp. 1380–1438, tr. in Austin Flannery, *More Post-conciliar Documents*, vol. 2, pp. 711–61.

> the anthropological order because the person to be evangelized is not an abstract being but someone subject to social and economic factors. There is also a connection in the theological sphere because the plan of creation cannot be isolated from the plan of redemption. There is, finally, a connection in the evangelical order, that is, the order of charity: for how can the new law be proclaimed unless it promotes a true practical advancement of man in a spirit of justice and peace.[1]

Paul went on learning throughout his pontificate, in great measure thanks to the Synod.

There was a grand ceremony in St Peter's to mark "ten years on", to which the "stars" of the Council, including those now eclipsed, such as Lercaro; those who, like Suenens, had reinvented themselves; those who plodded on, like König; and those whose advancement depended on Paul VI personally, for example Villot, former secretary of the Council. There was an aspect of leave-taking about this event: the next time these cardinals met would be for the conclave to elect his successor. Paul's thoughts turned to death.

But at the Angelus of 8 December 1975 – it was Monday and a public holiday in Italy – Paul was in playful mood. He wanted to share a "vision", a "dream". Obviously it was not a "vision" in the technical sense such as Pius XII would have claimed. He had been thinking about the feast of the Immaculate Conception and how, in the afternoon, he would go to the Piazza di Spagna, where according to tradition Our Lady would be crowned by a member of the Roman fire brigade. It is rather a daring feat, carried out with panache, having more to do with folklore and fun than mariology. Then he would go to the basilica of St Mary Major where Our Lady was known as *Salus Populi Romani* – salvation of the Roman people, popularly the "Madonna of the Snows". This was the cue for his open-eyed vision:

> How beautiful it would be if Our Lady, the Immaculate One, spread over Rome and the whole world a mantle of her snow, clear, astonishing, pure – the snow of her purity, innocence and beauty; and then supposing that as we came out of St Peter's we all had this transfigured vision of the world, and saw it covered with the whitest, softest, most angelic and spiritual snow.[2]

Of course, he pulls himself up with a start, it was only a distraction, and he was carried away by the magic (*incantesimo*) of the ceremony in

1 *Evangelii Nuntiandi*, 31.

2 *Insegnamenti*, pp. 1498–99.

St Peter's. But the Pauline "dream" was neither a flight nor an escape from the "real world". It carried with it the passionate prayer that "the face of the earth, now disfigured by so many passions and vices and sins, should be cleansed by the Holy Spirit".[1]

This moment of "epiphany" when everyday things are seen in a transformed light is the closest we will come to Montini's "spiritual experience". His best perceptions come in poetic images rather than abstract statement, and gather up the memories of a lifetime, recalling his youth in the Italian Alps, with the special hush after the first snowfall and the sense of a world made clean. Was he remembering January 1929 when St Peter's Square was covered in snow?

Now, 8 December in the year of grace 1975, the snow did not fall. The Holy Spirit's cleansing process (*Lava quod est sordidum*) could be perceived only by the eye of faith. The disfigured world was not yet transfigured. But it was *en voie de transfiguration*, caught up in the process.

There was still work to do before he died. A week later, on 14 December 1975, came the most important event in ecumenical relations with the Orthodox Church since the visit of Athenagoras in 1967. Metropolitan Meliton of Chalcedon visited the Vatican on behalf of the Ecumenical Patriarch, Dimitrios I. Meliton, an observer at Vatican II, was an old friend at home in international ecumenical circles who ought logically to have succeeded Patriarch Athenagoras on his death in 1972. But Turkish law required that the Patriarch be a Turkish citizen, which narrowed the field. Paul never established with Dimitrios the relationship he had enjoyed with Athenagoras, and Meliton remained the chief go-between.

So many memories crowded together on this 14 December 1975, memories of humiliations inflicted and clumsy rebuffs. As if to wipe the slate clean, Paul fell to his knees and, according to the official account:

> in an instinctive gesture of brotherhood, reconciliation and peace, kissed the feet of his guest. A meaningful and deep sign, according to the example of the Lord. The whole assembly understood the meaning of this gesture, and responded with prolonged applause.[2]

The reality was a little more confused. Not quite grasping what Paul was doing, Meliton sank to his knees as well and an obscure grappling ensued until Meliton understood what the arthritic Paul was trying to

1 Ibid. p. 1499.
2 Ibid. p. 1516.

do. He accepted the gesture with due humility. "Pope Paul," he remarked enigmatically, "has saved the papacy from itself."

The declaration "On Certain Problems of Social Ethics", *Personae Humanae*, was published by the Congregation for the Doctrine of the Faith on 29 December 1975. It made a rather sad Christmas present for Catholic homosexuals. It echoed *Humanae Vitae* in its title and in its argument. It said that Christian morality is based on *human* nature rather than the impersonal "nature" of the Stoics. Human persons are sexual beings, and their sexuality runs through the whole of life. This is the opening chord of *Personae Humanae*:

> The human person, contemporary scientists maintain, is so profoundly affected by sexuality that it must be considered one of the principal formative influences on the life of a man or a woman. In fact, sex is the source of the biological, psychological and spiritual characteristics which make a person male or female and which thus considerably influence each individual's progress towards maturity.[1]

This sounded a new note in the *magisterium* – the acknowledgement that the social sciences could help moral understanding. The study of women had led to the study of the human. It illustrated the need for an anthropology.

The male/female distinction can be made to serve many purposes. In *Personae Humanae* it was put to work to make the point that "sexual relations between persons of the same sex are necessarily and essentially disordered according to the objective moral order".[2] This was not what Catholic gays and lesbians wanted to hear. So there was an outcry. Paul showed he was out of touch with the modern world.

Yet the reasoning of the declaration was consistent. If, as *Humanae Vitae* taught, God's plan is that sexual relations should be at least "open to procreation", then homosexual acts do not conform to it. That is why they are "necessarily and essentially disordered". They cannot produce offspring. The male/female differentiation stressed at the outset of *Personae Humanae* can now be seen as reinforcing the case for heterosexual intercourse as the only form of sexual intercourse that is "fully and truly human", and that this truth "transcends historical circumstances".[3]

What was new was the admission that "constitutional" homosexuals existed, and an insistence that they should receive "kind and com-

1 *Personae Humanae*, 1, in Austin Flannery, *More Post-conciliar Documents*, 2, p. 486.

2 *Personae Humanae*, 8, in Flannery, p. 491.

3 *Personae Humanae*, 3, in Flannery, p. 487.

passionate" pastoral care. They were not to be bullied or persecuted. There were no grounds for homophobia. "Their culpability will be judged prudently" – and may be greatly diminished. But in the end "homosexual acts are intrinsically disordered, and may never be approved in any way whatsoever".[1] Nothing could be more clear. "Intrinsically" is a very tough, definitive word: it means of its very nature, and admits no exceptions. There is nothing indecisive or wishy-washy about *Personae Humanae*, any more than there was about its twin, *Humanae Vitae*. They stand or fall together.

But what was wholly new was a homosexual movement within the Church campaigning for acceptance of homosexuality as an equally valid expression of human love. One of the leaders of the movement, Donald Nugent, founder of New Ways Ministry, points out that after the American Medical Association statement in 1973 that homosexual orientation should be classified neither as a mental illness nor an emotional disorder, "the general trend was away from change of orientation therapy, and more towards therapy which helps promote self-acceptance, affirmation and learning of coping skills for inner- and intra-personal relationships in an often hostile social environment".[2] It all depends what you mean by "self-acceptance".

Pope Paul did not follow his usual practice of commenting on the document at this stage. However he alluded to it at the Angelus on Sunday, 28 December 1975 when he said that the Christian family today was under threat, having to cope with changing social customs but also certain "ideological currents" which sap the "constitutional principles of the family on which its happiness, stability and holiness [*sacralità*] are founded".[3] Homosexual relationships throw down the gauntlet to the Christian family.

But the story of the Holy Year should not end on this negative note. Cardinal Villot, who had been apprehensive, admitted it had been a great success, with 60,000 to 80,000 pilgrims crowding St Peter's Square every Wednesday. At seventy he was far more exhausted than Paul, who was seventy-eight. There had been spectacular marathons like the charismatic meetings and the ordination of 350 priests on the feast of Sts Peter and Paul.[4]

1 *Personae Humanae*, 8, op. cit.

2 Donald Nugent, "Sexual Orientation in Vatican Thinking", in *The Vatican and Homosexuality*, eds Jeannine Gramick and Pat Furey, p. 52. Nugent thinks the declaration was called *Persona Humana*. But it does not much matter since the whole tenor of the book is to say that the 1986 "Letter to Bishops of the Catholic Church on the Pastoral Care of Homosexual Persons" was worse than Paul VI's document.

3 *Insegnamenti*, 1975, p. 1574.

4 Antoine Wenger, *Le Cardinal Villot*, p. 139.

Betty Friedan had been surprised to find Paul so *human*, and his expression "so warm and caring". That was what all those who came close to him felt. We can now complete the Peter Nichols quotation:

> The Pope's manner is gentle, rather tense but kindly, and the most striking details of his presence are the way he holds his head to one side and the brightness of his eyes. His personality is striking at close quarters but it is not easily projected, with the result that the smaller the occasion, the more natural and impressive he is. But he loves crowds, and loves contact with throngs of enthusiastic faithful.[1]

During the Holy Year of 1975 a great many roads had led to Rome.

1 Peter Nichols, *The Times*, 4 June 1975.

37

Suspending an Archbishop

> I'm concerned about the Pope's head, which works well, not his legs, which don't. Didn't Erasmus of Rotterdam say that arthritis is the illness of those destined for longevity?
> (Mario Fontana, Paul VI's doctor)

Paul VI was no doubt consoled to know that his sufferings were sanctioned by Erasmus and glad to have a humanist doctor, after the poet-doctor, Ugo Piazza, who died on 5 December 1975. But apart from the pain it brought, his arthritis forced him to consider the question of resignation with a new seriousness. He had not left Italy since 1970. He was still hoping to go to Poland: Edward Gierek, Poland's new Communist Party leader, was not opposed to a visit, which would prove that the "normalization" of Church–State relations, so often talked about, was actually happening. But the decision did not depend on him. The "Big Brother" to the East feared that letting the Pope into Poland would have a destabilizing effect.

But more immediately the bicentenary of the United States in 1976 was being celebrated in Philadelphia with much tolling of the replica "Liberty Bell" and other spectacular festivities. A Eucharistic Congress was planned to coincide with the bicentenary celebrations to lend them a religious dimension. Clearly the Pope should go, just as he had gone to the Eucharistic Congress of 1964 in Bombay, and to Medellín in August 1968.

Moreover the Pope *wanted* to go to Philadelphia. But after consulting with Dr Mario Fontana, his personal physician, Don Pasquale Macchi and Archbishop Giovanni Benelli tried to dissuade him. A journey to the United States in August was inopportune, they argued. It was an election year, the campaign had already started with the New Hampshire primary, and he must not seem to interfere. Very well, Paul said, I will make sure my language embraces all parties. Macchi and Benelli thought up some more objections: he could not go to the United States without also visiting Canada, and probably Mexico as well. The projected visit was getting out of hand, and was exhausting even to contemplate. But he still wanted to go.

Then they came clean and told him the real reason: his health couldn't stand the strain of a long journey by air. Paul still wasn't convinced. A pope doesn't travel for fun, for pleasure, but for the good of the people of God. It was still no. But then he reasoned: if a pope is not fit enough to travel, he is not fit enough to do his job, *therefore for the good of the Church he should resign.*[1]

But once he started taking that line his advisers took the other tack. No, he must not even think of resigning: being unable to go through with a visit to the United States did not mean he was impeded in carrying out his work in Rome. Paul asked Benelli to get the Secretariat of State to set down in writing the reasons why he should not go to the United States. No one was in any hurry to do this. One morning he suddenly said to Macchi: "You haven't given me the memo I asked for on the Philadelphia visit. If I don't have it soon I'll decide for myself . . ." Macchi had no doubt that meant resignation.[2] Paul had already talked to the Abbot of Monte Cassino, and would end his days there as a Benedictine monk.

Macchi now tried to persuade him that journeys, though easily integrated into the papal mission, were not essential to it. His specific and irreplaceable role was to govern the Church. For this he needed a good mind and a generous heart, and he had both. There had been journeys enough – and their value as witness endured . . . Anyway, he had to conserve his energy for a possible visit to Poland, less exhausting and more necessary.[3]

He discussed that possibility with Cardinal Karol Wojtyla, Archbishop of Kraków, who preached the Curia retreat in March, later published as *Sign of Contradiction*.[4] It is an austere, pessimistic work, very conscious of the power of evil, and marks a break with the optimism of *Gaudium et Spes*. Paul listened wonderingly as the fifty-six-year-old Polish bishop spoke of God's infinite majesty and "the call to experience it in absolute quiet like Trappists in their monastery, like Bedouins in

1 The source for this episode is Carlo Cremona, *Paolo VI*, p. 238.

2 Ibid. p. 239.

3 Ibid. Cremona says that Macchi dictated these thoughts to him late into the night. He could only scribble them down.

4 Karol Wojtyla, *Segno di Contraddizione, Meditazioni*, Vita e Pensiero 1977. The Italian edition is given because it was this that influenced the second conclave of 1978. It has an introduction by Giuseppe Lazzati, Rector of the Catholic University of the Sacred Heart, in which he explains that Cardinal Wojtyla "spontaneously offered his text for publication". He makes it sound like a noble gesture.

the desert, and even like Buddhists". Then Cardinal Wojtyla quoted St John of the Cross, on whom he had written his first thesis:

> To attain to this which you know not,
> you must pass through that which you know not.
> To attain to that which you possess not,
> you must pass through that which you possess not.
> To attain to that which you are not,
> you must pass through that which you are not.[1]

It was like a Zen riddle.

Karol Wojtyla's retreat rather daunted the Curia. The Kraków archbishop conveyed his best wishes on Paul's eightieth birthday with the Polish phrase *Sto lat*! Paul remembered enough Polish to know it means: "May you live to be a hundred years!" His face fell at the prospect, but Wojtyla piously went on: "One should never set limits to divine Providence."[2] Paul stood rebuked. His own favourite phrase – which he claimed his father Giorgio got from Giuseppe Sarto, Bishop of Mantua, before becoming Pope Pius X – was "one cannot set limits to God's *mercy*".[3] There was a nuance.

But if he could not travel, then the members of the "new Curia", the Secretariat for Christian Unity, Non-Christian Religions and Nonbelievers could travel on his behalf. In 1973 he replaced Cardinal Paolo Marella with Sergio Pignedoli as President of the Secretariat for Non-Christian Religions, making him a cardinal that same year. Marella's spectacular inactivity was now excused on the grounds that the initial purpose of the Secretariat was study rather than contact, a time of "laying foundations"[4] rather than building anything. These were pious fictions. Pignedoli had a genius for friendship, knew something about Islam, having been pro-nuncio in East Africa, and gave himself a qualified staff: in charge of the Muslim desk was Fr Abou Mokh from Syria. Also available were the White Fathers (now called Missionaries of Africa), Jacques Cuoq and Maurice Borrmans, acknowledged experts on Islam.

In the summer of 1975 Pignedoli asked their advice. Adel Amer, an Egyptian working with the Arab League in Paris, reported that Colonel

1 Ibid. p. 25.

2 John Magee, "*La vita quotidiana de Paolo VI*", in *Modernité*, p. 140.

3 Ibid. p. 141.

4 Michael Fitzgerald, "Twenty-five Years of Dialogue", in *Islamochristiana*, 15, Rome 1989, p. 110. This is the annual review of the Secretariat (now Council) for Inter-Religious Dialogue; Bishop Fitzgerald, an English Missionary of Africa, is its secretary.

Muammar al-Gadaffi wanted to invite a Vatican delegation to his capital, Tripoli, for a seminar on Christian–Muslim relations: twelve a side, with not more than twenty "silent and attentive" observers looking on.[1] Though commonly regarded in the West as a revolutionary and bogeyman, Gadaffi presented himself as a Muslim integrist whose anti-Communism was unflawed. In a speech in Egypt he had declared: "I don't care whether the whole of Africa becomes Christian or Muslim; what I care about is stopping atheism and paganism in Africa."[2] Of course he could be expected to exploit the meeting to gain the utmost political advantage.

Fr Borrmans battled to have three African bishops at the meeting on the grounds that the further one got away from the cauldron of the Middle East and Israel the better the chances of dialogue. But already Colonel Gadaffi was changing the rules, cheerfully inviting Christians and Muslims to the former opera house – Libya had been an Italian colony – now renamed "the Theatre of Liberation". Instead of the twenty "silent and attentive" observers there were 500 people ready to stamp their feet and cheer. Gadaffi himself appeared out of nowhere, like a Bedouin, marched up to the stage and asked the Vatican delegation a tricky question: "Is the Vatican a *Christian* state?"

Pignedoli surveyed his team. None of them seemed keen to tackle this topic. Eventually Msgr Pietro Rossano made a gallant attempt to pack the history of the Papal States into five minutes. He did not think that the Vatican claimed to be based on the Gospels in the same sense the Muslim states claimed to be based on the Koran. Ha-ha, said Gadaffi, as though seeing a great light. The problem as in all Christian–Muslim dialogue was that both religions see themselves as definitive and final (*die letzte Religion*). Nevertheless there was in Tripoli a real exchange and progress in understanding on the religious level. Until, that is, the final "conclusions" were read out, very rapidly, in Arabic. One of them distinguished between Judaism and Zionism, describing the latter as "an aggressive and racist movement that was foreign to Palestine and the entire Middle East".[3]

Pignedoli strongly disapproved, Rossano was furious, but the press conference at which they could have explained themselves was cancelled. Most unfairly, the Italian press claimed Pignedoli had committed a gaffe sufficiently serious to rule him out of contention in the conclaves of

1 Maurice Borrmans, "*Le Séminaire du dialogue islamo-chrétien*", *Islamochristiana*, 2, 1976, p. 139. The definitive account of this extraordinary meeting.

2 *The Battle for Destiny*, Kalahari Publications, London 1967, p. 10.

3 Maurice Borrmans, op. cit. p. 158.

1978. Pignedoli soldiered on, sadder, wiser. There was no question of his resigning.

Neither did Paul resign, though it was Italy not Libya that put him on the rack. Throughout 1976 he was greatly preoccupied by the preparations for the first-ever congress of Italian Catholics. It was important by its theme "Evangelization and Human Promotion" which would have to apply the principles of *Evangelii Nuntiandi* to Italy; in particular it would have to address the problems posed by the dissident groups calling themselves "base communities". Second, it would have to reflect on the place of Catholics in Italian society after the divorce referendum, a clear instance of growing secularization. Third, it would be an expression of the growing self-awareness of the Italian Church as a local Church.

After the Holy Year it was the next task on the papal agenda. At his first general audience of 1976 he set it in the context of his universal mission:

> A new period of intense religious and pastoral activity opens for all of us who seek to be open to the "signs of the times" and who want to take advantage of the graces and resolutions of the Holy Year to give an impetus to a new and more fervent phase in Church life: we allude to the promotion of a new and more effective way of ordering our collective existence ... which has been called the "civilization of love".[1]

Ideally the Congress would apply the "civilization of love" to Italy. But the more preparations went on the more it seemed like a Platonic idea.

As Paul set out to scale this further peak of the pontificate he was riven by doubts and perplexities. For the Congress would open up a hornet's nest of problems. How were Italian Christians to be "present and effective" to society? What was one to think of those Catholics who scorned the Christian Democrats and worked with other parties?

What could be made of the Liga Democratica[2] which openly sided with the Communists? At least on this question the Italian Episcopal Conference (CEI) got a clear answer from Archbishop Benelli the *sostituto*: since Christianity and Marxism were ideologically incompatible, it followed that it was inconsistent with Christian faith to "adhere to or support movements which, in one form or another, are founded on Marxism".[3] But what chance was there of that line being obeyed? What position should the Italian Church take on the abortion legislation that was due to come before the Italian Parliament?

1 *Insegnamenti*, 1976, p. III. The "civilization of love" was his own coinage.

2 Sandro Magister, *La politica Vaticana*, p. 463.

3 Ibid. pp. 463–64.

But Paul's chief worry was that the Congress would become a vehicle for the "fringe groups" who were disturbing the peace of Italian Catholicism. Msgr Enrico Bartoletti, secretary of CEI, tried to reassure him: "Your holiness, if everybody does not take part in the Congress, it would be better not to hold it at all."[1] The Italian bishops were divided on whether Marxism had any positive value. Cardinal Pellegrino of Turin distinguished between Marxism as an ideology or philosophy and Marxism as "an instrument of analysis" that could be illuminating.[2] On the other hand Cardinal Ugo Poletti, Paul's Vicar for the Rome diocese, had called a conference on the "evils" of Rome in February 1974 which was designed to capture the city hall for the Christian Democrats.[3] But even apart from this dispute, how could one prevent the Bartoletti/Sorge conference from passing judgement on the policies and pontificate of Paul VI?

The unexpected death on 5 March of Msgr Enrico Bartoletti added to Paul's woes. It was a blow. He was one of the most promising theologians among the younger bishops, and Paul's most effective ally. He was associated with the "religious option" of Catholic Action, and the need to rethink evangelization in a post-Christian world.[4] The right wing, marshalled by Comunione e Liberazione and echoed by Archbishop Marcel Lefebvre, knew about his role in the Study Commission on Women and considered Bartoletti and those who thought like him "secularizing", feeble, defeatist and – they sometimes added – "Protestant" or at least "Protestantizing".

Though this mud was flung at the late Bartoletti, the real object of these attacks was Pope Paul himself. He felt keenly their injustice. But he left Italian affairs more and more to the substitute, Benelli, since Villot, Secretary of State, did not know the intricacies of Italian political life. Benelli blackballed the "obvious" successor to Bartoletti, Filippo Franceschi, Bishop of Ferrara, and "Higher Authority" nominated Luigi Maverna, known to be close to Benelli.[5]

One of the first acts of Benelli's appointee was to reconvene the Preparatory Committee of the Congress, "not so much with a view to continuing it, but to discuss whether it should take place at all." That

1 Bartolomeo Sorge, *Uscire del Tempio*, interviewed by Paolo Giuntella, p. 92.

2 Sandro Magister, *La Politica Vaticana*, p. 462. These remarks were made at the sanctuary of St Ignatius in the summer of 1975. Everyone seemed to have forgotten that these distinctions had been made in *Octogesima Adveniens* in 1971.

3 Ibid.

4 Giuseppe Alberigo, "*Santa Sede e vescovi nello stato unitario*", in *La Chiesa e il potere politico, Storia d'Italia, Annali* 9, p. 873.

5 Sandro Magister, *La politica Vaticana*, p. 478 fn. 49.

was the judgement of Sandro Magister who adds: "Only a decisive intervention by Cardinal Poma, President of CEI, was able to overcome the perplexities and fears of Paul VI."[1] But these fears were, in the end, overcome.

It is important to say that clearly because the revisionist "historians" of Comunione e Liberazione would later claim that the Congress took place *against the will* of Paul VI.[2] Were this true, it would show he was incompetent, not really in charge, a manipulated puppet-pope who had surrendered his authority to "others". The implication is that he ought to have followed his instinct and *resigned*, and that he stayed only because those who surrounded him – Benelli and Macchi are usually indicated – were serving their own interests.

The Conference did not begin until 30 October 1976. There was still the summer to be got through. His old mentor Don Galloni died on 6 June 1976 at La Montanina, the house that had belonged to the novelist Alessandro Manzoni. Paul's last letter to him had been full of his sadness at "defecting priests".

Don Pasquale Macchi now produced a "brilliant solution" to the Philadelphia problem or what to do about the US bicentennial. Paul would be whisked by helicopter to Bolsena where in 1283 occurred the "miracle of the Eucharist", which consisted of blood issuing from the consecrated elements. The miracle prompted Pope Urban IV to extend the feast of Corpus Christi to the whole Church the following year. The bloodstained corporal of Bolsena is kept in the cathedral of Orvieto, so from there Paul addressed the Americans on 8 August 1976 at six o'clock in the evening, thus concluding the 41st International Eucharistic Congress. He spoke an English that got more accented the older he got. He did his routine introduction: "It is the Bishop of Rome who speaks to you, the Successor of the Apostle Peter, the Pope of the Catholic Church, the Vicar of Christ on earth."[3]

This rehearsal of grand titles was not calculated to commend him to US Catholics at this point in their history. It was as though he were throwing down the gauntlet after *Humanae Vitae*. "We ask you to be silent," the strangulated voice went on, "to be silent now, and try to listen within yourselves to an inner proclamation!" It was an infelicitous speech that obscured the mystery of love and redemptive suffering that is the Eucharist. Perhaps his new English language secretary, Fr John Magee, spotted by Benelli when he was Nuncio in West Africa, was partly to blame.

1 Ibid. p. 465.

2 *Il Sabato*, 1–7 October 1988.

3 *Insegnamenti*, 1976, pp. 635–37.

Macchi's "brilliant solution" was in the event not such a good idea: a huge figure on a giant TV screen can seem very remote. In any case – though this was not a point Macchi would appreciate – Giovanni Benelli represented Pope Paul in Philadelphia and gave a good account of himself in an energetic speech.

What everyone remembered about Philadelphia was Benelli's embrace for both Mother Teresa of Calcutta and Dom Helder Câmara of Recife who shared the platform with him. This aroused the greatest enthusiasm for it seemed that the "official" or the "bureaucratic" Church was embracing the Church of charity, Mother Teresa, and of justice – Helder Câmara. By contrast Paul, in his ghostly appearance, sounded like a querulous old aunt intent on asserting his authority.

But was Paul not really in charge? In particular, was the Conference on the Italian Church held at EUR from 30 October to 4 November forced upon him against his will? The best answer to that came from Fr Bartolomeo Sorge SJ, editor of *Civiltà Cattolica*, who master-minded the assembly and gave its closing address:

> You have to be very naïve to imagine that a committee appointed by the Italian Bishops *could* organize an ecclesial meeting against the wishes of the Pope! All the more since the 1500 delegates were officially sent by their bishops of whom 120 were also present. Moreover Paul VI helped to prepare the Congress, devoting the five Wednesday audiences preceding the Congress to this theme, and insisting on celebrating the Congress Mass in St Peter's and pointedly calling it in his homily "*our* Congress".[1]

A sledge-hammer to crack a nut; but QED.

The Congress was not "against the will" of Paul VI. But his doubts and perplexities about it were not diminished by the fact that Cardinals Giovanni Colombo – his successor in Milan – and Albino Luciani – his successor as pope – as well as over half of the Italian bishops *deliberately stayed away*.[2]

Fr Sorge hoped the Conference would lead to what he called the "recomposition" of Italian Catholicism – that is, a reaffirmation of its unity after the débâcle of the divorce referendum. If their "political unity" (that is, the habit of voting for the Christian Democrats) could no longer be taken for granted, they should seek common ground in

1 *Adista*, 17–19 October 1988, p. 11.

2 Sandro Magister, *La politica Vaticana*, p. 478 fn. 49.

"cultural unity" on the pre-political level.[1] It does not seem that the concept of "recomposition", or the conference, had much practical result.

There was a magnificent concelebration in St Peter's to inaugurate it, in which Paul, like any aged priest, lamented the way the modern world in its dizzy-making headlong course

> seems to rebuff our attempts to interest it in religious matters, so rapidly judged and dismissed as superfluous, remote, foreign, hostile, *dépassé*, while at the same time, unconsciously and often with *Angst*, still yearning ardently for that ineffable and life-giving truth which we have the responsible privilege of possessing.[2]

This sounded like a confession of failure. Moreover Paul in his maturity would not have used that final word: Christians do not possess the truth, it possesses them.

The most disturbing speech at the Congress was that of Franco Bolgiani, an historian considered "close" to Cardinal Michele Pellegrino of Turin. His theme was "Thirty Years of Italian Catholicism". Any judgement on the years 1946–76 would have to involve some assessment of the present pontificate, now evidently approaching its end.

What was Bolgiani's verdict on the Pope who, now seventy-nine, was privately thinking of resignation? He was damned with faint praise and praised with faint damns. Tribute was paid to his past: "It was important that the new pope should be someone who in many years of silent and shrewd (*accorta*) meditation, when the horizon was closed, had worked prudently so that intellectual forces counted for something in the Church, and hope was not extinguished."[3] That referred to Montini's role under Pius XII in the 1950s.

What about his pontificate? Bolgiani thought it began well with the opening to dialogue in *Ecclesiam Suam* and the progressive views of *Populorum Progressio* ("so unwelcome to conservative Catholics"). The visits to the Holy Land and the United Nations scored good marks and the meetings with Patriarch Athenagoras and other ecumenical leaders were highly commended. But then Bolgiani concluded: "These writings and gestures were followed by undoubted signs of adjustment and

1 For an account of what *recomposizione* might mean, see Giuseppe Alberigo, "*Santa Sede e vescovi nello stato unitario*", in *La Chiesa e il potere politico, Storia d'Italia, Annali* 9, p. 874 fn. 22. Alberigo sees it as a feeble concept, little more than a way of papering over the cracks after the disarray manifested by the divorce referendum.

2 *Insegnamenti*, 1976, p. 893.

3 *Modernité*, p. 217.

changes of direction."[1] The pontificate of Paul VI was a promise unfulfilled.

Bolgiani concedes that ecumenism was one of the successes of the pontificate. The work of ARCIC continued as the most advanced theological dialogue, its even tenor hardly disturbed by the prospect of the Anglicans ordaining women. ARCIC was discussing *ministry*, not *who* exercised it. So the brief exchange of letters between the Archbishop of Canterbury and the Pope did not greatly perturb ARCIC. On 10 February 1976 Dr Coggan wrote:

> We believe . . . that unity will be achieved within a diversity of legitimate traditions because the Holy Spirit has never ceased to be active within the local churches throughout the world. Sometimes what seems to one tradition to be the legitimate expression of such diversity in unity will appear to another tradition to go beyond the bounds of legitimacy.[2]

This was the first time that the Anglican Communion had presented itself as a "local church" (or a group of local churches) within the universal Church. It seemed to suggest, interestingly, that unity had already been achieved.

Paul VI replied on 23 March 1976, expressing his sadness at "this new obstacle on the way to reconciliation, this new threat along our path".[3] Yet he did not think, and did not say, that the quest for unity was therefore blocked for all time.

ARCIC was justified in commenting on this 23 March 1976 letter that "the principles on which its doctrinal agreement rests are not affected by such ordinations (that is, of women); for it was concerned with the origin and nature of the ordained ministry and not with the question of who can or cannot be ordained".[4] Was this disingenuous, perhaps deliberately so?

Even if we leave that question aside as unanswerable, the "elucidation" ARCIC provided seemed reasonable: "Objections, however substantial, to the ordination of women are of a different kind from objections raised in the past against the validity of Anglican orders in general."[5] *Apostolicae Curae* of 1896 declared Anglican orders to be

1 Ibid.

2 Christopher Hill, "The Ordination of Women and Anglican–Roman Catholic Dialogue, "*Women Priests?* ed. Alyson Peberdy, Marshall Pickering 1988, p. 2. This is in a Women and Religion series edited by Janet Martin Soskice.

3 *Insegnamenti*, 1976, p. 666.

4 ARCIC, *The Final Report*, 1982, p. 44.

5 Ibid.

invalid by defect of form and intention. That was not the objection that was now being raised against the ordination of women.

The Commission on the role of women had already been disbanded on 31 January 1976, "its mission being complete and its final recommendations submitted to the Pontifical Council for the Laity".[1] That was the official version. In practice they went into Rosemary Goldie's archives, whence they were dispensed to students of good will. One could speak of a diffused effect of the Commission which, however, ended with Paul's death.

Thanks to the Anglicans, ARCIC remained the only forum in which the question of women's ordination stayed alive for Catholics on the official level. This remained true even after the publication of *Inter Insigiores* of 15 October 1976. Indeed one can argue that the relatively cautious and non-absolutist tone of *Inter Insigiores* was inspired by a reluctance to reject out of hand the Anglican precedent of the ordination of women. It does not say that the non-ordination of women is *de jure divino*, which would have excluded it for all time.

Joseph Ratzinger, at this date teaching theology at Regensburg, worked on the document and thought it could have been put more strongly. His 1984 judgement was that it was "very well prepared even though, like all official documents, it is marked by a certain dryness: it goes directly to the conclusions without being able to justify all the individual steps leading to them with the requisite fullness of detail".[2]

Whatever one thought about that, the question posed at the Assisi meeting of November 1975 remained to be resolved: how can Churches with women priests and those without them be reconciled in sacramental fellowship? That question, far from going away, had been made more acute by the increasing numbers of women being ordained in the Anglican Communion, especially in Canada and the United States.

Inter Insigiores was accompanied by a commentary (believed to be by Belgian Dominican Father Jerôme Hamer, then at the Congregation for the Doctrine of the Faith) which related it to the Paul VI – Dr Coggan correspondence. This usefully confirmed that the Anglican–Roman Catholic dialogue was the right context for appreciating the on-going debate.

It also, no doubt unintentionally, brought out some of the features of *Inter Insigiores*, which meant that future dialogue on this subject was not totally in vain. A meeting was planned for Versailles in February

1 Joel-Benoit d'Onorio, "*Paul VI et le gouvernement central*", in *Modernité de Paul VI*, p. 619.

2 Joseph Ratzinger, *The Ratzinger Report*, Ignatius Press, San Francisco 1985, p. 93. This comes at the start of a chapter curiously called "Women, A Woman".

1978 to consider the ecclesial consequences of the Anglican ordination of women.

Inter Insigiores said that women's ordination was to be rejected in accordance with the constant tradition of the Church. But at the same time it admitted that this was the first statement on the topic, and therefore that "tradition" was here being used in a rather special, not to say quixotic, sense. There was no constant tradition *against* women's ordination. The question had simply not arisen before. It was "untraditional" only by default.

Inter Insigiores also assembles the biblical, sacramental and symbolic arguments against women's ordination in what can only be described as a gingerly fashion: "It seems useful and opportune to *illustrate* this norm by showing *the profound fittingness* that theological reflection discovers. It is not a question here of bringing forward a demonstrative argument but of clarifying this teaching by *the analogy of faith*."[1] Hence the present tense used by *Inter Insigiores* was considered highly significant: "The Church, in fidelity to the example of the Lord, does not consider herself authorized to admit women to priestly ordination."[2] That did not sound like a definitive statement for all time.

But – to repeat – the question at this date was not whether the Catholic Church was about to ordain women (it was clearly not). It was whether the ordination of women by another Church with which it was seeking union created an insuperable barrier to such union.

That was certainly not the view of the Catholics present at the Versailles meeting in February 1978. A little-known note of Yves Congar stated:

> Two things may be seen as grounds for hope:
>
> 1 Those who ordain women do not think that they are departing from tradition.
>
> 2 The exclusion of women from the priesthood in the declaration *Inter Insigiores* is not a *de jure* definition (nor is it based on one).[3]

So there was still something left to discuss. Dr Donald Coggan, Archbishop of Canterbury, would visit Paul in 1977. The view that the ordination of women was a "legitimate development" of tradition and "an expansion of eligibility" was gaining ground in Anglican circles. Opposed as he was to women's ordination Paul had a keener sense than his successors of the complexity of situations and a reluctance to commit

1 Austin Flannery OP, *More Post-conciliar Documents*, vol. 2, p. 338. Italics supplied by Canon Christopher Hill.

2 Ibid. p. 332.

3 Christopher Hill, "The Ordination of Women in Anglican–Roman Catholic Dialogue", in *Women Priests?* p. 4.

the Church to irrevocable courses of action. If this made him seem hesitatant or dilatory, that is to his credit.

But in the areas he knew best he acted decisively. With the nomination of twenty cardinals on 24 May 1976 Paul completed the electoral college that would elect his successor. It was his last big consistory. Pope John used to boast of having created the first African cardinal. But here, at a stroke, were five out of twenty, one of whom was scarred with tribal marks while another was the son of a chief who had fifty wives.

Among the new African cardinals was a Jesuit, Viktor Razafimahatratra from Madagascar. Having been bishop of a small and unimportant diocese in the south of the island, he was surprised to hear from the Nuncio that he had been appointed Archbishop of Tananarive. He asked for time to make a retreat to think it over. "You can have fifteen minutes," said the Nuncio. (That was the time St Ignatius said he would need to get over the news of the suppression of the Society of Jesus.) Four days later the Nuncio called again. Good, thought Viktor, they've had second thoughts and thought better of it. But the Nuncio's first words were: "And you have also been made a cardinal."

The same news caused a shock to another Jesuit, Lawrence Picachy of Calcutta, who cheerfully accepted that, being less famous than a nun in his diocese, he was always referred to as "Mother Teresa's bishop". Neither Picachy nor Razafimahatratra could afford the expense attached to the consistory, and the Congregation for the Evangelization of Peoples had to foot the bill. The Brazilian Aloisio Lorscheider added a Latin American dimension. Beyond any doubt it was Paul's most adventurous and Third World consistory. Paul concelebrated with them on the feast of the Ascension, 27 May, and gave them all a ring, saying in Latin, "Receive this ring from Peter, and know that through the love of the Prince of the Apostles, the love of Christ is strengthened."[1]

This consistory was widely seen as a papal response to the book of Fr Walter Bühlman OFM, *The Coming of the Third Church*, who argued that the days of Rome as the centre of the Church were numbered and that already the initiative had passed to the Third World. The book cost Bühlman his teaching post in Rome, but if matters were that bad it was no doubt time to depart. Even among the new European cardinals there were men who understood the emphasis on the Third World and welcomed it. One such was Basil Hume OSB, Abbot of Ampleforth, who had accepted the position of Archbishop of Westminster only when Paul said it was a question of obedience. Nearly all mediaeval archbishops in England were Benedictines, but Hume was the first monk to hold this post since the restoration of the hierarchy in 1851.

1 *Insegnamenti*, 1976, p. 415.

Hume went into his first meeting in his Benedictine habit. Paul advanced on him, arms outstretched, and said, "*Benedetto colui qui viene nel nome del Signore*" (Blessed is he who comes in the name of the Lord). This was a play on *Benedictus, benedetto, blessed*. It also recalled his motto: *In nomine Domini* (In the name of the Lord). Hume, slightly alarmed at the prospect of speaking Italian, was reassured when the Pope said: "*Maintenant, parlons français.*" Paul was clearly in a hurry: Hume was created a cardinal just two months after being ordained bishop.[1]

Archbishop Marcel Lefebvre was suspended *a divinis* by the Congregation of Bishops on 24 July 1976. There was a sadness and inevitability about this measure. Lefebvre had gradually stepped up his provocations – almost as if he were daring Paul to act. He had opened his seminary at Ecône in a Swiss valley in 1971 and numbers grew steadily. In 1973 there were ninety-five and in the spring of 1976 a triumphant 110. He was warned in advance exactly what would happen if he went ahead with priestly ordinations at Ecône. His defiance was orchestrated by the media and was not without panache. So he was suspended. There was no alternative. But Paul was heavy-hearted.

He was subjected to a barrage of abuse this time from the right wing. His "campaign" against Lefebvre, wrote Rupert Scott, "is now generally admitted to have been an unjust, foolish misuse of Vatican authority".[2]

No one could say that who knew the story from Paul's perspective. We know exactly what he thought because he discussed the Lefebvre case with Jean Guitton on 8 September 1976 during their annual *tour d'horizon*. Though they tried to talk about Ronsard and poetry the conversation returned obstinately to Lefebvre. Paul said that Lefebvre had been "for thirteen years the greatest cross of my pontificate".

"For thirteen years": in other words Lefebvre had been a "cross" to be borne right from the start of his pontificate in 1963. Paul knew that Lefebvre never held the position of some conservatives that the Council itself was valid but that there were "excesses" in its application.

1 The source is Cardinal Basil Hume, to whom I am grateful. He also tells a delightful story about Rembert Weakland, then Abbot General of the OSBs, later Archbishop of Milwaukee. When Abbot General, Weakland took his mother to a private audience with Paul VI who lavished praise on Weakland, saying how fortunate she was to have such a wonderful, spiritual, learned, remarkable, etc. son. "Listen to that, Mom," said Weakland, "and he's infallible you know." Mom replied: "I've never had a crisis of faith before, but I sure have one now."

2 Generally admitted by whom? Presumably by those who agree with Scott's other remark: "There are many cardinals in the Roman Curia who are now prepared to admit that Paul VI's pontificate was the most disastrous of the century." Rupert Scott, "Tridentine Tribulations", *Spectator*, 25 June 1988. This was at the time of Lefebvre's excommunication when he took the further step of ordaining four bishops.

Lefebvre's position was that the Council itself was radically flawed and represented the invasion of the Church by the false values of the French Revolution. It celebrated "liberty" in the pernicious doctrine of religious freedom, "equality" in the erroneous doctrine of collegiality, and "fraternity" in ecumenism.

Paul VI could not forget the letter signed by Lefebvre which he received on 14 September 1964, on the eve of the third session, rejecting the principle of collegiality and warning the Pope that he would be betraying his heritage if he did not unilaterally reverse it now, immediately. Lefebvre included this letter in the book published that year, 1976, with the accurate title, *J'accuse le Concile.*

So from 1963 Lefebvre had been a thorn in the side of Paul who had shown considerable patience with him. When he did decide to act, his conscience was clear: "I've thought about it, I've tried everything, and if later on there is a schism, that will not be due to me but rather to the crazy almost morbid obstinacy of Msgr Lefebvre who tears the Church apart and scandalizes it by his disobedience."[1]

Guitton, who was not unsympathetic to Lefebvre – this enhances the quality of his reporting – pointed out that although he had tried personal letters and appeals, the one thing he had *not yet* tried was granting the personal audience Lefebvre had repeatedly requested. Paul replied: "Msgr Lefebvre is in open revolt. It is the revolt of a bishop who educates priests against me. If I welcome him here, he will very likely insult me, and distort my words afterwards."

That had been the experience of the intermediaries who had actually met Lefebvre. Whatever transpired in their meetings, Lefebvre always emerged convinced that he had uncovered yet further evidence of the masonic conspiracy gnawing away at the Church.

"I sent him messengers to plead with him in my name," said Paul, "and he rejected them." Nothing could replace a face-to-face meeting, said Guitton. "But how can I receive someone," Paul complained, "who said only yesterday in Besançon that he would kneel down before me only if I didn't insist on him first becoming a Protestant? How can I receive someone who says I am a modernist and a heretic?"[2]

Despite these misgivings Paul did receive Lefebvre on 11 September 1976, just three days after this conversation with Guitton. What had happened? Various intermediaries including Vincenzo Fagiolo and Don Domenico La Bellarte of the sanctuary of Padre Pio at San Giovanni Rotondo, had been trying to intercede for Lefebvre. Paul merely said:

1 Jean Guitton, *Paul VI secret*, p. 156.
2 Ibid. p. 155.

"See Don Macchi about that."[1] Evidently Paul did not expect anything to happen. Don Pasquale Macchi agreed in principle to seeing Lefebvre's latest emissary. But next day, 9 September 1976, Lefebvre himself arrived in Castelgandolfo and presented the Swiss Guard with a letter for the Pope. It said: "I have never had the intention of acting against the Church, still less of offending the Pope. I regret the suffering I have caused him by the positions I have taken."

Paul was "badly shaken (*ébranlé*)" on receiving this note, and rang Villot at the Secretariat of State. Paul seemed to want to go ahead with a meeting, as a last desperate effort to bring Lefebvre round, but he still doubted the archbishop's sincerity. Villot's advice was that he should under no circumstances see Lefebvre alone and that it was essential to have a witness. After discussing various candidates they settled on Msgr Giovanni Benelli.

Paul received Lefebvre the next day at 11 a.m. Benelli, who had been at Paul's side but not uttered a single word, phoned Villot with the gist of what had happened. The dominant feeling of the audience was of sadness. Lefebvre withdrew nothing, did not apologize and repeated his usual views. Paul received him with great severity. When Lefebvre advanced to embrace him, he refused, saying, "What have we here, a brother or an enemy?" Lefebvre's ploy soon became clear: if he were allowed freely to continue with his seminary at Ecône, then he would refrain from overt acts of opposition. Taken by surprise at this approach, Paul said, "I'll write to you."[2] That was all. Lefebvre left without either kiss of peace or blessing.

Villot was afraid that Lefebvre would exploit Paul's hesitation about a seminary that already had no canonical existence. Already Lefebvre had boasted to his sister, a nun at Albano near Castelgandolfo, that "it had taken him only two days to get the audience that his enemies had denied him for two years". The newspapers were interested, and Lefebvre would be giving interviews. The visit could not be denied. A laconic communiqué was inserted in *L'Osservatore Romano*. It said the Pope had invited Lefebvre "in strongly paternal fashion to reflect on the damaging situation he had caused the Church and on his responsibility before God to the faithful who follow him and to the entire Church".[3]

That of course did not stop the speculative stories in the press. The Vatican press officer, Fr Romeo Panciroli, issued *démentis* denying that Lefebvre had signed a document of submission before the audience or

1 Antoine Wenger, *Le Cardinal Villot*, p. 148. As a French bishop, Villot took a great interest in the Lefebvre case.

2 Ibid. pp. 148–49.

3 *L'Osservatore Romano*, 11 September 1976.

that the meeting had been long planned or indeed that there was any change at all or that Cardinal Villot's family had been Freemasons for two centuries.[1] In short, the audience was a mistake that made the solution of the Lefebvre affair more difficult. Don Macchi felt cheated: "*Sono stato ingannato*" (I was deceived) was his verdict.

It was not quite the end of the affair. Lefebvre repeated his demand to be allowed to say the Tridentine Mass and to form priests "as before the Council". He refused to give the written assurance that he accepted the Council and all its documents asked for by Paul in his letter of 11 October 1976.

Reflecting the whole affair Paul concluded that although the argument was ostensibly about the liturgy, it was really about the nature of tradition and the place of the living *magisterium*. He defended his liturgical reforms: "Not only have we maintained everything of the past but we have rediscovered the most ancient and primitive tradition, the one closest to the origins. This tradition had been obscured in the course of centuries, particularly by the Council of Trent."

Even so, the *canon* of St Pius V had been retained and given the first place. It is the *canon* that shapes the meaning of the act of worship.

Paul VI then approached the key question:

> The difference between the Mass of Pius V and the liturgy of the Council (sometimes called, I don't know why, the liturgy of Paul VI) is very small. Apparently the difference is a subtlety. But this so-called Mass of Pius V, as celebrated at Ecône, has become the symbol of the condemnation of the Council. I will never accept that one should symbolically reject the Council. If this exception were allowed, the whole Council would be subverted and, with it, its apostolic authority.[2]

The "Mass of Pius V," he remarked, has become like the white flag with the fleurs-de-lis of the French monarchists: a symbol of defiance.

Paul had submitted himself to the "apostolic authority" of the Council, and not unreasonably expected others to do the same. His position was always caricatured by Ecône apologists: they claimed he was appealing to his personal authority, rather than to the authority of the Church; and with equal injustice they charged that in constantly talking about "the" Council he was slighting the earlier Councils of the Church.[3]

Paul now knew that Lefebvre simply *did not wish* to understand. He

1 Wenger, *Villot*, p. 151. Instead of treating this accusation with lordly disdain, Villot made matters worse by elaborate replies.

2 Ibid. pp. 158–59.

3 *La Condamnation Sauvage*, p. 103.

saw him as a representative of that tenacious French right wing, born of Action Française, which saw the modern world in all its forms (the Reformation, Rationalism, the French Revolution, the Russian Revolution) as exclusively hostile.

What was lacking in Ecône was any sense of the development of doctrine. Guitton believed – and Paul VI agreed – that John Henry Newman was the hidden influence on Vatican II. Paul saw himself as responsible before history and God for a Council which he would not have called but over which he presided. In taking the name "Paul", Apostle to the Gentiles, he expressed his desire to reach out to the whole world. Religious liberty was a condition of the freedom of the act of faith; ecumenism was the way to heal the wounds of the Body of Christ; stress on what Christians have in common with the great world religions was not to fall into "indifferentism" but contribute to world peace. None of this was understood at Ecône. Lefebvre's real objection was to Paul's "modernity".

The failure of the audience with Lefebvre was Paul's greatest sadness. He had tried everything and been humiliated. What was left? The hope of repentance? Paul did not think that likely: "There would have to be a real change, a long process of maturation, a convergence of evidence, not only on the part of Msgr Lefebvre but on the part of his disciples. Then there would be a presumption of sincerity that I do not see at the moment."[1]

He did not expect to live long enough for that. And he was right.

1 Jean Guitton, *Paul VI secret*, pp. 159–60.

38

For Whom the Bell Tolls

> The real Pope Paul is not pessimistic, gloomy, indecisive, anguished. He is presented as such on the strength of a few words pronounced when he is dog-tired, perhaps having gone to bed at 4 a.m. or when he has received bad news about an American Jesuit theologian who has run off to get married. That's not the real Montini.
>
> (Giovanni Benelli, quoted by GIANCARLO ZIZOLA, *Panorama* 15 November 1982)

And the real Montini? Italians refer to popes by their surnames without any lack of respect. "He's not the tired, sick man you go on gossiping about," Benelli went on, "who should resign. Take his speech on 22 June 1975, ten years after the Council: that's the real Montini – the man who launched the reforms of Vatican II."[1] Zizola adds that Benelli was famous for being able to "exorcise Montini's anxieties" besides getting things done.

But now early in 1977 Paul VI took a decision that cost him a lot: he would let Benelli go, making him a bishop and a cardinal. Benelli would not have to undergo vicariously the fate he suffered by being excluded from the conclave of 1958. So this was good for Benelli. It also meant that he was admitting to himself that his pontificate had nothing more to do. He was wrong. But he began to dwell with thoughts of mortality, which for him were not gloomy. "Can one say Mass for a non-Catholic?" he asked John Magee one morning as they came out of the chapel. Magee hesitantly said "Well, er, yes, Christ died for all." "A good answer," Paul replied, "I've just said Mass for Hubert Humphrey. We can set no limits to God's mercy." He had picked up the news of Humphrey's death on the radio.[2] For the time being the decision about Benelli was kept secret, *in petto*.

Then on Monday, 21 February 1977 there was a wonderful occasion

1 Giancarlo Zizola, "*Il mio amico Onnipotente*", in *Panorama*, 15 November 1982, p. 95.

2 John Magee, "*La vita quotidiana*", in *Paul VI et la Modernité*, p. 141.

made for Benelli, who had always tried to find a role for the Holy See in the European Economic Community and sought to give it a "soul" – *un supplément d'âme*: an audience for its president, Roy Jenkins, and his *chef de cabinet*, Crispin Tickell. Jenkins consigns everything to his diary. It records:

> Paul VI was too frail happily to talk in French, so he talked in Italian and I talked mostly in English. Unfortunately this was pretty badly interpreted by a young monsignor from California. It was very much more informal than I had remembered when I previously had an audience with Pius XII over twenty years ago.
>
> The ceremonies going in and out are rather splendid with the Swiss Guards and the Papal Chamberlain still fully in operation. A group of about thirty *Mezzogiorno* bishops were waiting outside. It was not obvious to me (I had never thought about it previously) what to do when passing through a group of assembled bishops in this way. The best thing seemed to incline one's head gravely in one direction and then in the other. The impressiveness of my departure was, however, somewhat reduced, when one of them was heard to say in a strong stage whisper *è Callaghan.*[1]

In fact twenty-six bishops were present on this occasion, and they came from Campania. They were marshalled by Cardinal Corrado Ursi of Naples who made the usual flattering speech of homage.

However doddery Paul VI was by this stage, he managed to read out a speech which said that their region, known to antiquity as *Campania felix*, was undergoing the "rapid transformation of its old economic and social structures".[2] That could have provided matter for his earlier conversation with the President of the European Commission. The *mezzogiorno* or south of Italy was often considered as an "internal Third World", a stretch of Africa that had strayed into Europe. For the EC it was a "region" to be "developed". Paul said he felt for the bishops of Campania, and borrowed St Paul's words to express his empathy: "Who is weak, and I am not weak? Who is made to fall, and I am not indignant?"[3]

1 Roy Jenkins, *European Diary, 1977–1981*, Collins 1989, p. 51. The date was 21 February 1977. I have used the fuller version given in the *Observer*, 12 February 1989. Jim Callaghan was Prime Minister of the United Kingdom at the time. Lord Jenkins, now Chancellor of the University of Oxford, is quite unable to explain why Paul VI should be so reluctant to speak French. His frailness was not the answer.

2 *Insegnamenti*, XV, 1977, pp. 183–84.

3 Ibid. The Pauline text is from 2 Corinthians 11:29.

Paul's frailty struck Dr Garret Fitzgerald, Irish Foreign Minister, who followed up a Benelli hint and met the Pope on 25 March. Delayed by a complicated discussion on Ireland's unilateral fishing measures, Fitzgerald recalled that the last person to be late for a papal audience was Idi Amin. On arrival he heard voices from the Pope's library and assumed it was a last-minute briefing. But it was Paul himself, rehearsing his seven-minute address in French. It was uncompromising: "Ireland is a Catholic country, perhaps the only one left, and it should remain that way." There was no time to argue, even if Fitzgerald had been inclined to upset the ailing Pope. He merely remarked that an appallingly tragic situation existed in Northern Ireland to which "the Republic was trying to respond in a positive and Christian way".

Fitzgerald's account goes on:

> Before I could go any further, he intervened. He knew how tragic the situation was, he said, but it could not be a reason to change any of the laws that kept us a Catholic state. At that I more or less gave up. I left the audience somewhat shell-shocked. The tone and content of his remarks suggested I was a dangerous liberal intent upon destroying Catholicism in Ireland.[1]

He assumed that the Nuncio, the fiery Sicilian Archbishop Gaetano Alibrandi, was responsible for this depressing slander.

Fitzgerald found Archbishop Casaroli, head of the Council for Public Affairs, "polished and smooth" as ever. Casaroli pounced on his gratuitous remark that a united Ireland could be a federation or a confederation: "But in a federal state you could have divorce in one part and not in the other." Archbishop Giovanni Benelli, for his part, insisted that while Casaroli saw matters from a *religious* point of view, his task was to consider political implications:

> Would it not be important to pursue policies that would not lose us the Catholic vote? With as straight a face as I could I responded that I believed the Taoiseach was indeed concerned not to lose the Catholic vote – which was 96 per cent of the total. He seemed reassured. As we went down in the lift after the meeting, one of the officials accompanying me remarked that he sounded like a man thinking of standing for the Dail himself.[2]

1 Garret Fitzgerald, *All in a Life, an Autobiography*, Gill and Macmillan, 1991, pp. 186–87.

2 Ibid.

Fitzgerald was not to know that Benelli, on the verge of departure, was covering for the increasingly feeble Pope and was accused by the Curia of exceeding his brief.

Paul's frailty also struck the members of the Anglican delegation who came to see him on 27 to 30 April. This visit of Dr Donald Coggan, Archbishop of Canterbury, was the last of the great ecumenical visits to Pope Paul. It was widely regarded as something of a disappointment. Dr Coggan was usually blamed for "tactlessness" in calling for "Intercommunion now" in his sermon in the American Episcopal Church of St Paul's, via Napoli, on the evening of 28 April. It was said that his "Evangelical" background had let him down. He had clumsily failed to understand the "delicate" nature of relations with Rome.

Most of these judgements were unfair to Dr Coggan. He was more ecumenically minded than some Evangelicals. As President of the United Bible Society he knew and appreciated the work of Catholics like Walter Abbott SJ. The fact that Jean Coggan's mother had belonged to the Plymouth Brethren was neither here nor there; her father was a clergyman of the Church of England.[1] Moreover Coggan had been encouraged to raise the issue of intercommunion by Archbishop (then Bishop) Henry McAdoo, joint Chairman of ARCIC, and Bernard Pawley, Archdeacon of Canterbury.

True, one of his advisers, Dr John Moorman, Bishop of Ripon from 1959 to 1975, thought the visit unwise and inopportune: Paul VI was old, sick, and could not be expected to make binding decisions for the future; the ecumenical achievements of his pontificate were considerable and would remain; but top-level encounters that do not lead to some kind of visible progress in unity are a counter-productive anti-climax. But Moorman, though *an* Anglican authority on Rome, was not the only one.

Other advisers said: go ahead. The visit to Rome was part of an ecumenical journey that also took Dr Coggan to Constantinople to meet the Ecumenical Patriarch and Geneva to talk with the World Council of Churches. To omit Rome on such a journey would look like a snub.

So a Common Declaration, to be signed by pope and archbishop, was worked out in advance in conjunction with the Secretariat for Christian Unity. It took its stand on the Malta Report which set ARCIC's agenda, and listed what had been achieved in the eight years since then and what remained to be done. It was a practical, urgent recommitment to the nitty-gritty details of ecumenism on the local level. The Secretariat for Christian Unity, far from being worried by Dr Coggan's Evangelical

1 As Lord Coggan courteously pointed out to me.

theology, was gratified by it: it meant that Anglican ecumenism was not just confined to the "Catholic" wing of the Church.

Paul's brief speech in his library on the morning of 28 April 1977 mentioned the heroes of the abortive Malines conversations of the 1920s – Lord Halifax, Cardinal Desiré Mercier, Dom Lambert Beauduin OSB – and evoked Beauduin's famous formula for unity: "The pace of this movement has quickened marvellously in recent years, so that these words of hope, 'The Anglican Church united not absorbed', are no longer a mere dream."[1]

Though no doubt drafted by Cardinal Jan Willebrands and Msgr Charles Moeller, Paul VI willingly reached back in memory to canonize the phrase "united not absorbed" which was a condition of future progress. It was as important as his remarks about "sister Church" at the canonization of the English and Welsh Martyrs in 1970. Ecumenism inched forward in Paul's reign from nuance to nuance.

Dr Coggan's sermon that evening at St Paul's was in what he thought was the same vein. He did not *advocate* "wildcat" intercommunion (*l'intercommunion sauvage*), often denounced by Pope Paul, so much as pose a legitimate question about it:

> Has not the time now arrived when we have reached such a measure of agreement on so many of the fundamentals of the Gospel that a relationship of shared communion can be encouraged by the leadership of both our communities? I would go further and ask whether our work of joint evangelization will not be seriously weakened until we are able to go to that work strengthened by our joint participation in the Body and Blood of Christ. The day must come when together we kneel and receive from one another's hands the tokens of God's redeeming love and then directly go, again together, to the world which Christ came to redeem.[2]

Though Coggan was not to know it, this played straight into the hands of the curial conservatives, who watched every move of the Secretariat for Christian Unity in order to catch them out in unorthodoxy or – worse still – "indifferentism".

But behind Coggan's words, and explaining them, lay an experience. In February and March 1977 Dr Coggan toured the South Pacific. In Papua New Guinea the archbishop celebrated the Eucharist and preached at a teacher training college in Goroka. He was deeply moved

1 *Insegnamenti*, 1977, p. 405. See Sonya A. Quitsland, *Beauduin, A Prophet Vindicated*, 1973.

2 Edward J. Yarnold, *They are in Earnest*, p. 136.

because many of the Roman Catholics present, especially the nuns, received communion from his hands. Afterwards in the makeshift vestry the local Catholic bishop, the American Divine Word Father John Edward Cohill, gave the kiss of peace to Dr Coggan with tears in his eyes and said, "Next time you come, please God it will be better still." This incident made a deep impression on Dr Coggan, and he elaborated on it in the telling.[1] In his eyes it was further evidence that intercommunion was already happening, though sporadically and unofficially. Thus in Rome in his own mind he was simply asking for facts to be recognized, not "demanding intercommunion now".

This distinction was lost on the Italian press, which said Coggan had upset his host. But the sermon had no effect on the meeting next morning when Pope and Archbishop went through the Common Declaration and agreed to sign it the next day in the Sistine Chapel. Paul was flanked by Cardinal Jan Willebrands and Bishop Ramon Torrella Cascante. Coggan's aides, Bishop John Howe, Secretary of the Anglican Consultative Council, and Edward Knapp-Fisher, former Bishop of Pretoria, South Africa, were alarmed at how sick and feeble Paul appeared. He seemed unable to concentrate for very long. But he was happy with the statement.

The first hint of trouble came during a reception that evening at the Palazzo Doria Pamphilij where the Anglican Centre was housed. Fr Pierre Duprey phoned from the Secretariat for Christian Unity to say that "the Pope has changed his mind and has revised the text" (of the Common Declaration). It seemed discourteous to say the least to be unilaterally changing a joint statement at the last minute. The questions came thick and fast: Who had done this? What did it mean? Was Paul VI really in charge?

Next morning at eight at the English College Coggan and Knapp-Fisher conferred with Willebrands and Torrella Cascante about how to respond. The changes proposed did not have much rhyme or reason about them. The passage on "what had been achieved" was deleted. It looked as though someone wanted to show who was boss. But who would want to make that point? The Secretariat people, hardened by years of in-fighting, suspected their old adversary, Fr Luigi Ciappi OP. Although his grand title of Master of the Sacred Palace had been swept

1 He got into the habit of saying that when the local Roman Catholics had asked their bishop whether they might receive communion, he replied: "You must do what your conscience dictates" – "A very Anglican reply", Coggan would add. David Painter, Coggan's secretary at the time, says this exchange never happened. This is relevant in so far as it proves that the nuns' decision to receive Communion in Papua New Guinea was spontaneous rather than planned. Letter of David Painter to the author, 5 January 1987.

away in the reform of the Curia, Ciappi was still influential – he was made a cardinal two months later – and could sniff heresy or "indifferentism" a mile away. Another suspect was Fr Jerôme Hamer OP who had moved from the Secretariat for Christian Unity to the more congenial (for him) pastures of the Congregation for the Doctrine of the Faith. No one believed Pope Paul was responsible. Egged on by the Secretariat members, the Anglicans decided to oppose the changes.

But how could they get through to Pope Paul in time? Torrella Cascante knew the answer: call the *sostituto*, Msgr Giovanni Benelli. Unfortunately the telephone system of the English College chose this moment to break down. Torrella Cascante went out and phoned Benelli from a bar. Thus the comments on the changes reached Pope Paul at the eleventh hour, and were largely accepted without fuss. The duplicating machine at the Secretariat was set to work to produce 2000 copies of the tardily agreed statement. The Coggan party was sped through the streets of Rome with a police escort to meet their eleven o'clock deadline.

So, in reasonably unmutilated form, the Common Declaration was signed in the Sistine Chapel. Between Paul's first meeting with an Archbishop of Canterbury in 1966 and this meeting eleven years later there had been the three ARCIC documents, on Ministry, Eucharist and Authority. The joint statement said of ARCIC:

> Anglican and Roman Catholic theologians have faced calmly and objectively the doctrinal differences that have divided us. Without compromising their respective allegiances, they have discovered theological convergences as unexpected as they were happy ... The moment must soon come when the respective authorities must evaluate their conclusions.[1]

"Convergence towards Christ" was one of Paul's key phrases. "Unexpected" dealt neatly with those who, not having taken part in the process, did not appreciate the result. And it was vital to stress that they were not compromise texts.

This Common Declaration was the last act in Paul's dealings with the Anglican Communion. They had long recognized his special affection for them, and his competence: "It is an understatement to say that Pope Paul VI knew more than any other Pope about the Church of England.

1 *Insegnamenti*, 1977, p. 416. On the Anglican side, a positive evaluation was given by the Lambeth Conference of 1988, when the ARCIC Final Report was introduced by Dr George Carey, from 1991 Archbishop of Canterbury. On the Catholic side, that "evaluation" had to wait until December 1991. It was negative, and failed to recognize the originality of the method.

He was the only Pope who had given the necessary time and trouble to understand the Church of England.'[1]

Dr Coggan's visit, then, proved that Paul did not "change his mind on ecumenism" in his last years, as has been asserted. But again he looked very ill and his eyes lit up only when he saw an old friend, the ninety-year-old Jesuit Charles Boyer. "This is your day," said Paul to the man who had introduced him to Anglicans in the post-war period.

Back at the English College after the Common Declaration Dr Coggan was giving a press conference. Cardinal Willebrands, hot, flustered and still quivering from the "battle of the late changes", came into the office of the Rector, Fr Cormac Murphy-O'Connor, who said: "Your eminence, what you need is a stiff drink." "I do," said the Dutchman, "I do."[2]

There was a sequel to this story that was as unexpected as it was happy (to borrow the language of the Common Declaration). On the final Saturday morning Dr Coggan and some of his party visited the excavations in the crypt of St Peter's where the bones of the saint are said to be. As they emerged from this first-century experience, so different from the baroque Rome built over it, they found Benelli pacing up and down alone, obviously waiting for them.

Benelli wished to apologize "on behalf of the Holy Father" for the "difficulties" that had arisen. He often had this role of picking up the pieces caused by the ineptitude of others. But it was for the last time. In June 1977 Benelli was made Archbishop of Florence and a Cardinal.

The decision to part with his human dynamo was not unforced. On 17 May 1979, just two years before his death, Benelli met Giancarlo Zizola and told him the story:

> The Pope called me one evening to his private apartment. Tears streamed down his cheeks. He looked very old. His heart was weak. He knew that he could die at any moment. The tears were so abundant that they marked his blotter. Then he said that I should go to Florence because it was a post my service merited and because he didn't know how much longer he had to live.

1 Owen Chadwick, in *Anglican Initiatives in Christian Unity*, ed. E. G. W. Bill, SPCK 1967, p. 102.

2 Cormac Murphy-O'Connor, Bishop of Arundel and Brighton, though not the source of this story, confirmed its truth in a letter to the author, 31 January 1986. It seems fitting that he should now be co-chairman of ARCIC-II (sometimes known as Ben-ARCIC).

> He added that he would still want me to work with him, and that he would telephone me whenever necessary. Between the tears, he begged me to accept. So I accepted.
>
> It was painful to go. Paul and I were in such deep symbiosis that it was enough for him to start a sentence and I could complete it; a half-word was enough for me to understand his thought. We were two parts of a unity. The determining factor was the feeling he had that death was imminent. Yet he lived on for nearly two years, and it was a very hard time for him.[1]

What Benelli does not explain here is that he had enemies in the Curia who thought he had too much influence and wanted him removed. The more indispensable he thought he was, the more they sought to prove the contrary.

When Cardinal Villot summoned the 200 members of the Secretariat of State to make the prior announcement of Benelli's appointment as Archbishop of Florence, there was vigorous applause. After a studied pause, Villot went on: "And there is a second piece of good news – Msgr Benelli is to become a cardinal." This time the applause was dutiful rather than enthusiastic. It meant he would probably be back – perhaps as Secretary of State. But the diplomats accredited to the Holy See were sorry to see him go, and the Italian government gave him a farewell dinner.

One result of Benelli's unexpected and unforeseen move was the oddest consistory of the pontificate so far. It was also the last. It went against all the traditions to create one cardinal at a time: the favour would have been too obvious. So Benelli was joined by Joseph Ratzinger, Archbishop of Munich, Luigi Ciappi, the gaunt foe of the Secretariat for Christian Unity, Frantisek Tomasek of Prague and Bernardin Gantin from Benin, West Africa. It would be false to call the others makeweights – no doubt they were all in line for red hats anyway – but they made an incongruous line-up in the photograph. One explanation is that Paul not only allowed Benelli to choose between Turin and Florence but also to choose his fellow-cardinals.[2]

With Benelli gone, Paul considered his pontificate at an end. He had been preparing for death all his life and now, as it came closer, he was ready. On 30 June 1965 he had taken three sheets of notepaper embossed with the papal arms and written in his neat, clear handwriting:

1 Giancarlo Zizola, "*Il mio amico Onnipotente*", Panorama, 15 November 1982, p. 97.

2 Andrea Tornielli, "*Il Cardinale nella Tenaglia, Benelli 10 anni dopo*, 30 Giorni, August–September 1992, pp. 48–58.

"Some notes for my will. In the name of the Father, and of the Son and of the Holy Spirit."[1]

He took it out and read it again at Castelgandolfo in the summer of 1977. It was not so much a legal document as a prayer of gratitude, the summing up of a Eucharistic life. The tone was Franciscan throughout. He wanted to die "like a poor man" – *un povero*. He celebrated all the glories of creation as in St Francis' "Canticle of the Sun". Yet the prospect of leaving the things of this world did not make him undervalue them, rather the contrary. The trees and the mountains and Lake Albano seemed to acquire an enhanced value: "Now that the day draws to its close, and I must leave this wonderful and turbulent world, I thank you Lord."[2]

On Our Lady's Assumption, 15 August 1977, he wondered aloud whether he would ever celebrate this feast again with the people of Castelgandolfo. Visibly moved, he abandoned the solemn pontifical plural he always used and said: "I see the end of my life approaching. I see myself drawing close to the hereafter . . . and so I take this opportunity of this very happy meeting to greet and bless you all."[3]

He dragged Jean Guitton out to feed his favourite carp. He brought them dry bread every morning at eleven. He knelt by the pool and fed them individually. They were disturbed when Guitton's shadow fell upon them. "Get away," Paul whispered, "you're frightening my carp."[4] The water-lilies reminded Guitton of Monet's painting *Nymphéas* in the Tuileries. But Paul had never visited the Tuileries and would not do so now. He shushed Guitton: he was frightening the carp.

Then they walked along the 300-metre tree-lined avenue that Emilio Bonomelli, his fellow Brescian, had paved in the irregular Roman style. The Emperor Domitian had a palace on this site and believed in doing *mille passus* – a thousand paces – after lunch. Bonomelli, an historian as much as a gardener, had tried to make the park at Castelgandolfo a summing up of many possible styles from all over the world: so there was a French garden with hedges like soldiers on parade, the winding paths of an English garden, a Spanish orchard and Arab fountains pattering amid the palms.[5]

1 The full text was published, with facsimile in his own hand, in *L'Osservatore Romano*, 12 August 1978. It was unchanged from 1965, but on 14 July 1973 he had added a note which read: "I want my funeral to be as simple as possible and I want neither tomb nor special monument. A few offerings (prayers and good works)."

2 *Anni e Opere*, p. 229.

3 *Insegnamenti*, 1977, p. 764.

4 Jean Guitton, *Paul VI secret*, p. 167.

5 Ibid. pp. 167–68.

Never once did he complain of his health, Guitton reports.[1] The past was more vivid to him than recent events, but he did not dwell on it. If he remembered it, it was "to reflect on himself" in thanksgiving gratitude as St Ignatius advises, "so as to gather some fruit". The most striking "coincidence" of his life was that he was baptized on 30 September 1897, the day St Theresa of Lisieux, the Little Flower, died. When he wrote about this to the Lisieux Carmelites they told him that among Theresa's unpublished notes was the remark that after her death she would return "to the cradles of newly baptized babies".[2]

But it was the steely not the sentimental Theresa he evoked in his next remark. She had been to Rome and seen enough to be convinced of the mediocrity of many of its priests. Instead of being scandalized she resolved to compensate for their failures by an excess of love. Was this the key to Paul's own attitude? He had assimilated a passage from the *Histoire d'une Ame*:

> Considering the Mystical Body of Holy Church I couldn't find myself in any of the members described by St Paul, or rather I wanted to be in all of them. Charity provided the key to my vocation . . . I understood that the heart, that love enfolded all vocations . . . In the excess of my delirious joy I cried out: I have found my place in the bosom of the Church, and this place you have given me, my God: in the heart of the Church, my mother, I will be love. Thus I will be everything, and thus will my dream be realized.[3]

It was time for lunch.

Of Benelli's replacement, Msgr Giuseppe Caprio, he said: "He is very balanced and is devoted to me." True, but there was not the "symbiosis". Of the state of the Church he remarked that what was most lacking at the present time was "coherence" and he repeated the word. He poked mild fun at Cardinal Eugène Tisserant who was, in his view, better at analysis than synthesis and never quite managed to see things whole.[4] A lack of coherence?

In the papal chapel he showed Guitton the frescoes that Pope Pius XI had had painted by Rosen di Leopoli. They depicted scenes from the battle of Warsaw, 15 August 1920, the "miracle of the Vistula" when

1 Ibid. p. 143.

2 Ibid. p. 137.

3 Ibid. p. 138. Parts of this passage found their way into the Latin Breviary where, Guitton claimed, they sound more impressive and transform Thérèse's rather schoolgirl French into an oracle: "*Perspexi et agnovi amorem omnes vocationes in se concludere . . . In corde ecclesiae ego amor ero et ita ero omnia.*"

4 Ibid. p. 169.

the Red Army was driven back from the eastern suburbs of Warsaw. There was the chaplain, Father Skorupka, leading his troops.[1] Another bit of Paul's youth flashed by. It was his last meeting with Guitton.

But contemporary Communists still had to be dealt with. They were now queuing up to come to the Vatican, recognizing the Holy See as a factor for peace and the Pope as a "transnational actor". They did not expect a blessing, merely an assurance that they were a permanent fixture and that the Church would not seek to subvert them. The case of Hungary was particularly pertinent, for as long as Mindszenty was alive the memory of the illegitimacy and crimes of the Communist regime in 1948 and 1956 would be kept fresh. His death on 6 May 1975 at the clinic of the Brothers of Mercy in Vienna – he refused to live in Rome – removed one obstacle to *rapprochement* or what was called "normalization". But in his *Memoirs*, "the most readable book written by a bishop in the twentieth century, and the only autobiography by a cardinal to end with an attack on his Pope",[2] Mindszenty continued to heckle from the tomb.

Mindszenty's shade pointed accusingly at his successor and former secretary, László Lékai. Paul appointed him to the primatial see of Esztergom in February 1976 and made him a cardinal with what seemed like indecent haste in May that year. In Hungary and especially among the Hungarian diaspora *the* cardinal remained Mindszenty. Lékai talked the approved language of "peaceful co-existence", recognizing "realities", and recalled Lot's wife who was punished for "looking back". Lékai fixed his gaze on the future. This suited the pragmatic mood of Hungary, now into "goulash-Communism", having exhausted its stock of heroism in 1956. Its leader, János Kádár, had every reason to look forward with Lékai. For if he looked back he saw his betrayal of Imre Nagy and the other leaders of the 1956 revolution: he promised them an amnesty, only to hand them over to the Russians for execution. That explains why, unlike other Communist leaders, János Kádár never dared have a personality cult.

He had an audience with Paul on 9 June 1977. Achille Silvestrini, one of the architects of the Vatican's *Ostpolitik* in the Secretariat of State, claims that "the sacrifice of the intrepid pastor, Cardinal Mindszenty, opened the way for the appointment of bishops in all the dioceses of Hungary".[3] Silvestrini points to the critical note that crept into Paul's address to the bloody tyrant. This visit, he declared, was "the culmination of a long and not uninterrupted process of *rapprochement* over

1 Ibid. p. 169.

2 Owen Chadwick, *The Christian Church in the Cold War*, p. 72.

3 Achille Silvestrini, "*L'Ostpolitik de Paul VI*", in *Notiziario*, 20, p. 74.

fourteen years".[1] That was diplomatic understatement. The Pope went on:

> This policy of *rapprochement* and its results have been followed by many with watchful, often critical or at least puzzled eyes . . . Upon them depends, after the judgement of our conscience, the judgement of history . . . We believe that experience has confirmed the rightness of the way we embarked upon: the path of dialogue on realities, attentive to safeguard the rights and interests of the Church and believers, yet capable of understanding the concerns and the actions of the State in the domains that are proper to it.[2]

It cannot honestly be said that these words betrayed any great desire to "build socialism", which is what Kádár wanted to hear. They merely said that his *Ostpolitik* had been often misunderstood.

The old diplomat he was tendered a wily olive branch. He could not forget, he remarked, that the initiative that led to Helsinki 1975 came to the Holy See precisely from Hungary.[3] So it did: how Paul and Casaroli had puzzled over it in 1969. Now Kádár could feel vindicated, though how far he was happy with the human rights movement that resulted from Helsinki is another matter.

The real question this visit raised was not whether the Vatican was being soft on Communism, but whether Communist leaders any longer believed in the slogans they went on mouthing. Leszek Kolakowski, former Professor of Philosophy in Warsaw University, by now in exile in Oxford, judged Marxism no longer capable of inspiring creativity in art or philosophy or social thinking. It survived, therefore, only by its "institutional" content, which in turn depended on control of the secret police and the army. It was therefore fatally flawed, doomed. Governments without the consent of the governed could not last much longer.

Paul's state of health was beginning to worry Cardinal Jean Villot, his Secretary of State. With Benelli in Florence and Giuseppe Caprio, the new *sostituto*, playing himself in, Villot felt his own authority enhanced – all the more since he was already appointed *camerlengo* or chamberlain, the official who looked after the affairs of the Church after the death of a pope. His main, indeed his sole task, was to prepare the conclave to elect Paul's successor. The chamberlain did not think it right that Paul should be gadding off to Pescara by helicopter for a mere *Italian* Eucharistic Congress.[4] Villot went on:

1 Ibid.

2 *Insegnamenti*, 1977, p. 577.

3 Ibid. p. 578.

4 Antoine Wenger, *Le Cardinal Villot*, p. 211.

> The whole scene looks different now. Between 16 August and 3 September I had half an hour's conversation with the pope every day. He is lucid as ever, but his immediate and everyday concerns are about Italian matters . . . This is not a good situation. Of course, nobody notices because he still makes good speeches like the one he will give to the Parisian bishops on 24 September.[1] But that is because they are drafted by others and only revised by him. Everything is in slow motion. Sixteen ambassadors are waiting to present their credentials.[2]

Caprio wanted to get on with them. Feeling the absence of Benelli, Villot counselled patience. Paul, he said, was more exhausted by audiences than by ceremonies. But as a special concession to the Lebanon he would see that its new ambassador was in place before the canonization of Charbel Maklouf on 9 October.[3] St Charbel Maklouf was the first Maronite Christian to be canonized according to the Latin tradition.

That was – from Villot's point of vantage – the main event of the Synod of 1977 on the theme of *Catechetics in our Time*.[4] Otherwise this was the most modest, unadventurous, unnoticed, unnewsworthy, invisible and ignored Synod there had so far been. Even Msgr William H. Paradis, an expert in catechetics, confessed that most of the interventions were trite: "Many reflect things that have been said before, often in more appealing language. For the most part, they were couched in stiff ecclesiastical language that means nothing to almost everyone except professional Church people. The bishops were talking to one another and not to the world."[5]

Final judgement would have to wait, said Paradis, for the pontifical document that would sort out the confusion at the end of the Synod. That meant waiting till the pontificate of John Paul II.

The *ad limina* visit of the Irish bishops fell conveniently during the Synod. It concluded a series of fascinating back-stairs contacts. Dr Gar-

1 *Insegnamenti*, 1977, pp. 853–59. It is possible that Villot himself helped draft this speech which calls for the evangelization of different *milieux*: working class, scientific, intellectuals, students, p. 857.

2 Antoine Wenger, *Le Cardinal Villot*, p. 211.

3 He was as good as his word. On 7 October Antoine Fattal presented his credentials, *Insegnamenti*, 1977, pp. 915–16. Charbel Maklouf, a Maronite Catholic, known as the hermit of Annaya, had been beatified by Paul on 5 December 1965 at the end of the Council. Born in 1828, he died on Christmas Eve 1898.

4 The position-paper (known as *lineamenta*) was published in the *Tablet* in three instalments, 8, 15, 22 May 1976.

5 Wilfrid H. Paradis, "Synod verdict mixed: not final", *National Catholic Reporter*, 18 November 1977, p. 3.

ret Fitzgerald was the son of a Belfast Presbyterian mother, Mabel, and a Catholic poet-revolutionary, Desmond. We have already seen him in audience with the Pope. He became Foreign Minister in Liam Cosgrave's Fine Gael-Labour government in 1973, just after Ireland became a member of the European Community. In a paper on the future of Ireland he had written:

> The Irish problem is quite simply the fruit of Northern Protestant reluctance to become part of what they regard as an authoritarian southern Catholic state. This is the obstacle to be overcome. It is *their* fears that have to be resolved if tensions in the north are to be relieved, and Ireland is to be united.[1]

So the first condition of progress was to introduce "pluralistic" legislation, for example on divorce. Only in this way, he believed, could the rooted belief of the Northern Protestants that "home rule means Rome rule" be dispelled. But since the Irish Constitution[2] prescribed that legislation should reflect Catholic social teaching, any change would involve a referendum.

Fitzgerald, a powerful thinker, discussed these questions with Archbishop Agostino Casaroli whom he met at Helsinki in 1975 and at subsequent follow-up conferences. He thought Casaroli was sympathetic towards his idea of a "pluralism rooted in Christian fellowship, not in secular anti-clericalism" which could profit from the new spirit of ecumenism after Vatican II.[3] Benelli had served in the Dublin nunciature in 1950–51, and was therefore regarded as an expert on Ireland, also recognized the originality of his approach.

Fitzgerald had cunningly by-passed the nuncio in Dublin, the fiery Sicilian, Gaetano Alibrandi, who did not disguise his sympathies for the IRA and wanted to maintain unsullied the "Catholic traditions" of Ireland. Benelli arranged for Fitzgerald to have a secret audience with Paul VI on 25 March 1977, the feast of the Annunciation. Fitzgerald rehearsed his views on the future of Ireland.

By the time Paul came to address the Irish bishops on 10 October 1977 the cast-list had changed: Cardinal Conway died, Benelli was translated to Florence, and Fitzgerald was out of office. Paul spoke in Latin. Amid the customary clichés about Irish fidelity to the Church was

1 John Cooney, *The Crozier and the Dáil: Church and State 1922–1986*, p. 42.

2 Article 41 begins: "The State recognizes the Family as the natural primary and fundamental unit group of Society, and as a moral institution possessing inalienable and imprescriptible rights, antecedent and superior to all positive law." From this it concludes, 3, 2, that "No law shall be enacted providing for the grant of a dissolution of a marriage."

3 Cooney, op. cit. p. 45.

the observation that "the principles of the doctrine of Jesus Christ have been preserved in families, in parishes and in *society* itself".[1] That did not suggest any great enthusiasm for "pluralism", however nobly conceived. In view of Paul's grief at the divorce referendum in Italy, perhaps none was to be expected.

Paul was negative on another point that the Synod on catechetics was considering. Were denominational schools a good idea in the new ecumenical situation? Nowhere was this suggestion more relevant or poignant than in Northern Ireland where there had been many proposals – almost always from the laity – for "ecumenical schools" as the only answer to the problem of inbred bigotry. The bishops of Northern Ireland disagreed. They were there too, for ecclesiastically Ireland is already united and Armagh, seat of the Primate, is north of the border. Paul defended Catholic schools on the grounds that "through them, the outstanding inheritance of Ireland, that is, the Catholic faith as a treasury of civilization (*cultus civilis*), is handed on to posterity".[2]

True, he went on to praise the late Cardinal William Conway for introducing "the light of conciliar renewal to your people, as a column of peace and reconciliation in your land, and a consolation for the numerous afflictions of your nation, which we greatly love (*nobis adeo amata*)".[3] Touching, but one cannot avoid the feeling that the nuncio's victory over Garrett Fitzgerald did nothing to help solve Ireland's problems, which, today, remain as intractable as ever.[4]

With Poland, the other "Catholic country" at the opposite end of Europe, Paul showed greater percipience. Edward Gierek, first secretary of the Communist Party, requested an audience. The request granted, the audience took place on 1 December 1977. This encounter – or propaganda contest – can best be understood by asking what Gierek hoped to gain from it and then what Paul the diplomat sought to achieve.

Gierek, a bluff ex-miner from Silesia, was in the business of "managing" Poles since he could not honestly claim to lead them. He knew that Polish "dissidence" could not be crushed, since left to itself and offered a free choice the entire nation would be "dissident". In May 1977 he had imprisoned the striking workers of Radom. The only result was to stimulate the human rights movement, KOR, headed by Jacek Kuron

1 *Insegnamenti*, 1977, p. 935.

2 Ibid. p. 936.

3 Ibid.

4 Dr Garret Fitzgerald, now in the role of a European elder statesman and Catholic political philosopher, confirmed the outline of these events at the meeting of the Catholic Theological Association of Great Britain, Trinity and All Saints College, Leeds, September 1991. His lecture, "Christian Hope in Europe's Future", is published in *New Blackfriars*, January 1992, pp. 5–13.

and Adam Michnik, secular thinkers who nevertheless realized that "reform" in Poland depended on the support of the Catholic Church.

Gierek could not risk another clash with the alliance of workers, intellectuals and Catholics. So he went to Rome to seek a truce, some television pictures of himself shaking hands with Pope Paul, and an assurance that the Church would not throw its full weight into the post-Helsinki battle for human rights. It was humiliating for Gierek to have to come cap in hand, begging for support from the Pope. In his address of homage he claimed that his government had done much for the reconstruction of the country, the development of its industrial potential and for science and culture. "We attach great importance," concluded Gierek, playing his last, desperate card, "to the consolidation of the family and to the education of future generations".[1]

Paul was not duped by this. The "consolidation of the family" included not only abortion on demand but a "population policy" which granted living space – calculated in square metres – for only two children per family. He was icily polite. He recalled the Poland of his youth, its heroic work in reconstructing devastated cities as a "symbol of its unity and will to survive".[2] He was convinced that the Polish Church, since the millennium of 1966, had "contributed to the culture and moral education of the people" and was still "ready to make a positive contribution to Polish society".[3] Gierek waited anxiously for the catch.

"The Church," Paul went on, "does not ask for any privileges but only for the right to be itself, and the chance to develop without hindrance the action that is specific to it, according to its constitution and its mission." Thus if Gierk wanted diplomatic relations – and he did, so as to be able to leap-frog the unyielding Wyszyński and deal directly with the Vatican – he would have to pay a price. Finally Paul slotted the knife in, urging Gierek to implement the Final Act of Helsinki, which he had signed. So in the end Gierek got very little.

Paul's *Ostpolitik* could not be described as a sell out. Within two years of the meeting Gierek was gone and *Solidarnosc* became a power in the land. Then it was remembered that Cardinal Karol Wojtyla had given the Lenten retreat to the Roman Curia earlier that year. Was it possible that he had discussed Gierek's visit with the Archbishop of Kraków? It was more than likely.

Paul reached his eightieth birthday on 26 September 1977, and most commentators wrote anticipated obituaries and wondered whether he would resign. *L'Osservatore Romano* of 2 September 1977 carried an

1 *Insegnamenti*, p. 1122.

2 Ibid. p. 1118.

3 Ibid.

article by its new deputy editor, Don Virgilio Levi, explaining "why the Pope *could not* resign". He claimed that since only one pope in history had *spontaneously* resigned, resignation was clearly contrary to the apostolic tradition. At the same time he endeavoured to defend *Ingravescentem Aetatem* which excluded cardinals over eighty from the next conclave.

"Old men," Levi declared, "have a tendency to look backwards, to live in the past with their memories and sometimes their grouses," while the Church needs to forge ahead with the times. However, this did not apply to the pope, because he had the accumulated experience of the papacy to help him and, anyway, there were many *compos mentis* world statesmen who were older than him. Levi also made the extraordinary claim that while a bishop needs stamina, the papal office "demands not so much youthful energy as a swift and attentive mind, a heart full of charity, and well-tested experience . . ." One felt that Levi could have defended the proposition that black was "really" white.

Cardinal Franz König talked more persuasively on Austrian television. A retired pope, he said, would set up two "poles in the Church, the reigning pope and the retired pope, a situation that could create problems".[1] It was no secret, however, that if he *did* retire it would be to Monte Cassino.[2] Thus the wheel would have come full circle, and the Benedictine vocation denied him in 1916 would have been finally realized. Perhaps Benelli let slip the true reason why Paul did not resign: "He can't come down from his cross." To see him literally carrying the heavy cross on Good Friday in the Colosseum was to witness a parable of his idea of the papacy. And now the autumn of his life was drawing near.

1 *Tablet*, 8 October 1977.

2 Fappani-Molinari, *Montini Giovane*, p. 56.

39

The Secret of Transfiguration

> When you were young you fastened your belt about you and walked where you chose; but when you are old you will stretch out your arms, and a stranger will bind you fast, and carry you where you have no wish to go.
>
> (John 21:18 New English Bible)

Pope Paul VI was eighty on 27 September 1977. He was weary of life, and talked increasingly of death, of the death of others, of his own death. He compiled a *florilegium* of scriptural texts on death:

> *Tempus resolutionis meae instat* (the time of my departure has come) (2 Timothy 4:6)
>
> *Certus quod velox est depositio tabernaculi mei* (I know that the putting off of my body will be soon) (2 Peter 1:14)
>
> *Finis venit, venit finis* (The end comes, comes the end) (Ezekiel 7:2)[1]

In this mood, with the clock of time winding down and dusk approaching, he made an impulsive gesture which clearly showed that he considered his life dispensable. On 17 October 1977 a Lufthansa plane was hi-jacked at Mogadishu, Uganda, its assistant pilot was gunned down and the passengers were threatened with massacre. In a message to Cardinal Joseph Höffner, Archbishop of Cologne, later that day, Paul offered his own life in exchange for the hostages. "If it would help," he wrote, "we would offer our person for the freeing of the hostages."[2] The hostages were rescued in a breathtaking coup by Israeli commandos, so Paul's offer was not taken up.

No doubt his "gesture" was not very realistic – it would have been difficult to hand over and then conceal an elderly pope; but that does not make the self-offering insincere. It was quite enough to anger govern-

1 Jean Guitton, *Paul VI secret*, p. 28.

2 *Insegnamenti*, 1977, p. 962. The German was: "*Wäre es von Nutzen, so würden Wir sogar Unsere Person für die Befreiung der Geiseln anbieten.*"

ments holding to the absolute rule: never negotiate with terrorists. This was certainly the view of the Italian government which had to face the internal threat from the Red Brigades. Paul wondered about these sons and sometimes daughters of the bourgeoisie, veterans of 1968, who had schooled themselves to be hard and cruel. Aldo Moro was one of the few politicians who understood how deeply Italian politics were changed by 1968.

But this episode did not mean that he wanted to run away or evade responsibility. He recalled how Cardinal Giuseppe Pizzardo, his first superior at the Secretariat of State, used to have a special tray in which difficult or embarrassing problems remained until they were solved by life.[1] Paul disapproved. He never, at any time, used the excuse that tempts ageing popes as much as any other leader: "I will leave that problem to my successor."

He continued to be alert and responsive to the world about him. If he had been unable to do his work he would have resigned. There was no rest because the office could never be "suspended", bracketed out. He told Guitton:

> I go from challenge to challenge, I never have a moment's respite, never a moment's rest. And it will go on like that until my death. I don't want to go through a long illness like my predecessors. No one can understand that I have no future other than eternity, that is to say, judgement.[2]

In Montini the sense of responsibility and judgement went hand in hand.

Fr John Magee, an Irish Kiltegan missionary, had been his English language secretary since the end of 1976. Every morning Magee said Mass for the nuns who looked after the papal household, and then went up to serve Paul's Latin Mass. On Sundays they concelebrated together for the sisters in Italian.

Magee, plucked by Giovanni Benelli out of Africa, recounts his arrival in the papal household. No one briefed him about what to do or expect. Don Pasquale Macchi simply handed him a bunch of keys, saying: "There is a terrace up there. If you need a breath of air, take the lift." Suddenly Paul appeared. Magee wondered whether protocol demanded he should fall to his knees, and just stood awkwardly there. Paul saved him from embarrassment by saying in "perfect English": "Welcome to my house! I need you, I want you to come and stay with me in my house (*casa*), to work with me, to pray with me; and now let's

1 Jean Guitton, *Paul VI secret*, p. 80.

2 Ibid. p. 10: "*Personne ne peut comprendre que je n'ai d'autre avenir que l'éternité, c'est à dire le jugement.*"

go to lunch."[1] After that, protocol was abandoned and they got on wonderfully.

That same afternoon Paul noticed the bunch of keys. "You've already got the keys for the lift?" said the astonished Pope, "I have been in this house for thirteen years and no one ever gave me the keys." They went up in the lift and emerged on the sunlit terrace and admired the panorama. Magee had by now thought up an edifying answer to the question, "So you've already got the keys for this lift?" and timidly essayed, "These keys are as nothing compared with the keys that you bear." Paul looked him straight in the eye: "*Caro, caro, si,* yes indeed, how heavy are the keys in my pocket."[2] Did he mean the keys of St Peter?

One rainy Sunday afternoon Paul took Magee by the hand – "he could be quite childlike at times" – and led him up to a room he had never seen before: it was Paul's *private* library. These were the books, carefully annotated, that he had started collecting when he arrived in Rome in 1920. It was his habit to note the date he began a book, and when he finished it. This time Paul had his own keys. He opened a cupboard full of letters and photographs from his childhood that he showed with pride mingled with sadness.

Look, this is the house at Concesio, and here is the church where I was baptized. And look at all the letters *mamma mia* wrote to me when I came to Rome. There were photographs of his friends, of Cesare Trebeschi who died in a concentration camp, of Don Francesco Galloni the Alessandro Manzoni man, of Franco Costa who had just died. He had outlived all his contemporaries. "They've all gone," Paul said, "all gone, leaving me alone, and at my age I feel this solitude. When the friends of your own age, your contemporaries, your classmates are no more, you are really alone."[3]

Magee sought to comfort him by saying that one day there would be a grand reunion with his friends and what joy there would be. Paul looked suddenly very serious: "*Caro*, we must never presume on the mercy of God, we have to pray for it. It is not certain that I will go to Paradise. I have to ask for God's forgiveness and mercy – and so do you. Lord, remember me, when you come into your kingdom."[4]

1 John Magee, "*La vita quotidiana de Paolo VI*", in *Modernité de Paul VI*, pp. 135–36.

2 Ibid. p. 136.

3 Ibid. p. 139.

4 Ibid.

All gone, all dead, he keeps on saying. All the intellectuals who influenced him: Romano Guardini, Karl Adam, Jacques Maritain, the man of intellectual charity, all the priests . . . "all dead". And he alone is alive. It makes no sense.

He wanted no fuss for his eightieth birthday, and no public celebrations. "Let me keep it alone, in solitude and prayer, for the hour has come."

More and more he confided in Magee. "Do you want to know the secret of my spirituality?" he asked one day. Magee murmured something, but Paul was well away:

> We all – you, me, everyone – need a solid basis on which to build the edifice of a spiritual life. The foundation for me comes in two words, two concepts of St Augustine.
>
> The great mystery of God for me has always been this: that in my *miseria* I still find myself before the *misericordia* of God; that I am nothing, wretched; yet God the Father loves me, wants to save me, wants to haul me out of this *miseria*, something I'm incapable of doing left to myself.
>
> Then the Father sends his Son, a Son who represents God's mercy (*misericordia*), who translates it into an act of love towards me, an act of complete self-abandonment to the Father because he must save me too, wretched as I am. But a special grace is needed for this, the grace of conversion. I have to recognize God the Father's action in his Son in my regard. Once I acknowledge that, God can work in me through his Son: he gives me grace, the grace of baptism. After the grace of being reborn to God's life, my life becomes a tension of love, with God drawing me towards himself. And the loving hand of God draws me onwards towards his mercy, which raises me up when I fall; I have to fix my gaze on him to be drawn upwards, yet again.
>
> Always in all of us, there is this tension between my *miseria* and God's *misericordia*. The whole spiritual life of every one of us lies between those two poles. If I open myself to the action of God and the Holy Spirit and let them do with me what they will, then my tension becomes joyous and I feel within myself a great desire to come to him and receive his mercy; more than ever I recognize the need to be forgiven, to receive the gift of mercy. Then I feel the need to say *grazie, grazie, grazie*, thanks, thanks, thanks. And so my whole life becomes a *grazie* [*gratia*/thanksgiving/eucharist] to God because he has saved me, redeemed me, drawn me to himself

> in love. It is not anything I have done in my life that saves me, but God's mercy.[1]

That the *miseria* of the creature evokes the *misericordia* of the Creator was not the only Augustinian theme in Paul's spiritual outlook. It was, as he said, only the foundation.

Now Magee began to understand how Paul worked. Every Tuesday throughout his pontificate he would shut himself in his study to write, in his fine, elegant hand, his address for the Wednesday public audience. One of Magee's tasks was to supply him with the books he needed. Time and again Augustine figures on his list – never more than a single sheet of paper.[2]

His Augustinianism went deep. It began when he read the article *Augustin* – a treatise in itself – in the *Dictionnaire de Théologie Catholique*. "It is a rich vein that many exploit," he told Guitton, "without letting on."[3] He knew, because he had done so himself in 1930 to celebrate the 1500th anniversary of St Augustine's death at a time when it seemed that a new barbarism was hammering at the gates of Rome and overrunning Europe.

At lunch at Castelgandolfo he discussed with Guitton Augustine's conversation at Ostia with his mother, Monica, which led by degrees to "the vision of Ostia", an experience of ecstasy, being drawn out of oneself and into God. *Pondus meus amor meus* says Augustine: love is like the gravitational pull but upwards.[4] Paul translated that by "tension", not meaning taut like a bow-string but "tending-towards".

Ostia, once the Rome seaport from which Augustine left for Africa, was now no more than land-locked ruins. But all his life he had never been far from Augustine, baptized by St Ambrose during the Easter vigil of 387 in the crypt of Milan cathedral.[5] Ambrose, says Paul, "according to Augustine, his greatest discipline, had a remarkable fascination, a capacity for making himself understood, making himself loved. That was his charism."

It was Paul's charism too – on the level of personal contact, though not with crowds. His brother Francesco said of him: "If my brother the Pope has a weakness, it is that he retains as a public figure the virtues

1 Ibid. pp. 137–39.

2 Ibid. p. 138.

3 Jean Guitton, *Paul VI secret*, p. 82.

4 Ibid. p. 82.

5 Paul VI wrote three letters to Cardinal Giovanni Colombo, his successor in Milan, on St Augustine, St Ambrose and Alessandro Manzoni, author of *I Promessi Sposi*. Full text in *Notiziario*, 18, pp. 35–42.

of private life: these virtues lead him to do as much good as possible to those who have done him most harm."[1]

A text from St Ambrose can complete his *florilegium* on death: "*Ubi Petrus, ibi Ecclesia; ubi Ecclesia, nulla mors, sed vita aeterna.*" "Where Peter is, there is the Church" is often quoted; but Paul insisted on completing the quotation: "Where the Church is, there is no death, but eternal life."[2]

Paul returned to public life at the start of 1978 with a message of hope. He went to the basilica of St Mary Major to celebrate his tenth and last World Peace Day. He roused himself, now a patriarchal figure, for an ultimate appeal: "No to violence, yes to peace. If you want peace to reign in the world, you must make it reign in your hearts, in your families, in your homes, in your suburbs, in your cities, in your provinces, in your country."[3]

No story there, said the reporters in the press office, stifling a yawn. The usual stuff.

Yet at the time Paul was making this appeal against violence in Italy, a small group of ideologues was plotting to strike a blow at the heart of the Italian establishment by kidnapping Aldo Moro, leader of the Christian Democratic Party, and "putting him on trial" for the crimes of the capitalist state. Other candidates had been considered, such as Giulio Andreotti and Amintore Fanfani, but they had the disadvantage of living in the historic centre of Rome where security was tight and a quick getaway difficult. Moro lived in the suburbs and went openly to Mass at Santa Chiara with his family. The executive committee of the Red Brigades – even terrorists have their bureaucratic ways – decided finally on Moro in February, and fixed the date for mid-March.[4]

Paul had his annual bout of flu. It was bad enough for him to cancel his Wednesday general audience on 15 March but so as not to disappoint the 50,000 who turned up, he appeared at his window and urged them to prepare for Easter, the Passover, the transition to new life.

Next day Aldo Moro was seized as he left his home at via Pola. His escort of five were shot dead with brutal efficiency. So while Paul awaited his own death, Aldo Moro, the closest to him among the younger

1 Jean Guitton, *Paul VI secret*, p. 80.

2 *Notiziario*, 18, p. 41. This occurs in his letter to Cardinal Colombo, Archbishop of Milan, 3 December 1973, on the hundredth anniversary of the death of Alessandro Manzoni. Verdi's *Requiem* was written to mark the event. Since St Ambrose became a bishop in 373 it was also . . . but anniversaries lose their charm when there are too many of them.

3 *Insegnamenti*, 1978, p. 8.

4 I will follow the outline of events given by Leonardo Sciascia in *The Moro Affair*, 1987.

generation of Christian Democratic politicians in temperament, was in mortal danger.

Thus began for Paul an agony that went on for fifty-five days and sleepless nights. Where was Aldo? Was he alive? He sent telegrams to Cardinal Ugo Poletti, his Vicar for Rome, and to Eleanora Moro whom he had known as a student.[1] On 18 May the Red Brigades claimed full responsibility for Moro's capture and the murder of his escort. They were holding him in a "People's Court of Justice" in which he and the Christian Democratic Party would be put on trial.

On 19 May, Palm Sunday, Paul included the name of "Aldo Moro, so dear to us" in the list of prayer intentions, which ranged from the Lebanon to the Horn of Africa. "How many sufferings, how many deaths, what ruins," he lamented.[2] He speaks of the "renaissance of barbarism", and exactly the same phrase is used by Enrico Berlinguer, the Sardinian aristocrat who leads the Communist Party. Ironically Moro had been on his way to Parliament where, for the first time, the Communists were about to support a Christian Democratic-led coalition.

On 20 May in Turin where the trial of Roberto Curcio and his comrades is going on, the caged Red Brigades shout with glee, "Moro is in our hands!" They hoped they would soon be out of gaol as part of a deal to save Moro's life.[3]

But this merely stiffened the resolve of the government and in particular the Minister of the Interior, Francesco Cossiga, not to give in to or bargain with "terrorists". Democratic liberty demanded that blackmail and kidnapping could not be allowed to distort the course of justice. Paul reluctantly accepted this line, went doggedly through Holy Week, but what should have been the time of Paschal joy was turned to bitterness. Too much innocent blood had already been shed, he said, praying for the bodyguards and chauffeur whose deaths had been overlooked. He implored "the unknown authors of this terrifying deed to release their prisoner".[4]

On 31 March, after two weeks of floundering incompetence from the police, *L'Osservatore Romano* expressed the Holy See's willingness to take steps towards the solution of this "most painful occurrence". What the Holy See might actually do remained, at this point, a mystery. No one knew where Moro and his captors were. Were the Italian police just plain inefficient or was someone belonging to P2, the pseudo-

1 Carlo Cremona, *Paolo VI*, p. 257.

2 *Insegnamenti*, 1978, p. 217.

3 Sciascia, *The Moro Affair*, p. 8

4 *Insegnamenti*, 1978, p. 238.

masonic lodge of Liceo Gelli, anxious that Moro should die to prevent the political project on which he was engaged: cohabitation between the Christian Democrats and the Communists?

Meanwhile Moro's captors were not getting on very well in their interrogation. Mario Moretti, their leader, decided to "tell all" in 1984 (but without revealing names). Moro disappointed them. They wanted to unmask the links between the Christian Democrats, SIM, the Italian secret service, and the CIA and US multi-national corporations. Moro disappointed them by saying that he didn't really get on very well with the Americans, and indeed that they had "secretly threatened him". It followed that if Moro had no useful information to impart, they would have to fall back on their other goal of "earning recognition" through the exchange of prisoners.

There was an impasse. Though the government policy of "standing firm" was generally applauded, could not some deal have been done that might have saved the life of Moro? Was he just to be abandoned to his fate? Did one man have to die for the people? In the photographs that were released he looked increasingly tense and anguished.

Moreover Paul now had an additional motive for intervening. On 20 April 1978 the Moro family forwarded him a letter which directly appealed for his help. It chanced to be Moro's birthday:

> In this most difficult moment, I allow myself to appeal to Your Holiness with all respect and in profound hope so that with your lofty moral authority and Christian humanitarian spirit you may intercede with the competent authorities of the Italian government to find an equitable solution to the problem of the political prisoners and aid my return to my family.[1]

Paul could hardly ignore this. But Moro was asking him to put pressure on the Italian government, not to appeal to his captors.

Then, on the same day, there was a letter to Paul from Aldo Moro himself. Giulio Andreotti, the Prime Minister, recorded its existence in his diary for 21 April 1978:

> At 13h Msgr Casaroli arrived at my house. Last night someone had telephoned Don Mennini, curate at the church of St Lucy, to collect a folder; it contained two letters for the Moro family: one was for Zaccagnini [secretary general of the Christian Democratic party] and the other to be made public "for the

1 Facsimile in Giulio Andreotti, *A Ogni Morte de Papa*, opposite p. 132. The Red Brigades were holding Moro in the hope of securing the release of "political prisoners".

> Pope". Cardinal Poletti brought it to the Holy Father at 21.30, the family having decided not to publish it.[1]

Thus at 9.30 on the night of 20 April Moro's letter was on Paul's desk.

Moro, then, writing from an unknown place and under sentence of death, is arguing for his life:

> Most Holy Father
> In my difficult situation and mindful of the paternal kindness Your Holiness has so often shown me on many occasions notably when I was leader of FUCI, I dare to address Your Holiness in the hope that you will further in the most opportune manner a process that will lead to the exchange of political prisoners which would have positive effects for me and my unfortunate family which, for objective reasons, is at the heart of my anguished concern.
>
> I can imagine the fears of the government. But I must say that a great many governments have had recourse to this humanitarian practice and given the priority to saving human lives by exiling political prisoners, thus meeting security requirements. In any case, since they engage in guerrilla actions, exile is the only solution since there is no satisfactory way of holding them in prison on the national territory and I foresee terrible days ahead.
>
> Having seen in my prison a harsh article in *L'Osservatore Romano* against the solution of exile, I was very worried, for what voice other than the Church can break through the incrustations that have formed, and what humanism is there higher than Christian humanism? That is why my prayers, my hopes, as well as those of my unfortunate family, that Your Holiness was kind enough to receive some years ago, are addressed to you, the only one capable of inclining the Italian government towards an act of wisdom.
>
> My prayer is that you will repeat Pius XII's gesture in favour of the young professor Giuliano Vassali, who was in the same situation as me. Accept, most Holy Father, together with the thanks of those who would benefit from clemency, the assurance of my profound respect.[2]

1 Giulio Andreotti, *Diari 1976–1979*, Rizzoli, Milan, p. 211.

2 Antoine Wenger, *Le Cardinal Villot*, pp. 218–19. The letter was first published in *Panorama*, 5 December 1978, in a dossier on the Moro affair. It is said to be in the hands of Don Pasquale Macchi – which makes it curious that Macchi and the books he has inspired (Cremona, Saint-Ange) make no mention of it. Giuliano Vassali was a Socialist lawyer for whom Pius XII intervened with the Nazis in 1943.

L'Osservatore Romano, along with other papers, had cast doubt on the authenticity of some of Moro's letters from his dungeon, suggesting they were dictated by his gaolers to attain their own ends. But that was the authentic Moro style, complex, prolix, yet lucidly to the point.

Paul wanted desperately to respond positively to Moro's letter. But he had to follow the line of the Secretariat of State. Villot said: "It would be interference in the affairs of another country." Then Paul thought of appealing to President Leone. But he was a controversial figure, shortly to resign. Casaroli contacted Giulio Andreotti, the Prime Minister, who lived just over the Tiber across from the Castel Sant'Angelo. But he was adamant: no deals, no amnesty, no exile. The consequences would be too grave.

This was a dreadful blow for Paul. To be forbidden to intervene because this was "an Italian affair" made little sense. But his sense of constitutional propriety reasserted itself, leaving him with prayer as the only recourse. All he could do now was to appeal directly to Moro's captors.

Having omitted this essential background, Don Pasquale then describes what happened on the night of 21–22 April:

> Before supper he told me he was going to write to the Red Brigades. After the meal, the Rosary and Compline, he went to his study at 9.30 p.m. and worked till about 11.30. He had me take this draft to Msgr Casaroli [then head of the Council for Public Affairs of the Church]. After some thought, Msgr Casaroli suggested some slight modifications. Paul VI considered them, recollected himself in prayer and then came back to his desk. He re-copied the letter. He made me read it to him.[1]

Paul believed his letter would be more effective if it were in his own distinctive hand. Photocopies were distributed to the press next morning. They finished work and went to bed at 2.45 a.m.

This is what Moro's captors read in their hideaway:

> I write to you, men of the Red Brigades: restore Aldo Moro to freedom, to his family and to civil life.
>
> I don't know you, and I have no means of having any contact with you. That is why I write to you publicly, profiting from the interval before the deadline for the sentence of death you have pronounced upon him expires. He is a good and

1 Daniel-Ange, *Paul VI, un regard prophétique*, Editions Saint-Paul 1979, p. 100.

upright man, to whom no one can impute any crime, or accuse of lacking social sense or of failing in justice in the service of the peaceful harmony of society.

I have no mandate to speak to you, and I am not bound by any private interest in his regard. But I love him as a member of the great human family, as a friend of student days and – by a very special title – as a brother in faith and as a son of the Church of Christ. And it is in this supreme name of Christ that I make an appeal that you will certainly not ignore, an appeal to you unknown and implacable enemies of this decent and innocent man; on my knees I beg you, free Aldo Moro, simply, without conditions, not so much because of my humble and well-meaning intercession, but because he shares with you the common dignity of a brother in humanity, and because I would dare to hope that in conscience you would not want the cause of true social progress to be stained with innocent blood or tortured by superfluous suffering. We have already had to mourn and lament so many who died fulfilling their duty. We must all fear the hatred that degenerates into vendetta or slumps into desperation. And we must all fear the Lord who will avenge those who die without cause or fault.

Men of the Red Brigades, leave me, the interpreter of the voices of so many of our fellow-citizens, the hope that in your hearts feelings of humanity will triumph.

In prayer, and always loving you, I await for proof of that.

Paulus PP.VI.[1]

If literary style could convert the Red Brigades, Paul's letter should have done so. It belongs by right in any anthology of Italian twentieth-century writing. The eighty-year-old Montini, so often dismissed as querulous and irrelevant, finally spoke for the best of Italy.

Yet Paul was immediately criticized in public opinion and in some government circles for treating the "men of the Red Brigades" so wimpishly. They were the implacable "enemies of the state" and to accept their own self-designation was to grant them the "recognition" they craved. Popular opinion said they were not "human" at all, but "beasts" who had fallen below humanity. Some heartless critics said his praise of Moro was extravagant and unjustified. Others criticized the phrase "without conditions". Giovanni Moro, Aldo's son, was not sure his

1 *Anni e Opere*, pp. 225–26.

father would have accepted it. He could not expect to be released unconditionally; there would have to be negotiations of some sort.[1]

Don Pasquale Macchi's defence of Paul's letter is handicapped by his silence on Moro's letter to which it was a response. Paul addressed them as "men of the Red Brigades" because they were indeed "human beings, even if they had forgotten it . . . In this solemn and public appeal, Paul sought to remind them of the fact and call them back to humanity." Macchi also tries to explain what Paul meant by releasing Moro "without conditions". It meant there should be no negotiations which would "offend against the dignity of the State" by treating the Red Brigades as equals, as if they were on the same level as the State. To do that, said Macchi, would upset the "forces of law and order" who had sacrificed much to maintain the legal order and did not want to see it circumvented.[2] He meant simply that the police would not accept the release of any of their prisoners in exchange for Moro's life.

From his prison Moro addressed his colleagues with some bitterness, fully conscious of the irony of the situation – he had abolished the death penalty in Italy: "If you do not intercede, a chill page will have been written in the history of Italy. My blood will be upon you, upon the [Christian Democratic] party, upon the nation."[3]

Did he now include Paul VI in this charge? In a letter written to his wife, presumably between 27 and 30 April, he refers to an article by Virgilio Levi:

> I was distressed to see in *Il Giorno*'s editorial a reference to *L'Osservatore Romano* by the inevitable [Giancarlo] Zizola. In substance, No to the blackmailers. Thus through the medium of Signor Levi the Holy See, quite inconsistent with its former attitude, rejects its long humanitarian tradition by condemning today me and tomorrow innocent children to become the victims of this refusal to negotiate. This is terrible, unworthy of the Holy See. Since banishment is common practice in so many countries and even in the Soviet Union, one can't see why here it should be replaced by State slaughter. I don't know whether [Cardinal Ugo] Poletti could rectify this

1 Ferdinando Adornato, "*Non tradite mio padre*", interview with Giovanni Moro, *L'Espresso*, 15 May 1988. Giovanni was twenty when his father was killed. One of Aldo Moro's letters from his "prison" says to his wife, "Tell Giovanni what political life really is." Of all the Moros, Giovanni most resembles his father.

2 Carlo Cremona, *Paulo VI*, p. 260.

3 Sciascia, *The Moro Affair*, p. 66.

terrible mistake so contrary to the Holy See's normal practice.[1]

Alone in his cell Moro did not know where he was or what was happening off-stage. But the fear that Moro might die abandoned and thinking the Pope had done less than he might, impelled Paul to take his next initiative.

If there could be no exchange of prisoners, and if his direct appeal to the Red Brigades met with no response, could he not pay the ransom they were demanding? This was no longer a Secretariat of State matter, so from now on Macchi was the intermediary. He met Andreotti to "co-ordinate" policy. Was this "co-ordination" mentioned by Andreotti along these lines: "We will not release any political prisoners, but should you wish to ransom Moro we will not stand in your way"?

There remained the problem of how to get in touch with them. Macchi provided the telephone number of Msgr Georg Hüssler at Caritas Internationalis which they could use at any time. That seemed naïve to the Christian Democrats. They sent Giuseppe Lazzati, Rector of the Catholic University of Milan, to London to make contact with Amnesty International, who worked through the Apostolic Delegate, Archbishop Bruno Heim.

Did anyone actually make contact with the men who held Moro? Andreotti suggests that they did. Enter a new witness, *Monsignor* (not *Signor*) Virgilio Levi, then deputy director of *L'Osservatore Romano*. He told ANSA, the Italian news agency:

> The lines of Caritas International remained open to receive any request or proposal that might have saved the life of Moro. Naturally if there had been a demand for money the Pope would have done the impossible to put an end to this terrible evil. But it came to nothing because no contact was possible.

Asked about rumours that Paul VI had sought to raise money for Moro's ransom from Milanese and other Lombardy businessmen, Levi replied: "I don't know the details."[2]

That sounded like a reluctant yes. Don Pasquale Macchi adds: "There was no direct contact, but a serious attempt was made to convince Moro's gaolers within the framework of republican legality."[3] There was a flicker of hope after Paul's appeal and the suggestion of a

1 Ibid. p. 96. Carlo Cremona alludes to the draft of a letter to Paul VI written by Aldo Moro and found in a hideaway at via Montevenoso in Milan on 10 October 1990. "This sketch," he says, "was the basis of the letter the Pope read . . . In any case the document does not concern this biography. We have dealt with the subject to throw light on the sensibility and suffering of Paul VI" (p. 260). That seems faint-hearted.

2 ANSA, Italian Press Agency, 5 March 1988.

3 Carlo Cremona, *Paolo VI*, p. 261.

ransom attempt. Paul kept asking Macchi "Nothing new?" (*Nulla di nuovo*?) Cremona hints that some sort of contact was made, but that it was covered by the secret of the confessional.[1] There were rumours of a long-distance phone call from someone who had been in favour of answering Paul's appeal, but then had been ordered out of Rome and told to have nothing more to do with the affair. Moro's captors were divided among themselves.

But it was all in vain. Moro's fate had been settled. The body of Aldo Moro, leader of the Italian Christian Democrats, was discovered on 9 May 1978 in the boot of a red Renault halfway between the headquarters of the Christian Democrats and the Communists, riddled with bullets. Paul could not at first take in the news. Surely not this. He retired to his private chapel to be alone and pray.

The Moro family believed the Christian Democrats connived in the murder of their husband and father Aldo Moro. So on 13 May 1978 they absented themselves from the memorial service in St John Lateran, Rome's cathedral, "the head and mother of all churches".

If they had gone along they would have heard Paul upbraid God for allowing this appalling deed to happen. It was like Job reproaching the Lord for the ghastly mess of the world: "I will give free utterance to my complaint; I will speak in the bitterness of my soul" (Job 10:1). Once again the eighty-year-old Paul VI, never particularly popular in Italy, spoke for the nation, the *patria*.

It was not a voice of anger so much as distress and pain that Italy had sunk so low that young people should imagine that political violence could win anyone over. Their calculation was wrong. Moro's death had the contrary effect: it unified the political parties from left to right and meant the virtual collapse of the Red Brigades. So Paul's appeals to humanity had a delayed-action effect at least. Some Red Brigade members "repented" and made their confession – to a priest, not to the police. But Paul did not live to know this. For him the Moro tragedy had been the final twist in his crown of thorns, a last purification, a proxy agony. But it had also pulled him out of lethargy and given him a role that no politician could fulfil. Now he was free to get on with his own death.

That is not a fanciful idea. The German mediaeval mystics have a word *Gelassenheit*. It means something like letting go, but letting go in God. In that sense, holy men and women can choose the day of their death.

1 That is the only way to make sense of assertions such as: "The charity of the Church has always had secret ways to reach the cruellest of men, not using those compromised by the underworld, but intermediaries who like Good Samaritans to do good take the same paths as the criminals", ibid. p. 262.

The feast of Sts Peter and Paul, 29 June, was the fifteenth anniversary of his coronation. Henceforward no popes would be "crowned" and Paul had given his tiara away. He used the occasion to sum up and say farewell. "I have kept the faith," he says. He reviews his fidelity to the Church and to the Second Vatican Council. It is not a boast. "That was my duty," he says, "to be faithful. I've done everything. Now I've finished (*Ho fatto tutto. Ora ho finito*)." It remained only to quote Peter's words in John 6:68: "Lord, to whom shall we go? Thou hast the words of eternal life."[1]

He still had one more project that would remain unfulfilled. In September, he thought, he would go to Turin to see for himself the face of Christ on the Holy Shroud, "this face so true, so profound, so human, so divine, that we have always venerated", the face of Christ, the man of sorrows, "the expert in suffering".[2]

At the Angelus on Sunday, 9 July he said farewell to the city of Rome. Rome was not any more a "sacred" city, still less was it exemplary. With its violence and pollution and disorder it had become typical of the modern world. Yet it remained a symbolic city, the sign of unity "not only for the Italian people, but as the centre of the Catholic Church and the heir of an ideal type of civilization. Rome speaks to the world of fraternity, concord and peace."[3]

And today, he added, Italy had a new President, Sandro Pertini. Not to mention this, he said, would make him appear "a foreigner in his own country". The election of this Socialist President, though he did not say so, was Italy's response to terrorism, a closing of the ranks.

His penultimate audience on 26 July was a hymn to Christian friendship, quoting Cicero's definition of friendship in *De Amicitia* as "perfect agreement on all things, divine and human, accompanied by benevolence and love". But in Jesus this wonderful reality is "sublimated", not destroyed but carried to perfection, caught up in the life of the Trinity, Father, Son and Holy Spirit.[4]

In his last week he left Castelgandolfo only once. Call it whim or impulse, but he had to pray at the tomb of Cardinal Giuseppe Pizzardo at Frattocchie. We will never know quite why. Pizzardo had been his first superior in the Secretariat of State. At times he had treated Montini casually, harshly or unjustly. John Magee says: "By going to Cardinal Pizzardo's tomb to pray, it was as if he were saying: if there still remains

1 *Insegnamenti*, 1978, p. 524.

2 Daniel-Ange, *Paul VI, un regard prophétique*, p. 40.

3 *Insegnamenti*, 1978, p. 541.

4 Ibid. pp. 570–71.

some rust from that time. I want to free myself of it here, to be able to go cleansed before the Lord."[1]

His last audience, on 2 August, was about Christian joy. The tone was confidential, intimate. Why have the pilgrims come to Castelgandolfo? To see the Pope? Out of curiosity? Of course, they had really come to observe his state of health, sensing that this could be the last time they would see him. Perhaps they have come, he wonders a little doubtfully, to *listen* to the word of the Pope which has difficulty in making itself heard amid the babble of conflicting voices that come to us from all sides. In this confusion, he went on, faith brings direction and clarity of vision; but it must be "faith working through charity" (Galatians 5:6) which carries along with it "strength, joy, and the comfort of the divine life imparted to us".[2]

Next day, 3 August, Paul broke with precedent which says that popes do not receive heads of state while holidaying at Castelgandolfo. But since the head of state was Sandro Pertini, the newly chosen President of Italy, to Paul it seemed natural to extend this last courtesy to the country he loved.

Pertini described the audience himself. It began at 11.15 and lasted for two and a half hours, despite interruptions and flapping from "some prelate" (obviously Macchi) who kept trying to call the Pope away to other duties. They discussed the revision of the Concordat, and Pertini hoped he would give orders to his negotiating team to "abandon their intransigence and stop raising futile objections". The old Socialist unbeliever was famous for his bluntness. Then they chatted about old friends. Pertini knew Senator Lodovico Montini, of course, and Paul was delighted to discover that Franco Costa of Genoa, a friend from FUCI days, later Bishop of Crema, was Pertini's cousin.[3]

Over the next three days Pertini reproached himself for having stayed too long and exhausted an obviously sick man. Paul had a high fever the medical team could not explain, and therefore could not cure. Fr John Magee remembers the day well because he was just back from holiday in Ireland. Paul came to table, but didn't eat. He wanted to know all about Magee's holiday, and how his sister with the handicapped child was.

After the TV news that evening, they watched a Western because Macchi liked the genre. Magee goes on:

1 John Magee, "In Peter's House", *Thirty Days*, September 1988, p. 9.

2 *Insegnamenti*, 1978, pp. 585–87.

3 *Notiziario*, 5, p. 58. On 25 June 1982 a delegation from the Istituto Paolo VI in Brescia visited President Sandro Pertini in the Quirinale Palace, and he talked "with his usual cordiality" about Paul VI.

> Paul VI did not understand anything about the plot, and he asked me every so often, "Who is the good guy? Who is the bad guy?" He became enthusiastic only when there were scenes of horses. "The horse is the most beautiful animal that God has created," he said, "in Ireland you have some famous ones."[1]

He liked the horses in the commercials too. Then they said the rosary, and Magee went to bed.

Macchi stayed with Paul and read to him from Jean Guitton's *Mon petit catéchisme* and *Dialogues avec un enfant*. Paul made a remark Macchi found ominous and strange: "*Adesso viene la notte*" (Now the night comes).[2]

At 3 a.m. there were three rings on his bell. The convention was: one ring meant he was in his study, two he was in the bedroom, three he needed help. He needed help now as he sat on the edge of his bed, breathing with great difficulty. Macchi and Magee hoist him carefully into an armchair and give him oxygen to help him breathe. They summon the sisters. Macchi says to Magee: "You stay here by the Pope while I fetch the doctor." Already Paul is beginning to breathe more easily. To break the silence Magee says: "Your Holiness, should we pray together now?" Paul replies: "Yes, but not for me, pray *for the Church*." He repeats this all day.

The medical report says Paul is suffering from a fever caused by acute cystitis which makes the arthritis from which he has long suffered even more painful. He is treated with antibiotics. That evening Macchi and Dr Renato Buzzonnetti keep vigil with him. They dare not touch the alarm clock he bought in Poland in 1924. Only Paul knows how it works.

On Sunday, 6 August, the feast of the Transfiguration, on doctor's orders Paul does not get up. His eyes remain closed and he stirs uneasily in pain. "What time is it?" he asks Macchi. The room was in semi-darkness, the heavy curtains half-drawn and the shutters closed in the Italian manner to keep out the summer sunshine. "It's eleven o'clock." Paul opens his eyes and looks at his Polish alarm clock: it shows 10.45. "Look," he says, "my little old clock is as tired as me." Macchi tries to wind it up but confuses the alarm with the winder.

Paul needs to know the time because he does not want to miss the noon Angelus. It has already been announced that he will not appear at the window as usual. Now, propped up in a chair, he recites the Angelus

1 John Magee, "In Peter's House", *30 Days*, September 1988, p. 10.

2 Pasquale Macchi, "*Adesso viene la notte*, in *Notiziario*, 17, p. 121. I will follow this account of Paul's last hours, filling it out with the reports of Fr John Magee and Daniel-Ange (whose source was Macchi).

saying: "On this great feast of the Transfiguration, I want to recite the Angelus for all the faithful of the Church."

Then he is put back to bed and falls into a deep sleep which the bystanders hope will calm his fever. Dr Mario Fontana arrives at 2 p.m. Magee, at the bedside, feels the Pope wants to say something. "What do you want, Holiness?" he asks. Paul's answer, Magee says, was like a smile: "*Caro*, a little patience." Those were his last recorded non-liturgical words.

The chapel at Castelgandolfo is next door to the papal bedroom. The door is left ajar, Don Pasquale Macchi begins the Mass of the Transfiguration at 6 p.m. Paul clings to Magee's hand and joins in the Latin as though concelebrating. At the words of the creed "*Credo unam, sanctam, apostolicam ecclesiam*" he grips Magee's hand tightly and repeats in a strong voice, *apostolicam ecclesiam, apostolicam ecclesiam.*

Paul receives Communion under both kinds, his viaticum for the journey. As Mass ends Paul has a massive heart attack. It is as though he had exploded from within. Magee thinks he would have been thrown out of bed had his hand not been held. But now the grip weakens.

For another three hours Paul lingers on. Those who should be officially present – the secretary of state, the substitute, the Vicar of Rome – are summoned. So Jean Villot, Giuseppe Caprio, and Ugo Poletti duly arrive. Marco Montini, a favourite nephew, appears. Nobody thinks to call Giovanni Benelli, a cruel oversight.

The doctors continue to monitor temperature and blood pressure but there is not much more for them to do. Paul seems to be trying to say something. Macchi hushes everyone. Paul is murmuring repeatedly, faintly, as though for himself alone, "Our Father, who art in heaven . . ." By 9.30 p.m. even this ceases.

With everyone kneeling by the bedside, Cardinal Villot begins the prayers for the dying. Paul opens his eyes briefly, recognizes Villot, murmurs "*grazie*" and sketches a limp blessing before subsiding into a deep sleep, his last. There is no agony. Magee feels the pulse fading. At 9.41 the doctor says, "The Pope is dead." Then the Polish alarm clock went off.

He had one last message, scribbled on a pad by his bed, intended for the Angelus he was unable to recite at his window. He prays for all those who suffer, for the hungry, the unemployed, the sick. Then he rouses himself to say that "an incomparable destiny awaits those who have honoured their Christian vocation". And incomparable joy.

APPENDICES

Escape Plans

Appendix to Chapter 13

There is a vast amount of unreliable data about escape plans. Cardinal Pietro Palazzini "revealed" that Lamberto Stoppa, an engineer, had been charged with constructing an underground tunnel down which Pius XII might crawl to safety.[1]

Jacques Delaunay reports that Cardinal Manuel Goncalves Careijeira, then Patriarch of Lisbon, told the following tale to a Brazilian diplomat:

> In the spring of 1943 Pius XII expected to be arrested by the Gestapo when they arrived. He summoned Cardinal Careijeira to Rome, and gave him the following orders: "If I am arrested by the Germans, I will cease to be Piux XII and become Cardinal Pacelli once more. You will announce this news to the world and organize in Lisbon a conclave to elect the new Pope."[2]

That would have been a neat way of depriving Hitler of his prize. However Careijeira was still alive in 1967 and said Delaunay's story was "without foundation". Must one assume *cardinals* always tell the truth?

Ernst von Weizsäcker, German Ambassador to the Holy See at the time, in his *Errinerungen* (*Memories*) dismisses all talk of arresting the Pope as sheer allied propaganda. Much disinformation was flying about. But von Weizsäcker suddenly "remembers" what Pius VII said to an emissary of Napoleon: "You can arrest me if you like. But then you will have in your hands only an ordinary monk called Chiaramonti and not the Pope."[3] So it was the classic ploy when dealing with "tyrants", and a classic theme which figured in Montini's lectures at the Pontifical Academy. I suppose von Weizsäcker got it from Montini.[4]

1 *Thirty Days*, February 1988, p. 75.

2 Jacques Delaunay, *Grandes Controverses de Notre Temps*, Paris 1967.

3 Ernst Weizsäcker, *Memories*, p. 363.

4 For this material, thanks to Fr Robert Graham SJ of *Civiltà Cattolica*.

Appendix to Chapter 14

The Foreign Office, the Vatican and Marshall Aid

The new British minister to the Holy See, Victor Perowne, appointed on 4 June 1947, was briefed by Sir Francis D'Arcy Osborne on the Vatican's international role and the usefulness of Montini as a channel of communication. Both points were soon tested.

Ernest Bevin, Foreign Secretary, sent a telegram on 15 July 1947, suggesting there would be "a useful effect on US public opinion if *L'Osservatore Romano* were to publish an article expressing the interest of the Vatican in the forthcoming Paris Conference and emphasizing the importance of a European Plan and of American aid if economic chaos and consequent social upheaval are to be avoided".[1]

The Paris Conference was the European response to the speech by the US Secretary of State, General George Marshall, at Harvard on 5 June. Perowne discussed the Marshall Plan with Montini on 19 July: "Msgr Montini spoke to me spontaneously about the Pope's interest in the Conference, asking rather wistfully whether I thought there were any hope of the USSR and Spain participating."[2]

Perowne handed Montini a confidential Foreign Office report to help with the article.

Msgr Montini delivered what Bevin wanted, an article in *L'Osservatore Romano* on 27 July 1947. It endorsed the Marshall Plan unreservedly. The common good (*bonum commune*) of Europe demanded such a plan. It rejected the idea that it was a manoeuvre of dollar imperialism.

Far from being pleased, the Foreign Office was annoyed because the article had, in its views, made use of confidential information which could only have come from its telegrams to Perowne. Yet it was no secret that all the countries later known as "satellites" were forbidden by Moscow to take part in the Paris Conference. The offence of *L'Osservatore Romano* was to spell this out.

Thus the article noted that the Romanian Foreign Minister when refusing "could not resist adding that it did not represent the public opinion of his own people, 90 per cent of whom felt as he did". The Polish Prime Minister told the French Ambassador in Prague that Poland would willingly have accepted the Marshall Plan, had it been free to do

1 PRO, FO 380/122.

2 Ibid.

so. The rest of Eastern Europe was likewise obliged to swap interests for ideology. But you can't eat ideology.

Perowne went back to Montini to clear up this supposed *faux-pas*:

> When I saw Msgr Montini on 30 July he referred somewhat apologetically to the *Osservatore Romano* articles of 27 July which he described as rather muddled. He offered, should I so desire, to arrange for publication in *Il Quotidiano* of an article adhering more closely to the "useful suggestions" I had made when I visited him on 19 July. I accepted this offer, taking the opportunity to say that I should have preferred fewer details of the various governments invited to Paris and hoped that nothing of the kind would be repeated in *Il Quotidiano*. Msgr Montini concurred, but said that the Vatican had more than one source for the information.[1]

To save further *embarras* Sir Victor kept rigorously mum: he had said nothing to his French colleague Jacques Maritain, and "if approached by him or the press on the subject of the sources of the article, should plead ignorance".

The desired "corrective" article duly appeared in *Il Quotidiano*, the Catholic Action paper, on 3 August 1947, which shows the speed at which Montini could work. The "Carlo Adami" to whom it is attributed was in his office. It praised the initiative in economic co-operation already taken by the Benelux countries, and stated the principle on which the European Community would eventually be based: "It is clear that economic solidarity on a continental basis would protect the independence of European peoples far better than bilateral agreements concluded by one great power with so many countries, weak and needful of help as they are."[2]

The Soviet *niet* to the Marshall Plan was a tragic turning-point, whose consequences were unravelled only in the 1990s. The Poles felt particularly aggrieved that their "liberation" from Nazism had so quickly turned into a worse form of enslavement. The Iron Curtain became the frontier between plenty and shortage.

1 Ibid.
2 Ibid.

Appendix to Chapter 17

Montini and Fisher

After the meeting between Archbishop Montini and the visiting Anglicans in October 1956 there was an exchange of letters with the Archbishop of Canterbury, Dr Geoffrey Fisher. They can be found in the archives of the Council for Foreign Relations at Lambeth Palace. They have not been published before, and Edward Carpenter, in his massive work *Archbishop Fisher: His Life and Times*, is unaware of their existence. Though slight in content they represent an interesting "first".

Dr Fisher, a firm believer in the "ministry of the pen", wrote on 12 December 1956:

> Your Grace, dear Brother
>
> I have heard with the greatest appreciation of your kindness this summer to a number of clergy of the Church of England who were invited to visit your diocese. They returned with most enthusiastic accounts of your hospitality and Christian friendship and I hope you will allow me to write this short letter to say how much I appreciate this action. I am sure that such personal contacts as were enjoyed during this visit are the best way of creating that spirit of love and understanding between members of different theological traditions which is a prerequisite for closer unity in the future.
>
> I remain
> Yours very sincerely in Jesus Christ
> Geoffrey Fisher.

Montini's reply, dated 29 December, reached Lambeth on 4 January 1957. It is given in the somewhat literal translation prepared by Gage-Brown for Dr Fisher:

> Your Excellency
>
> I received with pleasure your letter of 12 December concerning the visit made to Milan by some members of the Anglican clergy last September.
>
> I thank your Excellency most heartily for your courteous words, and am glad to inform you that I have glad remembrances of these visitors, who were so good and nice (*tanti buoni e gentili*) and showed themselves to be animated by noble and devout sentiments.
>
> I express in my turn the wish that the spirit of charity and

the love of truth may produce with the grace of God even better fruits in the future.

To this wish – today, the feast of St Thomas of Canterbury – I add a special prayer.

I beg you to receive, your Excellency, the expression of my sincere respects, and I am in Jesus Christ

Your most devoted (*Suo devotissimo*)
+ G. B. Montini.

There are some nuances here. It was shrewd of Fisher to write about "different Christian traditions" (if he had said "Churches" he would have begged the ecclesiological question). In writing so naturally of "Anglican *clergy*" Montini just ignored *Apostolicae Curae*, the papal bull of 1896 which declared Anglican orders "absolutely null and utterly void". He also displayed "delicacy" by writing on the feast of St Thomas of Canterbury whom Fisher claimed to succeed.

Anglicans of this period worried a great deal about "recognition". This can be seen in a note Gage-Brown added to explain that Montini's choice of "your Excellency" as a form of address neatly side-stepped "the difficulty of committing himself on Anglican orders". This is most unlikely. It was the routine and proper way to address an archbishop in Italian.

Four years later his excellency Archbishop Fisher saw Pope John XXIII in the Vatican, the first Archbishop of Canterbury to visit a pope since the Reformation.

SELECT BIBLIOGRAPHY

Bibliography and sources

There exist two bibliographies of Giovanni Battista Montini, the first covering the Milanese period, the second his pontificate:

Antonio Rimoldi, *Bibliografia sull'episcopato Milanese del Card. G. B. Montini (1955–1963)* in *G. B. Montini arcivescovo*, NED (Nuove Edizioni Duomo), Milan 1983, pp. 347–56. = Arcivescovo (1983)

Paulus PP. VI (1963–1978): Elenchus Bibliographicus, collegit Pál Arato SJ, denuo refundis indicibus instruxit Paulo Vian (ed. Pál Arato SJ, completed and provided with indices by Paolo Vian), Publications of Paul VI Institute, Brescia 1981.

The publications of the Istituto Paolo VI in Brescia are also indispensable. They come in three forms, *Quaderni*, *Notiziario* and conference reports. For the pontificate, the essential collection of texts is *Insegnamenti*. See *Quaderni*, *Notiziario* and *Insegnamenti* for details.

In what follows I have confined myself to what proved useful.

Abbot SJ, Walter, *The Documents of Vatican II*, America Press, New York; Geoffrey Chapman, London 1966 (hastily done translations, with many errors and infelicities. See Austin Flannery OP for alternative).

Acta Synodalia Concilii Vaticani Secundi, Libreria editrice Vaticana (the official "Hansard" of the Council).

Actes et documents = *Actes et documents du Saint-Siège*, ed. Pierre Blet SJ, Robert A. Graham SJ, Angelo Martini SJ, and Burkhart Schneider SJ, Libreria editrice Vaticana, 11 vols.

Alberigo, Giuseppe, "*Santa Sede e vescovi nello stato unitario*", *La Chiesa e il potere politico, Storia d'Italia, Annali 9*, Einaudi, Turin 1986.

Alberigo, Giuseppe, ed., *Papa Giovanni*, Laterza, Rome 1987.

Alberigo, Giuseppe, ed., *Chiese Italiane e Concilio, esperienze pastorali nella chiesa italiana tra Pio XII e Paolo VI*, Marietti 1988. Includes a chapter by Gian Luca Potestà, "*L'episcopato di G. B. Montini a Milano (1955–1963)*".

Alexander, Stella, *The Triple Myth: A Life of Archbishop Alojzije Stepinac*, East European Monographs, Boulder, distrib. Columbia University Press 1987.

Andreotti, Giulio, *A Ogni Morte di Papa: I papi che ho conosciuto*, Rizzoli, Milan 1980 (Andreotti, ten times Prime Minister of Italy, begins "the Popes I have known" with St Pius X who knew his mother; he admits that foreign taxi-drivers never knew the name of Italy's President but could always name the reigning pope; stood up to *Signora* Margaret Thatcher).

Andreotti, Giulio, *Diari 1976–1979*, Rizzoli, Milan 1986.

Andrieux, Maurice, *Daily Life in Papal Rome*, Allen & Unwin, London 1968.

Anni e Opere di Paolo VI, ed. Nello Vian, introd. Arturo C. Jemolo, Istituto della Enciclopedia Italiana, Rome 1978 (this work covers Montini's whole life and provides essential bibliographical information).

Antonetti, Nicola, *La Fuci di Montini e di Righetti, Lettere di Igino Righetti ad Angela Gotelli (1928–33)*, AVE, Rome 1979.

Arrupe, SJ, Pedro, *Itinéraire d'un jésuite*, interviewed by Jean-Claude Dietsch SJ, *Le Centurion*, Paris 1982.

ASCV = *Acta Synodalia Concilii Vaticani Secundi*, Vatican Press. See above.

Barth, Karl, *Ad Limina Apostolorum*, EVZ Verlag, Zürich 1967.

Bartoletti, Enrico, "*La Question des Femmes et des Ministères Ordonnés*", unpublished memorandum presented personally to Paul VI at Castelgandolfo in August 1975. Thanks to Rosemary Goldie for making it available.

Blasier, Cole, *The Giants' Quarrel*, Pittsburgh University Press 1983.

Brachin, Pierre, "*Paul VI et l'Eglise des Pays-Bas*", in *Paul VI et la Modernité dans l'Eglise*.

Bugnini, Annibale, Abp, *The Reform of the Liturgy 1948–1975*, tr. Matthew J. O'Connell, Liturgical Press, Collegeville, Minnesota 1990 (*La Riforma liturgica 1948–1975*, Edizioni Liturgiche, Rome 1983).

Bullock, Alan, *Hitler and Stalin: Parallel Lives*, HarperCollins, London 1991.

Califano, Joseph A., "The President and the Pope: L.B.J., Paul VI and the Vietnam War", *America*, 12 October 1991 (this article is an extended version of a section of *The Triumph and Tragedy of Lyndon Johnson – the White House Years*, Simon and Schuster 1991. Califano was Johnson's top assistant for domestic affairs 1965 to 1969).

Campanini, Giorgio, "*Montini et Maritain*" in *G. B. Montini e la Società Italiana 1919–39*, CEDOC, Brescia 1983.

Capovilla, Loris F., *Giovanni XXIII, Quindici Letture*, Edizioni di Storia e Letteratura, Rome 1970.

Capovilla, Loris F., *L'Ite Missa Est di Papa Giovanni*, Messagero, Padua; and Grafica et Arte, Bergamo 1983.

Caprile SJ, Giovanni, *Il Concilio Vaticano II*, 5 vols, *Civiltà Cattolica*, 1965– (in the main the "chronicles" of *Civiltà Cattolica*'s Vatican specialist, but supplemented by material not otherwise available, often directly from Paul VI).

Caprile SJ, Giovanni, *Karol Wojtyla e il Sinodo dei Vescovi*, Vatican Press 1980.

Caracciolo, Nicola, interview with Princess Maria José, *La Repubblica*, 7 September 1983.

Carbone, Vincenzo, "*Il ruolo di Paolo VI nell'evoluzione e nella redazione della dichiarazione Dignitatis Humanae*" in *Paulo VI et il rapporto Chiesa-Mondo*.

Cardinale, Hyginus Eugene, *The Holy See and the International Order*, Colin Smythe, Gerrards Cross 1976 (the nephew of Don Giuseppe De Luca, was Apostolic Delegate in London and Nuncio to Belgium and the European Community).

Carpenter, Edward, *Archbishop Fisher: His Life and Times*, Canterbury Press, Norwich 1992.

Carretto, Carlo, *Letters to Dolcidia*, Fount, HarperCollins, London 1991.

Casaroli, Agostino, "*La Santa Sede e l'Europa*", *Civiltà Cattolica*, 19 February 1972 (did not let his office interfere with his help).

Casaroli, Agostino, "*Paolo VI e il dialogo*", *Il Regno*, 19/84, 11 November 1984.

Chadwick, Owen, *Anglican Initiatives in Christian Unity*, ed. E. G. W. Bill, SPCK 1967.

Chadwick, Owen, *Britain and the Vatican during the Second World War*, Cambridge University Press 1986 (the Ford Lectures given in the University of Oxford in 1981).

Chadwick, Owen, *Michael Ramsey: A Life*, Oxford University Press 1991.

Chadwick, Owen, *The Christian Church in the Cold War*, Penguin 1992.

Ciano, Galeazzo, *Diario 1937–1943*, ed. Renzo De Felice, Rizzoli, Milan 1980 (the first *complete* edition).

Clancy, John G., *Apostle for Our Time: Pope Paul VI*, Collins, London 1964.

Clark, Martin, *Modern Italy 1871–1982*, Longman, London 1984.

Clifton, Michael, *Amigo: Friend of the Poor*, Fowler-Wright, Leominster 1987.

Coleman, Dale, ed., *Michael Ramsey: The Anglican Spirit*, SPCK, London 1991 (consists of notes taken during Dr Ramsey's lectures at Nashotah House, a US Episcopalian seminary, in 1979).

Colombo, Giuseppe, "*Genesi, storia e significato dell'enciclica* 'Ecclesiam Suam' " in "*Ecclesiam Suam*", Brescia 1982.

Congar OP, Yves, *Challenge to the Church: The Case of Archbishop Lefebvre*, tr., pref. George Patrick Dwyer, Archbishop of Birmingham, Collins 1977.

Congar, OP, Yves, *Diversity and Communion*, SCM, London 1984.

Conzemius, Victor, Swiss historian provided anecdotes.

Cooney, John, *The Crozier and the Dáil: Church and State 1922–1986*, Mercier Press, Cork 1986.

Copleston, Frederick C., *Russian Religious Philosophy: Selected Aspects*, Search Press, London; University of Notre Dame, Indiana 1988.

Corbishley SJ, T., "The Pope and the Society", *Month*, April 1974 ("An unwillingness to listen is always the sign of a *weak* superior," wrote my former superior at Campion Hall, Oxford).

Cornwell, John, *Thief in the Night: The Death of Pope John Paul I*, Viking, London 1989 (*the* answer, and antidote, to David Yallop's meretricious book).

Cottier OP, Georges, "*Interventions de Paul VI dans l'élaboration de* 'Gaudium et Spes' " in *Paolo VI e il rapporto Chiesa-Mondo al Concilio*, Istituto Paolo VI, Brescia 1991.

Crehan SJ, Joseph, "The Papacy and the Holocaust", *Month*, November 1967.

Daley SJ, Brian, "Identifying Jesuits: the 32nd General Congregation", *Month*, May 1975.

Dallin, Alexander, *German Rule in Russia 1941–1945*, Macmillan, London 1981.

Daniel-Ange, *Paul VI, un regard prophétique*, Editions Saint-Paul 1979.

Davies, Norman, *God's Playground: A History of Poland*, vol. II, *1795 to the Present*, Clarendon Press, Oxford 1981.

de Brouker, José, *The Suenens Dossier: The Case for Collegiality*, Fides, Notre Dame, Indiana; and Gill and Macmillan, Dublin 1970 (grew out of the interview published in *Informations Catholiques Internationales*, 15 May 1969).

Deedy, jr., John G., "The Catholic Press and Vietnam" in *American Catholics and Vietnam*, Eerdmans, Grand Rapids 1968.

de Gaulle, Charles, *Memoires de Guerre*, Plon, Paris 1954.

de Laubier, Patrick, *Il pensiero sociale della Chiesa Cattolica*, Massimo, Milan 1986.

Delhaye, Philippe, "*Le Schéma de Zurich*" in *L'Eglise dans le monde de ce temps*, vol. I, Cerf 1967.

de Lubac SJ, Henri, *Les Eglises particulières dans l'Eglise universelle*, Aubier, Paris 1971.

de Lubac SJ, Henri, *Résistance chrétienne à l'antisémitisme: souvenirs 1940–1944*, Fayard 1988.

Denis, Henri, *Eglise, qu'as tu fait de ton Concile? Le Centurion*, Paris 1985.

De Rosa SJ, Giuseppe, "Learning the Hard Way: The Divorce Referendum in Italy", *Month*, August 1974.

Dhanis SJ, Edouard, and Jan Visser CSSR, *The Supplement to a New Catechism*, Search Press 1969.

Dick, Dr Jack, of Leuven University, provided information on Archbishop Jean Jadot.

Domenico, Roy, "The Vatican, the US and Vietnam in the Johnson Years", a paper delivered 13 October 1991 at the conference on Vatican Diplomacy in the Nineteenth and Twentieth Century, University of New Brunswick, Canada.

Dossetti, Giuseppe, "*Memoria di Giacomo Lercaro*" in *Chiese Italiane et Concilio*, ed. Giuseppe Alberigo, Marietti, Turin 1988.

Doyle OFM, Eric, "The Ordination of Women in the Roman Catholic Church" in *Feminine in the Church*, ed. Monica Furlong, SPCK 1984.

Duff SJ, Frank, in Hugh Morley OFM, *The Pope and the Press*, Notre Dame Press, Notre Dame, Indiana, 1968.

Dupuy, André, *La Diplomatie du Saint-Siege*, Téqui, Paris 1980.

Ellis, John Tracy, *Catholic Bishops*, Michael Glazier, Wilmington, Delaware, pb. 1984.

Erikson, Erik H., *Identity Youth and Crisis*, Faber, London 1968.

Falconi, Carlo, *Gedda e l'Azione cattolica*, Florence 1958.

Falconi, Carlo, *The Popes in the Twentieth Century*, Weidenfeld and Nicolson, London 1967.

Falconi, Carlo, *The Silence of Pius XII*, Faber, London 1970; and Little, Brown, New York.

Familiari = Giovanni Battista Montini, *Lettere ai Familiari 1919–1943*, ed. Nello Vian, Brescia 1986, 2 vols, Istituto Paolo VI (since the two volumes are numbered consecutively, I have given the page references only).

Fappani-Molinari = Antonio Fappani and Franco Molinari, *Giovanni Battista Montini Giovane, Documenti inediti e testimonianze*, Marietti, Turin 1979 (Montini remains "young" in their eyes until the death of his parents in 1943).

Faus, José Gonzalez, *Where the Spirit Breathes*, Orbis, New York 1989.

Finotti, Fabio, *Critica stilistica e linguaggio religioso in Giovanni Battista Montini*, Edizioni-Studium, Rome, Saggi/1 for the Istituto Paolo VI.

Fitzgerald, Garret, *All in a Life, An Autobiography*, Gill and Macmillan, Dublin 1991.

Flannery OP, Austin, *Vatican II: The Conciliar and Post-Conciliar Documents*, 1, 2 vols, Fowler Wright, Leominster vol. I, 1975, vol. II, 1982 (better tr. of Council texts than Abbott; indispensable collection of subsequent documents such as *Humanae Vitae*, *Evangelii Nuntiandi*, etc.).

Fogarty SJ, Gerald P., *The Vatican and the American Hierarchy from 1870 to 1965*, Michael Glazier, Wilmington 1985 (to whom be grateful thanks for reading through the entire MS of this book and eliminating sundry errors).

Fogazzaro, Antonio, *Il Santo*, ed. Anna Maria Moroni, Mondadori, Milan 1985 (placed on the Index of Forbidden books on 4 April 1906, and never removed).

Fontanelle, René, *His Holiness Pope Pius XII*, Catholic Book Club, London 1938.

Forgacs, David, ed., *Rethinking Italian Fascism, Capitalism, Populism and Culture*, Lawrence and Wishart, London 1986.

Fouilloux, Etienne, "*G. B. Montini face aux débats ecclesiaux de son temps*" in *Paul VI et la Modernité.*

Fouilloux, Etienne, *Les catholiques et l'unité chrétienne du XIXe au XXe siecle*, le Centurion, Paris, 1982 (the story of ecumenism seen from a French angle).

Francis de Sales, St, *Introduction to the Devout Life*, tr. and ed. John K, Ryan, Doubleday 1972.

Galilea, Segundo, "*Example d'une réception 'selective' et créative du Concile: l'Amérique Latine aux conférences de Medellín et de Puebla*" in *La Réception de Vatican II*, ed. Giuseppe Alberigo and Jean-Pierre Jossua, Cerf, Paris 1985.

Garzia, Italo, *Pio XII et l'Italia nella seconda guerra mondiale*, Morcelliana, Brescia 1988.

Garzonio, Marco, *Cardinale a Milano in un Mondo che cambia*, Rizzoli, Milan 1985 (interviews with Carlo Maria Martini SJ, Archbishop of Milan 1980—).

Giles, Frank, *Sundry Times*, John Murray, London 1986.

Giordani, Igino, and Luigi Sturzo, *Un Ponte tra due Generazioni, Carteggio 1924–1958*, pref. Gabriele de Rosa, introd. Paolo Piccoli, Editori Laterza, Milan 1986.

Giovetti, Paola, *Teresa Neumann*, St Paul, Slough 1990.

Giuntella, Maria Cristina, "*Cristiani nella Storia, Il 'caso Rossi' e suoi riflessi nelle organizzazioni cattoliche di massa*" in *Pio XII*, ed. Andrea Riccardi, Laterza 1984 (far and away the most illuminating article on Montini in the early 1950s, seen through his friend and protége, Mario Rossi).

Goldie, Rosemary, *The Church and the International Women's Year, 1975*, texts, Pontifical Church for the Laity, Vatican City.

Goldie, Rosemary, "*Paul VI, les laïcs et le laïcat*" in *Paul VI et la Modernité.*

Goldie, Rosemary, "*Bartoletti e il ruolo della donna nella Chiesa e nella società*" in *Un Vescovo italiano del Concilio, Enrico Bartoletti, 1916–1976*, Marietti, Genoa 1988 (supplied unpublished material on women).

Graham SJ, Robert, "Foreign Intelligence and the Vatican" in *The Catholic World Report*, March 1992 (Fr Graham has been most helpful to me: no one knows more about the wartime Vatican than he does).

Gray, Francine du Plessix, *Divine Disobedience: Profiles in Catholic Radicalism*, Hamish Hamilton, London 1970 (based on articles in *New Yorker*, about Ivan Illich, the Berrigan Brothers *et al.*).

Greeley, Andrew M., *The Making of the Popes 1978*, Andrews and McMeel, Kansas City 1978.

Greene, Graham, *Ways of Escape*, Bodley Head 1980.

Grootaers, Jan, *De Vatican II à Jean-Paul II, le grand tournant de l'Eglise catholique*, Le Centurion, Paris 1981.

Grootaers, Jan "*Une restauration de la théologie de l'épiscopat: contribution du Cardinal Alfrink à la préparation de Vatican II*" in *Glaube im Prozess, Für Karl Rahner*, Herder, Freiburg-im-Bresgau 1984.

Grootaers, Jan, "*L'attitude de l'archevêque Montini au cours de la première période du Concile*" in *Montini Arcivescovo* (1985).

Grootaers, Jan, "*Quelques données concernant la rédaction de l'encyclique 'Humanae Vitae'*" in *Paul VI et la Modernité*, 1985.

Grootaers, Jan, *Primauté et Collégialité, Le Dossier de Gérard Philips sur la Nota Explicativa Praevia*, Leuven University Press 1986.

Grootaers, Jan, "*L'opinion publique en Belgique et aux Pays-Bas*" in *Paulo VI e i probleme ecclesiologici al Concili*, Istituto Paolo VI, Brescia 1989.

Grootaers, Jan, "*Paul VI et la déclaration conciliare sur la liberté religieuse 'Dignitatis Humanae'*" in *Paolo VI e il rapporto Chiesa-Mondo al Concilio*, Istituto Paolo VI, Brescia 1991.

Grootaers, Jan, "*Humanae Vitae*" in *Dictionnaire d'histoire et de géographie ecclésiastiques*, Letourzey, Paris 1992 (this is the most careful and synthetic account of the origins, meaning and "reception" of *Humanae Vitae*).

Guardini, Romano, *Vom Geist der liturgie*, Herder, Freiburg 1922; *The Spirit of the Liturgy*, Sheed and Ward, London 1930.

Guarducci, Margherita, *Saint Pierre retrouvé*, Editions Saint-Paul, Paris-Fribourg 1974.

Guarducci, Margherita, *La Tomba di San Pietro*, Rusconi, Milan 1990.

Guitton, Jean, *Dialogues avec Paul VI*, Fayard, Paris 1967; tr. Anne and Christopher Fremantle, *The Pope Speaks*, Weidenfeld and Nicolson, London 1968 (raises the question: how much is reporting and how much is creative).

Guitton, Jean, *Paul VI secret*, Desclée de Brouwer, Paris 1979 (a different, more truthful book after Paul VI's death, a *retractatio* in the sense of St Augustine, p. 14).

Gutierrez, Gustavo, "*Le rapport entre l'Eglise et les pauvres, vu d'Amérique Latine*" in *La Réception de Vatican II*, ed. Giuseppe Alberigo and Jean-Pierre Jossua, Cerf, Paris 1985.

Häring, Bernhard, *Fede Storia Morale*, interviews with Gianni Lichieri, Borla, Rome 1989.

Hastings, Adrian, *A History of English Christianity 1920–1985*, Collins, London 1986.

Hastings, Adrian, ed., *Modern Catholicism: Vatican II and After*, SPCK, London; Oxford University Press, New York 1991.

Hebblethwaite, Peter, *The Council Fathers and Atheism*, Paulist Press, New York 1966.

Hebblethwaite, Peter, *Understanding the Synod*, Gill, Dublin and Sydney 1968.

Hebblethwaite, Peter, *The Runaway Church*, Collins, London 1975, pb 1978.

Hebblethwaite, Peter, "The Mariology of Three Popes", *The Way*, Supplement 51, Autumn 1984.

Hebblethwaite, Peter, *John XXIII, Pope of the Council*, Chapman, London 1984;

John XIII, Shepherd of the Modern World, Doubleday, New York 1985.

Heenan, John Carmel, *A Crown of Thorns: An Autobiography 1951–1963*, Hodder & Stoughton, London 1974. This was preceded by an account of his earlier life, *Not the Whole Truth*, Hodder & Stoughton 1971 (a *New Statesman* reviewer remarked he was "too clever by a quarter").

Henessy SJ, James, ed. "American Jesuit in Wartime Rome: The Diary of Vincent A. McCormick SJ, 1942–1945", *Mid-America*, January 1974, Loyola University, Chicago (Rector of the Gregorian University from 1934, McCormick moved into the Jesuit Curia at 5 Borgo Santo Spirito when the United States entered the war, where he found the German Jesuit Fr Robert Leiber, adviser to Pius XII. Thanks to Gerard Fogarty for making the McCormick diary available).

Hoffmann, Peter, *The History of the German Resistance 1933–1945*, MIT Press, Cambridge, Massachusetts 1977; English translation of *Widerstand, Staatsrecht, Attentat*, Piper, Munich, 1969.

Hoffmann, Peter, "*Non silet caritas inter arma*: Archbishop Angelo Roncalli and Ambassador Franz von Papen in Turkey during the Second World War" (thanks to the author for letting me see his MS).

Hume, Cardinal Basil OSB, Archbishop of Westminster: thanks for innumerable kindnesses and the thought that "when you are a cardinal, *who* made you a cardinal makes a great difference".

Insegnamenti = *Insegnamenti di Paolo VI*, vols I–XVI, Libreria editrice Vaticana; in addition there is an *Indice delle materie contenute nei primi dodici volumi di Insegnamenti de Paolo VI, 1963–1974*, which appeared in 1977 (contains everything said or written by Paul VI for the public: I have given the year rather than the volume number).

Johnson, Paul, *A History of the Modern World from 1917 to the 1980s*, Weidenfeld and Nicolson, London 1983.

Journet, Charles, *La Juridiction de l'Eglise dans la Cité*, Paris 1931.

Journet, Charles, *L'Eglise du Verbe Incarné*, Paris 1941.

Kaiser, Robert Blair, *The Politics of Sex and Religion*, Leaven Press, Kansas 1985. (Changed his name from Piser to Kaiser when he became *Time*'s Rome bureau chief, and lost his wife to Malachy Martin.)

Kasper, Walter, "*Ein Grundgesetz der Kirche, ein Grundgesetz der Restauration?*" in *Kein Grundgesetz der Kirche ohne Zustimmung der Christen*, Matthias-Grünewald, Mainz 1971 (from 1989 Bishop of Rottenburg/ Stuttgart, in which diocese lies the Tübingen Catholic Theology Faculty).

Kee, Alastair, *Marx and the Failure of Liberation Theology*, SCM and Trinity International, London and Philadelphia 1990 (reproaches liberation theologians with being *insufficiently* Marxist).

Kelikian, Alice A., *Town and Country under Fascism*, Clarendon Press, Oxford 1986.

Keneally, Thomas, *Schindler's Ark*, Hodder & Stoughton, London 1982.

Kennedy, Eugene, *The Now and Future Church: The Psychology of Being an American Catholic*, Doubleday 1984.

Keogh, Dermot, *The Vatican, the Bishops and Irish Politics 1919–39*, Cambridge University Press 1986 (thanks for unpublished articles).

König, Franz, *Where is the Church heading?* Interviewed by Gianni Licheri, Foreword by Cardinal Basil Hume OSB, St Paul Publications, Slough 1986.

Kotre, John, *Simple Gifts: The Lives of Pat and Patty Crowley*, Andrews and McMeel, Kansas City 1979 (kiss-and-tell-all about the papal birth-control commission).

Küng, Hans, *The Church*, Burns and Oates, London 1967, admirably tr. Ray and Rosaleen Ockenden.

Küng, Hans, *Infallible? An Inquiry*, Collins, London 1971 ("He writes with bitter antipathy towards Roman theology, the Roman Curia, and Pope Paul", Avery Dulles SJ in *America*, 24 April 1971).

Küng, Hans, *Judaism*, SCM Press, London 1992 (a masterwork).

Lai, Benny, *Les secrets du Vatican*, Hachette, Paris 1983 (the *confidant* of Cardinal Giuseppe Siri and the leading authority on Vatican finances in the nineteenth century: more gossip than secrets).

Lamb, Richard, *The Ghosts of Peace*, Michael Russell, Salisbury 1987.

Lamet SJ, Pedro Miguel, *Arrupe, una explosión en la Iglesia*, Ediciones Temas de Hoy, Madrid 1989 (as honest a book as the circumstances would allow).

Latz, Dorothy, 22 September 1971, supplied the reference to St Angela Merici in *Voce*, Autumn 1972.

Laurentin, René, *Bilan de la Troisième Session*, Seuil, Paris 1965.

Laurentin, René, *Bilan du Concile*, Seuil, Paris 1966.

Laurentin, René, *Nouveaux ministères et fin du clergé*, Seuil, Paris 1971.

Laurentin, René, "*Paul VI et l'après-concile*" in *Paul VI et la Modernité* (these entries indicate my debt to Laurentin, but something happened to him in the 1980s when he became the apologist for Medjugorje and other Marian apparitions).

Leonardi, Robert, and Douglas A. Wertman, *Italian Christian Democracy: The Politics of Dominance*, Macmillan, London 1989 (possibly the dullest book ever written: indispensable).

Leprieur OP, François, *Quand Rome condamne*, Plon/Cerf 1989 (the priest-worker movement seen from the inside via the Dominican archives).

Lernoux, Penny, *People of God: The Struggle for World Catholicism*, Viking, New York 1989 (a remarkably perceptive book by my colleague on the *National Catholic Reporter* who died of cancer on 8 October 1989, aged forty-one).

Letely, Emma, *Maurice Baring: A Citizen of Europe*, Constable, London 1991.

Levillain, Philippe, *La mécanique politique de Vatican II*, Beauchesne, Paris 1975.

Lichten, Joseph, "*Pio XII e gli Ebrei*", *Il Regno-Documenti*, 3, 1988.

McCormick SJ, Vincent A., *Diary*, see James Henessey SJ, ed.

McRemond, Louis, kept the "Irish dimension" before my eyes.

Mack Smith, Denis, *Mussolini*, Granada, St Albans 1983.

Mafai, Miriam, *Pane nero: Donne e vita quotidiana nella seconda guerra mondiale*, Mondadori 1988.

Magee, John, "*La vita quotidiana de Paolo VI*" in *Modernité de Paul VI*.

Magister, Sandro, *La politica vaticana e l'Italia 1943–1978*, Riuniti, Rome 1979.

Mahoney SJ, John, *The Making of Moral Theology: A Study of the Roman*

Catholic Tradition, Clarendon Press, Oxford 1987 (the Martin D'Arcy Memorial Lectures for 1981–82).

Maloney, Thomas, *Westminster, Whitehall and the Vatican*, Burns and Oates 1985.

Maritain, Jacques, *Humanisme intégral: Problèmes temporels et spirituels d'une nouvelle chrétienté*, Aubier, Paris 1936. Tr. M. R. Adamson, *True Humanism*, Geoffrey Bles 1938.

Martimort, Aimé Georges, "*Le rôle de Paul VI dans la réforme liturgique*" in *Le rôle de G. B. Montini–Paul VI dans la réforme liturgique*, Istituto Paolo VI, Brescia 1987, p. 59.

Menozzi, Daniele, "*L'Eglise et l'Histoire*" in *La chrétienté en débat*, ed. Giuseppe Alberigo, Cerf, Paris 1984.

Miccoli, Giovanni, "*Sul ruolo di Roncalli nella Chiesa italiana*" in *Papa Giovanni*, ed. Giuseppe Alberigo, Laterza, Rome 1987.

Milano, Gian Piero, "*Paolo VI e il principio della collegialità nel Sinodo dei Vescovi*" in *Paul VI et les Réformes Institutionelles dans l'Eglise*, Istituto Paolo VI, Brescia 1987.

Modernité = *Paul VI et la Modernité dans l'Eglise, Actes du colloque organisé par l'Ecole française de Rome*, Ecole Française de Rome and Istituto Paolo VI of Brescia, 1984.

Montini, G. Battista, ed. Cesare Trebeschi, *Lettere a un giovane amico*, Queriniana, Brescia 1978 (the ed. Cesare Trebeschi is the son of the "young friend", Andrea Trebeschi. Andrea perished in a concentration camp; Cesare became mayor of Brescia).

Montini, G. Battista, *Scritti giovanili*, Quericiana 1979, ed. Cesare Trebeschi (articles in *La Fionda*, the FUCI student magazine).

Montini, Giovanni Battista, *La preghiera dell'anima, le idee di S. Paolo, Colloqui Religiose*, pref. G. B. Scaglia, Istituto Paolo VI, Brescia, Quaderni dell'Istituto, 1, 1981. Originally published in *Studium*, 1931.

G. B. Montini et la società italiana 1919–1939, *Acta* of a seminar held at Brescia, 21–22 October 1983, Centro di Documentazione (CE.DOC).

Montini, Giovanni Battista, *Discorsi e scritti sul Concilio* (1959–1963), Istituto Paulo VI, Brescia, with Studium, Rome, Quaderni dell'Istituto, 3, 1983. Some of this material is in *The Church*, Palm Publishers, Montreal 1964. The principal texts are:

I Concilii ecumenici nella vita della Chiesa, a lecture at Passo della Medola summer school, 16 August 1960 (*The Church*, pp. 129–48).

Pensiamo al Concilio, pastoral letter for Lent, 22 February 1962 (*The Church*, pp. 149–92).

I Concilii nella vita della Chiesa, address to the Catholic University of Milan, 25 March 1962 (*The Church*, pp. 213–32).

Il Concilio ecumenico nel quadro storico internazionale, lecture to the Institute for the Study of International Politics, Milan, 27 April 1962 (*The Church*, pp. 193–212).

Roma e il Concilio, lecture in the Capidoglio, Rome, 10 October 1962 (not included in *The Church*).

Giovanni Battista Montini Arcivescovo di Milano e il Concilio ecumenico Vaticano

II, Preparazione e Primo periodo, Brescia 1985 = Arcivescovo (1985).

Montini, Giovanni Battista, *Sulla Madonna, discorsi e scritti 1955–1963*, ed. René Laurentin, Studium, Rome, and Istituto Paolo VI, Brescia 1988.

Moorman, John H., *Vatican Observed: An Anglican Impression of Vatican II*, Darton, Longman and Todd, London 1967 (Bishop of Ripon 1959–75, senior delegate observer at Vatican II, member of ARCIC 1969–81).

Morley OFM, Hugh, *The Pope and the Press*, Notre Dame Press 1968.

Moro, Renato, "The Catholic Contribution to the Constituent Assembly", paper at FUCI conference, Rome, 27 November 1986.

Murray SJ, John Courtney, "*La Libertà religiosa, materia di dibattito conciliare*", *Aggiornamenti Sociali*, April 1965 (this single entry does not do justice to his contribution to *Dignitatis Humanae*).

Neuner SJ, Joseph, ed., *Christian Revelation and World Religions*, Burns and Oates, London 1967.

Nicholl, Donald, "*Nostra Aetate*", *Modern Catholicism: Vatican II and After*, ed. Adrian Hastings, SPCK, London; Oxford University Press, New York 1991.

Notiziario = bulletin of the Istituto Paolo VI, Brescia, No. 1 appeared at Christmas 1979, and nos. 2–22 approximately twice a year since. The indispensable source for unpublished material from Paul VI; news of work in progress, manuscripts discovered, theses written, and so on.

Novak, Michael, *The Open Church*, Darton, Longman and Todd, London 1964 (a good book: but in the 1980's he became the well-heeled ideologue of Reaganonics and tried, unsuccessfully, to reduce Catholic Social Doctrine to it).

Nugent, Donald, "Sexual Orientation in Vatican Thinking" in *The Vatican and Homosexuality*, ed. Jeannine Gramick and Pat Furey, Crossroad, New York 1988 (is "Pat Furey" a *nom de guerre* for Don Nugent?).

O'Connor CSC, Edward D., *Pope Paul and the Spirit*, Ave Maria Press, Indiana 1978.

O'Donovan, Patrick, with a personal recollection by Robert Kee and biographical notes by Hermione O'Donovan, *A Journalist's Odyssey*, Esmonde Publishing 1985 (Cardinal Basil Hume, who knew him at Ampleforth, adds: "Patrick O'Donovan brought great distinction to whatever he wrote. I always read his work with interest and admiration").

Paoletti, Domenico, *La Testimonianza Cristiana nel Mondo Contemporaneo in Papa Montini*, pref. René Latourelle SJ, Miscellanea Francescana – CEFA, Rome 1991.

Papetti, Dr Renato, of the Istituto Paolo VI, Brescia: special thanks for access and answering my questions.

Pawley, Bernard, unpublished Rome Reports and other material, in Canterbury Cathedral Archives, quoted with permission of the Dean of Canterbury, the Librarian and Margaret Pawley, to whom the deepest thanks for access to this treasure trove.

Peri, Vittoria, "*Le radici italiane nella maturazione culturale di Giovanni Battista Montini*", *Archivum Historiae Pontificiae*, 22, 1984.

Piccioni, Donatella and Leone, *Antonio Fogazzaro*, Turin 1963 (a touching tribute from an older sister and brother team).

Pieris SJ, Aloysius, *An Asian Theology of Liberation*, Orbis, Maryknoll 1988.

Pimentet-Pinto, Francisco, Brazilian theologian, is the source of much Latin American information and advice.

Pollard, John F., *The Vatican and Italian Fascism 1929–32*, Cambridge University Press 1985 (a friend in need).

Poulat, Emile, "*Chiesa e Mondo Moderno*" in *Pio XII*, ed. Andrea Riccardi, Laterza, Roma-Bari 1984.

Prévotat, Jacques, "*Les Sources françaises de G. B. Montini*" in *Paul VI et la Modernité*, 1980.

Problemi Ecclesiologici = *Paolo VI e il Problemi Ecclesiologici al Concilio*, Istituto Paolo VI, Brescia 1989. The *Acta* of the colloquium held in Brescia, 19–21 September 1986.

Quaderni, published by Istituto Paolo VI, Brescia:

1. Giovanni Batista Montini, *Colloqui religiosi: la preghiera dell'anima, le idee di Sao Paolo*, 1981.
2. *Giovanni e Paolo, due Papi, Saggio di corrispondenza* (1925–1962), 1982.
3. Giovanni Battista Montini, *Discorsi e scritti sul Concilio 1959–1963)*, 1983.
4. Paolo VI, *Discorsi e documenti sul Concilio (1963–1965)*, 1986.

Quigley, Martin S., *Peace without Hiroshima: Secret Action at the Vatican in the Spring of 1945*, Madison Books, Lanham and New York 1991.

Quigley, Thomas E., ed., *American Catholics and Vietnam*, Eerdemans, Grand Rapids, Michigan 1968.

Quitsland, Sonya A., *Beauduin: A Prophet Vindicated*, Newman Press, New York 1973 (a new and fuller edition is promised).

Rahner SJ, Karl, *I Remember*, an autobiographical interview with Meinhold Krauss, SCM Press 1985, tr. Harvey D. Egan SJ.

Ramati, Alexander, *While the Pope Kept Silent: Assisi and the Nazi Occupation*, Allen & Unwin, London 1978.

Rendina, Claudio, *Il Vaticano, Storia e Segreti*, Newton Compton, Rome 1986 (a pop-book based on the "fancy that!" principle).

Rhodes, Sir Anthony, *The Vatican in the Age of the Dictators 1922–45*, Hodder & Stoughton, London 1973 (a pioneering work from an ex-diplomat who, though "not a Roman Catholic", did enough to secure a papal honour).

Riccardi, Andrea, *Il "Partito Romano" nella secondo dopo-guerra (1945–1954)*, Morcelliana, Brescia 1983.

Riccardi, Andrea, ed., *Pio XII*, Laterza, Roma-Bari 1984.

Rocca, Giancarlo, *L'Opus Dei, Appunti e Documenti per una Storia*, Rome 1985 (the work that first "exposed" Opus Dei to daylight – not that it made any difference).

Rossi, Mario V., *I Giorni della Onnipotenza, Memorie di un esperienza cattolica*, Coines Edizioni 1975 (thanks to Jan Grootaers for supplying this reference).

Sassoon, Donald, *Contemporary Italy: Politics, Economy and Society since 1945*, Longman, London 1986.

Schmidt SJ, Stepjan, *Augustin Cardinal Bea: Spiritual Profile*, Geoffrey Chapman, London 1971.

Schwalbach, Bruno, *Erzbischof Conrad Gröber und die nationalsozialistische Diktatur*, Badenia, Karlsruhe 1985 (thanks to Dr Peter Mödler for this reference).

Sciascia, Leonardo, *The Moro Affair* and *The Mystery of Majorana*, Carcanet, Manchester 1987.

Scoppola, Pietro, *La "Nuova cristianità" perduta*, Studium, Rome 1985.

"Serafian, Michael", *The Pilgrim*, Michael Joseph, London 1964 (this *nom de guerre* conceals Malachy Martin, and it is far and away his best book).

Seton-Watson, Christopher, *Italy from Liberalism to Fascism 1870–1925*, Methuen, London 1967.

Sharkey, Michael, ed., *International Theological Commission: Texts and Documents 1969–1985*, foreword by Joseph Cardinal Ratzinger, Ignatius Press, San Francisco 1989.

Shehan, Lawrence, A., *A Blessing of Years: The Memoirs of Lawrence Cardinal Shehan*, Notre Dame Press 1982.

Silvestrini, Achille, "*L'Ostpolitik de Paul VI*", *Notiziario* 20, pp. 70–83.

Soetens, Claude, "*Chinois avec les Chinois*", *Louvain*, July–August 1990 (on Father Vincent Lebbe).

Sorge SJ, Bartolomeo, *Uscire del Tempio*, interviewed by Paolo Giuntella, Marietti, Genoa 1989.

Stacpoole OSB, Alberic, "The Institutionalisation of the Church in the Middle Ages", *Ampleforth Journal*, Autumn 1968.

Stacpoole OSB, Alberic, ed., *Vatican II by those who were There*, Geoffrey Chapman, London 1988.

Stacpoole OSB, Alberic, "Montecassino 1989" in *Priests and People*, May 1990.

Stacpoole OSB, Alberic, monk of Ampleforth Abbey, read through the entire manuscript of this book, scrupulously, punctiliously, to whom grateful thanks.

Stehle, Hansjakob, *Die Ostpolitik des Vaticans*, Piper, Munich 1975. Tr. as *Eastern Politics of the Vatican 1917–1979*, Ohio University Press 1981.

Stehlin, Stewart A., *Weimar and the Vatican 1919–1933: German-Vatican Diplomatic Relations in the Interwar Years*, Princeton University Press 1983.

Stehlin, Stewart A., "The Emergence of a New Vatican Diplomacy", *The Holy See in the Modern Age*", University of New Brunswick, Canada, October 1991.

Steinberg, Jonathan, *All or Nothing: the Axis and the Holocaust 1941–1943*, Routledge, London 1990.

St John-Stevas, Norman, *The Agonising Choice: Birth Control, Religion and the Law*, Eyre & Spottiswoode, London 1971.

Sturzo, Luigi, and Mario Sturzo, *Carteggio 1924–1940*, 4 vols, Storia e Letteratura, ed Gabriele De Rosa, Rome 1985 (the correspondence of Luigi Sturzo in exile in Notting Hill, London, with his brother, Bishop of Armerina).

Suenens, Léon-Joseph, *Co-responsibility in the Church*, Burns and Oates/Herder and Herder, London 1968.

Suenens, Léon-Joseph, *A New Pentecost?* Darton, Longman and Todd, London 1975. Tr. from *Une Nouvelle Pentecôte?* Desclée de Brouwer 1974.

Suenens, Léon-Joseph, *Memories and Hopes*, ET Veritas, Dublin 1992.

Tardini, Cardinal Domenico, *Pio XII*, Tipografia Poliglotta Vaticana 1960.

Tasca, A., *Nascita e avvento del Fascismo*, 2 vols, Laterza, Bari 1965.

Tucci SJ, Roberto, "*Introduction historique et doctrinale à la Constitution Pastorale*" in *L'Eglise dans le monde de ce temps*, II, Cerf, Paris 1967 (helped me more than I, or he, can say).

Turi, Tommaso, *Laicità e Laicato nel Pensiero di Giuseppe Lazzati*, Pontificia Universita Laterenense 1990.

Vaillancourt, Jean-Guy, *Papal Power: A Study of Vatican Control over Lay Catholic Elites*, University of California Press, Berkeley 1980 (a work of "sociology" which, as its title indicates, is somewhat passionate).

Valier, Maria Luisa Paronetto, "*Una fiera contesa per cosa da nulla: La crisis del Circolo romana della FUCI nel 1933*", *Studium* 22, 1981, pp. 25–44.

Veuillot, Pierre, *Notre Sacerdoce, Documents Pontificaux de Pie X à nos jours*, Lettre-préface de son excellence Monseigneur Montini, Pro-Secrétaire d'Etat de sa Sainteté pour les Affaires ordinaires, Editions Fleurus, Paris 1954.

Villani, Giulio, *Il vescovo Elia Dalla Costa*, Florence 1974.

Wall, Bernard and Barbara, *Thaw at the Vatican*, Gollancz, London 1964. Barbara Wall (née Lucas), daughter of Sir Wilfrid Meynell, also supplied information on life in Rome in 1940 and 1963.

Walsh, Michael J., *The Tablet: A Commemorative History*, Tablet, London 1991 (librarian of Heythrop College, University of London, to whom thanks are due for answering my many bibliographical queries, reasonable and unreasonable, with both courtesy and efficiency).

Wenger AA, Antoine, "*Cinq Audiences de Paul VI*", *Notiziario*, 18.

Wenger AA, Antoine, *Le Cardinal Villot (1905–1979)*, préface de René Rémond, Desclée de Brouwer, Paris 1989.

White, Robert J., Director of Neurological Surgery at Case Western Reserve University, Cleveland, Ohio, provided valuable information on Paul's knowledge of medical morals.

Wilhelm, Maria di Blasio, *The Other Italy*, Norton, London 1989.

Wilson, Andrew H., *Hilaire Belloc*, Hamish Hamilton 1985.

Wilson, Edmund, *Europe without Baedeker*, Hogarth Press, London 1947.

Wiskemann, Elizabeth, *Europe of the Dictators*, Fontana History of Europe, Collins, London 1966.

Wojtyla, Karol, *Milosc i Odpowiedzialnosc*, Znak, Kraków 1960; *Amour et Responsabilité: étude de morale sexuelle*, pref. Henri de Lubac SJ, Stock, Paris 1965; tr. as *Love and Responsibility*, Collins 1981, with a new introd. by the author.

Wojtyla, Karol, *U Podstaw Odnowy*, Polish Theological Association, Kraków 1972. Tr. P. S. Falla, *Sources of Renewal*, Collins 1980.

Woodruff, Mia, widow of Douglas, editor of the *Tablet*, shared her memories of Montini from 1945 onwards over lunch at Marcham Priory, Oxfordshire in the summer of 1988. Though well over eighty and half blind, her mind was as alert as ever.

Wynn, Wilton, *Keepers of the Keys, John XXIII, Paul VI and John Paul II: Three who Changed the Church*, Random House, New York 1988 (veteran *Time* magazine writer and courteous southern gentleman who joined the Church he had reported on since 1962 in the pontificate of Pope John Paul II).

Yarnold SJ, Edward J., *They are in Earnest: Christian Unity in the Statements of Paul VI, John Paul I, John Paul II*, St Paul Publications, Slough 1982 (founder member of ARCIC's book is graced by a preface from Dr Robert Runcie, then Archbishop of Canterbury).

Zamoyski, Adam, *The Polish Way*, John Murray, London 1987.

Zizola, Giancarlo, *L'Utopia di Papa Giovanni*, Citadella editrice, Assisi 1973. Tr. as *The Utopia of Pope John XXIII*, Orbis, New York 1978.

Zizola, Giancarlo, *Quale Papa?* Borla 1977.

Zizola, Giancarlo, "*Giovanni Benelli: Il mio amico Onnipotente*", *Panorama*, 15 November 1982.

Zizola, Giancarlo, *Nel Basso dei Ciela*, Garzanti, Rome 1985.

Zizola, Giancarlo, *Il microfono di Dio, Pio XII, Padre Lombardi e i cattolici italiani*, Mondadori 1990.

Zizola, Giancarlo, to whom, over the years, I attribute my Italian education.

Zuccotti, Susan, *The Italians and the Holocaust*, Peter Halban 1987.

Index